Third Edition

AMERICA IS

HENRY N. DREWRY   THOMAS H. O'CONNOR   FRANK FREIDEL

CHARLES E. MERRILL PUBLISHING CO.
A Bell & Howell Company
Columbus, Ohio
Toronto • London • Sydney

Staff

Editorial

Project Director	Cheryl Currutt
Project Editors	John Lawyer, Brenda Smith, Donald Lankiewicz, Myra Immell
Project Assistants	Thomas Photos, Jacquelyn Whitney
Free-lance Editing and Indexing	Mary Jo Cavallaro Baumeister

Production

Designers	William Walker, Larry Koons
Cartographer	June Barnes
Project Artist	Katie Bookwalter White
Project Assistants	Jeff Kobelt, Lisa Brush, Shirley J. Beltz, Susan Myers, Timothy A. White, Dennis Smith
Photo Editors	Susan Marquart, Russell Lappa

ISBN 0-675-01867-6

Published by
CHARLES E. MERRILL PUBLISHING CO.
A Bell & Howell Company
Columbus, Ohio 43216

Printed in the United States of America

Preface

*Before we can set out on the road to success, we have to know
where we are going, and before we can know that we must determine
where we have been in the past.*

John F. Kennedy

The actions that people did or did not take in the past have made your present and will influence your future—just as you are the makers of American history for tomorrow's citizens. So this study of America is mostly a study of its people—their needs, wants, hopes, and choices. It was written to help you see more clearly the connections among people, places, events, and ideas. The information in this book is presented in the order of time so that you can put the many parts of American history into useful order.

America Is has 29 chapters grouped into 9 units. Each unit title can be used to describe what the United States has meant to its people at different times in its history. The chapters include photographs, maps, charts, quotations, skill and concept features, and profiles of famous and not-so-famous Americans. In the margins of each chapter are questions to guide your study. There are review questions at the end of each main section and Chapter Reviews, with questions ranging from simple recall of facts to a more thoughtful examination of ideas. Included in the chapter-end material is a section on skills to help you read the maps, graphs, and diagrams. At the end of each unit is a Unit Review that includes a time line of key events, a summary of major understandings, a list of suggested projects, and a short bibliography of enjoyable books for further reading.

America Is also contains 13 special features on American towns and cities to help you relive history from the Algonquin village of Secota to the "Space City, U.S.A." of Houston. Firsthand accounts of social, cultural, and economic aspects of American life are included.

At the back of the book, you will find several special features. There is a glossary to help you remember definitions and an index to help you find the page numbers for specific names and topics. There are also fact charts on the States of the Union and on the Presidents and Vice-Presidents. Copies of the Declaration of Independence and the Constitution (with annotations that will aid you in understanding more about the American political system) also appear.

The authors wish to express their thanks to the many students, teachers, and consultants who have made suggestions for changes based on their use of the first edition of *America Is.*

Contents

Maps

Authors

Henry N. Drewry is Lecturer with the rank of Professor of History at Princeton University. He taught for 14 years in secondary schools before joining the university. Drewry has coauthored several books and articles and has received the Harvard University Prize for Distinguished Secondary School Teaching. He is Director of the Princeton University Teacher Preparation Program and spends Sabbaticals in secondary schools teaching social studies.

Thomas H. O'Connor is Professor of American History and former chairman of the Department of History at Boston College. He has written many books and articles, including *The Disunited States: The Era of Civil War and Reconstruction* and *Lord of the Looms.*

Frank Freidel is Bullitt Professor of American History at the University of Washington and Charles Warren Professor Emeritus of American History at Harvard University. He has written more than 20 history books and is the author of *The Presidents of the United States,* published by the White House Historical Association.

Reviewers

Dorothy Bachmann
Social Studies Consultant
Educational Development Center
Paramus, New Jersey

William J. Burkhardt
Curriculum Coordinator
Northeast Junior High School
Bethlehem, Pennsylvania

Dorothea B. Chandler
Curriculum Consultant, Retired
Torrance Unified School District
Torrance, California

Walter Gordinier
Instructor of History
Nazareth Academy
Rochester, New York

Dona McSwain
Social Studies Department Chairman
West Stanley High School
Oakboro, North Carolina

Milt Olson
Social Studies Teacher
South Junior High School
Moorhead, Minnesota

Diane Rasserty
Social Studies Department Chairman
South Seminole Middle School
Casselberry, Florida

William Rayner
Social Studies Teacher
Altimira School
Sonoma, California

Richard Ross
Social Studies Teacher
Ada Middle School
Ada, Oklahoma

Prologue

History can help a person learn about the past, understand the present, and prepare for the future. Most current political, economic, and social conditions in the United States took a long time to develop and are continuing to change. History traces the development, following all the twists and turns that affected it along the way.

To begin to understand the present American political system, for example, consider some of the major political developments in the nation's past and ask questions about them. What was life in the colonies like under British rule? Why were the colonists unhappy with British rule? What kind of government did Americans set up for themselves? How did a free and open society in the United States affect the way that government worked? What divided the American people, leading to a civil war? How did America's relations with the world affect its foreign policy?

Similarly, the American economic system and American society can be considered. How did the United States industrialize? Why was business organized? Why was there conflict among races of people? Why was the United States called a nation of immigrants?

Even the most far-reaching study of history may not provide complete answers. There are some historical facts that are clear, simple, and upon which historians easily agree. There are other aspects of history that are not clear and upon which historians may never agree. These usually concern judgments involving correct and incorrect decisions. The important thing is that history raises questions and aids in providing a structure for answering them. Evaluating facts and weighing evidence are valuable skills for making sound and reasonable decisions.

America Is tells the story of the United States and its people. It follows a development from America's distant to recent past. It provides a framework for learning about the way things were, understanding the way things are, and preparing for the way things may be in the United States.

UNIT

I

AMERICA IS

Opportunity

Opportunity has been a way of life for people coming to America from the start. Thousands of years ago, people from Asia moved slowly overland into Alaska, hunting and gathering more food. Beginning in the fifteenth century, people from Europe and Africa traveled by sea to the New World. They believed that America offered a place to lead their own lives. With great areas of land and many natural resources, opportunities for people in America seemed to be unlimited.

The First Americans 1

About 42,000 years ago, ice covered one third of the earth's surface. The level of the oceans was lower, too. How did the Ice Age help make it possible for people to come from Asia to North America?

Many people around the world have a general view of America as a new land. They think of it as a recent discovery with a fairly brief history. Nothing could be further from the truth. The roots of American history stretch far back into the past. To understand the land and its peoples, it is necessary to go back and look at the earth tens of thousands of years ago.

1. The Beginning

The earth is very old and continues to go through many changes in the way it looks. These changes usually happen over long periods of time. This is especially true during the parts of earth history known as the Ice Ages. Then the general climate of the earth slowly grows cold. The moisture escaping from the oceans and seas, which usually returns as rain, falls mostly as snow. It becomes packed into *glaciers*—heavy, giant sheets of solid ice that move slowly across the land. With less rain returning to them, the oceans are lower than before and more land shows.

1.1 The Land Bridge. The latest Ice Age began about 70,000 B.C., reached its peak about 40,000 B.C., and ended about 10,000 B.C. Glaciers covered the most northern parts of Asia, Europe, and North America at different times during this Ice Age. The oceans then were much lower than they are today. Sometimes land showed between Asia and North America. It formed a *land bridge* which is now covered by the waters of the Bering Strait.

What is a land bridge?

Small bands of people in Asia *migrated*—moved from one place to settle in another—as land was covered and uncovered by the glaciers. Some migrated north and east when the earth's climate grew warmer. They followed the herds of animals moving slowly into newly opened lands, and their lives depended on their skills as hunters. The herds of moose, elk, and caribou were the people's major food. The animals and their hunters drifted into the land bridge area. Over hundreds of years, they migrated across it and into parts of what is now Alaska. They were the first people in the Western Hemisphere.

Why did people cross the land bridge?

1.2 Early People in America. The spread of people over the Western Hemisphere took many thousands of years. Some areas became free of ice during the warmer stages of the Ice Age. People moved through these areas into the body of North America. Some followed the rivers and streams toward the east. Others moved south and west along the Rocky Mountains. And there were some groups that moved farther south through Middle America deep into South

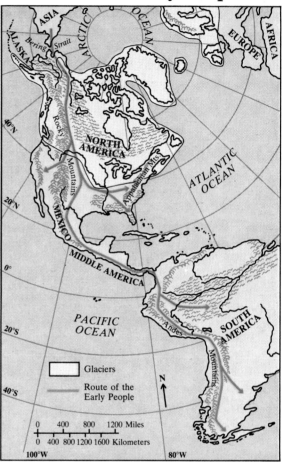

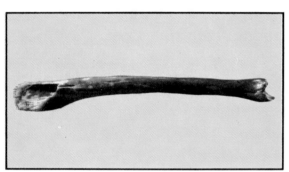

When scientists tested this caribou-bone scraper (bottom) found in Alaska, they proved that people lived there by 25,000 B.C. The duck decoy (top) was probably made in the Great Basin about 2500 B.C. What factors affected where the early Americans lived and what tools they made for hunting and working?

What is a culture?

America. By some 10,000 years ago, people were living in many places throughout North and South America.

When people moved, they sometimes entered new areas with very different kinds of weather, animals, and plants. The people developed different *cultures*—ways of life—to adjust to the areas in which they lived. The early people hunted such animals as giant buffalo and hairy elephants called mastodons. They chipped flint to make thin, sharp spear points to kill these animals. The people were mostly hunters, but they also fished and gathered some plants, seeds, and roots.

1.3 The Beginning of Farming. With the end of the Ice Age came the end of the largest Ice Age animals—giant buffalo and mastodons. People then hunted smaller game such as moose, elk, deer, and rabbits. In the warmer southern climates, the growing seasons were longer than in the north. There was a large supply of wild plants, and people gathered them for food.

What kind of animals did people hunt after the Ice Age?

In these warmer climates, the early people developed *agriculture*—the planned growing of food. As early as 8000 B.C., those in what is now Mexico learned to plant seeds and grow some kinds of food for themselves. Corn, beans, and squash were among the first plants grown. They soon became the people's basic plant foods. Pumpkins, gourds, potatoes, and avocados were also grown. Later there were many other crops, including tobacco which the people smoked, chewed, and sometimes ate.

People gained more control over their food supply when they learned to grow plants. Groups settled near fields and gardens and formed small villages. There they grew enough food to store some for later use. Because they no longer had to spend as much time searching for food, people could work on other things. As life became more complex, some of the larger groups developed organized societies. This was a long and gradual process that took thousands of years.

How did people gain more control over their food supply?

1. Where was the land bridge which the early people used to cross into the Western Hemisphere?
2. Why did the early people in the Western Hemisphere develop different cultures?
3. After the Ice Age, how did the early people get food?

2. People of Middle and South America

Between 300 and 1500 A.D., three groups of people in Middle and South America rose to power. The groups all had large populations and highly developed societies. While they were alike in some ways, each developed its own unique culture.

2.1 The Mayas. From about 300 to 900 A.D., the Mayas formed a great culture in Middle America. They had settled in the area of the Yucatán Peninsula (now southeast Mexico, Guatemala, and Honduras). There they made their living by farming, mostly growing corn. Most Mayas lived in one-room houses with thatched roofs.

Where did the Mayas settle?

Religion was the strongest force in the lives of the Mayas. They worshiped things in nature such as spirits of the sun, rain, and animals. Groups of Mayas lived near scattered religious centers, each ruled by a priest. In these centers, the Mayas built huge stone pyramids. On the flat tops of these were small temples and sculptures.

Who ruled Mayan everyday life?

The priests ruled the everyday lives of the people. The Mayan farmers supported the priests with their crops, and this gave the priests time to work out new ideas. The Mayan priests were very interested in measuring time. They studied the movement of the sun, moon, stars, and planets, and from this, they formed an accurate, 365-day calendar. The priests set up a system of numbers based on twenty with the place value of zero. The Mayas also had a system of writing in which small pictures stood for words.

What are some possible reasons for the decline of Mayan culture?

Mayan culture began to lose strength about 800 A.D. There may have been an epidemic or some natural disaster. The farms may have worn out the soil so it did not produce as many crops for food. Or there may have been wars among groups of Mayas or with outsiders. By about 1000 A.D., the Mayas had abandoned many of their religious centers. Some people drifted into the dense jungles while others stayed in the northern part of the Yucatán Peninsula.

2.2 The Aztecs. During the next few hundred years, another society rose to power. Its culture included large cities with many people and a well-ordered government. It began with a small group of hunter-warriors in the center of Mexico. In time, they took over nearby groups and formed an *empire*—many different peoples and lands ruled by one government or leader. The Aztec empire, led by a ruler who was all-powerful, later covered most of central and southern Mexico.

What is an empire?

In the early 1300's, the Aztecs set up a capital city, Tenochtitlán, built on an island in a lake. The people found a way to bring fresh water to the city from springs on the mainland. They built canals and raised streets of hard earth running through the city. The major canals and roads led to a central square, where the Aztecs built large pyramids with temples and sculpture on their flat tops. They put their markets, shops, government buildings, and great stone palaces around the square. The Aztecs had many flower gardens and a zoo with hundreds of kinds of birds and animals. By the early 1500's, nearly 100,000 people lived in the capital city.

Most Aztecs lived by farming. Corn was their most important crop, but they also grew beans, squash, peppers, cotton, and tobacco. The farmers grew enough food for themselves and for the government leaders and others in the capital. Aztec *artisans*—skilled workers—made pottery and wove cloth. They made jewelry from gold, silver, and

What are artisans?

Reading the Chapter
SKILL

One way to make your study of history easier is to look at the structure of the reading material. Begin with a careful look at the title of each chapter. Look at the sections and the subsections which divide it. The title and the headings form a guide to the ideas you should get from the reading. In this way, the outline previews the reading like a preview of a movie or a television program. Going through the outline before you read lets you know what to expect. After you read the material, use the outline to check your recall.

Use this chapter as an example. Follow the outline formed by the title, section headings, and subsection headings.

Title—The First Americans
Section heading—
1. The Beginning
Subsection headings—
1.1 The Land Bridge.
1.2 Early People in America.
1.3 The Beginning of Farming.
Section heading—
2. People of Middle and South America
Subsection headings—
2.1 The Mayas.
2.2 The Aztecs.
2.3 The Incas.

Section heading—
3. People of North America
Subsection headings—
3.1 The Southwest.
3.2 The Plains.
3.3 The Great Basin and California.
3.4 The Northwest Coast.
3.5 The Far North.
3.6 The Arctic.
3.7 The Eastern Woodlands.

You should be able to answer the following questions before you read the chapter.

1. What is the chapter about?
2. What is discussed in each of the three major sections?
3. Into what groups are the people of North America divided?

Looking over the outline can also raise some questions that reading the chapter will answer. Here are some possible questions.

1. When did people first come to the Western Hemisphere?
2. Who were the Mayas, Aztecs, and Incas?
3. Which people lived in the various geographic areas of North America?

By examining the title, section headings, and subsection headings, you can better understand the chapter. Follow this structure as you read each chapter in this book.

This two-headed serpent is a piece of Aztec jewelry probably worn across the chest. Artisans used turquoise as well as gold, silver, and jade for carving. Why was jewelry important in the Aztec economy?

jade. Aztec traders contacted many peoples and brought goods such as rubber, cacao, gold, and jewels into the Aztec capital.

Religion was a very important part of Aztec life. The people had many gods, and one of the most powerful was the war and sun god. The Aztecs believed that they must make human sacrifices to this god so that the sun would rise each morning. Thousands of people each year were put to death for that reason.

Why did the Aztecs make human sacrifices?

The Aztecs fought many wars to expand their empire. They took over new lands and forced the people to send goods to Tenochtitlán every year. The Aztecs also fought to get captives for the sacrifices. Some of the conquered peoples were angry about sending their wealth and their people as sacrifices to the Aztec capital. Sometimes they rebelled, and by the early 1500's, the empire began to weaken.

2.3 The Incas. Sometime after 1200, another great empire was formed in the Western Hemisphere. The Incas lived in the Andes Mountains of South America. By the middle of the 1400's, they ruled lands stretching in a narrow strip over 2,000 miles (3,200 kilometers) long from what is now southern Colombia to the middle of Chile. The heart of the Inca empire was in the mountains of Peru.

What things did the Incas raise?

Inca farmers grew many kinds of crops, among them grains and potatoes. They also raised llamas for meat and wool. All the land was controlled by the government. Most people, living in small stone houses, farmed the land for themselves and the government. The government in turn made sure that no one went hungry. Some of the land farmed by the Incas got little rain, so they built stone-lined canals to bring water to those fields.

The Incas also worshiped the sun, and they believed that their ruler was a direct descendant of the sun. As a living god, the ruler could do no wrong. The ruler's wishes were laws that directed the daily lives of the people. Under the ruler was a council of state with four members. Each was in charge of one quarter of the empire. There were many other levels of officers down to the village leaders. The government kept a *census*, or count, of the number of people in each part of the empire.

What did the Incas believe about their ruler?

Cuzco was the capital city of the Incas. It had a central square with temples and palaces around it. Inca artisans carefully shaped the stones in these buildings so that they fit together perfectly without cement. Sometimes they decorated buildings with thin sheets of gold. The artists

The Inca city of Machu Picchu (left) stretched along a ridge in the Andes Mountains. A highway system crisscrossed the Inca empire (right). How did these engineering accomplishments help make the Inca powerful?

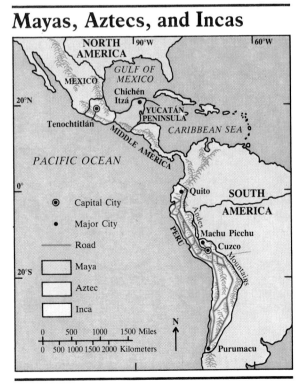

Mayas, Aztecs, and Incas

also used gold, as well as silver, copper, and bronze, to make ornaments. The Inca crafts included pottery and cloth woven from cotton and wool.

How did the Incas link their empire together?

The government built a chain of highways to link all parts of the empire. These carefully built roads crossed the high Andes Mountains. The Incas hung strong vine bridges across deep valleys and dug tunnels through the steepest mountains. They put inns and way stations along the routes. Over these roads, the Incas sent runners in a message service. In this way, the ruler kept in touch with all parts of the land.

Some groups of people willingly joined the Inca empire. Others were added to it by war. New members were carefully drawn into Inca life. They were taught the Inca religion and offered the same benefits and duties as other Incas. Groups who would not accept the Inca plan were moved to areas where they were not dangerous to the empire. Government leaders tried not to cause hardships because of the move.

What led to unrest in the Inca empire?

The Incas had the largest and most highly organized group in the Americas with an all-powerful ruler. In the early 1500's, the Inca ruler died without stating who should rule next. A bitter fight broke out between two groups, each claiming the throne for its leader. In the following years, there was unrest throughout the Inca empire.

1. What three groups of people developed great cultures in Middle and South America?
2. Where did each of the three great cultures develop?
3. What are some of the accomplishments of each group?

3. People of North America_____

For hundreds of years, the people of Middle and South America built their great cultures. At about the same time (from 100 B.C. to 1500 A.D.), other groups lived in the area that is now the United States and Canada. These people were spread out across the land, from the hot south to the cold north, from the Pacific to the Atlantic. Their cultures also were influenced by the *environment*—surrounding land, water, and air—in which they lived.

What influenced the cultures of the peoples living in North America?

3.1 The Southwest.   Most of the land is hot and dry in the southwest part of what is now the United States (Arizona, New Mexico, Utah, and Colorado). It has thin, rocky soil. In the northern part of this area are steep-walled canyons and flat-topped hills. The southern part is flat desert country.

The Hohokam were one of the early peoples who lived in this area. They probably had migrated from northwest Mexico around 300 B.C. By 100 B.C., they were settled near the middle of Arizona. The Hohokam farmed the land, building long canals to bring water from the rivers to the dry fields. Many years later, the Hohokam were followed on the land by the Pima and Papago peoples.

Who were the Hohokam?

North of the Hohokam lived another group known as the Anasazi, "the Old Ones." About 900 A.D., these people began to construct apartmentlike buildings in which villages of people lived. The group later was given the name Pueblo, from a Spanish word for village. The buildings, also later called *pueblos*, were very large, sometimes several stories high. They were made of stone or *adobe* (sun-dried brick) and were built into steep cliff walls or on *mesas*—the flat tops of high hills. People entered their pueblos by climbing ladders to openings in the flat roofs. The ladders could be pulled inside for protection.

What was used to build the pueblos?

Each pueblo formed a separate town independent from the others. Two of the Pueblo groups were the Hopi of Arizona and the Zuñi of

The Hopi people lived in these cliff pueblos in Arizona around 1150 A.D. They climbed up and down the cliff by toeholds cut in rock. They farmed nearby fields and hunted. Why did the Hopi build villages in cliffs?

New Mexico. In each group, a council of elders chosen by the priests set up rules and judged crimes. The Pueblos were a peaceful farm people, fighting only to protect themselves and their homes. Their major crops were corn, beans, and squash. They also grew cotton and wove cloth and blankets of many colors. The Pueblos made many kinds of baskets and pottery with black-on-white designs. Pueblo men and women shared the farm work equally. Women had a special place in Pueblo life, for they controlled the fields and were the leaders of their families.

What was the role of women in Pueblo life?

Water was very important to the Pueblo people. Their land was hot and dry, and they needed rain to make their crops grow. The Pueblos had many religious ceremonies to ask for rain during the year. These were held in the *kiva*, a round underground room. The kiva also was used as a meeting and working room for the men of the village.

How did the Apaches differ from the Pueblos?

Two other groups moved into the Southwest by about 1200 A.D. The Apaches and the Navahos came from northern Canada. They were warlike peoples who often raided the Pueblos, taking food and goods. The Apaches moved throughout the Southwest, not staying long in any one place. Their homes, called *wickiups*, were frames of thin poles covered with animal skins. They could be put up and down quickly.

The Navahos gradually began to settle near the Pueblos. They lived in *hogans*—small, round houses of mud and logs. The Navahos learned farming and weaving from the Pueblos. They also borrowed many parts of the Pueblo religion. One of these was the art of sand painting. To do this, the Navahos took sand, bits of minerals, and seeds of many colors and arranged them into a picture. They used these paintings in the ceremonies they held to cure sickness.

What and where is the Great Plains?

3.2 The Plains. Near the center of North America is a large area known as the Great Plains. It stretches from southern Canada to southern Texas. The eastern part of this area has rich soil. The western part, where the soil is not so rich, is a broad grassland.

Many different groups of people lived in this land. Among those who lived in the eastern part were the Dakota and other Sioux, and the Pawnee, Mandan, Osage, and Omaha peoples. They were farmers and hunters who set up small villages along rivers and streams. They made their homes of log frames covered with dirt and brush. The women took care of the crops, growing corn, beans, squash, and tobacco. The men hunted deer, elk, buffalo, and other big game.

What did the peoples of the Great Plains hunt?

The Blackfoot, Crow, Cheyenne, and Comanche lived in the western Plains. Their homes, known as *tipis*, were cone-shaped. They were made of poles covered with buffalo hides. These people hunted buffalo for food, clothing, and fuel. Sometimes hunters dressed in animal skins and crept up on their prey. Other times they tried to drive

Mandan people built villages along rivers and streams. Women fished and planted gardens. Men hunted and traded. Why were boats important in the everyday lives of the Mandan?

herds over cliffs or into narrow valleys where they were trapped. After the kill, the people carried the buffalo meat and skins to their homes or camps on *travois*—small platforms, each fastened to two poles. Sometimes the people used dogs to pull the travois.

The many groups living on the Plains often met each other as they hunted and traveled across the area. They sometimes traded food and other goods. Many languages were spoken by the Plains peoples. So they developed a set of hand signals for important words or phrases. This sign language allowed them to communicate with those who spoke a different language.

How did the different peoples of the Great Plains communicate with each other?

Their religions, centered around spiritual power, were very important to the Plains people. Sometimes people fasted for several days so that they might see visions of spirits. Every year, some groups gathered for the Sun Dance, a ceremony to keep away enemies and famine. As part of it, the men danced in a circle always facing the sun. Sometimes men tortured themselves to show how brave they were.

3.3 The Great Basin and California.   The Great Basin is a large area between the Rocky Mountains and the Sierra Nevada Mountains. It covers much of the present state of Nevada, as well as parts of California, Idaho, Utah, and Wyoming. The land is mostly a desert, too dry for farming. Only a few groups of people lived in this area, among them the Ute, Paiute, Shoshoni, and Nez Percé. These people lived in small family groups. They were always on the move, searching for food. They found pine nuts, seeds, and roots from a few wild plants. They also ate insects, rabbits, and other small animals.

Why did many groups live in California but only a few in the Great Basin?

Between the Great Basin and the Pacific coast, in the California area, the land is very different. The weather is mild, and many groups of people lived there, including the Modoc, Chumash, Yokut, and Pomo. These people lived in brush shelters and settled in small villages. Food was easy to get in the California area. The people hunted small game and caught fish. There were many kinds of wild plants, and the people ate seeds, berries, nuts, and roots. Acorns, one of their main foods, were gathered, pounded into flour, and washed to remove their acid. The flour was then used to make a kind of bread or mush.

The people of the Great Basin-California area made baskets and used them to gather, store, and sometimes cook foods. They wove the rushes used to make the baskets in many styles, sometimes with very tiny stitches. They often decorated the baskets with patterns of beads, feathers, and shells.

3.4 The Northwest Coast. The Northwest Coast stretches along the Pacific Ocean from northern California to southern Alaska. It is rich in natural resources. Dense forests grow in the mild, rainy climate. Many groups of people, such as the Haida, Tlingit, Chinook, and Nootka, lived there. They built strong houses of wooden posts and boards. The houses were large enough for as many as 50 people.

What was the main source of food for the peoples of the Northwest Coast?

The Northwest Coast people lived in small villages close to the ocean beaches. They made huge seagoing canoes up to 60 feet (18 meters) long. The people got most of their food by hunting sea animals and by fishing, generally for salmon. There was plenty of food, and the people sometimes traded some of it for goods from other groups.

The great forests were very close to the villages, and the people had many uses for wood. Besides their homes and canoes, they made carved boxes, wooden tools, and ceremonial masks. Outside their houses, they put large wooden posts called *totem poles*. These were carved with figures of faces and animals. The poles showed the history of the family and the titles of the family leader.

Village society was generally divided into four groups, based on wealth. The slaves were at the lowest level. They were people who had been captured in war. Next came the average people and above them, the nobles. At the top were the chiefs, the richest people in the villages.

What was a potlatch?

A chief sometimes gave a special feast, called a *potlatch*, which lasted for several days. During it, the chief gave away or destroyed many things such as canoes, blankets, and large sheets of copper. The potlatch proved how rich the chief was, and he kept his high level in the village.

3.5 The Far North. From the middle of Alaska stretching across Canada to the Atlantic is the Far North—a land of long winters and short summers. There are many lakes and streams there, as well as huge evergreen forests. A few groups of people lived in this area, the Tanaina, Cree, Ottawa, and the Ojibwa who are also called Chippewa. Small bands lived and hunted in family groups. They set up wood frame homes and covered them with bark, brush, or animal skins.

Who lived in the Far North?

Most of the Far North is very cold, and plants are scarce. People there lived on meat, sometimes pounded, mixed with berries, and dried. They hunted moose, deer, and beaver, and they caught fish. In the summers, the people used canoes made of wood poles and bark. In the winters, they had wooden snowshoes for traveling on the snow.

The people of North America formed many groups with varied ways of life. The major cultures are divided according to geography. What did the peoples within each section have in common?

People of North America

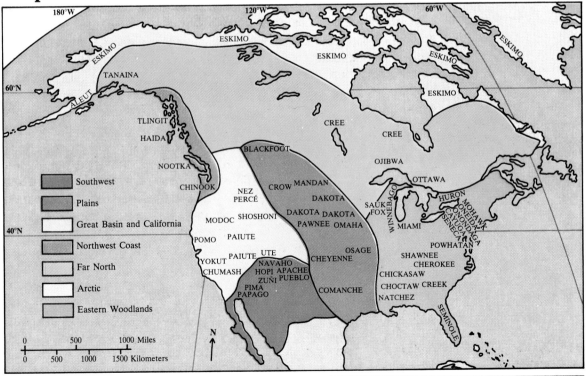

3.6 The Arctic. The land of North America that is nearest to the North Pole is known as the Arctic. In the west, it begins with the Aleutian Islands off the southern coast of Alaska. It stretches around Alaska and across northern Canada to Greenland in the Atlantic Ocean. The Arctic is one of the coldest areas of the world. Snow covers the land up to nine months each year. Most kinds of plants and animals cannot live so far north.

Two groups of people found ways to live in this harsh land. A small group called the Aleuts lived on the bare, foggy Aleutian Islands. They were a branch of a larger group, the Eskimos, who lived all across the area of the Arctic. The two groups had many of the same ways of living. But their languages and some of their customs were different.

What were the differences between the Aleuts and the Eskimos?

The people of the Arctic lived near the sea, and from it they got most of their food. They caught fish and hunted sea animals like whales, seals, and walrus. The people used two kinds of boats, both made of wood frames covered with animal skins. One of them, the *kayak*, was like a canoe and held one or two hunters. The other, the *umiak*, could hold about ten people. The Eskimos also tamed and used dogs to pull sleds across the ice and snow. In the Arctic, there was little wood that could be used for fires. So the people there sometimes ate meat raw.

For what did Arctic people use animals?

The Arctic people used the animals they killed for many things besides food. The skins were used for the many layers of clothing the people wore in the great cold. The people made goggles of bone with narrow slits to protect their eyes from the bright sun on the snow. They also used bone and ivory to make harpoons, hooks for fishing, knives, and needles. The Eskimos carved lamps from soft rock found in the Arctic area and burned seal oil in them. They used the lamps for light, heat, and some cooking.

The Arctic people built houses to protect them from the weather. Most Eskimos used animal skin tents in the short summers. In the cold winters, they made houses of sod, stone, and driftwood. Some of them built houses from blocks of snow. The Aleuts sometimes built houses under the ground, like basements. These had frames of whale bones or driftwood and were covered with grasses.

What were some Eskimo beliefs?

The people who lived in the Arctic had little contact with the people to the south. The Eskimos lived in small family groups which sometimes joined together for hunting. Eskimos believed that they should help each other to live in the harsh climate. It was important to them that each person live in peace with others in the group. The Aleuts lived in small villages on the islands. Each village was led by a chief, and all villages on an island were governed by one ruler. The Aleuts had slaves, most often people taken from nearby islands during raids.

3.7 The Eastern Woodlands. The area known as the Eastern Woodlands stretches from the Great Lakes and the St. Lawrence River in the north to the Gulf of Mexico in the south. From east to west, it covers the area between the Atlantic coast and the Mississippi River. The northern part has cold winters, and the whole area has warm summers. There are lots of rivers in the Eastern Woodlands, and plenty of rain falls on the land.

Many groups of people lived in this wide area. Different groups known together as the Iroquois lived in the northeast. Others like the Fox, Miami, Shawnee, Sauk, Huron, and Winnebago lived in the Great Lakes area. The Choctaw, Chickasaw, Cherokee, Creek, Powhatan, Natchez, and Seminole peoples lived in the southeast. And some groups lived in the center area in the Ohio and Mississippi river valleys. The Eastern Woodlands people got their food by hunting, fishing, farming, and gathering parts of wild plants. Many of them grew corn, beans, squash, and tobacco. Those who lived in the Great Lakes area harvested a kind of wild rice that grows there. And in the north, people made maple sugar from the sap of maple trees.

Most of the groups of the Eastern Woodlands lived in villages ruled by chiefs. Some people built fences around their villages for defense. They were made of logs set together on end and pointed on the top. Most people lived in *wigwams*, small, rounded buildings covered with sheets of bark. A few groups made their homes from poles and clay. The

Where was the Eastern Woodlands?

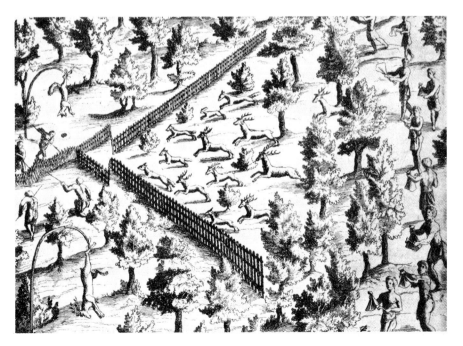

Deer provided many of the Eastern Woodlands people with clothing, food, and tools. The Huron hunted deer using traps. How was this way of hunting similar to the way buffalo were hunted in the western Plains?

The First Americans 19

Who lived in long houses?

Iroquois homes were large, rectangular buildings called **long houses**. They built them with wood poles and bark. A dozen or more related families lived in a long house, each with its own separate section.

The Eastern Woodlands people made many beautiful and useful things. Wood was carved into bowls and tools, and some pottery was made. In the southeast, the people wove cane and wicker baskets. People near the Great Lakes hammered copper to make works of art and small figures used in their ceremonies. The Ohio and Mississippi valley groups were well known for their crafts. These people made bowls, jars, and figures using bone, shells, and copper. Many of their pieces were shaped like animals.

Why was religion important to the people of the Eastern Woodlands?

Religion was important to the people of the Eastern Woodlands. Beliefs in spirits of nature guided their lives. Their feasts and ceremonies were often tied to the growing of food. For example, the Green Corn Dance of the Creek people honored the first corn crop of the year. Groups in the north were guided by dreams of supernatural beings. Many groups had dances and ceremonies to cure sickness. Members of one Iroquois group wore carved and painted wood masks as they worked to cure those who were ill.

Groups in the central part of the Eastern Woodlands built large hills of earth as part of their religion. As early as 600 A.D., the Hopewell people in the Ohio Valley area built these **mounds** in round, square, or animal shapes. The Hopewells used the mounds as places to bury their dead, sometimes as many as 1,000 in each. Around 1000 A.D., people in the Mississippi Valley were building temple mounds. These flat-topped mounds had small temples or chiefs' houses on them.

Some Eastern Woodlands villages, like those of the Creek people, had central plazas with meeting houses, public squares, and fields where ceremonies were held. Iroquois villages had groups of long houses. Women had an important role in Iroquois life. They controlled the land and the houses, both of which passed from mother to daughter. Iroquois women chose the **sachems**, or chiefs.

Why did women have an important role in Iroquois life?

War was common among the people of the area. Sometimes groups fought to show how brave they were. At other times, they fought to capture slaves. The Iroquois adopted some of the slaves, but they also put many others to death. To fight common enemies or solve common problems, some Eastern Woodlands groups formed **alliances**—unwritten partnerships for a specific purpose. Most of these did not last.

What did the Iroquois do to stop fighting among neighboring groups?

By about 1400, Iroquois leaders wanted to stop the bitter fighting among neighboring groups. So leaders of five groups in what is now New York formed the League of the Iroquois. These allies were the Cayuga, Onondaga, Oneida, Mohawk, and Seneca peoples. Each of

This serpent mound was built by Hopewell people 400 years ago. It winds a quarter-mile. Mounds were used for burial and other religious purposes. How do the mounds show the Hopewell people's concern with death?

them sent chiefs to a general council. There they discussed wars and other matters of the Woodlands peoples. Anyone could speak at the meeting. Each chief had one vote, and all of them had to agree before action was taken. The council handled only matters that involved all of its members. It could not bother the governing of any separate group. By the middle of the 1500's, the League of the Iroquois was one of the largest and strongest groups in the lands north of Mexico.

1. Who were some of the people living in the various geographic sections of North America?
2. How did ways of life differ among the people of North America?
3. Why was the League of the Iroquois formed?

4. Conclusion

The idea of America as a new land with a short history is obviously false. The Western Hemisphere is very old and has changed in geography and climate as conditions on the earth have changed. For tens of thousands of years, many groups of people, each with their own special habits, customs, languages, and ways of life lived there. They were living all across the land of North and South America when the first Europeans sailed westward across the Atlantic Ocean.

Chapter 1 Review

Main Points

1. The first people in America entered by way of a land bridge from Asia.
2. Over a long period of time, these early peoples moved to all parts of North and South America.
3. The early people were mostly hunters. By 8000 B.C., however, agriculture was beginning to be developed by some groups.
4. People gained control over their food supply when they learned to grow plants. Because they did not have to spend so much time searching for food, some people settled together forming villages, towns, and cities.
5. Between 300 and 1500 A.D., the Mayas, Aztecs, and Incas developed advanced societies in Middle and South America.
6. The cultures of the early Americans were influenced by their environment.
7. The early peoples in North America lived in the following geographical areas: the Southwest, the Plains, the Great Basin and California, the Northwest Coast, the Far North, the Arctic, and the Eastern Woodlands.

Building Vocabulary

1. Identify the following:

Ice Ages	Tenochtitlán	Hohokam	Sun Dance
Mayas	Incas	Pueblo	Eskimos
Aztecs	Cuzco	Sioux	League of the Iroquois

2. Define the following:

glaciers	census	wickiups	kayak
land bridge	environment	hogans	umiak
migrated	pueblos	tipis	wigwams
cultures	adobe	travois	long houses
agriculture	mesas	totem poles	mounds
empire	kiva	potlatch	sachems
artisans			alliances

Remembering the Facts

1. When did the first people on the American continents probably arrive?
2. From what continent did the first people come, and how did they reach the Americas?
3. How did the early people get the food they needed?
4. What new way of providing food was developed among the early people in the Western Hemisphere?

5. What were the three great cultures of Middle and South America?
6. Where did the Mayas live? the Aztecs? the Incas?
7. What kinds of food did they eat?

8. In what seven geographic areas did the early people in North America live?
9. What did early people in North America use to build their homes?
10. What was the purpose of totem poles?

Understanding the Facts

1. How did the Ice Age make it possible for people to travel by foot to the Americas from another continent?
2. How did geography and climate affect the lives and cultures of the peoples of North and South America?

3. How important was religion among the early people in the Americas?
4. Why did the people living on the Plains develop a sign language?
5. Why was the League of the Iroquois important?

Using Maps

Reference Maps. A map which shows various features such as oceans, continents, lakes, rivers, mountains, countries, and cities is called a reference map. To help readers, people who draw maps use symbols for the different features which the map shows. Symbols are used to show features created by people as well as natural features. The meaning for each symbol is found in the map key.

Before you look at a specific reference map, answer the following questions about geography in general.

1. What is a continent? an island? a peninsula? a mountain? a plain?
2. What do continents, islands, peninsulas, mountains, and plains have in common?
3. What is an ocean? a sea? a lake? a river?
4. What do oceans, seas, lakes, and rivers have in common?

5. How do continents differ from islands? How do oceans differ from seas?
6. Can you name any types of land or water areas that are not listed here?

After you have answered these questions, study the reference map and its key on page 11. Then answer the following questions.

1. What area of the world does the map show?
2. What is represented by each of the different symbols in the key?
3. Do the symbols which make up the key show features created by people or natural features?
4. Why is it important to be able to locate the geographic features shown on a reference map?

New World–
New Opportunities

2

Juan de la Cosa was a navigator on one of the ships during Columbus' first voyage in 1492. In 1500, he drew one of the earliest known maps of the New World. How accurate does the map appear to be?

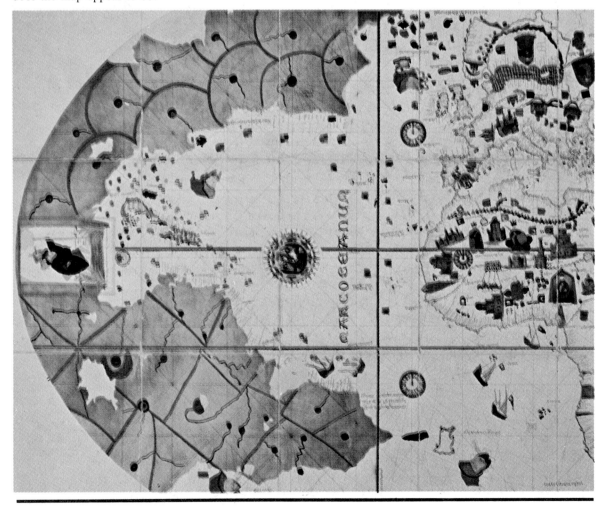

The Western Hemisphere is very large, and people have lived on the lands there for many thousands of years. But most of the people in Europe during the 1400's knew nothing of that area or its peoples. Most Europeans of that time had no idea how big the world is. Their maps showed Africa as a small peninsula and Asia as a large landmass. But they did not show the lands of the Western Hemisphere at all.

1. Backgrounds and New Beginnings

Some Europeans had explored less known areas of the world as early as the 800's. One of the first groups to sail far into the Atlantic Ocean came from the northern countries that are now Denmark, Sweden, and Norway. These Norse (North) people are also called Vikings. Sailing west in their sturdy ships, the Vikings found the islands of Iceland and Greenland and left settlers on them. About the year 1000, a group led by Leif Ericson sailed west from Greenland. They came to the coast of North America and stayed there for a short time. Little news of these adventures reached other people, however. During the next few hundred years, most Europeans were interested in the lands around and east of the Mediterranean Sea.

Who were the Vikings, and what did they do?

1.1 The Growth of Trade.   From about 1100 to 1250, Europeans took part in religious wars in the Middle East. In these wars, called Crusades, Christians tried to drive Muslims out of such Holy Land cities as Jerusalem and return them to Christian rule. The wars were not generally successful, but they helped to bring about great changes in the world. European soldiers came home knowing more about the geography and peoples of the Middle East. They also brought with them spices, silks, fine cottons, and other goods from these eastern Mediterranean lands. The goods were rare and costly in Western Europe at the time, because they came from the faraway lands of India, China, and Southeast Asia.

What were the Crusades?

A strong trade grew between Europe and Asia in the 1300's. To take part in the trade, Western Europeans dealt with traders of the Middle East and Central Europe. The Middle East merchants had a *monopoly* (exclusive control of the trade) because they alone knew the safe routes to the Far East. In turn, they traded only with a few merchants in Europe, mostly those of Venice and Genoa in Italy. The goods changed hands many times along the trade routes. Each time, the

Why was there a monopoly on trade between Europe and Asia?

Trade Routes in the 1400's

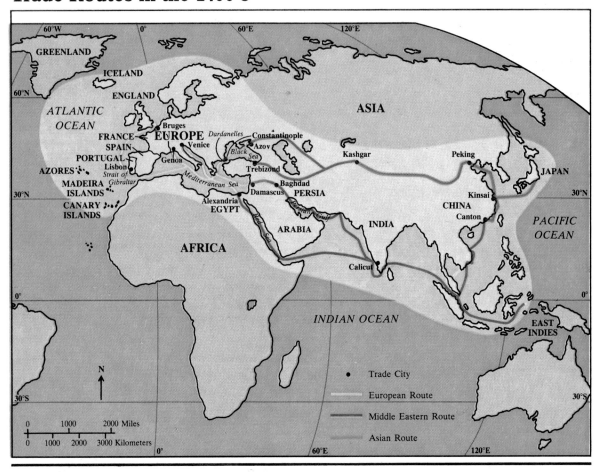

A system of water and land routes of trade linked the known world in the 1400's. Merchants controlled each of the many routes. In which cities did Asian, Middle Eastern, and European traders exchange goods?

prices were raised to cover the merchant's costs and to add some profit. Western Europeans wanted to avoid high prices by trading directly with Asian merchants. They could increase their own profits by finding a new route to the Far East.

Little was done about finding a new route until the early 1400's. Then a group of Muslims known as the Ottoman Turks rose to power. They took over the Middle East, swept through North Africa, and put Eastern Europe in danger. In 1453, the Turks captured Constantinople, a city at the crossroads of Asia and Europe. Trade was endangered because the Turks controlled much of the land and the known sea routes between Europe and the Far East. Western Europeans became more determined to find their own routes to Asia.

1.2 A New Route to the Far East. By the 1450's, some countries in Europe were changing from a collection of small kingdoms into large national states. Countries like Portugal, Spain, France, and England were slowly becoming unified under strong leaders. They had their own separate languages and systems of laws. They had large national armies and rich treasuries. Some of them could pay to have explorers find new trade and to set up *colonies*. These are settlements in other lands made by people still tied to the rule of their home countries. In the early 1400's, too, there were great improvements in sails and shipbuilding. New kinds of sailing tools made travel into unknown areas much safer than before.

What was happening in Europe during the 1400's?

Portugal was the most able of the western seagoing countries. Its sailors had been to the Madeira and Canary islands as well as the Azores in the Atlantic Ocean. The son of the Portuguese king, Prince Henry the Navigator, started a school in 1419. Navigators, sailors, ship captains, mapmakers, and others came there to study the sea and to try out new sailing tools. Using their ideas, Portuguese sea captains took ships south along the coast of Africa. The Portuguese had two aims. One was to find

Explorers used the astrolabe (left) and stars to determine latitude and time. The compass (right) was used for direction. How did these new kinds of sailing tools make ocean travel safer?

a route around Africa to Asia and the Far East trade. The other was to find the source of African gold which long had been a part of the Mediterranean trade.

In 1488, Bartolomeu Dias successfully rounded the southern tip of Africa and returned to Portugal. Ten years later, Vasco da Gama led three ships around the tip, crossed the Indian Ocean, and reached the northwest coast of India. After many years of searching, the Portuguese had found their own route to Asia.

Who was the first European to sail around Africa?

1.3   The African Continent.   Europeans had known very little about Africa south of the Sahara Desert. As the Portuguese slowly made their way down its coast, they found that Africa was not a small peninsula. It was a huge land of many peoples, languages, and cultures. Some Africans had strong kingdoms with important cities of trade and learning. At different times, the kingdoms of Ghana, Mali, and Songhai rose to power. They lay in the center of important trade routes that ran from North Africa to the West African coast. For that reason, they were known as the Middle Kingdoms. Their people had richly developed cultures. Gold, salt, ivory, leather, iron, and other African goods passed through their markets. The Muslim traders who came from North Africa also brought the ideas and teachings of their religion to the Middle Kingdoms. Many people there accepted parts of the Muslim religion, adding them to their own religious beliefs.

What were the Middle Kingdoms?

In Africa, the Portuguese raided and took what they wanted from small camps or villages that were not protected. When they came to areas under powerful kingdoms, they worked to set up peaceful trade. In 1441, a Portuguese sea captain returned from Africa with a valuable cargo. He had captured several Africans to sell as slaves. The slave trade, an old way of life in Europe and in Africa, was very profitable. Other sailors and merchants in Portugal became interested in this new source of slaves. Within ten years, Portugal became the European center for trade in African goods and in African slaves.

1.4   The Voyages of Columbus.   Portuguese explorers found a way to reach Asia by sailing south then east around Africa in 1498. Earlier, a sailor named Christopher Columbus had suggested another route. Columbus wanted to sail directly west from Europe to reach Asia. Some people at that time believed that such a voyage was possible. They knew that the earth was round, but they did not know how big it really is. Columbus expected to find China and India about 2,400 miles (3,840 kilometers) to the west, on the other side of the Atlantic. Actually, China and India are over 10,000 miles (16,000 kilometers) west, with the huge lands of the Western Hemisphere and the Pacific Ocean in the way.

What did Columbus want to do?

Christopher Columbus (left) was certain that Asia could be reached by sailing west from Spain. Fernando Magellan (right) proved it could be done. Why did Columbus fail to reach Asia while Magellan succeeded?

Columbus was an Italian who had worked as a sailor and mapmaker in Portugal. He tried to get the Portuguese to finance a trip to prove his idea. They refused. A few years later, Columbus was able to get the help he needed from Spain's rulers, Queen Isabella and King Ferdinand. At sunrise on August 3, 1492, three small ships—the *Niña*, the *Pinta*, and the *Santa María*—sailed from the harbor of Palos, Spain. They were bound for Asia.

After a short stay at the Canary Islands in September, the ships sailed west into the Atlantic. Five weeks later, a lookout from one of the ships spotted land. On October 12, 1492, Columbus and his sailors went ashore to an island they named San Salvador. It is part of the group in the Caribbean Sea now called the Bahamas. Columbus believed that he had come to the Indies Islands off the southeast coast of Asia. He called the people he found living there Indians. From that island, Columbus sailed to some of the others in the Caribbean. He did not find the Asian cities of trade that he expected, but Columbus took some of the Indians back to Spain.

The islands that Columbus reached are now called the West Indies, and he returned there three times in the next ten years. The news of his travels spread to other countries in Europe. "When treating of this country," wrote an Italian historian in 1494, "one must speak of a new world, so distant is it. . . ." A few years later, Amerigo Vespucci also explored the area for Portugal. He believed that these lands were part of a new continent which "it is proper to call a new world." In 1507, a German mapmaker gave the name America to these lands in honor of Vespucci, who had identified them as separate continents.

For whom was America named?

1.5 Dividing the World.   Soon after Columbus' first trip, ships from both Spain and Portugal were sailing far west into the Atlantic. These two countries were strong rivals. To prevent trouble between them, the Spanish rulers asked for help from the pope, the head of the Catholic church. Both Spain and Portugal were Catholic countries, and their rulers agreed to follow the pope's decision.

So in 1493, Pope Alexander VI drew an imaginary line, called the Line of Demarcation, around the world. Newly found lands not under control of a Christian leader to the west of the line would go to Spain; those lands east of it would go to Portugal. A year later, the two countries signed the Treaty of Tordesillas setting the line at 370 leagues (about 1,250 miles or 2,000 kilometers) west of the Cape Verde Islands in the Atlantic. A Portuguese sea captain, Pedro Alvarez Cabral, was blown off course on a voyage around Africa. He landed on the east coast of South America in 1500. Because of the treaty, Portugal was able to claim the area, now called Brazil. The lands found by explorers for Spain became an empire over much of the Western Hemisphere.

Who drew the Line of Demarcation? For what reason?

How did Portugal come to claim Brazil?

1. What events led to greater trade between Europeans and the people of the eastern Mediterranean?
2. Why were European nations interested in finding an all-water route to Asia?
3. How was Portugal able to take the lead in searching for new routes to Asia?
4. Why did Christopher Columbus call the people he met in the New World "Indians"?

2. Spain in the New World_____

Spain's rulers encouraged their people to follow the western routes of Columbus. They wanted to find the route to Asia, but they became even more interested in making claims on the new lands across the Atlantic. Almost all the news brought back from these lands had reports of great amounts of gold to be found there.

2.1 Early Spanish Explorations.   On his first trip to the New World, Columbus also had landed on the island which is divided today between Haiti and the Dominican Republic. He had named it Española (Hispaniola) and had written this description of it:

> *Its mountains and plains, and meadows, and fields, are so beautiful and rich for planting and sowing, and rearing cattle of all kinds, and for building towns and villages. The harbors on the coast, and the number and size and wholesomeness of the rivers, most of them bearing gold, surpass anything that would be believed by one who had not seen them.*

Columbus had set up a post on the island. It served as a base for Spaniards who explored other islands and the nearby mainland. In 1496, they built a new city named Santo Domingo and used it as the Spanish capital of the area.

In 1508, Juan Ponce de León sailed with soldiers to the island of Puerto Rico and took it over. By 1511, the Spaniards had taken several islands to settle, including Jamaica and Cuba. Ponce de León explored other areas and, in 1513, reached a land he named Florida (from the Spanish word meaning "full of flowers"). He searched there for gold and other treasures and tried to set up a Spanish settlement. The Indians of Florida drove the Spaniards out and killed Ponce de León in 1521. In 1565, the Spaniards started a settlement in Florida near the place where Ponce de León had first landed. Named St. Augustine, it was the first lasting European settlement in what is now the United States.

What was the first permanent European settlement in what is now the United States?

While Ponce de León and others searched the islands of the Caribbean, Vasco Nuñez de Balboa landed on the shore of what is now Panama in Central America. With soldiers, he traveled across Panama and reached the Pacific Ocean in 1513. Balboa and his force were the first Europeans to see this great ocean from its American shore. Their travels across Panama showed that the land was narrow in some places. This encouraged other explorers to keep looking for a way to reach Asia by going through or around America.

2.2 The Voyage of Magellan.   One of those explorers was Fernando Magellan. Magellan and his crew set out from Spain with five ships in September 1519. They reached Brazil and sailed south along its coast. By the following spring, Magellan found the strait which now bears his name at the tip of South America. The ships sailed through it and headed north into the Pacific Ocean to the Philippine Islands. Magellan was killed there, and most of his ships were wrecked. Another captain, Sebastián del Cano, brought the one remaining ship through the Indian Ocean and around Africa to Europe. On September 6, 1522, the *Victoria* and its valuable cargo of spices arrived in Spain after a

Who led the voyage which sailed around the world?

European Explorers

Explorers	Dates of Activity	Achievements
Bartolomeu Dias	1488	Sailed around the southern tip of Africa
Vasco da Gama	1498–1503	Reached India by sailing around the southern tip of Africa
Amerigo Vespucci	1497–1504	Explored the eastern coast of South America
Pedro Alvarez Cabral	1500	Landed in Brazil
Christopher Columbus	1492–1504	Explored the West Indies and the Caribbean
Vasco Nuñez de Balboa	1513	Reached the Pacific Ocean
Juan Ponce de León	1513–1521	Explored Florida
Hernando Cortés	1519–1536	Explored and conquered Mexico
Fernando Magellan	1519–1522	Led first expedition to sail around the world
Francisco Pizarro	1530–1537	Explored and conquered Peru
Hernando de Soto	1539–1542	Explored southeastern North America to the Mississippi River
Francisco de Coronado	1540–1542	Explored southwestern North America
Giovanni da Verrazano	1524	Sailed along the Atlantic coast of North America
Jacques Cartier	1534–1541	Explored St. Lawrence River valley
Samuel de Champlain	1603–1615	Explored St. Lawrence River valley
Louis Joliet and Jacques Marquette	1673	Explored along Mississippi River
La Salle	1669–1682	Explored from the Great Lakes to lower Mississippi River
Henry Hudson	1609–1611	Explored Hudson River and Hudson Bay areas

Major European Explorations

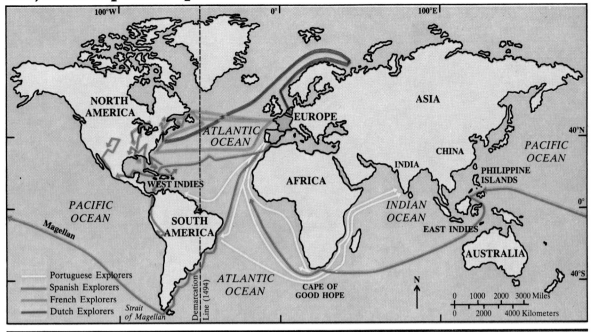

The governments of Portugal, Spain, France, and Holland supported the early voyages of exploration which led to colonization and settlement. Why did so many explorers start from just a few countries?

voyage around the world. The trip begun by Magellan proved that Christopher Columbus was right. Europeans could reach the Far East by sailing west.

2.3   The Conquest of Mexico and Peru.   In the same year that Magellan sailed from Spain, Hernando Cortés and 700 soldiers sailed from Cuba to the coast of Mexico. They landed near what is now Vera Cruz. Cortés wanted the Aztec land and gold for himself and Spain.

On his way into Mexico, Cortés met other Indians ruled by Montezuma and the Aztecs. Some of them, hoping for freedom, joined Cortés. The army moved on, invited by Montezuma to visit Tenochtitlán. Many Aztecs thought that Cortés might be the god mentioned in their histories. If so, they believed, no defense was possible against him. The Spaniards also marched to the city with horses, guns, and cannons—things unknown to the Indians.

What did the Aztecs think about Cortés?

Tenochtitlán was a wonderful sight to the Spaniards with its palaces, streets, water systems, and busy markets. They were amazed by the gold and silver used by the Aztecs, who did not seem to value it as

New World—New Opportunities   33

An Aztec artist drew this picture of the Spanish conquest of Mexico in the early 1500's. In what ways did the Spaniards hold an advantage in the fighting?

highly as the Spaniards did. Cortés put Montezuma into prison where the Aztec ruler died. By 1521, the Spanish army had defeated the Aztecs and taken over their empire. Mexican gold and silver were soon on their way to Spain. The Spaniards destroyed Tenochtitlán, with its places of human sacrifice, and built their own Mexico City in its place.

In 1530, another *conquistador* (Spanish for "conqueror") set out from a base in Panama. Francisco Pizarro led an army of 180 soldiers south. They cut their way through the jungles to the mountains of northern Peru. The army reached the Inca empire in 1532, and Pizarro captured its ruler, Atahualpa. Atahualpa gave the Spaniards great amounts of gold and silver for his freedom, but they murdered him. The army took over the government and began sending Inca treasure to Spain. Pizarro visited the Inca capital of Cuzco in the mountains. But in 1535, he chose a place on the coast to begin the Spanish city of Lima. In a short time, Spanish rule was spread over much of South America.

How did Spain gain control of much of South America?

2.4 Expanding the Empire.   News of the treasures taken by Cortés and Pizarro led others to the New World. Some searched for gold in the lands north of the Caribbean and across the Gulf of Mexico.

In 1539, Hernando de Soto took 600 soldiers into Florida. They marched west through the lands that later became Georgia and Alabama and reached the Mississippi River in May 1541. The army crossed the river and moved on, returning to it the following spring. There de Soto died of a fever, and the soldiers buried his body in the Mississippi. Explorations by de Soto had failed to turn up gold or silver. But they did give Spain a claim to the entire Gulf area and the lower part of the Mississippi Valley.

Francisco Vásquez de Coronado looked for gold farther west. He was searching for the "Seven Cities of Cibola." These were supposed to be whole cities made of gold. Beginning in 1540, Coronado's army traveled through the lands which later became Arizona, New Mexico, Texas, Oklahoma, and Kansas. They did reach the pueblos of the Zuñi Indians, but there was no gold. They were, however, the first Europeans to see the Grand Canyon, and their travels added a great sweep of land to the empire claimed by Spain.

How did Spain gain control of the Southwest?

2.5 Spanish Colonies. Spain set up many government offices at different times to look after its claims in the New World. One of these, the Council of the Indies, was formed in Spain in 1524. It made laws, administered justice, directed the army, and took care of finances for the empire. To govern the lands and people in the Americas more closely, Spain later formed colonies there. One, called New Spain, was formed in 1535, and its capital was Mexico City. It covered the West Indies, the Philippines, Venezuela, and all the lands claimed north of Panama. Another colony was Peru, formed in 1542, with its capital at Lima. It covered Panama and all the Spanish claims in South America except Venezuela. The governments in the colonies were headed by *viceroys* who were direct representatives of the Spanish crown.

Who looked after Spanish claims in the New World?

The crown owned the land in the colonies, according to European ideas, by claims and conquest. So the Spanish rulers also could give parts of it away. They gave large areas to the explorers and to other Spaniards who came to the New World. The Indians who lived on the lands were made to farm the fields and work the mines. In return, the Spanish owners were to give the Indians food, shelter, and clothing. They also were to protect and teach them. This plan soon became a system in which a few Spaniards owned huge areas of land worked by many Indian slaves.

A great number of Indians died fighting the Spaniards. Others died from European diseases or from slave work. The land system in the Spanish colonies depended on large numbers of workers to be profitable. By the early 1500's, most of the Caribbean Indians were dead, and the landowners wanted more slaves. So Spain allowed sea

What did the Spanish land system in the New World require?

Spain's empire in the New World was first settled by soldiers and missionaries. Estevanico, a black guide, and others led explorers and settlers through unknown areas. What seems to be the relation between the Spaniards and the Indians?

captains to bring them directly from Africa to the West Indies. Many African kingdoms did not want to supply this greater number of slaves. But the European countries used their stronger weapons and armies to capture slaves and enforce their wishes. By 1560, there were nearly 100,000 African slaves in the New World.

2.6 Spanish Missions.   Catholic priests were among the first people to follow the explorers to the New World. They came as *missionaries*—church workers sent to teach the Indians Christianity and to make them members of the Catholic church. The missionaries also taught the Indians Spanish ways of farming and making goods. Some, like Father Bartolomé de las Casas, tried to protect the Indians from cruel soldiers and landowners. But in most cases, they failed.

What did the missionaries do?

As the Spanish empire spread in the late 1500's and 1600's, the plan of setting up missions went with it. By the late 1600's, there were missions in Arizona and the southern part of California. Father Eusebio Kino, sometimes called "the priest on horseback," set up several missions there. In the late 1700's, Father Junípero Serra added to the mission chain as far north as what is now San Francisco.

How large was the Spanish empire in the New World?

By the middle of the 1500's, Spain had established the outlines of a colonial empire in the New World which was larger in size than the empires of Egypt, Persia, Greece, or Rome. From the Mississippi River, Florida, and Mexico in the north, to Cape Horn in the south,

Analyzing Pictures
=SKILL=

The pictures that appear all the way through this book contain special information. They aid your understanding of each chapter. The pictures identify the focus of the material, and they make the book more interesting.

Look carefully at each picture to analyze its content. The steps you can take to analyze the picture are simple.

1. Look at the picture to get a general sense of what the subject is about.
2. Read the caption which goes with each picture.
3. Decide if the picture is a drawing, a painting, or a photograph. (There will be no photographs before the mid-1800's when photography was developed.)
4. Decide, if possible, whether a drawing or a painting was done by someone who lived at the time or someone who lived at a later time.
5. Decide whether a picture is a posed portrait or an unposed photograph.
6. Consider the main theme and the general message of the picture.
7. Identify the main focus of the picture.
8. Consider how the figures in the picture support the main theme.
9. Consider how the use of color or lack of color supports the theme of the picture.
10. Decide why you think the picture is used at its location in the book.

Using such a list can make understanding pictures easier. As an example, use the above list to analyze the picture on page 36. Also, consider the following questions.

1. Two of the figures are soldiers. One is black; the other is white. What does this tell about the people who explored the area?
2. Three of the figures are Indians. What does their position in the picture tell about the way they were viewed by the artist and by the other figures in the picture?
3. Three of the figures are Catholic missionaries. What does this picture tell about their roles and importance to Spanish exploration?

As you look at the other pictures in this book, develop your own lists of questions.

from the Caribbean islands in the east, to the California missions in the west, Spain controlled the Atlantic and the Pacific.

1. Where did the Spaniards explore in the New World?
2. What did the Spanish explorers hope to find in Mexico and Peru?
3. How did the Spaniards control the large areas they took over in the New World?
4. What did the missionaries teach the Indians?

3. France in the New World

Portugal and Spain were the first Western European countries to make gains in their search for new routes to the Far East. By the middle of the 1500's, Portugal had set up many valuable trading posts in Africa and Asia. During the same years, Spain explored the lands across the Atlantic and brought back large amounts of gold and silver. News of these adventures quickly reached other European countries. Their rulers wanted a part of the Asian and African trade. They also became very interested in the lands and treasures of the New World.

3.1 Early French Voyages. Spain used soldiers, ships, and settlements to protect the areas it claimed in the New World, especially in Middle and South America. Spain's defenses were weak farther north. In 1523, Francis I, king of France, hired Giovanni da Verrazano to search that area for a route, a Northwest Passage, through North America to Asia. Verrazano reached the coast of North Carolina in the spring of 1524 and sailed up to what is now New York Harbor. He did not find a Northwest Passage but went as far as Nova Scotia before returning to France.

What were the early French explorers seeking?

From 1534 to 1541, Jacques Cartier made three trips to North America for France. He, too, was looking for the Northwest Passage. Cartier explored the area around the Gulf of St. Lawrence and the St. Lawrence River. He did not find a way to the Pacific. The lands he explored were called Canada by the Indians who lived there. Cartier claimed these lands for the French king.

After Cartier's trips, French exploration came to a sudden halt for two reasons. First, Verrazano and Cartier had failed to report any signs of gold or silver. The French government did not want to spend more money on costly trips without some proof that they would bring treasure. Second, France was caught up in civil wars that lasted nearly

40 years. In 1589, a powerful leader defeated his rivals and came to the throne as Henry IV. Under his rule, France again turned its interest to North America.

3.2 French Settlements.   The reports of Verrazano and Cartier had carried news of the forests, fish, and great numbers of fur-bearing animals in North America. Leaders in the fur business in France were very interested in these reports. With the king's permission, they hired Samuel de Champlain in 1603 to lead a group who would start fur-trading posts in eastern Canada. Beginning that year, Champlain made several such trips through Canada. He founded a settlement at Quebec in 1608, setting up a trading post and building a fort there. He also made allies of Huron and other northern Indians.

Who founded the first French settlements in Canada?

In the spring of 1609, Champlain's group explored the area south of the St. Lawrence River with some Huron and other Indian warriors. They moved into northern New York, reaching a lake which Champlain named for himself. Near there, the group met some members of the Mohawk family of the Iroquois—longtime enemies of the other northern Indians. There was a short fight with no clear winners, although the Mohawk were greatly surprised by the French guns. From then on, the Iroquois thought of the French as enemies, too.

The French found the League of the Iroquois to be powerful enemies. Because of them, the French did not move south to explore and settle the Atlantic coast area that is now the United States. Instead,

Why did the French not explore and settle the Atlantic coast area?

The French began to settle Canada in the 1600's. This map makes more sense turned upside-down, with Florida in the bottom left corner. What did the French artist hope to show in the detail of this picture?

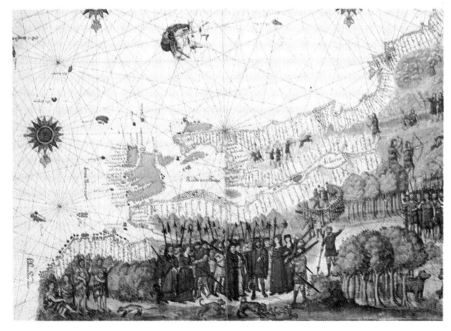

they moved west along the St. Lawrence River. Champlain also explored the Ottawa River farther west and crossed into Georgian Bay. He entered Lake Huron in 1615 before returning east by way of Lake Ontario. Champlain spent the next 20 years encouraging other French people to live and work in Canada.

3.3 French Missions.   Catholic missionaries were among those who followed Champlain to Canada. They set up missions as the Spaniards had done, working first from a base near the northwest tip of Lake Huron. They worked well with the Hurons but were not as successful with other Indians, especially the Iroquois. The Iroquois looked upon the French missionaries as great enemies. They tortured and killed some of them, like Father Isaac Jogues, and set out to destroy their allies. By the middle of the 1660's, the Iroquois had destroyed the mission base and had scattered the Hurons into the forests. The Hurons were never again a powerful Indian group, but the missionaries did not leave the Indian lands. They believed strongly that it was their duty to make the Indians members of the Catholic church.

With whom did the French missionaries work?

3.4 New France.   The French government was eager to make lasting settlements in North America. To do this, it gave control of the area to a private group called the Company of New France in 1627. It was also called the Company of the Hundred Associates because 100 people paid to start the company. The company agreed to bring 300 settlers a year to the New World in return for a monopoly on the fur trade there.

The plan under the company did not work very well. In 1663, the French king took back control of the lands called New France and

French missionaries and fur traders traveled the St. Lawrence River, the Great Lakes, and the Mississippi River, exploring and expanding New France. How did French relations with the Indians differ from that of the Spaniards?

appointed three officials to run it from Quebec. A governor, usually a French noble, was generally in charge. An *intendant* was head of the sovereign council, the appointed lawmaking and judicial body. A bishop took care of all church matters. Several of the people who held these offices turned out to be able leaders. Jean Talon, the first intendant, helped the fur traders and farmers. He also improved defenses against the Iroquois. Count Frontenac served as governor from 1672 to 1682. He was able to defeat the Iroquois, ending their threat to French settlements. Frontenac also encouraged exploration into western lands.

Who ran New France under the king?

3.5 Into the Great West. As eastern Canada became more settled by the French, missionaries and fur traders moved farther west. They heard stories from the western Indians about a large body of water. The French thought it might be the Northwest Passage. Explorers set out to find it and to add lands to the empire of France.

Two explorers, Father Jacques Marquette and Louis Joliet, set out to find the Northwest Passage in 1673. Starting at the top of Lake Michigan, they traveled down to the Mississippi by way of the Fox and Wisconsin rivers. Marquette and Joliet made their way down the Mississippi more than 1,000 miles (1,600 kilometers), to where it was joined by the Arkansas River. There they decided that the river would take them south to the Gulf of Mexico instead of west to the Pacific Ocean. They returned to Lake Michigan by way of the Illinois River.

Who were the first French to explore the Mississippi?

Another French explorer, Robert Cavelier, Sieur de la Salle, also traveled in the Great Lakes area. He explored a little of the Ohio land south of Lake Erie and saw Niagara Falls between it and Lake Ontario. La Salle took the Illinois River from south of Lake Michigan to the place where it joins the Mississippi. Traveling down that river, he reached the point in 1682 where it flowed into the Gulf of Mexico. La Salle claimed the lands on both sides of the Mississippi and the rivers which joined it for France. He named the area Louisiana in honor of the French king.

3.6 The Nature of New France. By the end of the 1600's, France claimed a three-part empire in North America. The northern area, Canada, ran from Nova Scotia west along the St. Lawrence to the Great Lakes. The southern part, Louisiana, ran north and south from the central Mississippi Valley to the Gulf of Mexico. The middle area took in the rest of the lands between the Mississippi and Ohio rivers. These lands were not as large as the huge Spanish empire in the New World. But the French had the largest empire in North America. It had thousands of rivers and lakes, making travel easy and communications quick. The French built forts along the borders of their empire.

What was the nature of New France?

La Salle (1643–1687)

PROFILE

At age 23, Robert Cavelier, Sieur de la Salle, settled in New France. There he traded furs and farmed near Montreal. From his Indian trading partners, he heard stories of the great rivers and lakes to the west.

La Salle had a strong spirit of adventure and a desire to expand the boundaries of New France. He sold his land in 1669 to finance a trip to explore the Ohio River. For the next 18 years, La Salle and a party of explorers traveled through the Great Lakes area and down the Mississippi River. La Salle reached the mouth of this great river in 1682 and claimed the entire Mississippi Valley for France. He named this huge territory Louisiana in honor of King Louis XIV of France.

La Salle wanted to establish a colony at the mouth of the river. So he returned to France, gathered 200 colonists, and sailed for America in 1684. The ships sailed too far west and landed on the Texas coast. When La Salle tried to lead the settlers over land to the Mississippi River, they could not find the way. After many difficulties, the colonists rebelled and returned to France.

Because of La Salle, France held a great empire in the heart of North America. Eventually, other explorers moved into the Mississippi Valley, and France established permanent settlements.

The French government screened all French people who wanted to go to North America. It made sure they were loyal to France and to the Catholic faith. New France did not have a large population. Some French people stayed along the Atlantic coastline and fished in the waters of Newfoundland and Labrador. Others farmed the land in small family plots. Many French people worked closely with the enormous network of Indian groups whose canoes carried valuable furs up and down the rivers and lakes to the various trading posts. French settlers who hunted and trapped alone in the deep forests of the far north became known as *coureurs de bois* (French for "forest runners"). Many of them joined Indian groups and followed Indian ways of life.

Although the number of French settlers remained small, they had strong unity and order. This gave the French an advantage against other

European countries which were interested in colonies. The French could also count upon large numbers of northern Indians to help them. They got along well with most Indians. The French were interested mostly in the fur trade, not in making the Indians work mines or fields. With a loyal band of settlers, a number of Indian allies, and a network of forts, the French intended to remain in North America for a long time.

What advantages did the French have in colonizing the New World?

1. Who was the first French explorer in the New World?
2. Where did the French make settlements?
3. What did French settlers hope to find in the New World?
4. Who claimed the Mississippi River Valley for France?

4. Other Europeans in the New World

While Spain and France were carving out their empires in the New World, other European nations were also eager to get their share of whatever wealth and resources America might have to offer. There was still some territory left unexplored along the Atlantic coast. It lay between the Spanish holdings in Florida and the French trading posts along the St. Lawrence River.

4.1 The Dutch in North America.   During the late 1500's and early 1600's, the Dutch carried on a very busy trade with Asia. They formed the Dutch East India Company in 1602 to manage it. Like other Europeans, the Dutch were interested in a faster, western route to Asia. In 1609, the company hired Henry Hudson to cross the Atlantic and search for the Northwest Passage. Hudson sailed his ship, the *Half Moon*, along the coast of North America and into a river which he named for himself. Although Hudson failed to find a route to Asia, the Dutch claimed the land along the Hudson River. They sent others to explore the area. The Dutch built a fort and trading post at the northern end of the river (now Albany, New York) in 1614. Another post was built on Manhattan Island at the southern end of the Hudson.

How did the Dutch acquire claims in the New World?

In 1621, the Dutch West India Company was formed to handle trade and settlements in America and Africa. Three years later, Dutch ships brought families to settle in the American colony they called New Netherland. They made several settlements along the Hudson and on the islands around its mouth. In 1626, Peter Minuit bought Manhattan Island from the Indians for about $24 in trading goods. The name

Who was responsible for the Dutch settlements in the New World?

European Claims in North America 1650

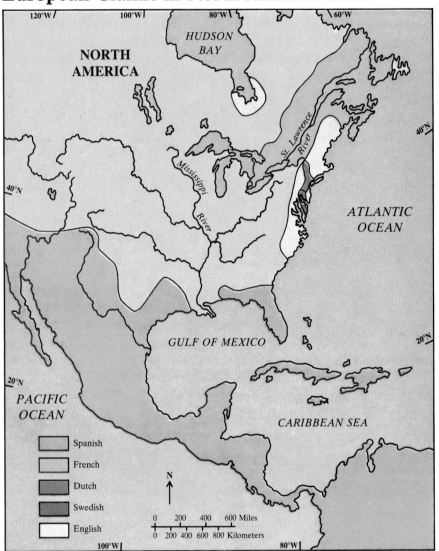

The Spanish, French, Dutch, Swedish, and English had land claims in North America by 1650. Why were some countries able to claim more land than other countries?

Manhattan was changed to New Amsterdam. It became the capital of New Netherland and was a major Dutch trading center. The company and the people were interested most in the fur trade. The population of New Netherland remained small.

How long did the Swedes have a colony in the New World?

4.2 New Sweden. People from Sweden also came to North America in the late 1630's. They built a few forts and settlements along the Delaware River, just south of New Netherland. The Dutch had

44 New World—New Opportunities

While the Spaniards searched for gold and the French searched for furs, the Dutch wanted new lands for trade centers. Ports like this one in New Amsterdam were links in a worldwide network of Dutch trading companies. How did the settlers in New Amsterdam improve harbors to protect their ships?

claimed this land but had not settled it. The main Swedish settlement was Fort Christina (now Wilmington, Delaware), and the colony they called New Sweden grew up around it.

Few people came from Sweden to the colony. Those who did planned to work in the fur trade. That caused trouble between New Sweden and New Netherland during the 1640's. In 1655, the Dutch took over New Sweden and ended Swedish rule in North America.

1. Where did the Dutch settle in the New World?
2. Where was New Sweden?

5. Conclusion _____

During the 1500's and 1600's, most of the major Western European powers made settlements in the Americas. The Portuguese claimed Brazil, and the Spaniards ruled an empire from western South America to California. French land claims swept from the Gulf of St. Lawrence to the Gulf of Mexico. Both the Dutch and the Swedes had settled colonies along the Hudson and Delaware rivers. The English also thought about overseas colonies in the late 1500's. They turned to the only area that was not protected by major settlements—the Atlantic coast of what is now the United States.

Chapter 2 Review

Main Points

1. During the 1400's, most Europeans did not know about the land and peoples of the Western Hemisphere.
2. The desire for more trade led Europeans to seek new routes to Asia after the Ottoman Turks cut off routes through the Middle East in 1453.
3. In the late 1400's, Portuguese navigators reached Asia by sailing around Africa.
4. Christopher Columbus landed in the Western Hemisphere when he attempted to reach Asia by crossing the Atlantic Ocean.
5. Spain led all other European nations in exploring the Western Hemisphere.
6. Portugal, France, Holland, Sweden, and England joined Spain in establishing settlements on the continents called the Americas.
7. European interests in the New World included gold, trade, land for colonies, and the desire to teach Christianity to the Indians.
8. With strong weapons and armies, Europeans were able to take the land of the peoples they met in America.

Building Vocabulary

1. Identify the following:

   Leif Ericson
   Crusades
   Middle Kingdoms
   Christopher Columbus
   Indians
   Line of Demarcation

   Fernando Magellan
   Montezuma
   Francisco Pizarro
   Council of the Indies
   Northwest Passage

   Samuel de Champlain
   Company of New France
   La Salle
   Henry Hudson
   Fort Christina

2. Define the following:

   monopoly
   colonies
   conquistador

   viceroys
   missionaries

   intendant
   coureurs de bois

Remembering the Facts

1. Why did Europeans want to go to Asia?
2. What country supported Christopher Columbus in his search for an all-water route to Asia?
3. Where did Columbus land on his first voyage to the New World?
4. What was the major accomplishment of Juan Ponce de León? Vasco Nuñez de

Balboa? Fernando Magellan? Hernando Cortés? Francisco Pizarro? Hernando de Soto? Francisco Vásquez de Coronado?

5. What did the Spanish explorers do when they met the Aztec and Inca peoples in Middle and South America? What did the people there do?

6. What were the main interests of Spain in coming to the New World?

7. What was the major accomplishment of Giovanni da Verrazano? Jacques Cartier? Samuel de Champlain?

8. What were the main interests of France in the New World?

Understanding the Facts

1. What developments in Europe and the Middle East led Europeans to seek an all-water route to Asia?

2. How did Christopher Columbus' plan to reach Asia differ from the Portuguese plan?

3. Why was Spain successful in establishing an empire in the New World?

4. Why did French exploration in North America stop for a while after the voyages of Cartier?

5. How were the Spaniards and the French different in the treatment of the people they met in the New World?

6. Why did the Dutch come to North America? Why did the Swedes?

Using Maps

Thematic Maps.   A map used to show information about a specialized subject is called a thematic map. The subject could be economic, political, social, cultural, or almost anything that can be expressed geographically. Areas of the map are usually colored to show elements of the subject of a thematic map.

The theme of the map on page 44 is the American land claims of various European nations. Answer the following questions about this thematic map.

1. What is the date of the land claims shown on this map?

2. Which color represents the area under Spanish control? French control? Dutch control? English control?

3. Which nation had the largest claims in North America?

4. Which nation claimed land in the Caribbean?

5. Which nations had claims to part of what is now the United States?

English Settlement in North America 3

English activity in exploration increased toward the end of the sixteenth century. Many people in England wanted to share in the glory of expansion. How did the English hope to benefit from exploration?

England is located on an island separated from the continent of Europe by a narrow channel. Part of its coast also faces the Atlantic Ocean. English leaders knew that Spain was building a rich empire across the ocean during the 1500's. They were eager to share in the wealth of the New World. But for much of the sixteenth century, their attention was centered on events in England and in Europe.

1. English Backgrounds

During the last half of the 1400's, the English had been caught up in several civil wars over the throne. The Wars of the Roses, as they were called, ended in 1485, and the noble who finally won was Henry Tudor. He came to the throne as King Henry VII and worked to restore law and order to the country. He also encouraged English business and trade and improved the country's money system.

What were the Wars of the Roses?

1.1 Claims and Conflicts. Henry VII showed interest in the New World shortly after the first voyage of Christopher Columbus. He hired an Italian sea captain called John Cabot in 1497 to explore part of the new lands for England. Cabot sailed to the shores of Newfoundland and traveled the coast as far south as what is now Delaware. Henry VII did not have money to follow up Cabot's explorations. But from those voyages, England later made its claims to the lands which one Spanish official had called "the cold and frozen North."

Which English monarch first showed interest in the New World?

During the reign of Henry's son, Henry VIII, there was also great unrest in England over religion. Like most Europeans, the English people were members of the Catholic church headed by the pope in Rome. In the 1520's, Henry VIII had a disagreement with the pope. As a result, Henry persuaded Parliament (the English lawmaking body) to break church ties between England and Rome. In 1534, Parliament passed the acts that set up the Church of England, or the Anglican church, and made the English monarch its head. In the next years, there was much bitter conflict in many parts of the kingdom. Some people wanted to remain Catholic, some followed the Church of England, and some adopted other forms of Protestant worship.

1.2 The Rule of Elizabeth. In 1558, Queen Elizabeth I, one of Henry's daughters, came to the throne of England. She was a strong ruler who firmly established the power of the crown. She worked to create religious as well as political unity in the country. Elizabeth made the Church of England a single, national church. All loyal English

What did Elizabeth I do?

English Settlement in North America 49

people were expected to belong to it. She also strengthened the English economy. She encouraged *manufacturing*—making goods by hand or machine—and promoted the sale of English wool to other countries.

Elizabeth also supported the growth of English sea power. For some time, England had been a rival of Spain, Europe's leading sea power and a strong Catholic country. In the mid-1500's, conflict between the two countries grew. With Elizabeth's approval, English sea captains raided Spanish treasure ships returning from the Americas, taking their cargoes. Sir John Hawkins and Sir Francis Drake were two of the most successful of these English "sea dogs," or raiders. Setting out in 1577, Drake sailed through the Strait of Magellan, north along the Pacific coast to what is now San Francisco Bay, and on around the world. He was the first English captain to do so, and he brought much gold and silver from Spanish ships back to England with him.

1.3 Early Exploration and Settlement.   During the late 1500's, England became richer, safer, and stronger. More English sailors explored and mapped the lands along the north Atlantic coast of North America. In 1576, Martin Frobisher sailed to Baffin Land, west of Greenland, and entered what is now called Frobisher Bay. John Davis explored most of Baffin Bay in 1585. A few years later, John Knight explored much of Newfoundland and Labrador. All of these sea captains were searching for the Northwest Passage to Asia. They did not find it, but they did claim the areas they explored for England.

Little by little, Queen Elizabeth took more interest in North America. In 1583, she sent Sir Humphrey Gilbert and five ships to find a place on the coast of North America for settlement. A colony there could serve as a base for England against Spain. Gilbert's ships arrived safely in Newfoundland. The plans for a settlement, however, were put off when Gilbert was lost at sea on his return trip. The following year Elizabeth asked Sir Walter Raleigh to look in other parts of North America for lands suited for colonies.

Raleigh sent several groups to explore the lands farther south. He named part of the area Virginia in honor of Queen Elizabeth, who was called the "Virgin Queen." In 1587, Raleigh sent about 150 men and women led by John White to start a settlement on Roanoke Island. There a baby named Virginia Dare was born—the first English child born in the New World. The first supply ships from England did not return to Roanoke for three years. When they arrived, all the colonists were gone. Searchers found only the letters CRO cut into a tree and the word CROATOAN carved into a doorpost.

The supply ships for the "lost colony" had been delayed by events in Europe. The rivalry between England and Spain over the years had

What explorers established English claims in parts of Canada?

For whom was Virginia named?

Major English Explorations

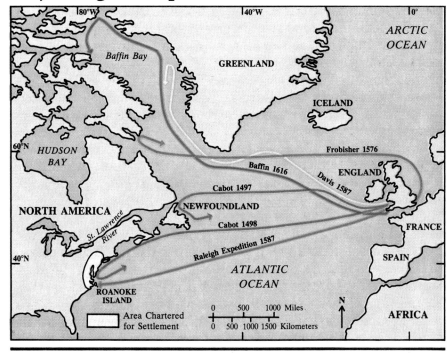

Most English explorers of the late 1500's and early 1600's were looking for a way around or through North America. They searched for the Northwest Passage. Only Raleigh's expedition led to settlement. How were the other explorations later used by the English to claim more of North America?

grown into war. King Philip II of Spain was very angry about the sinking of Spanish ships and the stealing of their gold by English "sea dogs." In 1588, he sent a great *armada*—fleet of warships—against England. The Spanish Armada, once in the narrow channel, was scattered by heavy storms. The guns of the smaller English ships greatly damaged the heavy Spanish vessels. With the defeat of the Spanish Armada, England became Europe's major naval power.

How did England become Europe's major naval power?

1. Which explorer provided the basis for England's claim to land in the New World?
2. What actions by the English led to war with Spain?
3. Where was the first English settlement in the New World?

2. First Permanent Colonies _____

The English still had not established a lasting settlement in the New World when Queen Elizabeth died in 1603. The English crown passed to her cousin, James Stuart, who was also King James VI of Scotland. He took the title James I of England and ruled both kingdoms. The new king was unpopular with the rich English nobles and had little money of his own. He wanted New World trade and settlements, but he could not pay to start colonies. Instead, he encouraged private (nongovernment) trading companies to do so.

2.1 Joint Stock Companies.   Most individuals, like the king, could not afford to start colonies by themselves. They chose to form groups called *joint stock companies*. In these, the head of the group asked the king for a *charter*. It was an official paper giving permission for settlements and trade in a certain area. It also allowed the company to sell shares to raise money for settlement. The *investors*—people who bought shares in the company—expected to make a profit from the trade carried on by the settlers. The charter also set some of the rules for the colony, often allowing the company to set the rest.

What is a joint stock company?

In 1606, James I granted a charter forming two joint stock companies known together as the Virginia Company. They were to settle the lands claimed by England in North America. One joint stock company, the London Company, was granted rights to settlement of the southern area including what is now North Carolina and Virginia. The other company was the Plymouth Company. It was given the northern region, most of which is now known as New England.

2.2 The Jamestown Settlement.   The London Company was the first to make a lasting English settlement in North America. It sent a group of 105 colonists to explore the area around the Chesapeake Bay. There, in the spring of 1607, the colonists started a settlement and called it Jamestown in honor of the king. It was the beginning of the colony of Virginia.

What was the first permanent English settlement in the New World?

Disease and lack of food killed more than two thirds of the colonists in their first few months. Those who lived seemed more interested in searching for gold and silver than in planting crops. Two supply ships from England arrived in Jamestown the next year, but the settlers still faced very hard times. The colony survived mostly because of Captain John Smith. Smith was a soldier who served as the colony's leader. He forced the settlers to work, especially at growing their own food. Smith also bargained for food from the powerful chief of the Powhatan Indians. The chief, called Powhatan by the settlers, controlled 200 villages near Jamestown. The Indians could have crushed the settlers, but Powhatan chose to trade rather than to make war.

Who was the leader of the Jamestown colony?

As time passed, the London Company sent more farmers to the Virginia colony. They planted crops and raised herds of animals on the

Land Grants, 1606

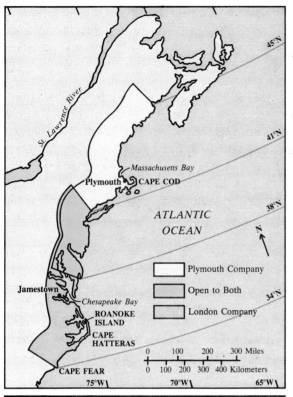

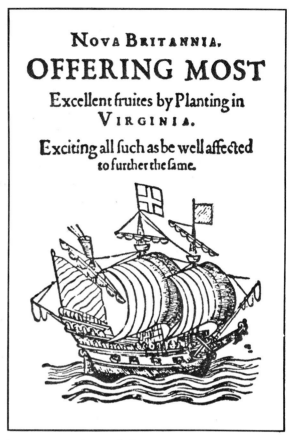

Both the Virginia Company and the London Company tried to attract settlers to their land in the New World. This advertisement was published in 1609. What did these companies have to offer a future settler?

lands they got from the Indians. About 1612, a settler named John Rolfe began planting fields of Indian tobacco. In a few years, tobacco became an important crop that brought high prices in England. Rolfe married Pocahontas, the daughter of Powhatan, in 1614. For a while, relations between the Indians and the settlers were friendly. The Virginia colony grew as thousands of men and women came to settle there. Then beginning in 1619, disease swept through the colony, killing nearly 4,000 settlers. During this time, the Powhatan Indians and the colonists fought over the land. After many battles, the colonists slowly gained control of the area.

During the early years, a lasting government began to take form in Virginia. By their charter, the owners of the London Company in England had the right to name a governor and a council to run the colony. All land belonged to the company, and the settlers worked it for

What crop became important for the Virginia economy?

Jamestown was well established by the 1630's. Trade with the Indians and the firm leadership of John Smith had helped it survive. How was its location near water also important to its growth?

What was the first legislature in the English colonies?

the company. The land policy did not work well, and in 1619, the company began granting land to individuals. That same year, the settlers were also given a voice in the running of the colony's government. They elected representatives to a *legislature*—lawmaking body—called the House of Burgesses. These people could pass laws, but those laws could be *vetoed,* or put aside, by the governor. The laws could also be vetoed by the London Company. Although its power was limited, the House of Burgesses was the first representative form of government in North America.

The London Company made little profit from the Virginia colony. Its leaders in England ran the company badly and quarreled bitterly among themselves. In 1624, James I took away their charter and brought Virginia under direct royal control. From then on, the king named the governor as well as members of the governor's council. The House of Burgesses continued as the elected legislature.

2.3 The Plymouth Colony. The Plymouth Company became the Council for New England in 1620, with the right to grant land to settlers for colonies. The first people to take advantage of this left England for America not only for money and land, but also for the kind of religious freedom they could not find in their homeland.

Many English people did not like the forms of worship that Queen Elizabeth had established for the Church of England. They believed that she had kept too many *rituals,* or forms of service, from the

Catholic church. Some who joined the national church wanted to work to make it better or to "purify" it. Because of this, they became known as Puritans. Others wanted to separate from the church, and they were known as Separatists. James I looked upon persons who were not followers of the Church of England as dangerous troublemakers. He made life so hard for the Separatists that a group of them left England in 1608. They settled in Holland where they stayed for 11 years.

How did Puritans and Separatists differ?

The Separatists heard about the success of the Jamestown colony in Virginia. After returning from Holland to England, they received a charter to start a settlement in that area of America, too. In 1620, the *Mayflower* set sail from England with 35 Separatists and 66 other passengers aboard. These people were also called Pilgrims because they were travelers in a strange land. They were headed for Virginia, but strong winds blew their ship farther north. They landed in New England just north of Cape Cod Bay, in what is now Massachusetts.

The Pilgrim leaders, including William Bradford and Captain Miles Standish, realized that they had not reached Virginia. Some of the people were upset, saying that they had only been given the right to settle and set up a government in Virginia. In order to prevent any possible trouble, 41 passengers of the *Mayflower* signed a **compact,** or agreement, to set up a civil government and to obey its laws. This Mayflower Compact was the basis for government in the colony. It said:

What established the basis of government for Plymouth?

> *We, whose names are underwritten . . . Having undertaken for the Glory of God, and Advancement of the Christian Faith, and the Honor of our King and Country, a Voyage to plant the first colony in the northern Parts of Virginia; Do . . . solemnly and mutually in the Presence of God and one another, covenant and combine ourselves together into a civil Body Politic, for our better Ordering and Preservation . . . .*

In late 1620, the Pilgrims began building a small settlement. They called it Plymouth after the town in England from which they had sailed. Their first winter was a hard one. Half the colonists died from the cold, illness, or the lack of food. Their lives became somewhat easier in the spring. They began to plant the large fields left by Indians who had died in an epidemic. They received help from Squanto, a Pawtuxet Indian. Squanto had been taken to England earlier by an explorer. He had lived there for a time and could speak English. Squanto stayed with the Pilgrims, teaching them useful Indian ways of living in the wilderness. The settlers also made a peace treaty with Massasoit, chief of the nearby Wampanoag Indians. It lasted for over 40 years.

Who aided the Pilgrims?

In time, the Pilgrims got an official land grant from the Council of New England. They governed themselves for the next 70 years with

Forty-one passengers of the *Mayflower* signed the Mayflower Compact on November 21, 1620. Why did the Pilgrims need the agreement?

almost no outside control. Plymouth became a small, independent settlement in New England with its own elected governor and council. Life was never easy in Plymouth, but the settlers made a fair living by farming, fishing, and trading.

Why did the Puritans come to the New World?

2.4 Massachusetts Bay Colony. A number of educated and wealthy Puritans in England formed the Massachusetts Bay Company in 1629. They received a charter and a grant of land in America. The Puritans took their charter with them when they left for America. They did not want to be controlled by people in England, as the colonists in Jamestown had been. The Puritans wanted to be independent and to govern themselves according to their own ideas.

More than 1,000 settlers arrived in Massachusetts in 1630. They founded Boston and several other towns. Many of these settlers died during the first hard winter, and some returned to England in the spring. People came to the colony in great numbers in the next few years, however. By 1640, the population was about 16,000.

The Puritans practiced in Massachusetts the type of religious life they had wanted in England. They set up a congregational form of worship. In it, each congregation was an independent group which chose its own minister and decided its own local church policies. The Puritan places of worship were called *meeting houses*. They were used for both religious services and day-to-day activities of government.

John Winthrop, the governor, and the other leaders tried to keep Massachusetts government in the hands of a small group of important Puritans. The legislature was called the General Court. It passed a law in 1631 that only members of the Congregational church could become voters. Few people were allowed to become church members, so the number of voters was limited. Beginning in 1634, the voters in each town chose three people to represent them in the General Court. This set up a form of representative government.

How did the Puritans restrict political rights?

2.5 Rhode Island and Connecticut. There were many restrictions on life in the Massachusetts Bay Colony. Because of this, many settlers decided to leave and start their own settlements elsewhere. One of the first to go was Roger Williams. He had been a minister in Salem, a town north of Boston. Williams believed that people should be able to worship as they pleased and that the church and the government should be separate. He also spoke out against taking land from the Indians.

Who was the first to speak out against Puritan practices?

Massachusetts leaders were angered by Williams and decided to send him back to England in 1635. Williams and five friends fled into the forests and made their way south to Narragansett Bay. Williams bought a nearby piece of land from the Narragansett Indians and started a settlement he called Providence. Religion was not used as a basis for voting, and people did not have to pay taxes to support the church.

Some other people from Massachusetts followed Williams into the area south of Boston. One of them was Anne Hutchinson, whose religious views also upset the Boston leaders. Hutchinson founded a settlement to the south of Providence. Before long, there were several settlements in the area. Roger Williams went to England in 1643. He received a charter for the various settlements the next year, and they became the colony of Rhode Island.

How did Rhode Island become a colony?

Other groups from Massachusetts moved west toward the Connecticut Valley. The Reverend Thomas Hooker led a group who established Hartford and several other towns. Their plan for government was called the Fundamental Orders of Connecticut. It allowed more voters to take part in the affairs of the settlement than did Massachusetts Bay. Other Massachusetts Puritans founded the town of New Haven in 1637. The king of England granted a charter in 1662 which joined New Haven and Hartford and set up the colony of Connecticut.

2.6 The Colony of Maryland. Charters to set up colonies such as Virginia and Plymouth had been given by English kings to private groups. The kings also gave charters to some of their rich friends. These people became known as *proprietors,* and they were given large areas of land in America. There they founded *proprietary colonies.* The

What was a proprietary colony?

Thomas Hooker and his followers (left) moved into Connecticut in 1636. Anne Hutchinson (right) moved to Rhode Island in 1638. Why did both people leave the Massachusetts Bay Colony?

Who founded the first proprietary colony?

proprietors most often stayed in England. They chose officials to lead their colonies and had direct control over them.

The first proprietary colony founded in North America was Maryland. It was a result of efforts of a Catholic English noble. George Calvert, the first Lord Baltimore, wanted land in America to gain wealth for his family and to be a refuge for fellow Catholics from England. Charles I granted the Calvert family a large piece of land north of the Potomac River near Virginia in 1632. It became the proprietary colony of Maryland.

The first group of some 200 colonists arrived in Maryland in the spring of 1634. From the beginning, the colony did well. The climate and soil were ideal for farming. A representative assembly gave the people a voice in the running of their colony. People of many religions came to live in Maryland. By the mid-1600's, there were more Protestants than Catholics. To protect religious freedom for both groups in Maryland, the Toleration Act was passed in 1649. It granted freedom of worship to all people who believed in Jesus Christ. Catholics lost much of their political power, however, as the number of Protestants grew in Maryland.

2.7 Maine and New Hampshire. As early as 1622, the areas north of Massachusetts had been settled by people from that colony. In 1629, the area was given to two English citizens who later became proprietors. Sir Ferdinando Gorges received most of Maine, while John Mason got New Hampshire. The king wanted these territories in safe, trustworthy hands for two reasons. He wanted to control the huge forest areas of Maine and New Hampshire. Great amounts of lumber, tar, pitch, and resin were needed by the English navy for building and repairing ships. The king also hoped that the two colonies would weaken the power of Puritan Massachusetts.

Why did the crown want Maine and New Hampshire to be proprietary colonies?

Things in Maine and New Hampshire did not work out as the English hoped. Over the years, Massachusetts Bay slowly and quietly bought up the holdings of the Gorges family. It took over Maine as well as the colony of Plymouth in 1691. Massachusetts also tried to buy New Hampshire from members of the Mason family. To prevent this, New Hampshire was changed in 1679 from a proprietary colony to a *royal colony,* one under the direct control of the king. It was the first royal colony in New England.

How did Massachusetts gain control of Maine?

1. How were the first settlements financed?
2. What hardships did the first settlers face?
3. Which two religious groups formed settlements in Massachusetts?
4. How was the colony of Maryland different from the other early colonies?

3. Later Colonies

While the first English colonies were being started in North America, relations between Charles I and Parliament broke down. Both sides raised armies and began a civil war in 1642. The forces of Parliament slowly gained power and defeated the royal army in 1646. Charles I was executed in 1649. For the next 11 years, England did not have a king. The leader was a member of Parliament, a Puritan named Oliver Cromwell. His title was "Lord Protector." During this period, no new colonies were founded in America. Those which had already been set up were allowed to handle their own affairs. Then in 1658, Cromwell died. English leaders invited the oldest son of Charles I to be king in 1660. He took the throne as Charles II. The period that followed proved to be a very active time of English colonization in America.

What caused a break in the English colonization of America?

Reading Time Lines
SKILL

Knowing the relation of time to events is important to studying history. Time lines can help to show that relation. The first time line below marks the period during which England started its colonies in North America. Each of the 13 colonies is labeled at a particular section of the time line when it was founded. Study the time line, and answer the following questions.

1. Which colony was founded first?
2. Which of the colonies was last?
3. In which century were most of the colonies founded?
4. How is Georgia different from the rest of the colonies?

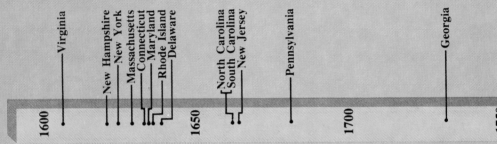

Time in relation to people is often expressed in generations. The time line below covers the same period of time as the one above. It is about several generations of the Adams family of Massachusetts. Beginning with Henry Adams in England, it continues to the birth of John Adams, who became the second President of the United States.

1. How many generations of the Adams family lived during this time?
2. How was John Adams related to Henry Adams?

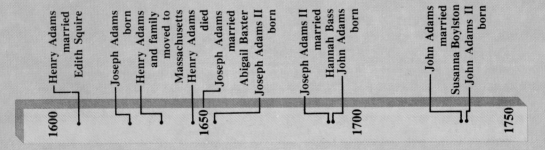

3.1 The Carolina Grant. Three years after Charles II took the throne of England, he granted eight nobles a large piece of land in America. This proprietary colony of Carolina ran from the southern border of Virginia to the northern border of Spanish Florida. The proprietors expected to make money as landowners, managing large estates producing olives, wine, silk, turpentine, and pitch.

Many people moved into the area of Carolina to live. The northern part was settled mostly by people who came from Virginia. They set up small farms, and tobacco was the main crop. The southern part of Carolina was settled mostly by people who were sent to the colony by the proprietors in England. Some founded the port settlement of Charles Town (later Charleston). The area grew rapidly and developed an active trade with England, the West Indies, and other colonies. The southern section broke away from the proprietors in 1719 and became the royal colony of South Carolina. Ten years later, the king took back the whole grant, and North Carolina also became a royal colony.

Who settled the Carolinas?

3.2 New York and New Jersey. By the early 1660's, the Dutch still held the areas of New Netherland and what had been New Sweden. This kept England from controlling the entire Atlantic coast from Spanish Florida in the south to French Canada in the north. Charles II set about to change that situation. He gave his brother James, the Duke of York, title to the entire area from Connecticut south to Maryland in 1664. He then sent four ships across the Atlantic Ocean to take the area from the Dutch.

The Dutch settlers first learned of these plans when the people living in New Amsterdam saw the powerful English ships anchored in their harbor. Seeing that fighting was useless, the Dutch allowed the English to take over. The English let the Dutch keep their own language, religion, customs, and ways of life.

Both the colony of New Netherland and the town of New Amsterdam were renamed New York in honor of the Duke. James, in turn, gave the area between the Hudson and Delaware rivers to two friends, Lord John Berkeley and Sir George Carteret. This area became the colony of New Jersey. It soon attracted many nearby settlers because of its generous land terms. With the addition of New York and New Jersey, the English empire in North America ran in a single, unbroken line along the Atlantic coast from Maine to South Carolina.

For whom was New York named?

3.3 Pennsylvania. After England took New York and New Jersey, it was 17 years before another English colony was set up in America. The colony of Pennsylvania, chartered in 1681, was the work of William Penn. Penn was a member of the Society of Friends, or

Dr. Alexander Hamilton (1712–1756)

===PROFILE===

In the 1700's, travel in the colonies was not easy. Every trip took careful planning. Transportation and roads were poor, and there were few maps. Each colony had different money, and robberies were frequent.

On the morning of May 30, 1744, Dr. Alexander Hamilton, a medical doctor, and a servant named Dromo set out from Annapolis, Maryland, to tour the colonies. They traveled on horseback, and their trip took them as far north as York in Maine. On the way, they visited Baltimore, Philadelphia, Trenton, New York, Providence, Boston, and New Haven. By the time they returned on September 27, Hamilton and Dromo had seen more of the colonies than most of the people living in America.

Hamilton described the trip as covering about 1,600 miles (2,560 kilometers).

Hamilton kept careful records of the people he met and the places he visited. He described the growing unity in colonial America. Americans of different colonies appeared to him to be more alike than people in different parts of some European countries.

After the trip, Hamilton continued to practice medicine, and he served in Maryland's colonial legislature. Hamilton is best remembered, however, for writing about his travels. When it was published, his book was one of the most accurate first-hand accounts of colonial life in the mid-1700's.

Quakers. This group believed that people did not need established churches or ministers to worship God. They did not approve of war and refused to serve in the army. They also refused to pay taxes to the government or the Church of England. Because of their beliefs, Quakers were often persecuted.

Who settled Pennsylvania?

William Penn asked Charles II for land in America where Quakers and people of other faiths could worship God in their own ways. The king owed a debt to Penn's father and gave Penn a grant of land west of the Delaware River in 1681. It was called Pennsylvania (Penn's woods).

Settlers from many countries with many religions came to Pennsylvania. Quakers from England, Presbyterians from Scotland,

William Penn signed treaties with the Indians and tried to honor them. How did peace between the Delaware Indians and the Pennsylvania colonists affect the growth of the colony?

Catholics from Ireland, Huguenots (Protestants) from France, Calvinists from Holland, Lutherans from Germany, and many others established settlements there. Only eight years after its founding, Pennsylvania had over 11,000 settlers. They produced large amounts of wheat, flour, beef, and pork. The main city, Philadelphia, was a settlement of brick houses, with a planned system of streets. Philadelphia was the largest and busiest city in the English colonies by 1750.

Why was Penn given a land grant?

3.4 Delaware. Pennsylvania had no outlet to the Atlantic Ocean. So William Penn got a grant from the Duke of York in 1682 for an area called Delaware, first settled by the Swedes. Delaware was governed by the leaders of Pennsylvania for almost 20 years. People from Delaware elected their own representative assembly in 1701. For some years after that, the two colonies were separate but shared the same governor.

Why did Penn seek a grant from the Duke of York?

3.5 Georgia. The last English colony in North America was established 50 years after Pennsylvania was founded. James Oglethorpe, an English reformer, wanted to create a refuge for people who were in English prisons because they could not pay their debts. The English government saw this as a chance to set up a military defense against the Spaniards in Florida. So in 1732, George II granted Oglethorpe a charter for the land between the Savannah River and the Florida border. The colony, named Georgia after the king, grew slowly. Some of the debtors refused to work and ran away. Oglethorpe's plans to produce wine and silk failed to work out, and the people spent much

Why did Georgia grow slowly?

English Settlement in North America 63

time fighting the Spanish. In 1752, the king took over, and Georgia became a royal colony.

1. How did England gain control of New York and New Jersey?
2. Which group established the colony of Pennsylvania?
3. Who founded the colony of Georgia? Why?

4. Governing the Colonies _____

During the early 1600's, England did not have a definite plan for governing the colonies. Jamestown, Plymouth, Massachusetts Bay, Rhode Island, and Connecticut all began without direct involvement of the crown. As years went by, most of these colonies took care of their own affairs. The proprietary colonies, too, were not firmly controlled by the English government. Although the king personally appointed the proprietors and was supposed to approve all decisions, he seldom knew what was going on across the ocean. In a short time, colonies like Maryland and New Hampshire had few close ties with the crown.

What did Charles II do to gain more control over the colonies?

4.1   Royal Colony Government.   By 1660, the English colonial system in America was made up of many different settlements spread out along the Atlantic coast. It was a loose grouping with no real unity. Charles II decided to take a more active role by forming royal colonies. In these, the governor and the members of the council (the upper house) were chosen by the crown. The assembly (the lower house) was elected by the colonists. The governor, with the council and the assembly, governed the colony by the crown's rules. In this way, the crown took part directly in the governing of a royal colony.

Why did the British have trouble governing the colonies?

Even with the growing number of royal colonies, England was having trouble with so many different colonies spread over such a great area. The people were used to leading their own lives and making their own rules. They had run their own assemblies and selected their own representatives. They chose their own church leaders, built their own ships, and set up their own defense. They often failed to pay their taxes to England. They fought with governors they did not like and refused to obey English laws. These problems were more common in the New England colonies which were not royal colonies. They had strong local assemblies and did not regard the authority of England very highly.

4.2   The Dominion of New England.   Charles II died in 1685 and was succeeded by his brother James, the Duke of York. James II

Settlement in the Thirteen Colonies

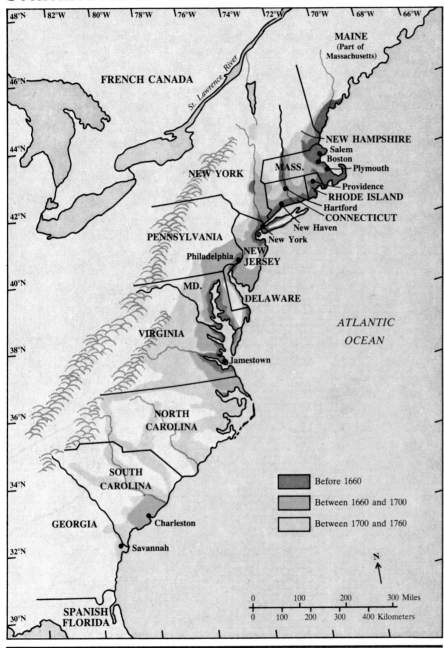

By 1760, about 95 percent of the colonists lived in rural areas, usually on farms or in small villages. The other 5 percent lived in cities. How was expansion affected by a growth in population? What might have motivated settlers to move farther west over this period of time?

The Colonies

Colony Date Founded	Original Founder	Reasons Founded	Type of Government
Virginia **1607**	London Company	Expand trade	Charter (1606–1624) Royal (1624)
Maine **1622**	Ferdinando Gorges John Mason	Profit for founders from trade and fishing	Proprietary (1622–1691) Part of Massachusetts (1691–1820)
New Hampshire **1622**	Ferdinando Gorges John Mason	Profit for founders from trade and fishing	Proprietary (1622–1641) Part of Massachusetts (1641–1679) Royal (1679)
New York **1624**	Peter Minuit	Expand Dutch trade	Dutch Colony (1624–1664) Proprietary (1664–1685) Royal (1685)
Massachusetts **1629**	Massachusetts Bay Company (Puritans)	Expand trade Religious freedom	Charter (1629–1691) Royal (1691)
Connecticut **1633**	Thomas Hooker	Expand trade Religious freedom	Self-governing Charter (1662)
Maryland **1634**	George Calvert	Profit for founder from selling land Religious freedom	Proprietary (1634–1691) Royal (1691–1715) Proprietary (1715)
Rhode Island **1636**	Roger Williams	Religious freedom	Self-governing Charter (1644)
Delaware **1638**	Swedish South Company	Expand Swedish trade	Swedish Colony (1638–1655) Dutch Colony (1655–1664) Proprietary (1664–1682) Part of Pennsylvania (1682–1701) Self-governing Charter (1701)
North Carolina **1663**	Anthony Cooper John Colleton William Berkeley	Profit for founders from trade and selling land	Proprietary (1663–1719) Royal (1719)
South Carolina **1663**	Anthony Cooper John Colleton William Berkeley	Profit for founders from trade and selling land	Proprietary (1663–1719) Royal (1719)
New Jersey **1664**	John Berkeley George Carteret	Profit for founders from selling land	Proprietary (1664–1702) Royal (1702)
Pennsylvania **1681**	William Penn	Profit for founder from selling land Religious freedom	Proprietary (1681)
Georgia **1732**	James Oglethorpe	Profit for founder Refuge for debtors Military defense	Proprietary (1732–1752) Royal (1752)

immediately went ahead with a plan to reorganize the colonies. The governments of New York, New Jersey, Connecticut, Rhode Island, Plymouth, Massachusetts Bay, New Hampshire, and Maine were joined to form the Dominion of New England. This was meant to create a strong, unified area on the border of French Canada. It was also supposed to bring Puritan colonies like Massachusetts under control.

The Dominion of New England was headed by a powerful governor, Sir Edmund Andros, appointed by the king. Andros was assisted by a council whose members were also appointed. He was a capable manager, but his style quickly made bitter enemies. Andros angered important Puritan leaders in Boston by refusing to accept Congregationalism as the official religion. He angered citizens by limiting them to one town meeting a year. He angered almost everyone when he raised taxes without going through the local assemblies.

How did Andros anger the people?

4.3 The Glorious Revolution.   Events in England put a sudden stop to the Dominion of New England. The English people drove out the unpopular James II in 1688. They asked his daughter Mary and her husband William to be joint rulers. This change was called the "Glorious Revolution." When news of it reached the colonies, some people in Boston rose up against Governor Andros. In April 1689, they put him and his council in prison and the Dominion ended.

What was the Glorious Revolution?

William and Mary agreed to give Massachusetts a new charter, but they made some changes. Although they insisted that the governor still be appointed by the crown, they did agree that the council could be chosen by the lower house. They also did away with the religious requirements for voting in the Bay Colony. The right to vote and to hold office became based on property ownership rather than on church membership. For the most part, however, things went back to the way they had been in Massachusetts and the other colonies.

1. What was a royal colony?
2. Why was the Dominion of New England created?

5. Conclusion

English plans for colonial organization and unity had failed by the early 1700's. The English colonies throughout North America were still as separate and divided as they had been during the 1600's. Each colony generally kept to itself and had its own government. Religions, points of view, and ways of doing things often differed. The colonies had no central government, capital city, or ruler—except the ruler of England who lived 3,000 miles (4,800 kilometers) away across the Atlantic.

Chapter 3 Review

Main Points

1. England was slow to enter the race for colonies in the New World because of political unrest at home.
2. During the reign of Queen Elizabeth I, England became the leading European naval power.
3. Between 1607 and 1732, England established colonies along the east coast of North America.
4. The English colonies were set up by joint stock companies, by proprietors, or by the English government.
5. English colonies were settled by people looking for land, money, and religious freedom.
6. The Glorious Revolution in England put an end to the English plan to centralize the colonial government.

Building Vocabulary

1. Identify the following:

John Cabot	Powhatan	John Winthrop	William Penn
Parliament	House of Burgesses	Roger Williams	Dr. Alexander Hamilton
Sir Francis Drake	Puritans	Anne Hutchinson	James Oglethorpe
Spanish Armada	Mayflower Compact	Toleration Act	Dominion of New England
Jamestown			

2. Define the following:

manufacturing	charter	vetoed	meeting houses
armada	investors	rituals	proprietors
joint stock companies	legislature	compact	proprietary colonies
			royal colony

Remembering the Facts

1. What delayed English efforts to establish colonies in the New World?
2. When did England begin to settle colonies in North America?
3. Which of the English colonies were set up by joint stock companies? by proprietors? as royal colonies?
4. How did Indians aid settlers at Jamestown and Plymouth?
5. Which colonies were started by people who left the Massachusetts Bay Colony?
6. Which English colony was first settled by the Dutch? How did the English government gain control of it?
7. How did England try to organize the governing of the colonies?
8. How did the Glorious Revolution in England affect the colonies?

Understanding the Facts

1. Why was tobacco important to the colony of Virginia?
2. Why did the Pilgrims, Puritans, and Quakers disagree with the Church of England?
3. Why was the Mayflower Compact important?
4. Why did people leave the Massachusetts Bay Colony?
5. Why did England want control of New Netherland and New Sweden?
6. Why did England plan to centralize the northeastern colonial governments under the Dominion of New England?

Using Maps

Longitude and Latitude. Because of the huge size of the earth, a way of easily identifying locations is needed. One way to do this is to draw two types of imaginary lines circling the globe. When maps are drawn, these lines are added, too.

One set of these lines runs north and south from north pole to south pole. These are called meridians, or lines of longitude. The distance between them is measured in degrees east or west of the prime (original) meridian. The prime meridian is labeled 0°. Since England was a world leader in exploration and mapmaking when the system was set up, the prime meridian runs through England.

The second set of lines runs east and west, but they do not come together at any one point. These are called parallels, or lines of latitude. The prime parallel is the equator, and it is labeled 0°. Latitude is measured in degrees according to the distance north or south of the equator.

By using these lines, we can identify any place on the earth as being at some degree east or west longitude and some degree north or south latitude.

Examine the map on page 65, and answer the following questions.

1. Between which lines of north latitude is the colony of Virginia?
2. Which line of west longitude runs along the eastern coast of Virginia?
3. Which parallel divides the Pennsylvania colony from the Maryland colony?
4. What is the one colony which lies entirely west of 80° west longitude?
5. Which colonies are crossed by the parallel at 40° north latitude?
6. Between which parallels do the English colonies lie?

Secota 1584-1587

ATLANTIC OCEAN

Albemarle Sound

36°N

ROANOKE ISLAND

Secota

Pomeiock

Croatoan

CAPE HATTERAS

Pamlico Sound

N

35°N

0 ... 10 ... 20 ... 30 Miles
0 ... 10 ... 20 ... 30 ... 40 Kilometers

Secota was a Powhatan Indian town near Roanoke Island in what is now the eastern part of North Carolina. In 1584, it was part of the land which Queen Elizabeth asked Sir Walter Raleigh to colonize for England. Raleigh hired Arthur Barlowe to lead the first group of English explorers to the area.

At different times, several groups were sent to explore and settle the area which became Virginia and North Carolina. John White drew pictures of the Indians, their towns, and the plants, fish, and birds which he saw on his trips. Barlowe, White, and a third explorer, Thomas Hariot, wrote down their descriptions of the new land for the people back in England. By reading the descriptions and looking at the pictures, Americans today can get an idea of how some earlier Americans, the Indians, lived in the 1580's.

Early Towns

Their towns are small and few, . . . a village may contain but ten or twelve houses— some perhaps as many as twenty. . . .

The houses are built of small poles . . . covered from top to bottom either with bark or with mats woven of long rushes. . . .

In one part of the country a . . . chief . . . may govern a single town, but in other parts the number of towns under one chief may vary to two, three, six, and even to eight or more. The greatest [chief] we met governed eighteen towns, and he could [get together] seven or eight hundred warriors. The language of each chief's territory differs from that of the others. . . .

Secota

Those of their towns which are not fenced in are usually more beautiful [like] Secota. The houses are farther apart and have gardens. . . . They also have groves of trees where they hunt deer, and fields where they sow their corn. In the cornfields they set up a little hut on a [platform], where a watchman is stationed. . . . He makes a continual noise to keep off birds and beasts. . . .

They also have a large plot . . . where they meet with neighbors to celebrate solemn feasts. . . . In the [smaller gardens] they sow pumpkins . . . and just outside the town is the river . . . from which they get their water.

The People

The chieftains of Virginia wear their hair long, tied in a knot close to the ears. . . . One long bird's feather is stuck into the [top] and a short one above each ear. They hang large pearls in their ears. . . . Their [faces and bodies] are painted. . . . Around their necks they have a chain of pearls . . . and upon their arms they wear bracelets. . . .

They are dressed in cloaks made of finely cured skins. . . .

The women of Secota [dress in] deerskins. . . . Their hair is cut short in front, somewhat longer at the back, and falls softly to their shoulders. . . . Their foreheads, cheeks, chins, arms, and legs are chalked, and the pattern of a chain is pricked or painted around their necks. . . .

The priests of the town . . . are [very old] and have greater experience than the ordinary [people]. Their hair [also] is cut in a crest on the top of their heads; the rest of it is short and falls over their foreheads like a fringe. Earrings adorn their ears. They wear a short cloak made of fine rabbit skins. . . .

They have sorcerers . . . whose [spells] often go against the laws of nature. For they are very familiar with devils, from whom they [get] knowledge about their enemies' movements.

[These men] shave their heads entirely, except for the crest, which they wear as the others do. A small black bird is [tied] above one of their ears as a badge of office. . . .

The [people] pay great attention to the sorcerer's words, which they often find to be true.

Planting Crops

The soil in the fields around Secota was very rich. Because of the long warm seasons, the Indians were able to bring in three crops of corn a year. To prepare the land for planting: They simply break the upper part of the ground to raise up the weeds, grass, and old stubs of cornstalks with their roots. . . . After the weeds have dried in the sun for a day or two,

John White, governor of Roanoke Island, was also an artist. His watercolors provide a look into the everyday lives of the people of Secota. How does White's painting show Secota was a well-planned town?

[they are] *scraped up into many small heaps and burned. . . .*

Then they sow the seed. For corn they begin in one corner of the plot and make a hole with a [stick]. *They put four grains into each hole . . . and cover them with soil. The seeds are planted in rows. . . . between the holes . . . the* [Indians] *sometimes set beans and peas. . . .*

Secota Cooking

Their women have the greatest skill in making large earthen pots, which are so fine that not even [the English] *can make any better. These are carried around from place to place just as easily as our own brass kettles. They set them up on a pile of earth and then put wood underneath and* [light] *it, taking great care that the fire burns evenly on all sides. They fill the pot with water, then put fruit, meat, and fish into it, and let it boil together as in a* [stew]. *. . . When it is cooled, they serve it in small dishes. . . .*

Catching Fish

They have a [special] *way of fishing in their rivers. As they have neither steel nor iron, they* [tie] *the sharp, hollow tail of a certain fish . . . to reeds or to the end of a long rod, and with this point they spear fish both by day and by night. . . . And they make traps with reeds or sticks set in the water. . . .*

It is a pleasing picture to see these people wading and sailing in their shallow rivers. They [do not] *desire to pile up riches. . . .*

Religion and Law

The people of Secota had many gods. Some were more important to them than others. They believed that their chief god had always lived. He had created the world and then had made other gods to help him create and rule everything else.

Then he made the sun, the moon, and the stars. . . . The [Indians] *say that the waters of the world were made first and that out of these all creatures . . . were formed.*

As to the creation of [people], *they think that the woman came first. She* [had] *children fathered by one of the gods, and in this way the* [Indians] *had their beginning. But how many ages or years have passed since then, they do not know, for they have no writing or any means of keeping records of past time. . . .*

Temples were set up where the Indians worshiped their gods. They made human shapes of the gods, or idols, and prayed and sang to them.

Shown here are various ways the Secotans caught fish. The lighted fire in the canoe attracted the fish at night. What other methods did they use?

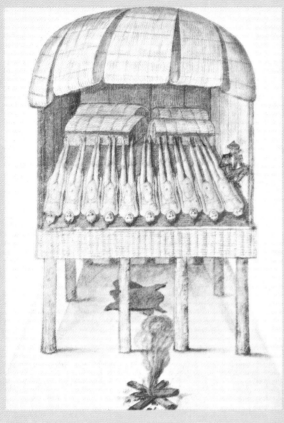

The bodies of dead chiefs were placed on platforms like this. How was the concern for death used to maintain law and order in Secota?

Under the [platform] *lives one of their priests, who is in charge of the dead and* [says] *his prayers night and day. He sleeps on deerskins spread on the ground, and if it is cold, he lights a fire.*

. . . the belief in heaven and the fiery pit makes the [people obey] *their governors and behave with great care, so that they may avoid* [pain] *after death and enjoy bliss. Evil-doers have to pay for their crimes in this world, nevertheless.* [Stealing] *. . . and other wicked acts are punished with fines, beatings, or even with death. . . .*

A Strange Sickness

As the English people stayed on in Virginia, the Indians of Secota and some of the other towns began to turn against them. At the same time, strange things began to happen in the towns which were visited by the English. Hariot wrote that:

. . . within a few days [after we left a town] *the people began to die very fast. In some towns twenty people died, in some forty, in some sixty. . . . And the strange thing was that this occurred only in towns where we had been. . . . The disease . . . was so strange a one that they did not know anything about it or how to cure it. . . .*

[The Indians believed] *that more of our* [people] *would yet come to this country to kill them and to take away their homes.*

Their religion taught them that humans have souls which do not die. After the body died, the soul of a good person would go to heaven. The soul of a bad person would go to a pit called Popogusso, at the farthest end of the world. There it would burn forever. Most of the bodies were buried, but for the chiefs:

. . . they build a [platform] *nine or ten feet high. . . . They cover this with mats and upon them lay the dead bodies of their chiefs* [after the bodies are specially treated]. *. . . Near the bodies they place their idol, for they are* [sure] *that it keeps the bodies of their chiefs from all harm.*

1. Where was Secota located?
2. What role did the sorcerers play?
3. What did the people of Secota look like? What did they wear?
4. What did the people of Secota eat?
5. How did the people of Secota believe the world was created?

Plymouth 1620~1650

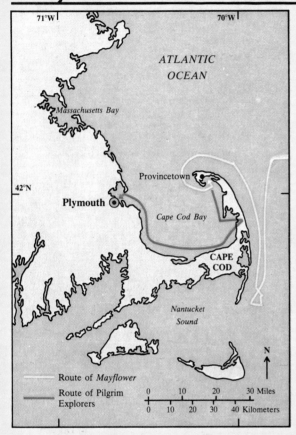

Route of *Mayflower*

Route of Pilgrim Explorers

After 65 days at sea, the *Mayflower* reached the coast of America at the beginning of winter in 1620. The crew, knowing they were too far north, sailed down the coast toward Virginia. The weather was so terrible that they turned back to Cape Cod Bay.

Using small boats from the ship, some of the passengers explored the land for a place to live. They finally found an area they named Plymouth where much of the land had already been cleared by Indians. It had a river and a hill where they could build a fort for safety. The passengers decided to settle there.

The *Mayflower* stayed for the rest of the winter because of the weather and the need for repairs. Many of the passengers lived aboard the crowded ship while they were building houses on the land. Among those settlers who came to Plymouth in 1620 were:

Captain Myles Standish and Rose his wife. . . .

Francis Cooke and his son John; but his wife and other children came afterwards. . . .

Mr. William Mullins and his wife and two children, Joseph and Priscilla; and a servant, Robert Carter. . . .

A Record

William Bradford, a Separatist, was chosen by the Pilgrims to be governor of Plymouth in 1621. He wrote a history, or record, of the many years of hardship that the Pilgrims faced in America. That history still exists today, and from it, people can learn who the Pilgrims were and what happened to them. Bradford was a leader in the settlement for more than 35 years. Much of the information on the following pages comes from his record.

A Hard Beginning

The settlers had a very hard time at first. They had only a few small boats, and the winter winds and rains made the harbor's water very rough. It was not easy to move their goods to land, and it took weeks to get their small houses built.

But that which was most sad . . . was, that in two or three months' time half of their company died, especially in January and February, being the depth of winter, and [needing] *houses and other comforts; being* [sick] *with . . . diseases which this long voyage . . . had brought upon them. So as there died some times two or three of a day . . . of 100 and odd persons,* [only about] *fifty remained. . . .*

All this while the Indians [were watching] *them, and would sometimes show themselves . . . but when any approached near them, they would run away. . . .*

Spring

But about the 16th of March, a certain Indian came boldly amongst them and spoke to them in broken English, which they could well understand. . . . His name was Samoset. He told them also of another Indian whose name was Squanto . . . who had been in England and could speak better English. . . .

Samoset came to visit the Pilgrims again and brought Squanto, Chief Massasoit, and others with him. The Pilgrims and the Indians

The Pilgrims landed in bad weather in the winter of 1620. What special problems did a winter landing present to the Pilgrims?

exchanged gifts and made speeches which Squanto translated. The visit ended after a peace treaty with Massasoit was signed. When the other Indians returned to their homes, Squanto stayed with the Pilgrims to help them learn about the new land.

New Ways for New Land

In a small village like Plymouth, everyone had to work hard for food—hoeing corn and other crops in the summer, digging clams and catching fish in the winter. The Pilgrims were not very skilled in farming and fishing at first. For example, Plymouth Harbor was filled with fish, but they had not brought hooks small enough to catch them. Squanto taught the Pilgrims Indian ways to fish and farm. He showed them where and how to trap and catch fish. He also taught them how and when to plant corn in hills, using fish for fertilizer. Governor Bradford wrote about Squanto's ways.

All which they found true by trial and experience. Some English seed they sowed, as wheat and [peas], *but it came not to good, either by the badness of the seed or lateness of the season or both, or some other* [trouble].

More Problems

Since they were poor people, the Pilgrims had needed help to come to the New World. The Plymouth Company's investors had paid for the voyage and for supplies. But, in return, the settlers had to spend their first seven years working for the company as a group, with common land and property. All of the profits, or extras, from their farming, fishing, and trading went back to London. And the Pilgrims did not like working common fields to fill a common warehouse, with no time to work for themselves and their families.

Pilgrims and Indians celebrated the first Thanksgiving in the New World. How did the Indians help the Plymouth colonists survive?

For the young men, that were most able and fit for [labor] *and service,* [were unhappy] *that they should spend their time and strength to work for other men's wives and children without any* [extra credit]. . . . *this was thought* [unfair]. . . .

In 1623, the common use of land began to change. That year, each family was given a piece of land for planting corn. Bradford wrote that:

This had very good success, for it made all hands very [busy], *so as much more corn was planted than otherwise.* . . . *The women now went willingly into the field, and took their little ones with them to set corn; which before would* [make believe] *weakness and inability.* . . .

Beginning to divide the land among families settled one problem. The trouble of paying back the Plymouth Company lasted for years. The settlers were not good enough at fishing to make a lot of profit, although the demand for dried cod was great in Europe. Most of their profit came from fur trading with the Indians from Cape Cod to Maine. In 1626, their debt was set at about $9,000. By the time they finally paid it off in 1648, the Pilgrims had sent the Plymouth Company furs and other goods worth about $100,000!

Growing

Plymouth, though small, was becoming a stronger settlement by 1627. The chief trading agent of the Dutch West India Company was very pleased with it during his visit that year. He reported that:

New Plymouth lies on the slope of a hill stretching east towards the sea-coast. . . . *The houses are constructed of clapboards, with gardens also enclosed behind and at the sides with clapboards, so that their houses and courtyards are arranged in very good order, with a stockade against sudden attack; and at the ends of the streets there are three wooden gates. In the center, on the cross street, stands the Governor's house, before which is a square stockade upon which four patereros* [guns] *are mounted, so as to enfilade* [cover] *the streets.*

Troubled Times

In the 1630's, many Puritans came to settle in the Boston area. The Pilgrims did make some money by selling cattle and other goods to the new people. But the growth of towns to the north of Plymouth, around the better Boston Harbor, also had a bad effect on the Pilgrim settlement. Soon, fewer ships came into their harbor, and trade fell off. Their fields, worked by the Indians long before the Pilgrims had arrived, were not so rich as some of the newer land. And as children grew up, there was no more land for

Plymouth buildings had walls of rough pine logs filled in with clay. How do the buildings of Plymouth compare to those of Secota?

Captain Standish his wife died in the first sickness and he married again and [has] *four sons living and some are dead. . . .*

Francis Cooke is still living, a very old man, and [has] *seen his children's children have children. After his wife came over with other of his children; he* [has] *three still living by her, all married and have five children, so their increase is eight. And his son John which came over with him is married, and* [has] *four children living. . . .*

Mr. Mullins and his wife, his son and his servant died the first winter. Only his daughter Priscilla survived, and married with John Alden [a *Mayflower* passenger]; *who are both living and have eleven children. And their eldest daughter is married and* [has] *five children. . . .*

Governor Bradford himself died in 1659, but Plymouth did continue. The town grew slowly and, in 1691, became part of the larger Massachusetts Bay Colony. As for the children of the Pilgrims, they also continued to grow in number. Some of them moved out into every part of America.

them near their parents. Some of the first settlers and many of their children began to move farther away. New towns and churches were started in other parts of the settlement. In 1644, the people talked about moving the whole settlement to better land on Cape Cod. Finally, some of the Pilgrim families did move to a place called Nauset. Governor Bradford wrote:

And thus was this poor church [Plymouth] *left, like* [a] *mother grown old and forsaken of her children . . . her* [older people] *being most of them worn away by death, and these of later time being like children* [married] *into other families, and she like a widow left only to trust in God. Thus, she that had made many rich became herself poor.*

Catching Up

In 1650, Bradford reported again on the families who had first come to Plymouth:

1. Where did many of the passengers of the *Mayflower* live during the first winter in Plymouth? Why?
2. Who was William Bradford?
3. Who paid for the Pilgrims' trip to the New World?
4. Compare the diet of the Indians of Secota to that of the Pilgrims of Plymouth.
5. Locate Secota and Plymouth on the maps. From their general locations, compare their climates. What problems would the colonists of Plymouth have that the Indians of Secota would not have?

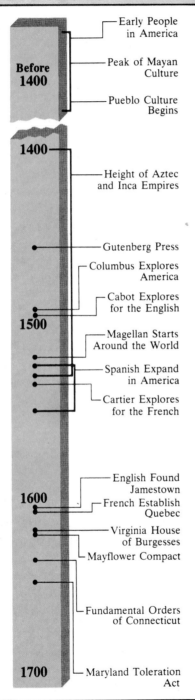

Before
1400

- Early People
  in America

- Peak of Mayan
  Culture

- Pueblo Culture
  Begins

1400

- Height of Aztec
  and Inca Empires

- Gutenberg Press

- Columbus Explores
  America

- Cabot Explores
  for the English

1500

- Magellan Starts
  Around the World

- Spanish Expand
  in America

- Cartier Explores
  for the French

- English Found
  Jamestown

1600

- French Establish
  Quebec

- Virginia House
  of Burgesses

- Mayflower Compact

- Fundamental Orders
  of Connecticut

1700

- Maryland Toleration
  Act

Summary

1. People first entered the Western Hemisphere across a land bridge between Asia and North America.

2. Over centuries, these people settled in all areas of North and South America.

3. Some of the early people established high levels of civilization and strong political units while others lived in small villages or moved from place to place as hunters.

4. European interest in the Western Hemisphere began with ocean voyages in the fifteenth century.

5. In 1492, Christopher Columbus landed in America while looking for an all-water trade route to Asia.

6. Europeans soon realized that Columbus had discovered a New World, with opportunities for adventure, riches, and land for empire.

7. In taking advantage of New World opportunities, Europeans conquered some groups of Indians and took the land of other groups.

8. Spain became the leading nation in exploring the New World, establishing a large empire in Central and South America and in the southwestern part of what is now the United States.

9. Portugal and France also set up empires, while Sweden and Holland had small areas of North America.

10. The English were late in entering the race for land in the New World, but in 1607, they began colonies along the Atlantic coast of North America.

Unit Questions

1. Why did the early people in the Western Hemisphere develop different cultures in the areas of North and South America where they settled?
2. What developments in Europe made it possible to begin sea voyages to unknown parts of the world in the fifteenth century?
3. How did Europeans become interested in Africa in the fifteenth century? Why did they remain interested in the years which followed?
4. What was wrong with the plan of Christopher Columbus to reach Asia by sailing west across the Atlantic Ocean?
5. What were some of the reasons that Europeans were able to enslave Indians and Africans?
6. What attracted people in the Old World to the New World?
7. Why did the English settle along the Atlantic coast of North America?
8. What were some of the differences in the groups of people and the reasons for settlement in the English, French, and Spanish colonies in America?
9. What were some of the reasons for the growth of a spirit of independence among the English colonies in North America during the 1600's?

Suggested Activities

1. Compare the reports of the first space explorers with the reports of the early explorers to the New World.
2. Select one group of Indian people. Describe the area in which they lived, and show how the environment influenced their way of life.
3. Examine atlases and list the titles of three reference maps and three thematic maps of North America.
4. Gather information on the Dutch or Swedish colonies in North America. Report on how you think these colonies might have survived against the English.

Suggested Readings

Armstrong, Virginia. *I Have Spoken: American History Through the Voices of the Indians*. Chicago: Swallow, 1971. Opinions of the European settlement of the New World are given from the points of view of various American Indians.

Brown, Richard. *The Human Side of American History*. Boston: Ginn & Company, 1962. Personal accounts of great and small events in American history.

Lavine, Sigmund. *The Houses the Indians Built*. New York: Dodd, Mead, & Co., 1975. Differences in the cultures of various Indian groups are shown through a study of their homes, buildings, and shrines.

Loeb, Robert. *Meet the Real Pilgrims: Everyday Life on Plimouth Plantation in 1627*. Garden City, New York: Doubleday, 1975. Looks at the lives of the Pilgrims in early New England.

Independence

Independence was a spirit that became evident early in the history of the American people. Far from established rules and restrictions on life in the Old World, people began to make their own laws and develop their own ways of doing things in the New World. When the freedom to be independent was threatened, American people fought to defend and preserve it. The spirit of independence contributed to the emergence of a new nation, government, and culture that was separate from the old.

Colonial Society 4

Bethlehem, Pennsylvania, was the main settlement in North America of one of the Protestant groups, the Moravians. This view of it was drawn in 1757. How did most settlers in the English colonies make a living?

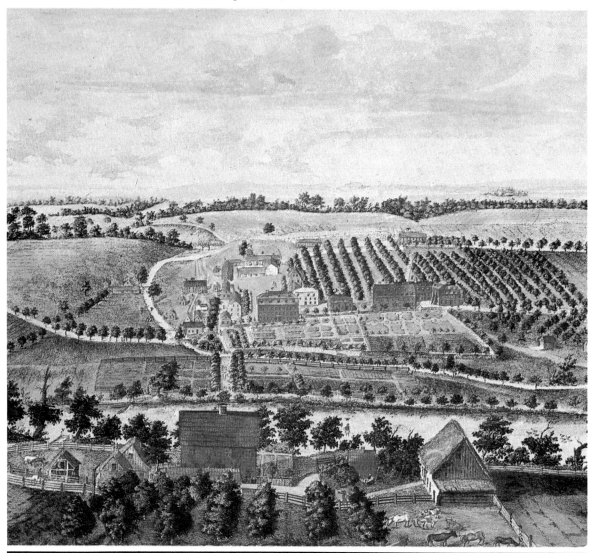

The English took more than 100 years to build their colonial empire in North America. Starting with Jamestown in 1607, they founded a string of colonies along the Atlantic coast. By the 1730's, the English had 13 colonies, stretching from French Canada in the north to Spanish Florida in the south. The 13 English colonies were different from each other in many ways. They had their own local governments and their own ways of life. The people who settled in the colonies had come to the New World for many different reasons. All of these people added to the growth and variety of American culture.

1. The People of the English Colonies_____

People from several countries *immigrated* to (came to live in) the English colonies of North America. By 1700, the colonies had about 250,000 people. This number increased ten times in the next 75 years. By 1775, the population of the English colonies was about 2.5 million. Most of the people were white Europeans who wanted to come to the New World. They hoped to have religious freedom, to escape poverty, and to find new ways of improving their lives. Some who arrived in the colonies were forced to come. This was especially true of the black people from Africa.

How much did population grow over time?

1.1   The English.   About 60 percent of the white settlers in the English colonies were of English nationality. They brought many English ways with them, and their language became the common one in the colonies. Most of them belonged to one of the Protestant religious groups.

The largest group of settlers were members of the middle class. They lived in *rural* (country) areas, where they farmed small plots of land. Some worked as blacksmiths, carpenters, or stonecutters. Some lived in the few *urban* (city) areas along the Atlantic coast, where they worked in shops, on ships, or with machines. A small number of colonists from England were members of the upper class. In the northern colonies, they became merchants, ministers, doctors, and lawyers. In the southern colonies, they were wealthy *planters*, owners of large farms known as plantations.

What were English settlers like?

1.2   The Scots.   The next largest group of English-speaking white settlers (about 14 percent) were Scots. Many came from southern Scotland, where they had worked as weavers and mechanics. The largest single group of Scots in America were the so-called Scotch-Irish. They were Scots whom the English government had forced to resettle in the province of Ulster in northern Ireland. They had been treated harshly by the English and hated by the Irish. They sought peace and safety in America. Most of the Scots who first came to America settled in Pennsylvania. In the early 1700's, some moved farther southwest, toward the mountain valleys of the Appalachians.

Why did Germans come to America?

1.3   The Germans.   One of the largest groups of non-English-speaking Europeans to come to the 13 colonies (8.7 percent) were Germans. The Germans left their homeland in the early 1700's to escape war and hunger. Most settled in Pennsylvania's Susquehanna Valley around Lancaster and York. Sometimes they were called Pennsylvania Dutch because the German word for "German" is *Deutsch.* The political freedom offered by Pennsylvania, together with the richness of the land, provided opportunities for many Germans to become successful. Most became well-to-do farmers. A few made a profitable living making and selling wagons and hardware.

1.4   Other European Settlers.   In addition to the Germans, there were several other groups of non-English-speaking European settlers. The Dutch (3.4 percent), located mostly in the Hudson Valley region of New York, contributed many things to American life. Their brick houses with tile roofs were stronger than the wooden planks and shingles of most colonial houses. Their pottery, kitchenware, and iron hardware were both well designed and useful. The French settled in many colonies. Making up about 1.7 percent of the population, they provided America with many artists and artisans. Swedes and Finns, 0.7 percent of all colonists, established settlements throughout the Delaware Valley. They developed ways to build log cabins that later became popular among settlers moving farther west.

What were some contributions of non-English-speaking European settlers?

1.5   The Africans.   The beginning of the black population in the English colonies came in 1619 when a Dutch ship left 20 Africans in Jamestown. Before the end of the century, many more Africans were brought to the colonies. They were captured in wars or kidnapped by slave traders along the coast of West Africa. Their trip to America was a terrible ordeal. Slave ships were horribly crowded, and people were poorly fed. Thousands of Africans died on the ships before reaching America.

When did blacks first come to America?

During the colonial period, Africans became the largest single non-English group in the English colonies. In 1700, there were more than 25,000 slaves. By 1750, there were over 235,000. And in 1775, there were some 500,000 slaves in the English colonies—about 20

Colonial Population, 1630–1780

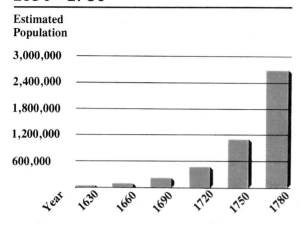

Percent of Nationality Groups, 1775

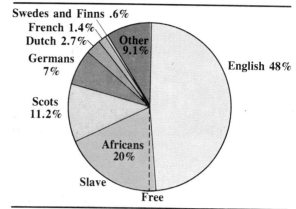

Total colonial population increased 100 times between 1630 and 1720. How much did it increase between 1750 and 1780? What percent of the total population did each nationality group make up?

percent of the total population. Just as the white population had grown ten times between 1700 and 1775, so had America's black population.

1. From what countries did the various people in the English colonies come?
2. Where did the people of various national backgrounds settle in the colonies?
3. How did the trip to the New World of blacks differ from that of whites?

2. Life in the English Colonies

The people who came to live in the various parts of the English colonies had many different manners and customs. Gradually, the immigrants to the New World began to form a way of life that was different in many ways from the one they had in the Old World. They began to shape an American way of life.

2.1 Work Roles. The vast majority of white settlers in the English colonies worked as farmers. Land formed the economic base of

What did the vast majority of colonists do for a living?

Skilled working people like those shown here were in great demand in the colonies. Hat makers (left) or a weaver (right) could make a good living. Why was each important to settlers living in the colonies?

colonial America. Where the soil was fertile and the climate favorable, farmers prospered. Where the soil was rocky and the climate cold, the land produced little beyond what a family needed to eat.

Since most people lived on farms, colonial cities remained small in size. They were important, however, as trade centers. Through them came manufactured goods from other English colonies and from England. Merchants were key figures in colonial cities. They brought in goods the colony needed and sold what the colony produced. Mills, factories, and iron-making furnaces were set up in many cities to produce goods for trade. Producers hired artisans to make shoes, furniture, silverware, and tools. The most important manufacturing activity, centered in New England, was shipbuilding.

Many people who came to the English colonies did not arrive as farmers, merchants, artisans, or manufacturers. They came as *indentured servants*. These were people who bound themselves to work for someone in America for a set number of years, usually five to seven. In exchange for their labor, the servants' passage was paid to the colonies by the person for whom they were to work. Once the term of service was completed, the servant was free. Most indentured servants were people who wanted to go to America but did not have enough money to make the trip. Gottlieb Mittelberger, who came from Germany in 1750, described the buying of indentured servants:

What was an indentured servant?

This is how the [sale of] human beings on board ship takes place. Every day Englishmen, Dutchmen, and . . . Germans come . . . on board the newly arrived vessel that has brought people from Europe and offers them for sale. From among the healthy they pick out those suitable for [their] purposes. . . . When an agreement has been reached, adult persons . . . bind themselves to serve for three, four, five, or six years, according to their health and age. The very young, between the ages of ten and fifteen, have to serve until they are twenty-one, however.

Many parents . . . must . . . sell their children as if they were cattle. Since the fathers and mothers often do not know where or to what masters their children are to be sent, it frequently happens that . . . parents and children do not see each other for years on end, or even for the rest of their lives.

The first Africans to come to the English colonies came as indentured servants. They helped to provide the workers needed on large farms, especially in the southern colonies. These servants were supposed to work out their terms of service and then get their freedom, just as the white

Many people who came to the colonies arrived as indentured servants. With the demand for more workers, black people from Africa were imported as slaves. Why did large farms, like this tobacco plantation, need so many workers?

Anne Bradstreet (1612–1672)
Phillis Wheatley (1753?–1784)
PROFILE

Few women were well known during colonial times. Most were known because of their husbands. There were some exceptions. Two of these were Anne Bradstreet and Phillis Wheatley. Both were born in the Old World, both lived in Massachusetts, and both were well educated. Both were also poets who were popular in America and Britain.

Bradstreet was born in Britain in 1612. In 1630, she sailed for America with her parents and husband. Bradstreet found life in Massachusetts Bay Colony to be difficult. Bradstreet maintained a house at the edge of the wilderness and raised eight children. She also found time to write poetry.

Bradstreet's early poems reflected mostly her Puritan religion. Later she wrote more personal poems. In a poem praising Queen Elizabeth I, Bradstreet expressed some thoughts on being a woman.

She hath wip'd off the aspersion
  [slander] of her Sex,
That women wisdom lack to play the
  Rex [ruler]. . . .

In 1650, a book of Bradstreet's poems was printed in Britain. *The Tenth Muse Lately Sprung Up in America* was the first volume published by an American poet.

Phillis Wheatley was born in Africa about 1753. In 1761, John and Susannah Wheatley bought her as a slave in Boston. The Wheatleys taught her to read and write. She also learned history, geography, and the Latin classics.

In 1766, Wheatley wrote her first poem. It was to King George III when he repealed the Stamp Act.

And may each clime with equal
  gladness see
A monarch's smile can set his subjects
  free!

In 1773, Wheatley was freed and went to Britain where she met other writers. There her first book, *Poems on Various Subjects,* was published. At the time, there were few volumes of poems by Americans, and this was the first by a black woman.

Wheatley was not a typical slave. Neither Anne Bradstreet nor Phillis Wheatley were typical women. Few women and almost no slaves were as well educated. Still fewer became published poets. Bradstreet and Wheatley were the exceptions.

servants did. A Virginia law in 1661 made black indentured servants' terms of service "continuous." This meant most Africans became servants for life. A 1663 Maryland law made black indentured servants *slaves*, people who were the property of their owners.

How did blacks become slaves?

2.2 Outlooks. The family was the cornerstone of colonial society. Most family groups in America were very large, especially those on the farms. A single household might contain a father, mother, brothers, sisters, grandparents, uncles, aunts, and cousins. Because of war, sickness, accidents, and the lack of proper medical care, the death rate was very high. It was common for a person to marry two or three times. And it was not unusual to have a household of 14 or 15 people. For farmers, a large household meant a steady source of labor.

What were features of the colonial family?

Under the English system of laws in the colonies, women had few political or civil rights. Women did not have the right to vote and could not participate in government. Generally, they were limited by law in owning property. Women, however, took on a great many responsibilities. Many worked alongside their husbands on the farms. Some managed farms by themselves when their husbands died or were away at war. A number of women operated taverns and inns. A few colonial

Old Burton Church, Virginia, is a typical eighteenth-century colonial building. This scene shows wealthy landowning families arriving for religious services. What part did religion play in the lives of the colonists?

governments did allow women to own property, inherit money, and hold licenses to operate businesses.

How important was religion in colonial America?

One of the most important influences on colonial life was religion. In some colonies, religious leaders were also the government leaders. Religion for most colonists was something that affected their daily lives. In colonial society, particularly in the Puritan colonies, emphasis was placed on hard work. It was considered a serious offense to waste time. English colonists believed that God rewarded those who worked hard and punished those who did not.

1. What was the economic base of colonial America?
2. How did people in the colonies make their livings?
3. What were some of the influences on colonial life?

3. Regions in the Colonies

There were many reasons why settlers in the English colonies shared similar ways of life. There were also reasons why some parts of the colonies were quite different from other parts. The English colonies were not all located in one small geographic area. They did not all have the same kind of climate, soil, and land formations. The colonies ran all the way from the Canadian border with its cool temperatures to Spanish Florida with its warm climate. This area contained three major regions—the New England Colonies, the Middle Colonies, and the Southern Colonies. In each of these, the people developed their own political systems, economic structures, and social patterns.

Into what regions were the English colonies divided?

3.1 The New England Colonies. The colonies in the New England region—Connecticut, Rhode Island, New Hampshire, and Massachusetts including Maine—had certain features in common. The people there were almost all of English background. Congregationalism, with strict Puritan beliefs, was the major form of worship. Congregations built meeting houses and elected their own ministers. Religion and politics were local matters in New England. Each town ran its own affairs. The *town meeting*, a gathering of all eligible voters, was the usual way in which political issues were debated and laws passed. Most adult males participated. Those who were not members of the Congregational church, however, were not allowed to vote.

What colonies made up the New England Colonies?

Why was education important to New England colonists?

Education was considered very important in the New England Colonies. The colonists believed that their children should be able to

Harvard College was founded in Cambridge, Massachusetts, in 1636. It was the first college in colonial America. Why was it established? What was the purpose of most colonial colleges founded later?

read and understand the Bible. In 1647, Massachusetts passed a law providing for a tax-supported public school system. Even before that, in 1636, Harvard College was founded in Cambridge, Massachusetts, near Boston. It was the first English colonial college, and it was built to train Congregationalist ministers. In 1701, Yale College in New Haven, Connecticut, and in 1769, Dartmouth College in Hanover, New Hampshire, were founded for the same reason.

Many of the people in the New England Colonies had small farms. They worked the land usually with the help of family members, including children. Much of the land was hard and rocky and not easy to farm. Farms produced little more than the people who lived there needed. So, many people also found work in seaport towns. Shipbuilding and fishing became important to the New England economy, and foreign trade increased greatly.

People in New England traded with such European countries as England, Portugal, Spain, and France. Trade with the British, French, and Spanish West Indies was also important. Molasses was brought into New England from the West Indies. Much of it was made into rum. Rum was shipped across the Atlantic Ocean to Africa. On the coast of West Africa, it was exchanged for slaves, and the slaves were shipped back across the Atlantic to the West Indies. There the slaves were sold, and part of the income was used to buy more molasses which was then

With whom did the people of New England trade?

Colonial Society 91

Colonial Trade Routes

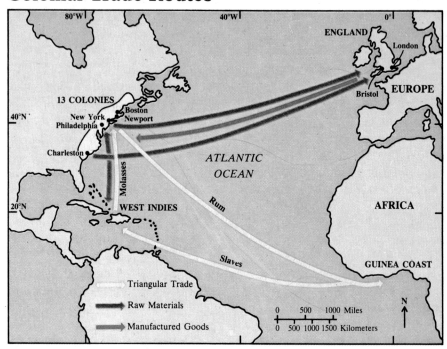

The flow of trade between the colonies and England involved raw materials from the colonies for goods made in England. Notice also the triangular trade routes. What three areas did this trade connect? What goods were traded?

brought to New England. This routine became known as the *triangular trade*.

What colonies made up the Middle Colonies?

3.2   The Middle Colonies.   The people in the Middle Colonies—New York, New Jersey, Pennsylvania, and Delaware—were quite different in their national backgrounds and religious beliefs. The Scots were mostly Presbyterian. The largest religious group among the Germans, Finns, and Swedes was Lutheran. The Dutch were Reformed, Lutheran, and Catholic. Most of the French were Huguenots (Protestants). Quakers, Baptists, and Methodists were mainly English and Welsh. The Jews who settled in New York and Philadelphia in the 1600's were Spanish and Portuguese.

Differences in nationality and religion prevented close political cooperation in the Middle Colonies. Town meetings were not used. Instead, decisions were usually made by government officials in an elected colonial assembly.

Who ran education in the Middle Colonies?

Public education in the Middle Colonies was not widespread. There were a number of schools and academies, usually run by private or church groups. Several schools of higher education were founded in the 1700's. The College of New Jersey, started in 1746 by the

Presbyterians, later became Princeton University. The Philadelphia College was chartered in 1754 and later became the University of Pennsylvania. The Church of England set up Columbia University in New York City in 1754. And the Dutch Reformed Church founded Rutgers University in 1766 in New Jersey.

Farming was the main way of making a living in the Middle Colonies. The size of the farms varied. There were the huge estates of the Dutch in New York. There were the small farms of the Germans and the Scots in Pennsylvania. Because all the farms produced mostly grains—corn, wheat, rye, barley—the Middle Colonies became known as the "Bread Colonies."

What was grown in the Middle Colonies?

The land of the Middle Colonies was more fertile than that in New England. It produced more than enough for the people who lived there to use. Farmers sold their surplus goods. Three important rivers—the Hudson, Delaware, and Susquehanna—which cut through the area were ways for farmers to move these goods to the merchants in the coastal cities of New York City, Philadelphia, and Baltimore.

During the colonial period, manufacturing in the Middle Colonies was usually done by people in their homes. Family members spun and wove textile goods, and artisans worked with iron, glass, and paper. Outside the home, other industries grew up. Sawmills produced large amounts of lumber, mills provided flour, and ovens baked bricks for building homes.

A ready supply of trees helped shipbuilding become a profitable industry in the colonies. Shipyards in the New England and Middle colonies built ships for trade and fishing. What kinds of skilled people did a community need to build ships?

Rice Hope, a Carolina plantation, was typical of the large farms in the South. Dr. William Read owned Rice Hope. What were the major crops grown by planters like Dr. Read?

What colonies made up the Southern Colonies?

3.3 The Southern Colonies. In the Southern Colonies—Maryland, Virginia, North Carolina, South Carolina, and Georgia—one religion and one social group dominated the area. The Church of England (in America known as the Episcopal church) was the leading religion. Political life was directed by planters.

The scattering of people over the large area of the Southern Colonies made it difficult to organize a public school system. Children of planters were usually taught at home by tutors. The other children worked on the farms and received little formal education. The only college in the Southern Colonies was William and Mary, founded in Williamsburg, Virginia, in 1693.

Farming was by far the most important way of life in the Southern Colonies. There were many small farms throughout the area, especially in the western valleys. Farmers there grew corn, grains, fruits, and vegetables. They usually worked their own land and lived on what they grew.

Who controlled southern political and business life?

A handful of planters ruled the southern political and business life. They controlled most of the farming and the *exporting* (sending out goods) and *importing* (bringing in goods) from other countries. The tobacco, rice, and *indigo* (a vegetable dye used on cloth) grown on the plantations of the Southern Colonies were in great demand in England. The planters made a large profit on these crops because they did not have to pay the slaves who were forced to work their large plantations. The wealth of most planters was in land and slaves. But they often had little cash for the things they needed. So, although southern planters were wealthy, they were also generally in debt.

3.4 The Western Frontier. The number of people in the three major regions grew rapidly. As this happened, more and more settlers moved west into the fresh lands on the outer limits of the colonies, called the *frontier*. In the 1600's, this meant the eastern foothills of the Appalachian Mountains. By the early 1700's, people from Pennsylvania, Virginia, and North Carolina pushed farther west. They passed through gaps in the Alleghenies and the Blue Ridge Mountains and moved into the lands of the Ohio Valley.

Where was the frontier?

Life on the frontier was hard and rugged. There were no luxuries, fine manners, or fancy clothes. Most frontier settlers lived isolated lives. Families had to rely on themselves for their material and spiritual needs. They cleared their own land and built their own one-room cabins. They made their furniture, raised their food, and made most of their clothes. There were no schools, and children had little formal education. Frontier families were usually very large. Children had regular duties on the farm and in the home.

What was life like on the frontier?

1. How were the geographic regions of the colonies different from one another?
2. What early colleges were established in each region?
3. What colonial products were in demand in England?

4. From Conflict to Unity

Threats and dangers from outside often cause people with different points of view to work together for their common safety. This is what happened to many of the English colonies in North America. People there still had different religions, different local political systems, and different ways of life. But they found they had to work together if they were to solve common problems.

What dangers did the people in the English colonies face?

4.1 The Settlers and the Indians. Most settlers in the English colonies fought with many Indian groups almost from the moment they arrived. As more settlers came to the colonies, they took over land where the Indians had lived and hunted for hundreds of years. The Indians saw the land being taken away and their ways of life being destroyed. So they often fought back. In 1622, Indians killed nearly one third of the settlers at Jamestown. The settlers answered the attack with a long series of wars against the Indian groups in Virginia. They destroyed Indian crops and burned their villages to the ground.

What was the basic cause of trouble between the Indians and colonists?

In New England, the Pequot Indians united in 1637 to drive out the settlers along the Connecticut River. The colonists struck back, killing over 500 men, women, and children in a Pequot camp. In 1643, the colonists of Massachusetts Bay, Plymouth, Connecticut, and New Haven joined together in the New England Confederation. A *confederation* is a loose union of people or groups for shared support and action. The New England Confederation was formed to protect the member colonies against the French and Dutch settlements as well as against the Indians. It was an early example of colonists working together for protection.

Several Indian groups in New England joined together under a Wampanoag chief known as "King Philip." In the summer of 1675, they set out to drive the settlers from the land. The Indians attacked settlement after settlement. After the death of King Philip in the spring of 1676, the fighting gradually ended. But the war made longtime enemies of the northeastern Indians and the New England settlers.

In Pennsylvania, William Penn and his Quaker followers established good relations with the Indians at first. The settlers usually abided by the terms of treaties. But later they, too, found it easy to force the Indians west. When the Scots and other groups began moving into the western lands during the early 1700's, fighting became more frequent between the settlers and the Indians there. Conflict between the two groups continued all through the colonial period. It provided a powerful force in pulling colonists together for their common defense.

4.2 The Colonists and the Crown. During the time of settlement, the English did not pay much attention to their colonies. The colonists were allowed to handle their own affairs. After King Charles II came to the throne in 1660, however, the English government decided to set up stricter rules and regulations. It wanted to use the colonies to increase wealth in England. The government began to follow a policy of *mercantilism.* According to this policy, the colonists were to produce raw materials not found in England. They were supposed to sell these raw materials only to England. In addition, the colonies were not to make anything they could buy from England.

To enforce this policy, many laws were passed in England to control colonial trade. The Navigation Acts of the 1660's listed such colonial products as tobacco, cotton, indigo, and turpentine which must be exported to England only. The English government ruled that colonists could import only English goods. All goods traded between the colonies and England had to be carried on English or colonial ships. One of the most profitable businesses in the colonies was the sugar trade with the West Indies. In an effort to stop the colonists from trading with

Who made up the New England Confederation?

What was the basic cause of trouble between the colonies and England?

Checking Points of View
SKILL

Historians have seen the American Indian from many points of view. Their attitudes are usually based on the popular opinion of their time. Here are two selections written at different times in American history.

Michel Guillaume Jean de Crèvecoeur in 1775 described what sometimes happened in the colonies after the French and Indian War. During the war, Indians captured some of the colonists' children.

Many an anxious parent I have seen last war, who at the return of the peace, went to the Indian villages where they knew their children had been carried . . . ; when to their [great] sorrow, they found them so perfectly Indianized, that many . . . chose to remain; and the reasons they gave me would greatly surprise you: the most perfect freedom, the ease of living, the absence of those cares . . . which so often [are with] us . . . made them prefer that life of which we entertain such dreadful opinions. . . .

Allan Nevins had another way of looking at the Indians in 1927.

They were physically of fine [build], strong and active. . . . Their chief [kind] of wealth consisted of their herds of ponies and of their weapons. . . . they were quite unable to understand the desire of the white man to [take over] any part of the earth. Their government was simple and, in a sense, democratic, [made up of] a leadership of chiefs who [gained] their [offices] by skill and courage and whose [authority] was most [strictly] exercised in time of war or other emergency.

These proud, stern, and really [frightening] peoples . . . had many faults but . . . [their] courage and [bravery] touched even their enemies to [admire them]. . . .

Having read these selections, answer the following questions.

1. What does each historian seem to be saying about the Indians?
2. What would make them each have a different point of view?
3. What can you say about people who write history, after reading these descriptions?
4. Can you think of other subjects over which historians might have different opinions?

Colonial Economy

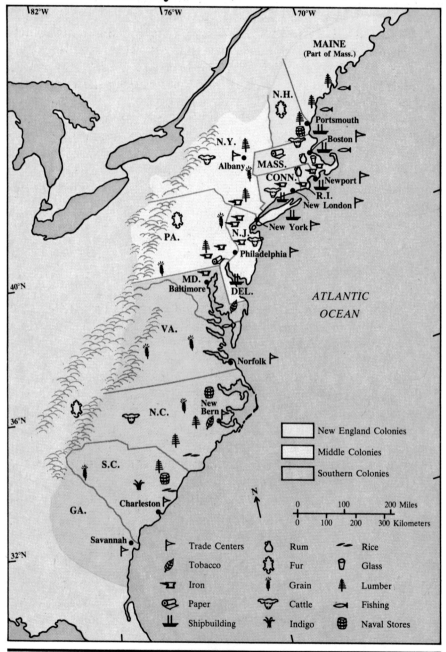

The colonies could not export enough raw materials to pay for the manufactured goods from England they needed. So colonists set up their own industries. How did the colonies differ in economic development?

the French and Spanish West Indies, England passed the Molasses Act of 1733. It made the colonists pay more for sugar, molasses, and rum imported from any place outside English territory.

Mercantilist laws also put restrictions on colonial manufacturing. The Woolen Act of 1699 stopped the colonists from exporting wool products. The Hat Act of 1732 and the Iron Act of 1750 also limited manufacturing. These laws were designed to keep colonial manufacturers from competing with English manufacturers.

Mercantilism hurt some colonial economic interests, but it also benefited them in several ways. Some colonists had a monopoly on the sale of several major crops—tobacco, rice, and indigo. Merchants took part in a trade that was closed to other countries. And during the era of almost constant wars at sea, colonial ships were protected by the powerful English navy.

How did mercantilism benefit the colonists?

Despite these benefits, merchants, traders, and leaders in business had reacted against the English laws by finding ways to avoid them by the early 1700's. Colonies carried on their own trade with foreign countries. They imported manufactured goods directly into the colonies. They used their own ships to smuggle tea from Holland, textiles from France, wine from Portugal, and molasses and sugar from the West Indies. The colonists were slowly uniting against the economic rules laid down by the English government.

4.3   The British and the French.   The third major threat to British colonial security was the presence of the French in North America. They had started building their empire at the same time the British started theirs. In 1608, one year after the founding of Jamestown, the French had started a settlement at Quebec. Both countries wanted to extend their empires, and they sometimes claimed the same lands in North America.

Why was there friction between the French and the British in North America?

In the late 1600's and early 1700's, the British and the French engaged in a series of wars to see which would be the leading world power. The fighting took place in many parts of the world—in Europe, India, the West Indies, and North America. In America, these wars became known as King William's War (1689–1697), Queen Anne's War (1702–1713), and King George's War (1744–1748). The French and their Indian allies raided frontier settlements in the Middle Colonies and New England. Colonists, in turn, attacked French posts along the Canadian border.

The rivalry between Britain and France finally became a worldwide struggle that once again involved Europe and India, as well as North America. The fighting began in America over the question of whether France or Britain owned the Ohio Valley. In the spring of 1754, the governor of Virginia, Robert Dinwiddie, sent 21-year-old George Washington and a small military force to stop the French from building Fort Duquesne, near present-day Pittsburgh, Pennsylvania. The French with Indian allies drove Washington off, and the French and Indian War began.

What was Franklin's Plan of Union?

To discuss action and defense, leaders from Maryland, Pennsylvania, New York, and the New England colonies met at Albany, New York, in June 1754. At this meeting, Benjamin Franklin of Pennsylvania suggested a Plan of Union. Under this plan, the colonies would join together under a president general named by the king. A grand council would also be created, elected by the colonial assemblies. Together with the king and the president general, it would make laws for the colonies.

Where did the French and Indian War begin?

Franklin's Plan of Union was turned down by the colonies and by the English government. The colonial governors did not want to lose power to a president general. The colonial assemblies did not want to share their authority with those outside their own areas. The king did not want still another set of leaders in America. So the colonies remained as separate as before. When fighting broke out in 1754, the colonists found themselves at war with the French.

In 1775, French soldiers and their Indian allies attacked a British force under the command of General Braddock (center) in Western Pennsylvania. What caused a conflict between the French and the British?

At first, the French and Indian War went badly for the British and the colonists. British General Edward Braddock and his soldiers were sent against the French at Fort Duquesne in 1755. Braddock and his soldiers, however, never got there. On the way, the French surprised them, firing from behind trees and bushes. Braddock was killed, and the British were defeated. This loss opened up the entire frontier to attacks by the French and their Indian allies. The British government and the colonies could not agree upon a course of action.

Things changed greatly in 1758, when William Pitt was put in charge of the British war effort. By using money and the army wisely, Pitt was able to change the course of the war. British forces took the offensive. They defeated the French in a number of battles during 1758 and 1759. In the fall of 1759, British General James Wolfe defeated General Louis Montcalm and his French forces on the Plains of Abraham, a plateau near the city of Quebec. The British captured Quebec, and the following spring, they captured Montreal. After suffering serious defeats in Europe, India, and the West Indies as well, France finally agreed to surrender.

What events led to defeat of the French by the British?

In 1763, Britain and France signed the Treaty of Paris. It officially ended the series of wars around the world and set down peace terms. According to the treaty, Britain received from France all of Canada and all the lands east of the Mississippi River. Britain also got all of Spanish Florida, since Spain had helped France in the war. Spain had been given Louisiana in 1762 to encourage it to join the war on the side of France. The Treaty of Paris marked the end of France as a colonial power in North America.

What were the terms of the Treaty of Paris of 1763?

1. Why was there conflict between the Indians and the settlers?
2. How did mercantilism affect the colonies?
3. Why were the French a threat to British colonial security?

5. Conclusion

There was rejoicing in the colonies over the end of the French and Indian War. The French were no longer a threat. Britain had succeeded in defending its claim to all the land of North America east of the Mississippi River. Its empire now extended from Hudson Bay in the north to the tip of Florida in the south. The young English king, George III, was hailed by the colonists. Yet in the next dozen years, events in colonial America would lead to war between Britain and the colonies.

Chapter 4 Review

Main Points

1. People who settled in the English colonies came from many different parts of Europe and Africa.
2. Most Europeans who immigrated to the colonies wanted to come. Most Africans came against their wills.
3. All of the people in the colonies contributed to a new American culture.
4. English culture most influenced the colonial way of life.
5. Life in the colonies varied with the differences in geography.
6. The English colonies can be divided into three groups—New England Colonies, Middle Colonies, and Southern Colonies.
7. Fear of the Indians, French, and Spanish and disagreements with the English encouraged unity among the colonists.
8. The French and Indian War began in 1754. After several defeats, the French surrendered and signed the Treaty of Paris in 1763.

Building Vocabulary

1. Identify the following:

   Anne Bradstreet
   Phillis Wheatley
   New England Colonies
   Congregationalism
   Middle Colonies

   "Bread Colonies"
   Southern Colonies
   New England Confederation
   King Philip
   Fort Duquesne

   Franklin's Plan of Union
   General Edward Braddock
   General James Wolfe
   General Louis Montcalm
   Treaty of Paris

2. Define the following:

   immigrated
   rural
   urban
   planters
   indentured servants

   slaves
   town meeting
   triangular trade
   exporting

   importing
   indigo
   frontier
   confederation
   mercantilism

Remembering the Facts

1. Why did Europeans settle in the English colonies? Why did Africans?
2. What were the two largest national groups in the English colonies?
3. How did most of the people in the colonies make a living?
4. Why was a large family an advantage in colonial society?

5. Which rights did men have under English law that women did not?
6. In which region of the colonies was public education most widespread? Which region grew mostly grain?
7. Where was the colonial frontier in the early 1600's? in the 1700's?
8. Why was the New England Confederation formed?
9. How did the colonists react to mercantilism?
10. How was William Pitt able to change the course of the French and Indian War?

Understanding the Facts

1. Why did the American culture develop differently from those cultures of the people who settled the colonies?
2. How did indentured servants differ from slaves?
3. Why did the colonial regions develop various ways of doing some things?
4. What threats and dangers caused the colonists to seek to unite in some of their actions?
5. How did the English hope to profit from the colonies?
6. How did the British win the French and Indian War?

Using Maps

Keys and Legends. Thematic maps contain various codes or keys to provide information or tell the story of the theme. A list of the keys with their meanings is called a legend.

Examine the map on page 98, and read the legend in the lower right corner. The legend contains keys which give information on the three major regions of the colonies and the various major products of the colonies.

On the map, the keys show the map symbols for the location of a region, a country, or an item. Notice that some of the keys are symbols and some are colors. After you have studied the map, answer the following questions.

1. Which color on the map shows the Southern Colonies?
2. Which color shows the Middle Colonies?
3. Which color shows the New England Colonies?
4. Which region in colonial America produced the most iron?
5. In which region were most of the trading centers located?
6. Which colonial region was closest to good fishing waters?
7. Which trading centers were closest to the supplies of naval stores?
8. What was produced in quantity in all regions of colonial America?

Winning Freedom 5

England's colonial empire was more loosely controlled than those of other European nations during the Age of Colonization. By the mid-1700's, the colonists and the British government had drifted quite a bit apart. Why?

The end of the French and Indian War in 1763 marked a turning point in relations between Britain and its American colonies. Britain decided to tighten its controls over the colonies, and the colonists disagreed with the change in policy. Each side found it hard to see the other's point of view. In the years that followed, the colonists and the British government drifted farther apart.

1. The Road to Rebellion

To the people of the colonies, the British victory in the French and Indian War brought a new feeling of security. The French threat had been ended, and the power of the Indians along the frontier had been greatly weakened. Victory also meant to American colonists that they no longer had to depend on the British military for their defense. Most colonists were proud of being part of the British Empire. But when the war was over, they looked forward to living their own lives as free as possible from Britain.

Following victory in the French and Indian War, what did the colonists expect?

For more than a century and a half, the British government had been too busy to control the colonies strictly. There had been political quarrels in Britain and a series of wars with France for almost 75 years. After 1763, Britain was at peace, and it turned its attention to the American colonies.

1.1 New British Policies. Britain changed the way it treated the colonies because of the needs it had after the French and Indian War. The war had cost a great deal of money, and the British government faced large debts. Many leaders in Britain felt that the colonies should help pay a part of the debts. They said that the war had been fought in large measure to protect the colonies from the French and their Indian allies.

What did the British do?

The British government also had to decide how to handle the land west of the Appalachian Mountains. British traders and merchants wanted the Indians to control it to guarantee them a continued supply of furs. The British government wanted to stop the spread of settlement west of the mountains. Keeping the colonies along the Atlantic coast would make them easier to control and would reduce Indian-white tensions.

In 1763, George III formed a new group of advisors under the leadership of George Grenville. With the king's support, Grenville introduced new policies for the colonies. One idea was to have the colonies strictly obey the Navigation Acts. These laws, passed in the late 1600's, were to limit colonial trade only to Britain. The colonies had been trading with other areas, and this was illegal. In addition, Grenville introduced a new series of laws. These laws together are known as the Grenville Acts.

1.2 The Grenville Acts. The Grenville Acts included several separate parts. Three of these resulted in much disagreement between Britain and the colonies. The first was the Proclamation of 1763. It prevented colonists from settling west of the Appalachian Mountains. Indian groups living in the area were to be left to themselves in order to protect the valuable fur trade.

The second was the Sugar Act of 1764. Grenville wanted to raise more money from colonial trade. So he placed a tax on sugar, wines, and coffee and set up a plan to enforce the collection of the tax on

Some people in Boston burned stamps to protest the Stamp Act (left). The Sons of Liberty used signs (bottom right) to keep people from using them. Examples of British stamps are shown here (top right). What was the Stamp Act?

molasses. More British navy ships were to patrol the American coast to stop smuggling. People caught smuggling were to be tried in naval courts rather than civil courts. The naval courts had no juries. In the past, colonial civil juries often did not convict people accused of smuggling.

The third major part of the Grenville Acts was the Stamp Act, passed in 1765. According to this, people had to buy stamps to put on all newspapers, pamphlets, contracts, wills, and certain other printed materials. The money raised from the sale of the stamps was to be used to help pay for British soldiers stationed in the colonies.

What acts were included in the Grenville Acts?

1.3 The Colonial Response. The British leaders felt they were right in passing the Grenville Acts. The colonies, on the other hand, felt that the British government took improper steps to control them. A storm of protest broke out in the colonies over the Grenville Acts. Many colonists insisted that Britain was trying to ruin colonial trade. They also felt they had the right to settle on land west of the Appalachian Mountains. And colonists protested against what they thought was illegal British taxation.

Part of the disagreement was over the meaning of representation in government. Voters in England selected the members of Parliament to represent all the people of the British Empire. These members did not represent a certain town, county, or area. This was called *virtual representation.* In the colonial legislatures, the idea of *direct representation* had developed. This meant that people of a certain area selected a representative who worked for that area. No American colonists sat in Parliament. Therefore, the colonists felt that they were not represented. In attacking the Stamp Act, Patrick Henry of Virginia stated that "taxation without representation is tyranny!"

What was at the core of the disagreement between the colonies and Britain?

The one part of the Grenville Acts which created the most protest was the Stamp Act. It was the first act passed that was not a tax on trade. Rather, it was a *direct tax,* or one which must be paid to the government and is not included in the price of goods. Colonial merchants and leaders were determined to force the British government to repeal the act.

What is a direct tax?

Measures were taken against the policies of the British government. The colonists organized a *boycott*—they refused to buy British goods. People were told not to buy the tax stamps. Also groups were formed to scare tax officials. Delegates from nine colonies met in New York City in October 1765 to discuss the Stamp Act. This meeting was known as the Stamp Act Congress. The congress stated that no taxes had ever been passed for the colonies except by their own legislatures. They called upon the British government to repeal the Stamp Act.

What is a boycott?

This cartoon is titled "The Horse America, Throwing His Master." It was published in the 1770's. Do you think it was drawn by a British or colonial cartoonist? Why?

Parliament repealed the act in March 1766. British merchants complained that Americans had stopped buying their goods, and they pressured British officials to change the law. The boycott had worked. But the British government did not completely back down. Parliament passed the Declaratory Act which let the colonists know that the British government had the right to pass laws for the colonies in all cases.

1.4   The Townshend Acts.   Relations between Britain and the colonies began to improve until George III selected new advisors. In 1767, Charles Townshend, a member of the group, proposed a series of taxes that would help raise money from the colonies. These were the Townshend Acts. New naval courts were set up, and taxes were placed on lead, paper, paint, glass, and tea. Townshend also proposed that money collected be used to pay certain British officials in the colonies. In the past, these officials depended upon money voted to them by the colonial legislatures. Because the colonial legislatures controlled the salaries, they had a great deal of influence on British officials.

What were the provisions of the Townshend Acts?

A new round of protests began over the passage of the Townshend Acts. New boycotts of British goods were started. Letters of protest were sent to Parliament. The Massachusetts legislature called for the other colonial legislatures to unite against the Townshend Acts. The colonists protested that they should not be taxed by Parliament since they were not represented there. They also viewed as dangerous the paying of officials with money raised from the new taxes.

Into what groups did the colonists divide?

As the conflicts between the British and the colonists increased, the American people divided into two groups. Those colonists who supported a possible break with Britain were called *patriots*. Those who remained loyal to England were called *loyalists*. In some colonies, patriot groups known as the Sons of Liberty were formed to enforce the boycott of British goods and to scare British officials stationed in the colonies.

On the night of March 5, 1770, a crowd of people led by the Sons of Liberty gathered in the streets of Boston and threw snowballs at a British guard. Other soldiers arrived to help the guard and were attacked by members of the crowd with sticks and pieces of ice. Some of the soldiers shot into the crowd, killing three people and wounding several others. A trial later determined that the soldiers were acting in self-defense. Patriot leaders, like Samuel Adams of Massachusetts, used the so-called Boston Massacre to increase dislike of the British. The clash had little impact outside of Massachusetts, however.

What was the Boston Massacre?

At the same time as the Boston Massacre, new leaders in Parliament forced a repeal of the Townshend Acts except for the tax on tea. The tea tax was kept to let the colonies know that the British leaders felt that they had the right to pass such laws. With the repeal came a period of calm for the next three years.

Paul Revere's engraving of the Boston Massacre appeared in *The Boston Gazette* in 1770. Note the "Butcher's Hall" sign over the customs house to the right. How did this engraving turn many colonists against the British?

1.5 The Boston Tea Party.   In 1773, the British government passed a law aimed at saving the East India Company from going bankrupt. This huge trading company was important in India and elsewhere in the British Empire. British officials feared that if it went bankrupt, it might hurt the British economy. So Parliament passed the Tea Act.

Under the plan, the company could ship 17 million pounds of unsold tea directly for sale in America. Other importers of tea had to land their product in England first and had to sell it to merchants there for resale. This added to the cost of the tea. Parliament wanted the East India Company to be able to sell its tea much cheaper than anyone else. The idea that the East India Company was to have a monopoly of the tea trade angered merchants in the colonies. They asked themselves what was to keep the British leaders from giving the same advantages to other companies for other goods.

When was the Boston Tea Party?

From South Carolina to Massachusetts, there were riots and even destruction of East India Company tea. On the night of December 16, 1773, the Boston Sons of Liberty, dressed as Mohawk Indians, dumped the tea cargo from three ships into Boston harbor. This famous "Tea Party" was the patriots' response to the British tea policy.

1.6 The Intolerable Acts.   The British leaders were shocked and angered by the Boston Tea Party. Many feared that the destruction of the tea was a direct threat to the authority of the government. They felt that the colonies must be shown that Britain did not intend to put up with those kinds of actions without an answer.

What were some provisions of the Intolerable Acts?

Members of Parliament moved in the spring of 1774 to punish Massachusetts for destroying the tea. A series of laws were passed that became known in the colonies as the Intolerable Acts. These measures closed the port of Boston to shipping until the people had paid for the tea they had destroyed. Parliament also put Massachusetts under control of the royal governor, suspending the colonial legislature. The laws prevented any British official from being tried in a colonial court. They also made it possible for British troops to be *quartered*—given a place to live—in private homes.

Why did the Quebec Act anger the colonists?

Another law, the Quebec Act, angered colonists even further. This law permitted French Canadians to keep their laws, their language, and their Catholic religion. It also stated that lands west of the Appalachian Mountains and north of the Ohio River belonged to Canada, not to the American colonies. This law was meant to keep the colonists from moving into the Ohio Valley.

1.7 The Continental Congress.   The passage of the Intolerable Acts pushed the colonists further away from Britain. American leaders called for a meeting to discuss ways to deal with the British government. The Virginia House of Burgesses asked each colony to send delegates to Philadelphia for a Continental Congress which could plan the next move.

Where did the First Continental Congress meet?

Representatives from every colony except Georgia met in the First Continental Congress in September 1774. They were deeply worried by the British actions but were divided in their ideas for meeting the crisis.

Which issues and events were important in pushing the British and the colonists into war? How were British policies short-sighted? How were the colonists economically motivated? How could the war have been prevented?

Events Leading to the Revolution

British Actions	Year	Colonial Actions
Parliament issued the Proclamation of 1763	1763	Colonists ignored the proclamation and continued to move westward
Parliament passed the Sugar Act to raise money from colonial imports	1764	Colonists protested new taxation without colonial representation in Parliament
Parliament imposed the Stamp Act to help pay for the British troops stationed in the colonies	1765	Colonists organized a boycott of British goods and the Sons of Liberty were formed to enforce the boycott
Parliament repealed the Stamp Act and passed the Declaratory Act to assert its authority	1766	Colonists welcomed the repeal of the Stamp Act and did not protest the Declaratory Act
Parliament passed the Townshend Acts to raise more money from colonial imports	1767	Colonists organized new boycotts after violent protests in Massachusetts
Parliament stationed more soldiers in Boston	1768	Colonists in 12 of the 13 colonies refused to import British goods
Parliament repealed the Townshend Acts except for a tax on tea	1770	Colonists clashed with British soldiers in Massachusetts, leading to the so-called Boston Massacre
Parliament passed the Tea Act, giving the monopoly on the tea trade to the East India Company	1773	Colonists protested the act and members of the Boston Tea Party destroyed a cargo of tea on a British ship
Parliament passed acts to close the Boston port, to suspend the Massachusetts charter, to house soldiers in colonial homes, and to prevent colonists from moving into the western frontier	1774	Colonists answered the so-called Intolerable Acts by calling a Continental Congress and by establishing a Continental Association to enforce a boycott of British goods
Parliament declared Massachusetts in a state of rebellion and sent soldiers to Lexington and Concord, Massachusetts	1775	Colonists called a Second Continental Congress and established a Continental Army

Some like James Duane of New York and Joseph Galloway of Pennsylvania hoped to ask the king for help. If George III would aid them, they would remain in the British Empire. They believed there were still some advantages to being tied to England and under Parliament's rule. Patriots like John Adams of Massachusetts and Patrick Henry of Virginia took the view that Parliament had no authority over the colonies. Even these patriots, however, were willing to try to make peace before starting to fight.

What steps did the First Continental Congress take?

The First Continental Congress took two major steps. As some delegates wished, a letter of grievances was sent to the king. The letter accepted the British leaders' right to govern colonial trade, but it asked the leaders to repeal laws which had been passed since 1763. These were the laws to which the Americans objected.

In a more extreme move, the First Continental Congress created a Continental Association. It was to enforce a boycott of British goods until Parliament repealed the Intolerable Acts. Some patriots burned British goods and tarred and feathered loyalists who would not join the boycott. Imports from England dropped to almost nothing.

1.8 The Final Break.   George III and the British leaders were determined not to back down again. They wanted British soldiers in America to enforce the laws. Early in 1775, British General Thomas Gage in Boston learned that patriots were collecting guns and ammunition and storing them at Concord, Massachusetts, near Boston. Gage, recently made governor of the colony, planned to take military action to stop them.

Why did the British march on Lexington and Concord?

On the evening of April 18, Gage sent 800 soldiers to seize the military supplies. Patriots in Boston heard of the move and sent Paul Revere and William Dawes to warn the patriots at Concord. The British soldiers arrived at Lexington, a town between Boston and Concord, at dawn. They were met there by 70 *minutemen*—patriot soldiers who could be ready for duty at a moment's notice. Shooting broke out, and eight minutemen were killed. At Concord, there was more fighting, but it ended by noon and the British were turned back to Boston. Meanwhile all the minutemen of the countryside had been called to arms. On the 15-mile march back to Boston, they shot at the British from behind trees and stone walls. The British march became a retreat.

What did the Second Continental Congress do in the spring of 1775?

With the fighting at Lexington and Concord, a war had started. A Second Continental Congress met in Philadelphia on May 10, 1775. The delegates named George Washington of Virginia as commander-in-chief of colonial armed forces, the Continental Army. For those still hoping for peace, the delegates sent to George III one last appeal—the Olive Branch Petition. George turned it down, and he declared that the

Reading Primary and Secondary Sources
SKILL

Among the important sources of information for historians are written records. They establish facts and help to interpret meaning. These records may be firsthand, or primary, sources which tell the author's own ideas. Others are secondhand, or secondary, sources which tell about other people's ideas. The two selections that follow tell about Paul Revere's part in the battles of Lexington and Concord.

Henry Wadsworth Longfellow wrote the poem "Paul Revere's Ride" in 1860.

Listen, my children, and you shall
  hear
Of the midnight ride of Paul Revere,
On the eighteenth of April, in
  Seventy-five;
Hardly a man is now alive
Who remembers that famous day and
  year.
He said to his friend, "If the British
  march
By land or sea from the town to-night,
Hang a lantern aloft in the belfry arch
Of the North Church tower as a signal
  light,—
One, if by land, and two, if by sea;
And I on the opposite shore will be,
Ready to ride and spread the alarm
Through every Middlesex village and
  farm,

For the country folk to be up and to
  arm."

Another source about Revere's ride is Paul Revere's own writing.

I set off upon a very good horse; it was then about 11 o'clock, and very pleasant. After I had passed Charlestown Neck, . . . I saw two men on horseback, under a tree. When I got near them, I discovered they were British officers. One tried to get ahead of me, and the other to take me. I turned my horse very quick, and galloped towards Charlestown Neck, and then pushed for the Medford Road. The one who chased me, trying to cut me off, got into a clay pond, near where the new tavern is now built. I got clear of him, and went through Medford, over the bridge, and up to Menotomy. In Medford, I awaked the captain of the Minutemen; and after that, I alarmed almost every house, till I got to Lexington.

Answer the following questions.

1. Which of the accounts is a primary source? Which is a secondary source?
2. Which of the accounts is a more reliable report of the event?
3. Why is it more reliable?

Americans were rebels. The time for appeals was over. The Second Continental Congress became a government for the patriots in revolt.

1. What were the restrictions the British placed on the colonists after 1763?
2. Why did the colonists object to British taxes?
3. How did patriots act toward the colonists who supported Britain?

2. The War for Independence

By early 1776, the independence cause was gaining support. Some colonists remained loyal to Britain, perhaps a majority in some areas. But a large number of patriots agreed with a pamphlet written by Thomas Paine called *Common Sense*. In it, Paine set down reasons why the colonies should become independent. Paine concluded, " 'Tis time to part."

2.1 The Declaration of Independence. On June 7, 1776, Richard Henry Lee of Virginia presented a resolution in the Second Continental Congress stating that "these United Colonies are, and of right ought to be, free and independent states. . . ." While the delegates talked about this idea, they named a committee of five to justify what American colonists were doing in their fight with Britain. Thomas Jefferson of Virginia, John Adams of Massachusetts, Robert Livingston of New York, Benjamin Franklin of Pennsylvania, and Roger Sherman of Connecticut made up the committee. Jefferson himself completed the final writing of what is known as the Declaration of Independence.

Who drafted the Declaration of Independence?

Jefferson wrote that all people are created equal and that all people have certain basic rights which no government can take away. He stated that all governments get their authority from the people. This was in opposition to the British government view that governments got their authority from one person, a king or queen. Jefferson also wrote that if a government did not protect the rights of the people, then the people could overthrow that government and make a new one. According to Jefferson, since George III did not protect their rights, the American colonists had the right to declare their independence.

What ideas were expressed in the Declaration of Independence?

On July 4, 1776, the delegates of the Second Continental Congress formally approved the Declaration of Independence. Copies of it were

Thomas Jefferson (right) composed the Declaration of Independence. Benjamin Franklin (left) and John Adams (center) made several suggestions, but it remained mostly Jefferson's work. What ideas about government did Jefferson write?

sent to all the colonies to inform the people. The colonists considered themselves independent, but they still had to fight and win a war to prove it.

2.2 The Early War. Both the Americans and the British had certain advantages and faced certain problems when war began. The colonial forces were fighting on their home ground and were close to their supplies. Many Americans knew how to handle weapons, which they used for hunting. On the other hand, they were seldom trained to fight in groups and to follow military commands. They also had a limited supply of guns and ammunition.

The British army was well trained and fully equipped. Their navy was the largest and the best in the world. Still, America was 3,000 miles (4,800 kilometers) from Britain. The British soldiers were far from

Thomas Paine (1737–1809)

PROFILE

One of the most effective writers on behalf of the patriot cause was Thomas Paine. He had come to America in 1774 from Britain. Working in Philadelphia as a journalist, he wrote appeals to take up the struggle against Britain.

In 1776, Paine published a pamphlet, *Common Sense*, in which he wrote that the rebelling colonists should cut their ties with the British government. Paine said that the cause of America was really the cause of all people, to overturn tyrant rulers. He demanded complete independence and the establishment of a strong union of the former colonies. *Common Sense* became the most widely read patriot pamphlet in the colonies.

During the war, Paine helped to lift the patriots' spirits by writing a series of papers titled *The Crisis*. The first of these began:

These are the times that try men's souls. . . . Tyranny, like hell, is not easily conquered; yet we have this consolation with us, that the harder the conflict, the more glorious the triumph.

After the colonies had won independence, Paine looked for other causes to champion. He urged revolt in Britain and in France. Paine spent his last years in the United States and died in 1809 almost forgotten by the American people.

home. The colonies were spread over a huge area, the land was rugged, and roads and means of communication were poor.

Where did the early fighting take place?

Early fighting took place on New England and the northeast area, especially around Boston. Soon after the fighting at Lexington and Concord, American soldiers narrowly lost the Battle of Bunker Hill. The fighting really took place on Breed's Hill, just north of Boston. Then in early 1776, the Continental Army under George Washington set up heavy guns and cannon at Dorchester Heights, hills to the south of Boston. British General William Howe in Boston realized that he could no longer hold the city. He took his troops out of Boston in March.

Thinking that the British would then attack New York, Washington moved his soldiers south to Long Island. The British landed in New York and, in a series of battles, defeated the Americans, driving them out of New York, through New Jersey, and into Pennsylvania. Late in 1776, the Americans crossed the Delaware River east from Pennsylvania into New Jersey. They surprised the enemy and defeated them at Trenton and at Princeton.

The British then made plans to defeat the Americans completely in the northeast during 1777. They wanted to gain control of the Hudson River Valley in New York. To do this, General John Burgoyne and his troops would march south from Canada to the Hudson Valley by way of Albany, New York. Another British force under Colonel Barry St. Leger with Indian support would march east from Lake Ontario to Albany. Still a third force under General Howe would move north from New York City to Albany. This attack would cut New England off from the rest of the colonies.

What was the British Plan of 1777?

The British plan was a failure from the start. General Howe sent forces to capture Philadelphia, instead of Albany. Although he did take Philadelphia, he did not help Burgoyne. With New England farmers rushing to the aid of the Continental Army, St. Leger's forces moving east from Lake Ontario were defeated. All alone, Burgoyne was then defeated at Saratoga in October 1777.

The American victory at Saratoga was considered the turning point of the war. It was important to Americans because it brought France into the war. Benjamin Franklin, who was the colonial representative to France at the time, used the news of victory to persuade the French to enter the war on the side of the colonies. France was a longtime enemy of Britain, and it saw the opportunity to work for Britain's defeat. From this point on, the French, who had already given secret aid to the Americans, began helping them openly. In 1778, French leaders signed a treaty of alliance promising guns, ships, and money to the American colonies.

2.3 Organizing the War. The victory at Saratoga did not solve all the problems the Americans faced. The Continental Congress had a hard time raising money to continue the war. It did not want to pass tax laws, as the British had done. Few colonial legislatures sent money. The government tried printing its own paper money, but most colonists considered it to have no value. The government finally had to borrow as much as $10 million from allied countries like France, Spain, and Holland. Private citizens also came to the aid of the Continental Congress. Wealthy individuals like Haym Salomon and Robert Morris loaned large sums of their money to keep the army in the field.

What problems did the Americans face during the Revolution?

The Major Campaigns of the Revolutionary War (1775-1777)

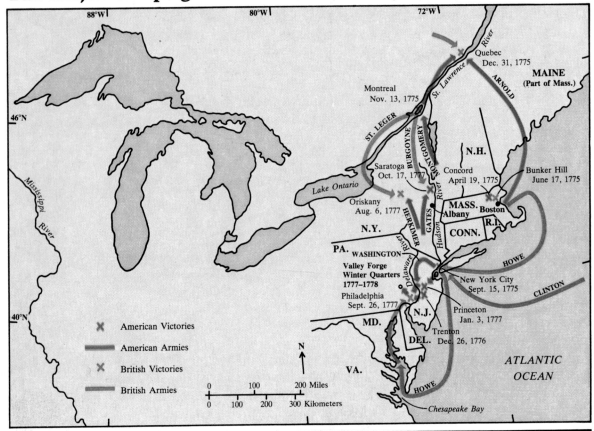

The British hoped to split the colonies by capturing the Hudson River Valley. Where did American armies defeat British armies to prevent the split? Where did British General Howe go instead of going north?

It was largely through the leadership of George Washington that the Continental Army held together. Officially, some 300,000 colonists served in the army during the war. Actually, Washington never commanded more than a few thousand at any one time. Most of his soldiers were often poorly fed and clothed. They suffered terrible hardships in their camp at Valley Forge, Pennsylvania, during the winter of 1777 and early 1778. Most of the men in Washington's army were farmers. They served a few months and then went home to help their families on the farms.

What role did women play in the war?

Few women took an active part in the fighting. Deborah Sampson, a white woman, disguised herself as a man and served in the Continental Army for several months. Deborah Gannet, a black woman, fought and was later cited for bravery. Some women joined their husbands in camp or on the battlefields, cooking and caring for the ill and wounded. Most women worked at home, tended the farms, ran the plantations, or managed the shops while the men were away at war.

2.4 The War in the West. In 1778 and 1779, there were a few battles west of the Appalachian Mountains. The British had forts important to the fur trade in the area. The Americans had settlements as far west as the Mississippi Valley. In an area along the Mississippi known as the American Bottoms, settlers established the towns of Cahokia and Kaskaskia. The British and their Indian allies attacked these and other settlements on the frontier.

To protect these colonists, George Rogers Clark gathered about 175 soldiers from Virginia to go into the western lands. Sweeping

Who fought the British in the West?

Prussian Baron von Steuben (left) discusses the war with Washington (right) during the harsh winter at Valley Forge. The baron was one of several foreign-born military officers fighting on the American side. Who was another?

John Trumbull painted "Surrender of Lord Cornwallis at Yorktown." Actually, Cornwallis' second in command surrendered to General Washington's second in command, General Benjamin Lincoln. When was the surrender?

through what today is Illinois and Indiana, Clark's forces overran British posts during the summer and fall of 1778. They struck at one fort, disappeared into the forest, and then struck at another fort miles away. With a victory at Vincennes in 1779, Clark established American control of the area between the Appalachian Mountains and the Mississippi River.

2.5 The War in the South. In the later part of the war, most of the fighting was in the south. British military leaders decided to capture the seaports of Charleston, South Carolina, and Savannah, Georgia. Loyalist support was strong in many areas of the south, and the British hoped to win the area.

Why did the British think they might win in the south?

As the British army moved inland, American soldiers in small groups tried to break up their advance. Forces led by Francis Marion, Thomas Sumter, and Andrew Pickens stole horses, destroyed supplies, and shot at marching soldiers. Despite some victories, the British were unable to hold any territory.

In 1780 and 1781, the Continental Army fought the British in several major battles, winning at King's Mountain and Cowpens, South

Carolina, and at Guilford Court House, North Carolina. After this last defeat, British General Charles Cornwallis retreated to Virginia. He moved to Yorktown on the Atlantic coast to rest his soldiers and get supplies.

Washington saw a chance to trap Cornwallis. He sent a large Continental force to block the British by land. They were joined by nearly 8,000 French soldiers under the command of the Marquis de Lafayette. Late in August 1781, a French fleet of warships blocked the British from the sea. Cut off from land and sea, Cornwallis surrendered his 7,500 soldiers to Washington. This American victory ended nearly all British hope for winning the war.

Who aided Washington at Yorktown?

The British captured major seaports in the South by 1780. They planned to capture more ports to supply the British armies as they moved north. Why did this plan fail for Lord Cornwallis at Yorktown?

The Major Campaigns of the Revolutionary War (1778-1781)

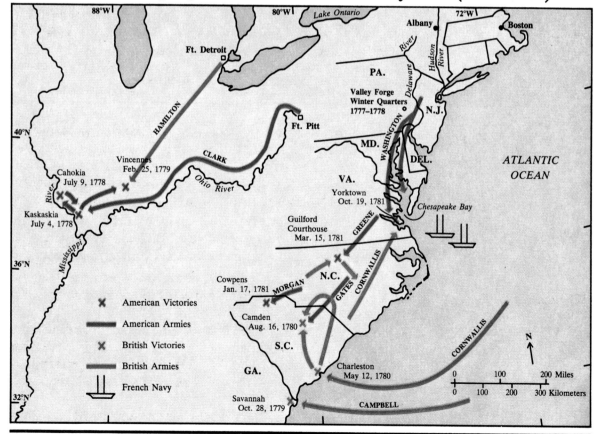

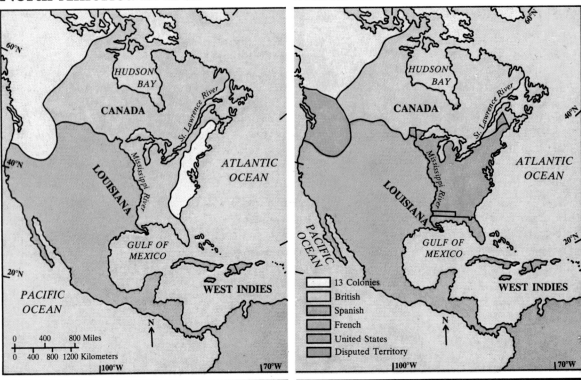

North America in 1763

North America in 1783

Legend (1783):
- 13 Colonies
- British
- Spanish
- French
- United States
- Disputed Territory

In 1783, which nation gained control of the area to the south of the United States? Which areas did Britain lose? Where were disputed areas after the Treaty of Paris in 1783?

2.6   The Treaty of Paris of 1783.   Some fighting went on over the next two years. In 1783, British and American leaders signed a treaty of peace in Paris, France, ending the war. According to the terms, Britain recognized American independence. The boundaries of the new country were set at Canada in the north, the Mississippi River in the west, and Florida in the south. Spain was given Florida, and both the United States and Britain could trade on the Mississippi. Americans also got fishing rights in the waters off Newfoundland and Nova Scotia. The 13 British colonies had become a new and independent nation.

1. Who was the commander of the Continental Army during the American Revolution?
2. Why was the Battle of Saratoga important to the Americans?
3. What was the last major battle of the Revolution?

3. The Meaning of Freedom

The American Revolution brought independence from Britain. It produced certain changes in the government, society, and economy. Independence also set in motion changes in the lives of the American people.

3.1 Political Results. The most obvious change after the Revolution was the absence of British officials in the new states. Former British political and military leaders went home. After the war, as many as 100,000 loyalists also left the country. Many settled in Canada and the West Indies.

What were the political results of the Revolution?

Each of the 13 colonies had formed state governments during the Revolution. These governments took over when British officials lost their control. Each new state was different from the others in some ways. But they did share certain ideas. The colonies had been using British law and political structures since they were chartered. And they continued to base their state governments in part on the British system.

The state governments had limited authority because the patriots feared what they saw as the limitless authority of the British government. They did not want their governments to be too strong. In many states, the office of governor was weak, keeping authority out of the hands of one person. Most of the authority was given to the state legislature and its members elected by direct representation.

The Revolution had brought about more demands for participation in government by more citizens. Some of the state governments were under the control of a small group of wealthy people. Voting rights based on wealth and land ownership were gradually relaxed, although they continued to be important in some states.

Women had hoped the war for independence would bring greater rights for them, too. It was a serious concern of Abigail Adams, writing a letter to her husband John at the Continental Congress.

> *Remember the ladies, and be more generous and favorable to them than your ancestors. Do not put such unlimited power into the hands of the husbands. Remember all men would be tyrants if they could. If particular care and attention is not paid to the ladies we are determined to foment a rebellion, and will not hold ourselves bound by any laws in which we have no voice, or representation.*

Despite the hopes of many women, they still could not vote or hold office in the years after the Revolution. In most states, the husbands of

Many of the colonists who supported Britain fled to British-held Canada (left). Some patriots (right) raised a "liberty pole" in celebration of the final break with Britain. How did the Revolution affect the colonists?

married women held legal control over their property and children. Black women as well as black men in America, most of whom were slaves, were unable to take part in political life.

3.2 Social Results. The Declaration of Independence emphasized the importance of human rights. This idea carried over into the American way of thinking after the end of the war. One area in which people applied the idea of human rights was in reforming the treatment of convicted criminals. Conditions in the prisons were improved, and laws which demanded the death penalty for minor offenses were repealed.

The human rights idea was not applied to the slaves, however. During the war, some 5,000 black Americans fought for the Continental Army. At first, many colonial leaders, including Washington, were against recruiting them. After fighting in many battles, Washington praised their bravery under fire. Many black slaves fought hoping to win their own freedom.

What were the social results of the Revolution?

After the war, Massachusetts and New Hampshire passed laws ending slavery. Several other states in the north freed slaves on a gradual basis. Within ten years after independence, every state except Georgia had either stopped or limited the importing of new slaves. Still, the market value of the American slaves increased. Some people in the north sold their slaves to owners in the south. Slave owners there were not willing to give up the advantages of using workers who did not have to be paid.

3.3   Economic Results.   By the terms of the Treaty of Paris, the United States became one of the largest nations in the world. Its borders stretched from the Atlantic Ocean in the east to the Mississippi River in the west. It was bound by the Great Lakes and Canada in the north and Spanish-owned Florida in the south. The land added to the original colonies made more space available for settlement.

What were the economic results of the Revolution?

After the war, the United States took an active role in world trade. America was no longer in business for Britain's needs alone, and its trade with other countries grew. People in manufacturing, which had increased during the war, found new markets in Europe.

The American Revolution led to the end of British restrictions on American trade and industry. It also brought economic problems. Because of the ways the Continental Congress paid for the war, the new government started out deep in debt to allies who had loaned it money. The government's attempt to print more money to meet financial demands lowered the value of the money already in use. America's economic fitness was tested from its start.

1. Why did the Americans limit the authority of the new state governments created during the war?
2. How were slaves affected by the American Revolution?
3. What were the economic problems of the new country after the war?

4. Conclusion

The American states in 1763 had been 13 separate and divided colonies. After the French and Indian War, the changing policies of the British government brought them together to protect what they saw as their natural rights to govern themselves. Their unity helped them to defeat the British in the War of Independence. The government which they set up during the Revolution served its purpose during the war. The question remained whether the 13 states could work together as one nation in peace.

Chapter 5 Review

Main Points

1. After the French and Indian War, Britain passed new laws to control the colonies.
2. The colonists considered the laws harmful to their economic interests.
3. Over several years, hostility mounted and led to open rebellion in 1775.
4. The colonists declared independence in July 1776.
5. After seven years of fighting, the colonial army defeated British forces and secured independence.
6. The Treaty of Paris in 1783 ended the war and set the territorial boundaries of the United States.
7. As a result of the Revolution, more free males began to take part in government.
8. There were few changes in the rights of women and of people held as slaves.
9. Because of large debts to allies who helped to pay for the war, the United States faced major economic problems at the end of the war.

Building Vocabulary

1. Identify the following:
   Grenville Acts
   Townshend Acts
   Boston Massacre
   Boston Tea Party
   Intolerable Acts
   General Thomas Gage

   Paul Revere
   Thomas Jefferson
   July 4, 1776
   Thomas Paine
   George Washington

   General William Howe
   Battle of Saratoga
   George Rogers Clark
   Marquis de Lafayette
   Treaty of Paris of 1783
   Abigail Adams

2. Define the following:
   virtual representation
   direct representation
   direct tax

   boycott
   patriots

   loyalists
   quartered
   minutemen

Remembering the Facts

1. How did the colonists respond to new British laws and regulations on colonial trade and industry?
2. Where did the First Continental Congress meet, and what was its purpose?

3. What was the role of the Sons of Liberty in the conflict with Britain? Why were such groups formed?

4. Which event was the formal statement of the colonists' demand to be independent?

5. What were the advantages and the disadvantages held by the British and the colonists in fighting the war?

6. Which European countries loaned money to the colonies to fight against Britain?

7. What were the main terms of the Treaty of Paris of 1783?

8. What political changes took place in the United States after the war?

9. How did the war influence the lives of blacks and women?

Understanding the Facts

1. Why did Britain change the way it controlled the colonies after the French and Indian War?

2. How were American trade and industry affected by laws passed by the British Parliament after 1763?

3. What were the various views of British policy among the colonists before 1776?

4. How were the colonists able to win the war?

5. How was American life changed as a result of the war and independence?

Using Maps

Tracing Routes. The map on page 118 shows the United States during the American Revolution from 1775 to 1777. The map on page 121 shows from 1778 to 1781. Symbols, names, and dates give information about the major battles of the Revolution from 1775 to 1781. Examine the maps, and answer the following questions.

In answering the questions, you must provide some information concerning directions. To help you, a symbol on the maps shows that north is the direction toward the top of the page. From this symbol, you can decide south, west, and east, as well.

1. Which keys or symbols show the routes followed by American soldiers?

2. Which army won the Battle of Bunker Hill on June 17, 1775?

3. Which direction did Washington's soldiers travel after leaving Trenton?

4. Where were Washington's troops during the winter of 1777 and 1778?

5. How far did Clark's soldiers travel from Fort Pitt to Kaskaskia?

6. Which direction did American soldiers travel to Yorktown?

7. Why was it a problem for Cornwallis to get supplies at Yorktown?

Forming a Union

6

In this painting of the Constitutional Convention by Thomas Rossiter, George Washington is shown presiding over the delegates. How did Americans govern themselves after they declared independence?

The people of the United States gained their political independence through the Revolution. Each of the former colonies became a state, and together, the states became a nation. Yet the future of the country was far from certain. It was still to be determined how well the states would be able to work together. Close to 3 million people, living along a coast stretching 1,200 miles (1,920 kilometers) from Georgia to Maine, had to learn to govern themselves as one country. There had been democracies before, such as the ones in ancient Greece and medieval Switzerland. None though had ever had so many people scattered over so large an area as the United States.

1. The Period of Confederation

During the colonial period, Britain had filled many of the needs of the American people—trade, defense, law, and order. The colonies had been part of a large and secure empire. After they had broken away from the empire, the 13 states tried to fill these same needs for the people. It was important that the new country quickly become strong and united.

1.1 The Confederation Government. During the war with Britain, the Second Continental Congress was the governing body for the rebelling colonies. In 1777, the congress drew up a plan for government. Known as the Articles of Confederation, the plan was put into effect in 1781. It set up a confederation among the 13 states. The Articles protected the freedom and independence of each state. It also provided a structure for governing the country as a whole.

What was the period following the Revolution called?

The Articles of Confederation set up a one-house congress with representatives from the states. In this legislature, each state had one vote. The Confederation congress had the authority to make war and peace. It also ran the postal service, coined money, set standards of weight and measure, and managed affairs with the Indian peoples. All 13 states had to agree before an *amendment* (a change in the provisions) could be made in the Articles of Confederation. During the time that the congress was not in session, a committee of states managed the day-to-day business of the nation. One delegate from each state made up the committee.

What could the Congress of the Confederation do?

1.2 Western Lands. After the Revolution, American settlers moved into the lands west of the Appalachian Mountains in great numbers. Thousands of people crossed the mountains into Kentucky and Tennessee. No definite plans had been made for this land or for the huge area north of the Ohio River, called the Northwest Territory. With the growing number of settlers, there was a need for order. To answer this need, the Confederation congress passed two *ordinances* (laws)— the Land Ordinance of 1785 and the Northwest Ordinance of 1787. They were based in part on an earlier plan of Thomas Jefferson.

How was land to be divided in the Northwest Territory?

The Land Ordinance of 1785 directed that the Northwest Territory be *surveyed*—examined and measured. The surveyors divided the land into townships along north-south and east-west lines forming six-mile squares. The townships were then divided into 36 sections of 640 acres. Each section was sold to one buyer. In each township, one section was set aside for the support of public education in the township.

Land in the Northwest Territory was to be sold at a price of at least $1 an acre. Because few settlers could afford to buy a whole section, land companies bought much of the land and resold it in smaller lots. The Confederation government often agreed to sell the land to these

Most American families west of the Appalachian Mountains lived in log cabins (left), and they worked small farms. First the land was cleared of trees (right). Then they planted crops. Why did settlers move to the frontier?

The Northwest Territory

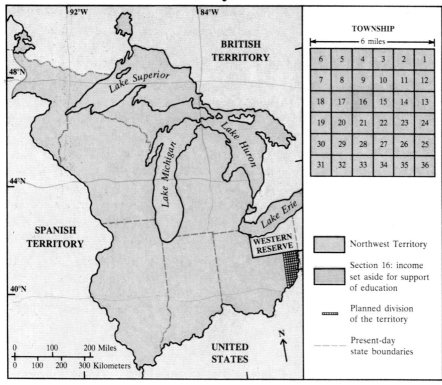

TOWNSHIP

6	5	4	3	2	1
7	8	9	10	11	12
18	17	16	15	14	13
19	20	21	22	23	24
30	29	28	27	26	25
31	32	33	34	35	36

6 miles

Northwest Territory

Section 16: income set aside for support of education

Planned division of the territory

Present-day state boundaries

Why was the area north of the Ohio River called the Northwest Territory? What states were formed from this area?

companies for only a few cents an acre because the government needed the money to operate.

The township system was not used in the area south of the Ohio River, basically because settlers already lived there. Lands in Kentucky and Tennessee had been divided at random, and the settlers there had set up local governments by 1785. The system established by the Land Ordinance of 1785, however, became the United States policy for organizing new lands.

Why was the township system not used in the South?

In addition to setting up a plan for selling land, the Congress of the Confederation took care of governing the Northwest Territory. It passed the Northwest Ordinance in 1787. This law directed that the congress name a governor, a secretary, and three judges to administer the area.

The ordinance also set up the steps which a territory was to take before becoming a state. Members of the congress agreed that not less than three nor more than five states would be made from the Northwest Territory. When there were 5,000 free adult males of voting age living in

How many states could be made from the Northwest Territory?

In this George Caleb Bingham painting, Daniel Boone (center) is shown escorting settlers through the Cumberland Gap. Boone blazed some of the early trails to the west. How did trailblazers make trips west easier?

the territory, they could elect a legislature for deciding local matters. When there were 60,000 free settlers in an area of the territory, the people could apply to the national government to have the area become a state. This system provided for organizing the Northwest Territory and other areas which would become part of the United States in the future. For this reason, the Northwest Ordinance was considered one of the most important acts passed by the Congress of the Confederation.

1.3   Problems of the Confederation.   The Articles of Confederation was the first United States *constitution*—a written plan of government. The government, guided by this plan, handled the problem of the western lands. Having no strong central organization, it was unable to handle other problems, however. The weaknesses of the Confederation plan of government were seen in both foreign affairs and business at home.

How did Britain create problems for the new nation?

One of the major problems in foreign affairs was relations with Britain. Despite the Treaty of Paris of 1783, British leaders stationed soldiers in forts in the Northwest Territory. Britain hoped to keep on good terms with the Indians in the area to save the fur trade for British merchants. The British government did not favor American trade with the British Empire either. Britain tried to keep Americans from trading directly with the nearby British West Indies, although smuggling kept such trade alive. Attempts to talk over trade agreements with Britain failed. Without British markets, there was a strain on the economy of the new nation.

Spain also created problems for the United States economy. Spanish leaders refused to allow Americans to use the port of New Orleans at the mouth of the Mississippi River. Without this port, western farmers could not ship their goods down the river to the Gulf of Mexico, then to European and other markets.

How did Spain create problems?

Americans were upset that their national government could not solve these problems. The members of the Confederation government complained that they needed funds to support an army or any other program. The government under the Articles of Confederation could not tax its citizens to raise money. The only taxing authority it had was to require postage for mail service. To keep the authority of the national government weak, the states often refused to give it money.

One of the most serious problems faced at home also concerned trade. The national government had no authority to control trade among the states. Each state set its own laws. One state could tax products coming in from other states. States argued over control of rivers and harbors. The people of New Jersey paid more for goods because most of their trade came through the port of New York. New York taxed the goods, and that added to the prices. In return, New Jersey taxed New York for a lighthouse built by New York on land owned by New Jersey. Similar disagreements arose between other states.

What was one of the most serious problems at home?

1.4 The Annapolis Convention. In March 1785, representatives from Virginia and Maryland met to discuss problems between the two states. At this conference held at Mount Vernon, they worked out ways of dealing with navigation rights on their shared waterways, the Potomac River and Chesapeake Bay. The Virginia legislature then invited all the states to send delegates to a larger convention on matters of trade among the states.

This conference met at Annapolis, Maryland, in September 1786. Delegates from only five states—New York, New Jersey, Delaware, Pennsylvania, and Virginia—came to this convention, however. Two delegates at the meeting, Alexander Hamilton of New York and James Madison of Virginia, were eager to have the states consider a complete

What was the purpose of the Annapolis Convention?

overhaul of the Articles of Confederation. The members of the Annapolis Convention adopted a report written by Hamilton to hold another convention in Philadelphia. This meeting was supposed to come up with ways to revise the Articles of Confederation so that the government would be able to deal more effectively with the problems of the United States.

1.5 Shays' Rebellion. The Confederation government's money troubles hurt mostly individual citizens. Business began to slow down after the end of the war with Britain. The prices of goods began to rise, and many people could not pay their debts. Taxes rose as the states

Daniel Shays led an army of discontented farmers in an uprising against Massachusetts authorities. At the right, Shays' followers seize the courthouse in Springfield. Many Americans supported the farmers' cause. What effect did Shays' Rebellion have on the country?

Daniel Shays (1747?–1825)

The years following the war with Britain were not easy for most American farmers. Markets shrank, and land taxes rose. Angry Massachusetts farmers organized to oppose some of the state tax laws. One leader of the opposition was Daniel Shays.

Shays had been a captain in the army and fought at Bunker Hill, Ticonderoga, and Saratoga. After the war, he returned to a home deep in debt. He and other landowners asked the state legislature to ease the land taxes. When no action was taken by the summer of 1786, Shays gathered a force of about 500 farmers in a march on the courthouse and armory in Springfield.

The Massachusetts militia stopped the advance and scattered the farmers. Some were arrested. But so many people felt sorry for the farmers' cause that Shays and his followers, at first sentenced to death, were pardoned in 1788.

Shays' uprising influenced the state legislature not to impose new taxes that year. It also passed laws making it possible for people who were bankrupt to keep their household goods and their tools. Equally important, the uprising demonstrated the weakness of the national government under the Articles of Confederation in maintaining a strong economy. After Shays' Rebellion, there came more support for a revision of the government. The plan to revise the Articles led to the framing of a new constitution.

---

tried to meet their debts and pay for government services. Farmers in states like Massachusetts began to lose their land to banks because they could not make mortgage payments.

In the summer of 1786, some landowners in western Massachusetts revolted against the tax laws. They seized local courthouses in order to keep judges from approving *foreclosures*—taking away of property due to failure to make payments on its debt. Daniel Shays, who had been a soldier in the Revolutionary War, led a group of farmers on a march to a courthouse and an armory in Springfield. The march, with its threat of violence, caused the state legislature to adjourn. Shays' force finally was

Where was Shays' Rebellion?

Forming a Union   135

broken up by the state militia in February 1787. This rebellion brought the economic problems of the country into much sharper focus.

1. What were the two major accomplishments of the Congress of the Confederation?
2. How did Britain violate the terms of the Treaty of Paris of 1783?
3. How was trade between states regulated?
4. What was the basic cause of Shays' Rebellion?

2. Making the Constitution_____

The convention in Philadelphia opened May 25, 1787, when enough delegates arrived to begin work. The meetings were held in the State House, where the Declaration of Independence had been signed. Attending the convention were 55 delegates, elected by the legislatures of 12 states. The leaders of Rhode Island were against any move to strengthen the government, so they did not send delegates.

Most of the convention members were young and came from the landowning upper classes. More than half were college-trained, and many were lawyers. Benjamin Franklin of Pennsylvania, who was 81 years of age, was the oldest. Jonathan Dayton of New Jersey, who was 26 years of age, was the youngest. Franklin and George Washington were the best known of the delegates. But there were some noted leaders not present. Samuel Adams had not been selected to attend. Patrick Henry refused to attend. Thomas Jefferson and John Adams were out of the country, serving as foreign ministers in France and Britain respectively.

Who did not attend the Constitutional Convention? Why?

2.1 Conflicting Plans of Government. An important question faced the delegates from the beginning of the convention. They had to decide if the Articles of Confederation should be improved or if an entirely new plan of government be written. Many of the delegates had received instructions to work only to improve the Articles. Other delegates felt strongly that a new plan of government was needed.

Who presented the Virginia Plan? the New Jersey Plan?

Four days after the convention opened, Edmund Randolph of Virginia presented 15 resolutions for discussion. These were known as the Virginia Plan and were meant **as** a design for a new national government. Debate over the Virginia Plan centered on the question of representation in the legislature. Randolph proposed that states not be represented equally. Rather, they should be represented according to either their population or the amount of money each contributed to the

Analyzing Sources of History
SKILL

Historians use many sources of information to understand an event. Written primary sources are often the most reliable record of what happened. Whenever possible, the historian tries to base an interpretation on these sources. Written primary sources include diaries, documents, eyewitness accounts, journals, letters, notes, and reports. These can be published or unpublished sources.

The following selections are written primary sources having to do with the Constitution. When the document was put before the convention on September 17, 1787, the delegates had various reactions.

James Madison of Virginia wrote very detailed notes during the convention. He recorded Benjamin Franklin's last speech to the delegates.

I confess that I do not entirely approve of this Constitution at present; but, sir, I am not sure I shall never approve it; for having lived long, I have experienced many instances of being [made], *by better information or fuller consideration, to change opinions even on important subjects, which I once thought right, but found to be otherwise. . . .*

On the whole, sir, I cannot help expressing a wish that every member of the convention who may still have objections to it would with me on this occasion doubt a little of his own [rightness] *and, to make* [clearly known] *our* [total agreement], *put his name to this instrument.*

George Mason of Virginia did not sign the Constitution. His objection to it is explained in a letter he wrote to George Washington on October 18, 1787.

There is no declaration of rights: (a bill of rights for individuals and states) and the laws of the general government being [higher than] *the laws and constitutions of the several states, the declarations of rights in the separate states are no security.*

Answer the following questions.
1. Which types of written primary sources are these selections?
2. What is Franklin's attitude toward the Constitution?
3. Why did Mason consider a declaration of rights important?
4. Which source would you consider to be more reliable? Why?

national government. With this plan, larger states would have more power.

The Virginia Plan showed clearly that many delegates were open to changing the structure of the government and not just revising the Articles of Confederation. But smaller states, like New Jersey, were against the Virginia Plan. New Jersey's William Paterson presented his own resolution. His plan, called the New Jersey Plan, insisted representation in the legislature remain the same as under the Articles. Each state would be represented equally.

What is a compromise?

2.2 The Great Compromise.   The issue of representation was a difficult one. It was settled by *compromise*—a settlement of differences by each side giving up part of what it wants. The delegates decided to have two houses of congress: the Senate and the House of Representatives. Each state was to have two Senators which were to be selected by its legislature. Small and large states, therefore, would be

As delegates signed the Constitution, Benjamin Franklin (center) observed a rising sun on the president's chair and a new day for the country. Not every delegate shared his view. Why did some delegates not sign the Constitution?

equally represented in the Senate. The number of delegates in the House of Representatives would be determined by the number of people in each state. Qualified voters in each state would elect their state's Representatives. The states with the most people would have a stronger voice in the House of Representatives.

What compromise was included within the Great Compromise?

Within this so-called Great Compromise was a second compromise which resolved a conflict between slave and free states. Slave states wanted to count all slaves when deciding the population for setting the number of Representatives in the House. Free states did not want slaves figured into the count. It was agreed that three fifths of the number of slaves should be counted to determine the number of Representatives. It was also agreed that the slaves were to be counted the same way in deciding each state's share of taxes.

2.3 Other Compromises. The Great Compromise helped to settle several problems facing the delegates, but there were still others to be solved. Many northern states wanted to give the national government authority to control trade. Southern states feared that such authority might be used to end the slave trade and to create high *tariffs* (taxes on imported goods). The delegates reached a compromise that was acceptable to northern and southern states. The national government was given the exclusive power to regulate trade among states and with other countries, including the power to tax imports. Congress could not, however, put a tax on any export. In addition, Congress could not interfere with the slave trade for 20 years.

What were some other compromises?

Other issues had to be resolved, too. For instance, the delegates decided that the national government was to have three branches or parts. In addition to the legislature, there was to be a national executive branch, headed by a president. The executive branch was to carry out the laws passed by the legislature. The third branch, a national *judiciary*, or court system, also was set up.

The convention met through the summer months of 1787. On September 15, the plan of government was completed. The majority of the delegates signed the Constitution of the United States on September 17. James Madison recorded the event:

> *While the last members were signing it, Dr. Franklin looked toward the president's chair at the back of which a rising sun happened to be painted, observed to a few members near him that painters had found it difficult to distinguish in their art a rising from a setting sun. "I have," said he, "often and often in the course of the session, and the* [changes between] *my hopes and fears as to its issue, looked at that behind the president*

without being able to tell whether it was rising or setting. But now at length I have the happiness to know that it is a rising and not a setting sun."

To whom was the Constitution first submitted?

The document was then sent to the Congress of the Confederation. That group submitted it to the states for their approval. Citizens elected special state conventions to consider the Constitution. Nine of the state conventions had to *ratify* (approve) it before the new government could be put into effect.

1. How did the Virginia Plan differ from the New Jersey Plan?
2. What was the Great Compromise?
3. What was the three-fifths compromise?

3. The Struggle for Ratification

Why was acceptance of the Constitution not certain?

Acceptance of the Constitution by the states was not certain. In each state, there were fierce debates over whether to approve the

Eleven states quickly ratified the Constitution, but North Carolina and Rhode Island did not. The *Massachusetts Centinel* urged their acceptance August 2, 1788. Why did this cartoonist want all states to ratify?

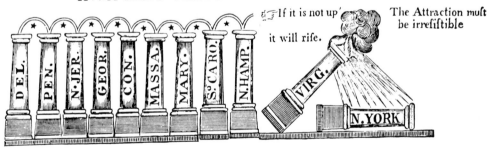

The Ninth PILLAR erected !
" The Ratification of the Conventions of nine States, fhall be fufficient for the eftablifh-ment of this Conftitution, between the States fo ratifying the fame." *Art.* vii.
INCIPIENT MAGNI PROCEDERE MENSES.

If it is not up it will rife.   The Attraction muft be irrefiftible

DEL. PEN. N.JER. GEOR. CON. MASSA. MARY. So.CARO. N.HAMP. VIRG. N.YORK

James Madison (left) and Alexander Hamilton (right) were two Federalist leaders who wrote articles supporting the Constitution. These articles were first published in New York in 1787. What were they called?

Constitution or to keep the Articles of Confederation. Some people feared the authority given to the national government. Many felt that their liberties and the rights of the states were more secure under the Articles of Confederation. They felt that, although the central government was weak, it was also safe.

3.1 Federalists and Anti-Federalists. Two different groups emerged in the struggle to ratify the Constitution. Those in favor of ratification were called Federalists, because they wanted a strong *federal* (national) government. Those against the Constitution were known as Anti-Federalists.

The ranks of the Federalists and the Anti-Federalists had people from every class, area, and economic interest. Well-known figures like George Washington and Benjamin Franklin favored ratification. James Madison, Alexander Hamilton, and John Jay carefully worded the Federalists' ideas in a series of articles for people to read in newspapers. Later the articles were bound together into two books called *The Federalist Papers*. Madison, Hamilton, and Jay tried to convince the people that the Constitution would provide a much better government

Who wrote The Federalist Papers?

Ratification of the Constitution

Date of Ratification	State	Vote
December 7, 1787	Delaware	Unanimous
December 12, 1787	Pennsylvania	46 For, 23 Against
December 18, 1787	New Jersey	Unanimous
January 2, 1788	Georgia	Unanimous
January 9, 1788	Connecticut	128 For, 40 Against
February 6, 1788	Massachusetts	187 For, 168 Against
April 28, 1788	Maryland	63 For, 11 Against
May 23, 1788	South Carolina	149 For, 73 Against
June 21, 1788	New Hampshire	57 For, 47 Against
June 25, 1788	Virginia	89 For, 79 Against
July 26, 1788	New York	30 For, 27 Against
November 21, 1789	North Carolina	194 For, 77 Against
May 29, 1790	Rhode Island	34 For, 32 Against

Which state convention was the first to ratify the Constitution? Which state was the last? Which states voted unanimously for ratification? Where was the Constitution narrowly approved?

than the Articles of Confederation. The Federalists were positive in their approach to the change, and they had the advantage of support from Washington and Franklin.

Many of those who were active in the move toward independence in the 1770's supported the Anti-Federalists in 1787. Patrick Henry, Samuel Adams, George Mason, and George Clinton were among those opposing a change in the national government. To them, the new constitution would destroy the rights of the states and individual liberties of the people. They felt that the Constitutional Convention had gone beyond its authority. It was to have improved the Articles of Confederation and nothing more.

What leaders opposed ratification?

3.2 Ratification. The decision to ratify or reject the Constitution began in the state conventions in the fall months of 1787. Before the year was over, Delaware, Pennsylvania, and New Jersey had approved the Constitution. Georgia, Connecticut, and Massachusetts ratified early in 1788. In Massachusetts, Federalist supporters had a tough time winning over the convention led by Samuel Adams. In a compromise measure with the Anti-Federalists, the Federalists promised to help pass a bill of rights as soon as a new government was set up under the Constitution.

What state was first to ratify the Constitution?

In 1788, enough states voted in favor of ratification to put the Constitution into effect. New Hampshire was the ninth and deciding state. New York and Virginia, however, had not yet acted. Without them, the Constitution would not have the broad support it needed to

Why was it important for New York and Virginia to ratify the Constitution?

succeed. After bitter debate, both states ratified the document during the summer of 1788. By the end of 1788, only North Carolina and Rhode Island had not voted on the Constitution. North Carolina voted in favor of it in 1789. Rhode Island held out until 1790, becoming the last state to approve the new plan of government.

3.3   The Bill of Rights.   One of the most important objections to ratifying the Constitution in many states was that it did not include a list of definite individual rights. Laws which limited the authority of the government over the individual had been written into the Constitution. Yet there were those who felt that these personal rights should also be spelled out. Before many of the states approved the Constitution, they insisted that such a list be added to it.

What was one of the strongest objections to ratifying the Constitution?

Soon after the new government began, these rights were written down by Congress. Called together the Bill of Rights, they were approved by the states and added as the first ten amendments to the Constitution on December 15, 1791. Among the basic rights guaranteed to all citizens were freedom of speech, freedom of religion, freedom of the press, and the right to a trial by jury. Also included were the right of assembly, the right to bear arms, and protection from cruel and unusual punishments. The Revolution had been fought for these rights, and Americans felt they must become part of the new government.

1. Why did the Anti-Federalists oppose the new constitution?
2. What was the purpose of *The Federalist Papers*?
3. How many states were needed to approve the Constitution?
4. What was the Bill of Rights?

4. Conclusion

American leaders created the Constitution of the United States in order to deal with problems which the government under the Articles of Confederation could not solve. A new plan of government was established to change the relationship of the national government to the states. It was also designed to better deal with important foreign problems. Like breaking away from British control, starting a new government in the United States was an uncertain venture. No one could say for sure that the new government would work successfully. But most Americans looked forward to trying government under the Constitution.

Chapter 6 Review

Main Points

1. The future of the United States was uncertain at the end of the war for independence.

2. The central government organized under the Articles of Confederation was a weak union in which each state had an equal vote in the national legislature.

3. The most important legislation passed by the Congress of the Confederation provided for the organization of the Northwest Territory and for the way new states could enter the Union.

4. Government under the Articles of Confederation was unable to handle many important economic problems.

5. Dissatisfaction with the Articles resulted in a convention in Philadelphia and a new plan of government.

6. The new constitution was the product of several compromises.

7. After much debate, the Constitution was ratified by all 13 states.

8. Soon after ratification, a Bill of Rights was added to the Constitution.

Building Vocabulary

1. Identify the following:
   Articles of Confederation
   Northwest Territory
   Annapolis Convention
   Daniel Shays

   Benjamin Franklin
   Virginia Plan
   New Jersey Plan

   Great Compromise
   Federalists
   Anti-Federalists
   Bill of Rights

2. Define the following:
   amendment
   ordinances
   surveyed
   constitution

   foreclosures
   compromise
   tariffs

   judiciary
   ratify
   federal

Remembering the Facts

1. What was the plan for government that was drawn up during the war for independence?

2. What were the provisions of the Land Ordinance of 1785?

3. What were the provisions in the Northwest Ordinance of 1787 for admitting new states?

4. What were the weaknesses of the Articles of Confederation?

5. What was the purpose of the 1787 convention in Philadelphia? What action did the convention take?

6. How did the delegates at the convention bring about agreement among people who had various views on what government should and should not do?

7. When was the Constitution ratified, and when did it go into effect?

8. What were some of the individual rights protected by the Bill of Rights?

Understanding the Facts

1. How did the colonial experience with the British government influence the kind of government established under the Articles of Confederation?

2. Why was the government under the Articles of Confederation not able to handle the problems facing the new nation?

3. How did the Great Compromise combine parts of the Virginia Plan and parts of the New Jersey Plan?

4. What were the major points of disagreement between the Federalists and the Anti-Federalists?

5. What was the purpose of the Bill of Rights?

Using Maps

Scale. Maps are drawings which give a small representation of a much larger area of the earth's surface. In an effort to make them as accurate as possible, reference maps and most thematic maps are drawn to scale. This means that a precise distance on the earth's surface is shown by a much smaller, but also precise, space on a flat surface.

The scale on a map tells the relationship to the actual size. It is usually given as part of the map key. For example, on the map on page 131, the miles of the earth's surface are shown by inches and centimeters.

Study the map, and answer the following questions.

1. On the map, one inch equals how many miles? how many kilometers?

2. Between which parallels of latitude is the Northwest Territory?

3. Between which meridians of longitude is the Northwest Territory?

4. What is the east-west distance across the Northwest Territory measured at 40 degrees north latitude?

5. What is the north-south distance across the Northwest Territory measured at 92 degrees west longitude?

6. What lake extends into the middle of the Northwest Territory? How long is it?

7. Which five states were organized from the Northwest Territory?

The Constitution

7

The Constitutional Convention met at Independence Hall in Philadelphia. What kind of document did the delegates write? What ideas about government did the document reflect?

The Constitution is the fundamental law of the United States. It provides an outline for the basic organization of the national government and sets procedures and limitations for its operation. As drafted by its Framers, the Constitution is a brief document, originally having less than 5,000 words. When drafted and ratified, the Constitution consisted of a short Preamble (introduction) and seven articles, or major sections. The Preamble states the general goals of the governmental system being formed by the Constitution. Articles I through III concern the organization, powers, and duties of the three branches of government—legislative, executive, and judicial. Article IV covers relations between and among the states. Article V provides for an amendment process. Article VI deals with miscellaneous items, and Article VII sets up the procedures for ratification.

What is the fundamental law of the United States?

How many Articles are there in the Constitution?

1. Basic Principles

At the heart of the Constitution lie a number of basic principles upon which the American political system rests. In forming their ideas about government, the Framers drew upon many sources in their political heritage, including British political philosophy and the ideals of the American Revolution.

1.1 Popular Sovereignty. In the United States, supreme political power rests with the people. Government gets its authority from them and acts only with their consent. This principle of *popular sovereignty* is clearly spelled out in the opening words of the Preamble to the Constitution, which states: "We, the people of the United States . . . do ordain and establish this Constitution. . . ."

From whom does government in the United States get its power?

1.2 Limited Government. Hand-in-hand with the idea of popular sovereignty goes the principle of *limited government*. Since the authority to rule comes from the people, then it follows that government may exercise only those powers granted to it by the people. No government in the United States—federal, state, or local—has unlimited power.

The Constitution prohibits both the federal and state governments from doing certain things. For example, Article I, Section 9 places several restrictions on the federal government. It cannot tax exports, suspend the writ of habeas corpus during peacetime, or grant titles of nobility. Article I, Section 10 says that the states cannot do such things as make treaties with other countries, coin money, or pass laws which void the obligations of contracts.

How is government limited in the United States?

The Constitution 147

Under the British system, Parliament makes and administers laws. The United States Constitution provided for a separation of powers. What is the function of each branch of the federal government?

What is the principle of federalism?

1.3 Federalism. The principle of *federalism*—the division of power between a central government and a number of state governments—grew out of the American struggle for independence from Great Britain. When the colonies revolted in 1775, they were rebelling against the rule of a powerful central government. The colonists insisted that such a government restricted their conduct of local affairs. After achieving independence, they were fearful of creating a strong central government in America.

The problems under the Articles of Confederation convinced many Americans that some form of government was needed other than a loose confederation of independent states. Therefore, the Framers of the Constitution provided for a system of government where political power is divided between the federal government and the states.

The federal government has how many branches?

1.4 Separation of Powers. The Framers of the Constitution not only divided the powers of government on two levels, but they also separated the executive, legislative, and judicial functions of the national government among three branches. This *separation of powers* was somewhat revolutionary at the time. In 1787, almost every nation in the Western world was ruled by a monarch. Even the British parliamentary system did not separate the basic functions of government. The British Parliament was both the maker and the administrator of laws.

The separation of powers is clearly stated in three articles of the Constitution. Article I, Section I says that "All legislative powers . . . shall be vested in a Congress. . . ." Congress cannot authorize any other agency or persons to make laws in its place. Article II, Section I provides that "The executive power shall be vested in a President. . . ." The President must see that the laws passed by Congress are carried out and can also recommend new laws. Though assisted by various agencies and bureaus, the President is solely responsible for the exercise of executive power at the national level. Article III, Section I provides that "The judicial power of the United States shall be vested in one Supreme Court, and in such inferior [lower] courts as the Congress may from time to time . . . establish." Judicial power includes interpreting, or determining the meaning of laws.

    1.5   Checks and Balances.   In drafting the powers and duties of each branch of the federal government, the Framers made certain that

How can the President check Congress and the Supreme Court? How can Congress check the Supreme Court and the President? How can the Supreme Court check the President and Congress?

System of Checks and Balances

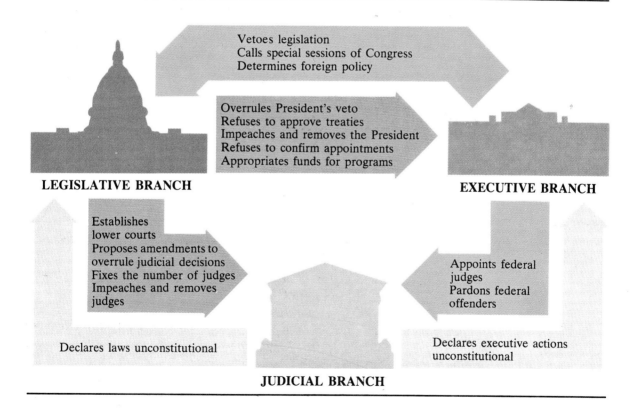

Vetoes legislation
Calls special sessions of Congress
Determines foreign policy

Overrules President's veto
Refuses to approve treaties
Impeaches and removes the President
Refuses to confirm appointments
Appropriates funds for programs

LEGISLATIVE BRANCH

EXECUTIVE BRANCH

Establishes lower courts
Proposes amendments to overrule judicial decisions
Fixes the number of judges
Impeaches and removes judges

Appoints federal judges
Pardons federal offenders

Declares laws unconstitutional

Declares executive actions unconstitutional

JUDICIAL BRANCH

no branch was totally independent of the other two. They set up a system of **checks and balances** by which each branch could restrain the power of the other branches. For example, although Congress has the power to pass laws, the President can veto any act of Congress. Congress, on the other hand, can pass a law over the veto of the President by a two-thirds vote of each house. The President has the power to make treaties and appoint ambassadors, judges, and other officials. But treaties and presidential appointments require the approval of the Senate.

1. What are the basic principles of the Constitution?
2. Are popular sovereignty and limited government related? How?
3. How are separation of powers and checks and balances related?

2. Other Principles

The principles described in Section 1 pertain to the very nature of the Constitution. That is, they describe the elements which make up the American political system. They are the root of the Constitution. In addition to the basic principles, there are a number of other principles that relate to the Constitution. Though these principles do not lie at the core, they are quite important.

2.1 Judicial Review. One of the great checks in the American governmental system is the principle of **judicial review**. This is the power of the courts to determine if acts of Congress or actions of the President are constitutional. Although the Constitution does not specifically provide for judicial review, it has become one of the most important functions of the courts. Alexander Hamilton wrote in *Federalist Paper #78*:

> *The interpretation of the laws is the proper and peculiar province* [responsibility] *of the courts. A constitution is, in fact, and must be regarded by the judges as, a fundamental law. It therefore belongs to them to ascertain its meaning as well as the meaning of any particular act proceeding from the legislative body.*

2.2 Supremacy of National Law. One principle noted in the Constitution is the **supremacy of national law,** or the concept that national law is superior to state law. Article VI of the Constitution contains the supremacy clause which states that "This Constitution, and the laws of the United States . . . shall be the supreme law of the land. . . ."

What are the two principles of supremacy?

2.3 Supremacy of Civilian Authority. The second important principle regarding supremacy is the idea that the military is subject to civilian authority. Although *supremacy of civilian authority* is not mentioned in the Constitution, it is shown by the fact that the President, a civilian, is commander in chief of the armed forces and only Congress has the power to declare war.

2.4 Additional Principles. There are other major principles which are part of the American political system. Among these are the rule of the majority, the recognition of minority rights, and respect for the worth and dignity of the individual. Although these principles have not been upheld at times, they have given meaning to the operation of government under the Constitution.

What are other important principles of the American political system?

1. How do the basic principles differ from other principles?
2. Which law is considered supreme, national or state?
3. What is the obligation of the majority to the minority?

3. Branches of Government

The Framers of the Constitution created three distinct branches of the federal government—legislative, executive, and judicial. Although unique for a national government at the time, this model of government was not unknown. The governments of the states, which had developed from those of the colonies, had such a form.

3.1 Congress. In a democratic system, perhaps the most important function of government is to make the people's will into public policy by means of law. The importance of this can be seen by the fact that the first and longest article of the Constitution deals with the legislative branch. In the American system, it is Congress which is the legislative branch of the federal government.

Who makes law at the national level?

Article I of the Constitution outlines the powers of Congress, the limits of those powers, and a variety of organizational and other matters. In Section I, the Framers created a *bicameral* (two-house) legislature. The lower house is the House of Representatives, and the upper house is the Senate. The creation of a bicameral legislature solved

This scene of the old House chambers was painted by Samuel F. B. Morse. Voters elect members of the House of Representatives every two years. What are the qualifications for being elected to the House of Representatives?

What are the qualifications of members of Congress?

the problem of legislative representation and was at the heart of the Great Compromise. Most Americans were familiar with the concept of a two-house legislature. All of the colonial governments except Georgia and Pennsylvania had two-house assemblies. The Framers also favored a bicameral legislature in the belief that one house would act as a check upon the other.

In addition to solving the problem of representation, the Framers had other decisions to make. One of these concerned qualifications for the members of Congress. They decided that members of the House of Representatives must be at least 25 years of age, citizens of the United States for 7 years, and residents of the states from which they are elected. Senators, on the other hand, must be at least 30 years of age, citizens for 9 years, and residents of the states from which they are elected. The Framers also decided that Representatives would serve two-year terms, while Senators would serve six-year terms.

The Framers wanted to make one house of the legislature more responsible to the will of the people and still provide a check on the pressures of public opinion. This was one reason why terms of office differed for Senators and Representatives. In addition, the Framers set up different methods of selecting members to the two houses. Representatives are elected directly by the voters. Although later changed, Senators were originally chosen by state legislatures.

There are still other differences between the House of Representatives and the Senate. Most of these deal with specific powers. For example, all *revenue bills* (tax bills for raising money and bills authorizing the spending of money) must be started in the House of Representatives. Only the Senate approves treaties and confirms presidential appointments. Each house has a different role in the impeachment process. The House of Representatives has the power to *impeach* (bring charges against) the President, Vice-President, and federal judges, and other civil (nonmilitary) officers of the United

What role does each house play in the impeachment process?

What changes were made in the functions of Congress? Who was the executive under the Articles of Confederation? What authority did the Constitution give to the Supreme Court?

Plans of Government

Articles of Confederation		Constitution of 1787
Unicameral legislature	**Legislative**	Bicameral legislature
One vote per state regardless of size or population		One vote per delegate with each state having equal representation in the Senate and represented according to population in the House of Representatives
Determine war and peace		
Send and receive ambassadors		Declare war
Make treaties and alliances		Tax and borrow money
Regulate value of coin		Coin money and regulate value
Set standards of weights and measures		Regulate commerce with foreign countries, between states, and with Indian people
Regulate trade and manage Indian affairs		Set standards of weights and measures
Set up and regulate post offices		Provide post offices and post roads
Direct land and naval forces		Protect copyrights and patents
		Set up minor courts
		Raise, support, and govern army and navy
		Call out militia to stop uprisings and invasions
		Govern the national capital
Committee of States serve when Congress is not in session	**Executive**	One person serves as President
Committee chosen by the Congress; presiding president chosen by Committee		Chosen by electors who are chosen by voters in the individual states
Specific powers authorized by Congress		Directs army and navy as commander in chief
Nine states must agree to the extent of the power		Pardons federal offenders, except in cases of impeachment
		Appoints ambassadors, judges, and federal officers
		Makes treaties and receives ambassadors
		Calls Congress into session in emergencies
		Executes all laws of the country
Congress can set up courts only to hear cases involving piracy or capture at sea	**Judicial**	Congress sits as a court for impeachment
Congress itself sits as a court in deciding disputes between two states		Supreme Court, plus minor courts set up by Congress, hear cases involving national laws, treaties, the Constitution, foreign nations and ambassadors, ships and shipping, two or more states, a state and citizen of another state, citizens of different states, and the national government

States. The Senate tries and removes that person from office upon conviction. Members of Congress are not subject to impeachment, but they can be expelled under the rules established by each house.

3.2 The Presidency.   One of the weaknesses of government under the Articles of Confederation was the lack of a strong executive. In drafting the Constitution, the Framers sought to correct this problem. They created the office of the Presidency and gave executive power to one person.

Who holds executive power at the national level?

In Article II, the powers and duties of the President are outlined. There is no clearly spelled-out definition of executive power. Because of this, there has been a continuing debate over the power of the Presidency. One side supports a strong chief executive who takes independent action, while the other side favors a President who follows the will of Congress more closely. Nevertheless, the Presidency has become a very powerful position. The power of the office can be seen by the many different functions of the President. For example, the President is the chief of state, or the ceremonial head of the national government. The President is also the chief administrator, the chief diplomat, the commander in chief of the armed forces, and the leader in suggesting new laws.

What are some of the roles of the President?

As the chief administrator, the President is responsible for carrying out and enforcing federal laws. Hundreds of federal departments, bureaus, agencies, and offices carry out the day-to-day affairs of the national government, under the control and direction of the President. The President has the power to issue executive orders to these offices which have the effect of law.

As the chief diplomat, the President is the leader in making American foreign policy. The President carries out this role through the power to make treaties, appoint diplomats, and give recognition to foreign countries.

As commander in chief of the army, the navy, the air force, and the militia of the states when called into federal service, the President is the nation's chief military officer. For the first time, the country had a single, overall military commander to organize the nation's defense in time of peace and direct the nation's military efforts in time of war.

As the leader in suggesting new laws, the President is the most important person in forming the nation's public policy. The President proposes, supports, and often pressures Congress to pass laws. The President is also required to review each bill approved by Congress.

The Framers wanted the method of selecting a President and the qualifications for office to be different from those for members of Congress. They decided that to become President, a person must be at

Responsibility

At the time the Constitution was written, citizens understood more about their duty toward government than about government's duty to protect their rights. Citizens in some European countries had no rights which the government respected. With this in mind, the Framers of the Constitution added a list of citizens' rights.

This does not mean citizens had no responsibilities. It means, however, that the Framers thought the citizens would take their duties toward government for granted. There seemed to be no reason to write them down.

Throughout the Constitution, the responsibilities are implied in various articles and amendments. Read the following selections from the Bill of Rights, and identify the implied responsibilities.

Congress shall make no law respecting an establishment of religion, or prohibiting the free exercise thereof; or abridging the freedom of speech, or of the press; or the right of people peaceably to assemble, and to petition the government for a redress of grievances.

A well-regulated militia being necessary to the security of a free state, the right of the people to keep and bear arms shall not be infringed.

The right of the people to be secure in their persons, houses, papers, and effects, against unreasonable searches and seizures, shall not be violated, and no warrants shall issue, but upon probable cause, supported by oath or affirmation, and particularly describing the place to be searched, and the persons or things to be seized.

Excessive bail shall not be required, nor excessive fines imposed, nor cruel and unusual punishments inflicted.

Answer the following questions.
1. What responsibility is implied in each of these selections?
2. Why would the failure of citizens to accept responsibility endanger their rights?
3. What happens in a democracy if the majority of the people must be forced to live up to their responsibilities?

What are the quali-
fications to be
President?

least 35 years of age, a resident of the United States for 14 years, and a native-born citizen. They also set up the electoral college as the method of selecting the President. It was designed to reduce the possibility of people making unwise choices through direct election. The Framers also felt that allowing Congress to choose the President would lessen the independence of the executive branch.

Under the electoral college system today, each state has as many presidential electors as that state has Representatives and Senators in Congress. The electors are chosen by methods set up by the legislatures of the states (by popular vote in all 50 states today). These electors, meeting in their own states in early December, cast their ballots for President (and Vice-President since the adoption of the Twelfth Amendment in 1804). The electors in each state are pledged to the candidate who receives the highest number of votes from the people in that state.

How is a President
elected?

Once the presidential electors have voted, the ballots are sealed and sent to Congress, where they are counted in early January. The person receiving a majority of the electoral votes is declared President. If no person has a majority, the House of Representatives chooses the chief executive from among the three candidates receiving the highest number of electoral votes. If no person receives a majority of electoral votes for Vice-President, the Senate makes the choice between the two leading candidates.

3.3 The Courts.   As noted by Alexander Hamilton in *The Federalist Papers:* "Laws are a dead letter without courts to expound and define their true meaning and operation." A major weakness of the Confederation government was the lack of a national court system. Under the Confederation government, the laws of the United States had been interpreted by each state as it saw fit. The Framers of the Constitution felt that a national court system was needed if the federal government was to be successful.

What was a major
weakness of the
Articles of
Confederation?

Article III provides the basis for the national judiciary. The organization is simple—one Supreme Court and such inferior (lower) courts as thought necessary by Congress. Congress established the basic court structure with the Judiciary Act of 1789.

The national court system exists side-by-side with the court systems of the states. Each of the court systems has its own *jurisdiction,* or authority to hear cases. Most cases in the federal courts begin in the lower courts. They can be appealed to higher courts—all the way to the Supreme Court. There are some cases, however, which begin in the Supreme Court and are decided there. To provide a stable system, and to keep judges from being removed simply because of an unpopular

What is jurisdiction?

James Madison (1751–1836)
John Marshall (1755–1835)

PROFILE

James Madison and John Marshall disagreed on foreign issues. They disagreed on affairs at home. But both helped to make the Constitution a workable plan for government.

In 1787, Madison was selected by the Virginia legislature to attend the Constitutional Convention. There Madison often showed a deep understanding of past governments, the Articles of Confederation, and the idea of federalism.

Madison favored a strong central government. He supported the new Constitution during the convention and through the ratification process. He served as a member of the Virginia Ratifying Convention. Madison also wrote essays for *The Federalist Papers*.

When the new government began, the voters of Virginia elected Madison to the House of Representatives. In Congress, he proposed to add the Bill of Rights to the Constitution. In 1801, President Thomas Jefferson named him Secretary of State. From 1809 to 1817, Madison was President.

John Marshall's contribution to the working of the Constitution came after the new government had been in operation for several years. In 1801, John Adams named Marshall Chief Justice of the Supreme Court.

The federal legal system was not well established when Adams appointed Marshall. The court had followed the British model. Marshall gave it a fashion of its own. In one ruling, he stated that the United States Supreme Court could decide if an act of the legislature was unconstitutional. This had been the practice in Britain and in the American state courts. Marshall, however, was the first to establish the practice for the federal court.

In disagreements between the federal and state governments, he ruled that the federal government was supreme. These decisions made the new government stronger. During 34 years as Chief Justice, Marshall made the federal government superior to the states and set up the federal judicial system as an equal branch of the government.

Both Madison and Marshall were strong leaders in the branches of the government that they served. Both desired to make the government under the Constitution succeed.

decision, federal judges are appointed for life, providing they properly carry out their duties.

1. What are the two houses that form the Congress?
2. Who elects the President of the United States?
3. Which court is the highest court in the United States?

4. Division of Powers_____

What is at the base of the American federal system?

At the base of the American federal system is the division of powers between the national and state governments. The Constitution was written in such a way as to give certain powers to the federal government, leave other powers to the states or to the people, and provide for the sharing of still other powers by both the federal and state governments.

What powers does the federal government have?

4.1 Delegated Powers. The federal government has only those powers delegated (given) to it by the Constitution and no others. There are three kinds of *delegated powers*—expressed, implied, and inherent.

Those powers known as *expressed powers* are formally stated in the Constitution. Examples of the expressed powers of Congress include laying and collecting taxes, borrowing money, regulating trade with foreign countries and among the states, and coining money. Among the expressed powers of the President are granting pardons for crimes against the United States and making treaties and appointments with the approval of the Senate.

What is the base of the implied powers?

Those powers known as *implied powers* are not stated directly in the Constitution, but are suggested or implied by the wording. The basis for the implied powers can be found in Article I, Section 8, which contains the Necessary and Proper Clause. This clause is sometimes called the "Elastic Clause." It states:

> *The Congress shall have power . . . to make all laws which shall be necessary and proper for carrying into execution the foregoing powers, and all other powers vested by this Constitution in the government of the United States, or in any department or officer thereof.*

Two examples of the use of implied powers of Congress are passing draft laws, which is implied by the power to raise armies, and selling treasury bonds, which is implied from the power to borrow money.

Those powers known as *inherent powers* belong to the federal government simply because it is a national government. The powers do not need to be spelled out in so many words. For instance, all national governments have the power to take action to defend their countries, to gain territory, and to regulate immigration.

4.2 Reserved Powers. The federal government is a government of delegated powers, while the states are governments of *reserved powers*. That is, the Constitution reserves to state governments those

What powers are exclusively federal? What powers are reserved to the states? What powers do the federal and state governments share? What powers are denied to the federal government? What are denied to the states?

Division of Powers

Powers Denied to the National and State Governments	Powers Divided Between the National and State Governments
Certain Powers Denied to the National Government: Tax exports Suspend writ of habeas corpus Grant titles of nobility	**Certain Exclusive Powers of the National Government:** Coin money Conduct foreign relations Regulate interstate commerce
Certain Powers Denied to Both the National and State Governments: Deny due process of law Pass ex post facto laws Pass bills of attainder	**Certain Concurrent Powers of Both the National and State Governments:** Levy taxes Provide for the public welfare Define and punish crimes
Certain Powers Denied to State Governments: Coin money Enter into treaties Void contracts	**Certain Reserved Powers of State Governments:** Create local governments Provide public education Direct automobile operation

powers not given to the federal government or denied to the states. For example, the states have the power to set up rules for the operation of public schools. The basis for reserved powers is the Tenth Amendment to the Constitution, which states:

What is the basis of the reserved powers?

> *The powers not delegated to the United States by the Constitution, nor prohibited by it to the states, are reserved to the states respectively, or to the people.*

What are "police powers"?

Probably the most important reserved powers of the states are their so-called *"police powers."* These are the ones that safeguard individual well-being. Under their police powers, states can forbid the practice of medicine without a license, require motor vehicle inspections, establish minimum wage and maximum working hour laws, prohibit gambling, and protect individual rights. Although states can restrict and regulate many things under their police powers, they cannot properly use these powers in an unreasonable or unfair way, nor can they violate constitutional provisions.

4.3 Shared Powers. There are still other powers which may be exercised by both the federal and state governments. These are called shared, or *concurrent powers.* Those powers not prohibited to the states by the Constitution may be used by the states at the same time as the federal government. Among the concurrent powers are the power to tax, to try those accused of crimes, and to provide money to build roads.

What are some limitations on power?

4.4 Limitations on Power. There are certain limitations on the powers of both the states and the federal government. For example, both the federal and state governments have the power to tax. However, neither level of government can tax the other. If this were possible, they might tax each other so heavily that they would destroy each other and the federal system.

Some powers, called *exclusive powers,* belong only to the federal government. Many of the expressed powers are also exclusive powers. Some exclusive powers, such as the coining of money, are denied to the states in the Constitution. If the states were allowed to hold certain powers, such as regulating trade among states, confusion might result.

1. What are the three kinds of delegated powers under the Constitution?
2. What powers are held by both federal and state governments?
3. What powers are held only by the federal government?

5. The Changing Constitution_____

The Framers of the Constitution realized that future problems of the country could not necessarily be solved with procedures set up in their time. They knew that as the country developed, it would be necessary to change and add to the Constitution. Because of this, they provided for a method of amending the Constitution.

5.1 The Amending Process. Article V states the ways in which the Constitution can be amended. Amendments can be proposed by a two-thirds vote in each house of Congress. Another method is by a national convention called by Congress at the request of two thirds of the state legislatures. To be adopted, amendments must be ratified by either the legislatures in three fourths of the states or by conventions in three fourths of the states. The first ten amendments were added to the Constitution soon after the federal government got started. Sixteen other amendments have been added since then.

How might amendments be proposed? ratified?

In 1789, the United States was a small agricultural country of 3.5 million people. Today the United States is a nation of 226.5 million people and a powerful industrial country. The amendments have allowed the Constitution to keep up with the changes caused by this

Realizing that their plans of government could not cover every situation, the Framers provided the means for change. This is the amendment process. How many ways can the Constitution be changed?

Amending the Constitution

Proposed by

Approved by

Congress
Two-thirds vote required in both Senate and House of Representatives

State Legislatures
Three fourths of all states required

or

or

National Convention
Congress calls a convention at the request of two thirds of the state legislatures

Special Conventions
Three fourths of all states required

growth. All 26 amendments were proposed by a two-thirds vote in each house of Congress. Only the original Constitution and one amendment have been ratified by state conventions. Some amendments, like the Twelfth, which altered the electoral college system, have changed original terms of the Constitution.

5.2 Informal Change.   In writing the Constitution, the Framers provided an outline of government. They left the many details of actual government operation to be added later by the various branches of government. Over the years, the Supreme Court, the Congress, the President, and political party practices have influenced the way in which the Constitution would be applied. In a number of cases, for example, Supreme Court rulings have defined and extended the meaning of the Constitution. In one case, the Supreme Court ruled that a person accused of a crime must be informed of certain basic rights, such as the right to remain silent and to have an attorney present during questioning. This ruling extended the provisions of the Fifth Amendment.

Through what means has the political system changed?

Congress, too, has added to basic provisions of the Constitution in order to change or expand the political system. For example, Congress was given the power to tax, but nothing was said about the kinds of taxes, how much they would be, who would pay them, or how they would be collected. All these things have been added through laws passed by Congress.

Like Congress, Presidents have interpreted their constitutional powers in many important ways. As an example, several Presidents, acting as commander in chief, have authorized the use of American military forces without a declaration of war from Congress. The most recent case is the Vietnam War.

Party practices and custom, too, have influenced the ways in which the Constitution has been interpreted and applied. Political parties were not mentioned by the Framers, but they have been an important part of the American political system since the 1790's. A custom that a President would serve no more than two terms was upheld until 1940, when President Franklin D. Roosevelt broke the tradition. The Twenty-second Amendment was then added to the Constitution. This amendment made the custom a formal part of the fundamental law of the land.

What custom became a formal amendment?

1. How does Article V provide for changing the Constitution?
2. What is the role of the Supreme Court in changing the Constitution?

6. Conclusion_____

The Constitution of the United States has provided the framework for the nation's government for nearly 200 years. It is the oldest written national constitution still in force in the world today. It has served as the model for the constitutions of many other nations.

The Constitution has lasted so long chiefly because of its flexibility. It was constructed in a way that permitted it to adapt to change and solve new problems. The Framers drew upon their knowledge and experience as they wrote the document. They were familiar with most of the old important historical documents—such as the English Magna Carta, the Mayflower Compact, and the English Bill of Rights. These and other political writings gave them ideas for the principles upon which the Constitution rests. They were aware of the forces at home and abroad which threatened the survival of the young nation. They also recognized the difficulty of writing a document which would guarantee the freedom of the people and still maintain order in the community. Their accomplishment is something in which all Americans can take pride.

After weeks of debate, a draft of the Constitution was submitted to the convention on August 6, 1787. Some discussion continued for another month. The document was signed on September 17. It went into effect in 1789. How does the Constitution continue to be more than just a written document?

Chapter 7 Review

Main Points

1. The Constitution is the fundamental law of the United States and provides for the organization of the national government.
2. Supreme political power rests with the people. The people elect representatives who operate the government.
3. Under the Constitution, government is limited to those powers granted to it by the people.
4. Under the Constitution, power is divided between state governments and the national government.
5. Within the national government, power is divided among the legislative, executive, and judicial branches.
6. Each branch of government has certain checks on the other branches to balance power within the national government.
7. There are a number of other principles besides those that are basic to the Constitution. They include judicial review, supremacy of national law, and supremacy of civilian authority.
8. According to the Constitution, some powers are held by the federal government only, some by the states or the people only, and some are shared.
9. The Constitution may be changed by adding formal amendments to it. It may also be changed informally by court interpretation.

Building Vocabulary

1. Identify the following:

   Framers
   Preamble

   electoral college
   James Madison

   John Marshall
   "Elastic Clause"

2. Define the following:

   popular sovereignty
   limited government
   federalism
   separation of powers
   checks and balances
   judicial review
   supremacy of national law

   supremacy of civilian authority
   bicameral
   revenue bills
   impeach
   jurisdiction
   delegated powers

   expressed powers
   implied powers
   inherent powers
   reserved powers
   "police powers"
   concurrent powers
   exclusive powers

Remembering the Facts

1. What is the source of supreme political power under the Constitution?
2. Which basic principle prevents government under the Constitution

from taking any action it might want to take?

3. What are the two levels of government provided for under the principle of federalism?

4. In providing for the separation of powers, what are the three branches of government in the Constitution?

5. What are the checks that each branch of government has over the others?

6. How do the two houses of Congress differ?

7. What is the role of the President of the United States with regard to the armed forces?

8. Because it is a national government, what are the powers held by the federal government?

9. What powers do the states have under the Constitution?

10. How can the Constitution be changed?

11. Where does the process of changing the written Constitution begin?

Understanding the Facts

1. How was the government created by the Constitution like the colonial government under Britain?

2. In what way was the government set up by the Constitution stronger than that of the Articles of Confederation?

3. How did the Framers of the Constitution attempt to prevent one branch of government from becoming too powerful?

4. Why would a revolution not be needed to change the Constitution?

Using Diagrams

Reading Diagrams. A diagram is a drawing which explains some idea. It is used instead of a written description or with a written description to make clear important points and relationships. The way a diagram is drawn is important to getting across the intended idea.

The diagram on page 149 concerns the government established under the Constitution. Read the title. Examine the drawing and its various parts. Read the written descriptions within the diagram. Then answer the following questions.

1. What does the diagram explain?

2. What are the three branches of government?

3. How does the diagram show the ways one branch of the government can check and balance another branch?

4. How can the legislative branch prevent a person, who was appointed by the executive branch, from taking office?

5. Which branch appoints the people who decide if a law is constitutional or not?

6. Which branch has the authority to remove the President from office?

7. What is meant by checks and balances?

Philadelphia 1750-1775

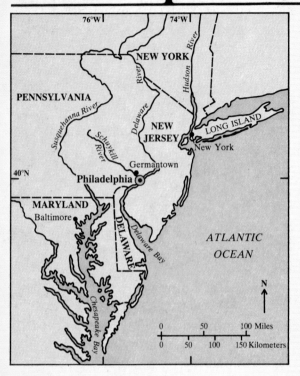

and other Christians in Philadelphia than there were Quakers. Several Jewish families also lived in the city, and many people did not belong to any particular church. The Quakers, however, continued to have a strong influence on the development of the city.

Earning a Living

Philadelphia quickly became a center of business for Pennsylvania and the other colonies. There were ironworks, flour mills, yards for building and repairing ships, carriage and wagon shops, and many different ways for people to earn their livings. Farmers brought produce from their rich fields to market. In the city's shops, they purchased candles, shoes, tools, and other goods.

Shipping and trade were the base of Philadelphia's economic growth. James Birket, a visitor to the city in 1759, reported on what he saw.

There is belonging to this town a great number of ships, and from here a very extensive trade is carried on to all the English islands in the West Indies for bread, flour, pork, hams, Indian corn, buckwheat oats, apples . . . shingles, hoops, bar iron . . . also livestock as sheep, geese, turkeys, ducks and fowl in great plenty; but some of their chief men . . . drive on a very large illegal trade with the French . . . for sugar and molasses, to the great damage of the honest and fair trader.

They have also a good trade for wheat, staves and other things, to Madeira, Lisbon, and several parts of Spain, to say nothing of that extensive trade between them and England for black walnut and other valuable wood of different kinds. . . .

William Penn laid out the plans for his Pennsylvania "city of brotherly love" in 1682. He located Philadelphia on the west banks of the Delaware River, not far from the Atlantic coast. The city grew quickly and, by the middle of the eighteenth century, was the largest and richest city in the American colonies.

The first settlers of Philadelphia were English Quakers, or members of the Society of Friends. They allowed all other Christians to come there and worship as they pleased. That freedom of religion drew many different groups of people from Europe, and the city's population continued to grow. By 1740, there were more Presbyterians, Anglicans, Roman Catholics, Baptists, Methodists, Lutherans,

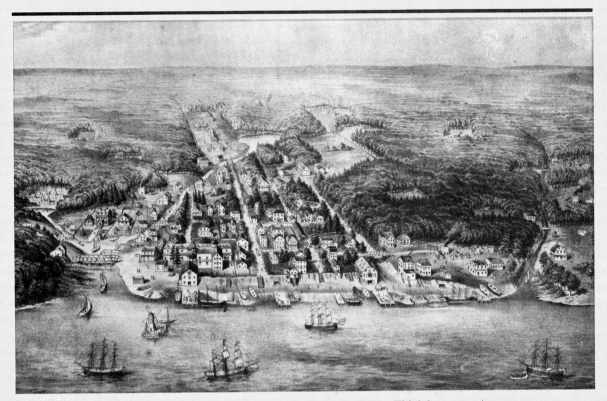

William Penn founded Philadelphia on the west bank of the Delaware River. This is how it looked in 1702. How did its location help its economic and physical growth by the middle 1700's?

Such a busy city could support workers with special skills. Painters, weavers, silversmiths, and cabinetmakers made things that were beautiful as well as useful. There was a need, too, for printed business and legal forms, government notices, and other useful items. By the time Benjamin Franklin arrived in 1723 to look for work, there were already two printers in Philadelphia. He went to work for one of them and, in a few years, became the city's most famous printer. Franklin, as others did, printed a newspaper, pamphlets, and a yearly almanac.

Families often continued to work in the same trade or profession for generations. The Bradfords, for example, were Philadelphia printers for more than 100 years. Cornelia Bradford, in 1740, became the first woman to be a successful printer and bookseller in the city. By the 1770's, presses were turning out seven different newspapers and thousands of books and pamphlets. Philadelphia's printers played a very important part in the exchange of ideas among the American colonists.

Self-improvement

Many of the people in the city enjoyed sharing ideas. Clubs were sometimes formed for "mutual improvement," as Franklin said of the Junto, a club that he and 11 of his friends started in 1727.

. . . we met on Friday evenings. The rules that I drew up required that every member, in his turn, should produce one or more queries [questions] on any point of Morals, Politics, or Natural Philosophy, to be [discussed] by the company; and once in three months produce and read an essay of his own writing, on any subject he pleased. Our debates were . . . in the sincere spirit of inquiry after truth. . . .

According to the social traditions of the times, only men belonged to these clubs. But women were sometimes the topic of the meetings. Carl Bridenbaugh, historian of colonial Philadelphia, wrote about a club that met in October 1766. Its members had chosen to discuss the question of women in politics.

After an animated and extremely serious discussion, in which it was conceded [agreed]

This advertisement appeared in a Philadelphia newspaper in the 1700's. What product is being advertised? Who is selling the product?

Juſt imported in the Ship **Myrtilla**, Captain Bolithe, from London, and to be ſold by

HANNAH BREINTNALL,

At the Sign of the Spectacles, in Second-ſtreet, near Black-Horſe Alley,

A Great Variety of the fineſt Chryſtal Spectacles, ſet in Temple, Steel, Leather or other Frames. Likewiſe true Venetian green Spectacles. for weak or watery Eyes, of various Sorts. Alſo Concave Spectacles, for ſhort ſighted Perſons; Magnifying and Reading Glaſſes; and an Aſſortment of large and ſmall Spy glaſſes and Bone Microſcopes, with magnifying and multiplying Glaſs, &c. &c. Pocket Compaſſes, of different Sizes. &c. ‖ 10 s. Tbctf.

that women have natural abilities equal to those of men, which might be improved by education, that their lively imaginations would "throw a subject into new lights," that their natural timidity [lack of boldness] would make for prudent [wise] decisions, and that Queen Elizabeth had proved an able ruler, the question was decided in the negative, on the grounds that the use of beauty and female arts would prejudice the public good and that active participation by the ladies [in politics] would "destroy the peace of Families."

Education

Education for women was not a common idea in all of the colonies. But the Quakers believed in a practical education for both boys and girls. Reading and writing were taught without charge if the children's parents were too poor to pay. Those who could pay were expected to do so. Philadelphia's first schools were started by the Quakers and other church groups. Within a few years, night schools opened for young workers eager to advance in business. Good private teachers could always find enough students to fill their classes.

In 1751, the Philadelphia Academy opened for the city's young men. It had been a special project of Franklin's, and he helped decide the subjects that were taught. Families from the lower and middle classes wanted their sons trained for business with English, bookkeeping, and other such practical courses. Upper-class families wanted their sons trained in the arts with foreign languages, philosophy, and classics. As a compromise, Franklin wrote:

. . . it would be well if they could be taught everything that is useful and everything that is ornamental. But art is long and their time is short. It is therefore proposed that they learn

those things that are likely to be most useful and most ornamental, regard being had to the . . . professions for which they are intended.

That same year, David Dove opened a private school for teaching girls some of the more advanced subjects. His school was very successful. Three years later, Anthony Benezet convinced the leaders of the Academy to permit girls to study the same subjects that the boys were offered, but in a separate building.

Benezet was also a pioneer in education for black people. A few black children had been attending the Quaker church schools. In 1750, Benezet opened an evening school for them in his home and paid for the supplies himself. He continued these classes until a group of Quakers took over the costs. They opened a free school to teach reading, writing, and arithmetic to black children in 1770. By the 1790's, Philadelphia had schools for black students taught by black teachers.

City Improvements

The rapid growth of business pushed the city's boundaries outward. The price of land within the city grew higher, and the noise of city traffic grew louder. To avoid the higher land costs, many smaller merchants moved to the edges of town. To avoid the noise and traffic, many of the richer families built their homes in areas outside the city. By the 1770's, Philadelphia had grown from a trade town to a metropolitan city with suburbs, or outlying districts of homes and small businesses.

Although many lived in the suburbs, the people worked to improve the appearance of the city. They supported many plans for the general public. Franklin and the members of the Junto were often involved in these projects. In his writings, Franklin described their "first project of a public nature."

Many of Benjamin Franklin's plans and projects benefited Philadelphia. How did Franklin help to improve city life?

Those who [loved] *reading were* [obliged] *to send for their books from England. . . .* [In 1731] *I* [proposed] *to render the benefit from books more common, by commencing* [beginning] *a public subscription library. . . . So few were the readers at that time in Philadelphia, and the majority of us so poor, that I was not able, with great industry, to find more than fifty persons, mostly young tradesmen, willing to pay down for this purpose forty shillings each, and ten shillings per annum* [year]. *On this little fund we began. The books were imported; the library was opened one day in the week for lending to the subscribers, on their promissory* notes to pay double the value if not duly returned. *The institution soon manifested [showed] its utility [usefulness], was imitated by other towns, and in other provinces.*

Fires were a problem in the city, and there was no organized way to fight them. In 1737, Franklin wrote and printed a paper about the different causes of fires. He also wrote about ways to deal with them.

This . . . gave rise to a project, which soon followed it, of forming a company [the Union Fire Company] for the more ready extinguishing of fires, and mutual assistance in removing and securing of goods when in danger. Associates in this scheme [plan] were presently found, amounting to thirty. Our articles of agreement [obliged] every member to keep always in good order, and fit for use, a certain number of leather buckets, with strong bags and baskets (for packing and transporting of goods), which were to be brought to every fire; and we agreed to meet once a month [to discuss] the subject of fires, as might be useful in our conduct on such occasions.

. . . this went on, one new company being formed after another. . . . The small fines that have been paid by members for absence at the monthly meetings have been [applied] to the purchase of fire-engines, ladders, fire-hooks, and other useful implements [tools] for each company, so that I question whether there is a city in the world better provided with the means of putting a stop to beginning conflagrations [fires]. . . .

More than 25 years after his first public project, Franklin was still working for the general good of the city. He had convinced the city leaders to keep the streets cleaned and patrolled at night for safety. But he believed that there was more to be done.

Our city, [though] laid out with a beautiful regularity, the streets large, [straight], and crossing each other at right angles, had the disgrace of suffering those streets to remain long [unpaved] and in wet weather the wheels of heavy carriages [plowed] them into a quagmire [deep mud], so that it was difficult to cross them; and in dry weather the dust was offensive. . . .

After some time I drew a bill for paving the city, and brought it into the Assembly. It was just before I went to England, in 1757 [on colonial business], and did not pass till I was gone . . . with an additional provision for lighting as well as paving the streets, which was a great improvement. It was by a private person, the late Mr. John Clifton, his giving a sample of the utility of lamps, by placing one at his door, that people were first [impressed] with the idea of enlighting all the city.

Social Improvements

As Philadelphia grew into a rich city, many of its successful people were interested in helping those who were not successful. At first, the Quakers were the strongest influence in this work. Soon church groups, business and social clubs, and many individuals were involved. They supported buildings to house and care for the old, the poor, the widows, and the orphans. They also collected money, food, and clothing.

Dr. Thomas Bond, helped by Franklin, opened a hospital to care for people who were sick and those who had mental illnesses in 1751. Bond needed Franklin's help to raise money because the idea of a hospital was new to most people. Many families of the lower and middle classes never went to doctors, and even the upper classes usually tried old family cures first.

Philadelphia also became a center of resistance to slavery. The Quakers taught that every individual had special dignity and that blacks were people, not property. Their ideas influenced others in the city. In 1775, the people of Philadelphia started the first anti-slavery society in America. Philadelphia was indeed the "city of brotherly love."

1. Who were the first settlers in Philadelphia?

2. What was the base of Philadelphia's economic growth?

3. What contributions did Franklin make to the development of Philadelphia?

4. Why did the suburbs of Philadelphia develop?

Philadelphia's population in 1775 was 40,000. At that time, it was larger than any city in England except for London. After the Revolution, it became the nation's capital. What attracted people to live and work in Philadelphia?

Unit II Review

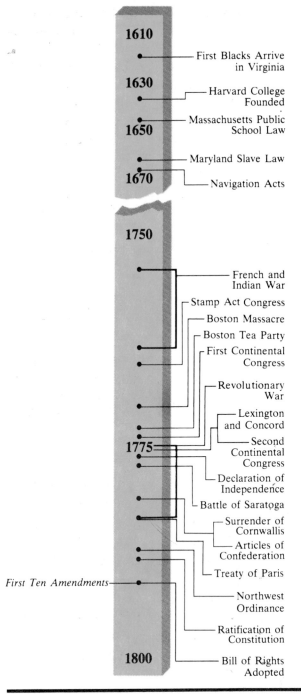

1610

First Blacks Arrive in Virginia

1630

Harvard College Founded

Massachusetts Public School Law

1650

Maryland Slave Law

1670

Navigation Acts

1750

French and Indian War

Stamp Act Congress

Boston Massacre

Boston Tea Party

First Continental Congress

Revolutionary War

Lexington and Concord

Second Continental Congress

1775

Declaration of Independence

Battle of Saratoga

Surrender of Cornwallis

Articles of Confederation

Treaty of Paris

Northwest Ordinance

First Ten Amendments

Ratification of Constitution

1800

Bill of Rights Adopted

Summary

1. The people of the English colonies came from Europe—especially the countries of England, Scotland, and Germany—as well as from Africa.

2. Although many groups contributed to the culture of the colonies, the English language and culture became the standard.

3. British victory in the French and Indian War freed the colonies from a major threat to their security and led them to hope for greater freedom.

4. Disagreements over political and economic matters developed between the colonies and Britain, leading to rebellion in 1775.

5. The colonies declared their independence from Britain, which they won after seven years of warfare.

6. Political rights for many men were expanded as a result of the Revolution, although there were few changes in rights for women or for those people held as slaves.

7. The government of the United States under the Articles of Confederation proved too weak to deal with the problems following the Revolution.

8. Dissatisfaction with the Articles of Confederation led to a convention of delegates from the states which drew up the Constitution as the fundamental law of the United States.

9. Under the Constitution, supreme political power rests with the people, who elect representatives.

Unit Questions

1. How were the experiences of people in the English colonies different from those in Africa and Europe?

2. What were some of the reasons for the development of three distinct regions in the English colonies?

3. How did the ways that the British government viewed their colonies in America differ from the ways that the colonists viewed themselves?

4. Why did the colonists, who thought of themselves as British citizens, revolt against their home country?

5. Why were the colonies able to defeat the powerful British army?

6. What were some of the most important social, political, and economic effects of the Revolution?

7. What were the boundaries of the United States as set by the Treaty of Paris in 1783?

8. How were experiences of Americans under British rule reflected in their distrust for strong central government under the Articles of Confederation?

9. Why did Americans decide to replace the Articles of Confederation with the Constitution?

10. What were the arguments for and against adopting the Constitution?

Suggested Activities

1. Imagine that you are a teenager who came from Europe or Africa during the late 1600's. In keeping a diary, what events might you describe?

2. Compare the Constitution with the rules of organization for one of your school groups. Identify the differences and similarities between the two.

3. As a class, compare life in eighteenth-century Philadelphia with life in your town today. How are they alike? How are they different?

Suggested Readings

Davis, Burke. *Black Heroes of the American Revolution.* New York: Harcourt Brace Jovanovich, 1976. Contributions of blacks in the American Revolution.

Depauw, Linda. *Founding Mothers: Women of America in the American Revolutionary Era.* Boston: Houghton Mifflin Company, 1975. Examines the roles of women in the American Revolution and the conditions which shaped their lives.

Forbes, Esther. *Johnny Tremain.* New York: Dell, 1969. The adventures of a young member of the Sons of Liberty during pre-Revolutionary days in Boston.

Perl, Lila. *Slumps, Grunts, and Snickerdoodles: What Colonial America Ate and Why.* New York: Seabury Press, Inc., 1975. Contains recipes and traces the changes in foods produced and eaten by the colonists.

UNIT
III

America is
Democracy

Democracy began as an outgrowth of a new and wide-open environment in the United States. Americans were free to move around the country and within social classes. They were no longer supposed to be grouped together according to ancestry, wealth, or education. Americans claimed that all people were created equal. It was believed that all Americans should be judged on their own merits. The democratic practice of government by all of the people in the United States was a developing process.

Testing the
New Government

George Washington receives a naval salute in New York harbor after his inauguration. Washington was the unanimous choice for the new office of President. What problems faced the United States and America's first President?

During the first few years after the Constitution was adopted, the future of the new nation was in question. The United States was not yet unified. Most people still felt they were citizens of a certain state rather than citizens of the United States. Many wondered whether the Constitution would work. Some people questioned whether America could last in a world of powerful, unfriendly countries.

George Washington voiced these worries when he said, ". . . the preservation of the sacred fire of liberty and the destiny of the [democratic] model of government . . . [depend] on the experiment intrusted to the hands of the American people." For better or for worse, however, this great American experiment was under way.

1. The Beginning

The Constitution provided an outline of government for the country's leaders. They began to create a working government, drawing on this outline plus their experiences in colonial government and the Confederation. As they set about their tasks, these leaders knew that their actions would serve as examples to be followed in years to come.

1.1 The First Election. As soon as the Constitution had been ratified, the new plan for government was set in motion. The first members of the Senate and the House of Representatives were elected. Then state legislatures chose *electors* whose task was to choose the President and Vice-President. In the country's first presidential election, George Washington was selected President, and John Adams was named Vice-President. Early in 1789, the new leaders of the country gathered in New York, the national capital, to begin work.

Who chooses the President?

1.2 The First Executive. As chief executive, President Washington thought his major task was to execute or carry out the policies set by Congress. In practice, the President also became a maker of policies. He did this by setting *precedents*—acts that would serve as examples in later situations. One of the first things Washington did was select people to head the executive departments newly set up by Congress. He named Thomas Jefferson of Virginia as Secretary of State, Alexander Hamilton of New York as Secretary of the Treasury, Henry Knox of Massachusetts as Secretary of War, and Edmund Randolph of Virginia as Attorney General. Washington met with these people and asked for their advice in government matters. They became the Cabinet, or body of advisors, and every President has had one.

What precedents did Washington set?

Washington also made policies in foreign affairs. He gained more power for his office in this field than was stated in the Constitution. It

George Washington (left) selected the first Cabinet—Edmund Randolph, Thomas Jefferson, Alexander Hamilton, and Henry Knox (from right to left). What area of responsibility did each Cabinet member hold?

How did Washington gain more power for the Presidency in foreign affairs?

said that the President was to make treaties with other countries with the help and approval of the Senate. At first, Washington tried to do this. When he was *negotiating* (trying to arrange terms) with a group of Indians, he asked the Senate's help. The Senators would not discuss the treaty while Washington was present. They wished to talk it over in private. Washington left, and from then on, he and the Presidents who followed him have negotiated treaties as they think best. Then they have sent the treaties to the Senate for approval.

1.3 A New Court System. One of the most important goals of the Framers of the Constitution was to make a strong court system. It would protect the rights of the people and keep them from being harmed by governments or by other people. To do this, Congress passed the Judiciary Act of 1789. It set up a system of courts that is still working, although sometimes the numbers of the courts have changed.

What courts were set up by Congress in 1789?

The lowest courts in this system were district courts set up to hear cases involving federal law. Next were the circuit courts which hear cases sent to them on *appeal*—the review of a lower court's findings by a higher court. This happens when there is some question about the first court's ruling. The Supreme Court is the highest court in the country and the last court of appeal. Washington chose John Jay of New York as the first Chief Justice of the Supreme Court.

1. Who was the first President to be elected under the Constitution?
2. What were the roles of Thomas Jefferson and Alexander Hamilton in the new government?
3. What was the highest court created by the Framers of the Constitution?

2. The Economy

Those who were forming the new government wanted it to be strong. To keep order at home and to be on equal terms with other countries, the United States had to have a strong economy. During Washington's first term, government leaders wanted to set up an economic program that would make the country prosperous. Alexander Hamilton, the Secretary of the Treasury, drew up such a program.

Who drafted this nation's first economic program?

2.1 Hamilton and the Debt. Alexander Hamilton saw that the new government had little money on hand and was deeply in debt. During the Revolution, the central and state governments had both borrowed money from their citizens and from other countries. These governments owed over $80 million. Hamilton thought that the federal government should repay the money owed to other countries and to its own citizens as well as the debts of the states. He believed that this money had to be repaid if the United States was to establish its credit.

Congress agreed to pay money owed to foreign countries. Conflict arose, however, over the plan to pay for the *domestic* (internal or within the country) debts. When the government had borrowed money during the Revolution, it had issued *bonds*—paper notes promising to repay the money in a certain length of time. After the war, many people believed that the government would not be able to pay off the bonds. So their value dropped, and they were bought by *speculators*—people who buy stocks, bonds, or land for the purpose of selling it for a profit later when the price goes up. Hamilton proposed that these bonds be *redeemed* (paid off) at their original value. Those people against the plan felt that the country should not give the speculators the benefit of a large profit. Hamilton convinced Congress that the debts must be paid.

What were the conflicts that arose over paying the debt?

Another part of the debt was owed by several states to American citizens. Hamilton wanted the government to *assume* (take over) these debts. Most of the southern states had already repaid their debts. Members of Congress from the South felt that citizens of their states should not be taxed to repay the debts of other states. A compromise was reached. Southerners agreed that the federal government would

Benjamin Banneker (1731–1806)

PROFILE

In 1771, Benjamin Banneker was a 41-year-old, black, Maryland farmer. That year, he seriously began to follow a lifelong interest in the sciences. He read about the earth and the heavens. With a simple telescope, he watched the sky. In 1789, he correctly predicted an eclipse of the sun. At a time when most American blacks were slaves and few were educated, Banneker was known as a mathematician and astronomer.

Banneker's talent drew the attention of Thomas Jefferson. It was Jefferson who told President George Washington that Banneker should be a member of the team to plan the new Federal District (later District of Columbia). He was the first black person named to a job by a President of the United States.

In 1791, Banneker began printing an annual almanac. It held not only scientific information, but also reports on social problems. In the 1793 edition, Banneker recommended what amounted to a department of the interior for the United States. He also planned for a league of nations to gain world peace.

Banneker saw his work as evidence that there was no connection between race and ability to learn. He believed his success was due to his free birth and education. In letters to Thomas Jefferson, he stated this and called for more democratic feelings toward blacks.

take over the states' debts. In return, people from the North agreed that the new capital of the United States would be built in the South. Until it was finished, the capital would be in Philadelphia.

2.2 A National Bank. Another part of Hamilton's plan proposed that the federal government establish a central bank for the United States. Hamilton did not want just one bank, but a national banking system. It would provide a place where the government could deposit its money. It would be large enough to lend money to the government as well as to private citizens. Finally, the bank would provide a sound currency.

When the bill to set up the Bank of the United States came up in Congress, there was much debate. Some people argued that the

What was the argument over establishing a national bank?

Constitution did not give the government the power to create a bank. A majority of Congress, however, agreed with Hamilton's plan, and the bank bill was passed in 1791.

2.3 A Tariff Proposal. Congress wanted to find ways to raise additional money for the federal government. In 1789, it passed a tariff act which placed *duties* (a kind of tax) on certain goods coming into the United States from other countries. Hamilton agreed with those who thought this was a good way to raise money. On December 5, 1791, he gave a *Report on Manufactures* to Congress. In it, Hamilton asked that Congress pass a *protective tariff*—a heavy tax on some manufactured goods imported into the United States. This would make foreign goods more expensive than those produced at home. Americans would then be encouraged to buy the cheaper goods made in the United States. This should encourage the growth of industry. Hamilton's report had little effect, although a slightly higher tariff was passed in 1792.

Why did Hamilton want a protective tariff?

2.4 The Whiskey Rebellion. In another proposal, Hamilton asked Congress to place an *excise tax* (tax on goods made and sold inside the country) on whiskey. On March 3, 1791, it was passed. Farmers in the frontier areas of the country thought the tax was very unfair. They often distilled grain into whiskey to sell, and it was a major source of money for them. Many of them began to avoid paying the tax.

Farmers in western Pennsylvania openly refused to pay the tax in 1794. Hamilton felt the authority of the new government was being

Where did the Whiskey Rebellion take place?

The first Bank of the United States was built in Philadelphia in 1795. Although Jefferson opposed it, Hamilton thought it would be a step toward creating a secure money system for the country. What was the purpose of a national bank?

A wagon load of whiskey sold for about $220. A wagon load of grain sold for about $36. An excise tax on whiskey meant less profit. Where did resentment toward the tax cause fighting between farmers and federal troops?

challenged. He wanted to show that the new government could enforce its laws. So Hamilton asked Washington to send troops against the resisting farmers. In October 1794, a force of about 13,000 militia marched into Pennsylvania to restore law and order. This show of force soon ended the "Whiskey Rebellion."

2.5 Opposition to Hamilton. Although Hamilton's economic plans were working, they had drawn strong opposition from the beginning. Perhaps the greatest disagreement was over the Bank of the United States. Thomas Jefferson thought the law setting up the Bank of the United States was unconstitutional because the Constitution did not specifically give Congress the power to set up a bank. He understood the Constitution to mean only what it actually said. His view was called a *strict construction* (narrow interpretation). Hamilton understood the Constitution to mean much more than it said. It gave Congress the power "to make all laws necessary and proper" to carry out its work. Hamilton felt this gave Congress the power to set up a bank. This view was called a *loose construction* (broad interpretation). The disagreement marked the start of two ways of understanding the Constitution.

Two political parties were formed out of these differences. One group was the Federalists, led by Hamilton. The other was Democratic-Republicans, usually called Republicans, led by Jefferson. Generally, Hamilton's followers favored a strong national government. They interpreted the Constitution broadly in order to give the federal government as much power as possible. Most Federalists believed that

Who led the opposition to Hamilton's policies?

What did each of the political parties favor?

people of wealth and education should hold office, and that the economy should be based on industry and trade as well as agriculture. Jefferson's supporters, on the other hand, favored the rights of the states, and they interpreted the Constitution strictly. They believed that average people should lead the country. They thought the economy should be based on agriculture with industry and trade less important.

1. Why did Hamilton insist on paying the national debts?
2. What was the purpose of the Bank of the United States?
3. Why did farmers in western Pennsylvania refuse to pay taxes?
4. Which political parties developed over disagreements on national economic policies?

3. Foreign Affairs

The world situation greatly added to the concerns of the new government. While trying to build a sound economy, it faced growing problems with European countries. Quarrels among these countries threatened to draw the United States into war. Great Britain still had trading posts in the American Northwest and had been capturing some American trading ships in the West Indies. Debates over these issues further divided the country's political parties.

3.1 Staying Neutral. When Great Britain and France went to war in 1793, the United States found itself in a difficult position. It had signed a treaty of alliance with France in 1778. But the United States did not want to fight another war with Great Britain. The possibility of war widened the differences between Jefferson, who favored the French, and Hamilton, who favored the British. In April 1793, President Washington issued a Proclamation of Neutrality. *Neutrality* means to not take sides in a conflict.

Why did Washington issue the Proclamation of Neutrality?

3.2 The Jay Treaty. The British would not accept America's neutral stand. They seized American ships carrying goods to France. They also began a policy of *impressment.* This meant they were stopping American ships and taking sailors off to force them to work on British ships. Often the British claimed that the sailors were really British citizens who had moved to America.

How did the British interfere with American trade?

Hoping to avoid war, Washington sent a peace mission to Great Britain in 1794. It was headed by John Jay, Chief Justice of the Supreme Court. Jay made a treaty with the British. By its terms, Britain agreed to pull out of its posts in the Northwest Territory. The United States

The British seized American ships when they suspected that the cargo was going to France. While on board, the British had American sailors pronounce certain words. If an American sailor spoke with an Irish or British accent, he was made prisoner and forced to serve in the British navy. How did the policy of impressment affect relations between the United States and Britain?

agreed that debts owed to British citizens from the Revolution would be paid. Americans who suffered losses from British seizures of ships were also to be paid for damages. The boundary with Canada in the northeast was to be surveyed and set.

Why were Americans upset with the Jay Treaty?

The Jay Treaty was approved by the Senate. It had prevented war with Great Britain, but it upset many Americans. Many were angry that the United States had not gained free trade with the West Indies. Others did not want the United States to repay debts owed to Great Britain from the Revolution. Those who were against the policies of Hamilton used the treaty to gain support for their views and further widened the gap between the political parties.

3.3 The Pinckney Treaty. When Spain learned about the Jay Treaty, its leaders decided to settle their differences with the United States. Because Spain had just signed an agreement with France, it faced war with Great Britain. Spanish officials feared that Britain and the United States might move against its territory in America.

What were the issues underlying the Pinckney Treaty?

Thomas Pinckney, the United States minister to Great Britain, negotiated a treaty with Spain, signed in October 1795. By its terms, Americans were guaranteed the right to navigate the Mississippi River and to use freely the port of New Orleans. They would also be able to transfer goods from river boats to oceangoing vessels without paying duties to Spain. In addition, Spain and the United States set the

Recognizing Main Ideas
SKILL

Some writers use the first sentence in a paragraph to present a main idea. Other writers give background information and conclude with the major point. There are also writers who do not state a main idea, leaving it up to the reader to decide.

Location alone does not determine the main idea for a paragraph, a chapter, or a book. Read the material, and ask what does most of the information explain or describe. When you can answer this, you have begun to identify the main idea.

Read the following selection about the Congress of the United States when Philadelphia was the capital city. It was written by a visitor to Congress in the late 1700's.

On entering the House of Representatives, I was struck with the convenient arrangement. . . . The size of the chamber was about 100 feet by 60. The seats in three rows formed semicircles behind each other, facing the Speaker, who was in a kind of pulpit near the center . . . and the clerk below him. Every member was accommodated for writing, by there being likewise a circular writing desk to each of the circular seats. Over the entrance was a large gallery, into which were admitted every citizen without distinction, who chose to attend; and under the gallery likewise were accommodations for those who were [invited]. But no person either in the gallery or under it, is suffered to express any mark of applause or discontent at what is dabbled; it being understood they are present in the person of their representative. This has been a great error in the new French government. An attempt, however, was once made to introduce it here (in March last) by clapping of hands, at a speech which fell from Mr. [Josiah] Parker. But the whole house instantly rose to resent it, and adjourned their business, being then in a committee and the galleries were closed.

Over the door I observed a bust of Dr. [Benjamin] Franklin, the great founder of their liberties, and [a Framer] of their present constitution.

1. What is the main idea of this selection?

2. Is the main idea stated, or must the reader determine it?

3. If it is stated, where does the writer present the idea?

4. Is all the other information used to explain or describe the idea?

boundary between Georgia and Spanish Florida at the 31st parallel. Many Americans were very pleased with the Pinckney Treaty.

3.4 Washington's Farewell. President Washington prepared to leave office in 1796. During his two terms, he had helped establish the new government on a solid foundation. But Washington was troubled. Matters with France were growing worse. The French had been angered by the Jay Treaty. Under the terms of the treaty of 1778, France and the United States were allies. Great Britain was France's enemy.

Why did Washington issue a Farewell Address?

President Washington was concerned over the possibility of war with France. In a Farewell Address written in September 1796, he urged future leaders to keep the United States independent when dealing with other nations. Washington said:

> *The great rule of conduct for us in regard to foreign nations is, in extending our commercial relations to have with them as little* political *connection as possible. . . .*
> *It is our true policy to steer clear of permanent alliances with any portion of the foreign world, so far, I mean, as we are now at liberty to do it. . . .*

Washington went on to admit that temporary alliances are sometimes necessary. Permanent alliances were to be avoided, however.

1. What war in Europe threatened United States neutrality?
2. How did the European war affect American trade?
3. What advice did Washington give in his Farewell Address?

4. The Adams Presidency

The United States faced many challenges following 1796. For the first time under the Constitution, George Washington was not leading the country. During the years from 1788 to 1796, however, the new government had proved it could work. A pattern had been set which promised success in dealing with the future.

4.1 The Election of 1796. The presidential election of 1796 was the first between political parties. John Adams and Thomas Pinckney ran for the Federalists. Thomas Jefferson and Aaron Burr ran for the Democratic-Republicans. The vote was very close. Many people were angry about the Jay Treaty and gave their support to the

Democratic-Republican party. When the votes were counted, Adams received a majority and was elected President. Jefferson received the second largest number of votes and became Vice-President. These two political rivals would share the highest offices in the land. But their first concern was the threat of war with France.

Who followed Washington as President?

4.2 The XYZ Affair. American relations with France had grown steadily worse during Washington's second term. The French had begun to do more damage to American shipping than had the British. President Adams was determined to avoid war. In 1797, he sent a peace commission to France. The three American commissioners were met by three people representing the French government. They demanded a loan for France and a bribe before allowing official talks to begin with the French government. The commissioners refused and returned to the United States. President Adams reported this to Congress, referring to the French officials as "X, Y, and Z." When news of the XYZ Affair became known, many Americans were angered. Congress voted funds to increase the size of the army and the navy. It seemed only a matter of time before war would break out.

4.3 The Convention of 1800. A sudden change in the French government helped relations between the two countries. In 1799, an American mission was greeted with friendship by the new leader of France, Napoleon Bonaparte. The Treaty of Morfontaine, better

John Adams (left) defeated Thomas Jefferson (right) in the 1796 presidential election. This campaign offered American voters a choice between political parties. Which party did each candidate represent?

What were the agreements made in the Convention of 1800?

known as the Convention of 1800, was signed by representatives of the two countries. The United States was released from the Alliance of 1778. In return, the French did not have to pay damages for the American shipping they had destroyed. War had been avoided.

4.4 The Alien and Sedition Acts.   Differences between the Federalists and Democratic-Republicans grew stronger as the election of 1800 drew near. The Federalists worried that they might lose the election. They were alarmed at the growth of the Democratic-Republican party. Much of it came from immigrants joining that party.

At whom were the Alien and Sedition Acts aimed?

In 1798, the Federalists in Congress passed several laws known as the Alien and Sedition Acts. These measures were intended to stop the Democratic-Republicans from gaining more power. One law increased the number of years needed for an *alien* (person who is not a citizen of the country in which he or she lives) to become a United States citizen. New immigrants then would not be able to vote for some years. In another act, the President was given the power to *deport* (send out of the country) any foreigner thought to be dangerous to the nation. The Sedition Act said that anyone guilty of *sedition*—the use of language to stir up rebellion against a government—could be fined and sent to prison. This law was aimed at a group of American newspaper writers who favored the Democratic-Republicans.

Why did the Democratic-Republican party oppose Jay's Treaty? Why did the Federalist party favor a pro-British foreign policy? Who would most likely support the Federalist party, a Pennsylvania wheat farmer or a Massachusetts banker? Who would most likely support the Democratic-Republican party, a South Carolina tobacco seller or a Kentucky blacksmith?

Political Parties in the 1790's

Federalist		Democratic-Republican
Favored government control by wealthy and educated citizens	Political Beliefs	Favored the selection of representatives by average citizens
Favored a strong national government		Favored a limited national government
Supported government aid to business, finance, and trade	Economic Beliefs	Supported no special favors to business; preferred farming
Favored a national bank		Favored sound state banks
Supported protective tariffs		Supported duty free imports
Favored British commercial ties and feared the French	Foreign Affairs	Sympathized with the French Revolution
Favored Jay's Treaty		Opposed Jay's Treaty
Strong in New England and seacoast areas	Sources of Strength	Strong in south, southwest, and frontier areas
Manufacturing interests, bankers, and merchants		Farmers, artisans, and skilled workers

The Alien and Sedition Acts were used by the party in office to fight their rivals. Although they did not last, they were laws made at a time when some people thought that strong political actions against the party in office were disloyal and illegal. Slowly people began to understand that party opposition was not only legal but valuable as a check on the party in power.

4.5 The Kentucky and Virginia Resolutions.   The Alien and Sedition Acts were attacked by Democratic-Republicans as unconstitutional. In 1798, Jefferson and Madison wrote papers protesting these acts. Jefferson's ideas were adopted by the legislature of Kentucky and Madison's by Virginia. These papers are known as the Kentucky and Virginia Resolutions.

Jefferson and Madison stated that the federal government had been formed by an agreement among the states. They believed in *states' rights*—that each state could decide when an act of the government was unconstitutional. A state could declare a law *null and void* (not binding). The Federalists disagreed. They stated that the government had been formed by the people, and that only the Supreme Court had the power to declare a law unconstitutional. No other state legislatures agreed with Virginia and Kentucky. The questions raised by this issue were important but left to another time to be answered.

What was the basic idea presented in the Resolutions?

4.6 The Election of 1800.   The Federalist party was badly divided by 1800. Hamilton and others were angry at President Adams, partly because he had made peace with France. Jefferson had won support for his attack of the Alien and Sedition Acts. In the election, a Democratic-Republican Congress was elected by a slim margin of votes. The results of the presidential election were in question for a while. Originally, the Constitution stated that electors would vote for two names for President. The person receiving the most votes would be President, and the person with the second largest number of votes would be Vice-President. In 1800, however, Jefferson and Aaron Burr, Republican candidate from New York, both received the same number of votes. The tie was settled in the House of Representatives where Jefferson was elected President. In 1804, an amendment was added to the Constitution to keep this from happening again. It said that electors would vote separately for President and Vice-President.

Who tied for the Presidency in 1800?

Who settled the issue?

1. Who became President after George Washington?
2. With which country was the United States involved in the XYZ Affair?
3. What was the purpose of the Alien and Sedition Acts?
4. Who won the presidential election of 1800?

Election of 1800

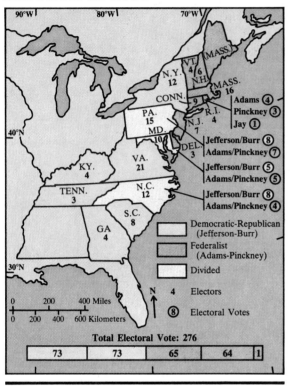

Total Electoral Vote: 276

| 73 | 73 | 65 | 64 | 1 |

REPUBLICANS

Turn out, turn out and save your Country from ruin!

From an *Emperor*—from a *King*—from the iron grasp of a *British Tory Faction*—an unprincipled banditti of British speculators. The hireling tools and emissaries of his majesty king George the 3d have thronged our city and diffused the poison of principles among us.

DOWN WITH THE TORIES, DOWN WITH THE BRITISH FACTION,

Before they have it in their power to enslave you, and reduce your families to distress by heavy taxation. Republicans want no Tribute-liars—they want no ship Ocean-liars—they want no Rufus King's for Lords —they want no Varick to lord it over them—they want no Jones for senator, who fought with the British against the Americans in time of the war.—But they want in their places such men as

Jefferson & Clinton,

who fought their Country's Battles in the year '76

A Federalist campaign poster (top right) maintained that Jefferson was unworthy to follow in the tradition of Washington. A Democratic-Republican notice (bottom right) said that the Federalists would lead the nation to ruin. Who won in 1800?

5. Jefferson in Office

When Thomas Jefferson was elected in 1800, it marked the beginning of many years of Democratic-Republican control in the United States. In an inaugural address made at his **inauguration** (ceremony of installing a person in office), Jefferson tried to quiet the fears of many Federalists who believed that he would make sweeping changes. He called upon all citizens to work together stating, "We are all Republicans, we are all Federalists."

Why did Jefferson think his election was a "revolution"?

5.1 The "Revolution of 1800." Jefferson liked to call his election the "Revolution of 1800." It showed that, in the United States, one political party could be defeated and the opposition party could take power peacefully. So far as policies were concerned, Jefferson's election was by no means a revolution. He continued the Bank of the United States and many of the policies of the Federalists. The biggest change he made was to cut government costs sharply, mostly by cutting money spent for the army and navy. He also ended the whiskey tax and raised money through customs duties and selling federal land.

5.2   Marbury v. Madison.   Early in Jefferson's first term, the Supreme Court decided one of the most important cases in American history. The Federalists had lost control of the executive and legislative branches in the election of 1800. They wanted to make their hold on the judicial branch stronger. Between the election and the inauguration, Congress added to the number of judges and court officers. President Adams then named members of his party to fill these posts.

When Jefferson took office, he told Secretary of State James Madison to hold the papers that would allow the new officials to start their jobs. William Marbury brought suit against Madison to make him turn over the papers on his appointment. The case came before the Supreme Court. Chief Justice John Marshall stated the opinion of the Court in 1803. He said Marbury had a right to the papers, but that the Court could not force Madison to turn them over to him. According to the Judiciary Act of 1789, the Court had the power to give such orders. Marshall said that the Court could not do so because that part of the Judiciary Act was unconstitutional.

Who declared an act of Congress unconstitutional?

✗ The case of *Marbury* v. *Madison* was the first time that the Supreme Court declared an act of Congress to be unconstitutional. In later decisions over the years, the Marshall Court said that the powers of the federal government were above those of the states in cases of constitutional law. All of these decisions made the judicial branch of the government as strong as the executive and legislative branches.

5.3   The Louisiana Purchase.   Soon after he became President in 1801, Jefferson learned that Napoleon of France was taking control of Louisiana away from Spain. Louisiana was a huge area stretching from the Mississippi River to the Rocky Mountains. The people of the West depended on the Mississippi River and New Orleans, the gateway to the sea, to get their goods to market. They were afraid that the French would close the Mississippi River and New Orleans to American use.

Napoleon had been planning to build a new French empire in North America. He had to give up those plans, however, when slaves on the Caribbean island of Santo Domingo revolted against French rule. Led by Toussaint L'Ouverture, they established the nation of Haiti. Without the island as a naval base, Napoleon feared that he could not hold Louisiana against the British. So he offered to sell Louisiana to the United States.

From whom was Louisiana purchased?

Although Jefferson favored the purchase, he was worried because the Constitution did not give the federal government power to buy land from a foreign country. As President, however, he did have the power to make treaties with the approval of the Senate. So he decided to sign a treaty to buy Louisiana. In April 1803, an agreement was signed for the purchase of Louisiana. The United States received claim to 827,000 square miles of land for $15 million. This new land doubled the size of the country at that time.

Who served as guides for Lewis and Clark?

5.4 Exploring Louisiana.   Very little was known about the area west of the Mississippi River. In 1804, President Jefferson sent a United States Army expedition under Captain Meriwether Lewis and Captain William Clark to explore the new territory. During their travels, they hired Sacajawea, a Shoshoni Indian, and her husband, Toussaint Charbonneau, a French fur trapper, to guide them. The

This map shows the extent of the Louisiana Purchase. The routes of the Lewis and Clark expedition are also shown. Which Americans benefited most from the purchase? How did the purchase affect the size of the United States?

Exploring the Louisiana Purchase, 1806

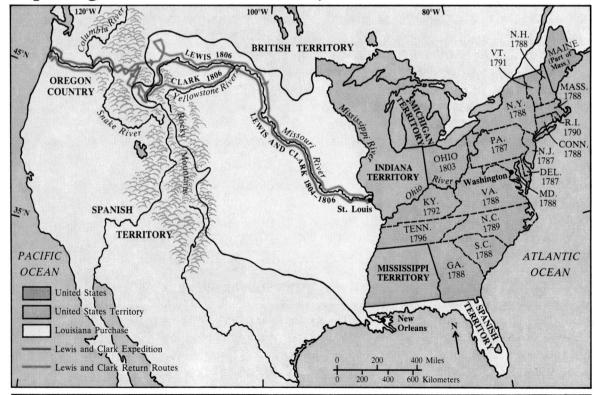

Lewis and Clark commanded an expedition of more than 50 people. Sacajawea, the only woman, joined the group as a guide. Ben York, Lewis' servant, was the only black. The others were soldiers, trappers, and volunteers. When was the trip?

group with Lewis and Clark made its way up the Missouri River and into the wilderness beyond. After crossing the Rocky Mountains, the expedition traveled down the Columbia River, reaching the Pacific Ocean in 1805. Lewis and Clark returned to St. Louis in 1806, bringing with them valuable facts about the lands west of the Mississippi. A whole new frontier was opened to American settlement.

1. What was the biggest change in government made by Thomas Jefferson as President?
2. What was the case in which the Supreme Court first declared an act of Congress unconstitutional?
3. Who led an expedition into Louisiana after its purchase in 1803?

6. Conclusion

The United States under the Constitution was a growing, changing country. In its early years, it faced many problems which the Framers of the Constitution had not expected. Some of the issues raised during these years would not be completely answered for years to come. But the new government had shown that it could withstand change and operate successfully. It had passed its first test. The nation had become established.

Chapter 8 Review

Main Points

1. As the first President of the United States, George Washington established many precedents.
2. Alexander Hamilton's economic program aimed to create a strong national economy.
3. Arguments over Hamilton's program led to the formation of political parties.
4. Foreign policy under Presidents Washington and Adams aimed to keep the United States neutral.
5. The Alien and Sedition Acts were passed in 1798. They were intended to stop the Democratic-Republicans from gaining more power.
6. The election of Thomas Jefferson as President in 1800 showed that control of government could pass peacefully from one party to another.
7. Under President Jefferson, the physical size of the United States increased with the purchase of Louisiana.

Building Vocabulary

1. Identify the following:

George Washington	Whiskey Rebellion	XYZ Affair
Cabinet	Federalists	Alien and Sedition Acts
Judiciary Act of 1789	Democratic-Republicans	*Marbury* v. *Madison*
Supreme Court	Jay Treaty	Toussaint L'Ouverture
Alexander Hamilton	Pinckney Treaty	Lewis and Clark Expedition
Benjamin Banneker		Sacajawea

2. Define the following:

electors	assume	impressment
precedents	duties	alien
negotiating	protective tariff	deport
appeal	excise tax	sedition
domestic	strict construction	states' rights
bonds	loose construction	null and void
speculators	neutrality	inauguration
redeemed		

Remembering the Facts

1. How was George Washington elected as first President?
2. When and where did the new national government begin its work?

3. What were the levels of federal courts created by the Judiciary Act of 1789?

4. What were the main points of Hamilton's economic program?

5. Which political party supported a strict construction of the Constitution? Which supported a loose construction?

6. What were the provisions of the Jay Treaty with Britain in 1794?

7. What did the United States gain in the Pinckney Treaty of 1795?

8. What was the XYZ Affair?

9. How was the tied election of 1800 settled?

10. What was the issue in the case of *Marbury* v. *Madison*?

11. Where did Lewis and Clark explore? Who went with them?

Understanding the Facts

1. Why was George Washington's Presidency important?

2. Why was a strong court system a goal of the Framers of the Constitution?

3. What was the purpose of the Bank of the United States?

4. Why did Jefferson and his followers oppose the plan for a national bank?

5. Why did political parties form in the United States?

6. How did the Pinckney Treaty help farmers in the western United States?

7. Why did Congress pass the Alien and Sedition Acts in 1798?

8. What was the significance of the "Revolution of 1800"?

Using Maps

Directions. It is important to know direction in order to use a map properly. North is the direction toward the North Pole. On most maps, north is usually at the top of the page. Many maps show a direction indicator for north.

Once you know north, you also know that east is to the right, west is to the left, and south is opposite north. For more precise directions, you can use the indicator to find northeast, northwest, southeast, and southwest. These are areas between the four basic directions.

Check your understanding of direction by using the map of the Louisiana Purchase on page 192 and answering the following questions.

1. Which direction from the United States was the Louisiana Territory?

2. Which direction provides the most direct route from Washington, D.C., to southern Louisiana?

3. When Lewis and Clark left St. Louis in 1804, which direction did they travel into Louisiana?

4. Which direction is New Orleans from St. Louis?

5. Which direction did Lewis and Clark travel along the Columbia River going toward the Pacific Ocean?

6. When Clark returned to St. Louis in 1806, which direction did he and his party take along the Yellowstone River?

The Growth of Nationalism

9

In 1812, the people in Philadelphia celebrated the Fourth of July. Less than half a century after Independence, the Fourth had become a national tradition. How did celebrating Independence Day help to form a national identity?

In the early 1800's, the future of the United States looked promising. The Constitution had proved to be a strong base upon which to build the new nation. The purchase of Louisiana more than doubled the size of the United States and gave people a huge new area in which to settle. Americans looked ahead confidently and expected to carry on their own affairs with no interference from Europe. They had created their own form of government, and they were beginning to create their own identity as a people.

1. The United States and Neutral Rights _____

President Jefferson began his second term of office in March 1805. He hoped to continue the policies which had brought peace and prosperity to the country during his first term. The United States had gained much from the long war between Great Britain and France. Both European countries bought American goods. Both allowed American merchants to trade with their West Indian islands. Things began to change, however, and foreign relations again became a major concern.

1.1   The Chesapeake Affair.   Between 1804 and 1806, France conquered much of Europe. Great Britain, a major enemy of France, controlled the seas. Each nation wanted to limit the other's trade. Both countries stated that they would attack ships heading for the other's ports. Great Britain began to *blockade* (close off) the American coast to stop American ships loaded with goods on their way to France. The British also continued to impress American sailors into the British navy. These acts interfered with *freedom of the seas*—the right of merchant ships in peace or war to move in any waters, except those belonging to a country. The British acts angered people in the United States.

What was the Chesapeake Affair?

In June 1807, the British warship *Leopard* sailed up to the American warship *Chesapeake*. The British demanded the right to search the American ship for *deserters* (soldiers or sailors who run away from their duty). When the American officer refused, the *Leopard* opened fire. Three sailors were killed, and 18 were wounded. Four other sailors were taken off the ship, accused of being deserters.

1.2   The Embargo.   After the attack on the *Chesapeake,* many Americans were ready for war. Jefferson, however, wanted to avoid it. He felt the country was not prepared to fight, because the Democratic-Republicans had reduced the size of the army and navy. Jefferson wanted to stop the British and French from harming

Ograbme, a snapping turtle, was a favorite cartoon character after 1807. Ograbme is embargo spelled backward. This cartoon shows a turtle grabbing a man who is trying to smuggle a barrel of tobacco onto a British ship. What did the Embargo of 1807 accomplish?

What is an embargo?

Against whom was the Embargo Act directed?

What acts were passed after the repeal of the Embargo Act?

American trade. He decided that the answer was to keep American ships from sailing the seas.

As a result, Congress passed the Embargo Act of 1807. An *embargo* is a law stopping all ships except foreign ships without cargo from leaving the country for foreign ports. Jefferson hoped to win the respect of Britain and France for American rights by refusing to sell them American goods. The policy did not work. The embargo hurt American trade even more than it did that of other countries. Harbors were crowded with ships, and thousands of workers were out of work. Prices dropped as goods had to be stored. Congress soon repealed the act.

James Madison became President in 1808. Soon after the election, the Non-Intercourse Act was passed. It allowed Americans to trade with any country except France and Great Britain. In 1810, Congress passed a new act. Under Macon's Bill Number 2, it was decided that if either Great Britain or France lifted their restrictions on American shipping, America would cut off all trade with the other country. Napoleon agreed to do this, and Madison gave orders forbidding trade with Great Britain. By 1812, Great Britain was so hurt by the boycott that the British repealed their restrictions on American shipping.

1.3   Trouble on the Frontier.   There was another reason why Americans were angry with Great Britain besides interference with trade and impressment. The British in Canada were helping the Indians fight American settlers along the western frontier. During this time, more and more settlers were crossing the Appalachian Mountains,

Tecumseh (1765-1813)

=PROFILE=

As settlers pushed west across the Appalachian Mountains, Indians of the Northwest Territory crowded together for support. They were afraid of losing their land and their ways of life. Tecumseh, chief of the Shawnee people, and his brother Tenskwatawa, the Prophet, tried to bring all the Indian people together to stop the advance of American settlement.

Tecumseh believed that all land, like water and air, belonged to all Indian people. He traveled and spoke with most of the Indian people east of the Rocky Mountains. A gifted speaker, Tecumseh urged the various groups to join together in a confederation. In this way, they could work as one to prevent the loss of their land and secure their future.

In 1808, Tecumseh and the Shawnee people were forced by settlers to move to Indiana from Ohio. While in Indiana, Tecumseh formed a plan of action that led to the Battle of Tippecanoe with United States soldiers in 1811.

When the War of 1812 began, Tecumseh believed that the British leaders were going to support his people's desire to protect their land in the Northwest Territory. So he and his followers joined the British soldiers against the Americans. The next year, United States forces defeated Tecumseh's soldiers at the Battle of the Thames, near Ontario, Canada. Tecumseh died in the battle, and with him, the dream of an Indian confederation died, too.

---

forcing the Indians to move farther west. As the Indians were crowded together, they were concerned about losing their lands and losing their ways of life.

Tecumseh, the chief of the Shawnees, and his brother, the Prophet, tried to unite several groups of Indians in 1811 in defense against the spread of white settlers. Many Indians along the frontier formed a confederation to try to prevent further loss of land. On November 7, 1811, American forces under General William Henry Harrison fought and defeated the Indians in western Indiana where the Tippecanoe River joins the Wabash River. The Indian defeat in the Battle of Tippecanoe was a major setback for Tecumseh's plans.

What did Tecumseh try to do?

1.4 The War Hawks. Many people in the West called for war against Great Britain. They thought that this was the way to stop the British aid to the Indians along the western frontier. Many were also convinced that Spain was giving aid to the Indians in the southeast. Great Britain and Spain were allies, and it seemed that the two countries were working against the United States.

Who were the "War Hawks"?

In 1810, several new members were elected to the House of Representatives. They voiced the demands of frontier people, stating that war was the way to protect American interests. Known as "War Hawks," they gained support for their views. Among them were John C. Calhoun of South Carolina and Henry Clay of Kentucky.

1.5 Madison's War Message. On June 1, 1812, President Madison sent a message to Congress. It asked for a declaration of war with Great Britain and stated his reasons. The British had impressed American sailors on the high seas, had blockaded the American coast, had interfered with trade, and had aided the Indians on the frontier. Although Congress was divided over the question of war, a majority in both houses voted in favor of the declaration. War was declared on June 18, 1812. The British had repealed their orders against American shipping two days before, but the news did not reach Congress in time.

What were the reasons for declaring war against Britain in 1812?

1. Who interfered with United States' freedom of the seas?
2. How was the Embargo of 1807 unsuccessful?
3. With whom did the United States go to war in 1812?

2. The War of 1812

Those Americans who were in favor of the War of 1812 felt that the United States needed to force Great Britain to respect American rights. Yet the country was not prepared for war in many ways. The army and navy were small and poorly equipped. Financing the war would be a major problem, because the Bank of the United States had been allowed to go out of existence in 1811. In addition, most of the people in New England were against what they called "Mr. Madison's War."

What problems did the United States face at the start of the war?

2.1 America on the Offensive. One advantage for Americans at the beginning of the war was that the British were fighting a war with France in Europe. Because of this, the British could not concentrate their attention on the trouble in America. The United States was therefore able to take the offensive in the first year of the war.

What problems did the British face?

A major American goal in the War of 1812 was to take over Canada. In the late summer of 1812, the United States planned a drive

Major Campaigns of the War of 1812

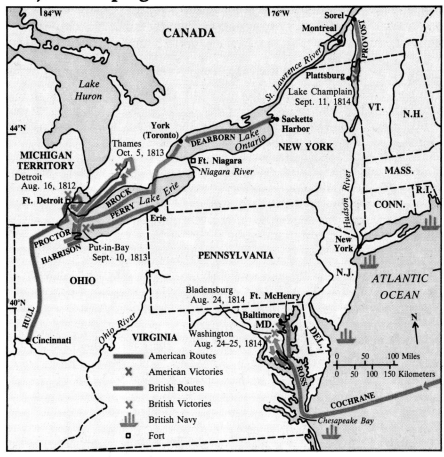

The major battles of the War of 1812 were widely scattered. Washington, the United States capital, and York, the Canadian capital at the time, were key military targets. What was each side trying to do? What was the purpose of the British blockade along the Atlantic coast?

on Canada. One attack was to be from Detroit, another along the Niagara River, and a third aimed at Montreal. All three attacks failed. Detroit fell to the British and Indians. British forces drove back two attacks across the Niagara River. The drive against Montreal ended when the New York militia refused to leave the United States.

The United States had few victories in 1812 except for those won by its small navy. Several American ships were sent out to harass and intercept the British fleet. The U.S.S. *Constitution* destroyed two British ships, earning the nickname "Old Ironsides." The British navy set up a blockade of the American coast early in 1813.

American forces were able to stop the British from taking the Great Lakes area in 1813. On September 10, naval forces led by Oliver Hazard Perry defeated the British at Put-in-Bay. Perry reported the

What was the American goal in the War of 1812?

Who was the hero of the Battle of Lake Erie?

The Growth of Nationalism 201

victory by saying, "We have met the enemy and they are ours." This victory gave Americans control of Lake Erie. On October 5, 1813, an army under General Harrison defeated a force of British and Indians at the Battle of the Thames in Canada. In the battle, Tecumseh was killed. With his death, efforts for a lasting Indian confederacy also died.

Why were the British able to take to the offensive?

2.2 Great Britain on the Offensive. By 1814, the British navy had almost complete control of the seas and commanded the coast of the United States. Until that year, they had been using most of their forces against the French in Europe. With the defeat of Napoleon in 1814, they turned their attention to the war in America.

On August 19, British forces landed on the coast of Maryland. They defeated an American army at Bladensburg, Maryland, and marched toward Washington, D.C. Several thousand American soldiers and government officers fled to Virginia. British soldiers entered Washington and burned the Capitol and the White House, home of the President. The British were acting in revenge for the burning of the Canadian city of York (Toronto) by Americans.

Where did the British attack?

Next the British decided to attack Baltimore. But they were not able to break down the defenses of Fort McHenry just outside the city. During the three-day shelling of the fort, Francis Scott Key, who watched the battle, wrote a poem titled "The Star-Spangled Banner." Later it was set to music and became the ***national anthem***—song of praise and patriotism—of the United States. About the same time, a British invasion along Lake Champlain was stopped by American naval forces under Captain Thomas Macdonough.

The bombing of Fort McHenry by the British led Francis Scott Key to observe the "rockets' red glare." Key felt so proud of the way the American forces held out that he wrote a poem. Later his poem was set to music and became the national anthem. How does a national anthem encourage patriotism?

After peace was signed but before the news of it arrived, Americans defeated the British at New Orleans. Andrew Jackson (far right on the white horse) became one of many national heroes during the War of 1812. Dolley Madison and Oliver Hazard Perry were others. How did heroes help a national pride to grow?

2.3 The Battle of New Orleans. After their failure to take Baltimore, the British prepared to attack New Orleans. They wanted to gain control of the entire Mississippi Valley. British ships sailed from the West Indies with 7,500 soldiers under Sir Edward Pakenham. American forces in New Orleans were led by General Andrew Jackson. Jackson had been fighting Indians in the Mississippi Territory since 1813. His troops had defeated the Indians at the Battle of Horseshoe Bend and had invaded Spanish Florida. They seized Pensacola in November 1814. Some of those who fought with Jackson in Florida were with him as he moved west to New Orleans.

Who commanded American troops in the Battle of New Orleans?

Most of the 5,000 American soldiers with Jackson, including two black battalions, had had little fighting experience. The British soldiers, on the other hand, were well trained and veterans of the war against France. They thought the Americans would not put up much resistance. Joining Jackson in New Orleans were several thousand other soldiers, including many from Kentucky and Tennessee and Jean Laffite from France. The British attacked on January 8, 1815. When the battle was over, about 2,000 British, including General Pakenham, had been killed or wounded. Less than 100 Americans had lost their lives.

The victory at New Orleans restored some of the national pride which had been lost because of earlier defeats. Many Americans felt they had won the war, but victory in this battle had no effect upon the war's outcome. Because of the slowness of communications, the Battle of New Orleans was fought after the treaty of peace.

What was unique about the Battle of New Orleans?

2.4 The Treaty of Ghent. In August 1814, five American representatives had met with British officials in Ghent, Belgium, to discuss peace. For over three months, the two sides could not come to terms. Finally, on December 24, 1814, an agreement was reached to end the war. Neither side could claim victory. Nevertheless, the United States became more independent from European affairs after the war.

What were the results of the War of 1812?

The Treaty of Ghent ended the fighting and brought peace. It said nothing, however, about the issues which had caused the war. It did not deal with impressment, blockades, or the United States' right to trade freely. It did return all land boundaries to what they had been when the war began. A commission was set up to decide the northeast boundary between the United States and Canada. Control of the Great Lakes and fishing rights were to be settled at a later date. The treaty was approved by the Senate on February 17, 1815.

2.5 The Hartford Convention. The war had been very unpopular in some parts of the United States. The area of the country most against it was New England. People there made their living by trade, and this was greatly hurt when the war began. New England was the only area of the country where the Federalists were in a majority, and the Federalists led the fight against the war.

What was the Hartford Convention?

When the war dragged on without a victory, New England Federalists became more and more bitter. In December 1814, they held a convention in Hartford, Connecticut. They met to discuss ways of taking action against the war. Some members of the group thought the New England states should *secede,* or break away from the United States. Few of the members agreed with this, however. After much discussion, a report was written. It stated that if a state found a federal law to be unconstitutional, it had the right to protect itself—to declare that law null and void. This idea had appeared earlier in the Kentucky and Virginia Resolutions written by Democratic-Republicans.

The report also included a list of amendments to be added to the Constitution. They would add to the powers of the states and take some power away from the federal government. Because they did not like James Madison, the members of the Convention wanted Presidents to serve only a single term in office. They wanted a two-thirds vote of both houses of Congress before war could be declared or new states could be added to the United States.

What happened to the Federalist party after the War of 1812?

The Hartford Convention sent representatives to Washington to present their demands to the government there. When they arrived, however, the people were celebrating news of the Treaty of Ghent and Jackson's victory at New Orleans. The Hartford Convention had met too late to have any effect upon the war. Later it was thought to have been disloyal to the United States, and the Federalists were looked upon as traitors. The power of the party was destroyed after the war.

1. Where were the major American victories in the war?
2. When was the treaty signed to end the war?
3. Which section of the United States opposed the war?

3. The National Spirit

The War of 1812 is sometimes called the "Second War of Independence." From 1789 to 1815, American policies had often been shaped by events in Europe. For 100 years after the Treaty of Ghent, the United States was more independent from Europe and was not directly involved in European wars. This gave Americans a chance to develop their own country. The end of the War of 1812 began a time of strong national pride under the Democratic-Republican party.

3.1 Nationalism and Politics. A spirit of nationalism was behind the message that President Madison presented to Congress in December 1815. *Nationalism* is a feeling of pride in the nation as a whole and loyalty to its goals. Madison called upon Congress to pass several measures to make the country strong and protect its independence. To give the country a sound money supply, Madison asked for a new Bank of the United States. He wanted a protective tariff to help American industry to grow. To improve transportation and help trade, he called for government money to build a system of roads and canals. To better protect the country, he asked that the army and navy be made larger.

What things did President Madison want Congress to pass?

It seemed to many people that the Democratic-Republicans had taken over much of the Federalist program. President Madison's ideas meant more power and responsibility for the federal government. However, many people were no longer against this and were in favor of the President's plans. By the time James Monroe took office in March 1817, much of Madison's program had been passed.

In 1816, Congress chartered the Second Bank of the United States for 20 years. When the first Bank had gone out of existence in 1811, many state governments had given bank charters to private individuals. These banks did not always have enough gold or silver to back up their paper money. Its value declined, creating an unstable financial situation. The Second Bank of the United States was strong and had many branches in different states. The money it issued was sound, and it had control over the less stable state-chartered banks.

Why was a new Bank of the United States needed?

How did the Tariff of 1816 protect American industries?

Congress also passed a new tariff in 1816. As the first real protective tariff, it placed high duties on foreign manufactured goods shipped into the United States. During the War of 1812, it had been hard to get some goods from Europe. As a result, many new factories had been built in America. After the war, the British sent large shipments of goods to sell in the United States. These goods were generally cheaper than those made in America. By having lower prices, the British hoped to drive the new American industries out of business. The Tariff of 1816, however, protected the new American industries by adding to the price of British products.

The building of a good transportation system was important to the United States. Farmers in the West and South needed roads and canals to carry goods to the East where a large amount went on to foreign markets. Northeastern manufacturers needed to move their goods to the West. However, the plan for building roads moved ahead slowly.

What road was built with federal aid?

Only one important route to the West was finished with federal aid. This was the Cumberland, or National, Road which was first planned in

The Erie Canal (left) was the first canal in America. It launched a boom in canal construction that lasted until the mid-1800's. New roads were also built during that time. A stagecoach (right) bounces along an unfinished portion of the National Road. Notice where the canals and roads are located on the map on the next page. How did farmers in the South get goods to markets along the Atlantic coast?

Principal Roads and Canals by 1840

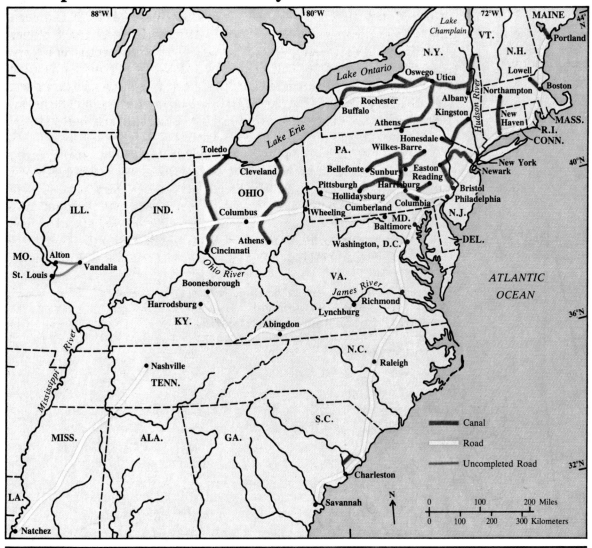

1807. Construction began in 1811, and by 1818, it joined the Potomac and Ohio rivers. Between 1822 and 1838, it was extended through Columbus, Ohio, and Indianapolis, Indiana, to Vandalia, Illinois. Bills for more roads and canals paid for by the federal government were thought to be unconstitutional by Presidents Monroe, Adams, and Jackson over the years. The idea of a national system of transportation had to be set aside for a time. Many of the roads and canals that were built were paid for by the states or by private companies.

3.2 Nationalism and the Courts. The judicial branch of the government strongly supported nationalism in the early 1800's. Chief Justice John Marshall was the leading figure in the Supreme Court. He had already stated his ideas about the role of the courts and judicial review in his opinion on the 1803 case of *Marbury* v. *Madison*.

In the case of *Fletcher* v. *Peck* in 1810, the Supreme Court ruled that acts of a state government could be voided if they violated provisions of the Constitution. In 1819, the Court ruled in *McCullough* v. *Maryland* that the state of Maryland could not tax the Bank of the United States. This ruling upheld the doctrine of implied powers and the supremacy of the national government. Marshall said that "the power to tax involves the power to destroy," and no state could destroy a national institution. In the case of *Gibbons* v. *Ogden* in 1824, the Supreme Court said that the state of New York could not grant a monopoly to anyone to run steamboats between New York and New Jersey. The opinion of the Court was that only Congress had the power to make laws governing **interstate trade,** or trade between or among states. All of these decisions added to the power of the national government over that of the states.

What idea was at the base of the Court's decisions in the early 1800's?

3.3 Nationalism and Foreign Affairs. A spirit of nationalism was shown in American foreign policy after the War of 1812. With the problems of Europe involving the United States less and less, the country turned its attention to the Western Hemisphere.

A new time of expansion began after the war. Spain and the United States agreed in the Adams-Onís Treaty of 1819 that Spain would *renounce* (give up) all claims to West Florida and would *cede* (yield or grant) East Florida to the United States. In return, the federal government agreed to pay claims of American citizens against the Spanish government up to $5 million. The United States also gave up its claims to Texas. The two countries also agreed to a boundary between the United States and the Spanish lands to the west.

What were the provisions of the Adams-Onís Treaty?

In the early 1800's, many Spanish colonies in Latin America had won their independence from Spain. Some European countries were thinking about returning these colonies to Spain or possibly taking them over. America wanted the colonies to stay independent. In December 1823, President Monroe announced what was later to become known as the Monroe Doctrine. He said that North and South America should no longer be thought of as "subjects for future colonization" by European countries. The United States would not interfere in European affairs, and Europeans were not to interfere in the affairs of the Western Hemisphere. Monroe's statement was a warning to European nations to keep "hands off" the newly independent Latin American countries. It

Why did Monroe announce the Monroe Doctrine?

Nationalism

Nationalism is a feeling of pride and devotion to a nation. The spirit of nationalism raises that nation above all others, promoting loyalty to its culture and interests. In the United States, American nationalism uniquely developed among people who came from various countries. These people became proud of the United States and loyal to it.

This feeling of nationalism grew in Mary Jane Watson in the 1820's when she came with her parents to live in Albany, New York. She wrote a letter in 1825 to her grandparents in England. She expressed her feelings about her new country and her confidence in its future.

My Dear Grandparents:
. . . It would be very agreeable for me to see my English friends, but I don't wish to return to England again. I like America much the best; it is a very plentiful country. A person may get a very good living here if they are industrious.

My father is doing very well and is very well satisfied to stay in this country. He has got a cow of his own and nine hogs. . . .

I have been very fortunate. I have got good clothes, and I can dress as well as any [upper-class woman] in Sedlescomb. I can enjoy a silk and white frock, and crepe frock and crepe veil. . . . You cannot tell the poor from the rich here; they are dressed as good as the other. . . .

We want Uncle William to come over to America. . . . [He] must . . . bring all . . . working tools. . . . Don't be discouraged now because some come back. Don't do as Mr. Rolfe did, step on shore and, before you know anything about the place, go right back again.

Any respectable person may get a good living by industry. It is a good place for young people; they can get good wages for their work. . . .

The people here are very good about education, much more than they are in England.

Mother and Father wish to be remembered to you. . . .
Your very affectionate granddaughter,
MARY JANE WATSON

1. How does Watson feel about her new home in the United States?
2. How does what Watson wrote in her letter show nationalism?
3. Why does Watson exaggerate the equality of life in America?

was also a warning to Russia not to move into the Pacific Coast area south of Alaska, which Russia held.

Americans were proud of Monroe's statement, but it was not greatly respected in Europe. At the time the Monroe Doctrine was issued, the United States could not really enforce it. For the most part, European nations left the Latin American countries alone because Great Britain had warned them away. The British had a strong trade with these countries and would use their navy to protect it. It was not until years later that the Monroe Doctrine became a powerful force in foreign affairs. In issuing the Doctrine, however, the United States had shown its political independence and its growing spirit of unity.

Who made the Monroe Doctrine effective in its early years?

1. How was the spirit of nationalism reflected in actions of Congress?
2. Which actions by the Supreme Court showed a feeling of nationalism?
3. How was American nationalism seen in United States foreign policy?

4. The Creation of a National Culture _____

The growing nationalism after the War of 1812 led to the rise of a truly American culture. From colonial times through the War of 1812, cultural life in the United States was strongly influenced by Europe, chiefly Great Britain. Long after they had won independence, Americans read European literature and admired European art and architecture. In the years after the War of 1812, however, Americans began to create their own art forms.

Who influenced American cultural life prior to 1812?

4.1 American Literature. During the country's first years, most American authors wrote about political matters. Many of them copied British writing because most people in the United States favored British literature. Few publishers would print the works of American authors. After the War of 1812, American authors were inspired by the national feeling. They began to form their own literature. They used settings, characters, and humor that were typically American.

Washington Irving of New York was one of the first authors to break away from British influence. He was also one of the first Americans to be widely read in Europe. The publication of his major work, the *Sketch Book,* in 1820 showed Irving's skill at short-story writing. In "Rip Van Winkle" and "The Legend of Sleepy Hollow," he

What was unique about Irving's writing?

President James Monroe (standing) discusses foreign policy with his Cabinet—John Quincy Adams, William H. Crawford, William Wirt, John C. Calhoun, Samuel L. Southard, and John McLean. What was the major contribution of the Monroe administration to foreign policy?

wrote about life in the Hudson River Valley. He used American forms of speech and action as well as America's history for his works.

One of the country's first major novelists was James Fenimore Cooper of New York. He wrote the "Leatherstocking" tales, including *The Last of the Mohicans, The Pathfinder,* and *The Deerslayer.* In these tales of the early western frontier, Cooper created an American folk hero in the character of "Leatherstocking." His adventure stories became well known in both America and Europe.

Other authors, such as William Cullen Bryant of Massachusetts, wrote poetry. Bryant expressed a love for natural beauty. His poem "Thanatopsis" appeared in 1817. In it, he suggested that by studying nature, people could better understand life and death.

Bryan's poetry expresses a love for what thing?

> *So live, that when thy summons comes to join*
> *The innumerable caravan, that moves*
> *To that mysterious realm, where each shall take*
> *His chamber in the silent halls of death,*
> *Thou go not, like the quarry-slave at night*
> *Scourged to his dungeon, but, sustained and soothed*
> *By an unfaltering trust, approach thy grave,*
> *Like one who draws the drapery of his couch*
> *About him, and lies down to pleasant dreams.*

With such poems as "Thanatopsis" and "To a Waterfowl," Bryant became famous on both sides of the Atlantic Ocean.

4.2 American Painting and Music.   Like literature, American painting in the country's early years was influenced by Europe. Well-known artists like Benjamin West, John Singleton Copley, and Gilbert Stuart had studied abroad and followed the British style of painting. They most often painted portraits.

After the War of 1812, American artists turned their attention to American themes. In the East, William Sidney Mount painted his Long Island neighbors at work and play. He showed them at barn dances, fishing in their boats, whittling wood, and bowling on the green. George Caleb Bingham left a vivid account of everyday life on the Missouri frontier. He pictured fur traders, riverboat workers, political speakers, and tax-paying citizens. George Catlin was one of several artists who lived and worked among the Indians. He painted scenes of their daily life, at trading posts and on hunting trips.

American painters also found inspiration in the rugged beauty of their country. Thomas Doughty of Pennsylvania was one of the first successful landscape painters and a leader of the "Hudson River

Who were some important American artists that contributed to the growth of the national spirit?

George Catlin (left) always attracted a crowd when he set up his easel. Catlin painted Four Bears (right), a Mandan chief, in 1832. How did Catlin and other artists contribute to what was known about Indians at the time?

School" of painting. This was made up of artists who liked to paint views of the Catskill Mountains and the Hudson River in New York. One of these artists, Thomas Cole of Ohio, became well known for his huge paintings of the mountains and forests of America. The public paid attention to the painting of this time. More Americans attended art shows and bought paintings to hang in their homes.

People also enjoyed the lighter side of cultural life. Almost every large city had more than one theater. Companies of players visited smaller towns, performing in barns, tents, or log cabins. Plays and musicals were most often a part of any steamboat trip. Families bought pianos to play tunes written by Americans. Stephen Foster was one such songwriter. "My Old Kentucky Home" and "O Susanna," written by Foster, were played, sung, or hummed by thousands. American music, like American literature and art, was created for all the people to enjoy.

What other cultural developments occurred in the years after the War of 1812?

4.3 American Architecture. Some Americans showed their pride in America in literature and painting. Others designed private homes and public buildings that would display the spirit of the nation. In the early years, American buildings had been copies of ones in Europe. After Americans had won independence, they wanted buildings in their own styles. At first, Americans borrowed from those of ancient Rome. This was called the "Roman Revival." Thomas Jefferson thought about Roman styles when he planned his home, Monticello, and buildings for the University of Virginia.

A Greek style followed the Roman style. This "Greek Revival" was partly due to American feeling about the Greek revolt against Turkey in 1821. Greek design became the model for public buildings all over the country, including the Capitol in Washington, D.C. It was also used for private homes, such as the plantation houses in the South.

1. What settings were used by American writers in the 1800's?
2. What were the themes of American painters after 1812?
3. Which styles were most used by American architects?

5. Conclusion _____

In the years after the War of 1812, Americans gained confidence in their own abilities and in the future of their country. The war was a turning point after which the American people began to establish a separate identity. The attention of the nation turned from Europe toward America. A new period of national growth and territorial expansion was about to begin.

Chapter 9 Review

Main Points

1. War between France and Britain brought prosperity and problems to America.
2. France and Britain both interfered with United States shipping and trade.
3. An embargo in 1807 failed to force France and Britain to respect the rights of the United States.
4. Under Tecumseh, a confederation of Indians tried to halt the western expansion of American settlers.
5. The United States fought a war with Britain between 1812 and 1814.
6. The Treaty of Ghent, signed on December 24, 1814, ended the war and set the peace terms.
7. Following the war, a spirit of nationalism influenced actions in domestic and foreign affairs.
8. The growth of nationalism led to the development of a unique American culture.

Building Vocabulary

1. Identify the following:

   Chesapeake   Andrew Jackson   Monroe Doctrine
   Tecumseh   Treaty of Ghent   Washington Irving
   War Hawks   Hartford Convention   "Thanatopsis"
   "Old Ironsides"   Cumberland Road   Thomas Doughty
   Oliver Hazard Perry   *McCullough* v. *Maryland*   Stephen Foster
   Francis Scott Key   "Greek Revival"

2. Define the following:

   blockade   national anthem   interstate trade
   freedom of the seas   secede   renounce
   deserters   nationalism   cede
   embargo

Remembering the Facts

1. How did war in Europe affect American trade in the early 1800's?
2. Why did the United States embargo its trade with foreign countries?
3. Which frontier conflict increased tension between Britain and America?
4. What were the major American victories of the War of 1812?
5. Why did people in New England oppose the war?
6. What were the provisions of the Treaty of Ghent in 1814?

7. Which Federalist ideas were adopted by President Madison and his party?
8. What were the provisions of the Monroe Doctrine?

9. Who was the first American author to break away from British styles?
10. What was the "Hudson River School"? Who was its leader?

Understanding the Facts

1. Why did the United States go to war with Britain rather than France?
2. How did poor communications influence both the start of the war and the Battle of New Orleans?
3. Why did the War of 1812 weaken the Federalist party?

4. Why was the War of 1812 called the "Second War for Independence"?
5. What change took place in American culture after the War of 1812?
6. What does the increased nationalism tell about the way Americans thought of themselves and their country?

Using Maps

Tracing Routes. Certain map skills are needed to gain information from a line of travel on a map. Knowing direction, using the scale, and reading the key make it possible to use a map to trace past events. Use the map on page 201 to answer the following questions about the War of 1812.

1. How are American troops shown on this map?
2. How are British troops shown?
3. What was the starting point for United States soldiers who took part in the western attacks on Canada?
4. Where did the Americans attack Canada?

5. How far did American troops travel on their way to fight in the Battle of the Thames?
6. From which direction did British soldiers move in their approach to Washington, D.C.?
7. How far did British soldiers travel overland to Washington?
8. Which places in the area of Virginia and Maryland, other than Washington, were attacked by British troops?
9. From which direction did the American navy approach York, Canada?
10. Which direction is Plattsburg, New York, from Montreal, Quebec?

The Age of Jackson   10

Andrew Jackson ushered in a new generation of political leaders. Electoral reform sparked greater participation. George Caleb Bingham captures the spirit in this painting, "Verdict of the People." Why was this time called the "Age of Jackson"?

The spirit of nationalism that swept the country after the War of 1812 led to a time of political unity. Because of this, the years that James Monroe served as President were called the "Era of Good Feelings." By 1816, the Federalist party had died, and in 1820, the Democratic-Republican candidate Monroe was reelected without opposition.

What was at the base of the "Era of Good Feelings"?

The political unity was short-lived, however. It had only existed on the surface. New forces were at work which would soon change the American political system. In 1828, these forces put Andrew Jackson in the White House. More than any other person, Jackson stood for the growing power of the American people in government. Because he was so important to the politics of the time, the years from 1828 to 1840 are known as the "Age of Jackson."

1. The Return of the Two-Party System

After the death of the Federalist party in 1816, the Democratic-Republicans dominated politics. But by 1824, the "Era of Good Feelings" was drawing to a close. Differences began to arise between groups in the party. Both the growing power of the common people and the rivalry among the major sections of the country created conflict in the years between 1824 and 1828. It was during this time that new parties began to take shape.

1.1 The Election of 1824. As the country grew, different sections—the Northeast, South, and West—began to form. Often they had different ideas and concerns. This gave rise to *sectionalism*—rivalry based on the special interests of different areas in a country.

What is sectionalism?

In 1824, each area offered its own candidate for President. Leaders in New England were most interested in business and manufacturing. They wanted John Quincy Adams of Massachusetts as President. People in the west wanted better transportation and cheaper land prices. Both Henry Clay of Kentucky and Andrew Jackson of Tennessee were from the West, although Clay thought of himself as a national figure. People in the South wanted lower taxes on imported goods. They backed either John C. Calhoun of South Carolina or William Crawford of Georgia. Calhoun later withdrew to run for Vice-President. All of the candidates called themselves Democratic-Republicans. The official representative of the party was Crawford.

None of the candidates won the necessary majority of electoral votes in 1824. For cases like that, the Constitution states in the Twelfth

Although John Quincy Adams (left) and Andrew Jackson (right) posed the same way for these portraits, they had little in common politically. Over what issues did Adams and Jackson disagree? How did they represent a split in their party?

Amendment that the House of Representatives is to choose the President from the top three. Because Jackson had received the largest number of votes, his supporters expected him to be chosen.

Henry Clay, who came in fourth, was out of the running for President. He asked his followers in the House to vote for Adams. Adams was close to Clay in his support of the American System. This was an economic plan that included a national bank, a protective tariff, and a system of roads and canals paid for by the federal government. With Clay's help, Adams was chosen President.

Who was elected President in 1824?

1.2 A Split in the Party. Shortly after taking office, President Adams named Henry Clay to be Secretary of State. Those people who followed Jackson were angry at this. They charged that a *corrupt bargain* had been made between Clay and Adams—that Clay had helped Adams win the election so that, in return, he would get a top post in his *administration*—the major offices in the executive branch of the government. In 1825, Andrew Jackson left the Senate and began to campaign for President. Members of Congress who supported Jackson worked against Adams and blocked most of his plans.

Why was there a split in the Democratic-Republican party?

Near the end of Adams' term in office, Congress passed the Tariff Act of 1828 to protect certain raw materials and woolen goods. People in the South were strongly against this measure as it would harm their direct trade with England. Northeastern manufacturers favored the tariff because it would protect American industry. Sectional differences like this led to a split in the Democratic-Republican party. Those favoring Jackson became Democrats, while Adams and his followers became National-Republicans. In 1828, there would again be two parties in the election.

1.3 The Election of 1828. Followers of Jackson were determined that he would win the election of 1828. They worked hard to gain support for him all over the country. People in the sections of the country backed Jackson for different reasons. Those in the South thought Jackson believed in states' rights. In the West, people hoped Jackson would use federal money to build roads and canals. They also expected that he would put an end to the Second Bank of the United States. The new Democratic party was strong in certain states of the Northeast, such as Pennsylvania and New York.

For what reasons was Jackson supported?

In the election of 1824, what section of the country voted for Andrew Jackson? What section voted for John Quincy Adams? How did Adams win the election of 1824? Where did Jackson gain support to win in 1828?

Election of 1824

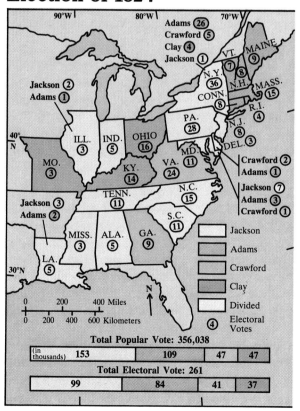

Total Popular Vote: 356,038

| (in thousands) | 153 | 109 | 47 | 47 |

Total Electoral Vote: 261

| 99 | 84 | 41 | 37 |

Election of 1828

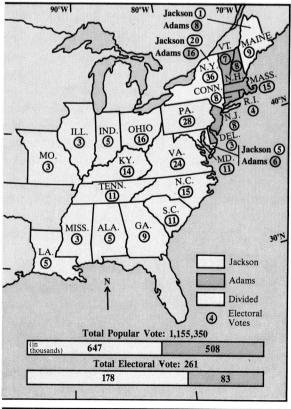

Total Popular Vote: 1,155,350

| (in thousands) | 647 | 508 |

Total Electoral Vote: 261

| 178 | 83 |

In 1828, Andrew Jackson received 178 electoral votes to 83 for John Quincy Adams. Jackson won the election with a clear majority. He was the first person from the West to become President. All former Presidents had been from Virginia or Massachusetts.

1. Who were the candidates for President in 1824?
2. Why was the North in favor and the South against a protective tariff?
3. Which party won the election of 1828?

2. Jacksonian Democracy

Thousands of people went to Washington, D.C., for the new President's inauguration. Many of them were average Americans who felt Jackson's election was a victory of the common people. For the first time, the votes of these people—from city workers to farmers—had played an important part in a national election. Jackson was felt to be more truly a choice of the people than any former President.

How was Jackson's victory in 1828 viewed?

2.1 The Jacksonian Ideal. Andrew Jackson stood for certain things which many Americans regarded with favor. He was an example of the frontier spirit and, like many others, had moved west into Indian lands. He had fought both the Indians and the British and was a military hero as a result of the Battle of New Orleans. He did not have the education or political experience of other Presidents. However, many people saw this as an advantage. Jackson seemed to prove that an ordinary American could become President.

2.2 The Growing Power of the People. Jackson became President at a time when greater numbers of people in the United States were able to take part in politics. The Constitution had allowed each state to decide which of its citizens could vote. Older state laws had limited voting to white males who owned property. Often there were also religious restrictions. Qualifications for *suffrage* (the right to vote) were first changed in the new states west of the Appalachian Mountains. Their laws allowed almost any white male citizen to vote or hold office. The laws of the eastern states changed more slowly.

Where were voting qualifications first changed?

Up to this time, the Presidency had been far-removed from control of the people. Candidates for President and Vice-President had been selected by party leaders in closed meetings, or *caucuses*. Then electors, picked by the state governments, selected the President and

John Floyd (1783–1837)

PROFILE

For most of his life, John Floyd actively supported political causes. He defended frontier interests. He encouraged Americans to settle the Oregon country. He was bitterly against Andrew Jackson. And he could not be moved from his stand for states' rights.

Floyd was born in the Kentucky territory. He studied medicine in Pennsylvania and settled in Virginia where his family first lived. In 1817, he was elected to the United States Congress where he fought for his causes, especially states' rights.

Floyd backed Jackson for President in 1828 because he thought Jackson would name him to a Cabinet post. When this did not happen and when Jackson showed his opposition to states' rights, Floyd became one of Jackson's main enemies.

On November 17, 1832, Floyd wrote in his diary:

Jackson is again elected . . . President of the United States. Should he still pursue his ignorant and violent course, which there is a strong probability he will do, we will never see another President of the United States elected.

Floyd left the federal government discouraged because not many there supported those things he did. Back home in Virginia, he was elected governor and kept up his objection to a strong national government. John Floyd felt the only way to guarantee states' rights was for states to secede from the Union.

Vice-President from among the candidates. By the early 1830's, candidates were nominated by convention, and citizens voted directly for presidential electors.

How were candidates nominated by the early 1830's?

The number of voters had grown by the 1830's, and their influence had become stronger. However, the greater democracy of the Age of Jackson did not extend to women, slaves, or Indians. In fact, while the laws were changing to allow more white males to vote and hold office, laws for slaves were becoming more harsh. Equal opportunity for each person in the country had yet to come.

2.3 The Spoils System. Soon after taking office in 1829, President Jackson began to put members of his own party in government jobs. He believed that changing the people who held these jobs would protect the government from dishonesty. It would also bring about greater democracy in the government. One of the people who agreed with Jackson, William Marcy of New York, was quoted as saying "to the victor belongs the spoils." So the practice of giving government jobs to political supporters came to be known as the *spoils system*. President Jackson called it "rotation in office." Jackson used the spoils system more widely than any former President. He set a pattern which would be followed for many years—sometimes with poor results.

Who coined the idea of a "spoils system"?

1. What did Andrew Jackson do before becoming President?
2. Which groups did not have the right to vote?
3. How did President Jackson use the spoils system?

3. Jackson's Use of Presidential Power_____

Andrew Jackson was liked by many voters because of his courage and daring in battle. As the leader of his party, he showed strong will in political battles. Jackson was thought to be a strong President and as such greatly influenced politics in the United States.

3.1 Executive Powers. Other Presidents had respected but not often used the powers of their office. George Washington had thought of himself as the chief executive whose job was to carry out the will of Congress. Jefferson had tried to act inside strict guidelines stated in the Constitution.

How did Jackson differ from earlier Presidents?

Jackson, on the other hand, believed in the powers of his office and did not hesitate to use them. All six former Presidents together had vetoed only nine bills passed by Congress. Jackson alone vetoed 12. Other Presidents had vetoed bills only when they thought them unconstitutional. Jackson vetoed them for political reasons as well. If a decision of the Supreme Court was different from his own views, Jackson felt he should have the last word. At first, few people knew what Jackson's views were on major issues. As events happened, the President's views became clear. Sometimes he was in favor of the rights of the states, and at other times the rights of the federal government.

3.2 States' Rights and Union. President Jackson's power was challenged shortly after he took office. Many people in the South were angry over the Tariff of 1828. During the summer of that year, South Carolina printed the "South Carolina Exposition and Protest." It was

Daniel Webster of Massachusetts (standing) speaks to the Senate. He is answering Robert Hayne of South Carolina (seated center, left of the Senator with his hand on his chin). What was the major issue of the Webster-Hayne debates?

later learned that Vice-President John C. Calhoun was its author. The paper said that each state could decide when an act of Congress was unconstitutional. If it so decided, the state could then declare the law null and void. This plan of *nullification* was much like that set forth earlier in the Kentucky and Virginia Resolutions. It had also been offered by New England Federalists at the Hartford Convention. To get a law passed once a state had nullified it, three fourths of the states would have to ratify it as an amendment to the Constitution.

What is nullification?

People in the South tried to win western support for nullification in 1830, during a debate in the Senate which began over western lands. People in the West were angry because of a bill which would limit the sale of these lands. Robert Hayne of South Carolina said that the Union was a joining of separate states. So the western states could nullify the bill if it became law. Daniel Webster of Massachusetts argued that the Union was a national government of all people in all states. He was against the idea of nullification. Webster said that only the Supreme Court had the right to decide if a law was constitutional.

What were Daniel Webster's thoughts on nullification?

The Webster-Hayne debates did not settle the question. No one was certain which side President Jackson would favor. In April 1830, leaders of the Democratic party held a dinner in honor of the late

Thomas Jefferson. At that dinner, Jackson offered a toast: "Our Federal Union: It must be preserved." It was clear that the President agreed with the views of Webster against nullification. Calhoun then rose to speak: "The Union, next to our liberty, most dear." This was a break between the two highest officers of the land. Jackson and Calhoun agreed on many things. But they had sharply different views on the major question of the right of a state to resist federal authority.

Why did Jackson veto the Maysville Road bill?

3.3 The Maysville Road Veto. President Jackson was a strong nationalist. He also believed in a narrow interpretation of the Constitution. Jackson believed in the absolute power of the federal government in its sphere. However, he wanted to limit that sphere. Shortly after the Jefferson Day dinner, he showed this point of view by vetoing the Maysville Road bill.

In May 1830, Congress passed a bill for the federal government to buy $150,000 worth of stock in the Maysville Road Company. This company planned to build a *turnpike*—a road built by a private company that charged a fee for using it—in Kentucky from Maysville to Lexington. This road would later connect with the National Road in Ohio. Jackson vetoed the measure on the grounds that the federal government should support only national projects. Since the Maysville Road would be built inside the state of Kentucky, it should be a state project. People in the West were upset. They had expected Jackson would favor *internal improvements*. This was a program of building roads, bridges, canals, and railroads during the early 1800's.

3.4 The Nullification Crisis. In July 1832, Congress passed a new protective tariff. It had lower rates than the Tariff of 1828, but people in the South were not pleased. In November 1832, the South Carolina government passed a bill to nullify the tariff acts of 1828 and 1832. It warned that South Carolina would secede from the United States if the government tried to enforce the law after February 1833. President Jackson was angry at these moves and prepared to send troops into South Carolina.

How was the nullification crisis resolved?

With the country facing a civil war, leaders worked out a compromise. Henry Clay drew up a new tariff which allowed for lower rates over a number of years. Congress also passed the Force Bill. It gave Jackson the power to use the army and navy to uphold federal law. Upon learning of the compromise, South Carolina withdrew its nullification bill. However, the trouble was only ended for a while. The ideas of states' rights and federal authority would arise again.

3.5 Jackson and the Bank. One of Jackson's biggest political battles was fought over the Bank of the United States. Like many

Reading for Detail
SKILL

It is important to be able to recognize the main idea of any paragraph, chapter, or book. In addition, it is important to understand the information which describes or explains an idea. If you try to put together a bicycle and do not understand the details of the instructions, the wheels might not turn or the gears might not shift.

The first step in reading for detail is to identify the major point. Once the point has been identified, the next step is to recognize the detailed information related to it. Sometimes it helps to ask questions about the main idea—who? what? when? where? how?

The following selection was written in 1832 by a British actor who visited the United States. In her journal, she wrote about a ten-hour carriage trip covering the 100 miles (160 kilometers) between New York and Philadelphia. Read the selection for the detail.

English eye has not seen, English ear has not heard, nor has it entered the heart of English people to conceive the surpassing clumsiness and wretchedness of these . . . inconveniences [coaches]. They are shaped something like boats, the sides being merely leather pieces, removable at pleasure, but which, in bad weather, are buttoned down to protect the inmates from the wet. . . . For the first few minutes, I thought I must have fainted from the intolerable sensation of smothering which I experienced. However, the leather having been removed, and a little more air obtained, I took heart of grace, and resigned myself to my fate. Away wallopped the four horses . . . and away we went after them . . . over the wickedest road, I do think, the cruellest, hard-heartedest road, that ever wheel rumbled upon. Through bog and marsh, and ruts . . . with the roots of trees protruding across our path, their boughs every now and then giving us an affectionate scratch through the windows; and, more than once, a half-demolished trunk or stump lying in the middle of the road lifting us up, and letting us down again, with most awful variations. . . .

1. Who was the traveler?
2. What were the roads and the coach like?
3. When did the writer travel?
4. Where was she traveling?
5. How did the writer feel about the experience?

Race over Uncle Sam's Course.
4th March 1833

In this anti-Jackson cartoon, the President and Martin Van Buren (left) ride a donkey in a race over the bank issue. They are losing to Henry Clay who supported the Bank of the United States. Actually, Jackson won his fight against the national bank. What was the bank issue?

Who was head of the Second Bank of the United States?

people from the West, he did not like banks and thought paper money was of no value. He had once lost most of his fortune because bank notes he accepted from a Philadelphia merchant were worthless. Jackson thought of the Bank as a monopoly used by the rich and powerful for their own gain. Although the government owned one fifth of its stock, control of the Bank was in the hands of the directors. Jackson said that the Bank was unconstitutional. In doing so, he was showing that he believed in the limited powers of the federal government. Jackson was also ignoring the Supreme Court's ruling in *McCullough* v. *Maryland*, which had upheld the implied powers of Congress.

Early in his first term, Jackson made his views on the Bank known. More and more people were against the Bank, and its head, Nicholas Biddle, became alarmed. He decided to take Henry Clay's advice and ask for a renewal of the Bank's charter four years early. Clay wanted to run for President in 1832. He thought that if Jackson vetoed the bill to renew the Bank charter, it would be unpopular with those who favored the Bank. So Jackson would lose the election. Congress passed the bill, and the President did veto it, attacking special interests and monopolies. Many Americans, however, agreed with Jackson's feeling about the Bank and were pleased by his vote. In 1832, Jackson was reelected by a wide margin.

After the election, Jackson set out to destroy the Bank. He ordered federal money removed from it and placed in certain state banks. These so-called *pet banks* printed large numbers of their own bank notes, often with little thought about the amount of *specie* (gold and silver coin) on hand to back them up. They used this money to start a credit boom. People borrowed the bank notes to buy government land. The land offices deposited this money back into the pet banks where it could be loaned to more people. *Land speculation* (buying up land to sell at a large profit) increased. It was a time of reckless spending and uncontrolled economic growth.

How did Jackson destroy the Bank?

Before Jackson left office, he acted to slow down the wave of land speculation. In July 1836, he wrote the "Specie Circular," which stated that only people who settled the land could pay for it with paper money. Everyone else had to pay for public lands with gold or silver.

1. How did President Jackson use the veto power?
2. Where was the strongest support for nullification?
3. How did President Jackson and Vice-President Calhoun differ on the major issues?
4. What brought about the nullification crisis?

4. Jackson and the Indians

Andrew Jackson was from a frontier state—Tennessee. He shared with many Americans at that time the view that the Indians were blocking settlement. As President, Jackson set up a plan for moving the Indian groups to lands west of the Mississippi River. Attempts to uphold the rights of Indians were opposed by the President.

4.1 Government and the Indians. The process of uprooting the Indians had been going on for a long time. Since the beginning of the nation, the United States government had promised to respect Indian rights. But settlers, desiring more and more land, kept moving west. Years of wars brought defeat to Indians trying to stop this advance. Speckled Snake, a Creek chief, spoke to his people in 1829:

When the first white man came over the wide waters, he was but a little man. . . . His legs were cramped by sitting long in his big boat, and he begged for a little land. . . .

When he came to these shores the Indians gave him land, and kindled fires to make him comfortable. . . .

But when the white man had warmed himself at the Indian's fire, and had filled himself with the Indian's hominy, he became very large. He stopped not at the mountain tops, and his foot covered the plains and the valleys. . . . Then he became our Great Father. He loved his red children, but he said: "You must move a little farther, lest by accident I tread on you. . . ."

Now he says, "The land you live upon is not yours. Go beyond the Mississippi; there is game; there you may remain while the grass grows and the rivers run."

Will not our Great Father come there also? . . .

Brothers! I have listened to a great many talks from our Great Father. But they always began and ended in this—"Get a little farther; you are too near me. . . ."

In 1830, with Andrew Jackson's encouragement, Congress passed the Indian Removal Act. It set up Indian resettlement west of the Mississippi River. The act also gave the President power to negotiate with the Indian groups. During Jackson's two terms, 94 treaties were made. The Removal Act did not say that federal troops could be used to aid in Indian resettlement. Few Americans, however, opposed the use of force against those Indians who refused to move.

4.2 Indian Removals.   Over the next ten years, the Chippewa, Menominee, Iowa, Sioux, Ottawa, and Winnebago Indians of the Great Lakes area signed treaties with the government and moved west. Some Indians, however, offered resistance to the government's policy. In 1832, the Sac and Fox Indians under Chief Black Hawk tried to return to their lands in the Wisconsin Territory and Illinois. In what became known as Black Hawk's War, army troops and the Illinois militia defeated the Indians. The Sac and Fox were forced to remain in the Iowa Territory.

In the Southeast, the states of Georgia, Mississippi, and Alabama passed laws stating that they had authority over the Indians and Indian lands inside their borders. These laws were aimed at the Creek, Chickasaw, Choctaw, and Cherokee peoples whose rights had been guaranteed by a treaty with the United States. The President, however, supported the states. The Chocktaw, Chickasaw, and Creek Indians moved west.

The Cherokee Indians were the last to leave their lands. Under several treaties with the United States, the Cherokees in Georgia had

Voter Participation, 1824–1840

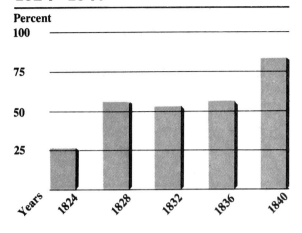

Percent of Eligible Voters, 1840

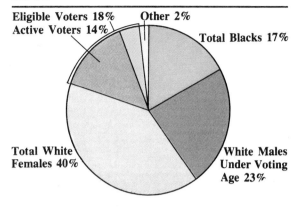

What was the increase in voter participation from 1824 to 1840? What were some reasons for the increase? What percent of the total population was eligible to vote in 1840? What percent was not eligible? What percent actually voted?

the Panic of 1837. They accused the President of following the policies of Jackson and doing nothing to end the depression.

5.3 Tippecanoe and Tyler Too. The Whigs hoped to win the election of 1840. They chose William Henry Harrison of Ohio, the hero of the Battle of Tippecanoe, to run for President. John Tyler of Virginia was selected as his running mate. As the Democrats had done with Jackson, the Whigs said that Harrison was an average American, hoping to appeal to many voters.

Jackson's policies of the 1830's had a further impact on the election of 1840. The Whigs knew that party leaders could no longer choose a candidate on their own. They had to win over large numbers of people who were allowed to vote. Rallies, parades, and slogans were used to gain support. The Whigs did not write a *platform*, or statement of the policies of the party. Instead, they campaigned with "Tippecanoe and Tyler too." The depression and the organization of the Whigs put Harrison in the White House. The election of 1840 showed how much the political process had changed in the Age of Jackson.

What was different about the election of 1840?

1. Which new political party was formed after 1832?
2. Whom did the new party nominate for President?
3. How did the Panic of 1837 help elect Harrison?

6. Conclusion

Andrew Jackson shaped the history of the time and was shaped by it. Jackson was able to settle, for a time, the question of nullification and states' rights. In the area of Indian affairs, he followed the general feeling of the times. Most Americans believed the Indians were in the way of their settlement and should be moved to the West. Important changes took place in the American political system during the Age of Jackson. Some began before Jackson took office. Others came during his term. One of the most important changes of the Age of Jackson was the greater number of people able to take part in political affairs.

Chapter 10 Review

Main Points

1. John Quincy Adams became President in 1824 in an election settled by the House of Representatives.

2. The election of 1824 led to a split in the Democratic-Republican party.

3. Andrew Jackson, elected in 1828, increased the power of the Presidency.

4. Democracy during the Jackson years provided a greater voice in government for white males. Women, blacks, and Indians did not benefit.

5. Sectional interests produced new conflicts during Andrew Jackson's Presidency.

6. Opposition to President Jackson led to the formation of the Whig party.

7. William Henry Harrison, the Whig candidate, became President in 1840.

Building Vocabulary

1. Identify the following:
   "Era of Good Feelings"
   American System
   Andrew Jackson
   John Floyd

   John C. Calhoun
   Webster-Hayne debates
   Force Bill
   "Specie Circular"

   Indian Removal Act
   Black Hawk's War
   Trail of Tears
   Whigs

2. Define the following:
   sectionalism
   corrupt bargain
   administration
   suffrage
   caucuses

   spoils system
   nullification
   turnpike
   internal improvements

   pet banks
   specie
   land speculation
   depression
   platform

Remembering the Facts

1. How was the President elected in 1824?

2. Which two political parties formed from the Democratic-Republican party following the election of 1824?

3. How was Jackson different from those who were President before him?

4. Which changes made it possible for more people to vote?

5. What was President Jackson's opinion of nullification?

6. Why did Jackson oppose the Bank?

7. What was the government's policy toward the Indians?

8. Which Indians fought against efforts to move them from their lands?

9. Why was the Whig party created?

10. What was the depression of 1837?

Understanding the Facts

1. Why did rivalries develop among various sections of the United States?

2. Why did Andrew Jackson think he had been cheated in the election of 1824?

3. Why did President Jackson replace government workers with members of his own political party?

4. When did Jackson act as a nationalist? as a supporter of states' rights?

5. Why did Jackson want the Indians to move west of the Mississippi River?

6. How did the Panic of 1837 influence the election of 1840?

7. Why did the Age of Jackson end?

Using Maps

Comparing Maps. Sometimes several maps are used together to show information about similar events at different times. By comparing what is shown on the different maps, additional information can be gained.

The maps shown on page 219 can be used this way. They show the voting patterns by states for the presidential elections in 1824 and 1828. Study each map. Compare the maps, and answer the following questions.

1. In which election did Andrew Jackson win the most states?

2. In which election did Jackson receive a majority of the electoral vote?

3. Which states did not support Jackson in both elections?

4. Where was Jackson's support strong in both elections?

5. Where was Jackson's support weak in both elections?

6. Which states divided their vote?

Washington, D.C. 1800-1825

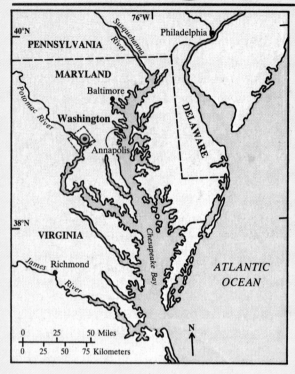

The United States government moved to the new federal city of Washington in 1800. In that year, the young city was a clear example of the difference that can exist between dreams and reality. In the dreams of government leaders, Washington was a magnificent capital with lovely parks, beautiful public buildings, and grand avenues. In reality, it was a small village of rough fields, half-finished buildings, and muddy paths.

There had been years of debate in Congress over the location of the nation's capital. No state wanted any other state to have special influence over the federal government. Congress had met in eight different cities, four different states. Moving became more difficult as the quantity of needed records grew. A compromise was finally reached that settled the question of a permanent location for the capital city. When southerners agreed to let the federal government assume the state debts of the Revolution, northerners agreed to have the capital along the banks of the Potomac River.

Two states gave land to the government to form the federal District of Columbia. There, only Congress had control. The District was free of any single state's influence. The capital, built in the District, was available to people from the North, the South, and the rapidly growing West.

Plans

President Washington selected the French engineer, Pierre Charles L'Enfant, to design the federal city in 1791. L'Enfant had come to America to serve in the Revolution. He wanted very much to design a great capital for the new nation. And on paper, his plans for the city of Washington were beautiful.

The survey work of marking the District's boundaries was done by Americans Andrew Ellicott and Benjamin Banneker. Banneker, a free black from Baltimore, was also an astronomer, mathematician, and scientist. The boundaries of the District of Columbia included the cities of George Town in Maryland and Alexandria in Virginia. The capital city itself was located next to George Town, on the Maryland side of the Potomac River. Later Alexandria and the lands across the Potomac were returned to Virginia.

L'Enfant planned Washington so that the three branches of the federal government were located in three separate areas of the city, according to their different constitutional duties. The building for the legislature, the Capitol, was on the highest point of land. A mile and a half away was the President's House, in the center of the executive area. From both of these, streets went out into the rest of the city. Pennsylvania Avenue was planned as a broad, stately connection between them. It would serve for ceremonial processions and would add dignity to the communication between the Congress and the President. The judicial building was to be in a third section of the city, away from these two main areas of traffic. The different buildings would be designed by different architects. By law, there could be no slave labor used to build the capital. Some slaves were hired out to do this work and earned money to buy their freedom.

Wide streets set Washington apart from other cities at the time. In Pierre Charles L'Enfant's plan, what were these boulevards designed to do?

Money Problems

President Washington and the early sessions of Congress did not set aside any money for building the city because they thought it would pay for itself. Government leaders expected many people to move into the area and buy expensive lots for their homes and businesses. Profits from those sales would be used to pay for the public streets and buildings. That idea did not work. Few people came to the city at first, and even fewer of them invested their money in it. The total number of people working for the federal government at that time was very small. It was not easy for others to earn a living in Washington. There was not much business in providing for the needs of those who worked for the government. Carpenters, stonemasons, and people in the building trades even had difficulty finding steady work. Life in the new federal city was certainly not as pleasant or profitable as it was in Philadelphia and the older American cities.

Moving In

With only three months left to serve in his term, John Adams moved into the President's House in 1800. Abigail, his wife, arrived in November and described the city in a letter to her sister.

As I expected to find it a new country, with Houses scattered over a space of ten miles, and trees [and] stumps in plenty with, a castle of a house—so I found it—The Presidents House is in a beautiful situation in front of which is the Potomac. . . . The country around is romantic but a wild, a wilderness at present.

I have been to George Town. . . . It is only one mile from me but a quagmire [deep mud] after every rain. Here we are obliged to send daily for marketing; The capital is near two miles from us. . . . but I am determined to be satisfied and content, to say nothing of inconvenience. . . .

Determined as she was, Abigail did mention some of the problems of living in a huge, unfinished house in another of her letters.

The house is upon a grand and superb scale, requiring about thirty servants to attend and keep the apartments in proper order, and perform the ordinary business of the house and stables. . . . The lighting [of] the apartments, from the kitchen to parlors and chambers, is a tax indeed [so may candles are needed] . . . we are obliged to keep [fires going] to secure us from daily agues [chills and fevers]. . . . bells [to call the servants] are [wholely] wanting, not one single one being hung through the whole house, and promises are all you can obtain. This is so great an inconvenience, that I know not what to do, or

George Washington inspects the unfinished President's House with architect James Hoban. Who was the first President to live in the White House?

how to do it. . . . if they will put me up some bells, and let me have wood enough to keep fires, I design to be pleased. I could content myself almost anywhere three months. . . . We have, indeed, come into a new country.

You must keep all this to yourself, and, when asked how I like it, say that I write you the situation [location] is beautiful, which is true. The house is made habitable, but there is not a single apartment finished. . . . We have not the least fence, yard, or other convenience . . . and the great unfinished audience-room [the East Room] I make a drying-room of, to hang up clothes in. The principal stairs are not up, and will not be this winter.

The Capitol

Members of Congress arrived in Washington after the fall harvest season. They found an unfinished Capitol with a few boarding houses close by it. One wing of the new building was almost completed. Its rooms were shared among the Senate, the House of Representatives, the Supreme Court, the courts of the District, and the new Library of Congress.

Unlike the members of the executive branch, the lawmakers usually came to their sessions alone. They left their families behind since Congress met for only a few months of the year. Most of the members lived in the boarding houses, and their social life generally centered around the dinner tables there. Travel around the city was difficult during the day and dangerous at night. There were no real streets, only fields and a few paths. In most areas, the ground was not even leveled to make walking easier.

Margaret Bayard Smith, wife of the city's first newspaper editor, wrote a letter that

During the War of 1812, 4,000 British soldiers attacked and burned Washington. How did the burning affect the future growth of the city?

described the dangers of traveling at night. Thomas Law, a friend, had built a new house:

This out-of-the-way-house to which Mr. Law removed, was separated from the most inhabited part of the city by fields and waste grounds broken up by deep gulleys or ravines over which there was occasionally a passable road. The election of President by Congress was then pending, one vote given or withheld would decide the question between Mr. Jefferson and Mr. Burr. Mr. Bayard from Delaware held that vote. He with other influential and leading members [of Congress] went to a ball given by Mr. Law. The night was dark and rainy, and on their attempt to return home, the coachman lost his way, and until daybreak was driving about this waste and broken ground and if not overturned into the deep gullies was momentarily in danger of being so, an accident which would most probably have cost some of the gentlemen their lives, and as it so happened that the company in the coach consisted of Mr. Bayard and three other members of Congress who had a leading and decisive influence in this difficult crisis of public affairs, the loss of either, might have turned the scales . . . and Mr. Burr [would have] been elected to the Presidency. . . .

Slow Growth

During Jefferson's administration, Congress did provide $3,000 to improve Pennsylvania Avenue and to plant trees along it. In general, however, little progress was made in completing the city. Poverty and unemployment were serious problems in Washington from its beginning. By 1802, 40 percent of the city's funds were used to help the poor.

The city's founders had expected a very rapid growth in population, especially by people with money to invest. But in 20 years' time, the total number of people who lived in the capital had increased by just 10,000 people, most of them poor. Free blacks were the only group within Washington that grew quickly in number. The city did allow slavery, and most citizens did not seem to have strong antislavery feelings. But Washington did not force slaves to leave the area when they were freed, as most of the southern states did. The city also had not made laws that stopped the growth of independent churches and schools for blacks. In general, most free black families felt safer in Washington than in other southern American cities. By 1820, the number of free blacks almost equaled the number of slaves. By 1840, their number was four times larger than the number of slaves.

The commerce and industry that was expected by the city's planners did not develop. George Town and Alexandria competed for most of the business in the District.

Congress seldom provided funds for work on the public properties. The experiment of establishing a magnificent federal city seemed to be a failure. Political scientist James Sterling Young suggests that the main problem was a lack of interest on the part of most Americans in a government that was located out of their way.

For the government of Jeffersonian times was not, by any candid [honest] view, one of the important institutions in American society—important as a social presence or important in its impact upon the everyday lives of the citizens. It was, for one thing, too new, an unfamiliar social presence in a society whose ways of living and whose organization of affairs had developed over a century without any national governmental institution. . . .

What government business there was was not, most of it, of a sort to attract any widespread, sustained [long lasting] citizen interest.

Growth was so slow for the capital that some people continued to believe that the federal government should move back to a larger city. To many people, the burning of Washington's government buildings by the British forces in 1814 seemed to be the final blow. Margaret Smith expressed those feelings in her writings:

Thursday. . . . This morning on awakening we were greeted with the sad news, that our city was taken, the bridges and public buildings burnt, our troops flying in every direction. Our little army totally dispersed [scattered].
. . . I do not suppose Government will ever return to Washington. All those whose property was invested in that place, will be reduced to poverty. . . .

Tuesday [August] 30. Here we are, once more restored to our home. . . . The blast has passed by, without devastating this spot. . . . The poor capitol! nothing but its blackened walls remained! 4 or 5 houses in the neighborhood were likewise in ruins. . . . We afterwards looked at the other public buildings, but none were so thoroughly destroyed as the House of Representatives and the President's House. Those beautiful pillars in that Representatives Hall were cracked and broken, the roof, that noble dome, painted and carved with such beauty and skill, lay in ashes in the cellars. . . . In the P.H. [President's House] not an inch, but its cracked and blackened walls remained. That scene, which when I last visited it, was so splendid . . . was now nothing but ashes. . . .

Recovery

But the government did return to Washington. That same September, President and Mrs. Madison moved into a house in the city, and the President worked from there. Members of Congress came back to the city for a special session. They met in the only government building that had not been damaged, the Post Office. There, after three weeks of debate, the House of Representatives voted 83 to 54 to keep the federal government in Washington. City bankers offered a loan to start the work of rebuilding. Three and a half months later, the Senate finally agreed.

Adams to Adams

In 1818, James and Elizabeth Monroe moved into the White House, as it was beginning to be called. Its outside walls had been freshly painted white to cover the marks from the British fire. Both wings of the Capitol were finished by then. Work had

The federal city in 1824 had many grand buildings like the Capitol. It also had many muddy streets. What problems faced lawmakers and their families from around the country who came to live and work in Washington?

begun on the center section. Washington still had no street lights, no sewer system, no city water system. Water was carried from wells in the center of the city or from the nearby creek. There were still open fields where cattle and hogs ran free. But there was a stronger feeling that the federal capital of Washington, D.C., was in place to stay.

John Quincy Adams moved into the White House just 25 years after his parents had lived in it. There was still no fence, but the grounds had been made smoother for walking. Most of the White House rooms were finished enough to be used. Louisa Adams, unlike Abigail, could use the great "audience-room" for public receptions instead of drying the family's clothes in it. A quarter of a century had passed since the government first moved to the District of Columbia. There was still a very strong contrast between the original dream and the reality of the capital city, but a beginning had been made. Washington, as a city, would move a little closer to the dream in the years to come.

1. What was L'Enfant's plan for the capital city?
2. Name the main street which connects the Capitol building and the President's House.
3. How did Congress expect to pay for the building of the capital city?
4. Where did most of the lawmakers live during their stay in Washington?
5. How was Washington affected by the War of 1812?
6. Compare the President's House which Abigail Adams lived in to that of her daughter-in-law, Louisa Adams.

Unit III Review

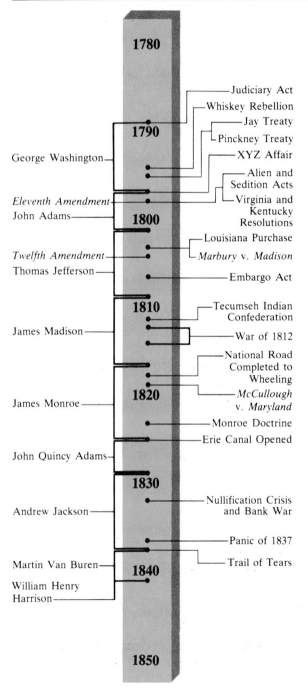

1780

1790
— Judiciary Act
— Whiskey Rebellion
— Jay Treaty
— Pinckney Treaty
— XYZ Affair

George Washington

— Alien and
  Sedition Acts
Eleventh Amendment
John Adams
— Virginia and
  Kentucky
  Resolutions
1800

— Louisiana Purchase
Twelfth Amendment
Thomas Jefferson
— *Marbury* v. *Madison*

— Embargo Act

1810
— Tecumseh Indian
  Confederation
James Madison
— War of 1812

— National Road
  Completed to
  Wheeling
1820
— *McCullough*
James Monroe
  v. *Maryland*

— Monroe Doctrine
— Erie Canal Opened

John Quincy Adams

1830

— Nullification Crisis
Andrew Jackson
  and Bank War

— Panic of 1837

— Trail of Tears
Martin Van Buren
1840
William Henry
Harrison

1850

Summary

1. It was not certain at first that the government of the United States would work under the Constitution because many people felt they were citizens of a state rather than of the nation.

2. Under the leadership of President Washington, who set many precedents for later leaders, the government was established on a firm foundation.

3. Because of disagreements over economic policies and foreign affairs, political parties formed around Thomas Jefferson and Alexander Hamilton.

4. The election of Thomas Jefferson as President in 1800 showed that in the United States, political power could be transferred from one party to another peacefully.

5. Under the Presidency of Thomas Jefferson, the size of the United States was doubled through the purchase of Louisiana from France.

6. The United States went to war with Britain in 1812, believing that the British were violating American rights at sea and turning the Indians on the western frontier against Americans.

7. The War of 1812 was followed by a new spirit of nationalism which helped to produce a unique American culture.

8. Democracy expanded for white men during the Age of Jackson, but women, blacks, and Indians benefited little.

9. Sectional differences became stronger during the Age of Jackson, challenging the power of the federal government.

Unit Questions

1. What major problems did the United States face during the first 50 years under the Constitution?
2. What cultural developments after the War of 1812 showed a greater emphasis of the people on democracy?
3. Who do you think won the War of 1812? Why do you think so?
4. What evidence can you give for the growth of nationalism and sectionalism in the country at the same time?
5. Washington, Jefferson, and Jackson are among the great American Presidents. What did each do that had a major influence on the government of the United States?
6. Why was Washington, D.C., made the capital of the country? How did it differ from the other cities which had served as the national capital?
7. What political parties existed in the first 50 years of the United States? Why did each develop?
8. Why did President Jackson, a strong nationalist, not support the position of the federal courts in the case of the Cherokee Indians against the state of Georgia?

Suggested Activities

1. Several new countries have come into existence during the last 50 years. Choose one and compare it with the first 50 years of the United States in terms of how it gained independence, its government, and its economy.
2. Write a poem or the lyrics of a song or draw or paint a picture which you think reflects American culture following the War of 1812.
3. Find out information about the major political parties in the United States today. Perhaps you could invite a representative from each of the major parties to speak to the class about their party's ideas and goals.

Suggested Readings

Blos, Joan. *A Gathering of Days: A New England Girl's Journal, 1830–1832.* New York: Charles Scribner's Sons, 1979. The journal of a teenager tells of life on a farm in New Hampshire.

Davis, Louise. *Snowball Fight in the White House.* Philadelphia: Westminster Press, 1974. Story of a children's Christmas party during the Presidency of Andrew Jackson.

Fisher, Vardis. *Tales of Valor.* Mattituck, New York: American Reprint/Rivercity Press, 1976. Traces Lewis and Clark's expedition into Louisiana.

Fleishman, Glen. *Cherokee Removal 1838: An Entire Nation Is Forced Out of Its Homeland.* New York: Watts, 1971. Looks at the actions taken to force the Cherokees out of Georgia.

UNIT
IV

AMERICA IS
Expansion

Expansion marked a course of history from the earliest days of people in America. The United States was made up of people who had moved to it from many places in the world. Many Americans remained on the move as the United States extended its political borders and grew economically. New reasons for moving continued to arise as new ways of getting there were developed. Advantages and disadvantages resulted from a rapid physical and economic growth in the United States.

The Promise
of America

11

Transcendentalists believed in the importance of self-reliance. Henry David Thoreau tried to live this belief near Walden Pond in Massachusetts. How did Thoreau symbolize widespread hope for a better America in the middle 1800's?

The greater democracy during the Jackson years was not just a matter of politics. There was also a spirit of equality and progress that made many Americans feel proud. They wanted to make life in the United States even better for all its people. A move toward reform began in the early 1800's and lasted through the first half of the century. These same years saw a flowering of American culture. The years from the 1820's through the 1850's was a high point for American literature.

1. The Spirit of Perfection

The American people had confidence that they could build a better future for America. They believed that people were able to perfect their lives. If each person could improve, then all society could improve. This spirit spread to more and more Americans in the 1820's and 1830's.

1.1 Changing Views on Religion. Religion was one of the bases of the reform movement. Many Americans were changing their ideas about religion. During the 1700's, some churches had taught that only a certain number of people—the *elect*—were chosen by God to be saved and go to heaven. As the country became more democratic, many churches began to teach that people had a duty to improve themselves and the world around them. In this way, they could be saved. These ideas encouraged people to make changes for the better.

How was religion changing in the 1800's?

Beginning in the 1820's, a number of *revivals*—meetings to make people more interested in religion—took place around the country. As part of this, preachers moved around the country giving sermons at large camp meetings most often held outdoors. One of the leading figures at the revivals was Charles Finney. He taught that good works were important, as well as faith. He said that with God's help, it was possible for people to live better lives. His teaching, and that of others like him, caused many Americans to support a wide variety of reforms.

What were revivals?

1.2 New Religious Groups. As more and more people began to change their ideas about religion, a number of new religious groups appeared in the United States. One of the largest was started in New York by Joseph Smith in 1830. It was the Church of Jesus Christ of Latter-Day Saints. The church members were called Mormons. Smith said that he had had *revelations* (special messages) from God. He taught those who followed him that they were God's chosen people. Smith also said that Mormon men could have more than one wife. The Mormons tried to set up ideal societies where they could live in their own way.

Who were the Mormons?

Mormons were often *persecuted* (treated cruelly) by other people for what they believed. They were forced to move several times. After living for a short time in Ohio and Missouri, they settled in Illinois. There in 1844, Joseph Smith was killed by an angry crowd. Brigham Young became the new Mormon leader. Driven from Illinois, the Mormons settled in Utah where they established Salt Lake City in 1847. During the next few years, they founded many towns and attracted thousands of new church members from Europe and the eastern United States.

Another new religious group began in western New York. William Miller said that the second coming of Jesus Christ would happen on a certain day in 1843. He asked people who followed him, known as Millerites, to prepare for that day. When the event did not take place on the day given, Miller said that it would happen sometime later.

1.3 A New Philosophy. Another base of the American reform movement was a *philosophy* (a set of ideas) developed largely by Ralph Waldo Emerson of Massachusetts. This was *transcendentalism.* Emerson believed that people could go beyond their limitations and perfect themselves and their society. Transcendentalists thought that every person was worthwhile, and that people had the ability to guide their own lives. Their philosophy was hopeful and encouraged the idea of progress.

What did transcendentalists believe?

Religious camp meetings were common in the 1830's. Large numbers of people gathered to practice their religion and encourage others to join them. Sermons at these meetings often visibly affected the people in the audience. Who was one of the leading revival preachers?

The Oneida Community, like most utopian experiments, believed that perfection could be gained through being industrious. Oneida produced a variety of goods, including silverware. What was the main purpose of utopian communities?

1.4 Utopian Communities. Some people wanted to remake, rather than reform, the world around them. They thought that the best way to practice their ideas was to withdraw from society into smaller groups. In the 1830's and 1840's, many of these groups set up ideal communities, or *utopias*. They were based on their ideas of how people should live together. Work, property, and wealth were shared.

In 1825, Robert Owen of Great Britain founded a community at New Harmony, Indiana. Brook Farm was started in Massachusetts in 1841. Several well-known transcendentalists lived there for a time. These settlements, however, did not last very long. In some other groups, like the Shakers, religion joined the people closer together. In 1842, the Amana Community was set up as a religious colony in New York. It later moved to Iowa, where its factories still turn out a variety of appliances.

What were some utopian communities?

1. How did religion influence the reform movement?
2. Which new religious groups were started during the middle 1800's?
3. What was transcendentalism?

Sarah Grimké (1792–1873)
Angelina Grimké (1805–1879)
PROFILE

The Grimké sisters played a major role in the antislavery crusade during the 1800's. They both wrote and lectured for the cause. But they were also identified with women's rights. The sisters were perhaps the first to present the case for women's legal and social freedoms in the United States.

Sarah and Angelina Grimké were born in Charleston, South Carolina. Their father was a supreme court judge in a state that strongly supported slavery. It might be expected that the sisters would have shared their father's and their state's views. Instead, they became abolitionists.

Living in South Carolina, they saw directly how owners treated slaves. The Grimké family itself owned slaves. Torn by the cruelty of slavery, the sisters left the South and moved to Philadelphia where they joined the Quakers. The antislavery activities of the Quakers fit the attitudes of the two women.

During the years that followed, they wrote and spoke against holding slaves. Angelina Grimké wrote an *Appeal to the Christian Women of the South*. Sarah Grimké wrote an *Epistle to the Clergy of the Southern States* asking for support for abolition. Because of their personal experience with the slave system, the Grimkés were believable. And because they were careful always to base their beliefs on the Bible, they were doubly effective.

The sisters spoke mainly to women's groups. But Angelina Grimké sometimes lectured to both men and women. Since women were not expected to speak in public to groups of both men and women, the sisters were criticized. Even other abolitionists objected to this activity.

When the Grimkés spoke of their right to speak before mixed groups, they hit at their basic rights as citizens. From this point, their activities included speaking for the rights of women as well as the rights of blacks. Sarah Grimké wrote newspaper articles on "The Province of Women." She also published the book *Letters on the Condition of Women and the Equality of the Sexes*.

Both sisters lived to see slavery ended after the Civil War. But much remained to be done before the rights they sought for blacks and women would gain widespread support.

2. Reforming American Society _____

The spirit of perfection led to the founding of ideal communities for some people. It had a different impact on the country as a whole. Many Americans believed that society could be improved by making its basic institutions better. During the early 1800's, reformers tried to improve almost every area of American life.

2.1 The Antislavery Movement. Slavery had become more and more rooted in American life since the country's beginning. Some people wanted to *abolish,* or put an end to, it. Known as *abolitionists,* they spoke out against slavery at a time most Americans accepted it.

Some abolitionists formed the American Colonization Society in 1817. They wanted to buy slaves, free them, and send them to a colony in Africa. Free blacks living in the United States would be sent there, too. The Society bought a strip of land on the west coast of Africa and named it Liberia, from a Latin word for "free." Several thousand freed slaves were sent there. The plan, however, was not very successful. It took a great deal of money, and the Society found it difficult to raise enough. Many blacks did not want to go to Africa. In New York, one group wrote:

What idea did the American Colonization Society put forth?

> *We are content to abide where we are. . . . The time must come when the Declaration of Independence will be felt in the heart, as well as uttered from the mouth, and when the rights of all shall be properly acknowledged and appreciated. . . . This is our home, and this is our country. Beneath its sod lie the bones of our fathers: for it, some of them fought, bled, and died. Here we were born, and here we will die.*

How did blacks react to the idea?

Most early abolitionists wanted to free the slaves slowly. At first, their groups had only a few members. The number grew, however, with the greater democratic feeling of the middle 1800's. One of the strongest supporters of abolition was William Lloyd Garrison. Garrison wanted immediate freedom for all slaves. He felt the government accepted slavery and the Constitution defended it. So Garrison refused to work through the political system. In 1831, he began publishing *The Liberator*, a newspaper which printed his views on slavery. In 1833, Garrison and several others started the American Anti-Slavery Society.

How did Garrison differ from other abolitionists?

Another group of abolitionists, led by Theodore Weld of Ohio, did not agree with Garrison. Weld had been influenced toward reform by Charles Finney. Weld wanted freedom for all slaves but thought it should be done gradually. Weld and his group were willing to use

Beginning in 1831, William Lloyd Garrison published *The Liberator* for 35 years. This is the newspaper masthead. How was the abolitionist movement, based on religious ideas, similar to other reform movements?

politics to gain their ends. In 1840, they formed the Liberty party and chose James G. Birney to run for President. Although the party did not last long, it played a role in the elections of 1844 and 1848.

Who was Frederick Douglass?

Many free blacks also worked against slavery. Some, like Frederick Douglass, had been slaves at one time. Douglass had taught himself to read and write before he escaped to the North. There he edited an abolitionist newspaper. He also gave moving speeches around the country for the American Anti-Slavery Society. Sojourner Truth had been a slave on a New York farm. After she was freed by state law in 1827, she traveled in the North, speaking for women's rights as well as against slavery.

Why were abolitionists unpopular?

For many years, abolitionists were unpopular in both the North and South. This was partly because of the prejudice against black people. *Prejudice* is an attitude or opinion about a person, group, or race which is formed without taking time or care to judge fairly. Angry crowds broke up many antislavery gatherings. In 1837, Elijah Lovejoy, an abolitionist publisher in Alton, Illinois, was killed while trying to save his printing press from being destroyed. The antislavery movement remained small during the 1840's and 1850's. Slowly, however, more and more people came to agree with the views of these people.

2.2   The Struggle for Women's Rights.   During the early years of America's history, women had few legal or political rights. They could not vote or hold public office. When a woman married, any property she held belonged to her husband. There were few educational opportunities, and most professions were closed to women.

In the 1840's, some people began to work to improve the position of women. Lucretia Mott and several other women had gone to London to attend an antislavery conference. They were not allowed into the meeting because they were women. So they decided to begin working for equal rights for women. In 1848, the first women's rights convention met in Seneca Falls, New York. Lucretia Mott and Elizabeth Cady Stanton had done most of the organizing for this meeting. Those attending wanted equal political, social, and economic rights for women. They wrote a statement modeled on the Declaration of Independence:

Who were some of the early leaders in the women's rights movement?

> *We hold these truths to be self-evident: that all men and women are created equal. . . .*
>
> *Now, in view of this entire disenfranchisement of one-half the people of this country, their social and religious degradation, in view of the unjust laws above mentioned, and because women do feel themselves aggrieved, oppressed, and fraudulently deprived of their most sacred rights, we insist that they have immediate admission to all the rights and privileges which belong to them as citizens of the United States.*

At first, gains of women's rights were small. However, the reformers did begin to draw people's attention to the cause.

Elizabeth Cady Stanton (left) and Lucretia Mott (right) organized the first women's rights convention at Seneca Falls, New York. What did those women attending the meeting hope to gain?

2.3 New Ideas on Education. Ideas about schools were also changing by the middle of the 1800's. Most schools before then were only for white children. In the South, general education for blacks was not allowed, although some slaves learned to read and write. There were also some independent schools for free black children. Elementary schools for whites were most often church schools. There children learned to read and write about their religions. Private schools were mostly for training young men as church, government, and business leaders. Those private schools and colleges often cost too much for most people.

The struggle to set up public education was not an easy one. Local and state governments were willing to set land aside for schools. But they often did not vote tax money to help run them. When they did, citizens without children objected. Wealthy parents often did not want to pay for the education of poor children. Church schools were opposed to education without religious training.

By the 1830's, this situation was changing. Many Americans began to agree that schools should be free to all children. Citizens needed to be able to read, write, and understand issues in order to vote. Farmers in the West, workers in eastern cities, and newly-arrived immigrants wanted their children to have the chance to improve their lives. There was an increase in the demand for public, tax-supported schools.

One of the most important leaders in the public school movement was Horace Mann of Massachusetts. Mann became the secretary of the Massachusetts Board of Education in 1837. He supported many reforms and laid the base for teaching as a profession. In Mann's day, many

What was education like before the mid-1800's?

Why was it difficult to set up public education?

Who was an important leader in the public school movement?

"The Mechanics of Arithmetic" are addition, subtraction, multiplication, and division. Why does this poster from the 1800's present problems in terms of fruits and vegetables? What other subjects did children at the time learn?

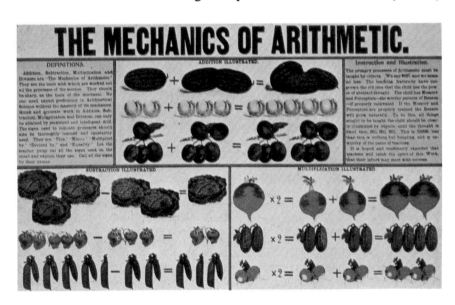

THE MECHANICS OF ARITHMETIC.

These women graduated from Oberlin College in 1855. Oberlin won nationwide attention with its views on women's rights and slavery. The college admitted women from its founding in 1833. What other schools were open to women?

teachers worked only part-time. They were often students in law or the ministry. Mann wanted well-trained, full-time professionals. He set up schools for training teachers and got higher salaries for teachers.

A number of new and better schools were started under Mann's direction. By 1860, the idea of free public schools was widely accepted in the northern part of the country. Most white children could receive an elementary, and often a high school, education. Private schools remained the major avenue of education in the South.

In the first half of the 1800's, efforts were made to give women more opportunities for education. Up to this time, women had generally not been allowed to enter schools of higher learning. In 1821, Emma Hart Willard opened a Female Seminary at Troy, New York. In 1837, Mary Lyon opened the Mount Holyoke Female Seminary in Massachusetts. A few colleges, such as Oberlin in Ohio, began to allow women to take courses. It took a long time, however, for most people to accept the idea of higher education for women.

What efforts were made to improve educational opportunities for women?

The books used by teachers and students during this period were also changing. Noah Webster, sometimes called the "schoolmaster to

America," tried to develop a uniform American speech. In 1828, he wrote a dictionary and a speller. Thousands of these books were sold all over the country. Webster and others, like William McGuffey, published readers that contained stories praising American life.

2.4 Helping People With Handicaps. Improving the lives of persons with handicaps began to receive more attention during the 1830's and 1840's. In 1817, the Reverend Thomas Gallaudet founded a school for people with hearing and speech difficulties in Hartford, Connecticut. It became a model for other schools in many parts of the country. In 1833, Dr. Samuel Howe set up the Perkins Institute for the Blind in Boston. This school also served as a model for others. Howe was a part of the antislavery movement and backed Horace Mann in his work to improve schools. In addition, Howe favored better care for people with mental illnesses.

Another person interested in the care of people with mental illnesses was Dorothea Dix. In 1841, Dix visited the Cambridge House of Correction in Massachusetts. She was shocked by what she saw there. People were treated as criminals and often kept in cages or chained. Sanitary conditions were very poor. Dix visited other jails and poorhouses, making notes of everything she saw. In 1843, she presented a report to the Massachusetts state legislature.

What changes were aimed at helping people with handicaps?

Slowly, things in Massachusetts improved, and Dix began visiting other parts of the United States. She helped set up a number of hospitals for people with mental illnesses. Dix also tried to get government aid for these hospitals. Congress passed a bill giving land grants to states to help in the care of those with mental illnesses. The bill was vetoed, however, by President Pierce. He felt that this care came under the powers of the states.

2.5 Prison Reform. In the early 1800's, many Americans became concerned about the cruel treatment of people who had committed crimes. Prison conditions were very harsh. Criminals, debtors, and people with mental illnesses were all housed together. There were long sentences for small crimes, and the death penalty was used often.

How did Auburn differ from earlier prisons?

In the 1820's, efforts were begun to reform the prison system. Pennsylvania built a new prison with a cell for each person. The Auburn Prison near Syracuse, New York, also had separate cells. It allowed the people in the prison time for meals and exercise. In time, those people were given the chance to take part in work and study programs. The emphasis shifted from punishment to reform. Dorothea Dix was one of the people who supported this change.

Population Density by 1850

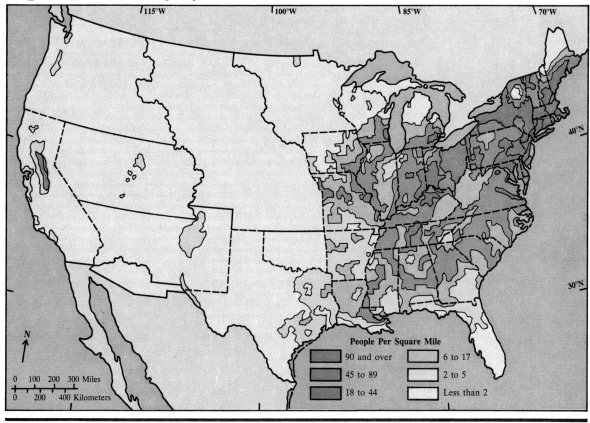

This map shows the average number of people living in every square mile of the United States in 1850. Where were most of the cities located? Where were most of the farms located?

2.6 The Temperance Crusade. One of the most powerful of the reform movements was the drive to limit or put an end to the use of liquor. Some people linked alcohol to crime, poverty, and other problems. They worked to win people over to the idea of *temperance,* or self-control, in drinking. Many groups were formed all over the country. And in 1826, the first national organization was founded. It was called the American Society for the Promotion of Temperance.

Some reformers believed that education was not enough. They wanted laws passed to stop the sale of liquor. One of the leaders in this drive was Neal Dow, the mayor of Portland, Maine. In 1851, largely because of Dow's work, Maine passed the first prohibition law. *Prohibition* means the forbidding by law of the manufacture, shipping,

What was the temperance crusade?

How did prohibition differ from temperance?

and sale of alcoholic beverages. Although other states passed laws like Maine's, many were later *repealed* (withdrawn).

1. Who were the abolitionists?
2. What came out of the women's rights convention of 1848?
3. What were the steps taken to improve education?
4. Who worked for reform for people in mental hospitals?

3. American Literature in the Reform Years _____

One of the greatest periods for American authors came during the years of growing democracy and reform. The writers of this time were often influenced by the democratic spirit and the spirit of perfection. They wrote about America and its people. They tried different forms and new ideas and themes.

What influenced American writers of the mid-1800's?

3.1 Transcendentalists. Ralph Waldo Emerson of Massachusetts was one of the most important figures in American thought in the first half of the 1800's. He spent much of his life writing and giving public speeches. In 1837, Emerson spoke at Harvard College. He urged Americans to look to the United States, rather than Europe, for their ideas. He also pointed out how important individualism, self-reliance, and self-improvement are. Many people thought of Emerson's speech as a kind of declaration of independence for American scholars.

Another leading American transcendentalist was Henry David Thoreau. Like Emerson, Thoreau believed in the supreme importance of individual freedom. In 1845, he went to live in a small cabin on the banks of Walden Pond near Concord, Massachusetts. He spent his time thinking and studying nature. Thoreau wrote one of his best works about his life there. Titled *Walden,* it was first printed in 1854.

In what did Thoreau believe?

Another transcendentalist author was Margaret Fuller. She grew up in New England and knew Ralph Waldo Emerson. In 1840, Fuller became the editor of a transcendentalist magazine, the *Dial.* Four years later, she went to New York where she wrote for a major newspaper. Fuller also wrote a book in favor of equal rights for women, titled *Woman in the Nineteenth Century.*

3.2 Poets and Novelists. Born in New England, Nathaniel Hawthorne wrote stories about his Puritan heritage. Hawthorne knew most of the leading transcendentalists and lived at Brook Farm for a time. However, he did not share the views of people there that all people could perfect their lives. His main concern was with the problem

How did Hawthorne differ from the transcendentalists?

Creativity

CONCEPT

Creativity can be defined as the ability to produce original ideas or things. No one seems to know why one person may be more creative than another. And no one seems to know why creative activity seems to occur at one place over a period of time. Some people say it happens when people recognize a need for something.

In the years between 1820 and 1850, a number of people in the United States recognized the need for a uniquely American literature. One of the literary figures of the time was Ralph Waldo Emerson. The selection which follows is from Emerson's *Nature*, published in 1836.

So shall we come to look at the world with new eyes. It shall answer the endless inquiry of the intellect,—What is truth? . . . What is good? . . . Then shall come to pass what my poet said; 'Nature is not fixed but fluid. Spirit alters, moulds, makes it. . . . Every spirit builds itself a house and beyond its house a world and beyond its world a heaven. Know then that the world exists for you. . . . Build therefore your own world. As . . . you conform your life to the pure idea in your mind . . . a

revolution in things will attend the influx of the spirit . . . [and] the advancing spirit [creates] its ornaments along its path, and carry with it the beauty it visits and the song which enchants it; it shall draw beautiful faces, warm hearts, wise discourse, and heroic acts, around its way, until evil is no more seen. . . .

On August 31, 1837, Emerson delivered "The American Scholar" speech at Harvard College. At that time, he said the following:

Not he is great who can alter matter, but he who can alter my state of mind. They are the kings of the world who give the color of their present thought to all nature and all art, and persuade men by the cheerful serenity of their carrying the matter, that this thing which they do is the apple which the ages have desired to pluck, now at last ripe, and inviting nations to the harvest. The great man makes the great thing.

1. What does Emerson think about creativity?
2. According to Emerson, what should be the world's view of the creative person?

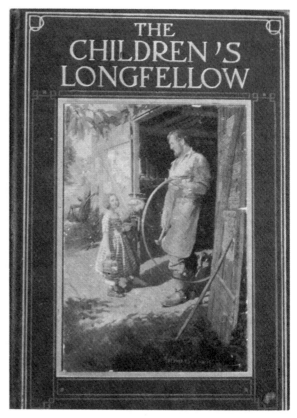

Novels by Herman Melville (left) and books of poetry by Henry Wadsworth Longfellow (right) were popular reading in the middle 1800's. How did literature contribute to a spirit of change in the United States?

of evil in people's lives. This is shown in such works as *The Scarlet Letter* and *The House of Seven Gables.*

Another novelist of the middle 1800's was Herman Melville of New York. He wrote adventure stories often based on his own experiences. Melville had a fairly gloomy view of human nature, as shown in one of his most famous works, *Moby Dick.* Set against the background of a whaling trip, the story deals with the struggle between good and evil. Melville's stories were complex, and he used a great deal of *symbolism,* or the use of one thing to stand for something else. For example, in *Moby Dick,* the white whale stands for evil. Many people had trouble understanding his writing, and Melville was overlooked for many years. Later he came to be thought of as one of America's leading authors.

Edgar Allen Poe wrote mostly poems and short stories. Poe was born in Boston and lived much of his life in Virginia. One of his poems, "The Raven," brought him to people's attention around the country.

Poe is thought of as the creator of detective stories. He also wrote horror tales, such as *The Pit and the Pendulum* and *The Murders in the Rue Morgue*. Poe's stories were complicated. He often used unhappy themes and wrote of the struggle between good and evil. More people read and liked Poe's work in later years than while he was alive.

What is Poe thought to have created?

Walt Whitman was another author of poems. He, perhaps more than any other author of this time, reflected the democratic spirit. Like the transcendentalists, he believed in the individual. One of his most important works was a group of poems called *Leaves of Grass,* first printed in 1855. In it, he praised the growing American nation. Whitman broke with the style of earlier poets. He wrote in *free verse*—poems which do not rhyme. This was one reason why he was not very popular while he was alive. After his death, Whitman became famous as the "Poet of Democracy."

What did Whitman reflect?

Henry Wadsworth Longfellow was one writer who was very popular during his lifetime. A New England poet, Longfellow used American themes in such widely-read tales as *The Courtship of Miles Standish* and *Song of Hiawatha*. Most of his works, including "The Village Blacksmith," appealed to the common people.

Why was Long-fellow popular?

Nearly as well known as Longfellow was John Greenleaf Whittier of Massachusetts. He wrote poems such as "Snow-Bound" and "The Barefoot Boy," based on New England life and legend. Whittier worked in the abolitionist movement, at times helping William Lloyd Garrison. Whittier's *Voices of Freedom* is a group of antislavery poems.

1. Where did Ralph Waldo Emerson think Americans should look for their ideas and themes?
2. Which authors of the middle 1800's reflected transcendentalism in their works?
3. What were some of the major literary works of this time?

4. Conclusion

The growth of democracy and the spirit of perfection influenced society and culture during the first half of the 1800's. Reformers worked to improve their society and shape American social institutions. These years were also important in the development of an American culture. The writers of the time created a national literature and set a standard which served to inspire later writers. These social and cultural forces helped to strengthen the bonds of national unity. However, disagreements over such problems as slavery were beginning, at the same time, to divide the nation.

Chapter 11 Review

Main Points

1. During the first half of the nineteenth century, Americans attempted to reform several aspects of their society.
2. Religion was an important factor in the reform movement of the period.
3. Changes in ideas about religion produced several new religious groups.
4. The movements to get equal rights for women and to abolish slavery made gains but remained small.
5. Public education was well established in the North by 1860. In the South, there were mostly private schools.
6. Major efforts for reform were concerned with the care of people with handicaps and people in prisons.
7. American literary figures wrote about America and its people.
8. American writers experimented with new literary forms.

Building Vocabulary

1. Identify the following:

   Charles Finney
   Mormons
   Ralph Waldo Emerson
   Brook Farm
   Sarah Grimké
   Angelina Grimké

   William Lloyd Garrison
   Theodore Weld
   Sojourner Truth
   Lucretia Mott
   Horace Mann
   Dorothea Dix

   Auburn Prison
   Neal Dow
   Walden Pond
   Margaret Fuller
   Edgar Allen Poe
   Walt Whitman

2. Define the following:

   elect
   revivals
   revelations
   persecuted
   philosophy

   transcendentalism
   utopias
   abolish
   abolitionists
   prejudice

   temperance
   prohibition
   repealed
   symbolism
   free verse

Remembering the Facts

1. Why did many Americans in the 1800's believe they could build a better future?
2. What did the transcendentalists believe about people's ability to perfect themselves and society?
3. Why did people establish utopian communities?
4. Who were the leading abolitionists, and what did they want to accomplish?
5. How were women's rights limited?

6. Which changes took place in public education during the early 1800's?
7. How were people with handicaps treated before the 1800's?

8. Which changes did reformers seek to make for prisons?
9. Who were the leading writers and poets of the middle 1800's?

Understanding the Facts

1. How did the revival movement influence reform?
2. Why did many Americans oppose the Mormons?
3. Why did some utopian communities fail while others lasted?
4. Why was the abolitionist movement small at a time when the country was becoming more democratic?

5. Why were many of the same people in several of the various reform movements in the eary 1800's?
6. Why was public education important in a growing democracy?
7. Why were some reformers opposed to the drinking of liquor?
8. How did the works of writers of this period reflect transcendentalism?

Using Maps

Demographic Maps. The ancient Greeks used the word *demos* to mean people. The Greek word *grapho* meant to write about a certain subject. Combining the two words forms the word *demography* which means the writing about human population.

A demographic map is a map that contains information about human population. The map on page 255 shows population density, the average number of people living in every square mile of an area. The information shown is for various parts of the United States in 1850. Study the map and its key. Answer the following questions.

1. Which section of the United States in 1850 was the most densely populated?
2. Was the most densely populated area north or south of the line of 40° north latitude?
3. Which section of the United States in 1850 was the least densely populated?
4. How would you describe the population for most of the area of the Mississippi River Valley?
5. Which was more densely populated, Michigan or North Carolina?
6. Was the area east of 85° west longitude more densely populated than the area to the west?

New Ways and New People

12

Manufacturing became more important to the American economy beginning with the establishment of Samuel Slater's mill in Rhode Island. How did the rise of industry change both economic and social life in America?

The United States, in the early 1800's, was an agricultural nation. It had been so since its beginning. Most of the people living in the United States were of British background and belonged to one of the Protestant churches. Major changes, however, were taking place that would alter American economic and social life. A new era was about to begin.

1. The Rise of Industry

In the years after the American Revolution, the United States imported most of its manufactured goods. Many Americans agreed with Thomas Jefferson's statement: "Let our workshops remain in Europe." Jefferson and others wanted the United States to stay a country of individually-owned farms.

During these years, some manufacturing was done in homes or small workshops. Manufacturing became more important to the American economy with the coming of the Industrial Revolution. This was a series of great changes that took place in *industry*—the making and selling of goods—starting in the 1700's. It began in Great Britain with new power-driven machines. It later spread to other countries around the world.

Where was manufacturing done in the late 1700's?

1.1 Beginnings in Textiles. As machines began to be used, products were made in factories instead of by one person at home or in a small shop. In the past, the people of the United States had mainly produced raw materials such as cotton, lumber, iron, and wheat. And until the 1800's, artisans like blacksmiths used hand tools to make their products. Shoes, saddles, hats, wagons, nails, flour, and books were all made by hand. People in England had carefully guarded their knowledge of manufacturing. Machinery or plans for it were not allowed to be taken out of the country.

In 1789, Samuel Slater came to America from Great Britain. He had worked in a cotton mill there and knew a great deal about the British *textile,* or cloth-making, machines. Slater had memorized the plans for the machines. With money from a Quaker merchant, Slater built some of these machines. In 1790, he started the first American textile mill on the banks of the Seekonk River in Pawtucket, Rhode Island. Water power was used to drive the machines in the early factories.

What was the first industry to become industrialized?

During the early 1800's, the country moved steadily away from the system of home manufacture. More and more work was done in the new textile mills. There were few of these, however, until the War of 1812. At this time, trade slowed down, and New England merchants began to

Why did New England merchants begin putting money into textiles?

What was the factory system?

put more money into textiles and less into shipping. They felt that people would buy American-made goods since European products were no longer available. The textile industry grew rapidly during and after the war.

1.2 The Factory System. Slater's mill at Pawtucket, Rhode Island introduced a new way to make goods. It was the *factory system*. Under it, workers came from their homes to buildings called factories where goods were made with power-driven machines. Making a product was divided into separate tasks. Instead of having one trained worker do all tasks, each task was done by a person with less training. Women and children, and later people from foreign countries, provided much of this unskilled labor, especially in the textile mills.

At Lowell, Massachusetts, investors set up what they called a model factory. They built boarding houses for the workers, who were mostly young women from New England farms. Hours were long, and the free time of workers was controlled. Time was set aside for some activities, such as the publication of a monthly magazine, *The Lowell Offering*.

Owners of textile mills (left) and other light industries employed many women. Women workers in Lowell, Massachusetts, published *The Lowell Offering* (right), a company magazine. Why did mill owners hire so many women?

Checking Fact and Opinion
=SKILL=

Fact and opinion are often difficult to separate. What a writer personally feels about a subject can flavor the writing. The reader must recognize the difference between fact and opinion and read with that in mind.

The following selection is from the travel journals of Josiah Quincy. During his lifetime, Quincy became a member of Congress. He also served as mayor of Boston and president of Harvard College. In 1801, he visited Slater's textile mill in Rhode Island. He described the mill scene, blending facts with opinion. As you read the selection, notice the various kinds of information Quincy included.

We found the proprietor very cautious of admitting strangers to view its operations, nor would he grant us the privilege until he had received satisfactory assurances that we were as ignorant and unconcerned about every thing relating to the cotton manufacture as he could wish. All the processes of turning cotton from its rough [form] *into every variety of marketable thread . . . are here performed by machinery operating by Water-wheels, assisted only by children*

from four to Ten years old, and one [supervisor]. *Above an hundred of the* [children] *are employed, at the rate of from 12 to 25 cents for a day's labor. Our attendant was very* [enthusiastic about] *the usefulness of this manufacture, and the employment it supplied for so many poor children. But an* [argument] *was* [given] *on the other side of the question . . . which called us to pity these little creatures,* [working] *in a* [crowded] *room, among* [fast machinery], *at an age when nature requires for them air, space, and sports. There was a dull dejection in the* [faces] *of all of them. This, united with the deafening roar of the falls and the rattling of the machinery,* [satisfied] *our curiosity.*

Answer the following questions.

1. Which facts did Quincy give about workers in the factory?
2. What was his opinion about using children as workers?
3. Which other opinions did Quincy express?
4. Which other facts are mentioned?
5. How can you tell what is fact and what is opinion?

Many Americans hoped that factories in the United States following the Lowell plan would be able to avoid the problems which came with the rise of manufacturing in Europe. The Lowell System, however, was not followed. In most other factories, conditions were as bad as those in Europe. Buildings were dirty, and pay was poor. Companies often cut wages as prices were brought down to encourage people to buy their goods. The factory system brought great change into the lives of a people used to farming their own land and making their own decisions.

In general, what conditions existed in the early factory system?

1.3 Inventions and Industry. In America, the need for new ways to do things produced a large number of inventions. The rapidly growing manufacturing in the 1800's was aided by the larger number of new machines. In 1800, there were 306 *patents*—licenses to make, use, or sell new inventions—registered with the United States Patent Office. By 1860, there were 28,000 new patents.

In 1793, Eli Whitney developed a machine to remove the seeds from cotton. The machine was called the *cotton gin* (short for "engine"). With it, workers were able to prepare more cotton for shipment to textile mills in a shorter time. The amount of cotton coming out of the South increased greatly, and plantation owners profited.

Why was Whitney an important inventor?

Whitney also used a new system of *interchangeable parts* in the making of firearms. These were parts which were exactly alike. If one part of a gun was damaged, another part of the same type could replace it. This discovery made *mass production* possible. This is a system of producing large numbers of an item quickly by using interchangeable parts. By the 1840's, many kinds of machinery, from clocks to farm equipment, were made in this way.

In 1839, Charles Goodyear discovered a way to cure rubber that made it able to stand great heat or cold. This process, *vulcanization,* made rubber practical for industrial use. In 1844, Samuel F. B. Morse finished his experiments with an electric telegraph by sending a message from Baltimore to Washington, D.C. The telegraph made it possible to send and receive news quickly. Elias Howe invented a machine in 1846 which could sew cloth faster than a person could by hand. Isaac Singer improved the sewing machine in 1851. This speeded up the manufacture of clothing. In 1851, William Kelly discovered a better way to make steel from iron ore. All of these and other inventions helped the growth of industry.

1.4 The Machine on the Farm. Machines had an effect on farming as well as manufacturing. Many of the new inventions made it easier to farm on a large scale. One of the most important was a mechanical reaper for harvesting grain. It was invented in 1831 by Cyrus

Isaac Singer's sewing machine (left) made mass production of clothing possible. With Cyrus McCormick's reaper (right) farmers could plant more crops each year. What other inventions helped to improve the American economy?

McCormick, who later set up a factory to manufacture reapers. In 1847, George Page built a revolving disc harrow which made the job of breaking up the earth for planting easier. John Heath invented a mechanical binder for grain harvesting in 1850. Many of these machines were later improved and had a greater impact on farming after 1860.

What impact did the inventions of the 1830's and 1840's have on farming?

1.5 The Iron Industry.   With more and more machines being used in farming and manufacturing, the need for iron grew. The United States had been producing iron in small mills for many years. The Lehigh, Susquehanna, and Delaware river valleys were early iron centers. Furnaces were set up near sources of wood, which was used in making charcoal. Charcoal was used to heat the furnaces that changed iron ore into crude iron.

In 1830, it was discovered that coal could be used instead of charcoal in making iron. The coal fields of Pennsylvania became an important source of fuel. By 1855, iron furnaces were using more coal than charcoal. By 1860, over 500,000 tons of crude iron were produced yearly by over 400 furnaces around the country. The United States became one of the leading iron producers in the world.

When did the United States become one of the leading iron producers in the world?

1. Who built the first textile machines in the United States?
2. Where was the first model factory system?
3. What were the major inventions of the middle 1800's?
4. Which product replaced charcoal in making iron?

2. A System of Transportation

In the early 1800's, it was not easy to get raw materials to factories, goods to markets, and food to the people cheaply and quickly. The rise of manufacturing and greater farming added to the need for better transportation.

2.1 New Roads. The United States had begun to improve transportation by building a system of roads. The National Road and similar projects were finished in the years from 1810 to 1860. By 1860, there were over 88,000 miles (140,000 kilometers) of hard-surfaced roads in the country. Road transportation was slow and costly, however. Goods were moved in wagons pulled by teams of horses. Wagons could carry only small loads and often made several trips.

What was one of the major road projects of the early 1800's?

2.2 The Canal Age. Farmers and manufacturers began to demand cheaper means of transportation. This led to a time of canal building, as boats or barges could carry larger loads at less cost. One of the most important projects during these years was the building of the Erie Canal. It was begun by the state of New York in 1817 and finished in 1825. The Erie Canal linked New York City with Buffalo on Lake Erie by way of Albany on the Hudson River. It opened the farms of the Middle West to the markets of the East.

What was one of the major canal projects of the early 1800's?

Tools used in building the Erie Canal (left) were powered by animals and groups of workers. To get canal boats over a rocky cliff, a double set of five locks (right) had to be built. Which cities did the Erie Canal link?

By the 1830's, canals were being dug all around the country, though mostly in the North. Pennsylvania developed a system of waterways connecting Philadelphia with other areas of the state. Ohio and Indiana had canals linking the Great Lakes and the Ohio River. New Jersey linked the Delaware and Raritan rivers. Both Virginia and Maryland built canals reaching from the Atlantic coast to farm areas in the western parts of those states. There were few important canals in the South. Several smaller canals were built to make it easier to travel on the rivers there. Generally, these rivers served the needs of the South.

2.3   The First Steamboats.   Neither the improvement of roads nor the building of canals solved the problem of slow transportation. In the early 1800's, however, different inventors began to develop new means of transportation which were also faster. The steam engine was invented by Thomas Newcomen by 1708. James Watt, a Scot, patented an improved engine in 1769. His work made the steam engine valuable as a machine for transportation.

Who built the first steamboat?

Robert Fulton of New York adapted the steam engine for use on a boat. In August 1807, Fulton's *Clermont* traveled from New York City to Albany. It was a trip of 150 miles (240 kilometers) up the Hudson River, and it took about 32 hours. Up to this time, boats had not been able to move easily upstream. Soon steamboats were being used in other parts of the country, especially on the Ohio and Mississippi rivers. By 1860, there were nearly 1,000 steamboats in service on the rivers.

Robert Fulton became the first to show that steamboats were a practical method of transportation. What was the name of Fulton's ship? How did his success affect river travel?

The first railroads in the United States linked nearby towns to improve existing means of transportation for goods and passengers. This painting shows the New Jersey Camden and Amboy Railroad in 1834. What other forms of transportation available in the middle 1800's are shown? Notice the railroad routes on the map on the next page. Where were most of the major lines?

2.4 The Coming of the Railroads. The steam engine was applied to land transportation at about the same time as it was being used in steamboats. An engineer in England, George Stephenson, built a steam-powered locomotive, *The Rocket*. It weighed five tons and could pull a load three times its own weight at 12 miles (19.2 kilometers) an hour. In 1829, *The Rocket* entered a contest with other kinds of locomotives and won. It set the pattern for future locomotive development. This was the beginning of the "railway era."

Who built the first steam locomotive?

In the United States, railroads, as well as early roads and canals, grew out of the commercial rivalry of eastern cities. Merchants in Boston, New York, Philadelphia, Baltimore, and Charleston promoted the building of railroads. They felt that this would bring them more trade. The first successful railroad in the United States was the Baltimore and Ohio. In 1830, Peter Cooper built the first steam locomotive in America, for the Baltimore and Ohio Railroad. It was called the *Tom Thumb*. In Charleston, South Carolina, *Best Friend of Charleston* carried passengers on the first scheduled steam-railroad run in 1830. Harriet Martineau, a visitor from England, wrote about several of her trips by train in the mid-1830's.

What was the first successful railroad in the United States?

. . . my journeys on [the Charleston and Augusta railroad] *were by far the most fatiguing of any I underwent in the country. The motion and the noise are distracting. . . .*

One great inconvenience of the American railroads is that, from wood being used for fuel, there is an incessant shower of large sparks, destructive to dress and comfort. . . . Some serious accidents from fire have happened in this way; and, during my last trip on the Columbia and Philadelphia rail-road, a lady in the car had a shawl burned to destruction on her shoulders; and I found that my own gown had thirteen holes in it. . . .

Nearly all of the early railroads were started to link ports on the east coast with areas farther west. Later they joined major cities

What area had the most developed railroad system by 1850?

Major Railroads in the 1850's

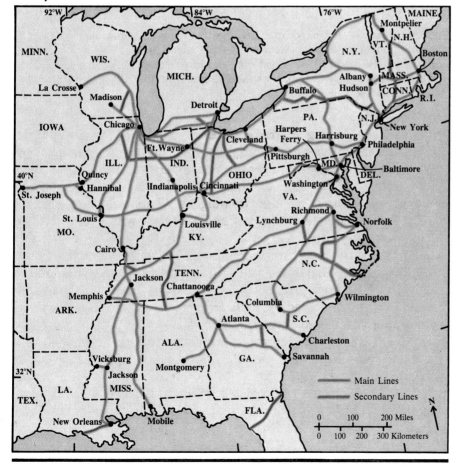

together as well. By 1850, New England had a system of railroads which connected nearly every city in the area. In 1852, the first railroad linking Detroit and Chicago was finished. The Rock Island Line built the first bridge over the Mississippi River in 1856. In the South, lines ran from Charleston and Savannah to Atlanta. However, there were not nearly as many miles of track in the South as in the North and Middle West.

By the mid-1800's, some 30,000 miles (48,000 kilometers) of track had been laid throughout the country. The United States, however, did not yet have a fast transportation system. Backed by different states and private merchants, railroad companies built lines in which the *gauge,* or distance between the rails, varied. This meant that at places where railroads of different gauges came together, goods had to be moved from one car to another. There were other problems, such as the lack of strong bridges and rails. In spite of these drawbacks, railroads were an important step toward faster, cheaper transportation.

With the growing number of railroads came a rise in related industries. There was a greater need for iron, timber, and coal. A communications system also developed along with the railroads. Telegraph lines were set up along the tracks, and the use of the telegraph improved railroad service. Messages could be sent from station to station giving the arrival and departure times of trains.

What were the major problems of railroads in the mid-1800's?

1. Why was good transportation important for the rise of industry?
2. Why did farmers need good transportation?
3. Which part of the country had the fewest miles of railroad?

3. The Growth of Cities

The factory system and the new industries in the middle 1800's led to a growing number of cities. Towns were built near factories because people had to live close to their work. Older cities grew, and new cities were started as the factories were built. There was a tremendous growth in the number and size of cities before 1860. In 1790, about 5 percent of the population lived in urban areas. By 1860, the number of people living in these areas had reached nearly 20 percent.

3.1 Old Cities and New Cities.   In 1790, there were only 24 places in the United States with over 2,500 people. As America began to industrialize, older cities grew. Between 1820 and 1840, New York City's population rose from 123,000 to 312,000. Philadelphia grew from

Population Growth, 1790–1860

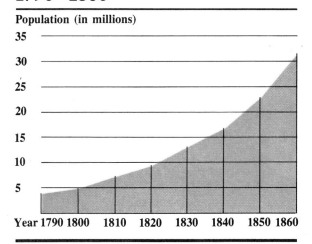

Population (in millions)

35	
30	
25	
20	
15	
10	
5	

Year 1790 1800   1810   1820   1830   1840   1850 1860

Total Estimated Population, 1860

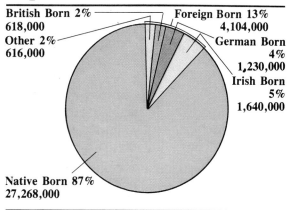

British Born 2%
618,000
Other 2%
616,000

Foreign Born 13%
4,104,000
German Born
4%
1,230,000
Irish Born
5%
1,640,000

Native Born 87%
27,268,000

How did total American population change from the time of the first census in 1790 until 1860? What percent of the population in 1860 was not born in the United States? Where were most immigrants born?

a population of 112,000 to 220,000. The number of people in Baltimore increased from 62,000 to 102,000, while Boston expanded from 42,000 to 93,000 people. New factories, the growth of commerce brought about by the railroads, and foreign trade all played a part in the growth of these older cities.

By 1830, new cities had been started in the West. Cincinnati, Pittsburgh, and Louisville all had populations from 10,000 to 25,000. These cities and others, like St. Louis, were located on rivers. They benefited from such improvements in transportation as the steamboat. Railroads were important to new cities of the West such as Chicago. Chicago was fast becoming one of the leading railroad junctions in the country. By 1860, it had a population of 109,000 and was growing rapidly. Altogether, by 1860, there were 392 places in the United States which had a population of 2,500 or more.

In general, how much did cities grow from 1790 to 1860?

3.2 Benefits and Problems. During the years from 1820 to 1860, people had both benefits and problems from city life. Education and jobs were easier to get than in rural areas. Many of the large cities had libraries, and some offered classes for adults. There were operas and plays for those who could pay to see them.

The growing urban centers, however, went beyond the ability of their governments to deal with certain problems. Larger cities stretched

What did cities do during the mid-1800's that created problems?

their borders beyond the point where water, sewage, and other services were available. There was much sickness in areas where poor people lived in crowded *tenements*—apartment houses generally without sanitation, comfort, and safety. The burning of coal made great clouds of smoke that hung over factory towns. In 1833, a visitor to Pittsburgh complained that the smoke caused so much dirt and soot that clean hands and faces were "objects of rare occurrence."

3.3   Improving City Life.   One of the major problems facing people who lived in cities was having enough water. City governments began building waterworks and dams to form *reservoirs*—places where water is collected and stored for use. In 1799, water from the Schuylkill River was carried through log pipes to an area of Philadelphia. With the opening of the Fairmount Waterworks in 1822, all parts of Philadelphia received water through a system of iron pipes. The problem of water supply also became serious in New York City. In 1842, the Croton Dam was built to form a reservoir for the city.

Most towns in the early 1800's did not have adequate lighting for the streets. At first, oil lamps were used. Later oil was replaced by coal gas. Boston began using coal gas for street lighting in 1822. New York City began its use the following year, and Philadelphia did the same in 1837. By the 1850's, gas lighting was common in most of the larger cities.

Another major improvement in city life was the development of professional police and fire departments. In the early 1800's, cities had poorly-paid *night watches*—people who lit the street lamps and called

What was a major problem that people faced living in cities in the mid-1800's?

What were night watches?

Every city lived in fear of fire because most buildings were made of wood. By the 1850's, many cities began to set up fire-fighting departments with public funds. Where was one of the earliest full-time fire departments?

Margaret Gaffney Haughery (1813–1882)

The career of Margaret Gaffney Haughery symbolizes both the drive for business success and the spirit of reform in America during the middle 1800's. Born in Ireland, Haughery's family moved to Maryland when she was five years old. At age nine, her parents died. She was brought up by neighbors, and she never learned to read or write. In 1835, she married. After moving to New Orleans, her husband left her, and her only child died.

Haughery worked at a laundry. She spent her free time with the children at a local orphanage. Using the money she saved, she bought several cows and started her own dairy business. By 1840, she had a dairy of 40 cows. In time, she used her profits to build a home for orphans. During her life, she helped to establish ten other homes for children and for elderly people.

In 1858, Haughery sold the dairy business and opened a bakery. She bought new, steam-powered machinery for it, making it the first bakery in the South to be run by steam. Later it became New Orleans' largest export business, producing and selling packaged crackers.

Even though she was a success in business, Haughery's simple way of life did not change. She liked to give help to people in need. Before she died, Haughery left a large amount of money to continue this help. Most people remembered her as "the Bread Woman of New Orleans."

out the hour of the night. They also sounded the alarm in case of fire. In 1844, New York City authorized a professional police force, and other cities soon followed this example. At first, fire protection for cities was provided by volunteer companies. A full-time fire department was formed in Cincinnati in 1853. This helped set a pattern of fire protection for other cities.

1. What was the largest city in the United States by 1840?
2. What were the benefits of city life?
3. What problems did the city cause?

4. The Changing Population

Many changes were taking place in the United States as the country industrialized. More people took jobs in factories and lived in cities. The population of the country was growing rapidly. There was also an increase in immigration to the United States from other areas of the world. When George Washington became President of the United States in 1789, the nation had nearly 4 million people. By 1810, the population had reached 7 million and by 1850, 23 million. Part of this growth came from a heavy flow of immigration beginning in the 1820's.

4.1 Increasing Immigration. During the years from 1820 to 1840, over 700,000 immigrants landed on the shores of the United States. Nearly 60 percent of these people were German or Irish. A second large movement of immigrants to the United States began in the 1840's. In 1846, the failure of the potato crop in Ireland started a *famine,* a general lack of food in an area causing starvation. During the next 15 years, more than 1 million Irish came to the United States. Thousands of Germans also came between 1840 and 1860. Poor harvest, lack of land and jobs, and desire for political freedom caused them to leave Germany in search of a better life. Altogether, well over 4 million people came to the United States in the years from 1840 to 1860.

What caused the Irish and Germans to immigrate to the United States in large numbers in the mid-1800's?

Many industries actively recruited foreign labor to come to the United States. This British drawing is titled "The Lure of American Wages." What does it suggest about the benefits of working in America?

4.2 Settling in America. The experiences of the immigrants when they arrived in the United States followed certain patterns. For the most part, people from Germany arrived with some money. Many were able to move to areas where land was available, such as the Middle West. Large numbers of German immigrants settled on farms in Illinois, Missouri, and Wisconsin. Thousands of Germans also settled in cities, especially in the West. Many set up their own businesses. By 1860, nearly half of the population of both Milwaukee and St. Louis was of German descent. Germans made up 30 percent of the population of Cincinnati.

When Irish immigrants landed in the United States, they generally did not have the money to buy farms or land. They often settled in eastern seaports, such as New York, Boston, Philadelphia, and Baltimore. In 1855, there were more than 50,000 Irish living in Boston. Nearly two thirds of the Irish immigrants to America settled in the northeast section of the country. Irish workers were important sources of labor around the country for the factories and for canal and railroad building.

Why did most Irish settle in eastern cities?

4.3 The Nativist Movement. During the 1830's and 1840's, a movement against the immigrants began in America. Members of the group were known as Nativists because they were native to, or born in, the United States. Most were Protestants of British background. Nativists feared competition for jobs from immigrants who worked for low wages. Nativists also believed that the country was in danger from the large numbers of Catholics coming there to live. Because most Irish immigrants were Catholics, the movement was largely directed against them. There were violent clashes in several cities between Nativist groups and Irish immigrants.

Why did a Nativist movement develop?

Nativists wanted only American-born Protestants to hold political office. They were against both foreigners and Catholics. In the 1850's, a national party was formed. When asked about opposition to immigrants, its members answered, "I know nothing." Because of this, they became known as the Know-Nothings. Under the name of the American party, the Know-Nothings participated in the election of 1856. They lost strength in the years after 1856. Issues like slavery began to push the question of immigration into the background.

1. From where did most of the immigrants come during the years between 1820 and 1840?
2. Where did most of these people settle?
3. Which political party was formed in opposition to the immigrants?

5. Conclusion

During the years from 1820 to 1860, the United States experienced a great deal of growth and change. Industry expanded with the introduction of power-driven machinery. Cities were established around newly-built factories. The coming of the railroad revolutionized transportation. Population increased as thousands of immigrants landed in the United States. By 1860, the "old" America had given way to a "new" America.

Chapter 12 Review

Main Points

1. In the first half of the nineteenth century, the United States began to develop industry as an important part of the national economy.

2. The factory system developed first in textiles and spread to other industries.

3. Numerous inventions aided in the growth of industry and transportation.

4. The rise of industry and the improvements in transportation led to the growth of more cities.

5. Life in the cities produced both benefits and problems.

6. Political opposition developed to the large number of immigrants who entered the United States.

Building Vocabulary

1. Identify the following:

   Industrial Revolution
   Samuel Slater
   The Lowell Offering
   Eli Whitney
   Samuel F. B. Morse
   Cyrus McCormick
   Erie Canal
   Robert Fulton
   The Rocket
   Margaret Gaffney Haughery
   Nativists
   Know-Nothings

2. Define the following:

   industry
   textile
   factory system
   patents
   cotton gin
   interchangeable parts
   mass production
   vulcanization
   gauge
   tenements
   reservoirs
   night watches
   famine

Remembering the Facts

1. What were the conditions in the early factories?
2. Which development made mass production possible?
3. How did inventions influence industry?
4. How were a person's rights to an invention legally protected?
5. What new methods of transportation were developed?
6. Which actions were taken to improve life in the cities?
7. What groups of people came to America from 1820 to 1860?
8. Why did Nativists oppose immigrants?

Understanding the Facts

1. Why was the textile industry the first to develop the factory system?
2. How did the factory system differ from the home workshop?
3. Which invention had the greatest effect on agriculture in the South?
4. What were the advantages of using the new inventions over the way things had been done?
5. Why was the iron industry important to most other industries?
6. What effect did new methods of transportation have on other industries?
7. How did the development of factories, farm machinery, and transportation effect the growth of cities?
8. How did the population change as the United States industrialized?

Using Line Graphs

Using Line Graphs. The left illustration on page 273 is called a line graph. A line is used to show the level of the subject of the graph during the years listed across the base line. The sweep and direction of the line provides comparison with the years before and after. The line graph also gives a sense of the trend or direction over the entire period shown.

Using the graph, answer the following questions.

1. What is shown by the graph?
2. How many people were in the United States in 1790?
3. What was the population of the United States in the most recent census before Andrew Jackson became President?
4. What was the population after President Jackson left office?
5. What was the increase in population between 1828 and 1836?
6. Did population become less, stay the same, or increase from 1790 to 1860?
7. Based on the information on the graph, why would you think that the population in 1870 would not be over 100,000,000 people?

From Ocean to Ocean 13

John Charles Frémont, the "Pathfinder," became a living sign of the spirit of manifest destiny. His adventures inspired many Americans to go west. What did people hope to find in the area west of the Mississippi River?

With the Louisiana Purchase in 1803, the United States gained its first area of land west of the Mississippi River. In the years following, Americans began to move into these lands as well as others in the West. Large areas of land were added to the United States in the 1840's and 1850's. Soon the nation extended from the Atlantic Ocean to the Pacific Ocean. Except for Alaska and Hawaii, the United States grew to its present size during these years.

1. The Westward Movement

Americans had begun to explore the lands west of the Mississippi River before many areas to the east of it were settled. The Lewis and Clark expedition of 1804 to 1806 gave people in the United States their first information about the Louisiana Territory. Soon other Americans were exploring and settling lands in the West. Moving across the Mississippi River into the huge area of the West presented exciting challenges and new problems to Americans and the United States.

1.1 Leading the Way West. The United States followed up the Lewis and Clark expedition with others. In 1806, Lieutenant Zebulon Pike traveled up the Arkansas River to the Rocky Mountains in Colorado. Pike's report gave new information about the West. It added to American interest in trade with the Spanish in New Mexico.

Where did Pike explore?

Another expedition was led by Major Stephen Long in 1819 and 1820. Long explored the Great Plains along the Platte River to the Rocky Mountains. Both Pike and Long reported that the Great Plains were not fit for settlement because of the lack of rainfall and trees. This led to the common belief that the Great Plains was a "Great American Desert." For years, people were not interested in settling there.

What were the early reports about the Great Plains?

Fur traders and trappers were an even more important source of information about the West. After the United States gained Louisiana, Americans became important in the western fur trade. Prior to that time, the French and Spanish had competed with the British for furs.

The trappers went into the mountains and river areas of the West for beaver. Some time during the year, they met with a representative of a fur-trading company to sell their furs. These furs were later sold by the companies to customers in the East or in Europe. Over the years, the trappers came to know the streams, rivers, mountain passes, and trails of nearly every area in the West. Such trappers as Jim Bridger and Jedediah Smith guided early settlers through the Rocky Mountains to Oregon and California.

1.2 Manifest Destiny. Americans moved into the lands west of the Mississippi River for the same reason that they had always moved west—for cheap and plentiful land. Large numbers of settlers started farms in Iowa, Arkansas, and Missouri in the 1820's and 1830's. By the 1840's, much of the Mississippi River Valley was settled, and interest began to grow in lands farther west.

What was the major reason people moved west?

Since colonial times, the settlers in America had believed that they had a right to the lands they settled. Most of them did not spend time talking about the westward movement. However, many would agree that it was helping to extend the democratic way of life. Political leaders and authors sometimes expressed ideas about the westward movement. They reflected the views of many Americans at the time.

What is meant by manifest destiny?

In 1845, a magazine editor first used the term manifest destiny. He wrote that it was the **manifest destiny**, or certain fate, of the United States to stretch from ocean to ocean. Many people in all parts of the country agreed with him. They were called **expansionists** because they wanted to expand the land area of the United States. People in business wanted ports on the Pacific coast where American ships could stop on their way to trade with Asia. Settlers wanted to live in the fertile lands of Oregon and California. American leaders did not want any European country to control these areas.

1. Who explored the West in the early 1800's?
2. How did the term manifest destiny come into use?
3. Which groups were in favor of expanding the area of the United States?

2. On to Oregon

Oregon was one of the areas in the West which attracted Americans. It included lands that are now the states of Oregon, Washington, Idaho, and parts of Wyoming and Montana. It stretched from a latitude of 54°40' in the north to 42° in the south—from the southern tip of present-day Alaska to northern California. Its boundary in the east was the Rocky Mountains and in the west, the Pacific Ocean. The area had been claimed at different times by several countries. Its rich soil, good rainfall, and mild climate became a strong attraction for American settlers.

2.1 Early Claims. In the early 1800's, Oregon was claimed by four different countries—Great Britain, the United States, Russia, and Spain. Spain gave up its claim to the area in the Adams-Onís Treaty of

1819. It set the boundary between Spanish lands and the Louisiana Purchase. After the Monroe Doctrine was issued in 1823, Russia gave up its claim to Oregon. By the late 1820's, only the United States and Great Britain were still trying to decide who controlled the area.

Both the United States and Great Britain claimed Oregon because both had explored the area and set up trade there. Traders from New England had sailed into the area toward the end of the 1700's. The Lewis and Clark expedition had traveled there. Also, John Jacob Astor's Pacific Fur Company had founded Fort Astoria on the Columbia River in 1811. This was the first permanent American settlement in the Oregon country. James Cook, an English explorer, had visited the Oregon coast in 1788. British claims were helped by the presence of the Hudson's Bay Company. Dr. John McLoughlin ran the company's business from a fort on the Columbia River. Until the 1840's, trappers working for the Hudson's Bay Company controlled the Oregon fur trade.

What was the basis of the American and British claims to Oregon?

2.2 The Canadian Boundary. Great Britain and the United States were not able to settle their differences over Oregon quickly.

Independence Rock in Wyoming was a popular resting place along the Oregon Trail. Many travelers scratched their names on the large landmark to document their journey. How long was the trip from Missouri to Oregon?

Routes to the Far West

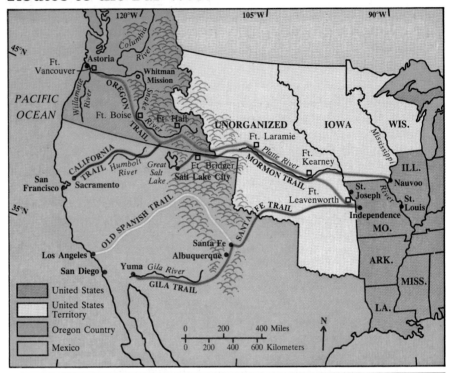

What forts were along the Oregon Trail? How long was the Santa Fe Trail? Where did the Mormon Trail begin and end? What towns were linked by the Gila Trail? Where was the Old Spanish Trail? What river flowed along a section of the California Trail?

What agreement helped to settle much of the U.S.-Canadian boundary?

They did, however, come to agree about the dividing line between the United States and Canada in the west. In the Convention of 1818, the boundary was set at the 49th parallel, running from the Lake of the Woods to the Rocky Mountains. The two countries also agreed to settle the question of Oregon at a later time. For a while, there would be a *joint occupation* of the territory. This meant that people from both the United States and Great Britain could settle in the area.

2.3 Oregon Fever. Events in Oregon soon began to favor the American claim. In the 1830's, missionaries from the United States, led by the Reverend Jason Lee, began to arrive. They settled south of the Columbia River in the Willamette Valley. Farther east on the Columbia River, Marcus and Narcissa Whitman founded a mission at Walla Walla. The experiences of the missionaries interested many people in the United States.

Beginning in the 1840's, "Oregon fever" gripped many Americans. In 1841, the first wagon train made the trip overland from Independence, Missouri, to Oregon. Soon other larger trains were making the 2,000-mile (3,200-kilometer) journey. These pioneers followed a path which came to be called the Oregon Trail. The wagon trains crossed the Great Plains, following the Platte River to Fort Laramie, some 600 miles (960 kilometers) from Independence. They crossed the Rocky Mountains at South Pass and went on to Fort Hall. From there, the settlers followed the Snake River to Fort Boise and on to the Columbia River. Moving along it, they made their way to the Willamette Valley. Many of these pioneers started farms there.

How did most pioneers get to Oregon?

In 1846, Francis Parkman traveled through the West. He wrote *The Oregon Trail* in 1849, describing what he had seen.

> *We were late in breaking up our camp . . . and scarcely had we ridden a mile when we saw . . . drawn against the horizon, a line of objects stretching . . . along the level edge of the prairie. An intervening swell soon hid them from sight, until, ascending it . . . we saw close before us the . . . caravan, with its heavy white wagons creeping on in slow procession, and a large drove of cattle following behind. Half a dozen . . . Missourians, mounted on horseback, were . . . shouting among them. . . . they called out to us: "How are ye, boys? Are ye for Oregon or California?"*
>
> *As we pushed rapidly by the wagons, children's faces were thrust out from the white coverings to look at us; while the careworn, thin-featured matron . . . seated in front, suspended the knitting on which most of them were engaged to stare at us with wondering curiosity. By the side of each wagon stalked the proprietor, urging on his patient oxen, . . . inch by inch, on their . . . journey.*

What was the journey to Oregon like?

The journey to Oregon took from four to six months. The people who made it faced dust, rainstorms, and sickness along the trail. Indians sometimes attacked, trying to stop the settlers moving through their lands. Snow was a danger once the wagon trains reached the Rocky Mountains. Often wagon wheels broke or metal tires fell off from the changes in temperatures.

Despite the hardships, there were soon 5,000 Americans living in the Oregon country. All of them lived south of the Columbia River, but they far outnumbered British people in the area. In 1843, they set up a temporary government. These settlers wanted the United States to stop sharing control of the area with Great Britain.

1. Where was the Oregon Trail?
2. Which countries had early claims to Oregon?
3. With which country did the United States jointly occupy Oregon?

3. The Southwest and California

Americans had become more interested in the land of Oregon in the 1840's. At the same time, they were looking to the lands south and west of the Louisiana Territory. These lands belonged to Spain until 1821, when Mexico declared its independence. The area had huge ranches and some mines, which were run by a few wealthy Spanish owners and their workers. The area served chiefly as a border to protect the lands of central Mexico. The Spaniards had not allowed people in these areas to trade with the United States. This began to change, especially after the new Mexican government took over. By the 1820's, Americans were trading and sometimes settling in Texas, New Mexico, and California.

3.1 Early Contacts in New Mexico. American trappers had sometimes gone into the settlements of New Mexico for food and supplies. The expedition of Zebulon Pike increased American interest in trade with this area. In 1822, William Becknell led a large caravan from Missouri to Santa Fe along what became known as the Santa Fe Trail. This marked the opening of regular trade between Americans and the people of New Mexico.

3.2 Americans in California. Early California was a land of missions and cattle ranches. Most of the people living there were

When did Mexico become independent?

What was the Santa Fe Trail?

As this painting suggests, California missions became centers of community life. How did the breakup of the missions affect the people who lived near them?

Mariano Guadalupe Vallejo (1808–1890)

PROFILE

During his life as a military and political leader, Mariano Guadalupe Vallejo saw California change from a thinly settled Spanish outpost into a well-populated American state. Vallejo was born, lived, and died in northern California.

In the 1830's, the Mexican government assigned Vallejo as the commander of a military post at Sonoma, north of San Francisco. His duty was to keep out settlers from the United States and to watch the Russian fur traders along the northern border of Mexican California. Vallejo owned a large section of land near Sonoma. Because of this and his position as military commander, he was one of the most powerful leaders in northern California. However, he could not stop the settlers coming from the United States. He decided to help them find places to settle, since he could not stop them.

In 1836, Vallejo supported his nephew, Juan Bautista Alvarado, in a rebellion against Mexico that led to the proclamation of the "free state" of California. When the United States went to war with Mexico in 1846, Americans with Vallejo's backing declared the Bear Flag Republic. After the war, when California became a state, Vallejo became an important state leader. He was a delegate to the state constitutional convention in 1849 and served in the new state senate.

Indians or the descendants of Spanish colonists. The first American contact with California was by way of the sea.

As early as 1795, ships from New England sailed California waters hunting sea otters. Sometimes these ships stopped to trade with the towns along the coast, although this was illegal. After the area became independent of Spain, an active trade in hides developed with Mexican ranchers. American merchants settled in towns such as Monterey, Los Angeles, and San Diego.

In the 1840's, people from the United States and Europe came to live in California. John Sutter, a Swiss settler, built a fort on the Sacramento River. A few Americans made their way overland to the fort by way of the California Trail. This trail had been started by

Who were the first Americans to settle in California?

trappers and began at Fort Bridger on the Oregon Trail. In a few years, several hundred Americans were living in California. There was talk of adding California to the United States.

During these years, the lands of the Catholic missions were broken up by the Mexican government. The Indians who worked for the missions were supposed to get part of the lands, but they received very little. The breakup of the missions and the large numbers of Americans moving into California affected the Indians. Many died from disease and lack of food. Their population dropped from more than 100,000 to fewer than 50,000.

3.3 Americans in Texas.   Texas interested the people in the United States chiefly because of its rich soil. In the early 1800's, southern cotton growers had begun migrating west from Virginia, the Carolinas, and Georgia. The soil in these states had become worn out. The farmers looked for better land in the Gulf regions. Louisiana, Mississippi, and Alabama became important cotton-growing states. In the 1820's, planters were looking to Texas as a real source of rich land on which to grow cotton, using slave labor.

Why were south-erners interested in Texas?

Stephen Austin started a settlement on the Brazos River in Texas in the early 1820's. Under an agreement made with the Mexican government, each of the 300 families which Austin brought to Texas received over 13,000 acres of land. Austin and others like him who brought settlers to Texas were known as *empresarios*—people who organize and take the risk for business deals. In 1825, Mexico began to accept all settlers who would swear their loyalty to Mexico and practice the Catholic religion. The population of Texas grew rapidly. By the early 1830's, there were 30,000 settlers from the United States living in Texas. Most were from the South, and many owned slaves.

3.4 The Republic of Texas.   Slavery and other troubles soon led to quarrels between the Americans in Texas and the Mexican government. Mexico had ended slavery and objected to the holding of slaves by Americans living in Texas. At the same time, Mexicans began to wonder whether loyalty of the Texas settlers was to the United States or to Mexico. They tried to stop more Americans from entering Texas.

What things caused quarrels between Americans in Texas and the Mexican government?

In 1834, General Antonio López de Santa Anna became president of Mexico. He wanted the government to control all of Mexico, including Texas, at a time when Texas wanted more freedom in local affairs. When the Texans rebelled in 1835, Santa Anna took steps to stop them. He crossed the Rio Grande with 6,000 soldiers. The main Mexican army under Santa Anna marched toward San Antonio. At the Alamo, a deserted mission in San Antonio, 187 Texans held out for several days against nearly 4,000 Mexican soldiers. The Mexican army

Where was the first battle between Texans and Mexi-cans fought?

In the Texas war for independence, Sam Houston (left) was the Texans' commander and first president of the republic. Fighting at the Alamo (right) inspired the Texas army. Why did "Remember the Alamo" become a rallying cry for Texas?

finally took the Alamo. In the attack, the defenders, including the famous frontier fighters Jim Bowie and Davy Crockett, were killed. A second Mexican force defeated a Texas army at the town of Goliad and killed over 300 prisoners. "Remember the Alamo" and "Remember Goliad" became important battle cries for Texans.

On March 2, 1836, Texans declared their independence. Sam Houston was placed in charge of the army. On April 21, 1836, Texas troops under his command won a victory that ended the war. They attacked and defeated the larger Mexican army near the San Jacinto River. Santa Anna was captured. He agreed to leave Texas with his army. Texans set up their own government like that of the United States. They chose Sam Houston as their first president.

Who commanded the Texas forces?

3.5 The Annexation Issue. Many Americans expected that Texas would be *annexed,* or added, to the United States after winning its independence. Over the next several years, however, the American government avoided the issue. Leaders feared war with Mexico since Mexico had not recognized the independence of Texas. They also did not want to stir up trouble over slavery. When John Tyler became President in 1841, he wanted to annex Texas but could not get Congress to agree. For several years, the people of Texas governed themselves.

In the election of 1844, James K. Polk became President of the United States. During the campaign, he had called for the annexation of both Texas and Oregon. Since most people living in Texas were Americans, they wanted Texas to be a part of the United States. Most people expected that when Polk took office in March 1845, Congress would approve the annexation of Texas. However, President Tyler got Congress to agree to annex Texas before Polk took office. On March 1, 1845, Texas became a state.

When was Texas annexed?

In his first message to Congress, President Polk called for an end to joint occupation of the Oregon country. He set up talks between both sides. The British government finally proposed the 49th parallel as the dividing line between British and American lands, except for the tip of Vancouver Island. On June 15, 1846, the Senate gave its approval. The United States annexed the area below the 49th parallel. These lands

When was the Oregon dispute settled?

Before the Oregon boundary settlement in 1846, who occupied the Oregon Country? How was the dispute finally solved?

Oregon Boundary

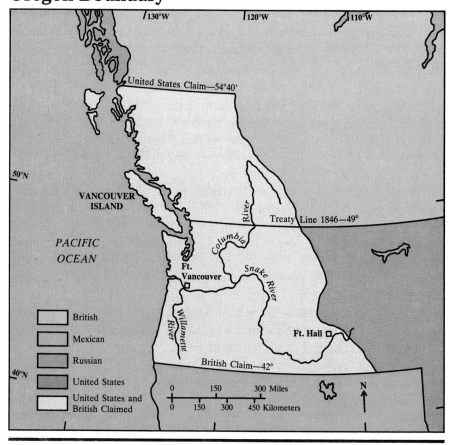

In this daguerreotype (an early type of photograph), American soldiers ride into a Mexican village. The Mexican War was the first American war to be photographed. Why was the Mexican War fought?

later became the states of Oregon and Washington. The final boundary with Canada had been set across the whole continent.

3.6 The Mexican War. Although the Oregon question was being settled peacefully, there was trouble with Mexico over the annexation of Texas. After Texas became a state, Mexico ended formal government relations with the United States. Conflict grew between the two countries over the Texas-Mexico border. The United States backed the Texas claim that its southern boundary was the Rio Grande. Mexico believed that it was farther north and east, along the Nueces River.

President Polk sent an agent to Mexico to talk about the border dispute and to try to buy California and New Mexico. When Polk heard that Mexican officials would not meet with this agent, he ordered General Zachary Taylor and his troops to the north bank of the Rio Grande. Mexico saw this as an invasion of its land. Polk began preparing a message asking Congress to declare war on Mexico for refusing to meet with his representative.

Before Polk could send the war message, however, word came that Mexican soldiers had crossed the Rio Grande and attacked American forces. The President sent a new war message to Congress. He wrote: "Mexico has passed the boundary of the United States, has invaded our territory, and shed American blood on American soil." On May 13, 1846, Congress declared war on Mexico.

What brought about a declaration of war against Mexico?

Once war had been declared, the United States Army acted quickly. General Taylor, known as "Old Rough and Ready," crossed the Rio Grande and made his way into northeastern Mexico in a series of hard-fought battles. He won an important victory at the Battle of Buena Vista in February 1847.

A second American army was led by General Winfield Scott. Scott was called "Old Fuss and Feathers," because he was such a careful planner. Scott's army moved down the east coast of Mexico by sea and landed at Vera Cruz. The Americans then marched inland and finally captured Mexico City, the capital, on September 14, 1847.

A third American army under the command of Colonel Stephen Kearny marched south from Fort Leavenworth, Kansas, to take Santa Fe. Part of this force then went on to California where a revolt had been staged in 1846 by Americans living there. Helped by Captain John C. Frémont and his United States soldiers, the rebels declared their independence from Mexico. They adopted a flag with a picture of a bear

Outside the original 13 states, how was each section of the country obtained? How many different ways did the United States use to gain land? By which means did the United States gain most of its land?

United States Expansion, 1853

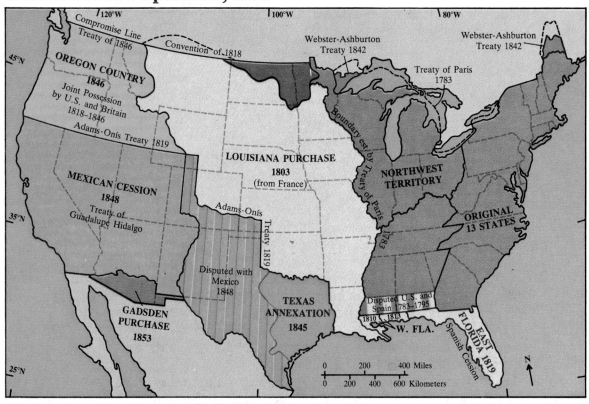

People came from many parts of the world to look for California gold. When was gold discovered in California?

on it as their symbol. For a few days, California became the Bear Flag Republic. Volunteers and sailors from the United States Navy under Commodore John D. Sloat soon took over much of California. There was some resistance from Mexicans living in California. But the Americans, including Kearny's troops, finished the conquest.

What was the Bear Flag Republic?

3.7 The Treaty of Guadalupe Hidalgo. As the war went on, some Americans began to demand more territory. A few even wanted to annex all of Mexico. Most Americans at least wanted to get California and New Mexico. The government also wanted Mexico to agree that Texas was part of the United States.

President Polk's agent in Mexico, Nicholas Trist, arranged a treaty that spelled out these terms. The Treaty of Guadalupe Hidalgo was signed early in 1848. The United States paid Mexico $15 million for all the land north of the Rio Grande and the Gila River. This area included the present states of California, Nevada, Utah, Arizona, New Mexico, Texas, and parts of Colorado and Wyoming. Several years later, the United States found that the best southern railroad route to the Pacific coast was south of the Gila River. In 1853, the United States paid Mexico $10 million for the strip of land that now forms the southern part of Arizona and New Mexico. This deal was known as the Gadsden Purchase. Including Texas, the United States had gained a huge area of over 1 million square miles. It had good soil, many natural resources, and ports on the coast of California.

Who arranged for the Treaty of Guadalupe Hidalgo?

3.8 The California Boom. Once the United States gained control over large areas of the West, Americans began moving into

Mobility

CONCEPT

Mobility means the process of moving or being moved. Americans in the 1700's and 1800's were characterized by movement. Artisans traveled from town to town to find work. Entire families moved to the frontier for more land.

Mobility can also mean a change in social or economic positions. This social mobility is the movement within a social class or from one class to another. Social mobility also has been characteristic of American life.

The discovery of gold in 1849 in California made many people rich, changing their social and economic status. The possibility of finding gold lured many people to the West. Read the following selections from the diary of Walter Colton, the founder of the first newspaper in California. Colton lived during the gold rush days.

Monday, May 29. Our town was startled out of its quiet dreams to-day, by the announcement that gold had been discovered on the American Fork [River]. The men wondered and talked, and the women too; but neither believed. . . .

Tuesday, June 20. . . . The excitement produced was intense; and many were soon busy in their hasty preparations for a departure to the mines. The family who had kept house for me caught the moving infection. Husband and wife were both packing up; the blacksmith dropped his hammer, the carpenter his plane, the mason his trowel, the farmer his sickle, the baker his loaf. . . . All were off for the mines. . . . I don't blame [them] a whit; seven dollars a month, while others are making two or three hundred a day! that is too much for human nature to stand. . . .

Thursday, August 16. . . . a man, well known to me . . . worked on the Yuba river sixty-four days and brought back, as the result of his individual labor, five thousand three hundred and fifty-six dollars. . . . a boy, fourteen years of age . . . worked . . . fifty-four days, and brought back three thousand four hundred and sixty-seven dollars.

Answer the following questions.

1. Which examples does Colton provide to show mobility as movement from one place to another?
2. How does he show social mobility?
3. Would the mobility of the people have been the same without gold?

these new lands. One event which drew people to the West was the discovery of gold. In 1848, James Marshall found gold on the property of John Sutter in California. Word spread rapidly. By 1849, large numbers of people were making their way from the East to California by ship or overland. This movement was called the *gold rush*. During 1849, more than 80,000 people came to California from Europe, Mexico, China, and the United States. They were known as *"forty-niners"* because of the year in which most of them came. Gold mining camps were quickly set up in the mountain valleys of central California. San Francisco grew up as an important trading center and source of supplies.

Why were the people participating in the California gold rush known as "forty-niners"?

At first, there seemed to be a great deal of gold. Miners often found it near the surface of the earth where it was easy to mine. Only a few people, however, became rich mining for gold. Many were disappointed and returned home. Some left to try their luck in other gold or silver booms in Nevada, Colorado, and later in Montana. Others settled down to farming or business. As a result of the gold rush, the population of California increased rapidly. It became a state in 1850. Similar opportunities would soon bring people to other areas of the West.

How successful were most miners?

1. Who started the trade between Americans and the people of New Mexico?
2. Who set up the first American settlement in Texas?
3. Who were the military leaders in the Mexican War?
4. What brought people to California in 1849?

4. Indians and the Westward Movement

The movement of people and the expansion of the United States into the lands west of the Mississippi River had a great influence on the Indians of the area. At first, there was little contact between the Indians and the newcomers. As time went on, there was greater contact with the growing numbers of trappers, miners, and settlers moving into the West. This affected the Indians' ways of life and caused the loss of more and more Indian land.

4.1 Changes in Indian Life.   The Spanish exploration and settlement in the West had brought many changes in the Indians' ways of life. One of the most important changes came with the introduction of horses into North America. The Spaniards brought horses with them when they explored the Great Plains in the 1500's. Through raids and trading with the Spaniards and each other, many groups of Indians

The introduction of what resulted in a major change in the Indians' ways of life?

acquired horses. With horses, they could hunt buffalo more easily and travel over larger areas of land.

Trade with trappers, hunters, and settlers became important to some groups of Indians. Often, new products were introduced by the traders. One of the most important of these was the gun, which greatly affected the Indians' method of warfare. When forced to move, Indians sometimes had to learn new ways of making a living. Those who had been hunters had to take up farming in order to survive. The greatest change for the Indians of the West was the same as for the Indians of the East—the loss of their land.

4.2   The Indians' Loss of Land.   The trappers who first went to the West did not fight with the Indians. Trappers often worked with them and sometimes married Indian women. They were not there to settle and farm, and so they did not threaten Indian land. As settlers followed the trappers into the lands on which Indian groups lived or used for hunting, conflicts grew. In the 1840's, the federal government was concerned with protecting the wagon trains moving through Indian

What was at the root of Indian-white conflicts?

George Catlin painted this scene of Plains Indians hunting buffalo. How did horses make the hunt easier? How did horses change the Indians' ways of life? Why was the buffalo important to the Plains Indians?

lands in the Great Plains. It built forts along the Oregon Trail and assigned army troops to them.

In 1851, the Sioux, Cheyenne, Arapaho, and several other Plains groups met with a representative of the United States government. They signed the Fort Laramie Treaty of 1851. Under its terms, the Indians were to receive payment from the federal government in exchange for the settlers' right to pass through their lands. Boundaries were set on the hunting lands of each group. A similar treaty was signed with the Comanches and Kiowas at Fort Atkinson, Kansas, in 1853.

The treaties set boundaries on the lands of the Indians. This made it possible for the United States government to begin keeping Indian groups within certain limits. Eventually, this policy would lead to *reservations,* or separate areas set aside or reserved for the Indians by the government.

What are reservations?

As more and more settlers entered western lands, the government pushed the Indians into ever smaller areas. As land was taken by settlers, many of those Indians who had already been sent from the East to areas of the West were made to move again. Some groups of Indians in more remote areas of Arizona, Montana, and other parts of the West, were not affected much in the years before 1860. However, conflicts continued in the years after 1860 that would affect Indians in all areas.

1. What was the effect of the horse on the Indian people of the Great Plains?
2. What was the significance of the Fort Laramie Treaty of 1851?

5. Conclusion

The huge amount of land added to the United States during the 1840's gave the country a great store of natural resources and provided land for new settlers. In the years before 1860, most settlers passed through the Great Plains and the Rocky Mountains on their way to the Pacific coast. Some also moved into the rich lands of the lower Mississippi Valley.

When the major part of the westward movement was over, the United States was a larger, more powerful country. On the one hand, expansion strengthened the feelings of nationalism. On the other hand, it led to division. The new lands added new states to the nation. This raised the question of slavery again. Balancing the interests of slave and nonslave states would become a greater problem than ever before.

Chapter 13 Review

Main Points

1. Many Americans came to believe that it was the manifest destiny of the United States to expand to the Pacific Ocean.
2. Americans were attracted to the West by the desire for land, gold, and adventure.
3. Settlers moved west over established trails into land occupied by Indians and claimed by Mexico and Britain.
4. American settlers in Texas revolted against Mexico and established an independent country.
5. In the 1840's, the United States annexed Texas and the Oregon country.
6. Mexico's objection to the annexation of Texas led to war with the United States.
7. As a result of victory in the Mexican War, the United States gained control of a huge amount of land north of the Rio Grande and the Gila River. Later it bought the area south of the Gila River in the Gadsden Purchase.
8. Contact with new groups moving into the West caused great changes in the Indians' ways of life.
9. Settlers forced Indians off the land in the West and onto reservations.

Building Vocabulary

1. Identify the following:

   Zebulon Pike | Santa Anna | Stephen Kearny
   49th parallel | Alamo | John C. Frémont
   Marcus and Narcissa Whitman | James K. Polk | Bear Flag Republic
   "Oregon fever" | Zachary Taylor | Treaty of Guadalupe Hidalgo
   Mariano Guadalupe Vallejo | Winfield Scott | Gadsden Purchase
   Stephen Austin | | Fort Laramie Treaty

2. Define the following:

   manifest destiny | empresarios | gold rush
   expansionists | annexed | "forty-niners"
   joint occupation | | reservations

Remembering the Facts

1. What was the role of explorers and trappers in the westward movement?
2. Why did merchants, settlers, and political leaders want to expand the United States to the Pacific Ocean?
3. Which route did Americans follow in traveling to Oregon?
4. What happened to the Spanish missions in California when Mexico gained its independence from Spain?

5. What did the Mexican government ask of Americans who settled in Texas?
6. How did Texas become independent? How did it become part of the United States?
7. What were the provisions of the Treaty of Guadalupe Hidalgo?
8. Which discovery in California attracted many Americans to that area?
9. What changes did the horse make in the lives of the Plains Indians?
10. What did the government do to protect settlers moving into Indian lands?

Understanding the Facts

1. What attracted Americans to the area west of the Mississippi?
2. With which countries did conflicts develop as Americans moved west?
3. Why did Texas want to be independent of Mexico? Why did it want to join the United States?
4. What were the causes of the war between Mexico and the United States?
5. How did the westward movement of Americans affect the Indians who lived west of the Mississippi River?
6. What was the government policy toward the Indians during the 1850's?

Using Maps

Longitude and Latitude. Laws and treaties often set boundaries in terms of longitude and latitude. One example of this concerned Oregon. The Oregon country in the early 1800's extended from the Rocky Mountains westward to the Pacific Ocean and from latitude 42° to 54°40'. It was claimed by both Britain and the United States. In 1846, an agreeable boundary for the huge area was set.

The map on page 290 provides information concerning the disputed area of Oregon. Review what you know about longitude and latitude. Study the map, and then answer the following questions.

1. Does the line 54°40' refer to north latitude or south latitude?
2. After the treaty of 1846, 54°40' set the boundary between which countries?
3. After 1846, 49° set the boundary between which countries?
4. After 1846, 42° set the boundary between which countries?
5. What is the distance north to south from 42° latitude to 49° latitude?

New Orleans 1845-1855

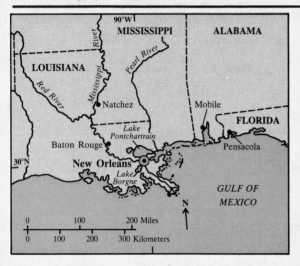

The French settlement of New Orleans was located about 100 miles (160 kilometers) from where the Mississippi River emptied into the Gulf of Mexico. During its early history, New Orleans had been controlled by first France, then Spain, then France again. In 1803, the United States had gotten New Orleans when it bought the Louisiana Territory from France. By the 1840's, New Orleans had become the third largest city in the country and a major southern port.

The Levees

The city was built on low land, almost as low as the river level in some areas. When northern snows melted in the spring, the river overflowed its banks and flooded many parts of the city. Early settlers began building walls of earth, or levees, to keep back the spring floods. In later years, more earth was added to the levees, and the walls grew high and wide. As the levees got wider, warehouses and roads were built on them. Ships and boats of all kinds were tied up at the docks along the levees. There the cargoes, or goods from the ships, were picked up or deposited. In New Orleans, the richest cargoes were usually those like Kentucky tobacco, Ohio flour, and cotton and sugar from plantations in Mississippi, Georgia, and Louisiana. Workers, called stevedores, moved the goods between the ships and warehouses. From New Orleans, the cargoes were carried in larger ships to the West Indies, Central and South America, Europe, and Africa. Goods brought to New Orleans from other countries were loaded onto steamboats and carried up the Mississippi River.

Visitors always found the levee exciting. Oakey Hall, from New York, wrote a description of the activity there in 1851:

A wilderness of ships and steamboats skirt it—if 'tis early morning. If but one short hour after sun-rise, the decks and wharfs are all astir, processions of loaded drays [heavy wagons] *are going by. . . . Thousands of hogsheads* [barrels], *bales, and bags and packages . . . sailors; stevedores; steamboat hands; clerks; planters; wealthy merchants too; running to and fro with* [many] *projects in their head. . . . A million dollars could not buy the articles of traffic* [trade goods] *taken in at one glance; articles of traffic that before twenty-four hours have gone by will all have disappeared. . . .*

French Influence

Although three different countries had controlled New Orleans at one time or another, France had the most influence over the culture and customs of the people. The children and grandchildren of the early French and Spanish settlers called themselves Creoles. They wanted to set themselves apart from the Anglo-Americans who came to New Orleans. The Anglos were Americans whose culture was most like the Anglo-Saxon people of Britain.

During the mid-1800's, the Creoles continued to follow French customs. French was the language used by the rich. People wore clothes designed after the latest French fashions and decorated their homes with French furniture. Many parents who could afford it sent their children to school in Paris.

The Code of Napoleon was the basis of Louisiana civil law, and legal proceedings were often conducted in French. Through the Creole influence, New Orleans became a center for opera and theater.

Many Peoples and Cultures

New Orleans was an exciting mixture of peoples. There were many blacks in the city, slave and free born. New Orleans was one of the country's main slave markets, yet there were about 10,000 free blacks living in the city. Some of them were very successful in business and the arts. Cecee Macarthy started an import business that was worth more than

Stevedores kept goods moving along the New Orleans levee. River boats carried products up and down the Mississippi River. Ocean ships sailed to and from foreign ports. What goods came through New Orleans?

$150,000 by the time she died in 1845. Armand Lanusse was a famous poet, and inventions of Norbert Rillieux were of value to the sugar industry.

As individuals, free white and black people often respected each other in New Orleans. Free blacks lived on the same city streets as whites. When they could afford it, they sent their children to private schools in America and France. As a group, however, the whites had almost all of the power and wealth. By the 1850's, more laws were passed to limit the rights of free blacks.

The demand for cheap labor drew many immigrants to New Orleans. Many died on the way or of yellow fever once they arrived in New Orleans. Since it had become illegal to import slaves from West Africa, those slaves that were already in New Orleans were too valuable to do heavy work. The European immigrants, especially the Irish, were hired to do the heaviest jobs of draining canals, paving streets, and improving the levees.

Northern visitors were often surprised by the way the people spent their Sundays. Bishop Whipple wrote in his journal:

. . . this is the day of military parade and review . . . a day of pomp and parade. . . .

Shops were open and singing and guitar playing in the streets, for which in New York or Philadelphia one would be put in prison.

Sunday was also a holiday for slaves in New Orleans. Many of them spent their time in Congo Square where they sang and danced in West African tradition. Some blacks in New Orleans continued to practice non-Christian religions brought from Africa and the West Indies. Most blacks attended Christian churches, usually Catholic, sometimes Baptist and Methodist. The Catholic church services were attended by whites and blacks together.

In other services, blacks usually were separated from whites. New Orleans also had a few churches that were only for blacks.

The Young People

Eliza Ripley wrote a book about her life in New Orleans. Her story has many examples of what it was like to grow up in that city.

In 1842 there was a class in Spanish at Mr. Hennen's house. . . . I was ten years old, but was allowed to join with some other members of my family, though my mother protested it was nonsense for a child like me and a waste of money. Father did not agree with her, and after over sixty years to think it over, I don't either. . . . years and years thereafter . . . while traveling in Mexico, some of the señor's teaching came [like a miracle] *back to me, bringing with*

Chocktaw Indians display produce in the French Market. What other nationalities made up the city's population, giving it an international flavor?

it enough Spanish to be of material help in that stranger country.

Ripley and her friends also had private lessons in music, singing, and dancing. Teachers were hired to give children lessons in polite manners. They were expected to learn how to walk gracefully and how to bow and curtsy properly. Ripley later wrote:

Is it any surprise that the miscellaneous education we girls of seventy years ago in New Orleans had access to, [ended] by fitting us for housewives and mothers, instead of [also teaching us to be] writers and platform speakers, doctors and lawyers . . . ?

The Homes

People had candelabras. . . . The candles in those gorgeous stands and an oil lamp on the [usual] center-table were supposed to furnish abundance of light for any occasion. . . . People sewed, embroidered, read and wrote and played chess evenings by candlelight, and except a few near-sighted people and the aged no one used glasses.

. . . Everybody in my early day had black haircloth furniture; maybe that was one reason red curtains were preferred. . . . However, as no moth [ate] it, dust did not rest on its slick, shiny surface, and it lasted forever, it had its advantages. [Many people had] a haircloth sofa, with a couple of hard, round pillows of the same . . . too slippery to nap on. . . .

Butler's pantry! My stars! Who ever heard of a butler's pantry, and sinks, and running water, and faucets inside houses? The only running water was a hydrant in the yard. . . .

Of course, every house had a storeroom . . . lined with shelves. . . . We had wire [boxes] on the back porch and a [metal-lined] box for the ice. . . . Ice was in

Many buildings in New Orleans are very decorative. Which group of people had the most influence on the culture of the people?

general use but very expensive. It was brought by ship from the North. . . .

The population of New Orleans had grown rapidly during the mid-1800's. The people who had lived there for many years were proud of their city.

"How do you like the city?" inquires an old resident. While you hesitate for an answer, himself replies:

"Excellently, of course; fine commercial advantages, eh?—the store-house of the Mississippi Valley—great destiny ahead."

1. Where was New Orleans located?
2. What is a levee?
3. What groups of people lived in New Orleans?
4. What did young people study during this period in New Orleans?

San Francisco 1845-1855

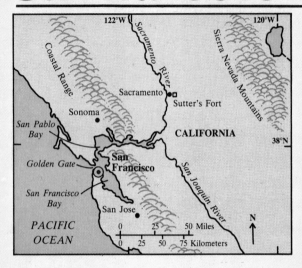

The city of San Francisco began as a village near a Spanish mission run by priests from the order of Saint Francis of Assisi. The village was often called the village of Saint Francis or *pueblo de San Francisco*. It was started halfway up the coast of California. It was built on an arm of land that reached out between the Pacific Ocean and a beautiful bay. A natural deep- water channel connected the bay to the ocean. This made San Francisco one of the finest and safest seaports in the world.

At the end of the Mexican War, California became part of the United States. Once people in the East learned about the rich soil and good weather, they began to move west.

Gold!

By the spring of 1848, the quiet growth of San Francisco ended. Gold had been discovered in the nearby Sierra Nevada Mountains.

San Francisco's *Californian* newspaper printed its last issue in May. In it, the owners wrote that the paper was closing down because they could not find anyone to work on it. Almost all of the 800 people living in the town had gone off to look for gold.

The whole country . . . resounds with the sordid [greedy] cry of gold! GOLD!! GOLD!!!—while the field is left half planted, the house half built, and every thing neglected . . . one man obtained one hundred and twenty-eight dollars' worth of the real stuff [gold] in one day's washing, and the average for all concerned is twenty dollars per [day]!

People arrived from all over the world—from South America, Europe, Australia, Asia, Mexico, and Canada. They traveled to California by land and by sea.

Golden Opportunities

As thousands of people came to California, new towns were started, and older towns became large cities. Those people who came by sea often landed first at San Francisco. Merchants in the city soon made it a supply center for the miners. One historian wrote in 1855:

A short experience of the mines had satisfied most of the citizens of San Francisco that . . . all was not gold that glittered, and that hard work was not easy. . . . They returned very soon to their old quarters, and found that much greater profits, with far less labor, were to be found in supplying the necessities of the miners. . . .

The miners' work was, in fact, hard and uncomfortable. They usually stood in cold streams for hours to wash, or separate, the gold from the mud and gravel. After the loose

Levi Strauss sold canvas work clothes called blue jeans to gold miners. What other businesses began to support the needs of gold miners?

"washing" or digging. Everyone who sold anything kept scales on hand to weigh the gold, valued at $16 an ounce.

One person from New York named Levi Strauss arrived in San Francisco in 1850. He had a roll of canvas cloth and some new ideas for making strong work pants. In a few years, miners and farmers alike were buying the famous "Levi's" work clothes.

It was a rare thing to find people doing the same kind of work in San Francisco that they had done before coming to California. People who had been farmers or bankers could as easily earn money as bankers and storekeepers. There seemed to be many different ways to get rich.

All That Glitters

According to some San Francisco historians, "the place and habits of the people" were odd or different because there were so few women and children.

There was no such thing as a home to be found. . . . Both dwellings and places of business were either common canvas tents, or small rough board shanties [poorly built sheds], *or frame buildings of one story. Only the great gambling saloons, the hotels, restaurants, and a few public buildings and stores had any pretensions* [claims] *to size, comfort or elegance. . . .*

City Government

Within a year following the gold rush, the population of San Francisco had grown from 2,000 to 25,000 people. This rapid growth caused the local government to be in a state of confusion. In 1849, there were three different city councils, each claiming to be the official one. A newly elected official discussed the city problems.

gold was taken up, the miners had to dig for the rest of it. They often slept on the ground at night and seldom cooked a good meal at camp. Most miners suffered from sore hands, sore feet, and sore stomachs. So they came into town for company and comfort, as well as for supplies and news from home.

In a short time, there was more gold in San Francisco than there were goods to buy with it. Storekeepers charged very high prices, and people paid them. Many people made very large fortunes without a bit of

Law and Order

There was no clear government authority to establish order or to enforce laws. San Francisco was sometimes a very frightening city. Stealing, mugging, and murder were common, and criminals often went unpunished. Fires were a constant danger because of so many canvas tents and wooden buildings. Whole sections of the city burned to the ground in a few hours. Many people believed that some of the fires were set in order to cover up a robbery or murder.

The citizens became angry over the lack of law and order. John Nugent encouraged the forming of a vigilante committee in his newspaper *Herald:*

We are here without jails, . . . without a police sufficiently strong for the circumstances; and . . . with these [shortages] *we have a bankrupt city and an incompetent council. On whom must we depend for relieving the town from the desperate and abandoned scoundrels who now infest it? There is clearly no remedy for the existing evil but in the strong arms and stout souls of the citizens themselves. . . . Let us then organize a band of two or three hundred Regulators, composed of such men as have a stake in the town, and who are interested in the welfare of the community. . . . If two or three of these robbers and burglars were caught and treated to lynch law, their fellows would be more careful about future* [robberies]. *. . .*

By early spring, 100 people formed a merchants' night patrol. They divided into street patrols and worked different areas of the city once a week on eight-hour shifts. This merchant patrol was the beginning of the vigilante group which would take the law into its own hands. In early June 1851, a constitution signed by 716 people stated the rules of

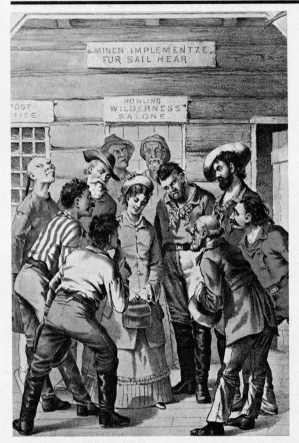

New arrivals in San Francisco were common. People came from all over the world to look for gold. Why were women and children a rare sight?

At this time we are without a dollar in the public treasury, and it is to be feared the city is greatly in debt. . . . You are without a single police officer or watchman, and have not the means of confining [holding] *a prisoner for an hour; neither have you a place to shelter, while living, sick and unfortunate strangers who may be cast upon our shores, or to bury them when dead. Public improvements are unknown in San Francisco. In short, you are without a single* [thing] *necessary for the promotion of prosperity, for the protection of property, or for the maintenance of order.*

San Francisco was a busy seaport by the middle of the 1850's. What became the economic base of the city after the gold rush years?

the vigilante committee. Money to run the group would come from donations from merchants, plus $5 from each member. Most members were well-educated and well-known in the community. They organized the vigilante committee like an army. Their headquarters was called Fort Gunnybags because of the barrier of sandbags placed on three sides of the building and piled eight feet high.

The committee organized a court, called the witnesses, and was judge and jury as well as executioner. Many people were worried about this means of handling the law. But the majority of citizens felt that it was the only way to restore order to the city. The committee was in existence twice during the 1850's. It captured, tried, and hanged several well-known criminals. It forced many others to leave the area. Although there were serious complaints against these groups because they had ignored the established system of law, no legal action was brought against the committee.

Gold to Goods, Again

By the middle of the 1850's, the California miner working alone had little chance of finding a rich strike. The gold was too deep in the earth to be taken out by hand. San Francisco had based its growth on the miners' gold. For a few years, the city suffered a panic and a depression as the supply of new gold grew smaller. Some miners went on to other western territories. Some returned, with or without gold, to their former homes. Many brought their families west and settled down in farming or business.

In the early years of the gold rush, the city was a wild and rough place. But almost overnight, San Francisco had changed from a quiet village into a major center of banking and trade. Ship captains from around the world continued to come to its excellent harbor. And the newly populated western lands continued to offer opportunities to people seeking adventure.

1. Who settled San Francisco?
2. Why is San Francisco such a good port?
3. Why did the population in San Francisco grow so rapidly?
4. Why were there so many fires in San Francisco?
5. Why was a vigilante committee formed?
6. How are San Francisco and New Orleans alike?
7. What kinds of people came to San Francisco and New Orleans? Why did they come?

Unit IV Review

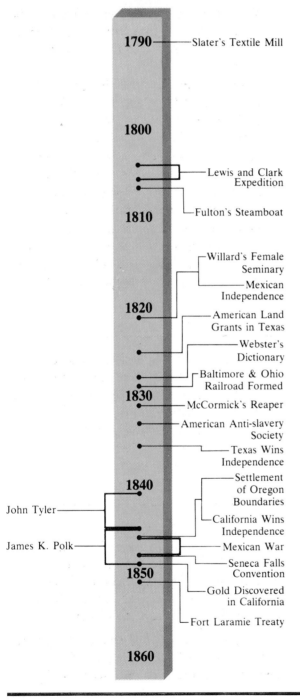

1790 —— Slater's Textile Mill

1800

Lewis and Clark Expedition

Fulton's Steamboat

1810

Willard's Female Seminary

Mexican Independence

American Land Grants in Texas

1820

Webster's Dictionary

Baltimore & Ohio Railroad Formed

1830

McCormick's Reaper

American Anti-slavery Society

Texas Wins Independence

Settlement of Oregon Boundaries

1840

John Tyler

California Wins Independence

James K. Polk

Mexican War

Seneca Falls Convention

1850

Gold Discovered in California

Fort Laramie Treaty

1860

Summary

1. The Age of Jackson saw a spirit of greater equality and progress which resulted in movements to improve American society.

2. The spirit of the Age of Jackson brought improvements in public education, better care for people with handicaps, reform of prisons, and demands for temperance, equal rights for women, and the abolition of slavery.

3. The early to middle 1800's was a period of major achievement concerning American literature, with American authors using new forms and themes to write about the country and its people.

4. The United States entered an Industrial Revolution in the early 1800's, beginning with the use of power-driven machinery in textile manufacturing.

5. New inventions helped to increase production in both industry and on the farm.

6. The rise of industry and improvements in transportation spurred major growth of American cities as immigrants and people from farm areas moved to them in search of better opportunities.

7. With a belief in manifest destiny and a desire for more land, Americans fought a war with Mexico, settled Oregon, and expanded their borders from the Atlantic to the Pacific.

8. With the exception of Alaska and Hawaii, the United States grew to its present size by 1853.

Unit Questions

1. Why was American literature in the 1800's, as expressed by writers such as Ralph Waldo Emerson, important to the development of the nation?

2. How were religion, philosophy, and the reform movements of the Jackson years related?

3. In what ways were the rise of industry, the development of a transportation system, and the growth of cities related to each other?

4. What section of the United States underwent the greatest changes as a result of the Industrial Revolution? What section or sections changed little and why?

5. What new territories were added to the country in the years from 1820 to 1850? In what different ways were they added?

6. Do you think that the changes in the nation to 1850 reflected more the philosophy of Thomas Jefferson or of Alexander Hamilton? Explain.

7. What circumstances or events before 1850 do you think clashed with the ideas of equality and progress as expressed in the Age of Jackson?

8. How do New Orleans and San Francisco reflect the expansion of the country in the mid-1800's? In what ways was each important to its section?

Suggested Activities

1. Find out information about when your school system was established. How is the system funded?

2. Using maps which show the country in the period from 1820 to 1850, decide where you would have built a railroad line. Between which points would it run? What would be its major function?

3. Find the size of covered wagons used in the 1840's. Make a list of important items which you think people needed for a move to the West.

Suggested Readings

Eggleston, Edward. *The Hoosier School Master*. Evanston, Illinois: McDougal-Littel & Co., 1977. Fictional account of the life of a rural school teacher in Indiana during the 1840's.

Flory, Jane. *The Golden Venture*. Boston: Houghton Mifflin Co., 1976. An 11-year-old girl's story of her trip and later life in the gold fields of the 1840's.

Nabokov, Peter (ed.). *Native American Testimony: An Anthology of Indian and White Relations. First Encounter to Dispossession*. New York: Thomas Y. Crowell Co., 1978. Firsthand accounts of Indians' views about relations with whites.

O'Dell, Scott. *Carlota*. Boston: Houghton Mifflin Co., 1977. The Mexican War as seen through the eyes of a young girl.

America
is
Division

Division *along economic, political, and social lines split the United States. Seldom before had a single nation of vast territorial expanse been made up of people with so many various backgrounds and outlooks. In a democratic society which encouraged free and open exchanges of ideas, differences were almost expected to occur. A variety of factors contributed to conflict and strife between people and regions. These same factors contributed to the difficulties in reuniting the nation.*

A Divided Nation

14

The North and South differed socially, economically, and politically. It was the conflict over slavery, however, that threatened to rip the two sections apart. Over what other issues did North and South disagree?

People in the United States had won a victory in the Mexican War and had settled the Oregon question. They had fulfilled what they thought of as the manifest destiny of their country. However, adding new territories also brought problems. The possibility of several new states in the Union raised the question of whether or not these states would allow slavery. Leaders in the North felt that it should not be allowed. Southern leaders, on the other hand, supported the spread of slavery. The struggle between the North and South became bitter, and there was talk of disunion and civil war.

1. Sectional Differences

Differences between the North and South did not begin or end with slavery. The two areas had been growing apart for more than 50 years. Social, economic, and political differences formed the background for the debate over slavery.

1.1 Social Differences. Different forms of social life had developed in the North and in the South. During colonial times, the sections shared certain social patterns. Most of the people were of British *heritage,* or background. They shared the same language, customs, and law. There were differences even then, however. In general, planters dominated social life in the South, while in the North, no single group set the pattern of living. Education was more widespread in the North than in the South.

How did the North and South differ socially?

In the years before 1860, the North changed more than the South, and the two areas became even less alike. The population of the North grew rapidly. Cities became important. Immigration brought a great variety of people to the northern states. The white population of the South grew slowly. Immigration into the South was also slow, and its impact was slight. The large number of black slaves in the South further set the two sections apart.

1.2 Economic Differences. The North and South also moved in different directions economically. In the early days of the United States, life in both parts of the country centered around farms and small villages. The South remained an agricultural area and did not develop much industry. Although most southern whites had small farms, the most important part of the southern economy was the large plantations. On them, tobacco, rice, sugar cane, and cotton were grown, using slave labor. Economic ideas changed slowly in the South. Southern leaders

How did the North and South differ economically?

The economy of the South was largely dependent on cotton picked by black labor. Notice the number of people who worked in the fields in this Currier and Ives lithograph. Why were so many people needed to produce cotton?

were generally against high taxes, government spending, and federal banks. They fought against raising tariff rates, since the South imported most of its manufactured goods.

After the War of 1812, the northern states rapidly began to build factories. Cities grew with the rise of industry. The building of factories required loans from banks. Northern leaders favored federal banks and government spending. They wanted government aid for building roads and making other transportation better. To protect the growing American industries, they favored higher tariffs on imported goods. While most people in the North also made a living by farming, industry was very important. Labor in the North was done by hired workers rather than by slaves.

1.3 Political Differences. In the country's early years, people in the North and South held similar political views. They believed in a constitutional form of government that placed limits on government actions and officials. They believed in a representative democracy in which government got its authority from the people. They also held a view of federalism that allowed each state to take care of its own affairs, while the federal government took care of national problems. In later

How did the North and South differ politically?

years, however, northern and southern states began to think differently about federalism.

One view was that the rights of states were above those of the federal government. This was the view first put forward in the Virginia and Kentucky Resolutions of 1798. It was later suggested at the Hartford Convention during the War of 1812 and by John C. Calhoun in his theory of nullification in the 1830's. As the debate over slavery became more bitter, many southern leaders came to favor the idea of states' rights. They depended on slavery for their wealth, and they felt that the federal government threatened it.

Northern leaders, on the other hand, supported the power of the federal government over that of the states. This view was stated in 1830 by Senator Daniel Webster of Massachusetts, when he argued with Robert Hayne against Calhoun's theory of nullification. People in the North thought that the federal government helped promote national unity and progress.

1. Which section developed an industrial economy?
2. In which section were slaves most important?
3. Which section strongly supported states' rights?

2. The Peculiar Institution

Slavery lay at the heart of the differences between the North and South. Southern whites called it the *"peculiar institution."* This did not mean that they thought slavery was strange or odd, but simply a way of life unique to the South.

What is meant by "peculiar institution"?

2.1 The Slave Trade. The first blacks brought to America were not slaves but indentured servants. They expected to be free after they had finished their terms of service. Later the status of indentured black servants was changed by law to that of slaves. The number of slaves grew slowly until 1713. Then the British took over the slave trade of North and South America, and the number of slaves grew rapidly.

What is the difference between slave and indentured servant?

The demand for slaves in the United States grew even more after the invention of the cotton gin in 1793 by Eli Whitney. In 1808, Congress stopped the importation of slaves. That year, there were about 1 million slaves in the United States. Despite the action of Congress, the system did not die out. Some slaves were smuggled into the country in the years after 1808, and the birthrate for slaves was very high. Between 1820 and 1850, the number of slaves rose from 1.5

million to over 3 million. Between 1850 and 1860, the number grew from 3 million to almost 4 million.

To where in the New World were most slaves brought?

Most of the slaves brought into the United States came from the west coast of Africa. Many of these landed first in the West Indies and later were moved north. Of the estimated 10 million slaves brought to the New World, one third went to Brazil, and many of the rest went to the Caribbean islands and parts of South America. Only about 5 percent of the people taken from Africa were brought to the United States.

2.2   People in Bondage.   Slaves were given a variety of tasks in the United States. Some worked in mines and others on the railroads. A small number of slaves worked as blacksmiths or carpenters in southern cities. The largest number of slaves, however, worked on plantations. Although some plantation slaves were household workers, most were field hands. They spent long hours growing tobacco, rice, sugar cane, and cotton. Solomon Northup, an escaped slave, told about work on one cotton plantation:

What did most slaves in the United States do?

> *The hands are required to be in the cotton fields as soon as it is light in the morning, and, with the exception of ten or fifteen minutes, which is given them at noon . . . they are not permitted to be a moment idle until it is too dark to see, and when the moon is full, they often times labor till the middle of the night. . . .*
>
> *The day's work over in the field, the baskets are . . . carried to the gin-house, where the cotton is weighed. . . . no matter how much* [a slave] *longs for sleep and rest—a slave never approaches the gin-house with* [a] *basket of cotton but with fear. If it falls short in weight . . .* [the slave] *knows that* [he or she] *must suffer. And if* [the slave] *has exceeded it by ten or twenty pounds . . .* [the owner] *will measure the next day's task accordingly.*

How were slaves considered property?

Slaves were most often thought of as property. They could be moved around and sold as their owners wished. The sale of slaves was done at *auctions*—public sales where goods or slaves are sold to the person who offers the most money for them. Often families were broken up when children were sold to different owners than those of their parents. Parents were often separated as well.

Every southern state had *slave codes,* or laws which controlled the lives of blacks. For slaves to learn to read and write was against the law, and their religious teaching was carefully watched. The daily lives of slaves were spelled out in detail. Punishments such as whipping, branding, and even death were given to slaves breaking these laws.

The number of southern whites who owned slaves was fairly small. Only about one fourth owned slaves or were members of a family which owned them. Also, most slave owners had a small number of slaves. In 1850, over one half of all slave owners had fewer than five slaves. Less than 1 percent had more than 100 slaves. Even the whites who owned no slaves were not in favor of ending the system, however. For the most part, these people believed that slavery was the only way to control blacks and allow blacks and whites to live together.

2.3 Forms of Slave Protest.   Although slaves had no rights, they were still able to work against the system of slavery. They made up songs and stories which helped them cope with their lives. Also, some slaves slowed down their work or damaged their tools. These things had to be done carefully and in secret for fear of punishment.

What forms did slave protests take?

Sometimes slaves revolted against their condition. These revolts almost always ended in failure, and most often resulted in death for those who took part. In 1800, more than 1,000 slaves led by Gabriel Prosser and Jack Bowler planned an attack on Richmond, Virginia. Their plans were discovered, and the leaders, along with some 14 other people, were put to death. In 1822, Denmark Vesey, a free black,

Slaves were regarded by many people as property which could be bought or sold. Like any product, they were advertised (left). Some slaves were sold by slave dealers (right). How was the sale of slaves most often done?

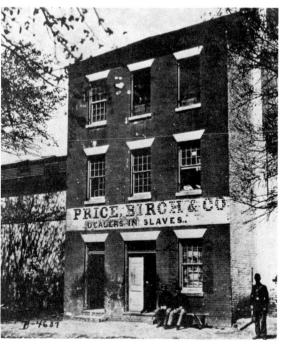

Slaves seldom won their freedom through the courts or by buying it. This painting is "Slaves Escaping Through a Swamp" by Thomas Moran. What risks did runaway slaves face if they were caught?

planned an uprising in Charleston, South Carolina. Again, the plans were discovered. Vesey and more than 30 others were put to death.

One slave revolt almost succeeded. It caused great fear among southern whites. The revolt was led by Nat Turner in 1831. Close to 60 white people were killed before Turner's rebellion in Southampton County, Virginia, was ended by state and federal troops. More than 100 blacks lost their lives in the fighting. A number of people, including Turner, were put to death. Fear of other slave revolts led whites to tighten controls over slaves.

Why did the Nat Turner revolt cause such great fear among southern whites?

Escape from slavery was also a form of protest. Since travel by slaves was closely watched, escape was difficult and dangerous. The chance of being caught was great. Slaves tried to leave the South and make their way north across the Ohio River or into Pennsylvania. They could be stopped by whites and asked for papers showing they could travel. Once an owner discovered a slave missing, a hunt began for the slave's capture and return.

What was the Underground Railroad?

Escaped slaves were not really safe until they reached Canada. They were often helped in their escape by people who were against slavery. These people served as *conductors* on a secret escape network known as the Underground Railroad. The slaves were led from one *station,* or safe place, to another until they reached safety. Harriet Tubman, herself a runaway slave, returned to the South many times and helped over 300 people escape to freedom.

2.4 Northern Attitudes Toward Slavery. The feelings of people in the North about slavery were mixed. Not all northern whites

Frederick Douglass (1817–1895)
PROFILE

In 1838, Frederick Douglass fled slavery in Tuckahoe, Maryland, for freedom in New Bedford, Massachusetts. In 1840, at a meeting of the Massachusetts Antislavery Society, Douglass told what freedom meant to him. He so impressed the abolitionists that they hired him to speak about his life as a slave. Douglass worked for the end of slavery and the end of unfair treatment of free black people everywhere.

Douglass wrote his autobiography in 1845. Because of his growing fame, he was concerned that some people might try to send him back to slavery. So he went to Europe for two years.

In England and Ireland, Douglass spoke to abolitionist groups.

With enough money from his book to buy his freedom, Douglass returned to the United States, settling in Rochester, New York. Douglass continued to work for the antislavery movement by starting a newspaper, the *North Star*. And he continued to oppose the discrimination he and other black people faced.

Douglass led attacks on separate seating for blacks and whites on trains and separate schools. He worked hard for equal rights for black people. Douglass was the leading supporter of liberty and justice for American black people in the 1800's.

---

were against it. Many, perhaps the majority, were prejudiced against blacks, both free blacks in the North and slaves in the South. Of the people who were against slavery, there were some who simply did not want it to spread into new territories or states. Others, the abolitionists, wanted an end to all slavery. Free blacks, such as Sojourner Truth and Frederick Douglass, went even further. They worked for equal treatment of blacks in America.

What were northern attitudes toward slavery?

2.5 Southern Response. The response of southern whites to the move to end slavery took several forms. At first, those people who favored slavery were most upset by abolitionists. Southern leaders felt that these people encouraged slaves to revolt. They tried to keep antislavery speakers out of their states. Post office workers in the South would not deliver mail about abolitionist ideas. In 1836, southern

How did southerners react to abolitionists?

members of the House of Representatives pushed through a *gag rule.* This law prevented the reading of antislavery petitions in the House.

As things grew worse between the North and South, southern leaders began to change their approach. They said that slavery was necessary to the economy of the South and the United States. They pointed out that the export of cotton paid for most of the country's imported goods. Southern whites also argued that slavery had existed in many societies in the past. They said that the working conditions in many northern factories were worse than those of the slaves. They pointed out that some factory workers earned barely enough money to live, while most slaves were well fed, clothed, and given shelter.

What arguments did southerners use to defend slavery?

1. What invention increased the demand for slaves?
2. How did the number of slaves in the United States change between 1820 and 1850?
3. Why did some people who did not own slaves favor slavery?
4. What were the goals of the abolitionists?

3. Slavery and Politics

Before the 1840's, leaders in both the North and South had tried to keep slavery out of politics. Neither of the major parties would take a stand on the issue. Both the Democrats and the Whigs drew support from all areas of the country, and they did not want to lose it. Arguments for and against slavery were presented, for the most part, by reformers or authors. Beginning in the 1840's, however, the slavery question came to dominate politics.

Why would the major parties not take a stand on slavery?

3.1 The Missouri Compromise. Representatives in Congress from the slave and free states had always looked out for the interests of their section. There was an uneasy balance of power in the Senate. Slave states and free states had been admitted in equal numbers and had equal numbers of Senators. In 1819, a bill had come up in Congress for the admission of Missouri as a state. Senator James Tallmadge of New York presented an amendment to the bill which would outlaw slavery in Missouri. Slaves already in Missouri would be *emancipated,* or set free. Southern representatives were against this idea. They felt it would upset the balance of power in the Senate in favor of the North. A deadlock resulted between northern and southern leaders in Congress.

Henry Clay of Kentucky played a major part in getting both sides to agree to a new compromise bill in 1820. In his plan, Missouri would be

Sectionalism

Slavery was at the heart of the sectional conflict which erupted in the 1840's. It often became an issue in debates in Congress. During the Mexican War, David Wilmot of Pennsylvania told the House of Representatives:

. . . we are fighting this war for Texas and for the South. I affirm it, every intelligent man knows it, Texas is the primary cause of this war; for this, sir, northern treasure is being exhausted and northern blood poured out upon the plains of Mexico. We are . . . cheerfully fighting this war for Texas; and yet we seek not to change the character of her institutions. Slavery is there; there let it remain. . . .

Now, sir, we are told that California is ours; that New Mexico is ours. . . . They are free. Shall they remain free? . . .

Slavery follows in the rear of our armies. . . . Shall this Government depart from its neutrality on this question and lend its power and influence to plant slavery in these Territories? There is no question of abolition here, sir. Shall the South be permitted by aggression, by invasion of the right, by subduing free territory and planting slavery upon it, to wrest

these provinces from northern freemen. . . .

Two years later, Robert Toombs of Georgia told the House:

. . . if by your legislation . . . [the North seeks] to drive us from the territories of California and New Mexico, purchased by the common blood and treasure of the whole people, . . . I am for disunion. . . . The Territories are the common property of the people of the United States. . . . it is your duty, while they are in a territorial state, to remove all impediments to their free enjoyment by all sections and people of the Union, the slaveholder and the non-slaveholder.

Neither person speaks out against the existence of slavery. After you have read these statements, answer the following questions.

1. What is it about slavery over which the two speakers differ?
2. What reflects different views based on the home states of these members of Congress?
3. What are the chances of compromise between the views expressed?

admitted to the Union as a slave state. To balance Missouri, Maine, which had been part of Massachusetts, would become a free state. Slavery would not be allowed in the rest of the Louisiana Territory north of latitude 36°30′, the southern border of Missouri. The Missouri Compromise settled slavery as a political question for the next 25 years.

3.2 The Wilmot Proviso and Popular Sovereignty. The question of slavery in new lands came up again when the United States went to war with Mexico. In August 1846, Representative David Wilmot of Pennsylvania put forth an amendment to a bill in Congress. It would outlaw slavery in any of the lands won from Mexico. Southern representatives were against the Wilmot Proviso, and it failed to pass.

In 1847, Senator Lewis Cass of Michigan came up with a plan called *popular sovereignty.* Under this plan, the people of each territory would decide for themselves whether or not to allow slavery. Cass' idea did not settle the problem.

3.3 The Free-Soil Party. In 1848, the Democrats chose Senator Cass to run for President. The Whigs chose General Zachary Taylor, who was well-known from the Mexican War, as their candidate. Neither party would take a stand against slavery. People in both parties who were strongly against slavery joined with members of the old Liberty party. They formed the Free-Soil party and asked Martin Van Buren to run for President. Members of the Free-Soil party favored the Wilmot Proviso, free homesteads for western settlers, and federal money for internal improvements.

Zachary Taylor was elected President in 1848. Although the Free-Soil party lost, it did serve to bring the question of slavery's expansion to the country's attention. Feelings on both sides grew sharper. When Congress met in 1849, the debate over slavery ended in another deadlock. Northern members refused to vote on any bills until slavery was outlawed in all new lands. Southern members refused to vote for any measure which would not allow slave owners to take their slaves anywhere they wished.

3.4 The Compromise of 1850. The deadlock centered around the lands recently won from Mexico. New states, formed from these areas, could upset the balance in the Senate between the North and South. To prevent trouble, Henry Clay came up with a compromise.

In the Compromise of 1850, California was admitted to the Union as a free state. This would balance Texas, which had been added as a slave state in 1845. The rest of the Mexican lands were formed into two territories, New Mexico and Utah. The people of these areas were to decide about slavery according to the popular sovereignty ideas of Cass.

New Mexico later voted to become a slave territory, and Utah voted to be free. The slave trade was stopped in the District of Columbia. A Fugitive Slave Act was passed. This called for the use of federal officers to catch *fugitive,* or runaway, slaves. Land claimed by both Texas and New Mexico was given to New Mexico. In return, Texas was paid $10 million by the federal government.

1. Which political parties were against the spread of slavery?
2. What was the purpose of the Free-Soil party?
3. What did the North and South gain from the Compromise of 1850?

4. The Road to Disunion

The Compromise of 1850 seemed to be a success. But it did not give the country a long period of peace. Both the North and the South were reaching the point where they were no longer willing to compromise. There were many events in the next ten years which kept the slavery issue before the American people.

Uncle Tom's Cabin (left) was written by Harriet Beecher Stowe (right) to promote the antislavery cause. Over 10,000 copies of it were sold in one week in 1852. Where did this book probably sell the best?

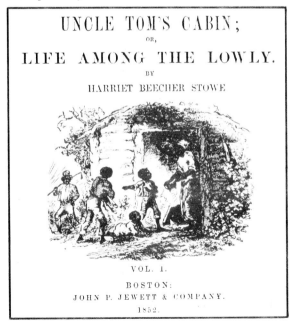

Why did the Fugitive Slave Act harden northern opinion against slavery?

4.1 The Fugitive Slave Act.   One thing which hardened northern opinion against slavery was the new Fugitive Slave Act. It said that federal law officers were to help catch escaped slaves. Anyone helping a slave could be fined or put in jail. The oath of a slave owner was all that was needed to prove that a black person was an escaped slave. No trial was allowed. In response to this act, many northern states passed *personal liberty laws*. These laws stopped state and local officials from obeying the federal fugitive slave laws.

Who wrote Uncle Tom's Cabin?

4.2 An American Best-Seller.   In 1852, a book was printed which greatly added to the tensions between the North and South. *Uncle Tom's Cabin* had been written by Harriet Beecher Stowe. It was a dramatic story of slave life. The book was a huge success, selling over 300,000 copies its first year in print. *Uncle Tom's Cabin* was also made into a stage play. Many people were moved by the story and joined the fight to end slavery.

What was the Kansas-Nebraska Act?

4.3 The Kansas-Nebraska Act.   The brief peace which resulted from the Compromise of 1850 came to an end in 1854. Senator Stephen Douglas of Illinois introduced a bill in Congress to organize the lands north of latitude 36°30' into the territories of Kansas and Nebraska. Douglas wanted the United States government to help build a railroad from Chicago to the Pacific Ocean. Once the area was organized, the government could give land to companies to build railroads. These companies could then sell land to settlers who would provide business for the railroads.

Douglas wanted to gain the support of southern members of Congress. He said that people in these new areas could decide about slavery on the basis of popular sovereignty. This would repeal that part of the Missouri Compromise which kept slavery from spreading into the area north of latitude 36°30'. Douglas' bill opened the slavery question in Congress again. Southern members favored the bill, while northern members hoped to defeat it. They were not able to do so, however. The Kansas-Nebraska Act became law in May 1854.

4.4 Bleeding Kansas.   Kansas became the center of the battle over slavery. Both the North and South wanted to control the area and sent people to live in Kansas. Antislavery business leaders, such as Amos Lawrence of Boston and Moses Grinnell of New York, formed groups to help people who wanted to move to Kansas. People moved into the area from the free states of Ohio, Indiana, and Illinois. Settlers favoring slavery moved into the area from Missouri.

During local elections, large numbers of people from Missouri crossed into Kansas. They voted for candidates favoring slavery and then returned to their homes. By 1856, there were two governments in the territory—one proslavery and one antislavery. Things in Kansas grew worse. In May 1856, people favoring slavery set fire to the town of Lawrence. Three days later, John Brown and several others killed five people at the proslavery settlement of Potawatomie Creek. In the 1850's, the territory became known as "Bleeding Kansas."

What events led to Kansas becoming known as "Bleeding Kansas"?

4.5   The Election of 1856.   The slavery issue brought the end of the Whig party. Many northern Whigs joined with members of the Free-Soil party and some antislavery Democrats to form another party in 1854. This new Republican party stood for the repeal of the Fugitive Slave Act and the Kansas-Nebraska Act. The party was not in favor of abolition, but it did want to stop the spread of slavery. It drew nearly all of its support from the North.

Against the background of violence in Kansas, the end of the Whig party, and the rise of the Republican party, the election of 1856 took place. The Democrats supported the Kansas-Nebraska Act and made no move against slavery. They chose James Buchanan of Pennsylvania to run. They hoped that he would appeal to people in both the North and the South. The Republicans chose John C. Frémont. They came out against the spread of slavery and for adding Kansas to the Union as a free state. Buchanan was elected President in 1856. The Republicans won a surprising number of votes. The election showed the rapid growth of the party, and this alarmed Southern leaders.

Who were the candidates in the election of 1856?

4.6   The Dred Scott Case.   During these years, many people feared that the Union was splitting apart. Leaders in the North and

The Battle of Hickory Point, near Lawrence, Kansas, intensified sectionalism. Fighting resulted when opposing forces struggled for control of Kansas. What forces fought for the territory?

South could not agree about slavery in the territories. The Supreme Court seemed to offer hope for a solution. It was considering an important case from a Missouri court about a slave named Dred Scott.

What was the Dred Scott case?

Scott was the slave of an army doctor who lived in Missouri. He had been taken by the doctor into Illinois, a free state, and into a territory (later Minnesota) where Congress had forbidden slavery. Scott believed that he had become free because of his stay in free territory. One Missouri court held that Scott was free, while the state supreme court ruled that he was still a slave. The case was taken to the Supreme Court of the United States.

Two days after President Buchanan took office in March 1857, the Supreme Court handed down its decision. Chief Justice Roger B. Taney gave the Court's opinion. He said that Scott was not a citizen. So he did not have the right to take a case to court. Taney denied Scott's claim that he was free. Taney also said that the Missouri Compromise was unconstitutional because Congress had no power to keep slavery out of territories. Slaves were thought of as property. According to the Fifth Amendment, a person's property could not be taken away without due process of law. Taney also said that Congress could not stop citizens from taking their slaves into free territories.

What was the Dred Scott decision?

Southern leaders hailed Taney's decision. They felt that it supported their views on the spread of slavery. Republicans and many northern Democrats were strongly against it. The Kansas-Nebraska Act had said that the people could decide about slavery in each territory. The Dred Scott case suggested that slavery could not be kept out of territories, even if the settlers voted against it.

4.7   The Lincoln-Douglas Debates.   Many Democrats, in both the North and South, hoped to see Stephen Douglas run for President one day. To them, he seemed the best hope for saving the Union. In 1858, Republican Abraham Lincoln ran against Douglas for election to the Senate from Illinois. Lincoln challenged Douglas to a number of public debates, hoping to win votes. The two candidates covered the important questions of the day.

The most important meeting of the two was at Freeport, Illinois. There Lincoln asked Douglas to explain his support of both popular sovereignty and the Dred Scott decision. Lincoln pointed out that the two positions were in conflict. Popular sovereignty meant that the people could decide whether or not to have slavery in their territories. The Dred Scott decision said that the government, and therefore the people, could not stop slavery in these areas.

What was the conflict that Lincoln asked Douglas to explain?

Douglas stated that the people could keep slavery out if they wished. If they did not pass laws to protect slavery, it would not last.

Expansion of Slavery

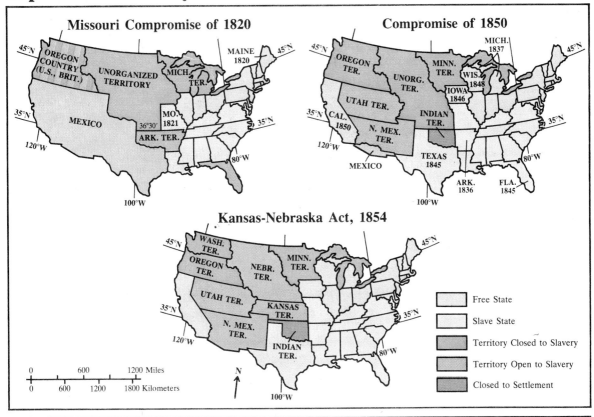

Missouri Compromise of 1820

Compromise of 1850

Kansas-Nebraska Act, 1854

Free State

Slave State

Territory Closed to Slavery

Territory Open to Slavery

Closed to Settlement

What resulted from the Missouri Compromise of 1820? How did the Compromise of 1850 affect the lands obtained from Mexico? Why did antislavery supporters oppose the Kansas-Nebraska Act of 1854?

Douglas won the election, but he lost much of his southern support for the Presidency. Lincoln, on the other hand, gained popularity in many parts of the North.

4.8 John Brown's Raid.   Bitterness between the North and South became even greater in the fall of 1859. John Brown, the Kansas abolitionist, formed a plan to give weapons to slaves and start a war for freedom. Brown and a small band of blacks and whites gathered at Harpers Ferry in what is now West Virginia. There they attacked the federal *arsenal,* a place where weapons are kept. United States troops under Colonel Robert E. Lee captured Brown and his followers after two days of battle. Brown and four others were hanged. The events at Harpers Ferry upset southern slave owners. They feared there would be

What was John Brown's raid?

other slave uprisings, planned by people from the North who were against slavery.

1. What was the Fugitive Slave Act?
2. When was the Republican party founded?
3. Why did many southern owners of slaves favor the Dred Scott decision?

5. The Final Break

In 1860, a presidential election was held. Judging by the election of 1856, the question of slavery would be central to the contest. Southern leaders were determined to see that the Republicans did not win. They thought the Republican party was a threat to their way of life.

5.1 Party Conventions. The Democrats held their convention in Charleston, South Carolina, only six months after the death of John Brown. Southern members feared that Stephen Douglas no longer favored slavery. They wanted him to accept a platform which protected slavery in the territories. When Douglas would not do this, delegates from eight southern states left, ending the convention. Northern Democrats met in Baltimore, where they chose Stephen Douglas. The southern Democrats later chose John C. Breckenridge of Kentucky.

What caused the split in the Democratic party in 1860?

Some Whigs and American party members also met at Baltimore. They formed the Constitutional-Union party. They wanted to gather support from both North and South and did not take a stand on slavery. John Bell of Tennessee was their candidate.

In May 1860, the Republican party convention opened in Chicago. With the Democratic party divided, they hoped to win. They chose Abraham Lincoln as their candidate. They wanted to stop the spread of slavery but did not demand that slaves in the South be freed.

5.2 The Election of 1860. The election was a four-way race among Lincoln, Douglas, Breckenridge, and Bell. Lincoln knew that he could get no support from the South and looked to the major cities in the North. As a result, he won 180 electoral votes from 18 free states. Breckenridge won 72 electoral votes from 11 slave states. Douglas and Bell finished far behind. The election showed how deeply the country was divided over slavery.

What did the election of 1860 show?

What was the southern response to Lincoln's election?

5.3 The Confederate States of America. Many southern leaders came to believe that *secession,* or withdrawing from the Union, was the only answer to Lincoln's election. On December 20, 1860, South Carolina voted to secede from the Union. Mississippi, Florida,

Election of 1860

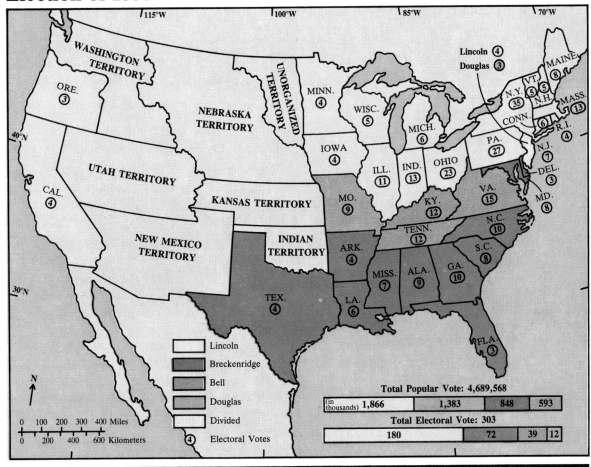

What section supported Abraham Lincoln in the election of 1860? Where was support for John C. Breckenridge the strongest? How was division in the United States over the slavery issue shown in the results of this election?

Alabama, Georgia, and Louisiana voted to leave the United States in January 1861. Texas withdrew in February.

Delegates from six of the seven states met in Montgomery, Alabama, in February 1861. They drew up a constitution for the Confederate States of America. It was much like that of the United States. Under this constitution, most of the power remained with the states. The Confederate congress could not pass laws against slavery or tariffs to protect industry. The delegates at Montgomery elected a president for a single six-year term. They chose Jefferson Davis of

With the election of Abraham Lincoln (left, seated at the far right) southern states began to leave the Union. The South organized under the leadership of Jefferson Davis (right, seated at the far left). When was the Confederacy established?

Mississippi for this office. Alexander Stephens of Georgia became the vice-president.

1. Who were the candidates for President in 1860?
2. Which states left the Union to form the Confederate States of America?

6. Conclusion

The social, economic, and political differences between the North and the South reached the breaking point over the question of slavery. The election of Abraham Lincoln in 1860 was seen by southern leaders as a signal to leave the Union. They believed that it was no longer possible to live in the same political system as the North. Southern people wanted their own system of government, with a society and an economy based on slavery. It remained to be seen whether the rest of the United States would allow the South to go its own way.

Chapter 14 Review

Main Points

1. For more than 50 years, political, social, and economic differences had been developing between the northern and southern sections of the country.
2. Views on slavery affected the way northerners and southerners came to feel about the nature of the Union.
3. Southern blacks often opposed slavery by revolting or trying to escape.
4. Northern abolitionists opposed slavery and its spread.
5. Owners of slaves considered slavery important to their way of life.
6. In spite of the efforts to compromise, slavery became a national issue.
7. After the election of Abraham Lincoln as President, seven southern states withdrew from the Union.

Building Vocabulary

1. Identify the following:

   Nat Turner
   Harriet Tubman
   Underground Railroad
   Frederick Douglass
   Henry Clay
   Missouri Compromise

   Wilmot Proviso
   Lewis Cass
   Zachary Taylor
   Compromise of 1850
   Fugitive Slave Act

   Harriet Beecher Stowe
   Stephen Douglas
   Dred Scott
   Abraham Lincoln
   John Brown
   Jefferson Davis

2. Define the following:

   heritage
   "peculiar institution"
   auctions
   slave codes
   conductors

   station
   gag rule
   emancipated
   popular sovereignty

   fugitive
   personal liberty laws
   arsenal
   secession

Remembering the Facts

1. What were the political, social, and economic differences which developed between the North and the South?
2. How many slaves were in the United States by 1850?
3. How were the lives of slaves restricted?
4. How did many slaves protest their bondage?
5. What were the abolitionists' attitudes toward slavery?

6. What were the efforts made to keep slavery from becoming a national issue on which people disagreed? What were the results?

7. How did the Kansas-Nebraska Act and the Dred Scott decision affect the efforts to compromise on the slavery issue?

8. What was the position of the Republican party on slavery?

9. Which event led southern states to secede from the Union?

Understanding the Facts

1. Why was states' rights tied closely to the slavery issue?

2. Why did the invention of the cotton gin increase the demand for slaves?

3. How was the life of a free person in the United States different from the life of a slave?

4. Why did neither major political party take a stand on the slavery issue before 1840?

5. Why did the compromises passed by Congress fail to prevent slavery from becoming a major issue in national politics?

Using Maps

Comparing Maps. Using two or more maps of the same area at different times can show change. The three maps on page 327 together show the expansion of slavery in the United States. Each map identifies the status of states and territories regarding slavery from 1820 to 1854. Study the maps, and answer the following questions.

1. Are these reference maps or thematic maps?

2. How many states existed in 1854 that did not at the time of the Missouri Compromise?

3. Were there more slave states or free states in 1820?

4. Were there more slave states or free states in 1850?

5. Were there more slave states or free states in 1854?

6. In 1854, was the total area of slave states and territories larger or smaller than the total area of free states and territories?

7. Considering the size of the area in which slavery was permitted, did the slave states gain or lose between 1820 and 1854?

8. Considering the number of states in which slavery existed, did the slave states gain or lose between 1820 and 1854?

The Civil War   15

Paul Philippoteaux painted this detail of the Battle of Gettysburg. During the war, one
of every four soldiers serving in the two armies was killed. Why was the Civil War fought
between the North and the South?

By early 1861, seven states of the lower South had seceded from the United States. The federal government faced a crisis. Allowing these states to leave would destroy the Union. But to save the Union, it might be necessary to use force. The use of force, of course, meant civil war for the nation.

1. The Opening Guns

Americans spent several anxious months from the election of Abraham Lincoln in late 1860 to the day he took office on March 4, 1861. Lincoln had not given his views about the South in public, and everyone wondered what he would do. Many people still hoped that a war between the North and the South could be avoided.

1.1 Lincoln's Inauguration. On February 11, 1861, Abraham Lincoln left his home in Springfield, Illinois, to begin the long journey to Washington, D.C. There had been reports that an attempt would be made on his life. So he entered Washington in disguise, after a secret train ride by night.

What did Lincoln try to do in his inaugural address? How?

In his inaugural speech, Lincoln tried to reassure the country. He said that he would do nothing to end slavery in the states where it already existed. He said that he believed the Union was *perpetual,* or everlasting, and that under the law, no state could leave it. Lincoln did not accept the secession of the lower South. To him, the Union was still unbroken. He said that he would carry out the law in all the states and protect government property in the states which were rebelling. Finally, Lincoln stated that he would preserve the Union at all costs.

1.2 The Fort Sumter Crisis. Early in 1861, the Confederate states had taken over many forts, arsenals, and navy yards in the South. Fort Sumter, on an island off Charleston, South Carolina, was one of the few remaining federal strongholds. The Confederacy thought of it as the property of a foreign power on southern soil.

Major Robert Anderson, commander of the fort, let President Lincoln know that he needed help. Lincoln knew that a relief ship sent to the fort might be taken as an act of war by the Confederacy. If he did not send relief, he felt that he would be failing in his duty as President. Lincoln finally decided to send a ship loaded with supplies only. He let South Carolina know what he had decided.

How did Lincoln try to handle the Fort Sumter crisis?

Southern leaders, however, saw this as an act of war. On the morning of April 12, 1861, Confederate cannons at Charleston opened fire on Fort Sumter. After 40 hours, soldiers in the fort surrendered. The firing on Fort Sumter marked the opening of the Civil War.

1.3 The Spread of Secession. The attack on the fort helped unify the North. Lincoln felt that the Confederate leaders, and not he, had taken the first step toward war. He issued a call for 75,000 volunteers for the army. The South saw this as a declaration of war. Jefferson Davis, president of the Confederacy, also called for volunteers to fight.

What did Lincoln do following the attack on Fort Sumter?

Until this time, eight slave states had remained with the Union. With President Lincoln's call for troops, Arkansas, North Carolina, Tennessee, and Virginia left the Union. This brought the number of Confederate states to 11. To the Confederates, Virginia was very important. Its large population and economy would benefit the South. With Virginia, the South also gained several experienced army officers, including Robert E. Lee. The capital of the Confederacy was moved from Montgomery, Alabama, to Richmond, Virginia.

Why was Virginia important to the Confederacy?

West Virginia seceded from Virginia in 1861 and was admitted to the Union in 1863. Some groups in Indian Territory backed the Union while others favored the Confederacy. What areas were the Union? What areas were the Confederacy?

Union and Confederacy

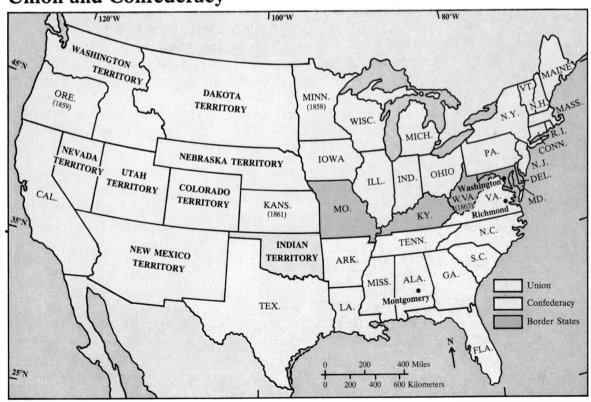

The remaining slave states—Missouri, Kentucky, Delaware, and Maryland—did not secede. These were the **border states,** located between the North and South. There, as in many other places, sentiment was divided. Part of Virginia, for example, refused to secede with the rest of the state. In 1863, 46 western counties joined the Union as the state of West Virginia. Even families were torn apart in this conflict, with some members joining the South, and others fighting for the North.

1.4 Union Plans and Advantages.

What was the Anaconda Plan?

The main goal of the leaders of the United States was to save the Union. General Winfield Scott was the commander of the Union army in 1861. He favored what was called the Anaconda Plan, after the snake which crushes its prey to death. The Union would blockade the Confederacy by sea from Norfolk, Virginia, to Texas. This would keep the South from sending out its cotton or bringing in supplies. Another part of the plan was to take over the Mississippi River and divide the South at that point. Also, the Union would invade the South and crush the Confederates there. On the foreign front, the North hoped to keep any European country from recognizing the Confederacy as a separate country. This would lessen the chance of outside aid for the South.

What were the Union's advantages?

The North had important advantages over the South. It had over twice the number of people and could raise large armies. Most of the factories which could make arms and other war supplies were in the North. Southern equipment often could not be replaced. The North had

Civil War armies used many innovations. In this drawing, Union soldiers set up telegraph lines. The telegraph improved communications among armies moving over great distances. Why were good communications important for an army to be successful?

Union and Confederate Resources, 1860

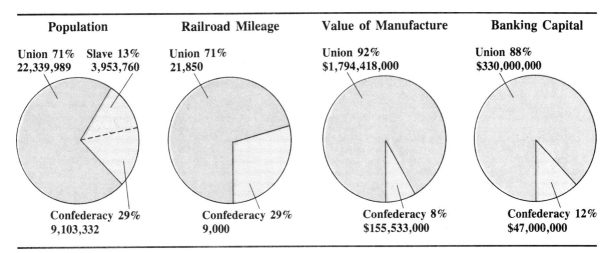

Population	Railroad Mileage	Value of Manufacture	Banking Capital
Union 71% Slave 13% 22,339,989 3,953,760	Union 71% 21,850	Union 92% $1,794,418,000	Union 88% $330,000,000
Confederacy 29% 9,103,332	Confederacy 29% 9,000	Confederacy 8% $155,533,000	Confederacy 12% $47,000,000

The Union had certain advantages over the Confederacy at the beginning of the war. These advantages were based on the resources of the two regions. How were most resources an advantage for the Union and a disadvantage for the Confederacy?

a better railroad system with more than 21,000 miles (33,600 kilometers) of track, to the South's 9,000 miles (15,300 kilometers). Finally, as the United States Navy became larger, the North gained the control of the sea.

1.5 Confederate Plans and Advantages.   The South also had certain advantages in 1861. The Confederates planned to fight a *defensive war.* That is, they would stay in their own area and defend it from attack. The South's army would be close to its cities and could get supplies easily. The soldiers would know the land in which they were fighting. Also, the South had many experienced military leaders. Army officers, such as Robert E. Lee, Thomas "Stonewall" Jackson, Joseph E. Johnston, and A. S. Johnston, had joined the Confederates.

What were the Confederacy's advantages?

Southern leaders hoped to get help from Europe, especially from France and Great Britain. They believed that British textile mills depended so much on southern cotton that Great Britain would aid the Confederacy to keep trade open. With European help, the South hoped to force the Union to recognize its independence.

1.6 The First Battle of Bull Run.   Many people in the North thought that General Scott's plan to defeat the South was not needed.

They thought that one quick victory over Confederate forces would end the war. President Lincoln gave in to the pressure for quick action. He allowed General Irvin McDowell to lead an attack on Richmond.

On July 16, 1861, McDowell's army of 30,000 marched out of Washington. They headed for the railroad junction at Manassas, Virginia. There, near a little stream called Bull Run, the Union soldiers met Confederate troops on the morning of July 21, 1861. The southern soldiers under General Pierre Beauregard defeated the Union troops. Retreat turned into flight as McDowell's soldiers headed back toward Washington. For the first time, people in the North began to see that it was going to be a long, hard war.

Why was the first Battle of Bull Run important?

1. When and where did the Civil War begin?
2. Which states had seceded from the Union after the start of the war?
3. Which slave states remained in the Union?
4. From which European countries did the Confederacy hope to get aid?

2. From Plans to Action

What did each side do following the first Battle of Bull Run?

After the Battle of Bull Run, both sides realized that their soldiers would have to have better training before battle. This was especially true of the North. The army of each side was larger than any before in America. The commanders of both the Union and Confederate forces had to learn how to direct groups of soldiers often numbering 50,000 or more. The months after Bull Run were spent in preparation as each side moved to put their plans into action.

2.1 The War in the West. The Union plan to take control of the Mississippi River met with more success than did the first campaigns in the East. On February 6, 1862, northern troops under Ulysses S. Grant moved up the Tennessee River. With the help of Union ships, they captured Fort Henry. Nearby Fort Donelson on the Cumberland River surrendered to Grant on February 16. The capture of these two forts opened much of the Confederate west to attack.

Who were the commanders at Shiloh?

Grant's army moved south on the Tennessee River to Pittsburg Landing, sometimes called Shiloh. On the morning of April 6, 1862, Confederates under General A. S. Johnston caught the Union army there by surprise. There was heavy fighting, and Grant drove the

The first encounter between ironclad ships happened in March 1862. The Union *Monitor* (left) clashed with the Confederate *Virginia* (right). As part of the Union navy, the *Virginia* had been named the *Merrimac*. What was the result of the battle of the ironclads?

Confederates off. After this Battle of Shiloh, Union forces controlled much of Tennessee and northern Mississippi.

2.2 The Naval Campaign. The most important task of the Union navy was to blockade the southern coast. At first, because there were few ships, this did not work well. *Blockade runners*—people who slipped goods through the blockade—were able to get through without much trouble. However, as the North began to build more and more ships, the blockade was tightened. Some ships were able to get to the South. But for the most part, the Union navy was able to stop southern trade. As the war went on, this had a disastrous effect on the South.

One real threat to the blockade was a Confederate ship, the *Virginia.* In 1861, this ship, then named the *Merrimac,* had been left by retreating Union forces. The Confederates recovered it and named it the *Virginia.* They turned it into an *ironclad,* a new kind of battleship covered with thick iron plates. The *Virginia* was based in Norfolk, which was blockaded by the Union navy.

What was the battle of the ironclads?

On March 8, 1862, the *Virginia* sank several Union ships in Norfolk harbor. The following day, the North sent in an ironclad of its own—the *Monitor.* The two ironclads shot at each other for five hours without doing much damage. The *Virginia* finally withdrew, and the blockade held. This had been the first battle between metal ships.

In April 1862, the Union navy under Admiral David Farragut took New Orleans. This limited Confederate use of the Mississippi River. Then Union troops took Memphis in June. This gave the North control of a great part of the Mississippi River.

What was the
Union's major ob-
jective in the East?

2.3 The War in the East.   The campaigns in the East were very important in the Civil War. The Union wanted to capture the Confederate capital at Richmond, Virginia. It also wanted to defeat the Army of Northern Virginia. This was the largest of the South's armies. Fighting against it was the Union's Army of the Potomac.

At first, there was a time of delays and no action. President Lincoln then ordered General George B. McClellan, who led the Army of the Potomac, to begin an operation to take Richmond. With the defeat of the *Virginia,* the Confederate navy could no longer prevent a move

How did the Union appear to be following General Winfield Scott's Anaconda Plan? Where did Confederate armies stop Union army advances? What was the purpose of the Union naval blockade?

Early Civil War (April 1861–July 1862)

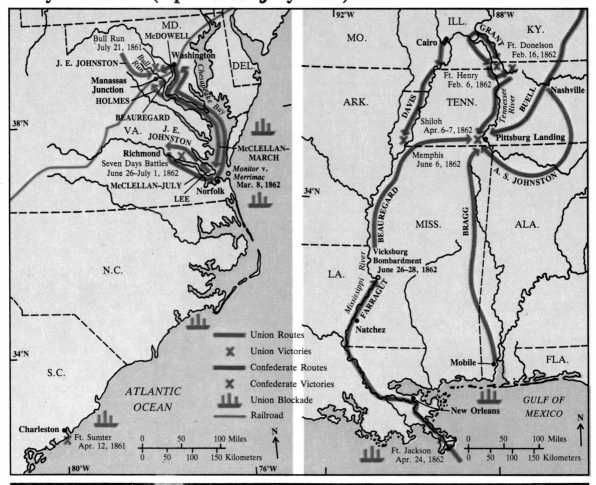

President Lincoln was an active commander in chief. In this Matthew Brady photograph, the President is shown visiting General George B. McClellan (facing the President) after the Battle of Antietam. Why did Lincoln consider Antietam an important Union victory?

against Richmond. So McClellan shipped over 100,000 soldiers by water to the peninsula between the York and James rivers in Virginia. Slow movement by the Union army allowed the Army of Northern Virginia, under General Robert E. Lee, to prepare defenses. After three months of fighting in this Peninsula Campaign, the Union army was forced back to the coast. The North had failed to take Richmond. President Lincoln replaced McClellan as commander of the Army of the Potomac.

Despite the change of command, northern forces in the East suffered one defeat after another. In August 1862, Lee defeated Union troops at the Second Battle of Bull Run. In September 1862, Lee decided to invade the North for the first time. He hoped that the sight of southern soldiers on Union soil might make Great Britain and France recognize and give aid to the Confederacy.

What did Lee hope to achieve by invading the North?

President Lincoln and other northern leaders were worried by the success of Lee's Army of Northern Virginia. Lincoln again made McClellan commander of the Army of the Potomac and ordered him to stop Lee. The two armies fought the Battle of Antietam in Maryland on September 17, 1862. Although McClellan did not win a clear victory, Lee's army withdrew to Virginia. More soldiers died during this one-day battle than during any other single day of the war. *Casualties,* or those people killed or wounded, were around 23,000.

2.4 The Emancipation Proclamation. President Lincoln believed that the war was being fought to save the Union, not to abolish

What was Lincoln's primary purpose in fighting the war?

slavery. In 1862, he wrote a letter to Horace Greeley of the New York *Tribune* explaining this view:

> *My* [main] *object in this struggle is to save the Union, and is not either to save or to destroy slavery. If I could save the Union without freeing any slave I would do it; and if I could save it by freeing all the slaves I would do it; and if I could save it by freeing some and leaving others alone I would also do that. . . . I have here stated my purpose according to my view of official duty; and I intend no* [change] *of my oft-expressed personal wish that all men every where could be free.*

Lincoln felt that making abolition the main goal of the war might divide the North. He did not want the slave states of Delaware, Maryland, Kentucky, and Missouri to leave the Union. As the move to end slavery grew stronger, however, Lincoln wanted to keep abolitionist support and still save the Union. He decided to take action against slavery in at least part of the South. This would help unite the North and hurt the Confederacy.

What did the Emancipation Proclamation state?

On September 22, 1862, shortly after the Battle of Antietam, Lincoln issued the Emancipation Proclamation. This **proclamation,** or official announcement, said that as of January 1, 1863, all slaves in Confederate lands would be "then, thenceforward, and forever free." This did not apply to the border states or to areas that had already been won back by the North. As Union armies took over more areas in the South, however, thousands of slaves were freed.

Nearly 200,000 blacks, most of whom had been slaves, joined the Union forces. Generally, they were not treated equally. They received lower pay and were often given jobs away from the fighting. However, during the last two years of the war, black soldiers took part in nearly every major battle.

1. Which western forts did the Union capture?
2. What were the early Confederate victories?
3. How active were blacks in fighting for the Union?

3. The War on the Home Front_____

The Civil War affected more people than any war in American history up to that time. It was no longer a matter of two small armies deciding the outcome, as in earlier years. The farms and factories on

The Civil War involved much of the population of both North and South. This drawing by Winslow Homer shows women filling cartridges at the Watertown Arsenal in Massachusetts. How else was the war supported on the home front?

How did the Civil War differ from earlier wars?

both sides had to provide the supplies needed for the huge armies and navies. Because of this, the war touched nearly every town and family in the country. It changed the lives of most Americans.

3.1 People at Home. For people in the North and the South alike, it was a terrible war. They were shocked by the large numbers of people being killed. While soldiers were fighting and dying on the battlefields, those at home did what they could to help the war effort.

In both the North and the South, women set up volunteer aid societies in churches, schools, and homes. They met to raise money, gather food, collect clothing, and roll bandages. Several women, such as Rose O'Neal Greenhow and Belle Boyd, became Confederate spies. In July 1861, Greenhow carried messages to Confederates about General Irvin McDowell's plans. This enabled the South to prepare for the first Battle of Bull Run. Belle Boyd was a messenger for Generals Beauregard and Jackson. She also smuggled medicines into the South and was a blockade runner.

At the beginning of the war, medical services were poor. The only real nursing care came from Catholic religious groups. In June 1861, the War Department made Dorothea Dix superintendent of nurses in the Union armies. Dix helped bring order into the hospitals of the North in spite of prejudice against women in the field of medicine. Clara Barton took medical supplies to the battlefields and nursed wounded soldiers. Mary Ann Bickerdyke brought sanitation and proper food to many Union army hospitals. By the end of the war, at least 3,200 women in both the North and South had served as nurses.

What women played important roles in medical improvements?

The Civil War   343

Clara Barton (1821–1912)
═══PROFILE═══

Clara Barton's goal in life was to bring comfort to people in trouble. In 1861, Barton began carrying supplies and nursing soldiers wounded in battle. Without help or encouragement from the government, she cared for the injured. She became known as the Angel of the Battlefield.

At the war's end, Barton set up an office to find information on the thousands of soldiers who were missing in action. In 1869, she traveled to Europe to recover from an illness. While in Switzerland, Barton learned of the International Committee of the Red Cross, which cared for the victims of war.

In 1881, Barton organized the American Red Cross. Under her leadership, this group raised money and expanded their efforts to aid victims of flood, fire, disease, and other disasters. Between 1881 and 1904, Barton provided relief without government help in 21 disasters. These included a forest fire in Michigan in 1881 and the Johnstown, Pennsylvania, flood in 1889.

The Red Cross goal was to get quickly to the scene of an emergency with relief—food, clothing, medicine, and materials for shelter. Because of Barton, the Red Cross provides relief in peace as well as in war.

3.2 Profits and Poverty.   Some people in the North gained much wealth because of the war. Farms in the Midwest became larger. The need for food grew because the soldiers had to be fed. Crop failures in parts of Europe made markets for American farm goods. Farmers bought more machines to replace workers who had gone off to war.

What was the status of farming during the war?

Some northern industries were hurt by the war, while others benefited from it. Certain textile plants, for example, had to shut down because there was not enough cotton. On the other hand, industries which made iron, cannons, movable bridges, and locomotives did well.

The prosperity brought about by the war was not spread evenly. Poor people and industrial workers usually did not share in the new wealth. Greater profits and higher taxes pushed up the price of many goods, such as food, gas, and firewood. Labor troubles grew as the war went on. Coal miners near Pittsburgh, dry-goods clerks in New York

City, shopkeepers in Boston, and newspaper workers in Chicago went on strike for higher wages during the war.

Life for people in the South was generally harder than for people in the North. Manufactured goods became scarce, and the price of food rose after the blockade was set up. Shortages became serious as the war dragged on. Butter sold for $15 a pound, bacon was $9 a pound, and potatoes sold for $25 a bushel. Sickness became a problem when the blockade cut off shipments of drugs and other medical supplies.

Why was life on the home front more difficult for southerners?

3.3 Soldiers for the Armies. At the beginning of the war, there was little problem getting enough soldiers to serve in the armed services. People were excited about the war. Enlistment tents were set up near busy streets, and recruits rushed to join up.

How did the South and the North get troops as the war continued?

As the war dragged on, the number of volunteers slowed. States offered *bounties*—payments of money to a person for entering the armed services. On April 14, 1862, the Confederate congress passed a law beginning the *draft*. This was a selection of people who would be forced to serve in the military. The Union did the same the following year. The draft was not popular, especially in some parts of the North. On both sides, those drafted could hire someone else to serve for them. Poor people, who could not hire substitutes, thought the draft was

"Come and Join Us Brothers" was a poster issued to urge more blacks to sign on for service in the Union army. Both North and South relied mostly on enlistments for the armed forces. How else were people persuaded to join the armies?

unfair to them. In July 1863, a draft riot took place in New York City. The crowds, 50,000 strong, burned many shops and attacked free blacks. Soldiers were brought in, and the riot ended after four days.

3.4   Financing the War.   Both the North and South were faced with the problem of finding enough money to pay for the war. The federal government borrowed money through the sale of bonds. It taxed the states and set up an income tax for the first time in America's history. It also issued paper money known as *greenbacks* that were not backed by either gold or silver. The government simply promised to redeem them in gold or silver at a later date. A national banking system was set up for the first time since the Age of Jackson.

What are greenbacks?

The South had more trouble paying for the war than the North did. Because it had to buy many supplies from Europe, the South ran out of cash early in the war. It hoped to raise money from European loans, using cotton and other cash crops as guarantees. Very little money, however, was raised in this way. The Confederate government set up a direct tax on the states, but it did not collect much money this way. The lack of cash became so great that the Confederacy began printing paper money which was not backed by gold or silver. The value of the money fell, and by the end of the war, it was almost worthless.

Why was it more difficult for the South to pay for the war?

3.5   Congress Without the South.   Republicans in the United States Congress took steps to pass laws which had been blocked before the war by southern members. Kansas came into the Union as a free state in 1861. Colorado, Nevada, and Dakota were admitted as free territories. Nevada then became a state in 1864. A new protective tariff for manufactured goods was passed. The Homestead Act of 1862 provided free land in the West for settlers. Also, two companies were chartered to build a railroad from Omaha, Nebraska, to California.

What territories were established during the war?

1. What were the roles of women during the war?
2. Which industries made a profit from the war?
3. How did the North and the South pay for the war?

4. The High Point of the Confederacy _____

Although the South had many problems, it continued to hold its own in the fighting. There were many people in the United States and in Europe who thought that the North would never be able to defeat the South. The fortunes of the Confederacy reached their high point in late

1862 and early 1863. Then events turned against the South, and the Union began the slow march toward victory.

4.1 Fredericksburg and Chancellorsville.   Shortly after the Battle of Antietam, President Lincoln again replaced McClellan as the Union commander in the East. General Ambrose Burnside led the Army of the Potomac in a march south to take Richmond. On December 13, 1862, the Union army attacked Lee's forces at Fredericksburg, Virginia. The Confederates were *entrenched,* or set up in a strong position, on a number of hills south of the town. They defeated the Army of the Potomac, with 11,000 casualties.

Who replaced McClellan as commander of the Army of the Potomac?

Once more, Lincoln changed commanders. In the spring of 1863, the Army of the Potomac under General Joseph Hooker again invaded Virginia. Hooker's forces clashed with Lee's Army of Northern Virginia near the town of Chancellorsville. The battle opened on May 2, and four days later, Hooker had to order his army to retreat. Lee had

Many volunteers on both sides were very young men who were drawn by the excitement of army travel. Where was the Confederate army's farthest northern advance? How far did McClellan's army travel from Washington to Antietam?

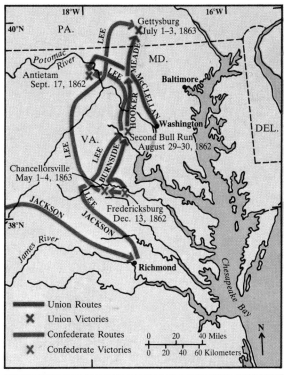

War in the East (1862–1863)

Union Routes
X Union Victories
Confederate Routes
X Confederate Victories

0   20   40 Miles
0 20 40 60 Kilometers

won another victory for the South. The losses on both sides were great, however. The South, in particular, had lost General Thomas "Stonewall" Jackson. Casualties for both sides were nearly 30,000.

4.2   The Battle of Gettysburg.   After winning at Fredericksburg and Chancellorsville, Lee decided to invade the North again. He believed that a southern victory on Union soil might force the North to give up the war. It might also persuade Great Britain and France to recognize the Confederacy.

What did Lee hope to accomplish by his second invasion of the North?

Lee's army marched north through the Shenandoah Valley of Virginia into Pennsylvania, heading for Harrisburg. From there, Lee hoped to be able to attack Philadelphia, Washington, or Baltimore. People all over the North were greatly worried. Lincoln replaced General Hooker with General George Meade and ordered him to stop Lee's army. The Army of the Potomac numbered nearly 100,000 against the Confederate army's 75,000.

On July 1, 1863, the two armies met near the small town of Gettysburg, Pennsylvania. For three days, the Confederate troops tried without success to break through the Union lines. On the afternoon of July 3 came the climax of the battle. General George Pickett led 15,000 soldiers against the heart of the Union's defense. "Pickett's Charge," as it was called, ended in failure.

What was Pickett's Charge?

Having suffered nearly 28,000 casualties, the Confederate army retreated. The Union losses were over 23,000 people killed or wounded. Lee's Army of Northern Virginia had suffered a major defeat in one of the most critical battles of the war.

4.3   The Fall of Vicksburg.   At about the same time that Lee was defeated at Gettysburg, General Ulysses S. Grant was fighting near the city of Vicksburg, Mississippi. On July 4, 1863, after a six-week siege, Vicksburg fell to Grant. The loss of Vicksburg cut off Arkansas and Texas from the rest of the South. With the fall of Vicksburg, the Mississippi River was completely in Union control.

1. What were the major battles fought in late 1862 and 1863?
2. Which battle stopped the Confederate invasion?
3. Why was the victory at Vicksburg important to the Union?

5. The Road to Appomattox

After the loss at Gettysburg and the fall of Vicksburg, events in the war more and more favored the North. Until these battles, Great

Using Speeches as Primary Sources
SKILL

On November 19, 1863, at least 50,000 people listened while President Abraham Lincoln spoke at Gettysburg, Pennsylvania. He was part of a dedication ceremony at a new national cemetery. In July, thousands had been hastily buried there after the Battle of Gettysburg.

The planners of the ceremony had invited Lincoln to come, but they did not expect him to attend while the war continued. Yet Lincoln wanted this opportunity to tell the people what he thought was the meaning of the war. He said:

Four score and seven years ago our fathers brought forth on this continent, a new nation, conceived in Liberty, and dedicated to the proposition that all men are created equal.

Now we are engaged in a great civil war, testing whether that nation or any nation so conceived and so dedicated, can long endure. We are met on a great battle-field of that war. We have come to dedicate a portion of that field, as a final resting place for those who here gave their lives that that nation might live. It is altogether fitting and proper that we should do this.

But, in a larger sense, we can not dedicate—we can not consecrate—we can not hallow—this ground. The brave men, living and dead, who struggled here, have consecrated it, far above our poor power to add or detract. The world will little note, nor long remember what we say here, but it can never forget what they did here. It is for us the living, rather, to be dedicated here to the unfinished work which they who fought here have thus far so nobly advanced. It is rather for us to be here dedicated to the great task remaining before us—that from these honored dead we take increased devotion to that cause for which they gave the last full measure of devotion—that we here highly resolve that these dead shall not have died in vain—that this nation, under God, shall have a new birth of freedom—and that government of the people, by the people, for the people, shall not perish from the earth.

Speeches are one kind of primary source. In studying a speech, it is important to think about more than just the words the speaker said. The following questions about the Gettysburg Address suggest some other things to consider.

1. When and where was it delivered?
2. Who was the audience?
3. Why did Lincoln make the speech?
4. According to Lincoln, why was the war being fought?

Last Phases of the War (1863–1865)

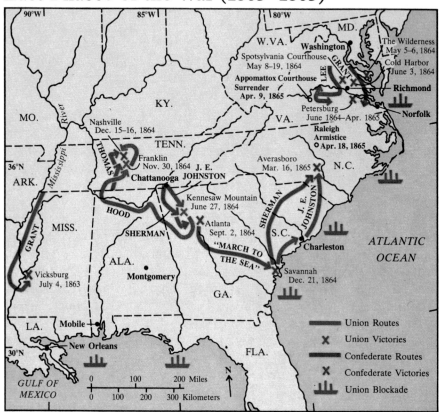

What did Grant accomplish by capturing Vicksburg? What was the purpose of Sherman's "March to the Sea"? Which series of battles in Virginia led to the Confederate surrender?

Britain had been thinking about recognizing the Confederacy. After the battles, it dropped the idea. Although the war was far from over, the advantage passed to the Union forces.

5.1 Grant in Command. In March 1864, after his success in the West, Grant was given command of all Union armies. He worked out a plan which would have these armies in the East and West working together. A large army under General William Sherman was to march out of Chattanooga, Tennessee, toward Atlanta. The Army of the Potomac would march on Richmond and Lee. The plan was designed to wear down the Confederates and destroy their will to fight.

What was Grant's plan for victory?

5.2 Sherman's March to the Sea. Sherman's army of nearly 100,000 soldiers left Chattanooga in May 1864, moving slowly toward Atlanta. Confederate troops under General Joseph Johnston tried to block the way but were forced back, greatly outnumbered. In September, Sherman's army entered Atlanta. The capture of the city was a great loss to the Confederacy. It was a major manufacturing center and the junction for several important railroads.

Sherman and his soldiers marched from Atlanta toward Savannah, Georgia and the Atlantic Ocean. Along the way, anything that might be used to help the South's war effort was destroyed. Crops, machinery, barns, and bridges were burned, and many miles of railroad track were torn up. On December 22, Sherman entered Savannah. From there, his forces moved north to join Grant in Virginia.

What was the "march to the sea"?

5.3   Grant Against Lee.   At the same time that Sherman was moving through Georgia, General Grant began the march toward Richmond. Grant knew that he had one important advantage—Union losses could be replaced, while those of the South could not. He felt that the war could be won if the larger and better-equipped northern army continued to pressure the Confederates.

What was Grant's advantage over Lee?

Grant led the Army of the Potomac into the wilderness area south of the Rappahannock River in Virginia. Lee's forces won the Battle of the Wilderness which took place on May 5 and 6, 1864. Grant then moved to the southeast and attacked Lee at Spotsylvania Courthouse. On June 3, Grant attacked Lee and was defeated at Cold Harbor. Near the railroad center of Petersburg, Virginia, the two armies dug in against each other again. Months of fighting followed. The number of casualties on both sides was very high in these battles, and Lee's army was slowly being reduced. In the spring of 1865, he decided to break away from Grant. Lee retreated west from Richmond only to find his

What battles took place between the armies of Grant and Lee?

General Robert E. Lee (right) surrendered the Confederacy's largest and most successful field army to General Ulysses S. Grant (left). As they met, officers from both sides were reunited with old friends and classmates. What did the Civil War accomplish?

army surrounded by federal soldiers. Lee knew his army could not continue to fight. The cause was lost.

On April 9, 1865, Lee and Grant met at the village of Appomattox Courthouse, Virginia. There the terms of surrender were worked out. Lee's forces laid down their arms and returned to their homes. A little over a month later, the last Confederate army under General Kirby Smith surrendered. The Civil War was over.

Who surrendered the last Confederate army?

5.4   With Malice Toward None.   Abraham Lincoln had been reelected President of the United States in 1864. As the war ended, he faced the task of rebuilding the country. He spoke of his plans in his second inaugural address.

What was the tone of Lincoln's second inaugural address?

> *With malice toward none, with charity for all, with firmness in the right as God gives us to see the right, let us strive on to finish the work we are in, to bind up the nation's wounds, to care for him who shall have borne the battle and for his widow and his orphan, to do all which may achieve and cherish a just and lasting peace among ourselves and with all nations.*

5.5   The Assassination of President Lincoln.   The plans of the President were cut short, however. On the night of April 14, 1865, only five days after Lee surrendered, President Lincoln went with his wife, Mary Todd Lincoln, to Ford's Theater. They were attending the play, *Our American Cousin.* There, Lincoln was ***assassinated***—killed by sudden or secret attack—by John Wilkes Booth, an actor who believed he was helping the Confederate cause. The death of Lincoln would prove tragic for the South. It lessened the chance for an easy peace.

Why was Lincoln's assassination a loss for the South?

1. Who commanded the Army of the Potomac in 1864?
2. When and where was the surrender?
3. When was Lincoln assassinated?

6. Conclusion

The Civil War was a turning point in American history. The North's victory saved the Union and ended the issue of federal authority versus states' rights. The war caused many problems, however. There were areas of the country which had to be rebuilt. There was great bitterness over the war. Sorrow had touched nearly every family in the country. About 2,400,000 soldiers had served in the two armies. Nearly 600,000 of them died. There was also the question of the freed slaves. It remained for them to become a truly equal part of American society.

Chapter 15 Review

Main Points

1. President Lincoln wanted to preserve the Union.

2. The Civil War began when Lincoln ordered supplies to Fort Sumter in South Carolina. Southern leaders then ordered an attack on the fort.

3. When Lincoln called for troops to put down the rebellion, Arkansas, North Carolina, Tennessee, and Virginia seceded. This brought the total of Confederate states to 11.

4. The Union had the advantages of a larger population, more industry, and better transportation.

5. The Confederacy had the advantages of better military leadership and shorter supply lines.

6. The Civil War was a long conflict with many casualties on both sides.

7. The Emancipation Proclamation laid the basis for freeing the slaves as the Union army took over areas formerly under Confederate control.

8. Many blacks fought in the Union army.

9. Many women in the North and the South took over jobs which had been done by men.

10. The Civil War ended when Lee surrendered to Grant at Appomattox Courthouse on April 9, 1865.

11. Lincoln was assassinated by John Wilkes Booth on April 14, 1865.

12. Lincoln's death lessened the chance for a peaceful rebuilding of the nation.

Building Vocabulary

1. Identify the following:

Abraham Lincoln	*Virginia*	Gettysburg
Fort Sumter	Emancipation Proclamation	William Sherman
Robert E. Lee	Belle Boyd	Appomattox Courthouse
Anaconda Plan	Clara Barton	John Wilkes Booth
Ulysses S. Grant		

2. Define the following:

perpetual	ironclad	draft
border states	casualties	greenbacks
defensive war	proclamation	entrenched
blockade runners	bounties	assassinated

Remembering the Facts

1. In his inaugural address, what was President Lincoln's position on slavery?

2. What were the plans of each side to win the war as soon as possible?

3. Why did the Confederacy think it would get financial aid from France and Britain?

4. Where were slaves freed at the time of the Emancipation Proclamation?

5. How did the war affect people on the home fronts?

6. Which political party controlled Congress during the war?

7. When did Lee surrender to Grant?

8. What were the major battles of the Civil War?

9. What prevented President Lincoln from putting his peace plan into operation?

Understanding the Facts

1. Why did Arkansas, North Carolina, Tennessee, and Virginia leave the Union in May 1861?

2. Why did the Union feel it was better prepared to win the war quickly?

3. Why did the Confederacy feel it was better prepared to win the war?

4. What was President Lincoln's purpose in the Emancipation Proclamation?

5. How did each section raise money and soldiers for the war?

6. How did those opposed to fighting avoid becoming soldiers?

7. Why was the Battle of Gettysburg important to both the North and the South?

8. Why did John Wilkes Booth assassinate President Lincoln?

Using Pie Graphs

Reading Pie Graphs. The illustrations shown on page 337 are called pie graphs. The circle, or the whole pie, represents the whole amount of the item being considered. The pie is divided into slices to show what percent of the whole is related to one group or another.

The pie graphs on page 337 consider several important economic factors. They compare the Union and the Confederacy at the time the Civil War began. Study each of the graphs, and answer the following questions.

1. In which of the matters considered is the Confederacy stronger than the Union?

2. In which of the matters considered is the Union stronger than the Confederacy?

3. Is the amount of money needed to fight a war a factor which favored the Union or the Confederacy?

4. Considering all four graphs, was the Union or the Confederacy better equipped to fight the war?

Rebuilding the Nation　16

On the night of April 2, 1865, the Confederate government abandoned Richmond. The city was left in flames. What plans were made for reuniting North and South and for rebuilding the Union?

President Lincoln and other government leaders in Washington faced a grave situation after Lee's surrender at Appomattox. The North's victory meant an end to the Confederacy. Still, the seceded states had to be brought back into the Union. There was the great task of rebuilding the many areas destroyed during the Civil War. And although nearly 4 million slaves had been freed, most of them had no clear idea how they would start making their livings. The United States tried to solve these issues in the years from 1865 to 1877, known as the Reconstruction period.

1. President Versus Congress

During the Civil War, Lincoln and Congress had often disagreed about government policy. Some Republican leaders thought the President should be harder on the South in the war. They also felt that Lincoln's plan for *reconstruction,* or rebuilding the Union after the war, was too soft on the South. This led to a struggle between the President and Congress. They could not agree over which branch of government should direct reconstruction and how it would be carried out. Things grew worse when Andrew Johnson took office following Lincoln's death.

1.1 Lincoln and Congress.   After the Union victories at Vicksburg and Gettysburg, President Lincoln had begun to make plans for returning the seceded states to the Union. In December 1863, he presented a *Proclamation of Amnesty and Reconstruction,* which outlined his plans. It said that southern whites should take an oath of loyalty to the United States. They would then be given *amnesty,* or a general pardon by the government. Confederate military and government leaders were not part of this plan. Once 10 percent of the people in each state who had voted in 1860 had taken the oath, that state could begin to form a new government. The new state governments had to recognize the freedom of blacks, but Lincoln did not push for further changes.

Many members of Congress thought Lincoln's plan was too mild. One group of Republicans were called Radicals because they wanted to make *radical,* or major, changes. Senators Charles Sumner of Massachusetts and Benjamin Wade of Ohio, as well as Representatives Thaddeus Stevens of Pennsylvania and Henry Winter Davis of Maryland, were Radical Republicans. They were most upset with Lincoln's plan.

Over what did Lincoln and Congress quarrel?

When did Lincoln present his plans on reconstruction?

How did Lincoln and the Radicals differ on their view regarding the Confederate states?

Lincoln felt that the southern states had never been legally out of the Union. So they still had all the rights of states. The Radicals, however, thought that the southern states had left the Union and should be treated as territories. Most Republicans also feared that the Democratic party would come back into power. They wanted to keep the southern states, which had been Democratic, out of the Union as long as possible.

The Radicals in Congress did not like the 10 percent part of Lincoln's plan. They felt it was not only too mild but also allowed the President, not Congress, to control reconstruction. In 1864, Arkansas, Tennessee, and Louisiana were ready to return to the Union under Lincoln's plan. Congress refused to seat their representatives.

Why did the Radicals not like Lincoln's plan?

In July 1864, Congress passed the Wade-Davis Bill. It said that a majority of the white male citizens in each seceded state should take an oath of loyalty to the United States. Then a convention could be held to set up a new state government. Only those who took an oath that they had never willingly aided the Confederacy could vote or serve in these state conventions. This barred anyone who had served as a member of a Confederate government or voluntarily fought for the South. Also, the new state constitution had to abolish slavery. Then, if Congress agreed, the state would be readmitted.

What was the Wade-Davis Bill?

Lincoln kept the Wade-Davis Bill from becoming law through the use of a *pocket veto*. A pocket veto occurs when a President fails to sign a

There were no immediate provisions made for slaves freed by the Thirteenth Amendment. Most blacks had neither jobs nor land of their own. Why did some blacks move to cities in the North?

bill presented to him by Congress within ten days of its recess. Lincoln's action further angered the Radicals, and the split between the President and Congress grew wider.

1.2 The Thirteenth Amendment.

What did the Thirteenth Amendment do?

Republicans were concerned that there were still slaves in the border states, in Tennessee, and in parts of certain other states. Lincoln's proclamation in 1863 led to the freeing of slaves only in those areas which were part of the Confederacy. So there were still slaves in some parts of the country. In January 1865, Congress passed the Thirteenth Amendment to the Constitution. It abolished slavery everywhere in the United States. The necessary 27 states ratified it, and on December 18, 1865, the amendment became law.

1.3 Johnson and Congress.

When Lincoln died, the task of reconstruction passed to Andrew Johnson. President Johnson had been born into a poor family in North Carolina and later moved to Tennessee. He entered politics and became known for defending the rights of poor farmers against the large plantation owners. As a Democratic candidate, Johnson was elected to the United States Senate in 1856. When Tennessee left the Union in 1861, he remained in the Senate. In 1864, Johnson was elected Vice-President of the United States.

As President, Johnson was at first on good terms with the Republicans. Because of his record, they thought that he would follow a firm policy toward the South. They were soon disappointed, however. Although Johnson did not like southern planters, he believed in states' rights and cared little about the freed slaves.

What was Johnson's plan for reconstruction?

In May 1865, Johnson set forth a plan of reconstruction much like Lincoln's. According to Johnson's plan, most southern whites would be pardoned once they had taken a loyalty oath. Leaders of the Confederacy and people who had at least $20,000 in cash or property would have to get a special pardon. Seceded states could hold elections for constitutional conventions. These conventions had to repeal their acts of secession. They also had to adopt the Thirteenth Amendment and refuse to pay the debts from the time they were Confederate states. Then new state governments could be formed and members of Congress chosen. By December 1865, the southern states had followed Johnson's plan and were ready to return to the Union.

1.4 Congressional Reaction.

How did Congress react to Johnson's plan?

The Radicals were angry because Johnson had formed a plan on his own. They thought that his plan, like Lincoln's, was too soft. The Radicals and other people in the North were also alarmed at the number of former Confederate leaders

Drawing Conclusions
SKILL

What most people in the North knew about the South they read in newspapers or heard in stories. What most people in the South knew about the North they also read or heard. Travelers and writers provided firsthand observations, and readers and listeners provided their own conclusions.

David Macrae, a well-known Scottish writer and church leader, toured the United States in 1867 and 1868. He later wrote a book called *The Americans at Home.* The following selections from that book describe the lives of some southern whites and some former slaves after the Civil War. Read the selections, and based on them, draw some conclusions about the South.

The South had not only wasted her population, but her material resources. I visited districts where the people . . . had dug up every potato in their fields, pulled every apple from their orchards, taken even the blankets from their beds, to make up and send to the . . . army.

. . . I heard of one lady who in January 1865 had 150,000 dollars in Confederate paper [money], and owned slaves that would have sold in 1860 for 50,000 dollars more in
gold. . . . *she had to go . . . to the [Freedmen's] Bureau shed . . . to get bread to keep her children from starvation.*

. . . Men who had held commanding positions during the war had fallen out of sight and were filling humble [jobs]. . . .

The old planters were . . . so poor that they were trying to sell a portion of their land in order to pay the tax upon the rest. . . .

All this talk about the [blacks] being happier in slavery I heard amongst the white people, but rarely if ever amongst the [blacks] themselves. Many of the poorest of them told me that they had to put up with coarser food . . . and poorer clothing . . . and that they had a hard struggle even for that; but the usual wind-up was,—"But thank the Lord, we're free, anyhow."

1. What is Macrae's view of white people in the South?
2. What is his view of the former slaves?
3. Based on this information alone, how would you describe the conditions in the South?
4. Why is one source of information often not enough to draw a proper conclusion?

who had been elected to office. When Congress met, the Republicans blocked the new southern members from taking their seats and prepared to defeat Johnson's plan.

1. Why was there conflict between President Lincoln and the Congress?
2. Who were the Radical Republicans?
3. How did Andrew Johnson view reconstruction?

2. Congressional Reconstruction

While President Johnson was putting forth his plan, Republicans in Congress were drawing up their own plan of reconstruction. They had several goals. The first was to return the southern states to the Union, but under tougher terms than those set by either Lincoln or Johnson. The second was to protect the freedom of blacks in the South. Once those who had been slaves had the right to vote, the Republicans stood to gain their support. This would help the Republicans stay in power. With these goals in mind, the Radicals moved to take charge of reconstruction.

2.1 The Freedmen's Bureau. In March 1865, Congress set up the Freedmen's Bureau. It aided all needy people in the South, although *freedmen*—men, women, and children who had been slaves—were its main concern. The Bureau helped blacks set up farms on abandoned lands. It drew up work contracts between black workers and white landowners. The Bureau also set up schools and courts for blacks. John T. Trowbridge, a visitor from the North, described one of the courts.

What did the Freedmen's Bureau do?

> *The freedmen's court is no respecter of persons. The proudest aristocrat and the humblest [worker] stand at its bar on an equal footing. . . .*
>
> *A great variety of business is brought before the Bureau. Here is a [black] man who has printed a reward offering fifty dollars for information to assist him in finding his wife and children, sold away from him in times of slavery: a small sum for such an object, you may say, but it is all he has, and he has come to the Bureau for assistance. . . .*
>
> *[Another] has made a crop; found everything—mules, feed, implements; hired his own help—fifteen men and*

The Freedmen's Bureau was set up to help former slaves adjust to freedom. The work of the Bureau included establishing schools. Why did freed blacks need a basic education?

women; managed everything; by agreement he was to have one half; but owing to an attempt to swindle him, he has had the cotton attached [legally taken away]. . . .

The Bureau was the only direct step taken by the government to help the South and the former slaves economically. In February 1866, Congress passed a bill to add to the powers of the Freedmen's Bureau. According to the bill, the Bureau would continue to work in the South. Blacks there would go on being protected by United States' soldiers. Johnson vetoed the bill on the grounds that it was passed by a Congress in which 11 states were not represented. Later a bill continuing the Freedmen's Bureau for two years was passed over his veto.

Why did Johnson veto the bill to add to the powers of the Freedmen's Bureau?

2.2 Black Codes and the Civil Rights Act. Soon after the end of the war, southern state governments had begun passing laws, called **black codes,** that limited the rights of blacks. The codes differed from state to state. But there were many similarities. Blacks were not allowed to vote. They could not testify against whites in court, nor could they serve on juries. Blacks could hold only certain kinds of jobs, generally in agriculture. Those who did not have a job were assigned to work for whites. With these restrictions, the lives of the freedmen were not much different from when they were slaves.

What were black codes?

Congress moved to protect the rights of blacks by passing the Civil Rights Act of 1866. This act aimed at protecting freedmen through the courts rather than by military power. Blacks were made citizens, and it became illegal to treat a person differently because of color. This was the first federal law to define citizenship and to safeguard civil rights within the states. President Johnson vetoed the bill on the grounds that it went against states' rights. Congress passed it over his veto.

What did the Civil Rights Act of 1866 provide?

2.3 The Fourteenth Amendment.

The Radicals in Congress feared that the Supreme Court might overturn the Civil Rights Act. To stop this, Congress made the act into a constitutional amendment. In June 1866, the amendment was sent to the states.

Why did the Radicals propose the Fourteenth Amendment?

The Fourteenth Amendment stated that all persons born in the United States (except Indians) were citizens of the United States and of the states in which they lived. No state could deprive a citizen of life, liberty, or property without due process of law. In addition, every citizen was entitled to equal protection of the laws. States that kept any adult male citizen from voting could lose part of their representation in Congress. Anyone who had sworn to uphold the Constitution and then taken part in a rebellion against the United States could not hold public office. Finally, Confederate debts were said to be illegal.

The only southern state that agreed to ratify the amendment in 1866 was Tennessee. That year Tennessee became the first seceded state to return to the Union. The other southern states felt that citizenship was a matter for each state to decide. They were supported by President Johnson and the northern Democrats. These states did not ratify the Fourteenth Amendment for two more years, until 1868.

When was the Fourteenth Amendment adopted?

2.4 The Reconstruction Acts.

President Johnson decided to go directly to the voters with his ideas about reconstruction. He hoped to talk the people into voting against the Radicals in the congressional elections of 1866. Johnson gave a number of strong speeches around the North in order to gain support. The Republicans, however, won more than a two-thirds majority in each house of Congress. As a result, they could pass any bill over Johnson's veto and so direct the course of reconstruction.

In March 1867, Congress passed the first of several Reconstruction Acts. Under these acts, the South (except Tennessee) was divided into military districts. Each of the five districts was headed by a general backed by soldiers. The generals were to see that the states held constitutional conventions. Delegates were to be chosen by all adult male voters. Confederate leaders were not allowed to vote or hold office. When the state constitutions had been accepted by Congress and enough of the new legislatures had approved the Fourteenth

What did the Reconstruction Acts provide?

Reconstruction of the South

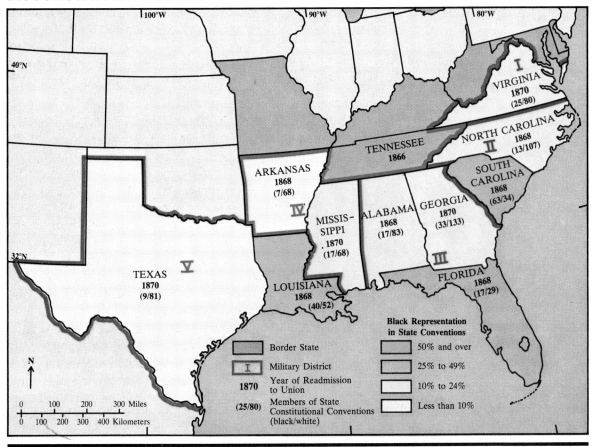

When did Congress pass the first Reconstruction Acts? What process did the former Confederate states follow for readmission into the Union? What was the purpose of establishing military districts?

Amendment, the states would be readmitted. By 1868, the amendment had been adopted. By 1870, all of the southern states had returned to the Union.

2.5 Johnson's Impeachment.   The struggle between Congress and Johnson was brought to a head by the Tenure of Office Act, passed in March 1867. *Tenure of office* means the length of time that a person can stay in office. This act stated that the President could not remove a person from federal office without the approval of the Senate. It was passed to check Johnson's power.

What was the Tenure of Office Act?

Johnson felt that the act was unconstitutional. He hoped to test the case in court. In February 1868, he removed Secretary of War Edwin

An officer of the Congress notified President Andrew Johnson of his impeachment (left). Tickets (right) were sold for the trial in the Senate. What was the result of the President's trial?

Why did Johnson remove Stanton from office?

Stanton from office. The Radicals then charged Johnson with breaking the law. The House of Representatives drew up 11 articles of impeachment against Johnson. Most of these were about the President not following the Tenure of Office Act.

The trial began in March 1868 with Chief Justice Salmon P. Chase presiding and the Senate acting as jury. Many people felt that Johnson was really being tried because he did not get along with the Radicals. The final vote came on May 16, 1868. With seven Republicans voting "not guilty," the final count was 35 to 19. This was just one vote short of the two-thirds majority needed to convict Johnson. Republican Senator Edmund G. Ross of Kansas cast the final and decisive ballot for *acquittal,* or a verdict of not guilty. Johnson served the rest of his term, but he had lost most of his influence.

What was the outcome of Johnson's impeachment?

1. Who was the Freedmen's Bureau meant to help?
2. How did the black codes restrict southern blacks?
3. Which southern state was the first to return to the Union?
4. Why was President Johnson impeached?

3. Reconstruction and the Postwar South _____

People all over the country held different ideas about reconstruction. This was especially true in the South. Opinions there were divided not only between blacks and whites but also among people of different political views. All of these groups had an important impact on reconstruction after the war.

3.1 Southern Blacks and Reconstruction.   Most of the blacks living in the South had been slaves before the Civil War. Afterwards, they were free, but most of them owned no land and had no money. Few could read or write. They hoped that reconstruction would bring them land and the chance for an education. These freedmen wanted to be able to vote and hold office in order to have an equal place in southern life.

Under the Reconstruction Acts, black people were allowed to vote for the new state governments. To protect their interests, blacks generally supported the Republicans. Blacks did more than vote, however. For the first time, they held public office in the South. Some black officials were appointed by the military governors. Others were

Robert Brown Elliot of South Carolina was a southern black elected to Congress during Reconstruction. What other black leaders filled key positions in state and federal governments?

Who were some
important black
leaders in the
South during
Reconstruction?

elected. Blanche K. Bruce of Mississippi, a former slave, was elected to the United States Senate. He had studied at Oberlin College in Ohio. Hiram P. Revels served as a Senator from Mississippi for one year. He had been trained for the ministry at Knox College in Illinois. Jonathan C. Gibbs, a Dartmouth College graduate, was secretary of state in Florida. He helped to set up Florida's public schools. Francis L. Cardozo, who had attended the University of Glasgow in Scotland, was secretary of state and later state treasurer in South Carolina.

In what state were
blacks a majority in
the state constitu-
tional convention?

Many blacks were elected to public office after the war. But they never really directed reconstruction in the South. Blacks were a minority in all southern state constitutional conventions, except South Carolina. There they outnumbered whites 76 to 48. In Mississippi, for example, there were only 17 blacks out of 100 representatives at the state convention. In Alabama, there were only 8 blacks out of 108. The percentage of blacks in the state legislatures was about the same, and their numbers grew smaller as time passed.

3.2 Southern Whites and Reconstruction.

Most southern whites accepted the defeat of the Confederacy and the abolition of slavery. They were not willing to go much further than that, however. They stood firmly against equal rights for black people. These southern whites did not want black people to vote or to hold office. They wanted blacks only to provide farm labor, under a system much like that of slavery. Most of them opposed the new Republican governments and anyone else seeking to help blacks.

What did most
southern whites
want for blacks?

3.3 Carpetbaggers and Scalawags.

The Republican party in the South was controlled, for the most part, by two groups. People from the North who moved into the South to take part in reconstruction were one group. Many of them carried their belongings in bags made of the same material as carpets. So they were called *carpetbaggers*. Some of them truly wanted to help, while others were just looking for opportunity for personal gain or adventure.

People from the other group were called *scalawags*. They were southern whites who worked with Reconstruction officials. Other southern whites thought of them as traitors. Some scalawags thought what they were doing was the best way to help the South. Others were thinking only of themselves. Some had been Whigs. They wanted to build up southern industry by working with northern Radicals. They hoped this would lessen the South's dependence on agriculture. Many people in the South did not want this change in their way of life. Many scalawags hoped that by influencing the votes of black people, they would reach their goals. When this failed, almost all of them left the Republican party.

3.4 Claims of Corruption. Many southern whites thought that the new governments in their states were corrupt. To prove this, they pointed to the growth of both state budgets and state debts. In South Carolina, for example, the public debt went from $7 million to $29 million in eight years. Taxes increased about 80 percent in Louisiana and almost 1400 percent in Mississippi. Southern whites generally put the blame on dishonest carpetbaggers and untrained blacks in government.

Why did people think there was corruption in the Reconstruction governments?

Although there was corruption in some state governments in the South after the Civil War, the same thing was true for many northern governments. Because of the needs of the people, large-scale spending was needed in the South. Bridges and buildings had to be replaced. Railroad lines had to be repaired and hospitals built. Public schools had to be set up. In 1860, there were only 20,000 children in the public schools of South Carolina. By 1873, there were about 120,000—both black and white. Social services of all kinds had to be provided, often for the first time.

Why was there large-scale spending?

3.5 The Ku Klux Klan. Many southern whites felt that freed blacks, with the help of northern Republicans, would destroy the South. These people wanted to keep white control in all areas. To do this, it was

With the economy of the South in near ruin, many southern whites moved west. How were those who stayed affected by Reconstruction?

"The First Vote" (left), from *Harper's Weekly,* shows a polling place in the South. In 1867, the Ku Klux Klan (right) was organized to frighten black voters from the polls. How else were blacks denied their rights?

necessary to stop northern support for the freedmen. They also wanted to keep blacks from voting and holding office. Since the Reconstruction governments, backed by the army, protected the voting and civil rights of all citizens, some whites turned to secret societies to achieve their goals.

What was the Ku Klux Klan?

One of the strongest of the secret groups was the Order of the Ku Klux Klan. It was formed shortly after the war in Pulaski, Tennessee, by Confederate soldiers. It quickly spread to many parts of the South. Robed and hooded, members of the Klan rode through the land trying to scare blacks and their supporters, especially agents of the Freedmen's Bureau. Blacks were kept from voting by threats, beatings, and sometimes killings.

1. What did the former slaves hope to gain from reconstruction?
2. Whom did southern blacks generally support during Reconstruction?
3. How did southern whites feel about new legislation during Reconstruction?
4. Why was the Ku Klux Klan formed?

4. The End of Reconstruction

By the late 1860's, Radical reconstruction was well under way in the South. It seemed likely to continue in the years ahead. In the 1870's, however, many Americans began to grow tired of the problems presented by reconstruction.

4.1 The Election of Grant. In 1868, the Republicans chose the Union army general, Ulysses S. Grant, to run for President. Democrats selected Horatio Seymour, former governor of New York. The Republicans stood by reconstruction, while the Democrats favored an end to it. They favored pulling United States soldiers out of the South. They wanted to pardon former Confederates and return all rights to the states.

What position did each party take in the election of 1868?

The campaign that year was a heated one. Republicans pointed to their war record. They reminded people that it had been members of the Democratic party in the South who had started the Civil War. Republicans claimed to have saved the Union. They pictured theirs as the party of patriotism.

The Republicans won the election of 1868. Grant won in 26 states, with an electoral vote of 214 to Seymour's 80. The popular vote, however, was much closer—3,012,833 for Grant and 2,703,249 for Seymour. Grant received around 400,000 votes from blacks. This showed how important the black vote could be.

In the North, many states had chosen not to let blacks vote, although the new state governments in the South had been forced to do so. This was changed by the Fifteenth Amendment. It said that no state could keep a person from voting because of color. The amendment was approved by enough states to become law on March 30, 1870.

What did the Fifteenth Amendment prohibit?

4.2 Grant and Reconstruction. Once in office, President Grant took a strong stand in favor of Radical reconstruction and black rights. He approved the Force Act, passed in May 1870, as well as the Ku Klux Klan Act of 1871. These laws gave Grant the power to use troops to end violence against blacks and Republican governments. Many arrests were made and the Klan began to lose its power.

Slowly, however, national backing for Radical policies began to weaken. By the end of his first term in office, President Grant had lost interest in sending soldiers into the South to protect Republicans and blacks. After his reelection in 1872, he stopped sending them.

4.3 Other Interests, Other Concerns. Congress, too, was becoming less concerned with supervising the South and helping the

Charlotte Forten (1837–1914)

In late 1861, Union army forces captured a group of islands off the coast of South Carolina and Georgia. Thousands of slaves had been left there as their owners fled from the northern soldiers. Many government leaders and abolitionists saw this as a chance to show that former slaves could live successfully as free citizens. The Port Royal Experiment gave educational and medical aid to the freed slaves on the islands. Charlotte Forten was one of the teachers who volunteered to help. She taught there from 1862 to 1864.

Forten was born in Philadelphia. She studied in Salem, Massachusetts, from 1854 to 1856. For two years, she taught elementary school there. In 1858, Forten moved back to Philadelphia where she lived with her family until going to Port Royal.

Forten kept a journal of her years on the Sea Islands. In it, she expressed her commitment to help the former slaves. She also reveals her own feelings as a young black woman growing up in a mostly white country.

This morning a large number—Superintendents, teachers and freed people, assembled in the little Baptist church. It was a sight that I shall not soon forget—that crowd of eager, happy black faces from which the shadow of slavery had forever passed. "Forever free!" "Forever free!" Those magical words were all the time singing themselves in my soul. . . .

What was occurring in the northern attitude toward reconstruction in the 1870's?

freedmen. For one thing, some of the most important Radical leaders were gone. By 1870, Davis, Wade, and Stevens had either retired or died. In May 1872, Congress passed an amnesty law. It allowed most former Confederate officials to vote and hold office. It also ended the Freedmen's Bureau.

The general public in the North had heard enough about reconstruction. There were other problems which attracted their attention. Among them were the Indian wars in the West, and a plan for the United States to buy Santo Domingo. There were also talks with the British over damage caused the North by Confederate ships built in Great Britain.

4.4 Scandals Under Grant.   Tales of scandal in the federal government under Grant also drew people's attention away from the South. Grant had been a great army leader, but he had not had much experience in politics. Some people tried to take advantage of this for their own gain.

Americans learned that in September 1869, Jay Gould and Jim Fisk, both millionaires, had bought enough gold to control its price. Fisk and Gould tried to get President Grant not to sell government gold. This would drive up the price of gold. Grant refused. Fisk and Gould then spread a rumor that the government had agreed not to sell, and the price rose. Fisk and Gould sold their supply of gold at a higher price. Soon after, the government released $4 million. This drove the price down and ruined many people. They blamed the government and President Grant for their losses.

What did Gould and Fisk attempt to do?

In 1872, the Crédit Mobilier scandal broke. The Crédit Mobilier construction company was formed by leaders of the Union Pacific Railroad. This company received contracts to build the railroad and charged very high prices. The costs were picked up by other stockholders in the railroad. The money, however, really went to the leaders and to some members of Congress who had accepted stock in the company for certain favors.

Who was involved in the Crédit Mobilier scandal?

Later in Grant's term, Secretary of the Treasury W. A. Richardson was found to be dishonest. He was forced to leave office. It was also discovered that President Grant's private secretary, Orville Babcock, was a part of what was called the "Whiskey Ring." This was a group of revenue officers and distillers formed to cheat the government out of tax money. By the time the Whiskey Ring was discovered, the government had lost millions of dollars. In 1876, the head of the War Department, W. W. Belknap, resigned from office. He was about to be impeached for taking bribes.

4.5 The Election of 1876.   These scandals hurt the Republican party, which had already lost most of its power in the South. By 1875, only three states—Louisiana, Florida, and South Carolina—remained under Republican control.

What southern states were under Republican control in 1876?

Against this background, the election of 1876 took place. At their convention, the Republicans chose Governor Rutherford B. Hayes of Ohio, a former Civil War general. The Democrats picked Governor Samuel Tilden of New York. Both candidates were interested in reform.

Who were the candidates in the election of 1876?

Tilden won a majority of the popular vote, but a question arose over the electoral vote. Both the Republicans and the Democrats claimed victory in South Carolina, Florida, and Louisiana. In Oregon, one vote was also in question. Congress set up a commission to award the votes. It had 15 members—five from the House, five from the Senate, and five from the Supreme Court. The commission finally voted eight to seven to give the 20 votes in question to Hayes.

How was the election decided?

The Democrats reached a compromise with the Republicans accepting the commission's decision. The Democrats accepted Hayes as President. In return, federal soldiers were removed from the South. The Compromise of 1877 was an agreement between northern Republicans and southern Democrats. It spelled the end of the period of Reconstruction.

Who won the popular vote in the election of 1876? Which candidate had the most electoral votes? What delayed the final outcome of this election? What made this election different from those before it?

Election of 1876

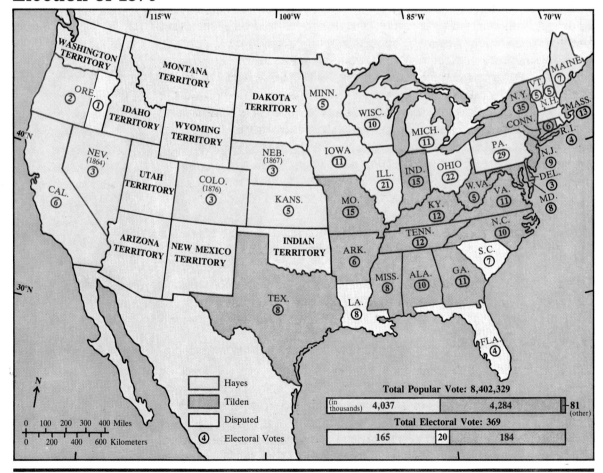

4.6 The Plight of Southern Blacks. The real losers in the Compromise of 1877 were southern blacks. The last Radical governments in the South were no longer protected by the federal government. They were soon taken over by the Democrats. People in the South called these Democrats the "Redeemers," or saviors, of the South.

As southern Democrats came into power, blacks began to lose their political rights. Some were kept from voting by violence. Others were threatened with the loss of their jobs or homes. Efforts were made to control those few who were allowed to vote.

It was almost impossible for blacks to prevent the loss of their rights because they did not have economic power. The Radical promise of free land had never been carried out, and most blacks had no cash or credit to buy land. Only a small number were able to rent farms. So many southern blacks had to hire out as laborers on farms or plantations owned by whites.

A system called *sharecropping* became the way of life for many freedmen. Instead of receiving wages or paying rent, blacks and some whites worked small pieces of land owned by someone else. In return, they received a share of a season's crops. Many landowners gave the farmers supplies and housing. Whatever the sharecroppers owed the landlord was taken out of their earnings at the end of the season. This system often put the sharecroppers into debt from which they never escaped.

What was the system of sharecropping?

1. How did President Grant view reconstruction?
2. What effect did the scandals during Grant's term of office have?
3. When did Reconstruction end?
4. How did the Compromise of 1877 affect southern blacks?

5. Conclusion _____

By the end of Reconstruction, the South was once more a part of the Union. Southern whites were again in control of southern state governments. Blacks had lost many of their newly gained political rights. The South had restored its economy. It had begun to industrialize, although agriculture was still important. Blacks, though legally free, were still workers tied to the land. Their struggle for equal rights would last for many years.

Chapter 16 Review

Main Points

1. President Lincoln and the Congress differed on how reconstruction of the South was to be carried out.
2. The Thirteenth Amendment, ratified in December 1865, freed all slaves.
3. Johnson's plan for reconstruction was much like Lincoln's.
4. Congress' plan for reconstruction would restore the South to the Union and protect the rights of former slaves.
5. The Fourteenth Amendment protected the rights of all people born or naturalized in the United States.
6. Conflict between Congress and President Johnson led to the President's impeachment. The Senate failed by one vote to convict Johnson of the charges.
7. Blacks voted and participated in the Reconstruction governments.
8. The Fifteenth Amendment was passed to protect the rights of blacks to vote.
9. Many people in the South opposed citizen rights for blacks. Blacks lost many of these rights when Democrats gained control of state governments in the South.

Building Vocabulary

1. Identify the following:

   Andrew Johnson
   Radical Republicans
   Charles Sumner
   Wade-Davis Bill
   Thirteenth Amendment

   Freedmen's Bureau
   Civil Rights Act of 1866
   Fourteenth Amendment
   Blanche K. Bruce

   Ku Klux Klan
   Ulysses S. Grant
   Charlotte Forten
   Crédit Mobilier
   Rutherford B. Hayes

2. Define the following:

   reconstruction
   amnesty
   radical
   pocket veto

   freedmen
   black codes
   tenure of office

   acquittal
   carpetbaggers
   scalawags
   sharecropping

Remembering the Facts

1. What was President Lincoln's plan for reconstructing the South?
2. Which slaves were freed by the Thirteenth Amendment?
3. How did Johnson become President? What was his plan for reconstruction?
4. What was the congressional plan for the reconstruction of the South?

5. Why was the Freedmen's Bureau organized?
6. What were the protections provided by the Fourteenth Amendment?
7. What was the role of the former slaves in politics during Reconstruction? In which states were they most active?

8. What did the Ku Klux Klan do against blacks and against the Radical Republicans?
9. What scandals broke during Grant's term as President?
10. What did the North and the South gain from the Compromise of 1877?

Understanding the Facts

1. How did presidential reconstruction differ from congressional reconstruction?
2. Why did Congress think President Johnson would follow a firm policy toward the South?
3. What charges were brought against Johnson by the House of Representatives? How were they decided?
4. Why did states in the South pass black codes?
5. Why was it important for blacks to vote? Why did southern whites object?
6. Why was there no major effort to provide land for freed slaves?

Using Maps

Thematic Maps. Maps are often used to show information on a variety of themes. They combine geographic information with information that could also appear in a table or on a chart.

The thematic map on page 363 deals with the reconstruction of the South after the Civil War. It contains geographic data and additional theme information. Study the map carefully, and answer the following questions.

1. What are the geographic divisions of the South shown on the map?
2. Which information on the map might have been placed in a chart?
3. Which military district shown on the map was composed of three states?
4. Which military district was composed of only one state?
5. Which state was not in any military district? Why not?
6. Which state had the largest number of black members of its constitutional convention?
7. In how many states did black members outnumber white members?
8. Based on the information in this map, who controlled the conventions that drew up the southern state constitutions?

New York 1860~1865

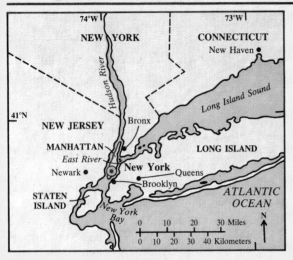

A group of American Indians sold an island off the northeastern coast of their lands to the Dutch West India Company in 1626. The Company had established a fort and trading post at the tip of the island which was located in a large bay. The island was named Manhattan after the Indians who sold it. The Dutch called the settlement New Amsterdam.

In 1664, New Amsterdam came under the rule of the English who changed its name to the City of New York. The English held it until the end of the Revolutionary War. The new government of the United States took its first census in 1790. By that time, Manhattan was home to more than 33,000 people. Under Dutch, English, and American rule, the city had grown as a center of trade.

In 1860, on the eve of the Civil War, New York was the biggest, richest city in the entire United States. More than 800,000 people lived on Manhattan, and hundreds of thousands more lived in nearby cities like Brooklyn, Queens, and the Bronx. Almost half the people living on the island had come to the United States from other countries. The City of New York was the biggest center of immigration in America.

First Impressions

In the spring of 1861, an English news writer visited the United States to report on the possibility of war between the North and South. William Russell's visit took him first to New York and then to other cities in the North and South. Russell returned to New York in July, after the war had started.

. . . the first thing which struck me was the changed [look] of the streets. Instead of peaceful citizens, men in military uniforms [crowded] the pathways, and [so many] United States' flags floated from the windows and roofs of the houses as to [give] the impression that it was a great holiday festival. . . . [In March,] it was very rarely I ever saw a man in soldier's clothes. . . . Now, fully a third of the people carried arms, and were dressed in some kind of martial garb.

The change in manner, in tone, in argument, is most remarkable. I met men to-day who last March argued coolly . . . about the right of Secession. They are now furious at the idea of such wickedness. . . .

Reactions

Once the question of war was decided, the people of New York joined in support of the Union cause. They acted quickly to organize and equip the soldiers, and they gave help to the families of those who volunteered to serve. There were thousands of volunteers, especially among the immigrant groups. To the poorest of them, army service meant pay. To most of the immigrants, it was also proof of loyalty to their new country.

Through religious, social, and government organizations, the people of the city played an important part in the war. They raised money for special payments to those who volunteered to join the army. They arranged for improved health care and sanitary conditions in the distant army camps. By the spring of 1862, people realized that "the show time of the war has passed away, and it has become a matter of sober business." Edward Dicey also wrote:

In many a house that I have been into, I have found the ladies busy in working for the army . . . but there is little talk or fuss made about it. There are few balls or large parties this season, and the opera is not regularly open. . . . but

Printing House Square was the center of the New York newspaper industry. What were some of the newspapers? What was their role in the Civil War?

work is plentiful, and the distress, as yet, has not gone deep down.

Young People

The daily lives of the younger people in the city changed little during the war years. Most of them kept up their studies, and Dicey was very impressed by the schools they attended.

The instruction is entirely [free]—everything, down to the pens and ink, being provided by the State. Education is not compulsory [required by law]; but the demand for it is so great that . . . the school benches are always more than filled. . . . The teachers in all the classes, except two or three . . . are women. . . . Reading, writing, ciphering [arithmetic], geography, grammar, history, book-keeping for the boys, and moral philosophy [the study of right and wrong] for the girls, were the [main subjects]. . . .

Besides the State schools, there are several free public schools, kept up by voluntary contributions [from church members]. . . . In the classes I went through . . . were representatives of almost every foreign nation . . . the majority were Germans, Irish, and [blacks]. . . . they learn to read and write [American English]. . . .

The Cost of Living

By the summer of 1863, the slow and deadly progress of the war had changed life for many of the city's people. Some of those in business became very rich from war trade. But the pay of ordinary soldiers was quickly spent by families as the cost of living increased. Taxes rose, rents went up, and food became very expensive.

Even the lowest-paying jobs became very important to the city's immigrants who held most of them. The Emancipation Proclamation had upset many workers, especially the Irish who had most of the unskilled, low-paying jobs. These people were afraid that freed blacks would come north to find work. Many of the workers had been the first to volunteer to fight for the Union. They were not so willing, however, to fight for the freedom of slaves.

The Draft Riot

Some political leaders and news writers in the city did not agree with the way President Lincoln ran the war. In 1863, they especially attacked the order to draft soldiers. The first list of drafted men was published on Sunday, July 12. It was made up mostly of poor people; many of them also supported the Democratic party. Some Democratic party leaders had

To protest the Conscription Act of 1863, some people in New York set fire to a building storing draft records. Why did people challenge the draft law?

claimed that it was unconstitutional for the government to force a state citizen to serve in a federal army. They charged that the number of Democrats on the draft list was too high.

Monday morning, a large crowd of people gathered in front of the draft office. Some of them believed that men had been drafted for political reasons. Others were afraid of losing their jobs to blacks. Many were tired of high prices and low pay.

By Monday afternoon, the crowd had changed into a violent mob. Men, women, and some children began to attack the draft office. They set fire to the records, books, and furniture. They beat the people who tried to stop them. From the draft office, the mob went to attack the shops and homes of antislavery leaders. They caught black people on the street and beat them, sometimes killing them. A home for black orphans was burned to the ground, and one child died in the fire.

After four days, the riot was finally ended with the help of federal and state soldiers and special groups of volunteer citizens. Many people had lost their lives, and over $1.5 million worth of property had been destroyed.

Joy and Sorrow

In some sections of New York, many people were making a great deal of money from the war. They enjoyed spending it. New theaters opened, and large new houses were built. Richly dressed men and women rode in expensive carriages along Fifth Avenue to Central Park.

George Templeton Strong, who lived on Manhattan all his life, recorded some of the events of April 1865 in his diary. Strong was walking down Wall Street on April 3 when the news came that Richmond had been captured by Union troops.

An enormous crowd soon blocked [the street]. . . . *Never before did I hear cheering that came straight from the heart . . . given because people felt relieved by cheering and hallooing. . . .*

I walked about on the outskirts of the crowd, shaking hands with everybody. . . . Men embraced and hugged each other . . . retreated into doorways to dry their eyes and came out again to flourish their hats and hurrah. . . .

It was not long, however, before joy turned into sadness. Two weeks later, Strong wrote:

April 15. . . . LINCOLN . . . ASSASSINATED LAST NIGHT!!!! . . . Tone of [angry] *feeling* [is] *very like that of four years ago when the news came of Sumter.*
. . . No business was done today. Most shops are closed and draped with black and white muslin [cloth].

Homecoming

As the war came to an end, soldiers who were not given other duties were allowed to go home. A news writer reported on their return to New York.

Some came by sea, but most by railways to Jersey City, and thence across the ferry to Pier No. 1. They landed near the open space by the Battery [the old Dutch fort area] *and marched up town. . . .* [Some freed blacks], *acting as water-carriers,* [walked] *in the rear. . . . Regiments known in the city were of course more warmly greeted than strangers passing through. . . . Heavy losses had been sustained. . . . The New York 52nd regiment, for example, came back less than three hundred strong, having had on its muster rolls, during the war, two thousand six hundred names.*

Broadway was a busy street in the 1860's. It was spared from battle during the war. How were the people of New York affected by the Civil War?

Many families had lost their fathers, brothers, and husbands. Some soldiers returned from the war badly wounded or crippled. These families faced a difficult future. Others looked at the rebuilding of the South as a new business adventure. They faced the future with confidence. The lives of the people of New York had been changed by the war in many ways.

1. What was the City of New York's original name?
2. Describe New York City on the eve of the Civil War.
3. Why did the immigrants volunteer for the Union army?
4. Describe Wall Street on April 3, 1865, when Richmond had been captured.

Atlanta 1860~1865

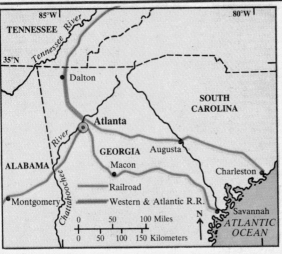

In the 1840's, two railroads in northeastern Georgia met at a town called Marthasville on the Chattahoochee River. Railroad promoters renamed the town Atlanta. The town began to grow very quickly. Property sales multiplied as new people came to start businesses. There was a medical college, but Atlanta did not have a public school system. White children attended private schools or took private lessons. There were very few free black families in the city, and slave children were not allowed to study. There were churches, factories, warehouses, banks, hotels, and restaurants. Doctors and lawyers settled in Atlanta, and newspaper offices opened. By 1860, Atlanta had a population of nearly 6,000 people and was one of the most important cities in the South.

Civil War Service

Atlanta was the chief supply center for the Confederate army during most of the Civil War. Its factories made many of the weapons used by the South. The four main railroad lines through the city carried soldiers and supplies to the front lines of the war. Some of Atlanta's people had moved north when the war first started. Many more of them stayed, raising money for weapons and supplies and caring for wounded soldiers. As the war dragged on, Atlanta grew so important to the Confederate cause that it became a main target of General Sherman's Union troops.

Early in the summer of 1864, Union soldiers pushed the Confederate troops into Georgia and across the Chattahoochee River. By July, General Hood's outnumbered troops prepared to defend Atlanta. Hood encouraged most of the families in the city to leave. Many of them did, and merchants and bankers sent their extra supplies to other cities for safekeeping. In August, Sherman's Union guns opened fire on the city.

Surrender

After several weeks of Union attack, the Confederates were forced to abandon Atlanta. Before leaving the city, Hood ordered his soldiers to burn all the army supplies that they could not carry with them. He did not want to leave weapons for the enemy to use. Sherman's soldiers entered Atlanta on September 2, 1864.

Sherman ordered the citizens to leave their homes and turned Atlanta into an armed Union camp. The city had been captured, but the war was not over. By November, Sherman's plans for marching through Georgia to Savannah were complete. He ordered his troops to destroy the railroad and telegraph lines and the bridges into northern Georgia and Tennessee. Atlanta was not to serve the Confederates as a supply base again.

When the Union troops prepared to leave the city, they gathered cattle and food supplies to take with them. Sherman told his officers that the army of more than 62,000 soldiers would have to "live off the land" when those supplies were gone. Orders were given to burn warehouses and factories before leaving the city. A Union soldier wrote about that day.

. . . it soon became [clear] that these fires were but the beginning of a general [blaze] which would sweep over the entire city and blot it out of existence . . . the soldiers [took] what they wanted before it burned up. . . . new fires began to spring up . . . noises rent the air . . . soldiers on foot and horseback raced up and down the streets while the buildings on either side were solid sheets of flame. . . . The night,

Union troops entered Atlanta in September 1864. Why was the capture and occupation of this southern city an important Union army objective?

for miles around was bright as mid-day; the city of Atlanta was one mass of flame. . . .

Coming Home

Three weeks after the Union army had burned Atlanta, General W. P. Howard of the Georgia troops came to inspect the damage. He reported to the governor:

Could I have arrived ten days earlier, with a guard of 100 men, I could have saved the State and city a million dollars.

There were about 250 wagons in the city on my arrival, loading with pilfered plunder [stolen goods]; pianoes, mirrors, furniture of all kinds, iron, hides without number, and . . . other things, very valuable at the present time. This exportation of stolen property had been going on ever since the place had been abandoned by the enemy.

Kate Massey from Atlanta wrote about some of the difficulties that families faced upon their return to the city.

People lived in anything they could find. Some families were housed in old freight cars. Some used discarded army tents. . . .
. . . A young woman [who needed a new dress] took several old ones, ripped, raveled, carded, spun, and wove them into new material. Then she made her dress. . . . Some children's shoes were made with wooden soles.

A few people found their homes unburned when they reached the city. Octavia Hammond wrote to neighbors about the condition of their property.

Your flowers are still alive and I think the grass lots have a notion to come up. If it were possible to [find] material we would have your lots enclosed for you to save them from wagons, horses and cattle. But the plank is not

General William Tecumseh Sherman made his mark on Atlanta by ordering it destroyed. What did Sherman hope to accomplish by burning the city?

loads of sand,—with piles of furniture and hundreds of packed boxes . . . with carpenters and masons,—with rubbish removers and house-builders . . . all bent on building and trading and swift fortune making.

Union Blue Again

By early spring, a few private schools had opened, and the medical college was preparing to hold classes again. But April was a month filled with bad news for the citizens of Atlanta. On the ninth, they learned that General Lee had surrendered to General Grant. On the twenty-sixth, General Johnston surrendered to General Sherman. For Atlanta, and for the whole South, the Civil War was over. Early in May, the city again became a military post for the United States army. This time, citizens were encouraged to stay and to continue rebuilding the city.

In many ways, the Union troops were helpful to the people of Atlanta. They were a strong influence on law and order, and they brought Northern money to the city. In the months that followed, the federal government was a great help to the poor of the city. Atlanta's leaders were concerned about the large numbers of Southerners who came to the city for help. The editor of the Atlanta *Daily Intelligencer* wrote in September about these people.

There is a population in and on the suburbs of this city . . . of families who have been stripped of everything, and whose [working men] went into the war and have never returned. . . . they simply exist. . . . With barely food [enough] to keep soul and body together. . . .

Others . . . were driven from their homes in other states and places, and have never been

to be had. . . . We have no garden at all, but I am afraid Ma will plant the front yard in cabbage, onions and peas. If she does I will [give you some]. . . .

Action!

Enough people had returned to Atlanta by December that regular elections were held for mayor and city council. The council then elected people to jobs like tax collector, city doctor, and police officers. The newly-elected treasurer reported that the city had less than $2 in cash. Supplies of money and goods were low, but the people of Atlanta had energy and courage. A visiting news writer reported on their activities a few months later.

From all this ruin . . . a new city is springing up with marvelous [speed]. . . . streets are alive from morning till night with . . . hauling teams and shouting men,— with loads of lumber and loads of brick and

able to return to them. . . . These people may be seen in any direction on the outskirts of town, and in the hurry and bustle of business it becomes us not to forget them. Strained, as our people are . . . surely something may be spared [for these others]. . . .

Another [group], *larger and increasing . . . are huddled together in most* [awful poverty]. *. . . our feelings are not so keenly aroused in their behalf. We* [mean] *the recently liberated slaves. . . .*

. . . the good of society, and the [lessening] *of crime, demand . . .* [we do something for them] *speedily!*

Freedom

Almost all groups of people faced hardships after the war. The recently freed slaves also faced terrible prejudice. Some white Southerners supported the ideas of freedom for blacks. Very few of them were willing to

Unlike New York, war ravaged both the city and the people of Atlanta. What did the people do to build a new city from the ruins of the old city?

accept the idea that any blacks should have full voting rights as citizens of the United States.

To most black people, freedom meant joy mixed with fear. Many came to the city because they had nowhere else to go. As Frederick Douglass said, "They were sent away empty-handed, without money, without friends and without a foot of land to stand upon."

A few black people had been trained in skills or as household servants. They often found work in the city, although they did not receive the same pay as white workers. Thousands of blacks had known only field work. They came to the city because they were curious or to find family and friends. Many came from fields ruined by war, and they needed the food that was given out by the army and the government.

Even with the terrible hardship they faced, blacks preferred their new roles as free people. Margrett Nillin, a former slave, explained when asked about it:

What do I like best, to be slave or free? . . . Well, it's this way, in slavery I own nothing and never own nothing. In freedom I can own the house and raise the family. All that causes me worry—and in slavery I had no worries—but I take the freedom.

1. How did Atlanta get its name?

2. What did the Union troops do in Atlanta during the war? after the war?

3. Describe the problems that faced the people of Atlanta after the war.

4. Compare the school systems of New York and Atlanta.

5. What roles did New York and Atlanta play in the Civil War?

Unit V Review

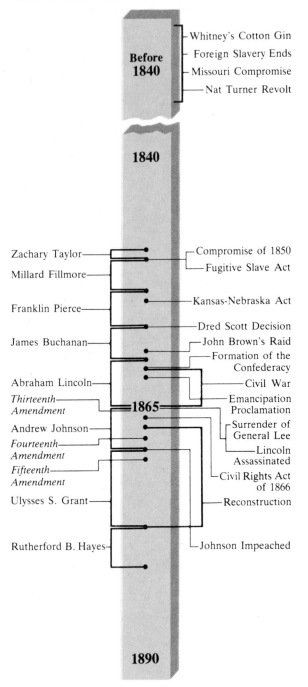

Before 1840
- Whitney's Cotton Gin
- Foreign Slavery Ends
- Missouri Compromise
- Nat Turner Revolt

1840

Zachary Taylor
- Compromise of 1850
- Fugitive Slave Act

Millard Fillmore

Franklin Pierce
- Kansas-Nebraska Act

- Dred Scott Decision

James Buchanan
- John Brown's Raid
- Formation of the Confederacy

Abraham Lincoln
- Civil War

Thirteenth Amendment
- Emancipation Proclamation

1865

Andrew Johnson
- Surrender of General Lee

Fourteenth Amendment
- Lincoln Assassinated

Fifteenth Amendment
- Civil Rights Act of 1866

Ulysses S. Grant
- Reconstruction

Rutherford B. Hayes
- Johnson Impeached

1890

Summary

1. Strong sectional differences had been developing between the North and South since the beginning of the nation.

2. The most important difference dividing the two sections—the institution of slavery—took on greater importance as the issue arose of slavery's expansion into new territories of the West.

3. Despite many attempts to keep the slavery issue out of politics, it became the leading question of the late 1850's, giving rise to the Republican party.

4. The victory of Abraham Lincoln and the Republican party in the election of 1860 was followed by the secession of 11 states from the Union.

5. The Union and Confederacy fought a long civil war which caused great loss of life and much damage in the South.

6. Following the Union victory in the war, wide differences in opinion arose over the efforts at reconstruction and over whether Congress or the President would guide reconstruction.

7. Congress, led by the Radical Republicans, took over reconstruction, passing laws to protect freed blacks.

8. Southern whites fought against rights for freed blacks, who were left without land or money to protect their position in southern society.

9. When federal support for freed blacks faded, white-controlled Democratic governments took over southern states, bringing an end to Reconstruction.

Unit Questions

1. Why did westward expansion before 1860 contribute to the sectional crisis between the North and the South?

2. Why did many Americans feel that slavery clashed with the ideas in the Declaration of Independence? How did white southerners deal with the ideas of slavery and the ideals of the Declaration of Independence?

3. How was the Republican party different from the Whigs or Democrats in its support? How was this important in 1860?

4. What were the major reasons why the North was able to win the war?

5. What was the position of the Confederacy toward President Lincoln's belief that the Union was perpetual? Did the position of the Southern states change during Reconstruction and how?

6. How did the Republican party use reconstruction for its own advantage?

7. What were the successes and failures of the war and reconstruction as far as the rights of blacks were concerned?

Suggested Activities

1. Write a brief statement showing how each of the following people might have reacted to news of the Dred Scott decision: a slave, a slave owner, a free black, and an abolitionist.

2. Locate poems and songs written during or about the Civil War. Try to include those which were about people from both the South and the North. Select several, and present them to the class.

3. Organize a discussion or class debate on the following—Do you think that reconstruction should have been controlled by Congress or the President?

Suggested Readings

Davis, Burke. *Mr. Lincoln's Whiskers.* New York: Coward, McCann, & Geoghegan, Inc., 1979. Discusses Lincoln's election as President and advice given him to grow a beard.

Ellis, Keith. *The American Civil War.* New York: G. P. Putnam, Sons, 1971. Discusses the leaders, battles, and events of the war.

Keith, Harold. *Rifles for Watie.* New York: Thomas Y. Crowell Co., 1957. The story of a young soldier during the Civil War.

Sterling, Dorothy. *The Trouble They Seen: Black People Tell the Story of Reconstruction.* Garden City, New York: Doubleday, 1976. Blacks give eyewitness accounts of reconstruction to Congress.

UNIT
VI

AMERICA IS
Growth

Growth has been a constant part of the
American experience. Beginning as a small
cluster of colonies on the Atlantic coast, the
nation physically expanded beyond the
Mississippi River to the Pacific Ocean. An
industrial revolution speeded up old areas of
economic growth and helped to create new ones.
The United States saw no limits to how much it
could grow and what it could achieve. The
American people formed one of the largest and
most powerful industrial nations in the world.

A Changing Nation

17

One of the best-known Currier and Ives prints of the West is "Across the Continent." It was painted by Fanny Palmer. What images does Palmer use to promote the benefits of the West?

The United States entered a period of great change after the Civil War. Large numbers of Americans moved to settle certain areas of the West for the first time. Many people, in the years between 1860 and 1890, experienced changes in their ways of life. The population of the country itself was also changing, as a new era of immigration brought millions of people to the United States.

1. Settlers on the Frontier _____

Huge new territories had been added to the United States during the 1840's. Some Americans already lived in those areas—that is, in California, Oregon, Texas, and other parts of the Far West. However, the frontier generally ran from Minnesota through Iowa, Missouri, Arkansas, and eastern Texas. Between this line and the Far West was a large area of land which included the Great Plains, the Rocky Mountains, and the Great Basin. In the years after the Civil War, more and more people moved into this area.

After the Civil War, what area was considered the frontier?

1.1 The Mining Frontier. New discoveries of gold and silver brought miners to the western frontier. A small mining boom occurred in Colorado in 1859. Other finds in that area over the next 30 years supplied new sources of mineral wealth. A huge deposit of silver, known as the Comstock Lode, drew miners to Nevada in 1859. Idaho became a center of mining activity in the 1860's. Between 1862 and 1868, discoveries were made in Montana. Mining also became important in New Mexico, Arizona, and the Black Hills of South Dakota.

Settlement of the mining frontier most often followed a pattern. Hundreds, sometimes thousands, of miners moved into an area and made claims. A mining camp was set up, from which a small town grew. Once a deposit was mined out, the town was often abandoned as the miners went to look for new claims. The empty, lifeless towns the miners left behind became known as *ghost towns*.

What was the pattern of mining settlement?

Gold and silver caused added interest in the West. Each find brought settlers, as well as miners, to the area. Many of them set up farms or started businesses. Important cities—such as Boise, Idaho; Helena, Montana; and Virginia City, Nevada—grew up near the mines. In addition, the precious metals from the West increased the wealth of the United States.

1.2 Ranchers and the West.

Where did cattle ranching first begin?

The large sweep of open land in the West attracted ranchers to the area. With its millions of acres of grass, it was well suited to raising cattle. At first ranches generally grew up around military posts or mining towns. Later they spread over the area.

The leading cattle-raising center was Texas. By 1865, there were about 4 million longhorn cattle in Texas. Descended from Spanish cattle brought into the area in the 1500's, these animals were better suited to the area than eastern stock. They could better withstand blizzards, drought, and certain diseases.

What led to a shift in the shipping of cattle?

In the 1850's, Texas cattle owners had driven small herds to Galveston and Shreveport for shipment by water to New Orleans, and on from there to the East. This method was both slow and costly. In the late 1860's, the first railroads were built into Kansas. Joseph McCoy, an Illinois cattle dealer, wanted to use the railroads to move Texas cattle to the East quickly and cheaply. McCoy made an agreement with officials of the Kansas Pacific Railroad. It stated that cattle brought to the town of Abilene, Kansas, would be shipped by train to eastern stockyards at certain rates. In 1867, 35,000 cattle were shipped from Abilene. In 1870, the number reached 300,000.

What was the long drive?

Bringing the cattle north from Texas to Abilene was called the *long drive*. It started in the spring, and the hardest work—caring for and moving the cattle—fell to workers called *cowhands*. They were usually young men, and many had been soldiers in the Civil War. Others were Mexicans or blacks, while some were Indians. The *trail boss* was the leader of the long drive. He bought Texas cattle, hired six to eight cowhands for every thousand cattle, and got six to ten horses for each cowhand. The drive north followed one of the cattle trails, such as the Chisholm Trail to Abilene or the Goodnight-Loving Trail to Wyoming. From there, most of the cattle were shipped to the East for beef. Cattle from Texas also were used to build up herds in Kansas, Nebraska, Wyoming, Colorado, Montana, and the Dakotas.

What caused the end to the open range?

By 1879, cattle raising had become a big business. However, as more people invested their money in cattle, more animals were bred than the land could support. This led to overgrazing of the *open range,* or unclaimed public grasslands. Conflicts over the use of the open range arose between large and small cattle owners as well as between cattle and sheep owners. There were also conflicts with people who wanted to settle and farm the land. Finally, two severe winters in 1885–1886 and 1886–1887 killed thousands of animals and brought an end to open-range cattle raising.

Slowly, the size of the herds was reduced. Cattle owners used barbed wire, introduced in 1874, to fence off their land into ranches.

Longhorns were tough animals bred to survive the harshness of extreme temperatures on the Great Plains. Their meat contained little fat. How did longhorn cattle raised in Texas reach consumer markets in the East?

The cowhands, who had once worked on the cattle drives, became ranch hands—fixing fences, branding cows, and living more or less in one place.

1.3 The Homesteaders. Another group also moved west in search of land. They were *homesteaders*—people who settled on land with plans to farm it. In 1862, Congress passed the Homestead Act. This act gave settlers 160 acres of land after they had lived on it for five years and improved it. Before this time, public land had generally been sold to raise money for the government. The Homestead Act gave land away in order to encourage settlement in the West. Many people from the East, and also some from Europe, rushed to accept the government's offer.

In earlier years, Americans had not settled the Great Plains. The area was thought to be unsuited for farming. By 1865, farmers were moving into the eastern areas of Kansas and Nebraska, on the edge of the Great Plains. The federal government, railroad companies, and private land companies soon began to promote settlement of the lands farther west.

The western part of Kansas and Nebraska was settled by homesteaders in the early 1880's. Thousands of farmers moved into the eastern Dakotas from 1868 to 1885. The population of the states of Minnesota, Kansas, Nebraska, the Dakotas, Colorado, and Montana

What was the Homestead Act?

Who promoted settlement of the Great Plains?

Western Land Use by 1890

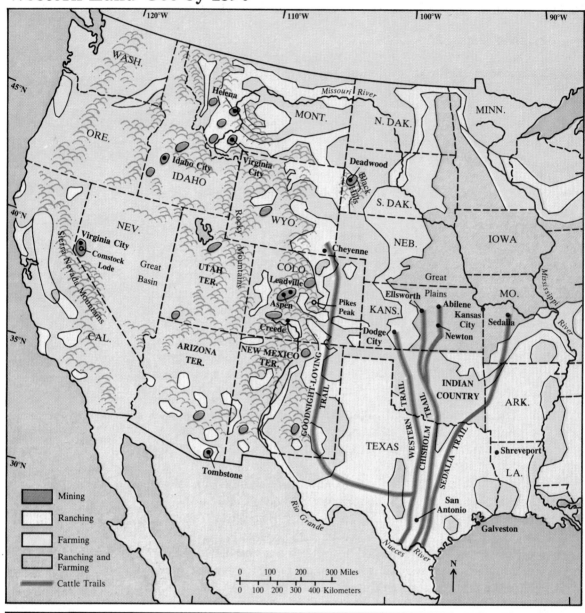

Under the Homestead Act, everyone who claimed land had to build a house on it. A house had to be at least 12 feet by 14 feet. It also had to have one door and one window. Notice the house on the next page. Of what does it appear to be made? Why was this material used? What were the major occupations of people settling the West? Where were more than one of these occupations done in the same area?

increased greatly. In the years from 1860 to 1900, more new land was opened for farmers than any time in the first 200 years of the country's history.

This land, especially on the Great Plains, presented problems never experienced before by American farmers. West of 98° longitude, there is little rainfall, few streams, and practically no trees. Drought is common, as are blizzards in the winter and insects in the summer. Faced with these problems, many homesteaders gave up and returned to the East or moved elsewhere. Those who stayed learned to survive. They used new steel plows to work the soil. They planted a new kind of Russian wheat which needed less water. They built windmills to pump underground water to the surface. These homesteaders also began to use *dry-farming*. This meant plowing deeply into the soil to bring up underground moisture.

What did farmers learn to do to survive on the Great Plains?

In spite of the problems, the homesteaders settled much of the remaining areas of the West. In 1890, the head of the census bureau of the United States stated that the frontier had closed. There were no longer any major areas of the West that had not been settled.

1. What were some of the most successful mining discoveries in the West?
2. Where were the leading cattle-raising centers?
3. What was the purpose of the Homestead Act?
4. What problems did farmers face on the Great Plains?

2. Indian Resistance and Federal Policy

What caused Indian life to change?

With the movement of settlers to Oregon and California in the 1840's, Indian life began to change. The coming of miners, ranchers, and farmers into the Great Plains and Rocky Mountain areas caused even greater changes. A long series of conflicts, lasting until the late 1880's, took place between the Indians and settlers in the West. These conflicts ended in the defeat of the Indians and the end of their traditional ways of life.

Upon what did Indians of the Great Plains depend?

2.1   The Plains Indians and the Settlers.   The Indians of the Great Plains depended upon the buffalo for food, clothing, and shelter. For many years, they had followed the herds as they moved over the Plains. Conflict arose, however, as the new settlers began to come into this area. In the 1850's, treaties between the federal government and certain groups of Plains Indians had set some limits on their hunting lands. As more miners, ranchers, and homesteaders moved into the West, it became difficult for the Indians to find the buffalo they needed.

The Indians were upset by the coming of the whites. They also were angry at the killing of large numbers of buffalo. Hunters working for railroad companies shot hundreds of buffalo to feed survey and track-laying teams. The animals also were killed for sport and for their hides, which had become popular in the East. The Indians tried to stop this killing, but the number of buffalo was quickly reduced.

What caused the Indian wars in the West?

2.2   The Last Indian Wars.   Fighting broke out between Indians and settlers in the late 1850's. Some Cheyenne and Arapaho groups attacked miners moving through Indian lands toward Colorado. Many Plains Indians fought against the whites in 1862 when government soldiers were pulled out of the West to fight in the Civil War. After the war, more soldiers were sent back to the West. The conflict between the government and the Indians continued.

In 1865, the army tried to build a road across Sioux land through central Wyoming to the gold mines in Montana. This led to the Red Cloud War, which lasted from 1865 to 1867. During this time, the Sioux, led by Chief Red Cloud, attacked many soldiers and miners along the road. In 1868, the federal government finally agreed to give up the project. The Sioux were guaranteed lands west of the Missouri River in South Dakota. They were also given hunting rights as far as the Bighorn Mountains in Wyoming.

In 1874, gold was discovered in the Black Hills of South Dakota. Miners by the hundreds came to the area. In 1875, the government broke its promise to the Sioux people and opened the Black Hills to

"The Song of the Talking Wire" was painted in the mid-1800's by Henry Farny. The telegraph poles are a physical sign of the settlers' westward movement. Over what issues did Indians and settlers come into conflict?

settlement. Many Sioux left their lands and camped near the Little Bighorn River in Montana. They were joined by some Cheyenne and Arapaho Indians. There were at least 2,500 warriors, led by Chiefs Sitting Bull and Crazy Horse.

The government ordered the Indians to return to their lands. When they did not do so, troops were sent to force them to move, in what became known as the Sioux War of 1876. One group of 264 soldiers was led by Lieutenant Colonel George Custer. They advanced against the Indians in the valley of the Little Bighorn. Custer and his troops were surrounded and killed by the Indians. When the news reached the East, large numbers of soldiers were sent West, and the Sioux fled the area. They later surrendered and were forced to return to their reservations.

What caused the Sioux War of 1876?

The Indians had few victories after the Battle of Little Bighorn. The United States government continued to send troops to force Indians onto reservations. In 1877, the government ordered the Nez Percé of the Wallowa Valley in eastern Oregon to move to a smaller reservation in Idaho. Led by Chief Joseph, a group of 800 men, women, and children tried to escape to Canada. They traveled for 15 weeks over 1,500 miles (2,400 kilometers). The group was caught by soldiers who had been sent to stop them some 40 miles (64 kilometers) from the border. After a battle, the Nez Percé surrendered. The Nez Percé were

Who was the leader of the Nez Percé?

sent to a reservation in Oklahoma. Chief Joseph, in advising his people to give up, had said:

> *I am tired of fighting. Our chiefs are killed. . . . The old men are all dead. It is the young men who now say yes or no. He who led the young men is dead. It is cold and we have no blankets. The little children are freezing to death. My people—some of them have run away to the hills and have no blankets and no food. No one knows where they are—perhaps freezing to death. I want to have time to look for my children and see how many of them I can find. Maybe I shall find them among the dead. Hear me, my chiefs, my heart is sick and sad. . . . From where the sun now stands Joseph will fight no more forever.*

Why did the army have difficulty in defeating the Apaches?

One of the longest Indian wars was fought between the army and the Apaches of the Southwest. The Apaches fought government attempts to force them onto reservations long after other Indians had given up the battle. The Apaches were some of the fiercest warriors ever faced by the army. They moved quickly in small bands, striking their enemies by surprise. Their knowledge of the rugged lands of New Mexico, Arizona, and western Texas gave them an advantage over the soldiers. The wars with the Apaches did not come to an end until the surrender of Chief Geronimo in 1886.

The Indian wars finally came to a close on the Pine Ridge reservations in South Dakota. In the late 1880's, a religious movement had spread to many of the Plains Indians. As part of it, a special dance called the Ghost Dance was performed. The people believed that after the dance, the buffalo would return and Indian lands would be restored. These beliefs alarmed settlers, who demanded that the army take action. In December 1890, soldiers tried to stop Sioux Ghost Dancers at Wounded Knee Creek on the Pine Ridge reservation. There was a brief fight, and more than 150 Sioux and some 25 soldiers were killed. Wounded Knee marked the end of armed conflict between the United States government and the Indians.

Where was the last armed conflict? Who was involved?

How had the government treated Indian groups before 1871? after 1871?

2.3 The Dawes Act. Until 1871, the United States government had treated different groups of Indians as separate nations. That year, Congress said that all Indians were to be *wards*—people under the care of a guardian—of the federal government. After that, efforts were stepped up to get the Indians to accept the ways of life of the white settlers.

There were people, however, who supported Indian rights. One of these was Helen Hunt Jackson, who wrote *A Century of Dishonor* in 1881. In it, Jackson spoke out against the government's harsh treatment

Sarah Winnemucca (1844–1891)

PROFILE

Settlers began to move into Nevada about the time Sarah Winnemucca was born in the 1840's. The area was the home of the Paiute Indians. The chief arranged for his granddaughter, Winnemucca, to live with a settler family. As a result, she learned to speak English and to appreciate the cultures of both the settlers and the Paiutes.

In 1859, silver was discovered at Comstock Lode. More settlers moved to Nevada and took over the land, forcing the Paiute people onto a reservation. Eventually, the settlers also took over the reservation.

About this time, Winnemucca's father became chief, and she became his interpreter and the Paiutes' speaker. For the rest of her life, Winnemucca pleaded the cause of her people for a homeland. She frequently received promises of improved treatment. But the promises were broken.

Winnemucca's life reflects what most Indian people in the United States experienced—defeat, mistreatment, and disappointment. Winnemucca failed to regain Paiute land holdings. Yet she remains important for what she tried to do.

of the Indians. Her book helped make other Americans aware of the problem, and certain reform groups were formed.

To answer the reformers' demands, Congress passed the Dawes Act in 1887. This act marked a change in the government's reservation policy. Up to 1887, Indians had been forced to live on reservations. The lands were held jointly by each traditional group. Under the Dawes Act, Indian families were given homesteads to farm. The plots would be held in trust by the government for 25 years. At the end of that time, the Indians would become full owners of the land and citizens of the United States. Indians who accepted these plots, however, had to promise not to associate with their traditional Indian groups. In this way, the government succeeded in breaking up these groups.

What was the Dawes Act?

Most of the Indians did not fare well under the Dawes Act. Reservation lands which were not divided into plots for the Indians were given or sold to settlers. So the Indians lost more than 60 percent of

Why did the Indians not fare well under the Dawes Act?

Indians forced onto reservations await supplies from United States government agents. How were Indians' traditional ways of life changed by government policy?

their remaining lands. Also, most of the Indians were not farmers, and they did not believe in individual ownership of property. For the most part, the Indians found it very difficult to adapt to white ways.

1. What effect did the decline of the buffalo have on the Plains Indians?
2. Where were major battles between the Indians and the federal government?
3. How did the Dawes Act change reservation policy?

3. Blacks in the Late 1800's

The late 1800's was a time of change for many Americans. This was especially true for blacks. They had made great gains right after the Civil War. Before Reconstruction ended, blacks began to lose their civil and political rights.

What was happening to blacks in the South after Reconstruction?

3.1 Losing the Vote. Many blacks had been denied the right to vote in the 1870's. Still, there were a few black voters in certain areas after the southern Democrats took control of the state governments. Beginning in the 1870's and continuing into the 1890's, the power of the Democratic party leaders in the South was challenged by other whites. These people were mainly poor whites who often owned small farms. They disliked the fact that the party leaders favored business, industry, and large landowners at the expense of poor white farmers.

For a short time, poor white and black farmers tried to work together. Most southern whites, however, soon came to feel that the right to vote should be taken away from the blacks. Without allies, there would be no chance of blacks gaining political power for themselves.

State leaders looked for ways to end black voting without violating such federal laws as the Fifteenth Amendment. Beginning in the 1890's, southern states began using two methods to keep blacks from voting. Voters had to pay a *poll tax,* or a tax to be paid at election time. They also had to pass a *literacy test.* This test was to prove that a voter could read and explain any part of the state constitution. Local voting officials, who were almost always white, determined whether a voter passed or failed the test. Blacks often did not have the money to pay the poll tax. Also, many of them did not have enough schooling to pass the literacy test. So they were kept from voting.

The poll tax and literacy test also would keep many poor whites from voting. To avoid this, other laws were developed. Beginning in 1898, many southern states wrote *"grandfather clauses"* into their constitutions. People who could not pass the literacy test or pay the poll tax could still vote if they, their fathers, or their grandfathers had been allowed to vote on or before January 1, 1867. Few, if any, blacks had been allowed to vote before 1867 so they did not qualify.

3.2 The Rise of "Jim Crow" Laws. Besides limiting the political rights of blacks, southern states passed laws to *segregate,* or separate, blacks from whites in everyday life. These laws came to be called "Jim Crow" laws. Blacks were segregated on railroads, steamboats, and other forms of transportation. They were not allowed to use the same hotels, restaurants, theaters, or parks as whites. Blacks were forced to attend separate schools and to use separate restrooms and drinking fountains in public places.

Such laws were not used before the Civil War because slavery defined the role of most blacks in the South. After the war, southern whites wanted to return to prewar life-styles. The "Jim Crow" laws were passed in an effort to do this. Segregation was not found only in the South, however. In both the North and West, blacks were kept from equal use of certain facilities by custom, rather than by law.

3.3 The Supreme Court and Civil Rights. Some people hoped that the laws and practices of segregation would be stopped by the Supreme Court. That hope was soon lost. During this period, the Court was very much in favor of states' rights. In 1873, the Court ruled in a series of cases known as the Slaughterhouse cases. The Court's decision said that although the Fourteenth Amendment did guarantee equal protection and due process to citizens, it applied only to certain

Why were blacks in the South being denied the right to vote?

What were "grandfather clauses"?

What were "Jim Crow" laws?

Why did segregation not exist before the Civil War?

What was the Supreme Court's attitude toward segregation?

situations. At other times, the rights of citizens were the responsibility of the states. The Court felt that the federal government had no power to decide what a state could or could not do to protect citizens' rights. In 1883, the Supreme Court ruled that the Fourteenth Amendment could not be used to stop segregation in private businesses. The Court said the amendment protected a person's rights against state actions only. It did not stop private individuals or companies from practicing segregation. Only state laws could do that.

A Supreme Court ruling on a Louisiana law added support to "Jim Crow" laws. Louisiana had passed a law requiring railroads to have separate cars for blacks. In 1896, Homer Plessy refused to leave a car for whites and was arrested. His case came before the Supreme Court as *Plessy* v. *Ferguson.*

What did the Plessy v. Ferguson *decision require concerning segregation?*

In May 1896, the Court ruled on the case. It said that segregation in itself was not illegal. In upholding the Louisiana law as constitutional, the Court put forth the idea that all that was necessary to make any form of segregation legal, and not in violation of the Fourteenth Amendment, was provision of equal facilities. In practice, facilities were seldom if ever equal. But the Court's basic statement remained in effect for nearly 60 years.

3.4   The Response of Black Leaders.   Black leaders did not always agree on what would be the best response to "Jim Crow" laws. One leader was Booker T. Washington, an educator and former slave. Washington founded Tuskegee Institute in Alabama and built it into an important college for blacks.

In September 1895, Washington gave a speech at a large fair in Atlanta. The address became known as the "Atlanta Compromise." In it, Washington said that he believed black people should work to gain economic security before seeking equal rights. Washington said:

What was Washington's view regarding the black response to segregation?

> *The wisest among my race understand that* [fighting for] *social equality is . . . folly, and that progress in . . . all the privileges that will come to us must be the result of . . . constant struggle rather than* [by force]. . . . *The opportunity to earn a dollar in a factory just now is worth* [much] *more than the opportunity to spend a dollar in an opera house.*

Washington asked southern whites to support *vocational,* or job, training for blacks. He also urged them to hire many of the black workers in the South. He did not press openly for equal rights.

Washington's views were popular with many white leaders in both the North and South. They saw this plan as an answer to problems between blacks and whites. Many whites believed that blacks should

William E. B. DuBois (left) was a key figure in forming the NAACP. Booker T. Washington (right) set up Tuskegee Institute in Alabama. What were the objectives that each black leader worked to accomplish?

serve as laborers and farmers with no equal rights. Washington, however, thought of his plan as only a temporary answer.

Some black leaders did not agree with Washington. One of them was William Monroe Trotter, a newspaper owner in Boston. Trotter felt that Washington's ideas betrayed blacks by not speaking out for their rights as citizens. He felt that it was wrong for a country based on democracy to deny a people their rights.

Who were important black leaders that did not agree with Washington's views?

The leading critic of Washington was William E. B. DuBois, a graduate of Fisk and Harvard universities. DuBois was very much against Washington's acceptance of segregation. He felt that whites had created problems by denying blacks equal rights. In 1903, DuBois wrote *The Souls of Black Folk*. He pointed out that it was up to whites and blacks jointly to solve these problems.

What was DuBois' view?

DuBois also disagreed with Washington's ideas about vocational training for blacks. He believed that talented blacks should receive the best possible education in all areas. These people would then become the leaders in the drive for black rights.

Two organizations were formed in the early 1900's by the groups led by DuBois and Washington. In 1909, DuBois joined with other blacks and whites to form the National Association for the Advancement of Colored People (NAACP). Their aims were to fight segregation, work for equal rights, and expand education for blacks.

Washington and many others supported the National Urban League, founded in 1911. Its main goal was employment for blacks.

1. How did "Jim Crow" laws affect black people?
2. What was at issue in the *Plessy* v. *Ferguson* case?
3. What groups helped blacks in the early 1900's?

4. A Growing and Changing Population

The population of America was also going through great changes in the early 1900's. In 1860, there were 31.5 million people in the United States. By 1900, the population had grown to 76 million people. A large part of this came from immigration. Between 1860 and 1900, 14 million immigrants entered the country. They brought their customs, languages, and religions to an already changing nation.

What was one cause of the huge increase in population in the late 1800's?

4.1 The "Old" Immigration. In the late 1800's, most immigrants who entered the United States were still coming from northwestern Europe. This movement was known as the *"old" immigration,* because these people came from the same areas as earlier immigrants. The largest group—nearly 3.5 million—came from Germany. Almost 2 million people arrived from Great Britain and nearly the same number from Ireland. Around 1.4 million people came from the Scandinavian countries of Denmark, Finland, Norway, and Sweden. Nearly 500,000 of them settled in the Middle West.

4.2 The "New" Immigration. Beginning around 1880, patterns of immigration began to change. More and more people entered the country from southern and eastern Europe. This movement was known as the *"new" immigration,* because up to that time few people from these areas had come to the United States. Between 1880 and 1900, about 100,000 "new" immigrants came to the United States each year. From 1900 to 1914, the numbers generally reached 500,000 a year.

What changes began to occur in immigration patterns in the 1880's?

Nearly 3 million Italians arrived in the United States between 1900 and 1914. During the same period, 3 million people from Austria-Hungary and almost 2.5 million people from Russia and the Baltic countries of Latvia, Lithuania, and Estonia came to America. Another 500,000 people entered the United States from the Balkan countries of Rumania, Bulgaria, Greece, and Turkey. Included in these groups were a large number of Poles.

Large numbers of "new" immigrants moved into the cities of the northeastern United States. They often sought jobs that had been

Pluralism

=CONCEPT=

From colonial times, the American population has been made up of various nationalities, races, and religions. The people who came to America tried to maintain their old world traditions while living in American society. Because of this, America became characterized by pluralism—several independent ethnic groups within a common society.

Despite the accepted idea of a pluralistic America, some Americans in the late 1800's felt that some immigrants would hurt the United States as a whole. There were hostile reactions to certain newcomers. A mood of fear led to many laws aimed at controlling immigration to the United States.

In 1896, Senator Henry Cabot Lodge of Massachusetts argued for a bill to establish a literacy test. The bill was designed to exclude all immigrants who could not read or write 25 words of the Constitution in any language.

It is found, in the first place, that the illiteracy test will bear most heavily upon the Italians, Russians, Poles, Hungarians, Greeks, and Asiatics, and very lightly, or not at all, upon English-speaking emigrants or Germans, Scandinavians, and French.

In other words, the races most affected by the illiteracy test are those whose emigration to this country has begun within the last twenty years and swelled rapidly to enormous proportions, races with which the English-speaking people have never hitherto assimilated, and who are most alien to the great body of the people of the United States.

President Grover Cleveland disagreed with Lodge's view and vetoed the bill.

It is said . . . that the quality of recent immigration is undesirable. The time is quite within recent memory when the same thing was said of immigrants who, with their descendants are now numbered among our best citizens. . . .

In my opinion, it is ⸱ . . . safe to admit . . . immigrants who, though unable to read or write, seek among us only a home and opportunity for work. . . .

1. Which groups did Senator Lodge hope to exclude? Why?
2. What was President Cleveland's argument opposing literacy tests?
3. What is the connection between the concept of pluralism and the idea of democracy?

Population Density by 1900

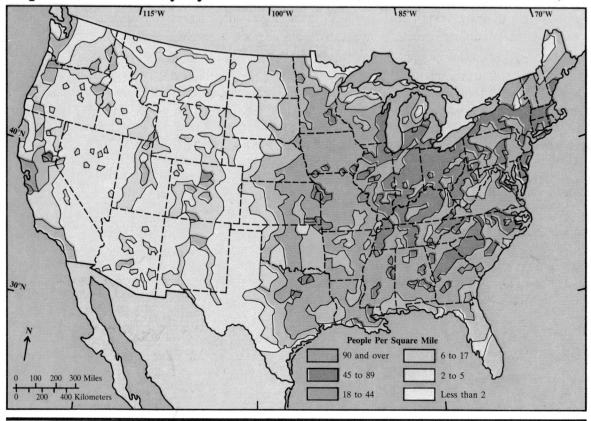

This map shows the average number of people living in every square mile of the United States in 1900. Where were most of the cities located? Where were most of the farms located?

Where did most "new" immigrants settle?

advertised in Europe by American businesses. Most of these immigrants were unskilled laborers. Some took jobs with steel manufacturers or the railroads. Others worked in the coal mines or in the garment industry. They tended to live among people from their own country who shared a common religion, customs, and language.

4.3 Asian Immigration. The first large group of people from China entered the United States in 1849 during the California gold rush. In the 1860's, Chinese workers played an important part in building the Central Pacific Railroad. More Chinese came in the 1870's. Many moved into the mining areas of the West. Some set up businesses in California, Nevada, and other western states. Even though Chinese immigration increased after 1860, only 300,000 Chinese entered the United States between 1820 and 1882.

Where did most Asian immigrants settle?

Some years later, people from Japan began entering the United States. They settled on the Pacific coast, mainly in California. Although some bought their own land, most took jobs as farm workers. By 1910, around 155,000 Japanese were living in the United States.

4.4 Reaction to Immigration. Many people born in the United States became alarmed at the large numbers of immigrants entering the country. They were disturbed because many of the immigrants had little education. Some Americans felt that because of this, these people could not take part in democracy. They also feared that the newcomers would take the jobs of American workers.

Why was there concern about immigration in the late 1800's?

In the East, there was reaction against people from southern and eastern Europe. Some people in the East did not like the fact that many of the immigrants were Catholic or Jewish. In the West, there had been opposition to Asian immigrants for some time. Their language, appearance, and customs were unfamiliar to most Americans.

In the late 1880's, a number of secret societies against immigrants were formed. Most were also against Catholics and Jews. One of the most important was the American Protective Association, started in 1887. Groups like this called for restrictions on immigration.

What was the American Protective Association?

4.5 Regulation of Immigration. In certain areas of the West, local laws were passed against the Chinese. Chinese could not hold certain jobs or marry whites. They were usually forced to live in certain parts of cities. As feelings against the Chinese grew, the federal government passed the Chinese Exclusion Act, the country's first law aimed at controlling immigration.

This cartoon was drawn by Joseph Keppler for his humor magazine *Puck*. It shows Uncle Sam welcoming people two by two from many countries onto his ark. Immigrants were welcomed for cheap labor by employers. Yet the newcomers were resented for working for low pay by many American workers. What special problems faced immigrants?

Immigration, 1861–1920

Immigration (in millions)

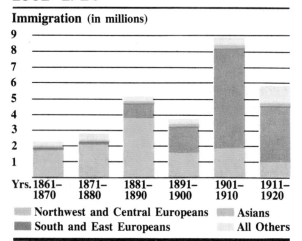

| | Northwest and Central Europeans | Asians |
| South and East Europeans | | All Others |

Population Growth, 1870–1920

Population (in millions)

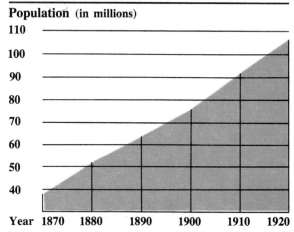

How did total American population change from the time of the census in 1870 until 1920? How did immigration change for each decade between 1861 and 1920? For each decade, where were most immigrants born?

What were the provisions of the Chinese Exclusion Act?

Passed in 1882, this act said that no Chinese worker could enter the country for the next ten years. This period was later extended. Nearly all of the Chinese wishing to enter the United States were workers. So the law stopped almost all Chinese from coming to America for some years. The law also said that the courts could no longer make Chinese people citizens of the United States. Two months later, Congress passed an act which restricted immigration in general. It said that criminals, people with mental illnesses, and people with no money or jobs could not enter the United States.

How were the Japanese immigrants made to feel prejudice?

The prejudice against Asians also was felt by the Japanese when they began entering the United States. They, too, were forced to live in certain areas. Local laws kept them from owning land. The federal government also tried to limit or to stop Japanese immigration through agreements with the government of Japan. In one of these, the San Francisco school board said it would end the policy of separate schools for Asian children. In return, the Japanese government said it would limit immigration to the United States.

1. From what countries did the "old" immigrants come?
2. From what countries did the "new" immigrants come?
3. From what countries did the Asian immigrants come?
4. From which countries was immigration restricted?

5. Conclusion

During the late 1800's, millions of immigrants came to the United States. They became an important source of labor for American industry. At the same time, blacks began to lose the rights they had gained during Reconstruction. By 1890, America's last frontier had been largely settled. The end of the frontier meant an end to the Indians' traditional ways of life. The railroads carried western products to the East. This helped feed the growing number of people in the cities, while the West's gold and silver helped pay for new industries. The United States was a leading industrial nation in the world.

Chapter 17 Review

Main Points

1. After the Civil War, the frontier disappeared as many miners, ranchers, and farmers moved to settle in the West.

2. Settlement of the West destroyed the western Indians' traditional ways of life.

3. Actions by state governments led to the loss of most black rights gained during Reconstruction.

4. The Supreme Court refused to protect the rights of blacks in cases before it.

5. By the end of the nineteenth century, many people migrated to the United States. A large number were from eastern Europe.

6. Anti-immigrant groups were formed, and laws were passed to regulate the entry of some immigrants.

Building Vocabulary

1. Identify the following:
   Comstock Lode
   Homestead Act
   George Custer
   Chief Joseph

   Helen Hunt Jackson
   Sarah Winnemucca
   Dawes Act
   "Jim Crow" laws

   Plessy v. *Ferguson*
   Booker T. Washington
   William E. B. DuBois
   Chinese Exclusion Act

2. Define the following:
   ghost towns
   long drive
   cowhands
   trail boss
   open range

   homesteaders
   dry-farming
   wards
   poll tax
   literacy test

   "grandfather clauses"
   segregate
   vocational
   "old" immigration
   "new" immigration

Remembering the Facts

1. Who moved into the West in the years after the Civil War?
2. What were the advantages of the Homestead Act for farmers?
3. How did Indians react to the efforts of settlers to take their land?
4. What did many state governments in the South do to prevent blacks from voting?
5. What was the Supreme Court decision in the *Plessy* v. *Ferguson* case?
6. How did DuBois and Washington differ in their views toward treatment of blacks?
7. What was the difference between "old" and "new" immigrants?
8. What actions were taken to regulate immigration?

Understanding the Facts

1. How did the Homestead Act change the way the federal government disposed of public land?
2. How did the United States fail to honor its treaties with the Indians?
3. How did the Dawes Act both help and hurt the Indians?
4. Why did people in the South want to keep blacks from voting?
5. Why were black citizens unable to prevent the loss of their rights?
6. Why did some Americans object to immigration from one country more than from others?

Using Bar Graphs

Reading Bar Graphs. The left diagram on page 406 is called a bar graph. Bars of various lengths are used to give information on the number of immigrants entering the country each decade (ten-year period) from 1861 to 1920. To read the graph, determine how far up the scale on the left each bar reaches. That will show about how many immigrants came to the United States during that decade. For each group of immigrants, measure the length of each color. Answer the following questions based on the information given on the bar graph.

1. How many immigrants came to the United States each decade shown?
2. In which decade was the largest amount of immigration?
3. In which decade was the greatest decrease in immigration from the previous decade?
4. For each decade, what area provided the most immigrants?
5. How did immigration change between 1880's and the 1890's?
6. What statement can be made about immigration between 1861 and 1920?

The Age of Big Business

Steelworkers in Bethlehem, Pennsylvania, use a Bessemer converter to refine iron into steel. This painting was done in 1895 by S. B. Shiley. How did American industry change in the years after the Civil War?

In the years from 1860 to 1900, the economy of the United States was changing. The process of industrialization, which had begun in the 1820's and 1830's, speeded up after the Civil War. The number and size of businesses increased. By 1900, certain large industries were so important to the American economy that this period became known as the "Age of Big Business."

1. Background to Industrial Growth_____

There were several things which made the growth of Big Business possible in the late 1800's. Some of them had been present in the early days of the United States. Others came with the changes taking place in American life.

What natural resources were important in the growth of Big Business?

1.1 Natural Resources. The United States had an abundance of natural resources. Some of them were needed for industrial growth. Coal, which was used as fuel to power steam engines in factories, was especially important. Large deposits were found in Pennsylvania, West Virginia, Kentucky, Ohio, and several other states.

Where was the first successful oil well drilled?

Other resources also aided the growth of industry in the late 1800's. Oil was used to lubricate machines and as a fuel for lamps. In 1859, Edwin Drake drilled the first successful oil well near Titusville, Pennsylvania. Before long, drilling began in Ohio and West Virginia. In 1865, over 2 million barrels of oil were produced.

Huge deposits of iron ore were found in upper Michigan as early as the 1840's. In 1855, the Soo canals opened. They made it possible for ships to pass between Lake Superior and Lake Huron. Iron ore then could be shipped through the Great Lakes to steel mills around Pittsburgh. Even larger deposits of iron ore were found in the Mesabi Range of Minnesota. This area was soon providing over one half of the country's supply of iron ore.

Where are the largest iron ore deposits in the country?

1.2 The Labor Supply. Another resource necessary to the growth of Big Business was labor. Between 1860 and 1900, the population of the United States grew rapidly. Because of this, the number of people seeking jobs grew as well. Former slaves were among those who joined the free labor market. In the late 1800's, some southern blacks began to seek jobs in cities.

Immigrants were another source of labor during these years. Between 1860 and 1900, 14 million people came to the United States.

They came to work in the clothing industry, on the railroads, and in the steel mills. The growing population served as a labor force for the growing industries. It also provided a large group of *consumers*—people who buy and use food, clothing, or any article which a producer makes.

What role did immigration play in the growth of Big Business?

1.3   The Importance of New Inventions.   New inventions also helped business to grow. Some inventors in the United States worked to make the production of goods easier. In the 1850's, Henry Bessemer of England and William Kelly of the United States separately discovered a new way to make steel from iron ore. This process made it possible to make more steel at less cost, and the steel industry grew rapidly.

How did inventions help increase industrialization?

Other inventors worked to improve communications. This especially helped people in business. In 1867, a typewriter was developed by Christopher Sholes. By 1873, the Remington Company was making typewriters on a large scale. The telephone, invented by Alexander Graham Bell, was introduced in Philadelphia in 1876. By the 1890's, the American Telephone and Telegraph Company had installed nearly 500,000 telephones in America's businesses and homes. In the early 1870's, Thomas Edison made some major improvements on the telegraph. Soon telegraph lines reached every part of the country and were used by business to carry out widespread operations.

Who were some important inventors of the late 1800's?

Thomas Edison also made other contributions. In 1879, he introduced the first practical electric light bulb. A short time later, he

Thomas Edison was called "The Wizard of Menlo Park." In his laboratory in Menlo Park, New Jersey, he experimented with new ways to improve industry. What were some of Edison's inventions?

invented a dynamo to generate electricity. Then in 1882, Edison set up the first central power plant in New York City. Electricity soon became an important source of power for homes, offices, and industry.

1. Where were the major production centers for coal and iron ore?
2. Which groups made up most of the labor force in cities?
3. Which inventions in the 1800's improved production and communication?

2. The Railroads

The first American companies to grow to a large size were the railroads. They served as a model for the development and organization of Big Business in the United States. The railroads were the first to develop ways of raising the money needed to run a large-scale business. They also were the first to develop ways to manage large companies.

What industry was the first to become Big Business?

2.1 Organizing the Systems. From 1860 to 1900, the railroad network grew rapidly. In 1860, there were just over 30,000 miles (48,000 kilometers) of track in the United States. By 1900, the total had risen to 193,000 miles (308,800 kilometers).

Railroads were built in every area of the United States. On May 10, 1869, the Central Pacific and the Union Pacific met at Promontory Point, Utah. This marked the completion of the first *transcontinental* (across the country, from coast to coast) railroad. In 1883, two other such railroads opened. One was the Northern Pacific, which ran from Minnesota to the Pacific Ocean. The other was the Southern Pacific, which joined New Orleans with Los Angeles and San Francisco. In 1889, the Santa Fe connected Chicago with Los Angeles. The Great Northern, following nearly the same route as the Northern Pacific, linked Minneapolis with Seattle in 1893.

When and where did the completion of the first transcontinental railroad take place?

Many smaller railroads were organized into giant systems to connect cities on the Atlantic coast to Chicago and St. Louis. This made it possible to ship goods and to travel to many places without changing railroads. By 1910, the New York Central and the Pennsylvania railroads each had over 10,000 miles (16,000 kilometers) of track. The Southern Railroad and the Louisville and Nashville Railroad each had over 5,000 miles (8,000 kilometers) of track.

2.2 Railroads as Big Business. Because of their growing size, the railroads faced certain problems. For one thing, they had to handle

Transcontinental Railroads

The Union Pacific advertised in Chicago its service which carried passengers "through to San Francisco in less than four days. . . . " What other railroads connected Chicago with cities on the west coast? What railroad linked New Orleans with the West?

hundreds of trains heading in different directions at different times of the day. They also had to buy thousands of rails, cars, and locomotives. They had to hire crews to lay and to repair track, as well as people to run the trains.

What problems did the railroads have?

Railroads also faced the problem of raising enough **capital** (money to operate). Few, if any, companies in the United States had over $1 million in capital until 1860. The railroads were the first companies to develop ways to raise large amounts of money from private investors. By 1860, there were several railroads with over $20 million in capital, and several others had $10 million.

To handle all of the problems they faced, railroads hired managers. These managers were the first to use long-range plans for spending. They studied the company to find out how its money was being spent and how to make better use of it. Many of these managers later took

What did railroads do to solve their problems?

jobs in other industries. In this way, they shared with others the methods they had used.

1. Which railroad lines crossed the United States west of the Mississippi River?
2. How were the railroads able to expand as an industry between 1860 and 1900?

3. The Rise of Industrial Giants

The growth of the railroad companies was closely followed by that of other businesses. Some companies grew so large and gathered together such huge amounts of capital that they soon controlled major areas of the American economy.

3.1 Rockefeller and Standard Oil. Oil refining was one industry that developed the same kind of large-scale operation as the railroads. At the end of the Civil War, John D. Rockefeller set up a *refinery*—a plant where crude oil is refined or changed into useable products—in Cleveland, Ohio. As a result of the oil boom in Pennsylvania, many people were building refineries. Rockefeller's

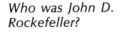
Who was John D. Rockefeller?

By the 1890's, John D. Rockefeller's Standard Oil Company of Ohio controlled about 80 percent of America's oil refining capacity. How did total oil production change between 1860 and 1920 to make Rockefeller America's first billionaire?

Petroleum Production, 1860–1920

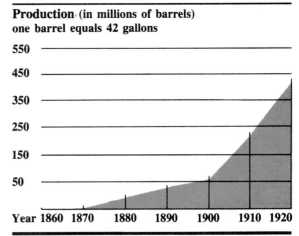

Production (in millions of barrels) one barrel equals 42 gallons

Year	1860	1870	1880	1890	1900	1910	1920

company was one of 30 in Cleveland. In 1867, he formed the Standard Oil Company. Within a few years, Standard Oil owned most of the other refineries in Cleveland as well as some in other cities.

To cut costs, Standard Oil made its own barrels, built its own warehouses, and had its own network of pipelines. To save even more money, Rockefeller made deals with the railroads that shipped oil products to market. Because he shipped larger amounts of oil than any other company, Rockefeller asked for lower rates. The railroads agreed because they needed Standard Oil's business. In Ohio, for example, Rockefeller's company paid only 10 cents a barrel for shipment, while all other companies had to pay 35 cents. The railroad also gave Standard Oil *rebates,* or refunds on its own freight costs.

What did Rockefeller do in the oil industry?

Because Standard Oil made and shipped its products for less, it was able to sell them for less. Smaller companies could not compete, and most of them sold out to Rockefeller. Others were driven out of business. Before long, Rockefeller controlled 90 percent of the oil refining business in the United States.

3.2 Carnegie and the Steel Industry. The steel industry also grew to become part of Big Business. One of the most important leaders in this industry was Andrew Carnegie. He had gained his business experience with the Pennsylvania Railroad. In the late 1860's, Carnegie turned his attention to steel.

Who was Andrew Carnegie?

Andrew Carnegie combined techniques of large-scale production and aggressive selling to improve the steel industry. How did total steel production change between 1860 and 1920 to make the United States the world's leading steel-producer?

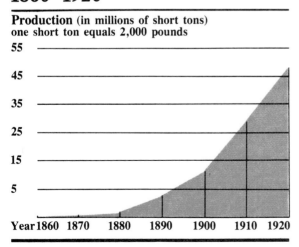

Steel Production, 1860–1920

Production (in millions of short tons)
one short ton equals 2,000 pounds

55	
45	
35	
25	
15	
5	

Year 1860 1870 1880 1890 1900 1910 1920

Carnegie invested money in the latest equipment and used the latest methods to make steel. Like Rockefeller, he sought ways to save money. Carnegie bought companies which supplied coal and iron ore as well as large mining areas of the Mesabi Range. He then bought boats to ship the ore to Pennsylvania. He built a railroad to carry it on from the Great Lakes to the steel mills around Pittsburgh. Because of these actions, Carnegie's costs were lower, and he could sell his steel for less. Other companies could not compete, and Carnegie soon controlled the industry.

Who formed United States Steel Corporation?

Carnegie retired from business in 1901. He sold his steel company to J. P. Morgan, a New York banker. Morgan combined other steel companies with Carnegie's to form the United States Steel Corporation. It had plants in many areas of the country, employed thousands of workers, and owned huge areas of land. United States Steel grew to become the first $1 billion company in the country.

3.3 Feeding the Nation. The meat-packing industry, too, was changing. Before the 1860's, cattle had been shipped by rail to cities around the country. There they were slaughtered and sold. Some business leaders felt that costs could be cut if the animals were slaughtered near where they were raised. Then the meat, rather than the whole animal, could be shipped to the cities. To do this, however, a way of preserving the meat during shipment had to be found.

What brought about the growth of the meat-packing industry?

This problem was solved in the 1870's when the refrigerator railroad car was introduced. Gustavus Swift owned a meat-packing company in Chicago. He built a large slaughterhouse and storage centers in some eastern cities. Animals were shipped to Chicago to be slaughtered. The meat was then moved east in the refrigerator cars. Before long, other companies followed Swift. The leading meat-packing companies—owned by Gustavus Swift, Nelson Morris, and Philip Armour—soon controlled the industry.

What is a corporation?

3.4 The Corporate System. The growth of Big Business led to the further development of certain forms of business organization. Most small businesses were started with money from one person's savings. This worked for small businesses. However, large businesses needed millions of dollars. To solve this problem, *corporations* (groups of investors who buy shares of stock in a company) were formed.

How does a corporation differ from other businesses?

In a corporation, stockholders receive *dividends,* or a share of the profits based on the number of shares they own. If a corporation fails, the stockholders lose only the money they paid for their shares. They are not responsible for any business debts. Stockholders, however, do not run the business. They choose a board of directors to do this. The board of directors generally sets policy for carrying on the corporation's

Corporation

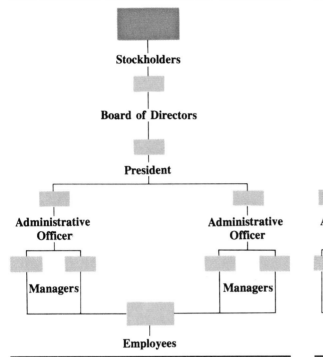

Stockholders

Board of Directors

President

Administrative Officer — Administrative Officer

Managers — Managers

Employees

Trust

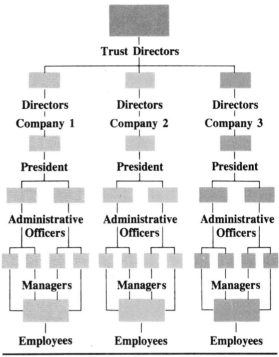

Trust Directors

Directors Company 1 — Directors Company 2 — Directors Company 3

President — President — President

Administrative Officers — Administrative Officers — Administrative Officers

Managers — Managers — Managers

Employees — Employees — Employees

Who controls a corporation? How could one person control a corporation? Who controls a trust? Using a trust agreement, how could one person control any number of other companies?

business. Day-to-day activities are handled by company officers who are selected by the board of directors. If one of the corporation's officers dies, the corporation does not come to an end. It continues to function under the board.

3.5 Pools and Trusts. One of the problems faced by businesses was competition from other companies. When businesses competed to sell their products, they tried to attract buyers by making goods more cheaply and lowering prices. When too many companies entered the same industry, however, more products were made than were needed. As a result, the products had to be sold at such low prices that the businesses did not make a profit.

Companies tried many ways of dealing with this problem. Rockefeller and Standard Oil decided to join other refining companies to form a *pool*. This was an agreement to divide up the market and

What did pools try to do?

Using Visual Evidence

SKILL

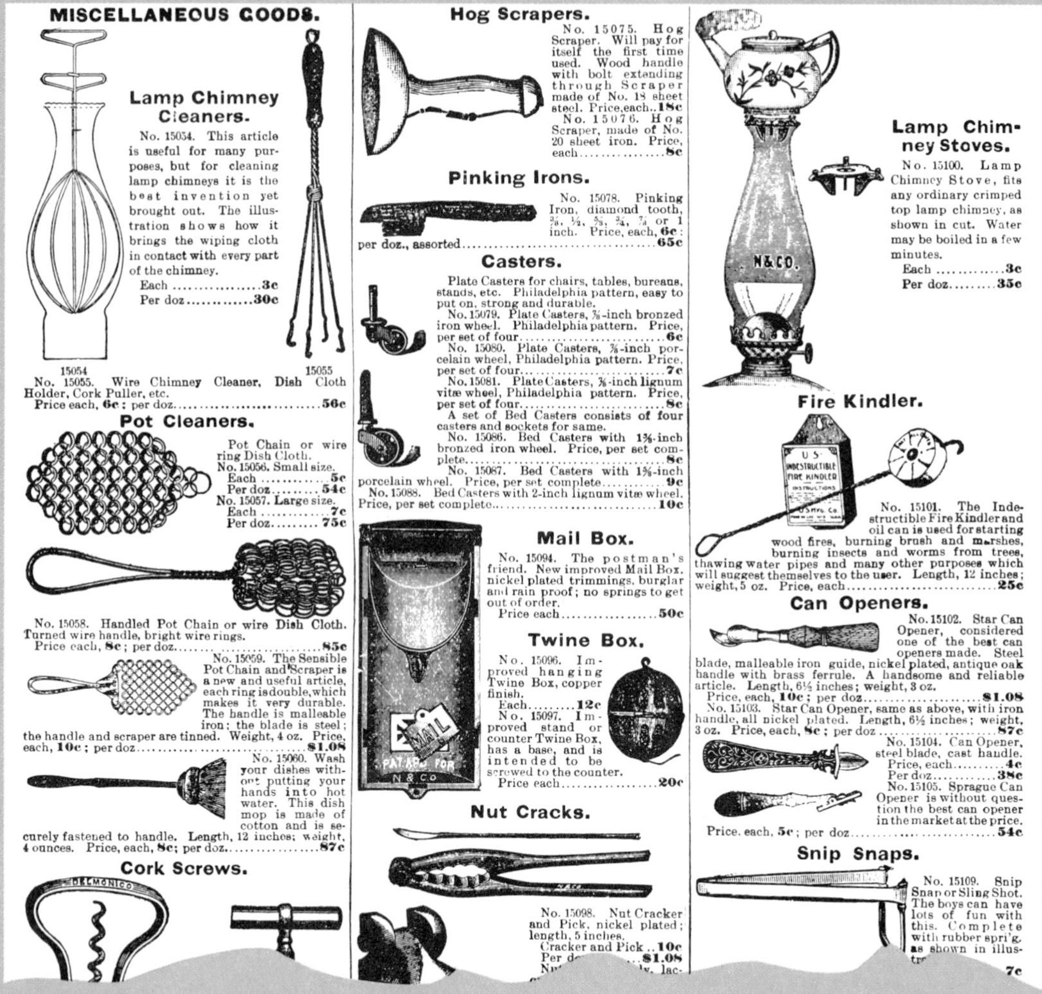

MISCELLANEOUS GOODS.

Lamp Chimney Cleaners.

No. 15054. This article is useful for many purposes, but for cleaning lamp chimneys it is the best invention yet brought out. The illustration shows how it brings the wiping cloth in contact with every part of the chimney.
Each **3c**
Per doz **30c**

15054 15055

No. 15055. Wire Chimney Cleaner, Dish Cloth Holder, Cork Puller, etc.
Price each, **6c**; per doz **56c**

Pot Cleaners.

Pot Chain or wire ring Dish Cloth.
No. 15056. Small size.
Each **5c**
Per doz **54c**
No. 15057. Large size.
Each **7c**
Per doz **75c**

No. 15058. Handled Pot Chain or wire Dish Cloth. Turned wire handle, bright wire rings.
Price each, **8c**; per doz **85c**

No. 15059. The Sensible Pot Chain and Scraper is a new and useful article, each ring is double, which makes it very durable. The handle is malleable iron; the blade is steel; the handle and scraper are tinned. Weight, 4 oz. Price, each, **10c**; per doz **$1.08**

No. 15060. Wash your dishes without putting your hands into hot water. This dish mop is made of cotton and is securely fastened to handle. Length, 12 inches; weight, 4 ounces. Price, each, **8c**; per doz **87c**

Cork Screws.

DELMONICO

Hog Scrapers.

No. 15075. Hog Scraper. Will pay for itself the first time used. Wood handle with bolt extending through Scraper made of No. 18 sheet steel. Price, each .. **18c**

No. 15076. Hog Scraper, made of No. 20 sheet iron. Price, each **8c**

Pinking Irons.

No. 15078. Pinking Iron, diamond tooth, $\frac{3}{8}$, $\frac{1}{2}$, $\frac{5}{8}$, $\frac{3}{4}$, $\frac{7}{8}$ or 1 inch. Price, each, **6c**; per doz., assorted **65c**

Casters.

Plate Casters for chairs, tables, bureaus, stands, etc. Philadelphia pattern, easy to put on, strong and durable.

No. 15079. Plate Casters, $\frac{7}{8}$-inch bronzed iron wheel. Philadelphia pattern. Price, per set of four **6c**

No. 15080. Plate Casters, $\frac{7}{8}$-inch porcelain wheel, Philadelphia pattern. Price, per set of four **7c**

No. 15081. Plate Casters, $\frac{7}{8}$-inch lignum vitæ wheel, Philadelphia pattern. Price, per set of four **8c**

A set of Bed Casters consists of four casters and sockets for same.

No. 15086. Bed Casters with $1\frac{3}{8}$-inch bronzed iron wheel. Price, per set complete **8c**

No. 15087. Bed Casters with $1\frac{5}{8}$-inch porcelain wheel. Price, per set complete **9c**

No. 15088. Bed Casters with 2-inch lignum vitæ wheel. Price, per set complete **10c**

Mail Box.

No. 15094. The postman's friend. New improved Mail Box, nickel plated trimmings, burglar and rain proof; no springs to get out of order.
Price each **50c**

MAIL
PAT. APD. FOR
N & CO

Twine Box.

No. 15096. Improved hanging Twine Box, copper finish.
Each **12c**

No. 15097. Improved stand or counter Twine Box, has a base, and is intended to be screwed to the counter.
Price each **20c**

Nut Cracks.

No. 15098. Nut Cracker and Pick, nickel plated; length, 5 inches.
Cracker and Pick .. **10c**
Per d... ...**$1.08**
N... ...ly, lac-

N&CO.

Lamp Chimney Stoves.

No. 15100. Lamp Chimney Stove, fits any ordinary crimped top lamp chimney, as shown in cut. Water may be boiled in a few minutes.
Each **3c**
Per doz **35c**

Fire Kindler.

U.S.
INDESTRUCTIBLE
FIRE KINDLER
INSTRUCTIONS
U.S. MFG. CO.

No. 15101. The Indestructible Fire Kindler and oil can is used for starting wood fires, burning brush and marshes, burning insects and worms from trees, thawing water pipes and many other purposes which will suggest themselves to the user. Length, 12 inches; weight, 5 oz. Price, each **25c**

Can Openers.

No. 15102. Star Can Opener, considered one of the best can openers made. Steel blade, malleable iron guide, nickel plated, antique oak handle with brass ferrule. A handsome and reliable article. Length, $6\frac{1}{2}$ inches; weight, 3 oz.
Price, each, **10c**; per doz **$1.08**

No. 15103. Star Can Opener, same as above, with iron handle, all nickel plated. Length, $6\frac{1}{2}$ inches; weight, 3 oz. Price, each, **8c**; per doz **87c**

No. 15104. Can Opener, steel blade, cast handle.
Price, each **4c**
Per doz **38c**

No. 15105. Sprague Can Opener is without question the best can opener in the market at the price.
Price, each, **5c**; per doz **54c**

Snip Snaps.

No. 15109. Snip Snap or Sling Shot. The boys can have lots of fun with this. Complete with rubber spri'g, as shown in illus- ...
7c

From the Sears, Roebuck catalog of the late 1890's, people can see the things Americans used in their everyday lives. This type of information is visual evidence.

1. Which items are unfamiliar today?
2. For what is each item used?
3. Which can be used today?
4. How do the prices compare to those of the same items today?

control prices. Each company would agree to buy so much crude oil and to sell only a certain amount of refined product. In this way, each company hoped to make a profit.

Pools were illegal, but it was difficult to prove their existence. They did not work, however, because the members could not force every company to join. There was also nothing to stop members from breaking agreements. As a result, Rockefeller looked for other ways to control competition.

Standard Oil was an Ohio company. By law, it was not allowed to own plants in other states or stock in out-of-state corporations. So in 1879, Rockefeller created the *trust*. Under this arrangement, stockholders from a number of companies gave their stock to a board of trustees. In return, they received trust certificates. Because the board held this stock, it could direct policy in all the companies. In this way, Standard Oil increased its influence on the oil business. Trusts also were set up in other businesses, resulting in the creation of monopolies.

How were trusts formed?

3.6 The Philosophy of Business.   Certain ideas supported the growth of Big Business. Together, they formed a philosophy for the leaders of American industry. One of the basic ideas of that philosophy was known as *laissez-faire*. This French term means "hands off." In business, it refers to an economy in which the government does not make rules for business.

What ideas did business leaders support?

Business leaders, like Rockefeller and Carnegie, believed in laissez-faire. They did not want the government to limit their activities. Some, like Carnegie, also thought that they should use part of their wealth for the good of society. Carnegie called this idea the *"gospel of wealth."* Business leaders felt that the economic system was democratic, and that a person's background was not important to success. Some of them also believed in *social Darwinism*. This refers to the idea that life was a struggle, and only the fittest survived.

To prove that their ideas were sound, leaders in business pointed to their achievements. Under their direction, the railroad system had grown rapidly. Between 1860 and 1890, capital invested in business had risen from $1 billion to almost $10 billion. As a result, the United States became the leading industrial nation in the world by 1900.

3.7 Business and Government.   Business leaders received support for their ideas from government. Both the Republicans and the Democrats in Congress favored laissez-faire. The Republicans, however, were more clearly thought of as the party of Big Business. They were, for the most part, in control of the Presidency from 1868 to 1900. The Supreme Court, too, generally favored the idea that government should not interfere with business.

What party strongly supported Big Business?

The Age of Big Business   419

Population by State, 1900

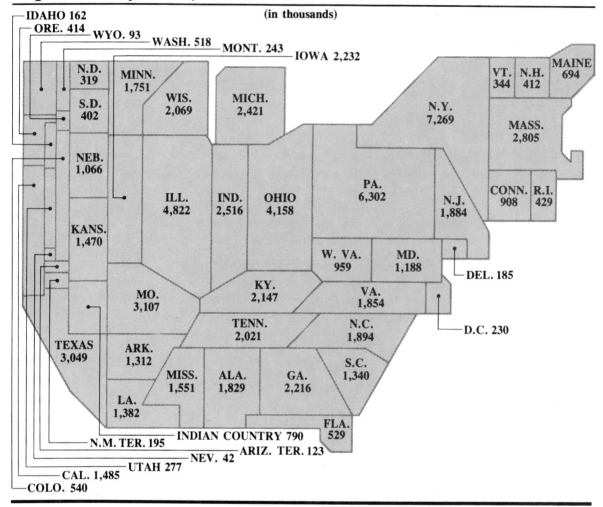

(in thousands)

IDAHO 162
ORE. 414
WYO. 93
WASH. 518
MONT. 243
IOWA 2,232
N.D. 319
MINN. 1,751
WIS. 2,069
MICH. 2,421
N.Y. 7,269
VT. 344
N.H. 412
MAINE 694
MASS. 2,805
S.D. 402
NEB. 1,066
ILL. 4,822
IND. 2,516
OHIO 4,158
PA. 6,302
N.J. 1,884
CONN. 908
R.I. 429
KANS. 1,470
W. VA. 959
MD. 1,188
DEL. 185
MO. 3,107
KY. 2,147
VA. 1,854
D.C. 230
TEXAS 3,049
ARK. 1,312
TENN. 2,021
N.C. 1,894
MISS. 1,551
ALA. 1,829
GA. 2,216
S.C. 1,340
LA. 1,382
FLA. 529
INDIAN COUNTRY 790
N.M. TER. 195
ARIZ. TER. 123
NEV. 42
UTAH 277
CAL. 1,485
COLO. 540

In 1900, which states had the largest number of people? Which states had the smallest? Which section of the United States was most populated? Which section was least populated?

This alliance of business and government led to both progress and corruption. Many people thought that society was not what it appeared to be on the surface. In fact, the writer Mark Twain called the late 1800's the *"gilded age."* He compared it to an object covered with gold paint.

1. How did John D. Rockefeller control the oil industry?
2. How did Andrew Carnegie cut costs in steel production?
3. What was the philosophy of business in the 1800's?

4. The Revolt of the Farmers

The rise of Big Business did not benefit all people. Groups of Americans began to complain about problems in the economic system for different reasons. Farmers were the first to feel the effects of economic change and to organize for reform.

4.1 The Plight of the Farmer. In the late 1800's, farmers in the United States were producing more than ever before. Between 1860 and 1900, the number of farms grew from 2 to 6 million. Annual wheat production jumped from 200 to over 665 million bushels. Corn production rose from less than 1 million bushels to over 2.5 billion bushels a year.

What problems did farmers face in the late 1800's?

The prices that farmers received for their crops, however, continued to drop. In 1869, a bushel of corn was 75 cents; in 1889, it was 28 cents. In 1866, a pound of cotton was 31 cents; in 1886, it was only 9 cents. Prices dropped partly because of competition from farmers in other countries. In the world market, American farmers had to compete against people in Canada, Australia, Russia, and South America. Rich farmlands in these countries were opened about the same time that American settlers were moving into the Great Plains.

While farm prices dropped, farm costs continued to rise. Because of this, many farmers in the Midwest, Great Plains, and South were deeply in debt. Farmers tended to blame manufacturers and bankers for their troubles. These people held most of the farm mortgages. They also set the prices of manufactured goods and controlled the railroads.

Farmers were especially angry at the railroads. In the 1860's, most had supported the building of railroads. By the 1880's, however, the railroads owned most of the warehouses and grain elevators that farmers used. This made many farmers, especially those in the Midwest and Great Plains, depend on the railroads for transportation. As a result, farmers had no choice but to pay the high rates charged by the railroads.

Why were farmers angry at the railroads?

4.2 The Grange Movement. A number of farm groups favored regulation of the railroads. One of these was the National Grange of the Patrons of Husbandry, or the Grange, formed by Oliver Kelley in 1867. It was set up to further farm interests, and in its early days, it was mainly a social group for the enjoyment of the farmers. By 1875, the Grange had over 800,000 members.

Who formed the Grange? for what purpose?

Through the Grange, members learned that they shared many of the same problems. Sometimes local groups of farmers combined their

While Oliver Kelley was working at the Department of Agriculture, he came up with an idea for a farmers' organization. At first, the Grange had mainly a social function. Meetings and parties provided welcomed breaks in daily farm routines. What else did Grange members do to improve life on farms?

What was the purpose of farmer cooperatives?

How did farmers attempt to regulate the railroads?

What was the Supreme Court's view toward the Granger laws?

money and set up a ***cooperative***—a business owned and operated by the people who use its services. These groups hoped to sell farm machinery, insurance, and warehousing to other farmers for lower prices than those charged by Big Business. Some of these efforts were successful, but they did not keep crop prices from falling.

As time passed, members of the Grange became more and more active in politics. They gained control of a number of state legislatures in the Midwest. Between 1870 and 1874, Illinois, Iowa, Minnesota, and Wisconsin passed laws to regulate the railroads and to supervise warehousing. These laws were known as Granger laws.

The railroad companies were against the Granger laws. They felt that states had no right to regulate interstate trade. Only Congress had that right. The railroad companies also said that states, by regulating rates, were taking away property (income) of the railroads without due process of law. This went against the Fourteenth Amendment.

In 1877, the Supreme Court heard the case of *Munn* v. *Illinois*. In it, the Court upheld a state law which set grain elevator rates. However, in 1886, the Court ruled against an Illinois law setting railroad rates. In *Wabash, St. Louis, and Pacific Railroad Company* v. *Illinois*, the Court held that Illinois could not regulate rates because the railroad company carried freight across several state borders. Only Congress could regulate rates for interstate carriers, not any state. Later the Court ruled that businesses were entitled to the protections of the Fourteenth

Thomas Watson (1856–1922)
PROFILE

As a member of the Georgia legislature from 1882 to 1890, Thomas Watson sought prosperity for all southern farmers. He did not want the farming economy of the South to become a victim to the industrial economy of the North.

Watson won the support of the Populist party, a black and white alliance of farming interests. It worked to elect him to the United States Congress in 1890. There he supported Populist ideas to benefit farmers.

Watson lost his reelection campaigns in 1892 and 1894. In 1896, he became the Populist party candidate for Vice-President with Democratic presidential candidate William Jennings Bryan. Many Democrats did not want Watson running with Bryan and did not support the ticket. Without the Democrats, Bryan and Watson lost.

The defeat changed Watson. In the 1900's, he spoke out against blacks, socialists, Jews, and Catholics—some of the same people who had helped elect him to office earlier in his career. Watson saw these people as representing the ideas and races of people that threatened prosperity for white southern farmers. Many people saw Watson as representing the racial and religious fears of his time.

Amendment. The Court's change in policy helped bring about the end to Granger laws and the Grange's influence in politics.

4.3 The Farmers' Alliances. During the 1890's, farmers formed other groups. In Kansas, Nebraska, Iowa, Minnesota, and the Dakotas, they joined the Northwest Alliance. In the South, white farmers joined the Southern Alliance, while black farmers formed the Colored Farmers' Alliance. In 1890, they won control of a number of state legislatures in the South and in the West. They also sent more than 50 members to Congress.

4.4 The Rise of Populism. After the elections of 1890, farm leaders, as well as some city workers, decided to form a new political party. In July 1892, they met in Omaha, Nebraska, where they started the People's party. Members of the new party were called Populists.

What was populism?

The Populists felt that Big Business controlled state legislatures. They wanted to return power to the citizens. They called for many government reforms. Among them were the use of the secret ballot and the direct election of United States Senators. Populists favored other measures as well. The *initiative* was a method by which citizens could propose new laws at any time. The *referendum* was a method that allowed citizens to vote to approve or defeat any bill brought up by the legislature. The *recall* was a way for citizens to vote on removing elected officials from public office.

What things did the Populists support?

The Populists also wanted to check the power of Big Business. They thought that the government should take over the railroad companies, telegraph companies, and steamship lines. They favored a *graduated income tax*—a tax system in which people with more money pay higher taxes.

In 1892, James B. Weaver was the Populist candidate for President. He received over 1 million popular votes. In 1894, Populist candidates received over 1.5 million votes. Most of the party's support, however, was in the Midwest, the Rocky Mountain area, and the South. In the South, black and white farmers worked together for a brief time before cooperation broke down. It did not seem that the Populists were strong enough to win in 1896.

1. What happened to farm prices between 1860 and 1900?
2. How did farmers organize?
3. Where were farmers' organizations strongest?

5. The Rise of American Labor

Farmers were not the only people concerned by the rise of Big Business. Workers of all types were affected. The growth of industry changed not only the way they worked, but also the way they lived. In the late 1800's, these people turned more and more to their own organizations for help.

5.1 Early Labor Groups. There had been a number of local labor organizations before 1860. Some of these were simply groups to help one another. They were generally made up of skilled workers, who often owned their own tools and their own shops.

Who belonged to the early labor organizations in the United States?

With industrialization, mills and factories employed greater numbers of people who needed little or no skill to do the work. Because these people could be replaced easily, they had little bargaining power with their employers. As Big Business grew, so did disputes between the workers and their employers. As companies grew larger, it was no longer possible to settle matters on a personal or even a local level. Because of this, workers began to form national *labor unions*. Through these groups, they tried to bargain with factory owners for better conditions.

In 1866, a number of trade unions, made up of skilled workers, joined together to form the National Labor Union. Its leaders wanted to make changes through political means. Most of the members, however, were interested in more immediate gains. After a few years, the National Labor Union broke up.

What was the first important national labor union?

5.2 The Knights of Labor.   In December 1869, the Noble and Holy Order of the Knights of Labor was founded by Uriah Stephens. The Knights was an organization of individuals rather than of trade unions. It was open to all workers, both skilled and unskilled. Mother Mary Jones, who joined the Knights in Chicago, wrote of her decision:

Who formed the Knights of Labor? Who could belong?

> *I learned that in 1865 . . . a group of men met in Louisville, Kentucky. They came from the North and from the South [and] a year or two before had been fighting each other over the*

Machinist Frank J. Farrell introduced Terence Powderly to the 1886 Knights of Labor Convention (left). How many members did the Knights have in 1886? When did membership in the AFL surpass that of the Knight's best year?

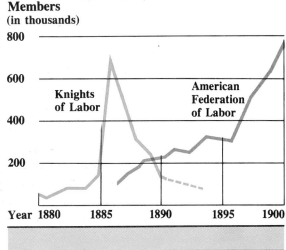

Union Membership, 1880–1900

Members (in thousands)

Knights of Labor

American Federation of Labor

Year 1880   1885   1890   1895   1900

question of . . . slavery. They decided that the time had come [for] *a program to fight another brutal form of slavery—industrial slavery. Out of* [their] *decision had come the Knights of Labor.*

. . . I decided to take an active part in the efforts of the working people to better the conditions under which they worked and lived. I became a member. . . .

What did the Knights of Labor favor instead of strikes?

In 1879, Terence Powderly was chosen leader of the Knights. He was a reformer who felt that workers should set up their own mines, factories, and railroads. Powderly and other leaders of the Knights were against the use of *strikes*—a refusal by workers to work until the company's owners agreed to their demands or offered an acceptable compromise. They favored settling disputes between owners and workers by negotiation. In spite of this, strikes became more common in the 1880's, partly because a few local unions held successful ones. During Powderly's years in office, the Knights grew rapidly. By 1886, it had over 700,000 members.

5.3 Haymarket Square. In 1886, workers all over the country struck for an eight-hour day. A strike was already in progress in Chicago against the McCormick Harvesting Machine Company. Strikers and police had clashed there in a street fight on May 3. A striker was killed, and several people were wounded. Union leaders called for a meeting the next day in Haymarket Square to protest the striker's death. Some *anarchists*—those people who wanted to do away with government—attended the meeting and made speeches supporting the eight-hour day. The police started to break up the meeting, and someone threw a bomb. It killed seven police officers and wounded many others. The police fired into the crowd and killed four more people.

What occurred at Haymarket Square?

Americans were upset by the news of violence at Haymarket Square. Some people blamed the anarchists, and their leaders were tried and found guilty. Although nothing linked the anarchists with the bombing, four of them were executed for murder. Many people also blamed the labor unions, mainly the Knights of Labor. Within a few years, the Knights lost a great deal of influence and most of its members.

Who was blamed for the violence?

5.4 The American Federation of Labor. As the Knights declined, another group rose. This was the American Federation of Labor (AFL), formed in 1886 by Samuel Gompers. The AFL was made up of skilled workers who belonged to national trade unions. Each of these trade unions remained more or less independent within the AFL. The AFL did not want to change society. Its goals were to gain better conditions for workers, such as higher pay and shorter hours. Gompers

Who formed the AFL? What were the AFL's aims?

and other leaders favored the use of strikes. By 1900, the AFL was the leading union in the country.

1. How did labor organize?
2. What actions could a union take to accomplish its goals?
3. What made the AFL different from other labor groups?

6. The Search for Justice

The rise of Big Business caused concern not only among farmers and workers, but also among other groups of Americans. More and more people began to speak out for reform.

6.1 Religion and Reform. In the late 1800's, many religious leaders began to work to improve people's living conditions. Churches in many parts of the country began giving aid to the poor. They set up nurseries and kindergartens. Both the Young Men's Christian Association (YMCA) and the Young Women's Christian Association (YWCA) grew rapidly. In 1880, the Salvation Army opened its first mission at Philadelphia. Soon others were opened in many cities.

What were some of the groups that tried to improve living conditions?

6.2 The Settlement House Movement. People also founded *settlement houses*. These were places where people could go to receive

What were settlement houses?

There were usually few outdoor places in crowded cities for people to relax. Some settlement houses offered recreation space and equipment for everyone to use. What other activities did settlement houses provide?

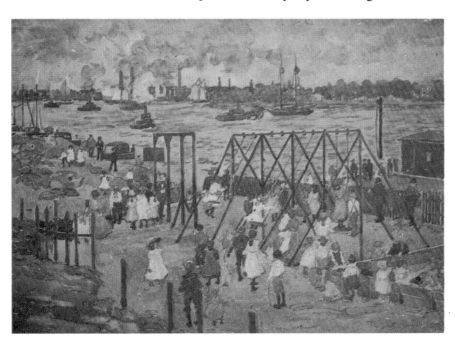

medical care and to get help in finding jobs. Immigrants could go to learn English. The first settlement house was established in London, England, in 1884. In the United States, the first settlement house was set up in New York City in 1886. Settlement houses were also founded in Chicago, Pittsburgh, Boston, and other large cities.

One of the most famous settlement houses was Chicago's Hull House. It was started by Jane Addams in 1889. Jane Edna Hunter, a black nurse from South Carolina, set up the Working Girls' Home Association in Cleveland, Ohio. It was founded to help black women find jobs in the city. Lillian Wald started Henry Street Settlement in New York. Wald was especially interested in providing free nursing care for the needy.

Who were some important settlement house founders?

What were some important works that urged reform?

6.3 The Literature of Protest. A number of authors during these years wrote works that urged reform. Henry George's *Progress and Poverty* came out in 1879. George wanted a single tax levied on those who owned land. George believed this would narrow the gap between the rich and the poor. Edward Bellamy's *Looking Backward,* printed in 1888, described a utopian America in the year 2000. In this society, profit making had been set aside, and wealth was shared by all. Jacob Riis did a study of life in the slums, *How the Other Half Lives,* in 1890. It showed a number of photographs Riis had taken in New York City. Slum life was also described in Stephen Crane's *Maggie: A Girl of the Streets. Wealth Against Commonwealth* by Henry Demarest Lloyd directly attacked the Standard Oil trust. All of these writings drew people's attention to the problems caused by Big Business.

1. What was the settlement house movement?
2. Who wrote about problems caused by business in the late 1800's?

7. Conclusion

The United States became the world's leading industrial nation during the "Age of Big Business." The rise of Big Business, however, created a new set of problems for Americans. By the end of the 1800's, opinion was divided about the economy. Supporters of laissez-faire believed that the economic system worked best when left alone. They also believed that the system was, for the most part, fair. Farmers, workers, and others believed that rules were needed to control Big Business and ensure justice for everyone. As the new century began, Americans continued the search for answers to the questions raised by these issues.

Chapter 18 Review

Main Points

1. By the beginning of the 1900's, the United States led the world in industrial production.

2. Abundant natural resources, a large labor force, and new inventions made industrial growth possible.

3. The railroads were the first companies to become large-scale businesses.

4. The oil and steel industries grew to dominate major areas of the economy.

5. The corporation developed as a way to organize business.

6. Pools and trusts created monopolies in some businesses.

7. Farmers and workers experienced difficulties which many thought were caused by business.

8. Farmers and workers organized to protect their own interests.

9. Efforts to reform business practices believed to have caused problems for farmers and workers had limited success. This was due largely to government's support of business interests.

Building Vocabulary

1. Identify the following:

Titusville	Gustavus Swift	Thomas Watson	Terence Powderly
Thomas Edison	Grange	Populists	Haymarket Square
Promontory Point	Granger laws	Knights of Labor	Samuel Gompers
John D. Rockefeller	*Munn* v. *Illinois*	Mother Mary Jones	Jane Edna Hunter
Andrew Carnegie			Jacob Riis

2. Define the following:

consumers	dividends	social Darwinism	recall
transcontinental	pool	"gilded age"	graduated income tax
capital	trust	cooperative	labor unions
refinery	laissez-faire	initiative	strikes
rebates	"gospel of wealth"	referendum	anarchists
corporations			settlement houses

Remembering the Facts

1. What made the growth of business possible in the late 1800's?

2. How did the railroads form a model of organization for other industries?

3. Which industries organized after the railroads did?

4. What was the purpose of a corporation? What were stockholders?

5. How did the idea of laissez-faire benefit business?
6. What did farmers and workers do to protect themselves against problems caused by the growth of industry?

7. What were some of the difficulties that farm organizations and unions encountered?
8. What reform groups attempted to improve living conditions in the cities?

Understanding the Facts

1. What is meant by "Big Business"?
2. Why did the railroad industry develop as the first business organization?
3. What were the benefits and problems in the way Rockefeller organized the oil industry?
4. How did the growth of business change the lives of workers?

5. How did business affect farmers?
6. What were the advantages of the corporation over other forms of business organization?
7. How successful were farmers in their efforts to regulate railroads?
8. How did the settlement houses help to improve life in the cities?

Using Diagrams

Reading Skewed Diagrams. All reference maps and most thematic maps are drawn to scale. They attempt to show shapes of land formations as they are. In this way, most maps make it possible to compare the size and shape of surrounding land areas. To compare something other than size and shape, a skewed diagram is often used. Skewing means distorting a geographic area according to what information is to be shown.

The diagram on page 420 is roughly how a map of the United States would look to reflect state population in 1900. It is drawn to provide a comparison based on population, and not on physical size and shape. Examine this special diagram, and answer the following questions.

1. How is it possible to tell if one state has more people than those around it?
2. Which two states appear to have the most people living in them?
3. Which states appear to have the fewest people living in them?
4. How does the population in the territories and the Indian Country compare to the population in the states?
5. Which section of the country appears to have the most people?

The Progressive Era   19

"The Bowery at Night" was painted by W. Louis Sonntag, Jr. It shows an area of New York City at the beginning of the twentieth century. What forms of transportation can be seen in the painting?

By the end of the 1800's, new and growing industries were bringing the American people more opportunities than ever before. Many Americans, however, searched for answers to the problems caused by industrialization. In the early 1900's, a wave of reform swept the United States. Because of the number of reforms made during these years, the period became known as the Progressive Era.

1. New Opportunities _____

The rise of industry led to the growth of cities. Many people moved to these cities looking for a chance to improve their lives. There they often found jobs, a better opportunity for education, and new ways to enjoy themselves.

1.1   Toward an Urban America.   After the Civil War, cities in the United States grew both in number and in size. Between 1860 and 1910, the urban population of the United States grew from a little over 6 million to over 40 million. In 1860, 20 percent of all Americans lived in cities with 2,500 or more people. By 1910, 46 percent of all Americans lived in such places. In 1860, there were only 16 cities in the United States with a population over 50,000. By 1910, there were 109.

This growth came from different sources. Many Americans left their farms for city life. They came to work in the new offices and factories. During the late 1800's and early 1900's, some southern blacks began moving to cities to find better jobs. At the same time, immigrants in search of a better life settled in the cities of the Northeast and Middle West.

1.2   Growing Educational Opportunities.   As the economy grew, so did interest in public education. In the 1870's, some states passed *compulsory attendance laws*. These laws required that children attend school for a certain part of the year. By 1900, 30 states had passed such laws.

More people became interested in higher education during the late 1800's. One of the reasons for this was the Morrill Act, passed in 1862. Under this act, states were given public lands to set up state colleges of engineering, teacher training, and agriculture. Meanwhile, the total number of colleges grew from about 500 in 1870 to nearly 1,000 in 1900.

During these years, educational opportunities increased for both women and blacks. By 1900, blacks had founded over 30 colleges, mostly in the South. Over 2,000 black students had graduated. By 1900, nearly 100,000 women were attending college.

To what extent did urban growth take place in the late 1800's?

What were the sources of urban growth?

What things helped foster a growth in education in the late 1800's?

1.3 Popular Sports. The growing interest in education was matched by a growing interest in leisure. Greater use of labor-saving machines at work and at home made it possible for people to have more free time. This time was spent in a number of ways. People attended and took part in sports events and other free-time activities.

What helped to bring about an increase in leisure time?

The most popular spectator sport was baseball. Baseball, as it is known today, was started by Abner Doubleday. In 1869, the first professional team, the Cincinnati Red Stockings, was formed. In 1876, teams from eight cities formed the National League, and in 1900, the American League was set up. The first World Series, between the Boston Red Sox and the Pittsburgh Pirates, was played in 1903.

When and where did professional baseball begin?

Football was nearly as popular as baseball. It had first been played between teams of students from the same school. Then in 1869, the first *intercollegiate* (involving two or more colleges) game took place between Princeton and Rutgers. The first professional game was played in 1895. In the 1890's, the game of basketball was invented by Dr. James Naismith in Springfield, Massachusetts.

The late 1800's also saw the beginning of the bicycle craze. This was partly due to the fact that a safer bicycle had been developed in 1888. It had two rubber tires of the same size filled with air. Older bicycles had had metal-rimmed wheels, a large one in front and a small one in back. By 1900, about 10 million Americans were riding bicycles. Clubs were

What brought about the bicycle craze?

Sports flourished in the early 1900's. Bowling—together with billiards, hiking, golf, croquet, tennis, and swimming—were popular activities. What was the most popular spectator sport at this same time?

formed, magazines carried articles on cycling, and roads were improved for riding.

1.4 Popular Music and Literature. Americans also spent time listening to music. John Philip Sousa and his band thrilled thousands with such marches as "The Stars and Stripes Forever" and "The Washington Post March." Sousa had been a director of the United States Marine Corps Band. He formed his own band in 1892 and took it on tour to cities around the United States and Europe. Ragtime also became popular in the late 1890's. It started with Scott Joplin's "Maple Leaf Rag." It was a long time, however, before ragtime was accepted as a serious form of music. By the early 1900's, many people were also becoming interested in *operettas,* or light operas. Two of the most popular were Victor Herbert's "Babes in Toyland" and Sigmund Romberg's "Student Prince."

What kinds of music became popular in the late 1800's?

Americans also were finding time to read. Writers such as Bret Harte, Louisa May Alcott, and Samuel Clemens, who wrote under the name of Mark Twain, were among the more popular authors of the late 1800's. Harte wrote adventure stories of the West, like *The Luck of Roaring Camp*. Alcott, who wrote *Little Women*, based her stories on the lives of young people in New England. Clemens had been a riverboat captain on the Mississippi as well as a journalist in the mining camps of the West. He wrote such works as *The Adventures of Tom Sawyer* and *The Adventures of Huckleberry Finn*.

During the late 1800's, newspapers became an important part of American life. Daily papers were printed in every major city. Several

Between 1860 and 1920, Americans steadily left the countrysides and moved into cities and towns. How did the percents of urban and rural population change during these years?

Urban Population

Year	Percent Rural	Percent Urban	Cities 2,500 to 50,000	Cities over 50,000
1860	80.2	19.8	376	16
1870	74.3	25.7	638	25
1880	71.8	28.2	904	35
1890	64.9	35.1	1290	58
1900	60.3	39.7	1659	80
1910	54.3	45.7	2153	109
1920	48.8	51.2	2578	144

foreign language papers also existed. Most small towns had at least weekly papers. As people's interest in day-to-day happenings grew, so did newspaper circulation. It jumped from 2.8 million in 1870 to 24.2 million readers in 1900.

What took place in the newspaper industry during the late 1800's?

1. What law did Congress pass to help the growth of American colleges?
2. What were the most popular sports in the late 1800's?
3. Who were some of the leading writers of this time?

2. The Struggle for Control

In the late 1800's, life was improving for many, but not all, Americans. Certain groups continued to demand government control of Big Business. Farm organizations began to seek reforms at the national level.

2.1 The Interstate Commerce Act. When state regulation of Big Business failed, farmers looked to the national government for a solution. In 1887, the Interstate Commerce Act was passed. This act stopped railroads from forming pools, giving rebates, or charging unfair rates. It set up the Interstate Commerce Commission (ICC) to oversee the railroads. It became the first *regulatory commission* (supervising agency) in the United States.

What was the first federal regulatory commission?

For the most part, the Interstate Commerce Act did not work well. The act failed to spell out what rates were fair and just. It also did not give the ICC the power to enforce its orders. Only the courts could make the railroads obey, and at the time, the courts often sided with the railroads. In spite of this, the Interstate Commerce Act did mark the beginning of federal regulation of Big Business.

2.2 The Sherman Antitrust Act. In 1890, Congress passed another law aimed at controlling Big Business. This was the Sherman Antitrust Act. It was the first federal law dealing with trusts and monopolies. The act said that any combination or contract made in "restraint of trade" (with the idea of limiting trade) was against the law. The Sherman Antitrust Act also proved to be weak. Congress failed to state clearly what was meant by "restraint of trade." Therefore, it was very hard to prove that businesses were violating the act.

What was the purpose of the Sherman Antitrust Act?

2.3 The Election of 1896. The struggle to control Big Business lasted through the 1890's. It had a strong effect on the election of 1896.

Jane Addams (1860–1935)

PROFILE

At age 29, Jane Addams took over the shabby Hull mansion in Chicago's tenement district. In 1889, she opened its doors to the poor and oppressed of the city. She renamed the mansion Hull House. By 1900, Addams provided social services to 2,000 people each day, offering recreation, entertainment, job training, and education.

Addams was raised in Illinois. Early in her life, she was determined to improve the world's way of living. Hull House was her way of beginning. It also served as a model for many more people who felt they could best help other people by working and living with them.

Besides Hull House, Addams found other ways to improve the world. She fought for legal protection of immigrants, for the regulation of child labor, and for women's suffrage. During World War I, she was the central figure in the international women's peace movement. In 1931, she shared the Nobel Peace Prize with Nicholas Murray Butler, president of Columbia University. Typically, Addams directed that her share of the prize money be used to help create a better life for all of humankind.

What was the major issue of the election of 1896?

What effect did being on the gold standard have on money?

A number of issues divided the reformers and the supporters of Big Business. The most important issue, however, was the money question.

In 1873, the United States had gone on the **gold standard.** This meant that paper money was backed by gold alone. Since gold was scarce, this reduced the amount of money in use and hurt farmers. They wanted paper money to be backed by silver as well as gold, a policy known as **bimetalism.** Money backed by both metals would have brought about **inflation,** or an increased money supply with a resulting rise in prices. Farmers then would have been able to pay off their debts more easily. Silver miners and their representatives in Congress backed the farmers. Those who favored the gold standard, on the other hand, believed that if the government used both silver and gold to back money, gold would drop in value. This, in turn, would weaken business and the economy.

In July 1896, the Democrats met in Chicago. People who favored silver soon took over the convention. As the delegates worked on the platform, William Jennings Bryan gave a moving speech:

> *You come to us and tell us that the great cities are in favor of the gold standard; we reply that the great cities rest upon our broad and fertile prairies. Burn down your cities and leave our farms, and your cities will spring up again as if by magic; but destroy our farms and the grass will grow in the streets of every city in the country. . . .*
>
> *Having behind us the producing masses of this nation and the world, supported by the commercial interests, the laboring interests, and the toilers everywhere, we will answer their demand for a gold standard by saying to them: You shall not press down upon the brow of labor this crown of thorns, you shall not crucify mankind upon a cross of gold.*

Following this speech, the Democrats agreed to support a money supply backed by both silver and gold. They also chose Bryan to run for President.

The choice of Bryan, as well as the Democratic platform, presented a problem for the Populists. The Democrats had, more or less, taken

Bryan was the candidate of what parties?

Whether William Jennings Bryan spoke in a big city convention hall or at a rural railroad stop, he attracted a crowd. He was a popular politician who never reached his goal of becoming President of the United States. To whom did Bryan lose the election of 1896?

over the Populist party's platform. So the Populists also chose Bryan, thinking that he had the best chance to win.

What was the Republican position in the election of 1896?

With the Democrats and Populists supporting bimetalism, the Republicans came out for the gold standard and a higher protective tariff. They selected William McKinley of Ohio as their candidate. McKinley won in 1896 with 271 electoral votes to Bryan's 176.

What helped to bring about an end to the Populist party?

During McKinley's term in office, the economy began to improve. Crop failures in Europe caused farm prices to rise. New gold found in Alaska made it possible to add to the country's gold reserves. This meant that the government could increase the money supply without minting silver. All of these changes helped to bring about an end to the Populist party.

1. What was the purpose of the Interstate Commerce Act?
2. How successful was the Sherman Antitrust Act?
3. Who wanted to increase the amount of money in use? Why?

3. The Beginnings of Progressivism

Shortly after the decline of the Populists, a new wave of reform swept the country. The reformers believed that their ideas would lead to progress and a better way of life for more Americans. Because of this, these people were called progressives. Although they drew support from some of the same groups as the Populists, there were differences. Progressivism, unlike populism, was centered in America's cities. Its leaders were doctors, lawyers, teachers, and owners of small businesses, rather than farmers.

Who were the reformers of the early 1900's?

3.1 Progressive Aims. The progressives did not have an organized group and often differed in their aims. Most progressives shared certain ideas, however. They wanted honest government, with power in the hands of the people. They wanted an active government, which would regulate Big Business. They also favored social reforms that would make life better for people. They worked to improve labor conditions for women, children, and other workers. The progressive aims, however, did not include improving rights for minority groups. Life for blacks, Indians, and Mexican Americans grew worse in some ways in this period.

3.2 Progressive Literature. In the early 1900's, certain writers pointed out the need for reform by pointing out corruption in

American life. Known as *muckrakers,* these authors criticized Big Business and government. One of the first was Ida M. Tarbell, whose *History of the Standard Oil Company* appeared in 1903. In it, Tarbell attacked Rockefeller's business practices. Another reform writer was Lincoln Steffens. In *The Shame of the Cities,* which appeared in 1904, Steffens wrote about corrupt practices in city government. In *The Jungle,* which was printed in 1906, Upton Sinclair examined the practices of the meat-packing industry. These works and others drew attention to the need for change.

Who were the muckrakers?

3.3 Progressivism at the Local Level.

Many progressive ideas were put into practice in the early 1900's. The major area to receive the attention at the local level was city government. It was often run by political bosses. The voters, influenced by the bosses, chose a mayor and a city council to run the government. Other important city jobs were filled with supporters of the bosses through the spoils system. These city officers often favored businesses in return for large gifts of money, which helped them to remain in power.

What did progressives seek to change at the local level? How?

Progressives wanted to break boss rule. One way was to change the form of city government. In 1901, one new form of government was set up in Galveston, Texas. The city had been hit by a tidal wave, and the mayor and council could not handle the situation. So the citizens elected a five-member commission to make laws for the city. Each of the commissioners was in charge of one city department, such as police, fire, or water services. The *commission form* of government allowed

Thomas Nast drew this cartoon of New York City's Tweed Ring, run by political boss William Marcy Tweed. The ring robbed the people of New York of millions of tax dollars. How did the progressives try to do away with dishonest boss rule in city government?

Progressive Governor Robert La Follette of Wisconsin speaks from the back of a wagon in 1897. His fiery enthusiasm attracted public support for many reform measures. How did reforms in Wisconsin compare with those in other states?

each person to take care of one area of government, rather than having one person—the mayor—responsible for all areas. Before long, about 400 cities had commission governments.

In 1908, another new type of government was formed in Staunton, Virginia. This was the *city-manager form* of government. Under the city-manager form, a professional manager is hired by the city council to take care of city business. In a short time, over 40 cities had hired managers.

How does the city-manager form of government differ from the commission form of government?

What progressive reforms were introduced in Wisconsin?

3.4 Progressivism at the State Level.   Progressives were also active at the state level. In Wisconsin, Robert La Follette was elected governor in 1900. Under La Follette, Wisconsin passed a number of progressive measures. One of these set up the *direct primary,* or nominating election. Through the direct primary, the voters selected candidates for public office. Up to this time, candidates had been chosen by party convention or caucus. Wisconsin also passed a *workman's compensation law.* It gave payments to workers hurt in industrial accidents. In addition, Wisconsin set up a commission to regulate the railroads inside the state and adopted a graduated income tax.

Other states, such as New York, New Jersey, Iowa, Missouri, and California, also passed progressive measures. In 1902, Oregon voted in the initiative and the referendum. By 1918, 20 states had passed similar laws.

1. Who were the leaders of the progressive movement?
2. Who were some of the writers of progressive works?
3. In which states were progressive reformers most active?

4. Roosevelt and Progressivism

The reforms that had begun in the cities spread to the state legislatures and then to the federal government. In the White House, progressivism found a supporter in Theodore Roosevelt. As Vice-President, Roosevelt became President when William McKinley was assassinated by Leon Czolgosz, an anarchist, in 1901.

Who was the first President to support progressivism?

4.1 Early Executive Actions. Roosevelt had strong ideas about government. He thought that government should protect the people, and he was willing to use his power to that end. Roosevelt also had certain ideas about business. He believed that the growth of Big Business, including trusts, was a natural part of the economic system. However, he was against those trusts which he believed did not work for the public good. He believed that the government should step in to regulate such trusts.

What were Roosevelt's views about trusts?

In March 1902, Roosevelt directed the government to file a suit against the Northern Securities Company. This company owned three major railroads in the Northwest. It was a *holding company*—one that owns controlling interest in other companies. In such a company, the board of directors owns, rather than holds in trust, the stock of the companies. The board directs the policy for the companies whose stock it owns. The Supreme Court finally ruled against Northern Securities and ordered it to be broken up. Roosevelt then ordered suits against Standard Oil, the American Tobacco Company, and other trusts. Soon Americans hailed Roosevelt as a "trustbuster."

How did Roosevelt become known as the "trustbuster"?

Before Roosevelt took office, government generally had sided with business against labor. Roosevelt wanted to show the federal government's influence on both. He found the opportunity to try this in 1902.

When Theodore Roosevelt (left) became President, he used his executive authority to preserve public lands. Here he enjoys Yosemite National Park with John Muir (right), a noted naturalist and presidential advisor. What law permitted the President to set aside land for public forests?

How did Roosevelt become involved in the coal strike of 1902?

In May of that year, a coal strike broke out in Pennsylvania. It dragged on and caused serious shortages of coal. In October, Roosevelt called the strike leaders and mine owners to a meeting at the White House. He asked them to settle their differences and end the strike. The workers agreed to go along with the decision of a government commission, but the mine owners refused. When Roosevelt threatened to use the army to run the mines, the owners finally agreed to settle. The miners failed to gain recognition of their union and received only a small pay raise. Roosevelt, however, had shown the federal government's power.

4.2 Roosevelt and Congress. After he was elected President in 1904, Roosevelt felt that he was in a better position to push progressive reforms. Turning first to the railroads, he got Congress to pass the Hepburn Act in 1906. This act strengthened the Interstate Commerce Commission by allowing it to fix railroad rates. Its rates could only be challenged through the courts.

What progressive legislation was passed under Roosevelt?

Also in 1906, the Pure Food and Drug Act was passed by Congress, with Roosevelt's backing. This act stopped the manufacture, sale, or transportation of foods and drugs which were not pure or not properly marked. About the same time, the Meat Inspection Act was passed. This set up federal inspection of all meat transported across state lines.

Asking Questions

=SKILL=

Historians use source material to answer questions they have about the past. The same material, however, can also raise more questions.

On March 25, 1911, a fire broke out in the Triangle Shirtwaist (a type of blouse) Company in New York City. The company was located on the eighth, ninth, and tenth floors of the Asch Building. The building had been constructed in 1901 and met all of New York's fire safety laws at the time. It had only one fire escape which ended on the second floor. More than 140 people died as a result of the March fire.

Max Rothen, a worker at the company, described attempts to stop the fire.

At the same time there were cries of "fire" from all sides. The line of hanging patterns began to burn. Some of the cutters jumped up and tried to tear the patterns from the line but the fire was ahead of them. The patterns were burning. They began to fall on the layers of thin goods underneath them. Every time another piece dropped, light scraps of burning fabric began to fly around the room. They came down on other tables and they fell on the machines. Then the line broke and the whole string of burning patterns fell down.

Samuel Bernstein, Triangle's production manager, described what he did during the fire.

I saw Louis Senderman, the assistant shipping clerk from the tenth floor. I hollered, "Louis, get me a hose!" . . . As I took the hose from him, I said, "Is it open?" But it didn't work. No pressure. No water. I tried it. I opened it. I turned the nozzle one way and then another. It didn't work. I threw it away.

Read the following questions, and decide which of them is answered by the material. Also decide which questions are raised by reading the material.

1. How did the fire start?
2. How did the fire spread?
3. How did people attempt to put out the fire?
4. Why were they not able to put out the fire?
5. How could the fire have been prevented?
6. Who was at fault in the death of the workers?
7. Did similar conditions exist in other clothing factories?
8. What should be done to prevent future fires?
9. How can you find the answers?

4.3 Roosevelt and Conservation. Roosevelt gave strong support to the *conservation* movement. The idea of conserving or saving natural resources began to grow in the late 1800's. Conservationists criticized the way America's resources were used. They were against wasteful lumber and mining practices. They believed that part of the forests and other places of natural beauty should be set aside for all people to enjoy.

What did conservationists want in the late 1800's?

One way in which Roosevelt furthered the cause of conservation was to set aside land for public forests. The Forest Reserve Act of 1891 had given Presidents the power to do this. Presidents Harrison, Cleveland, and McKinley had set aside some 47 million acres of land. Under Roosevelt, about 150 million acres of land were set aside.

Roosevelt also favored government development of natural resources. In 1902, he signed the Newlands Act. This law stated that money from the sale of public lands was to be used for irrigation projects in the West. Dams were built, and over 1 million acres of land were made suitable for farming.

What was the Newlands Act?

1. Why did the federal government file suit against the Northern Securities Company?
2. Which side did Roosevelt take in the coal strike of 1902?
3. What did Roosevelt do to conserve nature?

5. Taft and Progressivism

In 1908, Roosevelt supported William Howard Taft, his Secretary of War, for the Presidency. Taft was chosen by the Republicans and defeated Democrat William Jennings Bryan. Both of them had run as progressives. It appeared that Americans favored more reforms.

5.1 The Republican Split. Roosevelt and the progressives hoped that Taft would go on working for reform. They soon found they were at odds with the President, however. For one thing, Taft called on Congress to lower the tariff. But later he spoke out in favor of the high Payne-Aldrich Tariff that Congress passed in 1909. This angered the progressives.

How did Taft anger Roosevelt and the progressives?

Another matter also caused problems between Taft and Roosevelt and the progressives. Taft chose Richard Ballinger to be Secretary of the Interior. Ballinger favored opening public lands to business development. When Gifford Pinchot, the head of the Forestry Service,

Many children provided cheap labor in factories during the early 1900's. Fast-moving spools on this textile machine spin close to a young worker's unprotected feet. After 1912, who looked after the health, education, and working conditions of children?

spoke out against this, Taft fired him. Roosevelt was very angry because he had appointed Pinchot.

By 1910, the Republican party had divided into two groups—the "Old Guard" and the "Insurgents." The Old Guard was a conservative group, while the Insurgents favored reform. Taft, thinking that the Insurgents were out to destroy him, sided with the Old Guard.

What was the "Old Guard"?

In spite of this, progressivism made certain gains under Taft. In the area of conservation, Taft followed Roosevelt and added to the public forests. He went further than Roosevelt in fighting trusts, beginning nearly 80 antitrust suits. Under Taft, railroad regulation was made more effective. In 1910, he signed the Mann-Elkins Act, which improved the Hepburn Act and furthered the power of the ICC.

What progressive reforms were made under Taft?

Taft's years in office also produced certain social reforms. In 1912, the government set up the Children's Bureau to look into the health, education, and work conditions of children. Taft also backed progressive political measures like the Sixteenth and Seventeenth Amendments. The first set up a federal income tax. The second provided for the direct election of United States Senators. Although passed by Congress under Taft, neither amendment was ratified by the states to become law until 1913.

The Progressive Era 445

5.2 The Election of 1912. As the election of 1912 drew near, the Insurgents formed the National Progressive Republican League. They hoped to run Senator Robert La Follette for President. When La Follette became ill, they turned to Roosevelt. However, in Chicago at the Republican convention, the Old Guard forced the renomination of President Taft.

How did the Bull Moose party come into being?

The Progressives then met separately in Chicago and chose Roosevelt. In accepting the nomination, Roosevelt stated he was "as fit as a bull moose." After this, the party became known as the Bull Moose party. Its platform, formed mainly by Roosevelt, was called New

Who won the presidential election of 1912? What contributed to the defeat of the Republican party in this election? Which states voted for the Old Guard Republican candidate? Which states favored the progressive candidate?

Election of 1912

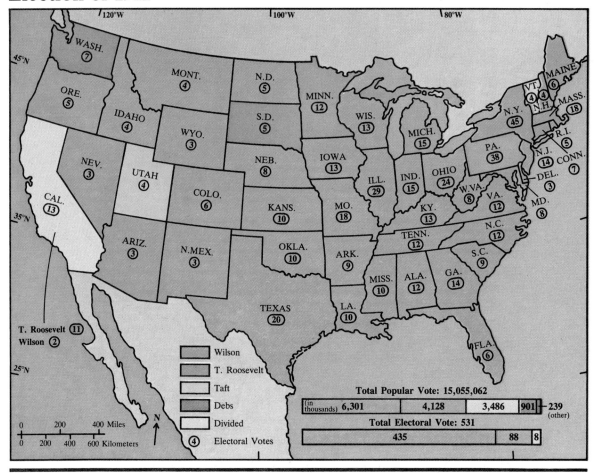

Nationalism. It set forth the idea that the government should act directly to promote the public good. This included regulating Big Business as well as protecting labor.

Because of the split in the Republican party, the Democrats hoped for a victory. Meeting in Baltimore, they chose Woodrow Wilson, the progressive governor of New Jersey, as their candidate. Wilson won the election with 435 electoral votes to 88 for Roosevelt and 8 for Taft. Again, the American people had voted for reform.

In what place did the Republican candidate finish in the election of 1912?

1. What caused a split in the Republican party during the Taft administration?
2. Which group did Taft support?

6. Woodrow Wilson and the New Freedom_____

Wilson's program, known as the New Freedom, called for sweeping changes. Wilson wanted to lower the tariff, reorganize the banking system, and make the antitrust laws stronger. He hoped all of these measures would restore free competition in the American economy.

6.1 Tariff Reform. Shortly after he took office, Wilson went before Congress to ask for a lower tariff. He was the first President since Jefferson to appear there in person. Representative Oscar Underwood offered a new bill that set lower rates. Passed in October 1913, the Underwood bill allowed goods made in other countries to compete with American products. It also brought lower prices for such raw materials as iron, steel, wool, and sugar.

What did the Underwood bill provide?

To make up for lost customs money, a graduated income tax was added to the bill. It had been made possible by the Sixteenth Amendment. It placed a 1 percent tax on all incomes over $4,000. An added tax of 1 percent was placed on all incomes from $20,000 to $50,000. The level reached 6 percent on incomes over $500,000.

6.2 Banking Reform. Wilson next sought reforms in the field of money and banking. After looking into the country's banking system, a House committee wrote a report. It noted that control of the banking system rested with a few powerful bankers. Wilson and the progressives hoped to break up this "money trust."

How did Wilson reform the nation's banking system?

In December 1913, Congress passed the Federal Reserve Act. This act set up the Federal Reserve System. It divided the United States into banking districts, each with a Federal Reserve bank. A Federal Reserve Board in Washington, D.C., governed the Reserve banks. All banks chartered by the federal government had to join the system. Each member bank had to put a certain amount of money into the Federal Reserve bank in its district. This *reserve requirement* helped protect people's deposits in member banks.

6.3 Trust Reform. Wilson wanted to bring an end to monopolies by Big Business. In 1914, with his backing, Congress passed an act setting up the Federal Trade Commission (FTC). The FTC's job was to check out all businesses which took part in interstate trade. It could order such businesses to stop practices which were not fair.

What were the provisions of the Clayton Antitrust Act?

Wilson backed the Clayton Antitrust Act, passed in 1914. With this act, businesses could not give rebates. They could not hold stock in other companies which were making the same product or in the same industry. The act also said that labor should not be thought of as a commodity and that labor organizations should not be viewed as illegal groups in restraint of trade. The act stopped the use of *injunctions*—court orders preventing a particular action—in labor problems unless the courts felt they were necessary to prevent violence.

Both the Federal Trade Commission Act and the Clayton Antitrust Act, however, were only partly successful. The courts still interpreted laws in a way that made them hard to enforce. And the courts continued to side with business against labor unions.

Joseph Keppler's cartoon, "Bosses of the Senate," shows a powerful trust representation in the upper chamber of Congress. At times, the Senate was known as the "millionaires club" because of the many industrialists there. What measures to regulate trusts were passed by Congress over this influence?

6.4 Reforms for Farmers. During Wilson's term of office, the government took steps to help the American farmer. In 1914, the Smith-Lever Act was passed. It set up a system of trained agents to advise farmers. In 1916, the Federal Farm Loan Act was passed. Under it, the country was divided into 12 districts, each with a Farm Loan Bank. The banks would loan money to farmers at lower interest rates than other banks. In 1917, the Smith-Hughes Act was passed. It provided federal money for education in agriculture and the trades.

What was the purpose of the Federal Farm Loan Act?

6.5 Reforms for Workers. Progressives under Wilson worked to improve life for workers as well as farmers. The La Follette Seamen's Act, passed in 1915, set up regulations to improve wages, hours, and working conditions for American sailors. In 1916, the Adamson Act set the eight-hour day for railroad workers in interstate trade.

The government also tried to regulate child labor. In 1900, nearly 1.7 million children under the age of 16 worked in factories and mines. Many states had already passed laws about hours and working conditions for children. In 1916, Congress passed the Keating-Owen Act. This was the first federal law to regulate child labor. It stopped certain goods from being shipped across state lines. These included goods made by children under 14 and products of mines using children under 16. It also included goods made by children under 16 who worked more than eight hours a day. Two years later, in *Hammer* v. *Dagenhart,* the Supreme Court struck down this law. The Court said it interfered with the states' right to regulate local manufacturing.

What were the provisions of the Keating-Owen Act? What happened to the act?

1. How did Woodrow Wilson change tariff rates?
2. What new banking system did Wilson start?
3. What laws were passed during Wilson's term of office to aid farmers and workers?

7. Conclusion

Like all reform movements, progressivism was only partly successful in doing what it set out to do. In the economic area, it did not end monopolies or the dominance of Big Business. However, state and federal agencies did, to a certain degree, standardize rules for business and end some of the worst business practices. Under the influence of progressivism, the government expanded its role in social as well as economic matters. The government, in fact, took more responsibility for the well-being of all Americans. This set a trend which was to continue long after the end of the Progressive Era.

Chapter 19 Review

Main Points

1. The rise of industry created both new opportunities and new problems for the American people.
2. Some groups demanded government control of business to solve problems.
3. Efforts to regulate business were not totally effective in the late 1800's.
4. Progressivism developed as an urban reform movement in the early 1900's.
5. Progressives wanted government to be in the hands of the people, and they wanted government to regulate business.
6. Progressive efforts for reform took place on the local, state, and federal levels.
7. Presidents Theodore Roosevelt, William Taft, and Woodrow Wilson promoted progressive ideas in varying degrees.
8. Progressive lawmakers were concerned with trust regulation, banking reform, and aid to farmers and workers.

Building Vocabulary

1. Identify the following:

Morrill Act
Abner Doubleday
Scott Joplin
Louisa May Alcott
Interstate Commerce Commission
Sherman Antitrust Act
Jane Addams

William Jennings Bryan
William McKinley
progressives
Ida M. Tarbell
Robert La Follette
Theodore Roosevelt

William Howard Taft
Bull Moose party
New Nationalism
Woodrow Wilson
New Freedom
Federal Trade
  Commission

2. Define the following:

compulsory attendance laws
intercollegiate
operettas
regulatory commission
gold standard
bimetalism

inflation
muckrakers
commission form
city-manager form
direct primary

workman's compensation
  law
holding company
conservation
reserve requirement
injunctions

Remembering the Facts

1. What new opportunities did increased industrial production provide?
2. How did Americans use their leisure time?

3. What efforts were made to regulate business in the late 1800's?
4. What did progressive reformers want to accomplish?
5. What types of city governments developed during the period?
6. How did Presidents T. Roosevelt, Taft, and Wilson act to regulate business?

7. How were children affected by progressive reforms?
8. Which progressive reforms became amendments to the Constitution?
9. How did farmers and production workers gain from progressive reforms?
10. Which groups of people were not helped by progressive reforms?

Understanding the Facts

1. How did industrialization help lead to increased popularity of sports, music, and literature?
2. Why did the Interstate Commerce Act and the Sherman Antitrust Act have little effect on business?
3. Why did the reduction of the amount of money in use cause problems for farmers?

4. Why were Democrats successful in electing Wilson as President in 1912?
5. What did the Federal Reserve Act do to the American banking system?
6. What was the message of reform writers such as Ida Tarbell, Lincoln Steffans, and Upton Sinclair?
7. How successful was the progressive movement in bringing about reforms?

Using Tables

Reading Tables.   One source of historical information is a collection of numbers called statistics. Statistics are often presented as individual bits of information. They also may be shown in groups of numbers called tables. Like graphs, tables are arranged in an orderly manner, providing the opportunity to compare various items.

Study the table on page 434, and answer the following questions.

1. What is the subject of the table?
2. What period of time does it cover?

3. In what groups are the statistics presented?
4. What percent of the American population lived in rural areas in 1860?
5. What percent of the population lived in cities in 1890?
6. When did more people live in cities than in rural areas?
7. How many cities under 50,000 people were there in 1870?
8. As more people began to live in cities, what happened to the total number of cities?

Chicago 1870–1895

Chicago began as a muddy swamp along the southern tip of Lake Michigan. The area had a strange odor because skunk cabbage grew nearby. The Potawatomi Indians called the area Chicagou, or "place of the skunk." The first permanent European settler was Jean Baptiste Point de Saible, a black fur trader from France. In 1779, he built a cabin and set up a fur-trading post. Settlers began coming into the area, and Chicago started to grow.

By 1870, Chicago had grown into a leading trade center for the corn, wheat, lumber, and meat-packing industries. It connected the east coast and the west coast by water and rail. It was easy to get lumber from the nearby forests in Michigan and Wisconsin. Most of the buildings in Chicago at this time were made of wood, and fire was a serious threat.

The Great Chicago Fire

In the fall of 1871, this threat of fire became real. Chicago had been without rain for almost three months. On Sunday, October 8, a fire started. Firefighters had little hope of stopping it. Most of their equipment had been destroyed in a fire the night before, and they were very tired. This new fire raged out of control until the morning of October 10, when rainfall finally put it out.

The path of the fire went through the business district of Chicago. Nearly 300 people died in the fire, and more than 100,000 lost their homes. Over $200 million worth of property was ruined. But the Chicago Relief and Aid Society, active in helping the poor since 1857, saw to it that no one went homeless or hungry that winter.

The people of Chicago began to rebuild their city. The city council passed strict rules about fireproof buildings. So brick and stone were used more often than wood. Many buildings followed the same style as those that had burned. Some Chicago architects, however, wanted to build something different and uniquely American. With the development of the elevator and the telephone, Chicago architects came up with a new kind of building—the skyscraper. Tall buildings soon changed the Chicago skyline, and the city continued to grow.

Economic Growth

During the depression of 1873, Chicago's economy, based on food products, thrived. People all over America needed food, and the grain stores and meat-packing industries in Chicago supplied it. The railroad played a major role in the meat-packing industry. It brought live animals to the Union Stockyards from the Great Plains and shipped them on to markets in the East.

Gustavus Swift, owner of one meat-packing company, shipped frozen beef east during the winter. In 1879, he came up with a way to ship frozen meat east all year long. Swift used a new railroad car called the Tiffany Refrigerator Car. Frozen beef became so popular that all the other packing companies began to use refrigerated cars, too. Shipment of meat increased from $65 million in 1870 to over $500 million in 1890.

The Heart of Chicago

Tens of thousands of people came to Chicago during the late 1800's. They included thousands of immigrants from Germany, Ireland, Italy, Greece, and many other countries. Black people moved there from southern states. The newcomers seldom found things as they had hoped. Jobs were hard to get. Work was not steady, and many people had to do jobs they had never done before. Pay was very low for working days that were sometimes 10 to 16 hours long.

Women and children often had to work in sweatshops to help their families live. These shops were usually found in the run-down tenement buildings surrounding the business districts. The bad lighting, lack of fresh air, and poor plumbing made working there very difficult. Some girls, 10 to 15 years old,

The Chicago fire of 1871 burned nearly 2,000 acres of the city. After it was destroyed, Chicago was rebuilt in a manner similar to other modern cities. What improvements were made in the second building of Chicago?

worked in clothes sweatshops. They averaged 50 cents a week for sewing on buttons or pulling out threads. If they did those jobs well, they sometimes moved up to sewing articles by hand and earned $2 or $2.50 a week as the older women did. Boys of the same age generally had jobs as messengers or errand runners.

Holding the same job for many years did not guarantee that a worker would keep that job. Mary McDowell wrote:

One of my best friends was a German cattle butcher who began work at eleven years of age on the "killing floor," where he worked for twenty-five years until his right arm began to shake from the constant [use] of a huge cleaver, more like a battle axe.

Workers butcher beef in a Chicago meat-packing plant. What factors contributed to Chicago becoming a major meat-packing center?

. . . after going twenty-five years on a "killing bed," where he had been one of the few skilled workers, receiving forty-five cents an hour, he [was] suddenly [fired] without any reason given by the boss, except that his right arm was shaking and that he was unable to keep up with the "pace maker," [leader] who was a giant. . . . "I understand now," he said, "why men are not sure of a job always, and why they organize, for at thirty-five I have reached my old age limit."

Housing was a serious problem. Most immigrants lived close to the business districts. The buildings in these districts were not kept in very good condition. The only water for some came from a pump in the yard. Garbage and waste matter often sat in the alleys behind the buildings. Still, owners charged high rents. Sometimes several families lived together in one room to help pay the rent. Others took in boarders.

A Helping Hand

There were people in Chicago who cared about the problems of the poor. Mary McDowell lived and worked in a settlement house there in the late 1880's. She wrote:

. . . the Settlement home was upstairs over a Day Nursery; every morning when it was barely light in the winter, I would be wakened by the cry of the little children who wanted the mother to stay at home and not go to work. Here again for the first time in my life I saw the meaning of the job and how wage-earning women had to carry two burdens—that of the home and that of the wage-earning world. In that day there was no child-labor law and the packing industry found useful the boys and girls of eleven years of age, and men and women and children had no limit to their day's work.

Jane Addams learned about settlement house work during a visit to London in 1888. What was the name of the settlement house Addams opened in Chicago?

very fond. He was a graduate of the Institute of Technology [in Greece], and drew very well. He had collected a large book of drawings and photographs. He thought that when he came to America, where we had no ruins, that we would be interested to hear about them. . . . He said he had sold fruit to Americans for years in Chicago, and that although he often had tried to lead the conversation to his beloved Acropolis [an ancient ruin in Athens], no one had ever seemed interested. He came to the conclusion no one in Chicago had heard of ancient Greece, nor knew that it had a wonderful history. . . . That man was disappointed and Chicago was losing something he could have given to it. I did not like to tell him we had become so snobbish in America that it did not occur to [us] that a shabby-looking foreigner selling apples could have his mind and heart full of the deathless beauties of ancient Greece. . . .

Jane Addams rented a mansion in the middle of the tenement section of Chicago in 1889. She named it Hull House and opened its doors to the neighborhood. At Hull House, immigrants could learn to speak English and other job skills.

The efforts of Jane Addams to help the newcomers did not stop at Hull House. She had a great respect for the immigrants and joined many groups to help change living conditions. She told of a Greek fruit seller and his impression of the people of Chicago:

For three years, in Greece, while he was saving money to come to America, he used to make drawings of ancient Athens, of which he was

The World's Fair

Many of the social problems that were affecting Chicago were also affecting the country as a whole. However, people in Chicago spent two years enjoying something special—the World's Fair.

On February 24, 1890, the United States Congress selected Chicago as the site for the World's Columbian Exposition to be held in 1893. Its purpose was to celebrate the 400th anniversary of Columbus' landing in America. Daniel Burnham was the chief architect of the fair. It was his decision to have all the buildings painted white, giving Chicago the nickname "The White City."

The fair had 50 foreign nations and 37 colonies participating as well as every state in the country. The fairgrounds were located in Jackson Park and Washington Park on a total of 1,037 acres of land. A reporter described the activity as construction started:

At the moment when this is being prepared for the press, the greater part of the Fair tract in Jackson Park is one-third enclosed by the waters of Lake Michigan and two-thirds by a tall fence six miles in length. Within that enclosure is to be witnessed a scene of extraordinary activity. Close at hand, as one approaches the site from the city, the second story of the Woman's Building already rises above the greenery, and as far as the eye can comprehend the scene the view is dotted with other white forests and thickets of new timber,

This watertower along Michigan and Chicago avenues was one of the few structures to survive the fire. Why were most buildings so easily destroyed?

marking the foundations and framework of the great buildings that the Commissioners are to erect as the nucleus and glory of the Fair.

Amusements were located on the midway of the fair. One of the most popular was the world's first ferris wheel, designed by George Ferris. For 50 cents, the fairgoer could ride around on the 250-foot wheel twice.

Another popular ride was the movable sidewalk. The fare for it was five cents. It went from one end of the Main Columbian Pier to the other. A total of 5,610 people could sit or stand on it and be carried along at different speeds.

More than 27 million people visited the Columbian Exposition. They went away impressed with the exhibits they had seen and with the city of Chicago. On November 1, 1893, the *Chicago Tribune* reported:

After six months of checkered experiences beginning with discouragements and closing with unexpected success, Chicago bids good-by to its Fair regretfully—a good-by that comes from the heart. The White City had become so attractive in its enticements, so regally beautiful in all its environments, so delightful as a pleasure resort, and so entwined with our municipal life . . . it is not easy to realize that all this beauty must fade away and pass forever from sight. . . . The only consolation is that Chicago has given to the world a vision of supreme beauty, which dims all past achievement and which challenges the future; that millions have looked upon it with delighted eyes; and that it has left enduring influences behind which will work for sweetness and light all over this broad land.

By the end of the nineteenth century, America was moving into a new age. The city

One of the best overall views of the Columbian Exposition was from the basket of an observation balloon. The giant Ferris Wheel can be seen in the distance. What other amusements attracted people to the fair?

of Chicago was also moving forward with continued growth in population and industry. The small, muddy swamp town had grown into a major American city.

1. Why did the Chicago fire of 1871 go out of control?

2. What were the living conditions of the poor in Chicago?

3. What services did Hull House and other settlement houses offer to the people of Chicago?

4. What was the purpose of the World's Columbian Exposition?

Unit VI Review

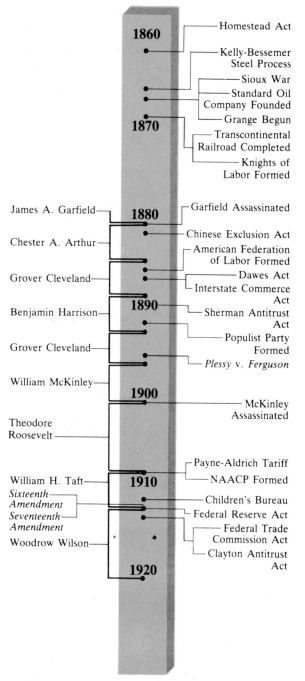

1860 — Homestead Act
— Kelly-Bessemer Steel Process
— Sioux War
— Standard Oil Company Founded

1870 — Grange Begun
— Transcontinental Railroad Completed
— Knights of Labor Formed

James A. Garfield — 1880 — Garfield Assassinated

Chester A. Arthur — — Chinese Exclusion Act
— American Federation of Labor Formed

Grover Cleveland — — Dawes Act
— Interstate Commerce Act

Benjamin Harrison — 1890 — Sherman Antitrust Act
— Populist Party Formed

Grover Cleveland — — *Plessy v. Ferguson*

William McKinley — 1900 — McKinley Assassinated

Theodore Roosevelt —

William H. Taft — 1910 — Payne-Aldrich Tariff
— NAACP Formed

Sixteenth Amendment — — Children's Bureau
Seventeenth Amendment — — Federal Reserve Act
Woodrow Wilson — — Federal Trade Commission Act
— Clayton Antitrust Act

1920

Summary

1. For the United States, the period from the end of the Civil War until 1900 was a time of great changes as a result of population growth, the settling of the last frontier areas in the West, and the rise of Big Business.

2. There were many important changes for groups of people, including the end of traditional ways of life for western Indians and the gradual loss of black rights with the rise of Jim Crow laws.

3. Large numbers of immigrants contributed to rapid population growth, with the "old" immigration of northern and western Europe giving way to greater "new" immigration from eastern and southern Europe as well as from Asia.

4. The American economy was transformed with the rise of huge business corporations that sometimes were able to create monopolies in some industries.

5. By 1900, the United States had become the leading industrial nation in the world, but such groups as farmers and industrial workers felt that they were not benefiting from the changes in the economy.

6. Problems of farmers gave rise to the Populists, while industrial workers became more active in forming labor unions to better their conditions.

7. During the Progressive Era, reformers at the local, state, and national level worked to correct some of the serious problems of an industrial society.

Unit Questions

1. What were some of the results of the settlement of the West for settlers, Indians, and the nation as a whole?

2. How was the treatment of Indian groups by the government in the late 1800's similar to or different from what it had been earlier?

3. Why did many whites feel that laws were necessary to segregate blacks and whites in the late 1800's when such laws had not been necessary earlier?

4. What were some of the benefits and some of the problems caused by the growth of Big Business?

5. What were the ideas of business leaders like Rockefeller regarding the role of government in the economy? How were these views different from those of reform groups such as the progressives?

6. Compare the Populists with the progressives by answering the following: Who supported each movement? What were some of the problems which each attempted to solve? What were some of the reforms each group supported?

7. Why did reformers find it necessary to organize on a national level and to have federal laws passed to regulate Big Business?

Suggested Activities

1. The frontier era of American history is said to have ended around 1890. As a group, make a list of new frontiers which you think are still ahead for the American people. Remember that frontiers can include knowledge as well as geography.

2. Using current newspapers, identify reforms which are currently being demanded. What group or groups will benefit? Who opposes the reforms?

3. Present a report to the class about a sports team, event, or famous sports figure from the period 1890 to 1910.

Suggested Readings

Katz, William. *Black People Who Made the Old West.* New York: Thomas Y. Crowell Co., 1977. Describes the life of blacks who moved west after the Civil War.

Lehmann, Linda. *Better Than a Princess.* New York: Elsevier-Nelson, 1978. The story of an immigrant child and her brother on their way to Missouri.

Sandler, Martin. *The Way We Lived: A Photographic Record of Work in a Vanished America.* Boston: Little, Brown & Co., 1977. Photographs of life in the United States from the Civil War to World War I.

Syme, Ronald. *Geronimo.* New York: William Morrow & Co., 1975. Describes the battle of the Indians to defend their land.

AMERICA
IS
Power

Power came to the United States with political strength and industrial growth. As it became powerful, the United States moved beyond its territorial limits in search of new markets and colonies. The United States began to compete with other world nations for more trade and more land. From this rivalry, the United States rose to take a major role in shaping world affairs. American influence in global matters made it necessary for people in the United States to be concerned for what went on in the world.

A New
Manifest Destiny

The United States' "Great White Fleet" toured the world between 1907 and 1909 to promote American naval strength. What role did a powerful navy play in America's plans for expansion?

The United States has been an expanding nation throughout much of its history. Manifest destiny carried the American people from the eastern seaboard to the Pacific. In the late 1800's, the United States became interested in a new kind of expansion. It began to acquire lands across the seas. This was a new manifest destiny. And because of it, the United States had to change the way it looked at foreign affairs.

1. The Stirrings of Expansion

Until the 1880's and 1890's, the American people paid attention mostly to what was going on at home. Americans were living through the changes of industrialization. They were fighting a civil war and settling the frontier areas of the West. They showed little interest in other lands. But by the end of the 1800's, Americans were looking overseas. Soon most were willing to go along with their government's involvement in the affairs of other countries.

Why did Americans pay little attention to foreign affairs during much of the 1800's?

1.1 Early Attempts. Americans had begun trading with other areas of the world long before the Civil War. In 1844, Caleb Cushing became the first American commissioner to China. Several years earlier, there had been a war between Great Britain and China. The British had made the Chinese open several ports to British trade. Cushing worked out a trade agreement with the Chinese to open the same ports to American ships.

How did the United States obtain trading rights in China?

Japan, on the other hand, had kept its ports closed to Western trade. The Japanese finally opened one port, Nagasaki, to the Spanish, Portuguese, and Dutch. The Americans, however, wanted to trade with Japan, too. In 1853, a fleet of American warships under Commodore Matthew Perry sailed to Japan. Perry convinced the Japanese ruler to open several ports to the United States the following year.

Who opened up Japan to trade?

An early supporter of American expansion overseas was William Seward, President Andrew Johnson's Secretary of State. At the time, Alaska was owned by Russia. In 1867, Seward convinced the United States government to buy Alaska from the Russians for $7.2 million. That same year, the United States also annexed Midway Island, in the Pacific west of Hawaii.

1.2 Expansionist Ideas. By the late 1880's, most of the industrialized countries of the world were looking for new markets for their goods. They also wanted new sources of such raw materials as oil, tin, rubber, and cotton. For these and other reasons, European

In 1854, Commodore Matthew Perry opened Japan for trade with the United States. This Japanese painting shows some of the many trading ships that sailed to Japan. Why did the United States expand its trade in Asia?

What were the basic reasons underlying the rise of imperialism?

How was social Darwinism applied to imperialism?

What did Alfred Mahan believe?

countries became involved in *imperialism*—spreading the rule of one country over that of another. Great Britain, France, Germany, Belgium, and other European countries were trying to divide Africa and parts of Asia into colonies. These powers began to build empires.

The ideas of social Darwinism were applied to imperialism. Many people believed that the powers were taking part in a struggle in which only the great and powerful survived. One way to survive was to build empires. Many Americans believed that the United States also should build an empire. Some Americans were eager to sell their goods around the world. Others had money they wanted to invest in factories, railroads, mines, and farms in other lands. Others believed it was their duty to bring Christianity to the people of other parts of the world.

Captain Alfred Thayer Mahan, head of the Naval War College at Newport, Rhode Island, was very much in favor of American expansion. He believed that for a nation to be great, it had to have a powerful navy. In 1890, Mahan wrote *The Influence of Sea Power Upon History, 1660–1783*. In this book, Mahan showed how important sea power had been in winning wars. He also wrote that nations needed colonies to serve as ports and coaling stations for ships.

1.3 Interest in the Pacific.   American and European interests turned to the islands of the Pacific. The United States and European countries hoped to set up bases there for their warships. The Americans also wanted to use certain islands as stopovers where steamships would take on coal for the long voyage from the United States to Asia and Australia.

Why did the United States want to obtain islands in the Pacific?

In 1878, the United States reached an agreement with local rulers for a naval base at Pago Pago in Samoa, a group of islands between Hawaii and Australia. Great Britain and Germany also had claims in Samoa. The three powers argued over control of the islands and came close to war. Finally, the United States and Germany divided control of the islands in 1899. Great Britain received land elsewhere.

Another group of Pacific islands in which the United States government was interested was the Hawaiian Islands. From the time the Americans began to trade with China in the late 1700's, these islands were important stops for the ships and sailors of many countries. During the 1820's, American missionaries started going to Hawaii to try to teach the people Christianity. Other Americans went to grow sugar and to trade. Before long, the Americans in Hawaii grew wealthy and were influencing the island government.

How did the United States become involved in Hawaii?

In 1890, the United States passed the McKinley Tariff. It put a tax on Hawaiian sugar. This made Hawaiian sugar more expensive than sugar grown in the United States. The act hurt Hawaii's sugar trade with the United States and brought the Hawaiian economy close to ruin. Americans in Hawaii wanted the United States to annex the islands. If

The pineapple industry (left) and other American commercial interests in Hawaii helped to bring an end to the rule of Queen Liliuokalani (right). Why were the Hawaiian Islands important to United States overseas expansion?

Hawaii were part of the United States, the tariff no longer would affect the sugar trade.

Who led the move for annexation?

But the Hawaiian ruler, Queen Liliuokalani, did not agree. She wanted to rid the Hawaiian government of American influence. The Americans staged a revolt in 1893 led by Sanford B. Dole, a judge. The American minister to Hawaii, John Stevens, brought in American naval forces for support. The Americans set up a new government, with Dole at its head, and asked the United States to annex Hawaii.

President Grover Cleveland sent a special representative to the island to find out what was happening there. The representative reported that Americans had been behind the revolt. The report said that most Hawaiians did not want Hawaii to become a part of the United States. As a result, the Cleveland administration refused to annex the islands. In 1894, the Republic of Hawaii was proclaimed, and President Cleveland recognized the new government of Hawaii. He refused, however, to annex the islands. They were not annexed until July 1898.

Why did the Cleveland administration prevent annexation?

1.4 Growing Involvement in the Caribbean.   At about the same time that the United States was involved in Hawaii, it also was expanding its influence in the Caribbean area. For a long time, the American government had felt that the area was necessary to the security of the United States.

How did the United States become involved in the Venezuelan boundary dispute?

In the late 1880's, the United States became involved in a dispute between Great Britain and Venezuela. Those two countries could not agree over the boundary between Venezuela and the British colony of Guiana in South America. The disagreement had been going on for years. But it grew worse when gold was discovered in the area. Venezuela asked the United States to settle the matter by *arbitration*—the hearing and deciding of a disagreement by a third party. But the British refused to support such an idea.

What position did Olney express in his message to the British?

In 1894, Secretary of State Richard Olney sent a message to the British. It stated that the United States was the supreme power in the Western Hemisphere. It had the right, under the Monroe Doctrine of 1823, to step in and settle any dispute which threatened the peace of the Western Hemisphere. At first, the British did not agree. But they had problems in other parts of the world and needed to stay friendly with the United States. In 1897, they agreed to arbitration. By 1899, the matter was settled, and American influence in Latin America and the Caribbean was greatly increased.

1. When did the United States begin to trade with Japan?
2. Where did imperialist countries set up colonies?
3. Which Pacific islands were taken by the United States?

Liliuokalani (1838–1917)
Emilio Aguinaldo (1869–1964)

PROFILE

Liliuokalani and Emilio Aguinaldo lived in lands where the United States expanded in the late nineteenth century. Their experiences help to explain the distrust which some people felt for Americans. Both objected to United States government control of their countries. As a result, they were removed from power.

Liliuokalani became queen of Hawaii when her brother died in 1891. From the start of her reign, her rule was weakened by a constitution forced on her brother by American business leaders in Honolulu. The constitution gave most authority to the American cabinet members.

When Liliuokalani tried to overrule the constitution with a royal decree, her opposition organized against her. With support from the American navy, the opposition took over government buildings, abolished the monarchy, and set up a new government. Liliuokalani was removed from office, and a republic was set up with Sanford Dole as president.

Liliuokalani tried to get support from the United States government to regain her throne. But war with Spain showed the islands' importance in the Pacific Ocean. In 1898, Congress voted to annex Hawaii.

Emilio Aguinaldo had a similar experience in the Philippines. In 1896, he led an uprising against the Spanish colonial rulers in his country. Aguinaldo successfully established a government and declared the Philippines to be independent in 1898. Conflict developed when the United States did not recognize Filipino independence. The United States replaced Spain as the colonial ruler of the Philippines.

Fighting between Aguinaldo's forces and American soldiers began in 1899 after a Filipino citizen was killed by an American soldier. Before it was over in 1902, the American government used 70,000 soldiers and spent $600 million to defeat Aguinaldo. In 1901, Aguinaldo was captured and jailed. After the fighting, he was released and returned to private life.

The activities of Liliuokalani and Emilio Aguinaldo came at a time when expansion was a major force in American politics. The United States used its power against their claims to be the leaders of their peoples.

2. The Spanish-American War

American interest and involvement in foreign affairs kept growing. By the 1890's, the United States was the leading industrial country in the world. Then in 1898, the United States went to war with Spain. As a result of that, the United States became recognized as a major world power.

2.1 Trouble in Cuba. By the late 1800's, Cuba and Puerto Rico were all that was left of the Spanish empire in the Western Hemisphere. The Cubans, eager to be independent, had revolted in 1868. The war went on for ten years before the Spaniards won it. In 1895, the Cubans revolted again. Many Americans had investments in Cuba and followed events there closely. Most of them sympathized with the Cuban rebels.

When did the Cubans first revolt?

What role did American newspapers play in the Cuban crisis?

The American public found out about what was happening in Cuba through the newspapers. Two New York newspapers, William Randolph Hearst's *Journal* and Joseph Pulitzer's *World,* competed with each other to sell ads and papers. Each tried to print the most shocking tales of Spanish cruelty in Cuba. This kind of reporting was called *yellow journalism.* The newspaper people thought this type of reporting would bring them more readers.

The Spanish general in Cuba, Valeriano Weyler, made all Cubans who lived in the countryside move to certain towns, which they could not leave. Weyler thought this would stop the people from helping the rebels. Conditions in these towns were terrible. Thousands of Cubans died from disease and starvation. The newspaper reports about such conditions shocked many Americans and turned them more against the Spaniards.

What effect did the de Lôme letter have on American-Spanish relations?

American feelings against Spain grew stronger in 1898 when the *Journal* printed a stolen letter written by Enrique Dupuy de Lôme, the Spanish minister to the United States. In the letter, de Lôme called President McKinley a "crowd pleaser" and hinted that he was a poor politician. Americans felt the letter was an insult to the United States.

Who blew up the Maine?

Then on February 15, 1898, the American battleship *Maine* exploded in the harbor of Havana, Cuba. The ship sank, and more than 250 crew members died. No one knew for sure who or what had caused the explosion. But newspaper headlines and many American politicians blamed the Spaniards. The cry "Remember the *Maine*" was heard everywhere.

In April, the United States Congress passed a resolution which demanded that the Spanish armed forces leave Cuba. Part of the resolution was known as the Teller Amendment. It said that once the United States had restored peace in Cuba, it would turn over control of the island to the Cuban people. On April 24, 1898, Spain declared war on the United States. The next day, Congress declared that the United States had been at war with Spain since April 21. On that day, part of the Atlantic fleet had been ordered to Cuban waters.

2.2 War With Spain. The actual fighting of the Spanish-American War did not start in Cuba. It started in the Philippines, which had been part of Spain's empire for more than 300 years. Two months before war was declared, Assistant Secretary of the Navy Theodore Roosevelt had ordered Commodore George Dewey to take the American fleet in the Pacific to the Philippines if war was declared against Spain.

Where did military action first take place?

Shortly after war was declared, Dewey sailed from his base in China. On May 1, 1898, the American ships sailed into Manila Bay. In a few hours, Dewey's ships destroyed the Spanish fleet there. The navy had to wait for the army to arrive before taking the city of Manila. In August, the Americans attacked by land and by sea, and the Spaniards surrendered Manila.

While some Americans were fighting the Spaniards in the Philippines, others were fighting them in Cuba. About 17,000

Commodore George Dewey's Asiatic Squadron steamed from Hong Kong to Manila Bay (left). Once in range of the Spanish fleet (right), Dewey told his captain "You may fire when ready, Gridley." When was the opening battle of the war?

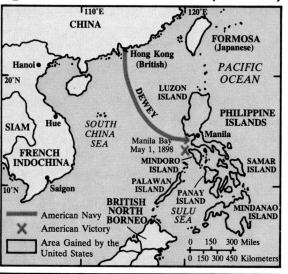

Spanish-American War (Pacific)

Spanish-American War (Caribbean)

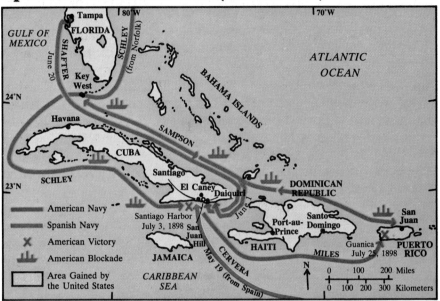

War in the Caribbean Sea began when Spanish Admiral Pascual Cervera's fleet encountered the American naval squadrons of Commodore William Schley and Rear Admiral William T. Sampson. When and where was this battle?

What important battles occurred in Cuba?

Who were the Rough Riders?

American troops had landed near Santiago, Cuba, and were trying to take the city. They were opposed by only a small part of the Spanish forces in Cuba. The American forces won two victories near Santiago, one at El Caney and another at San Juan Hill.

The charge up San Juan Hill was led by Theodore Roosevelt. Roosevelt had resigned his post in the Department of the Navy to take part in the fighting. As a lieutenant colonel, he led a cavalry regiment called the Rough Riders. This group was made up mostly of ranchers, cowhands, and Indians. Most of them had been recruited by Roosevelt himself.

Richard Harding Davis was an observer of the Spanish-American War in Cuba. He wrote about Roosevelt and General Hawkins at San Juan Hill:

> *General Hawkins, with hair as white as snow . . . was so noble a sight that you felt inclined to pray for his safety; on the other hand, Roosevelt, mounted high on horseback, and charging the rifle-pits at a gallop and quite alone, made you feel that you would like to cheer. He wore on his sombrero a blue polka-dot handkerchief . . . which, as he advanced, floated out straight behind his head. . . . Afterward, the men of his regiment who followed this flag, adopted a polka-dot handkerchief as the badge of the Rough Riders.*

The victories put the Americans in a position to take Santiago. A Spanish fleet led by Admiral Pascual Cervera y Topete tried to escape from the Santiago harbor. The ships were caught and destroyed on July 3 by American ships under Rear Admiral William Sampson. About two weeks later, on July 16, the Spaniards surrendered the city of Santiago.

Who led Puerto Rico's revolt against Spanish rule?

There was also fighting on the Spanish-controlled island of Puerto Rico. Like the Cubans and the Filipinos, the Puerto Ricans had tried to become free from Spanish rule. Led by Ramon Emeterio Betances, they had revolted in 1868 and declared the Republic of Puerto Rico. But the revolt failed, as did another one in 1897. In July 1898, American forces under General Nelson A. Miles occupied the island. In August, an *armistice*—an agreement to stop fighting—was signed by the United States and Spain.

2.3 The Treaty of Paris.   In October 1898, representatives from Spain and the United States met in Paris to talk over peace terms. No one from the Pacific or Caribbean colonies over whom the war had been fought were present. According to the peace terms, Spain allowed Cuba to become an independent republic under the protection of the United States. Puerto Rico and Guam, an island in the western Pacific, were given to the United States as payment for war damages. When President McKinley pressed to gain the Philippines also, the Spaniards were opposed. But they finally agreed to sell the Philippines to the United States for $20 million. On February 6, 1899, the United States ratified the Treaty of Paris.

How did the United States acquire Guam and Puerto Rico? the Philippines?

1. What areas in the Caribbean did Spain control?
2. Why did the United States navy attack Manila in 1898?
3. How long did the Spanish-American War last?
4. Where was the treaty that ended the Spanish-American War written?

3. Foreign Affairs in the Pacific and Asia

The Spanish-American War greatly changed the position of the United States in foreign affairs. By the beginning of the 1900's, the United States had its own overseas empire. Because of this, it had a strong interest in foreign affairs, especially in the Pacific and Asia.

3.1 Governing the Philippines.   The people of the Philippines expected to be given their independence after the Spaniards were defeated. Many Americans also favored independence for the islands. But President McKinley felt the United States should keep control.

When the Filipinos found out that they were not going to become independent, they revolted against American rule. The Filipinos were led by Emilio Aguinaldo who had earlier helped the Americans defeat the Spaniards. The Americans brought in more soldiers to hold off the Filipinos. In 1901, Aguinaldo was captured, and his revolution ended.

Who led the revolt by the Filipinos?

On July 4 of that year, the President named Judge William Howard Taft to be the first civil governor of the Philippines. Taft had headed a commission that had studied the situation in the islands. It had reported on how to set up a civil government there. The President also selected several Americans to serve in the upper house of the island legislature. The Filipinos elected the members to the lower house.

Who headed the first civilian government?

3.2 China and the Open Door. One reason the United States wanted to keep the Philippines was to have territory close to China. China was rich in natural resources. Its large population offered a good market for American goods. Constant fighting among different groups of Chinese had made the Chinese government weak. It was not strong enough to keep other countries out of China. Great Britain, Germany, Russia, Japan, and France claimed parts of China as their own *spheres of influence,* or areas of control over trade. Each country had special trading rights in its spheres and tried to keep others from trading there.

What was a sphere of influence?

American business people were afraid they might lose out on the China trade. At the same time, the British were concerned about how strong the Japanese were becoming in China. They wanted the United States to get all countries to agree to equal trading rights in China.

Who first wanted equal trade rights in China?

In 1899, Secretary of State John Hay sent messages to the major European countries and Japan. In these notes, Hay spoke of an Open Door policy in China. Hay wanted the countries to agree to keep Chinese ports open to all. He wanted them to guarantee equal railroad, harbor, and tariff rates for all. He also wanted them to allow the Chinese government to collect duties on all goods coming into and going out of China. Most of the countries hesitated to accept the plan. This did not stop Hay. In March 1900, when no countries had disagreed, Hay announced that all the powers had agreed to the Open Door.

What was Hay's Open Door policy?

Many Chinese did not like the changes foreign trade had brought to their country. They wanted all outsiders to leave China. Members of a Chinese secret society, which Westerners called the Boxers, led an effort to remove foreigners from the country. In 1900, they attacked foreigners living in the city of Peking. The siege lasted for eight weeks. American, British, German, Russian, Japanese, and French troops joined to rescue their people in Peking and put an end to the attack.

What was the Boxer Rebellion?

Imperialism
═CONCEPT═

The policy of extending one nation's influence over another nation is called imperialism. It can mean the actual occupation and rule. It can mean control either by diplomacy or military force. Imperialism can also mean the control of key aspects of a less powerful nation's economy.

Following the Spanish-American War, Filipinos fought against American soldiers in their country. These soldiers represented American rule. In the United States, many citizens argued both for and against keeping American rule over the Philippines.

President William McKinley later explained how he arrived at the decision to favor rule over the Philippines.

When . . . I realized that the Philippines had dropped into our laps I confess I did not know what to do with them. I sought counsel from all sides—Democrats as well as Republicans—but got little help. I thought first we would take only Manila; then Luzon; then other islands, perhaps, also. I walked the floor of the White House night after night. . . . And one night late it came to me this way—I don't know how it was, but it came: (1) That we could

not give them back to Spain—that would be cowardly and dishonorable; (2) that we could not turn them over to France or Germany—our commercial rivals in the Orient—that would be bad business . . . ; (3) that we could not leave them to themselves—they were [not ready] for self-government—and they would soon have anarchy and misrule over there worse than Spain's was; and (4) there was nothing left for us to do but to take them all, and to educate the Filipinos, and . . . do the very best we could by them. . . . And then I went to bed . . . and the next morning I sent for the chief engineer of the War Department . . . and told him to put the Philippines on the map of the United States . . . and there they are, and there they will stay while I am President!

1. Based on President McKinley's statement, what was the reason for United States imperialism in the Philippines?
2. How was McKinley's decision based on a sense of duty?
3. How was a business interest reflected in the decision?
4. How does McKinley reflect a sense of the new manifest destiny?

In the middle 1800's, foreign flags flew over the port of Canton. They showed the number of Western nations trading with China. Which countries do these flags represent?

What was expressed in the second Open Door note?

The United States was afraid that the other countries would use the Boxer Rebellion as an excuse to divide up China. In July 1900, the United States issued a second Open Door note. It stated that America would preserve the land and government of China as one nation. It also said that America would continue to support the idea of equal trade with China for all countries of the world.

3.3 Relations With Japan. Japan was important to the Open Door policy. Soon after the Japanese opened their country to trade in 1854, they began to industrialize and modernize their economy. By the early 1900's, Japan was one of the leading powers of the world. It had carved a sphere of influence out of China and had gained control of Korea. The Japanese also were interested in Manchuria, an area in northeastern China. But the Russians also wanted to control the area, and conflict arose. The United States was afraid that if either country gained too much influence, the Open Door policy would be in danger.

Why was Japan important to the Open Door policy?

In 1904, war broke out between Japan and Russia. By 1905, the Japanese clearly were winning the war. To bring about peace, President Roosevelt offered to hold talks between the two countries. Both sides agreed, and in August 1905, they met with him in Portsmouth, New Hampshire. Roosevelt later received the Nobel Peace Prize for his efforts. But the Japanese were not happy with the peace terms. They did not feel that they had received the cash and land they deserved from their victories over the Russians.

Who played a role in settling the Russo-Japanese War?

While the peace talks were going on, the United States and Japan worked out the Taft-Katsura Agreement of 1905. In it, the United

States agreed to recognize Japanese control of Korea. Japan agreed to make no move toward the Philippines. But relations between the United States and Japan were not good. Over the next few years, relations grew worse. The United States and Japan feared each other's power in Asian affairs.

1. Why did the United States keep control of the Philippines after the Spanish-American War?
2. Which countries were interested in trade with China?
3. What caused war between Japan and Russia in 1904?

4. United States in Latin America

When the United States won the Spanish-American War, it gained possessions not only in the Pacific, but in the Caribbean as well. American interest in the Caribbean had been growing before the war. After the war, the United States became the main power in the area.

4.1 Governing Puerto Rico. In 1900, the United States passed the Foraker Act. This act set up a government in Puerto Rico much like the one in the Philippines. A governor and 11 members of an executive council were to be selected by the President. Five of the council members had to be Puerto Ricans. The council would serve as the upper house of the legislature. The lower house would be elected by the people of Puerto Rico.

What was the Foraker Act?

Puerto Rican reaction to rule by the United States was mixed. Leaders like Betances were against it. But many business people were in favor of it. Under American rule, a great deal more sugar was grown for the American market. More farmland was bought by large sugar companies. This left less land for the small farmers. Many of them wanted Puerto Rico to be independent.

4.2 American Interest in Cuba. After the United States had helped to free Cuba from Spain, the Americans kept an active interest in the island's affairs. The United States government wanted to protect American investments there. It also wanted to make sure that no other country gained influence in Cuba.

In 1900, the Cubans held a convention to write a constitution for their country. In March of the following year, Congress passed the Platt Amendment. It was part of a bill that provided money for the operation of the army. The Platt Amendment said that Cuba had to agree to sell or *lease* (rent) land to the United States for naval bases. Cuba also had to

What was the Platt Amendment?

allow the United States to make sure that law and order were kept on the island. Further, Cuba could not borrow more money from a foreign power than it was able to repay. When the Cubans agreed to include the terms of the amendment in their constitution, American troops left.

Who was in command of the military government in Cuba?

The military government the United States had set up in Cuba under General Leonard Wood was very active. It helped make many improvements in living conditions for the people. Through the efforts of Walter Reed, an American army surgeon, it helped fight disease on the island. But the Cuban people still did not like the idea of the Americans running their affairs.

4.3   The Panama Canal.   During the Spanish-American War, the Americans found out how useful it would be to have a canal that cut across Central America, joining the Caribbean with the Pacific Ocean. Such a canal would allow navy ships to go from the Atlantic to the Pacific without going all the way around South America. With naval bases in Cuba and other Caribbean islands, the United States felt it could protect a canal in Central America.

Who first attempted to build a canal across Panama?

A French company under Ferdinand de Lesseps had started to build a canal across the Isthmus of Panama in 1881. The *isthmus*—a narrow strip of land between two larger bodies of land—connected North America and South America. At the time, Panama was part of

Planners took advantage of the Panama Railroad and natural waterways in deciding where to build the canal. What major body of water is part of the Panama Canal?

Panama Canal

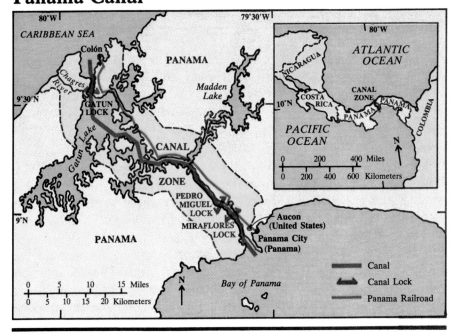

France started construction on the Panama Canal in the 1880's. The United States completed the project. When was the canal opened?

the country of Colombia. The Colombian government had given the French company the rights to build the canal. But in 1889, the French company ran out of money and had to stop work. Its right to build was about to run out, so the company offered to sell the right to the United States for $40 million.

The United States wanted a treaty with Colombia to build the canal. It also wanted Colombia to give it a strip of land along both sides of the canal. The United States offered Colombia $10 million. Representatives from the United States and Colombia tried to work out a treaty. But the Colombians thought that the price offered by the Americans was too low. The Colombians also feared that if they gave up a strip of land along the canal route, they might lose control over Panama.

Why were the Colombians against a canal treaty?

In November 1903, a group of people in Panama who wanted the United States to build the canal staged a revolt. American warships were sent to the area by President Roosevelt. They kept Colombian soldiers from landing in Panama and stopping the revolt. The Republic of Panama was declared and was recognized by the United States. Panama and the United States signed the Hay-Bunau-Varilla Treaty. It gave the United States the right to build a canal for $10 million. It also gave the United States a lease on a strip of land ten miles (16 kilometers) wide along the canal route. The treaty gave the United States sole control of the canal area "forever."

What did William Gorgas do?

The building of the canal was a huge undertaking. The route ran through jungle and over mountains. Colonel William Gorgas, an army doctor, worked to clear the canal area of *yellow fever,* a disease caused by a kind of mosquito. This allowed the work to continue. The canal opened in 1914. Although it was under the control of the United States, ships of all countries were allowed to use it.

4.4 Big Stick Diplomacy. Getting the right to build the Panama Canal was part of President Roosevelt's *big stick diplomacy.* Roosevelt liked to quote a West African saying: "Speak softly, and carry a big stick, you will go far." The saying was applied to his foreign policy. Roosevelt believed that the United States should be willing to use force (a "big stick") to protect American interests.

Where and how did Roosevelt use big stick diplomacy?

President Roosevelt was concerned that some Latin American countries were not paying the debts they owed to European countries. He thought the Europeans might try to use force to get what was owed them. He feared that once the European nations were in Latin America, they would stay and take over countries there. This had almost happened in 1902 when Great Britain, Germany, and Italy blockaded Venezuela to make it pay its debts. Venezuela had agreed to arbitration. But American leaders feared that the same thing would happen elsewhere.

President Theodore Roosevelt used big stick diplomacy (left) in United States' relations with Latin America. President William Howard Taft used dollar diplomacy (right). What did both Presidents try to accomplish?

The Venezuela crisis led President Roosevelt to announce in 1904 a *corollary,* or addition, to the Monroe Doctrine. The Roosevelt Corollary said that the United States might have to intervene in Latin American countries that did not pay their debts or live up to other agreements. The United States would use its *"international police power."* This meant it would take responsibility for preserving order and protecting life and property. It would keep European countries from interfering in Latin America, against the Monroe Doctrine.

What was the Roosevelt Corollary?

President Roosevelt put his corollary to work in 1905. That year the Dominican Republic could not pay the Europeans what it owed them. Americans took over the Dominican customs collection and payment of debts until the Europeans received their payment in full.

4.5 Dollar Diplomacy. In March 1909, William Howard Taft took office as President. He went along with Roosevelt's policy of bringing the United States into the affairs of other countries to protect American interests. He did, however, change the policy in some ways. He encouraged American business people to invest more in other countries. This added to American trade and brought more money into the United States and the other countries as well. It also put Americans in key economic positions in other countries. In this way, Americans would have a say in other countries without using force. Taft's foreign policy was called *dollar diplomacy.* He tried to use it both in Latin America and in China.

Who fostered dollar diplomacy? How?

To prevent European control in Latin America, President Taft wanted American banks to guarantee the debts of Latin American countries. In 1909, the United States government got American bankers to take over Honduras' debts to European countries. Much the same thing happened in Haiti in 1910 and in Nicaragua in 1911. To make sure that the banks were repaid, Americans took over customs collection. Then a revolution broke out against the Nicaraguan government. President Taft sent American marines to stop the revolt. American forces remained in Nicaragua until 1925.

Dollar diplomacy did not do as well in China as it did in Latin America. Secretary of State Philander Knox, however, was able to talk European countries active in China into allowing American bankers to join a group that was financing railroads there.

4.6 The New Freedom in Foreign Affairs. When Woodrow Wilson became President in March 1913, he promised to change the direction of American foreign policy. He hoped to use ideas like those behind the New Freedom reforms at home. Wilson wanted to end the use of military force and economic pressure by the United States. Instead, he wanted to use friendship, fair play, and democracy.

How did Wilson want to change American foreign policy?

United States Acquisitions, 1858–1917

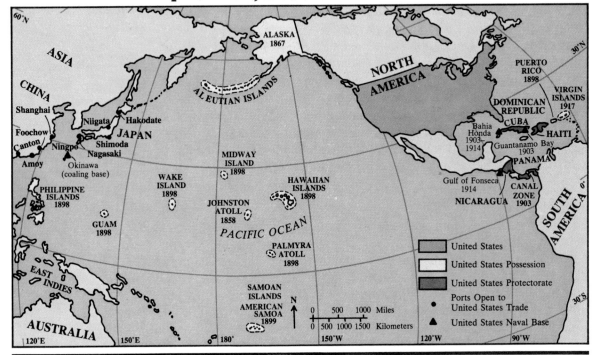

The United States acquired strategic areas of the Caribbean to protect the Panama Canal. Acquisitions of certain Pacific Islands linked the United States with Asian trade. What various ways did the United States expand in the world?

Where did Wilson use force?

President Wilson had promised to change American policy. But he did use force several times in the Caribbean. He used American troops to back governments he believed were democratic. He also used American influence against governments he felt were not democratic. In 1915, President Wilson sent soldiers into Haiti. In 1916, he sent them into the Dominican Republic.

President Wilson also obtained another Caribbean area for the United States. The Americans were afraid that Germany might use the Virgin Islands as a naval base. So in 1917, the United States bought the islands from Denmark for $25 million.

President Wilson felt he had good reason for using force in the Caribbean. But his use of force did not please the people of Latin America. Mexico had gone through several revolutions. In February 1913, the president of Mexico, Francisco Madero, was killed by agents of General Victoriano Huerta, the leader of the army in Mexico City. Huerta then made himself president of Mexico.

President Wilson said that Huerta had not become president legally. For this reason, the United States would not recognize Huerta's government or give it any aid. In 1914, President Wilson ordered the American navy to the Mexican city of Vera Cruz to stop a shipment of arms to Huerta's army. In the battle which followed, 126 Mexicans and 19 Americans were killed. War was prevented when leaders from Argentina, Brazil, and Chile helped to arrange a peace between the United States and Mexico.

What was the problem between the United States and Mexico?

General Huerta was forced to leave office in 1914. He was replaced by Venustiano Carranza, whose government President Wilson recognized. In Mexico, Carranza was opposed by other leaders. One of these was General Francisco (Pancho) Villa. He wanted to end Carranza's rule. In 1916, Villa began a campaign to win the support of the Mexican people. In January of that year, Villa's troops killed 18 Americans working in northern Mexico. Two months later, the soldiers crossed the border into the United States and killed 16 people in New Mexico.

President Wilson ordered General John Pershing to lead American forces across the border into Mexico to capture Villa. Nearly 15,000 American soldiers followed Pershing deep into Mexico. They did not capture Villa. And the fact that they were on Mexican land caused bitter feelings against the United States. By then, however, events in Europe had started to hold greater interest for the United States. In 1917, President Wilson ordered the American soldiers out of Mexico.

Why did General Pershing lead American forces into Mexico?

1. Who controlled the Puerto Rican government after 1900?
2. Why was the United States interested in Cuba?
3. Why did the United States want a canal across Panama?
4. How did big stick diplomacy compare with dollar diplomacy?

5. Conclusion

In the early years of the 1900's, the United States played a larger part in foreign affairs than it ever had before. Its possessions in the Pacific and in the Caribbean made the United States a major world power. In the Caribbean, the United States acted in the affairs of any country in order to protect American interests. All of this marked a major change in the direction of American foreign policy. But one thing which had yet to change was America's attitude toward affairs in Europe. The country had always tried to avoid getting into the troubles of Europeans. However, as a major world power, it was becoming more difficult for it to avoid problems elsewhere in the world.

Chapter 20 Review

Main Points

1. In the late 1800's, the United States became involved in expansion.
2. The Pacific and the Caribbean were the major areas of American interest.
3. America became a world power as a result of the Spanish-American War.
4. The United States obtained Puerto Rico, Guam, and the Philippines from Spain.
5. America wanted trade in China open to all nations.
6. America supported a revolution in Panama and gained the right to build a canal across the isthmus.
7. The United States protected its trade in the Caribbean and kept other nations from moving into the area.

Building Vocabulary

1. Identify the following:

   Matthew Perry
   William Seward
   Alfred Thayer Mahan
   McKinley Tariff
   Liliuokalani
   Emilio Aguinaldo

   Maine
   Manila
   San Juan Hill
   Rough Riders
   Ramon Emeterio Betances
   Open Door policy

   Boxers
   Taft-Katsura Agreement
   Panama Canal
   Hay-Bunau-Varilla Treaty
   Victoriano Huerta
   Francisco Villa

2. Define the following:

   imperialism
   arbitration
   yellow journalism
   armistice

   spheres of influence
   lease
   isthmus
   yellow fever

   big stick diplomacy
   corollary
   "international police power"
   dollar diplomacy

Remembering the Facts

1. What industrial countries became involved in expansion?
2. Why did some Americans think that the United States should build an empire?
3. How did Hawaii become part of the United States?
4. What caused war between the United States and Spain?
5. What were the provisions of the Treaty of Paris?
6. What did Filipinos do when the United States decided to keep control of the Philippine Islands?

7. Why were industrial countries interested in China?

8. What was the purpose of the Open Door policy?

9. How did the United States govern Puerto Rico and the Philippines?

10. How did the United States gain control of the area for building the Panama Canal?

11. What were the policies of Presidents Taft and Wilson toward Latin America?

Understanding the Facts

1. What was new about the "new manifest destiny"?

2. How were relations between the United States and Japan different from relations between the United States and China? Why?

3. Why was the Spanish-American War a short war?

4. How did Theodore Roosevelt's corollary vary from the Monroe Doctrine?

5. Why did the United States want to build a canal in Panama?

6. How was American foreign policy influenced by an interest in trade? How was it influenced by an interest in security?

Using Maps

Insert Maps. When a small section of the earth's surface is shown on a map, it helps to be able to locate it as part of a larger area. This is a smaller scaled drawing of the general area in which the small section appears. It is shown near the main map to provide a better perspective and a better sense of location.

An insert map is used with the map on page 476. Study the main map and the insert. Then answer the following questions.

1. What is the subject of the main map?

2. What area is shown in the insert?

3. What countries and bodies of water are shown on the insert map?

4. What is the approximate length of the Panama Canal? Which map is more useful for this?

5. What is the approximate length of Panama? Which map is more useful for this?

6. What general direction does a ship travel moving from the Caribbean Sea to the Pacific Ocean?

7. Why is the measurement for scale given on the main map not useful in measuring distances on the insert map?

A World at War   21

Mal Thompson painted this scene of American infantry fighting near Mezy, France, July 1918. It depicts the trench warfare of World War I. What impact did World War I have on the United States?

Because it had become a major world power, the United States had to face many new problems and take on many new responsibilities. Woodrow Wilson had been President for little more than a year when war broke out in Europe. At first, the war was fought only in Europe, but it soon spread all over the world. Before long, the United States found it had to decide whether or not to join the fighting.

1. Years of Uncertainty _____

From the time war broke out in Europe in the summer of 1914 until 1917, there was much uncertainty in the United States. The government's policy was to stay out of the war. But this became more difficult. Many things happened to test the country's will to remain neutral. Between 1914 and 1917, Americans were spending much of their time on problems brought on by the war in Europe.

When did war break out in Europe?

1.1 The Alliance System.   There had been trouble among the major industrial countries of Europe long before 1914. Both at home and elsewhere, the Europeans competed with one another for resources and markets. To protect their interests, they built up their armies and navies and formed alliances with other countries. Many signed treaties in which they promised to defend each other in case of war.

By the early 1900's, two alliances had formed in Europe. One was made up of France, Russia, and Great Britain and was called the Triple Entente. The other was made up of Germany, Austria-Hungary, and Italy and was called the Triple Alliance.

1.2 The Opening Guns.   Both Russia and Austria-Hungary wanted to control the Balkans. One of Russia's allies was Serbia, a small Balkan country whose people were Slavs. Serbia wanted to unite all Slavs in the Balkans and form independent Balkan states. Many Slavs lived in Austria-Hungary, and Serbia wanted them to join in its movement. Austria-Hungary, however, was against this. On June 28, 1914, Archduke Franz Ferdinand, the next in line to be emperor of Austria-Hungary, was killed by a Serbian student in the town of Sarajevo. Austria-Hungary said that the Serbian government had planned the killing. On July 28, Austria-Hungary declared war on Serbia. Russia began to ready its army to protect Serbia. Germany, an ally of Austria-Hungary, went to that country's aid by declaring war on Russia on August 1, 1914. Two days later, Germany also declared war on France.

How did World War I begin?

France and Germany had been enemies for a long time. By the time the war started, Germany had a plan ready to crush the French armed forces. Part of the plan called for the German army to march through the neutral country of Belgium. This would put the Germans behind the main French army. They could then take the city of Paris and ports on the English channel. But when Germany marched into Belgium, Great Britain declared war on Germany and rushed in to help France.

What brought Great Britain into the war?

The Germans' plan to take Paris failed. The French drove them back at the Battle of the Marne in September 1914. But the war was far from over. For the first time, machine guns were being used in the fighting. As a result, a new kind of warfare was developing. In the past, battles on land were fought mostly by the *infantry*—groups of soldiers trained to fight on foot. With the new weapons, this way of fighting did not work so well, and more battles were fought by *trench warfare.* *Trenches,* or ditches, formed defensive lines to slow down the enemy. Soldiers put up barbed wire in front of the trenches. A series of these defenses stretched across France from the border of Switzerland to the English channel. This kind of fighting led to a long, drawn-out war.

How did fighting in World War I differ from earlier wars?

By 1915, Germany, Austria-Hungary, and the Ottoman Empire (Turkey) were fighting as the Central Powers. Great Britain, France, Russia, Belgium, Rumania, Greece, Serbia, and Montenegro had formed the Allied Powers. Italy, which had been an ally of Germany, changed sides in 1915 and joined the Allies. Most of the fighting took place in Europe. But there also were battles in the Middle East and Africa. Naval battles took place on the major oceans of the world. As a result, the war became known as World War I.

Which nation switched sides?

1.3   The Problems of Neutrality.   When the war first began in Europe, President Wilson asked the American people to remain neutral "in thought as well as in action." That was hard for many people to do. There was much support in the United States for the Allies. Many Americans of British background sided with Great Britain. Other Americans reminded the people of the close ties between the United States and France since the American Revolution.

Why was there support for the Allied Powers?

At the same time, many Americans of German heritage sided with Germany. They felt it had been forced into the war by Russia and France. Still other Americans of Irish background did not like the British and were against American aid to Great Britain. And those Americans who had come from Austria-Hungary and the Balkan countries most often supported their former homelands.

What Americans supported the Central Powers in the early years of the war?

The United States government tried to remain neutral, although this became harder to do. At first, the war had slowed down American trade overseas. As the war went on, the countries fighting in it found they needed more food and clothing than they could make. They turned to the United States for these and other goods. This led to a sharp rise in American production of wheat, cotton, minerals, food, and *munitions*, or war materials.

Because the United States was neutral, it had the right under international law to trade everything but weapons and other munitions

World competition for new markets and colonies was widespread by the early 1900's. It was most active in the Eastern Hemisphere. Where were the major colonies of each colonial power?

Colonialism in the Eastern Hemisphere, 1914

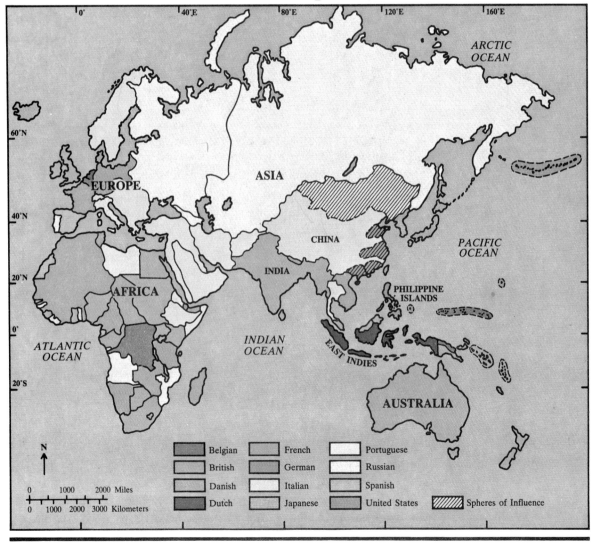

ARCTIC OCEAN

EUROPE

ASIA

CHINA

PACIFIC OCEAN

INDIA

AFRICA

PHILIPPINE ISLANDS

ATLANTIC OCEAN

INDIAN OCEAN

EAST INDIES

AUSTRALIA

N

Belgian	French	Portuguese
British	German	Russian
Danish	Italian	Spanish
Dutch	Japanese	United States

Spheres of Influence

0   1000   2000 Miles
0 1000 2000 3000 Kilometers

Some people wanted the United States to fight in World War I to protect America's national honor (left). Others wanted to protect American economic interests (right). What reasons did President Wilson give for declaring war?

What were America's rights under international law?

with whomever it wanted. But the British navy blockaded the Central Powers, which cut off much of the American trade with them. As a result, most of the American trade was with the Allies.

War loans were another link between the United States and the Allies. In September 1915, President Wilson agreed to allow Americans to make private loans to the countries at war. By April 1917, $2.3 billion had been loaned to the Allies and only $20 million to the Central Powers.

How did the Allies seek to gain American support?

The Allies wanted to win Americans over to their side. Since the British controlled the Atlantic cables that carried European news to the United States, the Allies used the cables to spread *propaganda*—information designed to help or harm a cause. The Allied news often showed the Germans as cold, cruel people whose victory would be bad for America and the rest of the world. Because of all these things—the trade, the war loans, and the propaganda—it was not easy for Americans to remain neutral. More and more the United States was becoming linked to the Allies.

1.4 Submarine Warfare. Ships had been used in battle throughout history. Over the years, ships at sea followed certain rules of international law during a war. Three steps were supposed to be taken before a warship could sink a merchant ship. A warning shot was to be fired to stop the merchant ship. A boarding party was to be sent over to check for war materials. And arrangements were to be made for the safety of passengers and crew.

What were the rules of international law regarding ships at sea before World War I?

In World War I, the British kept the German navy's surface ships tied up in port. So the Germans used submarines to sink enemy ships. The Germans said submarines could not follow the rules that governed other ships. Submarines had to stay underwater, because once they surfaced, they became easy targets to be destroyed. The Germans also pointed out that there was not enough room on submarines to keep people taken from enemy ships. On February 1915, the Germans announced that the water around Great Britain was a war zone. All enemy ships that entered the area would be sunk on sight. The Germans made it clear that neutral ships entering a declared war zone did so at their own risk.

What were the German arguments against such rules as they related to submarine warfare?

On May 7, 1915, a German submarine sank the British passenger liner *Lusitania* off the coast of Ireland. As the ship sank, 1,198 people died. Of the passengers who died, 128 were Americans. People in the United States were shocked and angered by the sinking. They paid no attention to the German charge that the *Lusitania* was carrying arms and munitions. President Wilson reacted by sending a strong protest.

What was the Lusitania, *and what happened to it?*

A few months later, a German submarine sank another British passenger ship, the *Arabic*. Two Americans were among those who were killed. Germany did not want to break relations with the United States. It promised to stop attacking passenger ships without warning.

On March 24, 1916, the Germans sank the French passenger ship *Sussex* in the English channel. Several Americans who were on board the *Sussex* were hurt. The incident angered Americans. They felt that the Germans had broken the promise they had made following the sinking of the *Arabic*. President Wilson warned Germany that unless it stopped its warfare against passenger and freight ships, the United States would break off relations. On May 4, Germany answered President Wilson by issuing the *Sussex* Pledge. In it, Germany said it would not sink any more passenger and merchant ships without warning. The pledge helped improve relations between Germany and the United States for a time.

What was the Sussex Pledge?

1. What were the alliances in Europe?
2. What was the immediate cause of war in Europe?
3. What was the position that President Wilson wanted the American people to take concerning the war?
4. What German weapon caused problems regarding international laws of the sea?

Carrie Chapman Catt (1859–1947)

PROFILE

Carrie Chapman Catt led the campaign for women's suffrage in the 1900's. She became president of the National American Suffrage Association in 1915. For most of her life, Catt worked for the right of women to participate in the election process.

Catt developed a three-way plan to give women the right to vote. Her plan supported an amendment to the Constitution. It also called for amending state constitutions and for gaining voting rights in state primary elections.

The women's right to vote movement lost some of its force during World War I. While many members wanted to put off their plan, Catt continued her attempts to convince Americans of the cause for women's suffrage.

After the war ended, Congress approved a women's right to vote amendment to the Constitution. In 1920, the amendment was passed by enough states to become law.

Along with her national leadership, Carrie Chapman Catt carried on less well-known work for women on the international level. Catt had called for the establishment of a League of Women Voters. She did not take an active part in it, however. She served to inspire other women to carry on the responsibility for all citizens to exercise their right to vote.

2. Preparedness and Pacifism

The fact that the United States was neutral did not stop most Americans from worrying about the future. They were not sure that the country would be able to remain neutral. Some were afraid that if the United States entered the war, its armed forces would be too weak to defend the country. They felt that, to be on the safe side, the United States should prepare for war. Other Americans, however, did not like that idea. They feared that preparing for war would make American entry into the war more likely.

2.1 Demands for Preparedness. Soon after the start of World War I, some Americans began to demand that the United States prepare in order to better defend itself against attack. This is called *preparedness*. In December 1914, these people formed the National Security League to campaign for national preparedness. In 1915, more groups were formed. At first, President Wilson was not interested. But when the *Lusitania* was sunk, he changed his attitude. In December 1915, Wilson asked Congress for more money to increase the size of the army and navy.

Why did some Americans make demands for national preparedness?

Over the next year or so, Congress acted in several ways. In June 1916, it passed the National Defense Act, which made both the army and the National Guard larger. The act also set up the Reserve Officer Training Corps, which allowed officers to be trained at colleges. Two months later, Congress approved funds to begin building new ships for the navy. In September 1916, Congress set up the National Shipping Board. It could buy, lease, or build ships for the United States government. The following month, Congress created the Council of National Defense. Its job was to see that private industry met the needs of the armed services.

What did the National Defense Act do?

2.2 The Pacifist Movement. Not all Americans were in favor of preparedness. Some were against it and any other movement which they thought could draw the United States into war. These people were called *pacifists*. They had been growing in numbers in many areas of the world even before World War I had started. Pacifists were against violence and war as a way of settling problems. They believed that any dispute could be settled in peaceful ways.

What Americans were against preparedness? Why?

American pacifists included Jane Addams and William Jennings Bryan. Bryan was Secretary of State when World War I began. Shortly after the *Lusitania* was sunk, he resigned his post. He was afraid that a strong message to Germany would lead the United States into war.

1. What was the purpose of the National Security League?
2. What was the pacifist movement?

3. The Road to War

The year 1916 was an election year in the United States. The Republicans chose as their candidate Charles Evans Hughes, a Justice of the Supreme Court. The Democrats renominated Wilson. They used the slogan "He kept us out of war." It caught the imagination of the

American people and helped Wilson win a close election. He received 277 electoral votes to 254 for Hughes.

After the election, Wilson tried to get the Allied Powers and the Central Powers to talk about peace. But his efforts failed because each side was sure it was going to win the war before long.

3.1 On the Brink. Any hopes President Wilson had for peace soon faded. German leaders had decided that they could win the war if their submarines could cut off trade between the Allies and the United States. Germany told the United States that beginning February 1, 1917, German submarines would sink on sight all ships in the Mediterranean and in the waters around Great Britain.

Why were the Germans willing to risk the consequences of a return to unconditional submarine warfare?

The Germans were not worried about the Americans entering the war. They were sure the war would be over before the United States could react. President Wilson, however, felt that Germany had violated the *Sussex* Pledge and broke off relations.

What was the Zimmermann note?

On March 1, 1917, a story appeared in the newspapers which angered many Americans and led them to call for war. The story was about a note sent to the German minister in Mexico by Arthur Zimmermann, the German Foreign Secretary. The Zimmermann note had been picked up by the British. They passed it on to the United States. In the note, Zimmermann told the German minister that if war broke out with the United States, he was to suggest an alliance between Mexico and Germany. He was to tell the Mexican government that if it joined Germany, Mexico would receive Texas, New Mexico, and Arizona—the area it had lost in the Mexican War. Zimmermann also suggested that the Mexicans talk Japan into joining them.

3.2 "A Fearful Thing." As pressure in the United States grew, Wilson and Congress tried to keep the country neutral. Then in March 1917, the Germans sank five American merchant ships. This again violated international law. On the evening of April 2, 1917, President Wilson asked Congress for a declaration of war. He said:

What were the nation's war aims as expressed by Wilson?

> *The world must be made safe for democracy. . . . We have no selfish ends to serve. We desire no conquest, no dominion. We seek no . . . material compensation for the sacrifices we shall freely make. We are but one of the champions of the rights of mankind. . . .*
>
> *It is a fearful thing to lead this great peaceful people into war, into the most terrible and disastrous of all wars, civilization itself seeming to be in the balance.*

Congress acted quickly. On April 4, the Senate voted 82 to 6 for war against Germany. Two days later, the House of Representatives

Allied Shipping Losses, 1914–1918

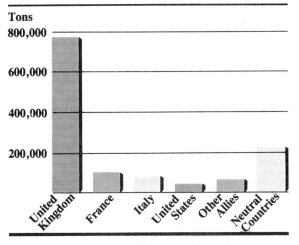

German submarines, or U-boats, did much damage in the course of the war. Some nations used the group convoy system to limit destruction. Which Allied nations suffered the greatest losses at sea during World War I?

voted 373 to 50 in favor of war. That same day, President Wilson signed the resolution, and the United States officially entered World War I. On December 7, 1917, the United States also declared war on Austria-Hungary.

1. Who was the Democratic candidate for President in 1916? What was his slogan?
2. What did Germany promise Mexico in the Zimmermann note?
3. When did the United States enter World War I?

4. America in World War I

The war that the United States entered in 1917 was different from any war in which Americans had fought in the past. Such weapons as machine guns, huge cannons, poison gas, and airplanes that carried bombs were being used in greater numbers than ever before. Battles were fought by thousands of soldiers at one time. People and industries had to organize to supply American soldiers fighting in Europe. The steps the government took to carry out the war was felt by all the people.

4.1 Wartime Industry and Agriculture. The United States had to make sure that the country met the needs of the military. To do this, the federal government set up agencies to regulate the country's economy. A War Industries Board was created in July 1917. The board was headed by Bernard Baruch. It had the power to fix prices, set standards, make sure of raw materials, and decide what goods should be produced first.

What agencies were set up to regulate the economy?

In August 1917, Congress passed the Lever Food and Fuel Act, which set up a Food Administration and a Fuel Administration. The Food Administration was headed by Herbert Hoover. Its jobs were to stop the waste of food and to make sure that more food was produced. The agency asked Americans not to eat meat on certain days of the week. In this way, there would be more meat to send to the Allies. It also set the price of wheat. Because farmers were pleased with the price, they began to grow more wheat than they had in the past. The Fuel Administration was headed by Harry Garfield. Its jobs were to find ways to save and to produce more electricity.

Who headed the Food Administration?

In December 1917, the federal government took over the railroads. Congress set up the United States Railroad Administration (USRA). Under the direction of William Gibbs McAdoo, the Secretary of the Treasury and President Wilson's son-in-law, the USRA controlled the track operated by close to 3,000 railway companies. It ran the railroads as a single system.

What was Wilson's son-in-law's post?

4.2 Wartime Labor and Immigration. Thousands of Americans left their jobs to join the military. Large numbers of people began to leave their homes in one part of the country to seek better jobs. Among these were many blacks and Mexican Americans.

Thousands of blacks left the rural South to find work in the North. There they worked in steel mills, coal mines, meat-packing plants, and other industries. More than 12,000 blacks found jobs with the Pennsylvania Railroad. Mexican Americans from the Southwest moved to cities in the Middle West. They found work in mills, mines, and factories there. By 1920, nearly 70,000 Mexican Americans were living east of the Mississippi River, and ten times that many lived in the western states.

What Americans moved to the cities of the North and Middle West during the war? Why?

Women became an important part of the American work force. Between 1915 and 1918, more than 1 million took jobs outside their homes. They worked in factories doing jobs that had been done by men. They also worked in new industries that had opened just to make military supplies. Women who had been working in business and industry before the war had a chance to move into better jobs which, for the most part, had been held by men.

What effect did the war have on women?

The need to produce more also affected immigration. When the war began in Europe, fewer Europeans came into the United States than had in past years. In 1917, new laws were passed which cut down the number of immigrants even more. The new laws stated that immigrants over the age of 16 had to be able to read. Persons from a special "barred zone," which included India, Siam, and Indochina, were not allowed to enter the country as immigrants.

What types of workers immigrated to the United States during the war?

But as the war dragged on and more Americans left the country to fight, America's need for workers grew. Food growers in the West asked Congress to allow all the farm workers who wanted to enter the country to do so. Growers hired Filipinos to work their fields in Hawaii. Mexicans were put to work in fields in California and other places.

4.3 Financing the War. It cost a great deal of money to fight World War I. The United States government had to find a way to raise

Many Americans played an active part in World War I. Some people on the home front worked in munition plants (left). A poster (right) reminded Americans to conserve for the war effort. How was the national economy affected by the war?

Film actor Douglas Fairbanks (left) called for Americans to buy war bonds at a rally on Wall Street. A poster (right), written in five languages, urged Hawaiians to buy war savings stamps. What laws provided for financing the war?

What was the Liberty Loan Act?

that money. In April 1917, it passed the Liberty Loan Act, which allowed bonds to be sold to the public. Huge rallies, parades, and speeches by *celebrities,* or well-known people from the world of sports and entertainment, helped persuade large numbers of Americans to buy war bonds. The sale of these bonds raised more than $20 billion for the war.

Six months later, Congress passed the War Revenue Act. It made income taxes the chief source of revenue during the war. The act also raised postal rates and taxes on certain goods, transportation, amusements, liquor, and tobacco.

What did the Committee on Public Information do?

At the same time the government was working to raise money, it was trying to gain public support for the war. To do this, the Committee on Public Information was set up. Headed by newspaper writer George Creel, it was made up of the Secretaries of State, War, and the Navy. The committee hired people to give talks and to write stories and articles. It also had movies, posters, and signs made in support of the war effort.

Laws were passed to stop people from doing anything to upset the war effort. One of the most important laws was the Espionage Act passed in June 1917. It set fines and prison terms for any person who helped the enemy, got in the way of military recruiting, or caused other persons to refuse to serve in the armed services. The act also gave the Postmaster General the power to hold back any kind of mail that spoke against the war effort.

The laws were strictly enforced. A. Philip Randolph and Chandler Owen were publishers of a newspaper called *The Messenger.* In 1918, they were sent to prison for writing an article that urged other black people not to support the war. The following year, the Espionage Act was put to a legal test. Charles T. Schenck, who was against the war, was convicted for passing out papers telling people not to join the armed services. Schenck appealed to the Supreme Court. Justice Oliver Wendell Holmes ruled that Schenck was guilty as charged. Holmes said that Schenck's actions were "a clear and present danger" to the United States in time of war.

What was Justice Holmes' ruling in Schenck v. the United States?

4.4 Americans to War. In May 1917, Congress passed the Selective Service Act, setting up a draft. The act said that all male citizens between the ages of 21 and 30 had to register with draft boards. The following year, the act was changed to include all male citizens between the ages of 18 and 45. The names of those who registered were placed in a *lottery,* or chance drawing. The people whose names were drawn had to serve in the army. About 24 million Americans, black and white, were registered under the draft. About 3.8 million of these were called to serve in the army.

How did the Selective Service Act work?

Once the United States had soldiers, it had to get them and supplies across the Atlantic. Before the Americans entered the war, the Allies had been losing ships faster than new ones could be built. American navy leaders, such as Admiral William S. Sims, got the Allies to use a *convoy system.* In it, small, fast warships called *destroyers* traveled with the supply ships. The destroyers carried weapons for use against submarines. They could protect the supply ships from attack.

What was a convoy system?

In June 1917, the first American soldiers arrived in France. Called the American Expeditionary Force, they were led by General John Pershing. At first, Americans were used only in small units and as replacements for some French and British soldiers. They did not take part in any important actions until May 1918, when they were rushed to Château-Thierry. There they helped the French stop a new German drive to take Paris.

Who was commander of the American Expeditionary Force?

What changes were taking place in the war in 1918?

In 1918, many changes were taking place in the war. Russia no longer was in the war. There had been a revolution there. The Bolsheviks had overthrown the government and set up a new Communist one. Their leader, Lenin, also had signed a separate peace with Germany at Brest-Litovsk. By that time, the American convoy system was working well and had badly damaged German naval plans. Allied morale, which had been at its lowest when America entered the war, had risen. Meanwhile, General Pershing had convinced the Allied military command to allow American soldiers to fight together as one army under him.

In what battles did American troops fight?

In June 1918, the Americans fought their first sizable action of the war at Belleau Wood. This was followed in July and August by the second Battle of the Marne, which many people feel was the turning point of the war. More than 85,000 American soldiers took part in the battle. The war lasted through the summer and into the fall, with Allied attacks at St. Mihiel and a large-scale attack in the Meuse-Argonne area. The success of these attacks convinced the Germans that they could not win the war. On November 11, they asked for an armistice. World War I had come to an end.

At the end of the war, there were more than 2 million American soldiers in France. Although they had taken part in the fighting for only a little over a year, 112,000 Americans had been killed or had died from disease. Another 237,000 had been wounded. The cost of the war to other countries was even greater. Russia, France, Austria-Hungary, and Germany all lost more than 1 million soldiers. Over 900,000 British soldiers had died. Italy, Rumania, and Turkey also had lost hundreds of thousands.

What contributions did the United States make to the war?

The United States had given more than just its people to the war. When Americans arrived in France, the Allies had been at war for several years. They had lost a great many soldiers who could not be replaced. Those still fighting were tired, and their morale was low. American entry into the war boosted Allied morale and gave the Allies an edge. The United States also made very important contributions of food and money. Much of the war materials from the United States had arrived too late to affect the outcome of the war, however. In most cases, the Americans had used British and French arms, French-made cannons, and French and British airplanes.

1. How were industry and agriculture affected by the war?
2. How did the war affect immigration?
3. How many American soldiers fought in the war? How many died?

Europe in World War I, 1914–1917

Where were German submarines most active during the war? Where were major battles on the western front fought? What were the major battles on the eastern front? When did the war in the east end? When was the last major battle on the western front?

5. A Plan for Peace

Long before the fighting was over, President Wilson began to prepare for the peace conference that would take place after the war. He believed that the war had been caused by secret alliances, national pride, arms races, and selfish imperialism. Wilson hoped to work out a peace treaty that would end these things and bring about peace.

5.1 The Fourteen Points. On January 8, 1918, Wilson went before Congress to offer a peace plan called the Fourteen Points. Basic to this plan was cooperation among all countries of the world. Among other things, the plan called for freedom of the seas in peace and in war,

Changes in Europe, 1919

The treaty ending World War I affected the political geography of Europe (left). It also affected politics in the United States. To what element of the Versailles Treaty (right) did many United States Senators object?

What were the major items of Wilson's peace plan?

an end to secret treaties and alliances, and equal trading rights for all countries. It also called for all countries to cut down the size of their armed forces and to allow people to choose their own forms of government. The fourteenth point called for the countries of the world to form a League of Nations. It would work to preserve world peace.

President Wilson believed that the idea of the League of Nations was the most important point in the peace plan. A great many Americans believed Wilson's plan was a good one. The German government agreed with them. The Germans thought the Fourteen Points would serve as the base for the final peace treaty.

5.2 The Versailles Treaty.   On November 18, 1918, President Wilson announced that he and his advisors planned to go to Paris. There they would take part in the conference that would prepare the treaty ending the war. In Paris, Wilson met the leaders of the three major Allied powers—Georges Clemenceau of France, David Lloyd George of Great Britain, and Vittorio Orlando of Italy. They made it clear that they had come to punish Germany. They refused to accept Wilson's Fourteen Points as the base for peace. After much talk, however, they agreed to make Wilson's League of Nations a part of the final treaty. The Treaty of Versailles was signed on June 28, 1919.

Who were the Big Four?

The German representatives were shocked when they saw the Versailles Treaty. Aside from the part that allowed for a League of Nations, it was very different from President Wilson's Fourteen Points. It stated that Germany alone was responsible for starting World War I. For this reason, Germany was to pay the Allies a huge sum of money for war damages. That sum later was set at $56 billion. Germany also had to agree to almost total *disarmament*—the reduction of weapons, military supplies, and armed forces by a government.

Why were the Germans shocked by the Versailles Treaty?

After the treaty was signed, President Wilson returned to the United States to present it for Senate approval. Wilson soon found out that a number of Senators did not want to approve it. These Senators were led by Henry Cabot Lodge of Massachusetts, William E. Borah of Idaho, and Hiram Johnson of California.

Some of the Senators were against the treaty because they felt it meant the United States would have to become a member of the League of Nations. They were afraid that if this happened, Americans would be drawn into foreign wars to protect other countries. They thought this would upset American foreign policy. Others were angry because President Wilson had not talked to Senate leaders before the treaty was drawn up. They wanted some changes made in the treaty.

President Wilson refused. He would not make changes affecting the League. Senator Lodge and his supporters also refused to change their stand. They said that unless the President made the changes they wanted, they would make sure the Senate did not approve the treaty.

In the summer of 1919, Wilson decided to take his case to the people. On September 4, 1919, he set out on a speaking tour of the Middle and Far West. In the course of 22 days, he traveled more than 8,000 miles (12,800 kilometers) and made 37 speeches in 29 cities. While speaking at Pueblo, Colorado, the President collapsed and was rushed back to Washington. There he suffered a stroke which left him disabled for the rest of his term in office and until his death in 1924.

What did President Wilson attempt to do to overcome Senate opposition to the treaty?

On November 19, 1919, the Treaty of Versailles came up for a vote in the Senate. President Wilson's efforts had done no good. The Senate defeated the treaty. In February 1920, it was brought up again. Wilson still refused to make changes, and on March 19, 1920, it again went down to defeat.

What was the final outcome of the Versailles Treaty?

Security

Some people say that they are secure. This might mean that they are safe, free from danger, fear, or anxiety. Nations try to ensure security with a strong armed forces. World War I, however, proved that strong armed forces are not enough.

During and after World War I, a means to ensure international security was suggested. Instead of using armed forces, international cooperation could be used. President Woodrow Wilson expressed this idea in a speech on January 8, 1918. He hoped all nations could agree on some principles to work together for world peace. In this speech, he presented his Fourteen Points.

I. Open covenants of peace, openly arrived at. . . .

II. Absolute freedom of navigation upon the seas . . . in peace and in war.

III. The removal, so far as possible, of all economic barriers and the establishment of an equality of trade conditions among . . . nations. . . .

IV. Adequate guarantees . . . that national armaments will be reduced to the lowest point consistent with domestic safety.

V. . . . impartial adjustment of all colonial claims. . . .

VI. The evacuation of all Russian territory. . . .

VII. Belgium . . . must be evacuated and restored. . . .

VIII. All French territory should be freed. . . .

IX. A readjustment of the frontiers of Italy. . . .

X. The peoples of Austria-Hungary . . . should be accorded the freest opportunity of autonomous development.

XI. Rumania, Serbia, and Montenegro should be evacuated. . . .

XII. The Turkish portions of the present Ottoman Empire should be assured a secure sovereignty. . . .

XIII. An independent Polish state should be erected. . . .

XIV. A general association of nations must be formed . . . for the purpose of affording mutual guarantees of political independence and territorial integrity to great and small states alike.

1. How does Wilson's security plan deal with the causes of World War I?
2. What are Wilson's suggested changes to ensure international security?
3. How does Wilson hope to maintain peace for the future?

The Versailles Treaty was signed in the Hall of Mirrors at the Versailles Palace in France. At the signing were the Big Four Allied leaders, (center, left to right) Vittorio Orlando of Italy, Woodrow Wilson of the United States, Georges Clemenceau of France, and Lloyd George of Great Britain. How was Germany affected by the treaty?

Wilson's last hope was that in the 1920 elections the people would elect a new Congress controlled by Democrats. Wilson's hope was shattered, however, when Warren G. Harding of Ohio and the Republican party won. That ended any idea of the United States joining the League of Nations. On July 2, 1921, Congress declared an end to the war with Germany and Austria-Hungary.

1. What was President Wilson's plan for peace?
2. Where did the Allies meet to draw up a treaty?
3. Which of the Fourteen Points did Wilson think was most important?
4. Who opposed the Versailles Treaty in the United States Senate?

6. Conclusion _____

With the defeat of the Versailles Treaty and the election of Warren G. Harding, one era in American history came to an end and another began. World War I marked the end of the United States staying out of affairs in Europe. But the final results of the war upset many Americans. They had gone to war with high ideals, hoping to make the world a better place in which to live. But the peace treaty showed them that the warring nations had not changed their ways. Because of this, Americans wanted to turn again toward a policy of noninvolvement.

Chapter 21 Review

Main Points

1. The United States tried to remain neutral when war started between the Allied Powers and the Central Powers in Europe.

2. The war raised questions concerning the rights of neutral nations.

3. Allied propaganda, German submarine warfare, and American business interests caused Americans to side with the Allies.

4. Some Americans wanted the country to prepare for war. Others were pacifists.

5. The United States entered the war in 1917.

6. Government agencies were created to organize the economy for war.

7. The United States supplied the Allies with war materials, and American soldiers fought in the war.

8. An armistice ended the fighting on November 11, 1918.

9. Most of President Wilson's plan for peace was rejected by the Allied leaders.

10. The Senate did not approve the Versailles Treaty because of disagreements over the League of Nations.

Building Vocabulary

1. Identify the following:

Woodrow Wilson	*Sussex* Pledge	Espionage Act
Triple Entente	Carrie Chapman Catt	Selective Service Act
Archduke Franz Ferdinand	National Defense Act	John Pershing
Central Powers	Zimmermann note	Fourteen Points
Allied Powers	War Revenue Act	League of Nations
Lusitania		Treaty of Versailles

2. Define the following:

infantry	propaganda	lottery
trench warfare	preparedness	convoy system
trenches	pacifists	destroyers
munitions	celebrities	disarmament

Remembering the Facts

1. Why did European nations create an alliance system?

2. What did Congress do in 1916 to strengthen the armed forces?

3. Why was it difficult for Americans to remain neutral during the war?

4. What did Germany do that led the United States into the war on the side of the Allies?

5. What were the wartime controls on industry and agriculture in the United States?

6. Where did industry get the increased number of workers it needed?

7. How did the government get the money it needed to finance the war?

8. How were people selected for the armed forces?

9. What part did the United States play in fighting with the Allies?

10. What were the major provisions of Wilson's Fourteen Points?

11. Why did the Senate oppose the Treaty of Versailles?

Understanding the Facts

1. What advantages and problems did war in Europe present for Americans?

2. What caused American policy to move from neutrality to participation?

3. How was Wilson's plan for peace accepted by the Germans? by the Allies? by the United States Senate?

4. How was life in the United States influenced by the war?

5. What did the election of Warren G. Harding in 1920 seem to say about the general attitude of the American people toward other countries?

Using Maps

Mercator Projection. If a tennis ball is cut into two pieces and one half is flattened on a table, it cannot be flattened totally without more cutting in some way. Mapmakers have the same problem. A mapmaker trys to show the surface of a round earth on a flat map. When only a small part of the earth's surface is shown on a map, there is no problem. Adjustments must be made when large land areas or the whole earth are shown.

In making adjustments from a round to a flat surface, mapmakers use a variety of systems or projections. Each system shows certain areas accurately, but none show true scale for every part of the earth.

Only a globe is an accurate reflection of the earth.

One of the frequently used systems is the Mercator Projection. With this projection, all parallels and meridians appear parallel to each other. Look at the map on page 487, and answer the following questions.

1. What parts of the earth's surface are closest to scale on the map?

2. What parts are most distorted?

3. Which land areas appear on the map to be larger than they really are?

4. Why do certain land areas appear to be unlike they really are?

Detroit 1900-1920

People who visited Detroit at the end of the nineteenth century saw a comfortable, midwestern town on a beautiful river. One visitor wrote:

The Detroit River . . . is one of the most beautiful water avenues west of the Hudson. It is from half a mile to a mile wide, [and] is always of a clear blue color. . . . It is, with reason, the pride of the city, and the ferry boats [moving] between Detroit and Windsor [in Canada] are of the most attractive type. In summer . . . musicians are engaged for the regular trips. . . . Whole families spend the day on the river . . . taking their dinner in baskets, as . . . a picnic. . . .

Memories

George Stark remembered his childhood during this time in Detroit.

We children were always told to [keep] our play to our own back yards, so we seldom played in our own back yards. We went "out in front." Mother never worried much about this

small disobedience, because there was no danger of us being run down by automobiles. There weren't any. . . .

In the late 1890's, the bicycle craze was at its peak. . . . The more daring of the ladies wore divided skirts, making it possible for them to ride men's bicycles, which, for some strange reason, were supposed to be faster. But what difference did it make, when the police would grab you if you went more than fifteen miles an hour. That was our speed limit. If you exceeded it, you were called a "scortcher" and the "scortcher cops" might get you. . . .

But what would one remember from the early days. . . . [We] would remember . . . the . . . chug of the horseless carriage which churned up the dirt roads in our neighborhood. . . . We didn't know that we were looking at the dawn of the machine age. . . .

The machine age in transportation soon changed Detroit into one of the leading industrial cities of the world.

Right Place, Right Time

Conditions were right for Detroit to become the auto capital. In 1900, Detroit was a rapidly growing city. It was well known for iron and steel production. Its location near the Great Lakes helped it to become a major center for building gasoline boat engines. The city had many workshops where people made engines and engine parts. There were also plenty of skilled workers who had experience making body parts for wagons and carriages.

Money to finance new ideas was also available in Detroit. Some people there had made great fortunes in mining, shipping, and lumber. By the end of the 1800's, their children were looking for new ways to make more money. The horseless carriage seemed like an exciting venture.

Another important factor was that many of the pioneers of the automobile industry lived in the Detroit area. People like Ransom E. Olds (Oldsmobile), Henry Ford (Ford Motor Company), William Durant (General Motors Company), David D. Buick (Buick), and Henry N. Leland (Cadillac) moved quickly to manufacture the automobile.

Growth of a City

With the growth of the automobile industry, the population of Detroit grew from 285,704 in 1900 to 465,766 in 1910. By 1920, the population almost doubled to 993,678, making Detroit the fourth largest city in the country. Many of its people were foreign-born. One Detroit resident observed that "every third [person] you meet in Detroit was born in a foreign country."

Automobiles were beginning to sell, and every company was trying to develop ways to produce more cars at lower costs. In 1909, Henry Ford came up with a plan to build only one model automobile, the Model T. The body would be exactly the same for all cars, and "any customer [could] have a car painted

Henry Ford drives his first automobile which he called the Quadricycle. The success of his first gasoline automobile eventually led to the founding of the Ford Motor Company. What other automobile pioneers lived in the Detroit area?

any color, so long as it [was] black." The Model T would cost $275.

Moving Assembly Line

The Ford Company could not keep up with the flood of orders for the Model T. To make the cars faster, Ford developed the moving assembly line in his plants in 1914.

The first step forward in assembly came when we began taking the work to the [people] instead of the [people] to the work. . . .

The principles of assembly are these:

(1) Place the tools and the [workers] in the [order] of the operation. . . .

(2) Use work slides or some other form of carrier . . . and if possible have gravity carry the part to the next [worker].

(3) Use sliding assembling lines by which the parts to be assembled are delivered at convenient distances.

The net result . . . is [less need] for thought on the part of the worker and [fewer] movements. . . . [Each person] does as nearly as possible only one thing with only one movement. . . .

It must not be imagined, however, that all this worked out as quickly as it sounds. The speed of the moving work had to be carefully

Ford introduced the first moving assembly line at his Highland Park plant. At this plant, he also announced the revolutionary five-dollar-a-day wage. How did Ford's new ideas change the automobile industry?

Detroit factories employed many immigrants. How did the city's determination to Americanize its foreign-born population affect these workers?

tried out. . . . *The idea is that [people] must not be hurried . . . [they] must have . . . not a single unnecessary second.*

A visitor to the Ford Motor Plant in 1914 described this scene.

Of course there was order in that place; of course there was system . . . "efficiency"—but to my mind, [not used] to such things, the whole room, with its [endless] aisles, its whirling shafts and wheels, its forest of roof-supporting posts and flapping, flying, leather belting, its endless rows of [twisting] machinery, its shrieking, hammering, and clatter, its smell of oil, its autumn haze of smoke . . . expressed . . . delirium.

Fancy a jungle of wheels and belts and weird iron forms—of men, machinery and movement—add to it every kind of sound you can imagine: the sound of a million squirrels chirking, a million monkeys quarreling, a million lions roaring . . . a million elephants smashing through a forest of sheet iron, a million boys whistling on their fingers, a million others coughing . . . imagine all of this happening at the very edge of Niagara Falls, with the everlasting roar of the [waterfall] as a [continuing] background. . . .

Fancy all this riot going on at once: then imagine the effect of its suddenly ceasing [stopping]. For that is what it did. The wheels slowed down and became still. The belts stopped flapping. The machines lay dead. The noise faded to a murmur: then to utter silence. Our ears rang with the quiet. The aisles all at once were full of men in overalls, each with a paper package or a box. Some of them walked swiftly toward the exits. Others settled down on piles of automobile parts, or the bases of machines to eat. . . . It was the lull of noon.

The Five Dollar Day

About this time, Ford also announced that he would pay $5 for an eight-hour work day. Until this, the pay for the average plant worker had been $1 a day for unskilled labor and $3.50 a day for skilled labor. Ford's announcement caused many people to change jobs. However, there were conditions that had to be met to earn this $5. The person had to be on the payroll for six months and be of good moral character. Ford checked up on his employees. He had a social service department which told the workers how to live and how to spend their money.

Effect on Economy

The automobile industry had become the only industry in Detroit. It had a major effect on the Detroit economy. The people of the city soon discovered that auto sales depended on the attitude and income of the consumer. Since the automobile was a durable, expensive item, the purchase of a new one could be put off for a year or two. This industry followed a boom-bust cycle, causing serious problems for Detroit in 1915. The editor of the Board of Commerce's magazine noted:

No such transition [change] from extreme depression to the greatest activity ever before occurred in the history of Detroit as in the months from April to October, 1915.

In April the Board of Commerce was just closing its self-imposed task of finding work for a host of the unemployed. At the opening of the year a large proportion of the factories were running on short time, and thousands of willing and capable men were seeking work in vain. . . .

Six months later there was a striking contrast in conditions. There was an actual scarcity [lack] of various kinds of skilled labor and no surplus of common labor. Some of the factories were running overtime, more men were employed than ever before, and no one who was able and willing to work needed to be out of a job.

One of the main reasons for this change was Detroit's determination to "Americanize" its foreign-born population. In the fall of 1914, factories had slowed down, and 80,000 people had lost their jobs. The Detroit Board of Commerce tried to find jobs and organized help for the people out of work.

One important fact that the Board of Commerce discovered was that most of the people who could not get jobs also could not speak English. Therefore, the forces of the city banded together to "Americanize" Detroit. Business leaders worked with schools and the Board of Commerce to encourage workers to learn English. Posters were placed on bulletin boards in factories, schools, churches, and libraries saying "Learn English and Get Better Pay." English lessons were given free. People from foreign countries were also encouraged to become American citizens.

On January 31, 1916, the Packard Motor Company made this announcement:

From and after this date, promotions to positions of importance in the organization of this company will be given only to those who are native born or naturalized citizens of the United States, or to those of foreign birth who have relinquished their foreign citizenship, and who have filed with our Government their first

Detroit's development depended on the growth of the automobile industry. How did Detroit change following World War I?

papers applying for citizenship, which application for citizenship must be [carefully] followed to its completion."

"America First" became the motto of the city.

Detroit and the War

In 1917, the United States declared war against Germany. Detroit played a major role in the war effort. About 65,000 men and women from the city entered the armed forces. The automobile industry made World War I the first motorized war in history. The production of automobiles slowed down. Ambulances, trucks, and staff cars began to roll out of Detroit. They were being assembled so quickly that the railroad transportation could not handle the supply. The state of Michigan built a concrete highway from Detroit to Toledo to move the equipment more quickly.

The assembly line meant that military supplies and materials could be manufactured quickly. The automobile plants made ammunition and guns. Even tin hats which soldiers wore came through the assembly line.

New ideas also came from Detroit. The Liberty engine was designed and made by the automobile industry. It was used in Allied aircraft. Ford began developing small, armored machines that looked like huge bugs. They were called Whippet tanks. Ford also manufactured the Eagle boats. These small, fast boats were used for patrol and antisubmarine warfare.

On November 11, 1917, when an armistice was signed, the people of Detroit stopped work and gathered downtown to celebrate. It was one of the largest celebrations to be held in Detroit. The state troops were called out to handle the crowd, but they soon gave up and joined in the celebration.

The war brought changes to the city. It stopped the immigration from Europe. People from the South, both white and black, came to take jobs in the factories. They, plus the soldiers returning from the war, created a housing shortage. Conditions in the city changed.

As the town grew, and more business was centered in the business section, the value of land increased, ground rents became higher, and only business houses came to occupy the central sections. [Living] quarters were driven farther and farther from the center. The well-to-do left first. They went to the outskirts . . . of the city. The old mansions came to be tenement houses; for by crowding, the laboring people were able to reduce the rent per [person]. As a result of this process the worst housing conditions are to be found about the business section. . . .

Following the war, factories began to make automobiles again. Detroit had become the major automobile manufacturing center of the nation. The sound of its first chugging automobile had turned into the booming roar of an industrial empire.

1. What conditions helped bring the automobile industry to Detroit?
2. What caused the growth in Detroit's population?
3. What major ideas did Ford introduce into the automobile industry?
4. How did the automobile industry affect the economy of the city?
5. How many people were out of work in 1914? Why did so many remain jobless? How did Detroit handle this problem?
6. What part did Detroit play in World War I? What had Detroit become following the war?

Unit VII Review

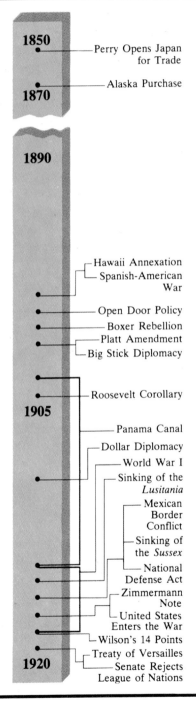

1850 — Perry Opens Japan for Trade

1870 — Alaska Purchase

1890

Hawaii Annexation
Spanish-American War
Open Door Policy
Boxer Rebellion
Platt Amendment
Big Stick Diplomacy

Roosevelt Corollary

1905

Panama Canal
Dollar Diplomacy
World War I
Sinking of the *Lusitania*
Mexican Border Conflict
Sinking of the *Sussex*
National Defense Act
Zimmermann Note
United States Enters the War
Wilson's 14 Points
Treaty of Versailles
Senate Rejects League of Nations

1920

Summary

1. New interests and ideas led the United States to a policy of overseas expansion in the late nineteenth century.

2. Victory in the Spanish-American War marked the rise of the United States as a major world power.

3. The United States acquired control of territories in the Caribbean and the Pacific which helped to extend American influence in world affairs.

4. Rivalry over empires and the development of military alliances led to World War I.

5. The official policy of the United States when the war started was one of neutrality, but the interests of the country favored the Allies.

6. Relations between the United States and Germany grew worse, with the United States joining the Allies and playing a major part in the victory.

7. President Wilson led attempts for a fair and just peace with his Fourteen Points, but these were rejected by the other Allied leaders.

8. The United States Senate turned down the Treaty of Versailles over the issue of the League of Nations, with Germany being forced to accept responsibility for the war and the League forming without American membership.

9. Many Americans wished a return to a policy of noninvolvement in foreign affairs, but American interests around the world made such a move impossible.

Unit Questions

1. What were some of the reasons why the United States changed its foreign policy to one of overseas expansion?
2. In what ways were the views of Americans about involvement in the Caribbean different from their views on involvement in the Pacific?
3. What were some of the differences and some of the similarities in the foreign policies of Presidents T. Roosevelt, Taft, and Wilson?
4. How were the naval policies of Britain and Germany the same during World War I? Why did the German policy lead to American entry into the war?
5. Do you think that the actions of the federal government toward the economy during World War I were closer to the ideas of laissez-faire or those of the progressives? Explain.
6. What were the contributions of the United States toward victory for the Allies in World War I?
7. What were the objections of some people in the United States toward participation in the League of Nations?
8. Between 1898 and 1918, with what countries did the United States fight wars and in what countries did it intervene for some reason?

Suggested Activities

1. Make a list of the areas outside of the continental United States which were taken over by the United States. Beside each, show the status of these areas today.
2. Find out what the Nobel Peace Prize is and how it started. Make a list of the winners and the reason why they got the award. Identify the winners who were Americans.
3. Prepare a report on the Panama Canal. Include the length of time it takes for a trip through the canal. Include a map, and show how much time is saved by using the canal instead of traveling around South America.

Suggested Readings

Bales, Carol. *Tales of the Elders: A Memory Book of Men and Women Who Came to America as Immigrants, 1900–1930*. Chicago: Follett, 1977. Stories with pictures of immigrants to the United States.

Hagedorn, Hermann. *The Rough Riders*. New York: Harper, 1927. Teddy Roosevelt's famous regiment in the Spanish-American War.

Jantzen, Steven. *Hurray for Peace, Hurray for War*. New York: Alfred A. Knopf, Inc., 1971. An account of the United States' influence in World War I in Europe.

Johnson, Hannah. *Picture the Past, 1900–1915*. Wooster, Ohio: Norman Lathrop, Inc., 1975. Descriptions and pictures of life in the United States at the start of the twentieth century.

Challenge

Challenge demanded response by American people living in a complex, free society in a changing world. Americans faced demanding tasks resulting from the United States' position as a world political and economic power. Global wars and economic depression were met with foreign and domestic policies designed to solve and prevent repeating challenges. New challenges remained, however, as the United States constantly changed within itself and changed in its relations with the world.

Life in the Twenties   22

This illustration is from Thomas Hart Benton's mural "Contemporary America." The subject is life in the 1920's. What seems to be the painter's impression of the decade that some people called the "Roaring Twenties"?

World War I had brought about many changes in American ways of thinking and in American ways of life. Some Americans began to feel there had been too much change. By the 1920's, many felt that the country should return to the practices and values of the past. President Warren Harding summed up the feelings of many Americans in his famous call for "normalcy."

> America's present need is not heroics, but healing; not nostrums [cure-alls], but normalcy; not revolution, but restoration; not agitation, but adjustment; not surgery, but serenity; not the dramatic, but the dispassionate; . . . not submergence in internationality, but sustainment in triumphant nationality.

1. Toward a More Peaceful World

Many Americans came away from World War I feeling angry and bitter. Some felt the Europeans had not given the United States enough credit for its part in the war. Others did not like the fact that Allied leaders had not used President Wilson's Fourteen Points as the basis for peace. Americans could not put World War I out of their minds. It had left them with a strong wish to stay out of future wars.

Why were Americans angry about World War I?

1.1 The Move for Disarmament. For the most part, Republicans had been against the Treaty of Versailles. They had not wanted the United States to become a member of the League of Nations. Still, they wanted to show that they did favor peace. Senator William E. Borah gave them a chance to do this. He asked the leading powers in the world to meet to talk about disarmament.

On November 21, 1921, the Washington Conference on the Limitations of Armaments began. Delegates from the United States, Great Britain, France, Belgium, Japan, Holland, Portugal, and China met in Washington, D.C. There, Secretary of State Charles Evans Hughes called for each country to take a holiday in the building of warships. He asked each country to remove some ships from service and to stop building others.

What meeting took place in Washington in 1921? What was its purpose?

The conference lasted until February 6, 1922. When it was over, nine treaties had been signed. One of these was the Five-Power Pact of 1922. In it, the United States, Great Britain, Japan, France, and Italy agreed to build no new warships during the next ten years. Each country also agreed to limit the total tonnage of its warships. The United States

What were the terms of the Five-Power Pact?

and Great Britain each agreed to limit theirs to about 500,000 tons, Japan to about 300,000 tons, and France and Italy to about 175,000 tons each.

1.2 Outlawing War. Many people were encouraged by what had happened in Washington. They felt that the time had come to outlaw war altogether. James T. Shotwell, a professor at Columbia University in New York City, talked to Aristide Briand, the French Foreign Minister, about the idea. Nicholas Murray Butler, the president of Columbia University, brought the matter to public attention in a letter to *The New York Times*.

Who suggested creating a pact to outlaw war?

In 1927, Briand suggested that the United States and France sign a pact to outlaw war between the two countries. Frank Kellogg, the American Secretary of State, agreed. But he felt that other countries besides the United States and France should be included.

On August 27, 1928, the Kellogg-Briand Pact, also known as the Pact of Paris, was signed by 15 countries. It stated that none of them would use war to settle any conflict that might arise among them. Before long, 62 countries had signed the pact. But it really was little more than a symbol. There was no way to enforce it. It did, however, give people around the world hope that there would be no more war.

Why was the Kellogg-Briand Pact not very effective?

1.3 New Policies Toward Latin America. In the late 1920's, the United States began to try to improve its relations with the countries of Latin America. Some Latin Americans had begun to speak out against the United States and its interference in the affairs of their countries.

In January 1928, delegates from North and South America met at the Havana Conference in Havana, Cuba. During this meeting, some Latin American delegates openly criticized the United States. They tried to, but could not, push through a resolution that said "no state has the right to intervene in the affairs of another."

Following the election that November, President Herbert Hoover went on a goodwill tour of Latin America. At the same time, Secretary of State Joshua Reuben Clark began a study of the Monroe Doctrine. He wanted to see if the Roosevelt Corollary supported the Monroe Doctrine. In a memorandum issued in December 1928, Clark held that it did not. Clark said that the Doctrine's warning that European powers could not intervene in Latin American affairs did not mean that the United States had the right to do so. Clark's note showed that the United States' policy toward Latin America was changing.

About what was the Clark memorandum written?

1.4 Easing Tensions With Japan. At the same time it was trying to better relations with Latin America, the United States also was working to better them with Japan. During the Washington Arms

Herbert Hoover took a pre-inaugural tour of Central and South America to improve the image of the United States. What was the Hoover administration's Latin America policy?

Conference, the United States and Japan had signed several treaties. One concerned a small Pacific area called Yap Island. It was an important terminal for communications cables across the ocean. Japan had taken the island from Germany during World War I. In the treaty, the United States agreed to honor Japanese control of the island, and Japan agreed to allow the United States cable rights.

What steps did the United States take to ease tensions with Japan?

Two other treaties were signed by Great Britain and France as well as by the United States and Japan. In these, the four powers agreed to respect each other's rights in the Pacific. They also said they would meet to settle any disputes that might arise there. The United States and Japan, along with the other seven powers that had met in Washington, also signed the Nine-Power Pact. In it, all agreed to observe the Open Door policy in China.

These treaties helped better relations between the United States and Japan. At the same time, however, they caused some problems. Japan did not like the fact that the Five-Power Pact did not allow it as great a tonnage of ships as the pact did the United States and Great Britain. Japanese military leaders felt that their navy should be the equal of any navy in the world.

What things continued to cause problems between Japan and the United States?

Then, too, the Japanese felt that many Americans were prejudiced against people of Japanese background in the United States. At the Paris Peace Conference of 1919, Japan had wanted to pass a resolution and have it become part of the final peace treaty. The Japanese resolution had stated that people of all races were equal. President Wilson had helped block the resolution. He said the Senate would not approve any treaty that contained it. The Japanese did not forget this. They saw it as a sign of American prejudice.

1. What agreements did the United States sign to limit the world's arms production?
2. What agreement outlawed war?
3. What was the purpose of the Havana Conference?

2. Intolerance and Civil Rights

World War I made some Americans want to avoid war above almost everything else. It also made some Americans *intolerant*—not willing to respect the beliefs, practices, or behavior of others. During the 1920's, this feeling was directed at several different groups.

2.1 The Red Scare. Part of the intolerance of the 1920's grew out of a fear of *communism*. Communists believe that through their government, the people own all property. There is no private ownership. The government, however, is supposed to meet the needs of all the people equally. Where the Communist party controls the government, it does not allow other political parties to exist. Communists believe that because the people share everything equally, they no longer will have to compete with one another. This, in turn, means that there will be no problems brought on by competition.

What were some beliefs of Communists?

In 1917, the Bolsheviks under Lenin overthrew the government of Russia and set up a Communist state. Since one of the goals of communism is to spread the system around the world, Americans began to fear that communism would spread to the United States. Because Communists were known as "reds" this became known as the *red scare*.

In 1919, a Communist party was formed in the United States. Some Americans felt that something had to be done. One such American was A. Mitchell Palmer, Attorney General of the United States. Under his direction, the Department of Justice went after people suspected of being disloyal to the United States. This included anyone thought to be a Communist. It also included many who spoke out for labor reform or any other unpopular idea.

What actions were taken during the red scare?

In many cities, the police raided places where they thought these people could be found. By early 1920, some 4,000 to 6,000 people had been rounded up and jailed. About 500 aliens were deported. Others were tried and convicted under state laws that forbade the support of certain unpopular ideas or the overthrow of the government.

2.2 From Fear to Intolerance. The fear of communism helped bring about a general fear of anything or anyone foreign or different. Because of this, much of the red scare was directed against aliens and new immigrants. Some Americans felt that these people were spreading ideas that could harm the American way of life.

Who were Sacco and Vanzetti? What happened to them?

On May 5, 1920, Nicola Sacco and Bartolomeo Vanzetti, who had recently come to the United States, were arrested. They were charged with a payroll robbery and murder. On July 14, 1921, Sacco and Vanzetti were convicted and sentenced to death. Their trial, however, led to debate in the United States and other places. Sacco and Vanzetti were anarchists. Many people felt that this was the reason they had been convicted. Others, however, felt they had received a fair trial and were guilty. In August 1927, after many appeals, Sacco and Vanzetti were executed. Their trial showed how divided Americans could be when the values held by most people conflicted with the rights of those in the minority.

Other groups also were the targets of prejudice during the 1920's. Many Americans were prejudiced against Jews, Catholics, and blacks and often discriminated against them. Many blacks had moved from the South to cities in the North, Middle West, and West during World War

Clarence Darrow (left) and William Jennings Bryan (right) take a break during the Scopes Trial in Dayton, Tennessee, in 1925. Darrow defended school teacher John Scopes, and Bryan led the prosecution in a trial that became a national sensation. The basic issue concerned what could or could not be taught in public schools. The trial pointed up the conflicting life-styles of the 1920's. When else did varying life-styles conflict in the 1920's?

I. They were viewed with mistrust and fear by many whites. During the war and right after it, attacks on blacks led to riots in such cities as Houston, East St. Louis, Chicago, Omaha, and Knoxville. Some blacks were killed, among them several World War I veterans, still in uniform.

A new Ku Klux Klan had been organized in 1915. It spoke out against blacks, Catholics, Jews, and foreigners. By 1924, the Klan claimed nearly 5 million members and was powerful in several state governments. The Klan used threats and violence against those who opposed it. It went after black business owners who might compete with white-owned businesses. It sometimes forced Japanese and Chinese people on the West Coast to sell their land at low prices. Its members wore masks at their public meetings so others would not know who they were. When some states passed laws forbidding masks, the Klan lost members. Publicity and government investigations into Klan activities also led to a loss of members. By 1930, its membership had fallen to less than 30,000.

What caused the rise of a new Ku Klux Klan? What brought about its decline?

What immigration laws were passed in the 1920's? What were their provisions?

2.3 Closing the Door. The growth of intolerance and fear led the United States to a new immigration policy. In 1921, Congress passed a law which set up a *quota* (a certain number) for people who wanted to move to the United States. It limited the number of new immigrants

Immigration laws in 1921 and 1924 set quotas. After the 1921 law was passed, some business leaders worked to loosen restrictions to allow more unskilled labor into the United States. How did both laws immediately affect total immigration?

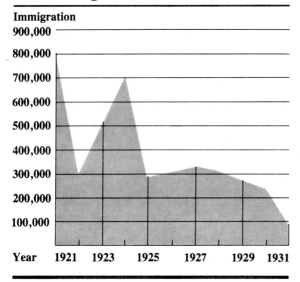

Effects of Quota Acts on Immigration, 1921–1931

from any country to 3 percent of the number from that country who had been living in the United States in 1910.

The new law, however, still did not please some people in Congress. In 1910, a great many eastern and southern Europeans had been living in the United States. Because of this, the 1921 law allowed a large number of people from those areas to enter the United States. In 1924, Congress passed a new law. It cut the quota to 2 percent and changed the year on which it was based to 1890. That year, fewer people from eastern and southern Europe had been living in the United States. The law also barred all Asian immigrants. Until this time, the wives and children of Japanese immigrants had been allowed to enter the United States under the Gentlemen's Agreement.

In 1929, the National Origins Act was passed. It said that only 150,000 immigrants could enter the United States each year. The number of people allowed from each country was based on the number from the area living in the United States in 1920.

The 1924 law had led to a shortage of workers on sugar plantations and farms. But the problem was taken care of in part by Filipino immigrants. They did not fall under the immigration laws because the Philippines were an American possession. By 1930, there were about 45,000 Filipinos in the United States and another 63,000 in Hawaii.

2.4   The Struggle for Civil and Political Rights.   Even with the intolerance shown by some Americans in the 1920's, gains still were made in the area of rights. Women, for example, had played an important part in the war effort. Partly because of this, many people pushed harder for women's suffrage. In 1919, Woodrow Wilson had asked Congress to amend the Constitution to give women the right to vote. In 1920, Congress passed and the states ratified the Nineteenth Amendment. It gave women that right.

What gains in rights were made in the 1920's?

In 1924, Congress passed an act that made citizens of all Indians living in the United States. The bill had been written by Senator Charles Curtis of Kansas. Curtis had Kaw and Osage Indian heritage. The act applied only to one third of the Indians, however. The other two thirds were already citizens. Some had become citizens through treaties or the Dawes Act of 1887. Others had done so by marrying citizens or by joining the armed services during World War I.

What bill was sponsored by Senator Curtis?

Once Indians became citizens, they were subject to local laws and to taxes. In the past, citizenship had caused many Indians to lose their lands because they could not pay their property taxes. This, plus a fear they would lose many of their traditions and ways of life, led some Indians to try to stop Curtis' bill from becoming law. Eight Indian groups protested to Congress and later to the League of Nations. In the

Why did some Indians not want Curtis' bill passed?

end, their protests did no good. All Indians living in the United States became citizens.

World War I had made many Americans more aware of their country and the opportunities it had to offer as well as its problems. This was especially true for Mexican Americans and blacks. Many of them had served as soldiers and worked in arms factories during World War I. Because of this, they expected to be treated as well as other Americans.

What conditions did Mexican Americans face after World War I? What did they do?

After the war, however, Mexican Americans found that many jobs were closed to them. Those jobs that were open did not offer any chance to move to better jobs. At the same time, new immigrants from Mexico kept arriving. This meant more competition for unskilled jobs. As a result, Mexican Americans who could not find the jobs they wanted usually ended up working for low pay, many as farm laborers.

In time, some Mexican Americans began to help others learn more about their political and legal rights. In 1921, the Order of the Sons of America was founded in San Antonio, Texas. It worked through political action to gain greater educational opportunities for people of Spanish and Mexican backgrounds. The Order and groups like it were at work in other areas that had large numbers of Mexican Americans.

Blacks ran into many of the same problems as Mexican Americans. For some blacks, the end of the war meant a loss of jobs when returning

Women in the 1920's demanded equal rights as American citizens (left). Many women gained job rights through the actions of professional and trade unions (right). What constitutional right did women win in 1920?

Ynes Mexia (1870–1938)

PROFILE

Ynes Mexia began a career as a scientist at age 55. For 13 years, Mexia traveled throughout North and South America gathering and classifying plants.

Mexia was born in Washington, D.C., where her father worked as a representative of the Mexican government. She grew up in Texas and went to school in Pennsylvania and Maryland. In 1908, Mexia moved to San Francisco, taking a job as a social worker.

In 1921, Mexia entered the University of California. There she showed an interest in the natural sciences, especially the science of plants called botany. During the summer of 1925, Mexia and other botanists from the University went to the Mexican desert. They returned with about 500 plant species, including *Mimosa mexiae,* named for Mexia by the botanist Joseph Nelson Rose.

Mexia decided to spend her life as a plant explorer. She led many plant study trips. She worked for the University of California and other groups and sold her rare plants to pay for the trips. Mexia discovered many new plants. She found mosses in Alaska and tropical plants in Mexico, Ecuador, Peru, and Brazil. She traveled as far as the Andes Mountains and the Strait of Magellan to look for plants. A friend once described Mexia as being "the true explorer type and happiest when independent and far from civilization."

white soldiers got their old jobs back. Some tried to earn a living by starting businesses. Many of them failed, however.

Blacks, too, had groups which tried to help them. In 1914, a Jamaican-born black named Marcus Garvey had started the Universal Negro Improvement Association (UNIA). During the 1920's, at least 500,000 people became members of the group. Garvey believed that blacks should become independent from whites. He encouraged blacks to look to Africa to find out about their backgrounds. In his newspaper *Negro World,* Garvey wrote about the history and achievements of the people of Africa. In 1923, Garvey was accused by the government of using the United States mail to trick people into giving money to the

What did Marcus Garvey believe?

UNIA. He was sent to prison. Many people felt the reason Garvey was found guilty was his leadership in the UNIA. Garvey was pardoned after two years, but he was forced to leave the country. His organization and his ideas of black pride and dignity continued after he was gone.

Another group that worked to help blacks was the NAACP. In the 1920's, it won two important cases before the Supreme Court. One was the case of Dr. O. H. Sweet, a black dentist. He had been attacked by a white mob for buying a home in a white neighborhood in Detroit, Michigan. When gunfire from Sweet's house killed one of the attackers, he was brought to trial. The Court ruled that Dr. Sweet had the right to defend himself from the threat of harm.

What two court cases in the 1920's were victories in safeguarding the rights of blacks?

The other case had to do with the rights of blacks to vote in primary elections. In many areas of the South, blacks had not been allowed to vote in these elections. In 1927, the Supreme Court ruled on the case of *Nixon* v. *Herndon.* The Court said that states could not keep blacks who wanted to vote from taking part in primaries.

1. What caused the red scare?
2. Against what groups was prejudice directed?
3. What countries were most affected by immigration quota laws?

3. Politics and the Economy

For many Americans, the 1920's were years of prosperity. The end of the war brought an end to government restrictions on business. It also brought a move away from regulations such as those of the Progressive Era. Business people pushed hard for free enterprise. They worked mostly through the Republican party. All three Presidents who held office during the 1920's were Republicans, and they supported the ideas of business leaders. President Harding summed up the general feeling when he stated that there should be "less government in business, and more business in government."

What party supported business in the 1920's?

3.1 The Politics of Normalcy. Elected in 1920, Warren G. Harding was a well-liked President. He named three well-qualified people to his Cabinet. They were Secretary of State Charles Evans Hughes, Secretary of Commerce Herbert Hoover, and Secretary of the Treasury Andrew Mellon. Harding also named others to government posts just because they were close friends. In the end, this led to

What scandals occurred in the Harding administration?

scandal. Attorney General Harry Daugherty and Charles R. Forbes, chief of the Veterans Bureau, for example, were tried for corruption.

The largest scandal, however, centered around Secretary of the Interior Albert B. Fall. When Harding took office, oil reserves on government land at Teapot Dome, Wyoming, and Elk Hills, California, were being held for the navy to use. Under Harding, the lands were given to the Department of the Interior. In exchange for money and other gifts, Fall leased the lands to private oil companies. This was illegal. In 1927, Fall was convicted in court, made to pay a large fine, and sent to prison.

How did the various regions of the United States differ according to agriculture and industry? Where was each type of agriculture most common? Where was each type of industry most common?

The United States Economy, 1920

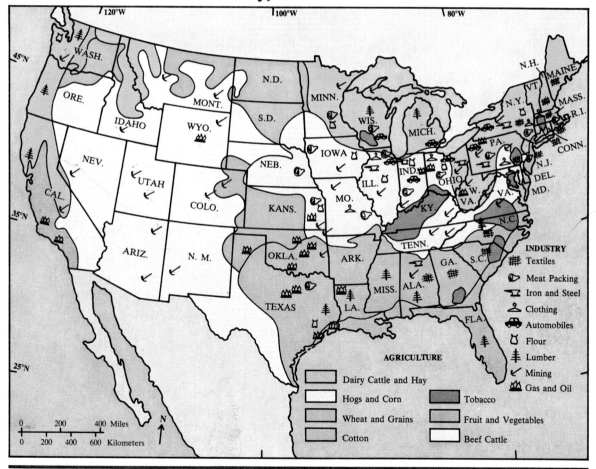

The pressure of these scandals was hard on the President, and he became ill while on a trip to Alaska. On August 2, 1923, while returning from the trip, he died in San Francisco. Upon Harding's death, Vice-President Calvin Coolidge became President. Coolidge was liked by business people and by the Republican party. When he ran for President in 1924, he won the election. Coolidge believed in thrift, hard work, and honesty. Business did well under Coolidge, and the newspapers spoke of "Coolidge Prosperity."

Coolidge decided not to run again in 1928. So the Republicans chose Herbert Hoover. Hoover had headed the Food Administration

Al Smith appealed to many urban voters. This urban swing for a Democratic candidate was not noticeable in the Hoover landslide victory, but it was the beginning of a shift in Democratic strength from rural to urban. Why did Smith lose?

Election of 1928

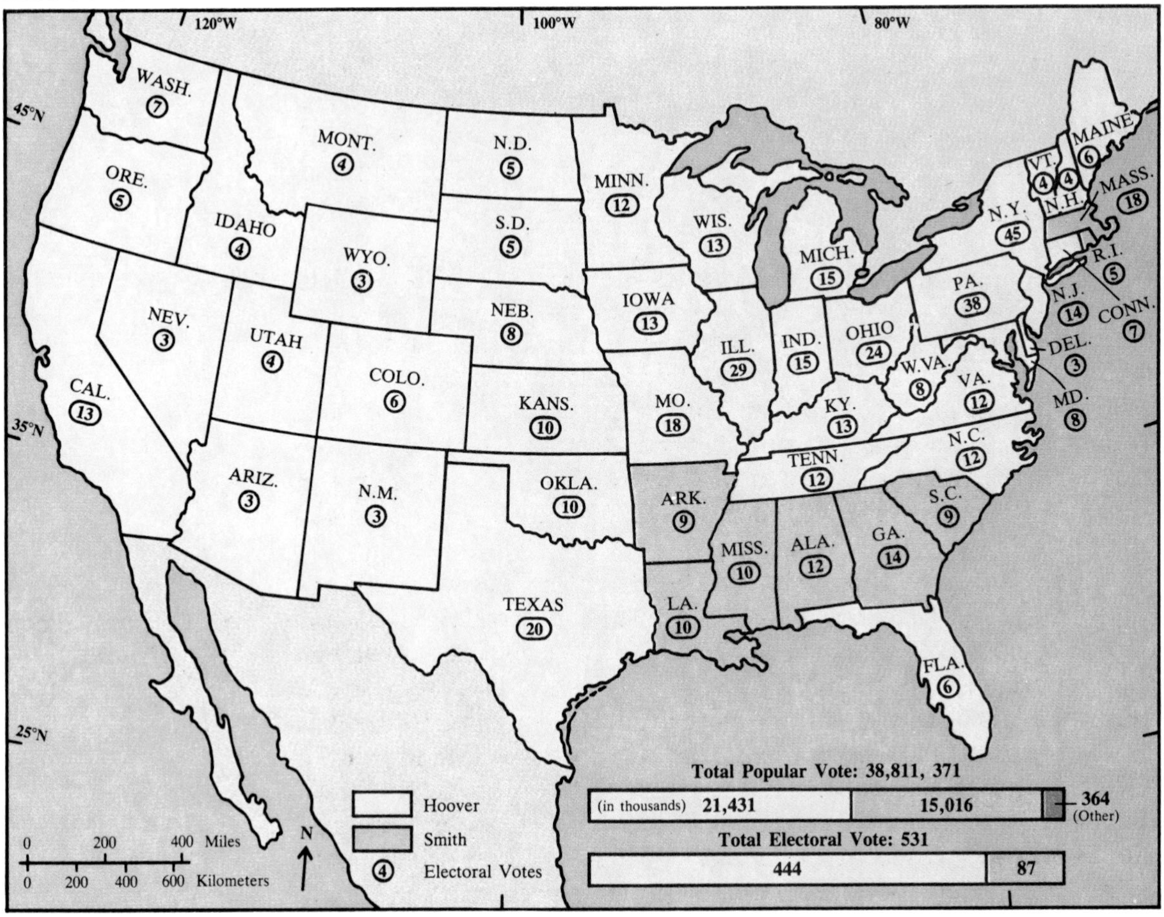

| 120°W | 100°W | 80°W |

WASH. 7
ORE. 5
IDAHO 4
MONT. 4
N.D. 5
MINN. 12
WIS. 13
MICH. 15
MAINE 6
VT 4
N.H. 4
N.Y. 45
MASS. 18
R.I. 5
S.D. 5
WYO. 3
NEV. 3
UTAH 4
NEB. 8
IOWA 13
PA. 38
N.J. 14
CONN. 7
CAL. 13
COLO. 6
KANS. 10
ILL. 29
IND. 15
OHIO 24
W.VA. 8
VA. 12
DEL. 3
MD. 8
ARIZ. 3
N.M. 3
OKLA. 10
MO. 18
KY. 13
TENN. 12
N.C. 12
ARK. 9
S.C. 9
MISS. 10
ALA. 12
GA. 14
TEXAS 20
LA. 10
FLA. 6

Hoover
Smith
④ Electoral Votes

0   200   400 Miles
0 200 400 600 Kilometers

Total Popular Vote: 38,811, 371
(in thousands) 21,431 15,016 364 (Other)
Total Electoral Vote: 531
444 87

and directed the country's European relief program during World War I. He was well known as an engineer and business leader. The Democrats chose Alfred Smith, the governor of New York, as their candidate. He was the first Catholic to be nominated for the Presidency.

Who were the candidates in the election of 1928?

Hoover and his party promised that if America stayed with the policies of free enterprise, the country would go on doing well. They also promised the American people "a chicken in every pot, a car in every garage." The Republicans won the election by many votes.

3.2 The Boom Economy. There was good reason for most Americans to think that prosperity would last. Following a short depression right after World War I, the economy had gotten better. During the 1920's, it kept growing. More goods were produced than in any time before in the country's history.

What was the status of the economy throughout the 1920's?

A major factor in the boom was the growth of new industries. One of the most important of these was the automobile industry. Inventors had been working for many years to develop a successful automobile. In 1893, Charles and Frank Duryea built the first successful gasoline-powered car in the United States. Soon people like Ransom Olds, Henry Ford, and David Buick began to manufacture cars. By 1930, 3 million Americans were making or selling automobiles. There were 23 million cars and 4 million trucks and buses in the United States.

Another industry that grew in the 1920's was *aviation*, or air transportation. The first successful airplane flight had been made in 1903 at Kitty Hawk, North Carolina, by Orville and Wilbur Wright. The airplane had been improved for use in World War I. After the war, not many people traveled by air. By 1927, that began to change. That year, Charles Lindbergh flew from New York to Paris in his plane, *The Spirit of St. Louis*. Lindbergh's was the first nonstop, solo flight across the Atlantic. It helped to get more people interested in air travel. Between 1928 and 1930, the number of people traveling by plane grew from 1,400 to 32,000.

Other factors also helped bring about a boom economy. Americans bought more *consumer goods*—products made for individual use. Many of these goods were electric appliances, such as vacuum cleaners, washing machines, and radios. To make enough electricity to meet the needs of all these new goods, the electric power industry grew greatly.

What factors helped to bring about a boom economy?

Advertising was another factor in the growth of industry in the 1920's. Business leaders wanted more people to buy more goods. So they set out to convince people they needed all kinds of products. Goods were advertised in newspapers and on radio. During 1925, more money was spent on advertising than on public education. Many people used credit to buy the things they wanted.

What part of the
economy did not
prosper?

Some parts of the economy did not do as well as others, however. Farmers had produced large quantities of food during World War I. The end of the wartime demand and the changing diet of Americans caused problems for farmers. While business boomed, agriculture did not.

3.3 Protecting American Business. While the economy was doing well, business people became more popular. The government did all it could to protect business interests. The Fordney-McCumber Tariff, for example, was passed in 1922. It raised tariff rates to protect American business from competition from other countries.

Business had friends in the federal government. One of them was Andrew Mellon, Secretary of the Treasury from 1921 to 1930. Mellon helped to have laws passed that lowered taxes for corporations and for the wealthy. Mellon believed that this would help the economy by freeing more money for investments.

The government also helped business in other ways. Neither the ICC, the Justice Department, nor the courts actively worked to see that laws against trusts and monopolies were obeyed. Because of this, there were a great many **mergers**. This was the joining together of two or more companies to form a larger company. In manufacturing and mining alone, around 8,000 companies were taken over in this way.

3.4 Holding Down American Labor. Business fared well during the 1920's, but labor unions did not. Because workers were badly needed for the war effort during World War I, the government had backed their efforts to organize. Wages rose, and the number of workers in the AFL grew from 2 million to 4 million.

Once the war was over, businesses wanted to hold down costs. Government at all levels took the side of business. By 1919, there was serious trouble between business and labor. That year, nearly 4 million workers took part in strikes or work-stoppages.

What was the most
serious strike of
1919?

The most serious strike began in September 1919 in the steel industry. Nearly 275,000 steel workers walked off their jobs. The number grew to around 350,000. To help crush the strike, the steel companies tried to scare many workers who were recent immigrants. The steel companies told these workers that if they did not go back to work, they would lose their jobs to other immigrants. The steel companies also took out newspaper ads in many languages, all of which said that striking was un-American. The companies also hired strikebreakers to take the place of many workers. Local police and state militias broke up workers' meetings. Because of all this, the steel strike finally was crushed.

When the steel strike failed, other business leaders also began to fight the unions. Many of them used a system they called the American

Abundance

How to produce enough food, clothing, and shelter for people to survive has been a problem for much of world history. Changes in the ways that goods were produced improved some conditions. In the years following World War I, however, many people in the world had little beyond what they needed to survive.

At this time, the United States was one of the wealthiest countries in the world. It also was a major industrial nation that had not been physically damaged by the war. Many Americans believed that the United States had reached a level of abundance of production. This would provide a high standard of living for all people, and it would do away with poverty.

In 1928, the Republican presidential candidate, Herbert Hoover, spoke in New York City about American abundance.

. . . our people are steadily increasing their spending for higher standards of living. Today there are almost nine automobiles for each ten families. . . . The slogan of progress is changing from the full dinner pail to the full garage. Our people have more to eat, better things to wear, and better homes. . . . Wages have increased, the cost of living has decreased. The job of every man and woman has been made more secure. We have in this short period decreased the fear of poverty, the fear of unemployment, the fear of old age; and these are fears that are the greatest calamities of humankind.

All this progress means more than increased creature comforts. It finds a thousand interpretations into a greater and fuller life. A score of new helps save the drudgery of the home. . . . We have steadily reduced the sweat in human labor. Our hours of labor are lessened; our leisure has increased. . . .

. . . all this . . . leads to a release of the energies of men and women from the dull drudgery of life to a wider vision and a higher hope. It leads to the opportunity for greater and greater service, not alone from man to man in our own land, but from our country to the whole world. It leads to an America, healthy in body, healthy in spirit, . . . youthful, eager—with a vision, searching beyond the farthest horizons, with an open mind, sympathetic and generous.

1. How was America abundant?
2. How did abundance benefit the United States?
3. How was American abundance to benefit the entire world?

Plan. Under it, companies in the same industry joined together. Each gave money to be used to keep unions out of their businesses. They hired strikebreakers and put spies in the unions. They also used the *blacklist*—a list that named workers who took part in union activities or strikes. They sent the list to other employers so that they would not hire those listed. Businesses also used *yellow-dog contracts*—agreements which workers had to sign before they took a job stating that they would not join a union.

These methods worked, and the unions lost members. Pay for workers as a whole went up in the 1920's. But it did not keep up with the growing prosperity of the rest of the economy.

1. What new industries developed in the 1920's?
2. How did government aid business?
3. What problems did organized labor have?

4. The Jazz Age

The 1920's was a time of sharp contrasts. This could be seen in the different life-styles of the American people. Many Americans did not accept the new ideas, and their lives went on much as before. Others, however, welcomed the chance for a change to a less-ordered life. A new kind of music called *jazz* became popular. It had syncopated rhythms and developed from ragtime and blues music. It soon became a symbol for some Americans, and the decade of the 1920's came to be known as the Jazz Age.

4.1 New Styles of Life. During the 1920's, new inventions freed people from certain tasks. The automobile allowed them to go places more often. Vacuum cleaners, canned foods, electric refrigerators, and gas ovens cut down on the time needed to do housework. Many women found they had more free time and greater freedom. They worked outside the home, went to college, and entered professions.

What inventions brought changes to the American life-style? How?

More Americans seemed to be doing things for fun. Stunts performed in automobiles and airplanes drew a lot of attention. Pilots flew around the country putting on air shows.

Some Americans did not follow the new styles of living. This was most true for people who lived in rural areas. They still felt that hard work, thrift, and religion were the best American values. They supported leaders who spoke out against the changing times and new values.

What was prohibition?

4.2 The Prohibition Years. The 1920's also brought a change in attitudes and laws about drinking alcoholic beverages. The Eighteenth Amendment, which had been ratified in 1919, went into

Advertising in the 1920's became the art of persuading customers to buy products. How were household appliances and automobiles presented to appeal to American consumers? How important was the name of a product?

effect in 1920. It made it illegal to make, transport, or sell alcoholic beverages. Several states had adopted such laws earlier, but this was the first federal prohibition law. Groups such as the Women's Christian Temperance Union had worked for years to have such a law passed.

Large numbers of Americans were not willing to accept the law. Some people began to make beer and liquor at home. Others smuggled it into the United States from Canada and Mexico. Nightclubs called *speakeasies* sold liquor even though it was against the law.

What did prohibition cause?

There were not enough federal or state agents to patrol all the borders of the United States. So the law became harder and harder to enforce. Smuggling soon became common and was taken over by gangsters like Al Capone, Dion O'Banion, and George "Bugs" Moran. They fought with one another for control. Each wanted to be the only one to sell alcoholic beverages in certain cities. Much of the profit they made was used to help them take over other kinds of businesses.

4.3 Literature of the 1920's. Both the excitement and the problems of the changing times could be seen in the literature of the

In general, about what did the authors of the 1920's write?

1920's. Many authors wrote about the sadness of modern life. One such author was Ernest Hemingway. In *The Sun Also Rises* and *A Farewell to Arms,* Hemingway's characters are people who are searching for values and the meaning of life.

Another author of the period was F. Scott Fitzgerald. Fitzgerald wrote about the carefree lives of the young and the wealthy. His works, *This Side of Paradise* and *The Great Gatsby,* helped to make him a symbol of the Jazz Age. Still another author was Sinclair Lewis. Lewis criticized people's dullness and their narrow views. He became best known for *Main Street* and *Babbitt.* Both of these are stories about small-town life. His novel *Arrowsmith* was about a doctor and his rise in society. In 1930, Lewis became the first American to win the Nobel Prize for Literature.

Claude McKay was another writer of this time. In 1922, his poems, "If We Must Die" and "To My White Friends," expressed objections many blacks felt about discrimination. His novel, *Home to Harlem,* dealt with life in that black community.

Some important poets also became well known during the 1920's. One was Edna St. Vincent Millay. She spoke out against traditional values in such works as "A Few Figs from Thistles" and *The Harp-Weaver and Other Poems.* Robert Frost showed the traditional side of American life in his poems about nature. One of his best-known poems was "Stopping by the Woods on a Snowy Evening." It appeared in the volume *New Hampshire* in 1924. Another poet was Countee Cullen. Cullen wrote in subtle form protesting the way blacks were treated. Among his well-known poems were "The Ballad of the Brown Girl" and "Copper Sun."

What was the Harlem Renaissance?

Countee Cullen and Claude McKay were part of a black cultural movement of the 1920's. It was called the Harlem Renaissance because so many important black writers and artists lived and worked in the Harlem area of New York City. *Renaissance* means a time when there is much artistic and intellectual activity.

4.4 Popular Culture. During the 1920's, new forms of entertainment appeared which were enjoyed by a great number of people. The radio was one of these. It became an important form of

Why was radio important?

both information and entertainment. Stations KDKA in Pittsburgh and WWJ in Detroit began broadcasting in 1920. Not long after that, the National Broadcasting Company (NBC) organized a group of stations into one network. By 1930, 12 million families in the United States owned radios.

Magazines such as the *Saturday Evening Post, Time,* and *Reader's Digest* grew in popularity. Motion pictures, too, made important gains.

In 1927, the first "talkie" was made with its sound track played on a phonograph. Soon millions of Americans were going to the movies every week to see such stars as Clara Bow, Janet Gaynor, and John Barrymore.

Organized sports became one of the more popular forms of entertainment for Americans. Baseball came to be known as the "national pastime." The names of such players as New York Yankees stars "Babe" Ruth and Lou Gehrig were household words. In football, college coach Knute Rockne's Notre Dame teams won 105 games and lost only 12 between 1919 and 1931. One of the best-known college players of the time was Harold "Red" Grange of the University of Illinois. At the same time, professional football players like Jim Thorpe helped their teams gain many fans.

Boxing matches also drew large crowds. Around 100,000 people paid a total of more than $2.5 million to see Jack Dempsey fight Gene Tunney in 1927. Tennis players—like Bill Tilden and Helen Wills—and

What happened to sports during the 1920's?

This detail of a mural was painted by Aaron Douglas. It is a symbolic view of a jazz musician, showing jazz as an important element in American black culture. Douglas and other black artists and writers contributed to a cultural movement in the 1920's. Why was this movement called the Harlem Renaissance?

George Wesley Bellows painted this scene of a memorable moment in 1923 at the Polo Grounds in New York. Luis Firpo knocked Jack Dempsey through the ropes in the first round. Dempsey returned to the ring to win by a knockout in the second round. He retained the heavyweight title which he held from 1919 to 1926. What other great athletes played during the decade of the 1920's?

golfers—like Bobby Jones and Walter Hagen—also did much to promote their sports all over the country.

1. Why was the 1920's called the Jazz Age?
2. What were some of the changes in American life-styles?
3. Who were some of the outstanding writers, sports figures, and entertainers?

5. Conclusion

The United States was a study in contrasts during the 1920's. More and more Americans were trying to get ahead by making more money. Americans also showed that they had a strong desire to "return to normalcy." At the federal level, normalcy meant government support for business. It meant a return to the kind of thinking that had gone on in the United States in the years before the Progressive Era. Most Americans did not notice that the economy was changing. Before long, the results of these changes offered American business, government, and labor leaders one of their hardest challenges.

Chapter 22 Review

Main Points

1. American foreign policymakers in the 1920's sought to prevent the United States from ever again becoming involved in war.
2. The United States made efforts to improve relations with Latin America and Japan.
3. Following World War I, demonstrations of intolerance were reflected in the red scare, revival of the Ku Klux Klan, riots against blacks, and immigration restrictions.
4. The Nineteenth Amendment to the Constitution gave women the right to vote.
5. In 1924, Congress made citizens of all Indians living in the United States.
6. Blacks and Mexican Americans organized groups to protect and promote their interests.
7. The federal government was controlled by the Republican party which was favorable to business and opposed labor.
8. The development of new industries contributed to the economic boom of the 1920's. The economic boom did not include agriculture.
9. New ideas and new life-styles in the 1920's conflicted with traditional patterns of life.
10. Outstanding literary works and new forms of entertainment provided cultural outlets for people.

Building Vocabulary

1. Identify the following:

Five-Power Pact	Order of the Sons of America	Charles Lindbergh
Kellogg-Briand Pact	Ynes Mexia	American Plan
Havana Conference	Marcus Garvey	Jazz Age
A. Mitchell Palmer	Andrew Mellon	Ernest Hemingway
Sacco and Vanzetti	Teapot Dome	Claude McKay
Nineteenth Amendment	Calvin Coolidge	Edna St. Vincent Millay
Charles Curtis	Kitty Hawk	Harlem Renaissance

2. Define the following:

intolerant	aviation	yellow-dog contracts
communism	consumer goods	jazz
red scare	mergers	speakeasies
quota	blacklist	renaissance

Remembering the Facts

1. What did the United States do to try to prevent future wars?
2. What was the American foreign policy toward Latin America?
3. How was prejudice and intolerance expressed during the 1920's?
4. What did immigration laws with quotas try to accomplish?
5. How did Indians become citizens? Why did some Indians not want this?
6. What groups worked to help blacks in the 1920's?
7. What was the attitude of the Republican party toward business?
8. What did business leaders do to weaken labor unions?
9. What were some of the new forms of entertainment during the 1920's? What older forms of entertainment became popular?

Understanding the Facts

1. How did World War I change the United States' relations with the rest of the world?
2. Why did the United States pass immigration quota laws? Which groups were affected most by them?
3. What ideas did Marcus Garvey make popular among black people?
4. How was prohibition accepted by the American people?
5. How did life-styles during the Jazz Age differ from traditional life-styles?

Using Maps

Thematic Maps. Thematic maps can show a variety of information about an area. It can be political, social, cultural, or economic, in addition to geographic. The map on page 527 shows the distribution of industry and agriculture in the United States in 1920. Industrial areas are shown with symbols. Agricultural areas are color keyed. Use the map to answer the following questions.

1. What seems to be the main industry of the South?
2. What is the Far West's main agricultural product?
3. Where is the center of meat-packing activity located?
4. Why are meat-packing plants close to the areas of cattle and hogs?
5. What is the principal industry of the Rocky Mountain area?
6. What states produce tobacco?
7. Where does there appear to be more industry than agriculture?

The Depression and the New Deal

23

The Great Depression ruined careers and sapped the vitality of many Americans. Life at a time when jobs were scarce was portrayed in "Employment Agency" by Isaac Soyer. Why did a decade of apparent prosperity end by 1929?

The economic boom in the United States came to an end in 1929. That year a depression set in which lasted through the 1930's. The worst economic collapse in American history, it hurt a great many Americans. For this reason, it caused many to change their ideas about the government and the economy. Long after the 1930's, the changes which took place during the depression still were influencing the American people and their government.

1. The Great Depression and Its Effects

Because it affected the country so much, the depression which started in 1929 is called the "Great Depression." At first, Americans thought that the depression would last only a short time. But they found out they were wrong, as millions of Americans lost their jobs. The confidence and hope of the 1920's were replaced by worry and despair. America's leaders faced a long, hard struggle as they tried to bring back a sound economy and the confidence of the country.

Why was the depression of the 1930's known as the "Great Depression"?

1.1 Danger Signals. The Great Depression did not happen overnight. The problems which led to it began in the early 1920's. One problem had to do with American farmers. In the years after World War I, farmers did not do well. They were producing more crops and other farm products than could be sold at high prices. So prices were low, and farmers made little profit. Since they made little money, they could not afford to buy new farm machinery or other manufactured goods.

What factors helped cause the Great Depression?

Another problem was that the greatest prosperity of the 1920's went to a small number of Americans who already were wealthy. The pay of industrial workers did not grow as much as they had hoped. Like the farmers, these workers could not buy many new goods. Factories were making more than could be sold. By the middle 1920's, the building industry, as well as several others, had begun to slow down.

What was the installment plan?

Because many people did not have enough cash to buy the big things they needed or wanted, they began to use the ***installment plan***. They bought goods on credit and made payments each month. This helped to keep the economy going. At the same time, however, it helped hide some problems. People sometimes bought things only to find out later that they could not afford to make the monthly payments.

Why did people buy stock in the 1920's?

1.2 The Stock Market Crash. Because they were so sure of the economy during the 1920's, many people bought stocks. Some of the buyers were speculators. ***Stockbrokers***—people who sell stocks—en-

Total Farm Net Income, 1919–1929

Dollars (in billions)

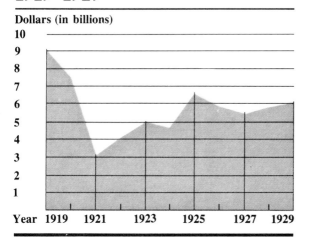

| Year | 1919 | 1921 | 1923 | 1925 | 1927 | 1929 |

Average Wages for Production Workers, 1919–1929

Cents Per Hour

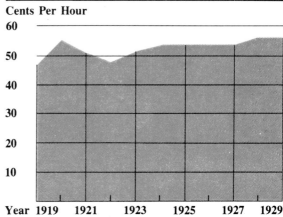

| Year | 1919 | 1921 | 1923 | 1925 | 1927 | 1929 |

Income on the farm (left) and in the factories (right) remained relatively low throughout the 1920's. So, workers used credit to make major purchases. How did this method of buying cause problems for American industries?

couraged this kind of buying by allowing people to buy stocks *"on margin."* This meant that people could buy stocks without paying the full amount of the purchase price. They paid 10 percent of the price and thought of the rest as a loan to be paid off later. When the price of the stock went up enough, the buyer would sell it at a profit and pay off the loan.

How did the stock market crash?

In October 1929, prices began to slip. Many investors began to sell their stocks before the prices fell further. People who had bought stocks "on margin" rushed to sell them before the prices slipped so low that they could not cover the amount of their loans. On October 29, 1929, about 16 million shares of stock were sold. Because so many people wanted to sell their stocks, prices plunged to a fraction of their old value. The stock market had "crashed."

What effect did the stock market crash have?

What happened in the stock market had an effect on other areas of the economy. Banks that had invested in the stock market lost a great deal of money. Those that had loaned money to people to buy stocks found that many people could not pay back the loans. With limited funds, many banks could not make loans. This led to less available credit. Since most people no longer could get credit, they bought less than before. Because fewer goods were being bought, industries began to produce less. Before long, fewer workers were needed, and people began to lose their jobs.

The stock market crash also was felt in Europe. Many countries there had not yet recovered from World War I. Since their economies were somewhat depressed, the crash had a key effect. European industry depended on loans from Americans. When the market crashed, European countries could not get credit. That led to a decline in world trade.

How many people were out of work at the height of the depression? When was that?

1.3   The Effects of the Depression.   By the early 1930's, the depression had become unlike anything Americans had ever known before. In 1932, almost 13 million Americans—nearly 25 percent of the work force—were without jobs. Thousands of others worked only a few hours each week. Unskilled workers and black workers were often the first to lose their jobs. Farmers who could not make their mortgage payments lost their farms.

Thousands of people began to wander around the country looking for work. Most had little or no money and no place to live. Before long, cardboard and tin shacks that served as homes sprang up in cities all over the country. These areas were called Hoovervilles. In some places,

The apple seller became a symbol for unemployment during the depression. The pennies received by this seller were his only income. What percent of the total work force was unemployed by 1932?

This St. Louis man was typical of thousands of people who lacked money to keep up rent or mortgage payments. He built his shanty from bits of tin, planks, and other assorted materials. Often these shanties were built close to one another, forming neighborhoods. What were these shantytowns called?

the local governments and groups of private citizens tried to raise enough money to care for these people. In other places, signs were posted that told travelers to keep moving because there were no jobs and no help. An author wrote this description:

> . . . those bleak settlements ironically known as "Hoovervilles" in the outskirts of the cities and on vacant lots—groups of makeshift shacks constructed out of packing boxes, scrap iron, anything that could be picked up free in a . . . combing of the city dumps: shacks in which men and sometimes whole families of . . . people were sleeping on automobile seats carried from auto-graveyards. . . . homeless people sleeping in doorways or on park benches, and going the rounds of the restaurants for leftover half-eaten biscuits, piecrusts, anything to keep the fires of life burning.

Things got worse in the middle 1930's when a serious drought hit the southern Great Plains. There had been too much grazing by livestock and too much plowing up of the sod. During the drought, the soil turned to dust, which was picked up and blown by the wind. The area became known as the *dust bowl.* Kansas and Oklahoma were hit especially hard. Because the land no longer could be farmed, families began moving elsewhere in search of food and jobs. Many moved to

Where was the dust bowl? How did it develop?

The Depression and the New Deal   543

Arthur Rothstein photographed this Oklahoma farmer and his two children fleeing a dust storm in 1936. What caused these dust bowl conditions over much of the southern Great Plains?

How did the government try to cut down the number of people needing relief?

California. But even with state and local help, there were too many people, too little money, and too few jobs.

Federal and state governments wanted to cut down the number of people seeking jobs or needing relief. Some people thought one way to do this was by sending Mexicans who were living in the United States back to Mexico. Between 1930 and 1940, more than 250,000 Mexicans were returned to Mexico. Most of the adults were Mexican citizens. But many of the children had been born in the United States and were American citizens.

To further help American workers without jobs, several members of Congress wanted to restrict immigration from other countries. To do this, Congress passed the Tydings-McDuffie bill in 1934. It called for Philippine independence in ten years. It also said that only 50 Filipinos could enter the United States each year. The act proved unnecessary, however. During the years of the depression, more people left the United States than came into it as immigrants.

1.4 Hoover and the Depression. When the stock market crashed in 1929, Herbert Hoover had been President for a little over six months. Like many Americans, Hoover felt the American economy would soon improve. He thought the problems could be solved by making business stronger. Hoover held meetings with business leaders to ask them not to cut workers' pay and to keep people working. He also helped start private relief agencies and asked city and state governments to do the same.

The one thing Hoover did not do, however, was allow the federal government to give direct aid to the people. He believed that it was up to the states and business to help the people as much as possible. Hoover was willing, however, to provide loans and other forms of indirect aid.

What was Hoover against regarding relief? Why?

In December 1931, Hoover suggested that a government agency be set up with the power to issue tax-free bonds and offer credit. Congress acted on Hoover's idea. In January 1932, it set up the Reconstruction Finance Corporation (RFC). The RFC had the power to loan money to banks, life insurance companies, building and loan groups, farm mortgage companies, and railroads. The government hoped that by keeping these businesses healthy, no more jobs or income would be lost. In July of the same year, the Relief and Construction Act was passed. It gave the RFC the power to give $1.5 billion in loans to set up state and local public works projects. It also gave the RFC more powers to help farmers.

What could the RFC do?

President Hoover tried hard to help the country recover. But he would not change his mind about direct federal aid to the people. He believed that a move of that kind by the federal government would destroy such longtime American values as self-reliance and individualism. Because of this stand, Hoover became less popular with many Americans.

An incident that took place in 1932 made matters worse. That summer, more than 15,000 World War I veterans marched on Washington, D.C. They demanded payment of a bonus which they were to receive in 1945. They said they would not leave until they got their money. While they waited, they built shacks and camped near the Capitol. When Congress refused to pay them, all but about 2,000 of the veterans gave up and went home.

Why did World War I veterans march on Washington?

President Hoover and others were afraid that the veterans who remained might cause trouble. When the Washington police tried to get them to leave, several people were killed. Soldiers led by General Douglas MacArthur finally scattered the veterans and destroyed their camps. This put an end to the trouble, but it also turned more Americans against Hoover.

1.5 The Election of 1932. The year 1932 was an election year. When the political parties met to name their choices for the Presidency,

What was the major issue of the election of 1932?

Election of 1932

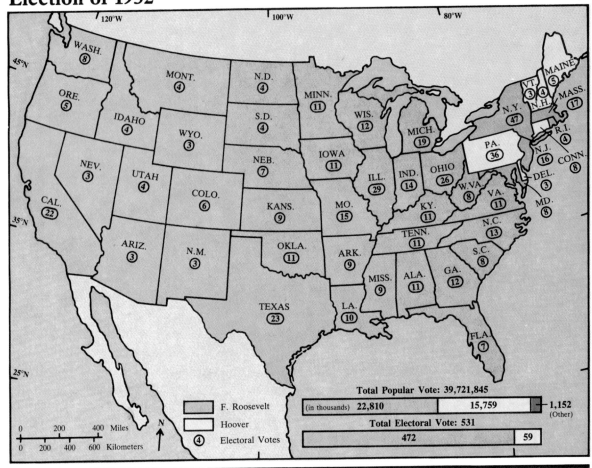

	F. Roosevelt		
	Hoover		
④	Electoral Votes		

Total Popular Vote: 39,721,845

(in thousands) 22,810	15,759	1,152 (Other)

Total Electoral Vote: 531

472	59

This map shows a significant Democratic victory. Compare this with the 1928 presidential election to see the extent of the Republican loss. What factors contributed to Herbet Hoover's defeat?

the big issue was the depression and what it had done to the economy. The Republican party again chose Herbert Hoover. The Democrats chose Franklin Delano Roosevelt, the governor of New York. Roosevelt had been stricken with infantile paralysis (polio) in 1921 and no longer could walk without braces and canes. Still, he remained very active in politics.

In the campaign, Hoover put the blame for the depression on world conditions. He said that his policies were beginning to change things for the better. Roosevelt promised a "new deal for the American people." He traveled around the country attacking Republican policies. Hoover, on the other hand, told the people that if Roosevelt and the Democrats won, "the grass will grow in the streets of a hundred cities, a thousand towns; the weeds will overrun the fields of millions of farms."

Roosevelt won the election of 1932. He got 23 million to Hoover's 16 million popular votes and 472 to Hoover's 59 electoral votes. The Democrats also gained control of both houses of Congress.

1. What problems did farmers and workers face during the 1920's?
2. What was meant by buying stocks "on margin"?
3. What effect did the depression have on jobs?

2. The New Deal: Emergency Measures

Once he was in office, President Roosevelt was willing to listen to and try new ideas. He was not against using emergency measures if he thought they would help make conditions better for Americans. The program Roosevelt and his advisors finally decided upon is called the New Deal. Two of its chief aims were relief and recovery.

2.1 Repealing Prohibition. One of the first measures that Roosevelt and the Democrats pushed through Congress had to do with prohibition. Many members of Congress did not feel that the law could be enforced. They felt if it were ended, the federal government not only would save money but also would make some by taxing liquor sales. On February 20, 1933, the Twenty-first Amendment was passed to repeal the Eighteenth Amendment. In December of the same year, it was ratified, and prohibition on a national level came to an end.

Why was prohibition ended?

2.2 The Banking Crisis. One of the first major problems President Roosevelt faced was a banking crisis. By the time he took office, more than 5,000 banks had shut down. Because of this, the American people had little faith left in the American banking system. More and more people began taking their money out of banks.

In March 1933, Roosevelt and Congress passed the Emergency Banking Act. It declared a four-day "banking holiday" for all credit unions, banks, and other loan institutions. During this time, all banking business was stopped. Only gold and silver licensed by the Treasury Department could be withdrawn or sent out of the country. Roosevelt hoped this would stop the banking crisis, and it did. By the time the holiday was over, so was the crisis.

How did Roosevelt handle the banking crisis?

The Depression and the New Deal   547

New Deal Legislation, First 100 Days

Date Enacted	Law	Purpose
March 9, 1933	Emergency Banking Act	Closed all banks to restore public confidence in government
March 11, 1933	Economy Act	Cut federal spending by reducing veteran's pensions and cutting federal salaries
March 31, 1933	Civilian Conservation Corps (CCC)	Created jobs for unemployed single men between the ages of 18 and 25
May 12, 1933	Agricultural Adjustment Act (AAA)	Paid farmers not to grow crops in order to raise farm prices and cut surpluses
May 12, 1933	Federal Emergency Relief Act	Provided money to states for relief of people in need
May 18, 1933	Tennessee Valley Authority (TVA)	Developed hydroelectric power in the Tennessee Valley to improve economic conditions
May 27, 1933	"Truth in Securities" Act	Required sellers of stocks and bonds to make public all important information about the nature of their securities
June 13, 1933	Home Owners' Loan Act	Created an agency to refinance individual home mortgages at low interest
June 16, 1933	Farm Credit Act	Created an agency to centralize all farm credit services for refinancing farm mortgages
June 16, 1933	Railroad Coordination Act	Attempted to rescue the railroad industry by enforcing consolidation and other economy measures
June 16, 1933	National Industrial Recovery Act (NIRA)	Stimulated business recovery by codes of fair competition
June 16, 1933	Glass-Steagall Banking Act	Forced commercial banks out of the investment business and created the Federal Deposit Insurance Corporation (FDIC)

On March 12, Roosevelt spoke to the American people on the radio. This was the first time a President had used the radio to reach the people. Roosevelt made such talks, which he called *fireside chats,* a regular event while he was in office. During his first chat, Roosevelt told the American people that their money would be safe in banks. His words gave the people more confidence in banks and in business.

2.3 Putting People to Work.   In 1933, 12.8 million people in the United States were out of work. Shortly after Roosevelt took office, he and Congress began working on ways to provide jobs or relief for all these people and their families.

On March 31, 1933, the Civilian Conservation Corps (CCC) was set up to provide jobs for men 18 to 25 years old. At first, it authorized work for 250,000 young men. Under the direction of army officers, its members replanted forests and built dams and roads. In return, they were paid $30 a month. By 1941, some 2 million young people were working for the CCC.

What was the purpose of the CCC?

The CCC was just the first of many programs. In May 1933, the Federal Emergency Relief Administration (FERA) was set up to give direct aid to the states. The FERA, headed by Harry Hopkins, had the power to give the states $500 million for work projects and relief. In November of the same year, the Civil Works Administration (CWA) was formed. Also led by Harry Hopkins, it gave jobs to 4 million Americans through late 1933 and early 1934.

In June 1933, the Public Works Administration (PWA) came into being. It was created to give work to people without jobs so they would be able to buy the products of farms and industries. The PWA was headed by Secretary of the Interior Harold Ickes and had $3.3 billion to spend. It gave the money to state and local governments to hire workers to build highways, public buildings, and dams.

What was the purpose of the PWA?

Despite paralysis, Franklin Roosevelt (right) vigorously attacked problems caused by the Great Depression. One problem was an increasing number of bank closings (left). On March 5, 1933, he ordered all banks closed for inspection. Sound banks were reopened March 13. Congress passed many economic measures in the first 100 days of the Roosevelt administration? What bills were passed? Why?

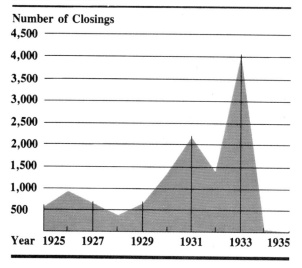

Bank Closings, 1925–1935

Number of Closings

*What program pro-
vided the first direct
federal aid in fur-
thering the arts?
How?*

In April 1935, the Works Progress Administration (WPA), later called the Works Projects Administration, was set up. It was headed by Harry Hopkins. The WPA provided work building playgrounds and hospitals. It also set up projects for actors, writers, and artists. These people created paintings and sculptures, as well as murals on public buildings. They gave plays and concerts. This was the first time the federal government had taken a direct part in furthering the arts.

2.4 Helping the Farmer. The New Deal also tried to help American farmers. In May 1933, the Agricultural Adjustment Act was passed. It set up the Agricultural Adjustment Administration (AAA).

*What was the pur-
pose of the AAA?*

The chief aim of the act was to raise farm prices by getting farmers to grow less. Farmers were paid not to plant crops on part of their land. The money used to pay them came from a tax on millers, meat packers, and other food industries.

The government also took other steps to help farmers. The Farm Credit Administration (FCA), for example, helped farmers get low interest loans. With them, farmers would not lose their farms to the banks that held the mortgages. Farmers who had lost their farms earlier also could receive loans.

*What was the pur-
pose of industrial
codes?*

2.5 Helping Industry. One of the most important parts of the New Deal was its plan to help industry. In June 1933, the National Industrial Recovery Act was passed. It set up the National Recovery

The Civilian Conservation Corps (left) employed men 18 to 25 years old. The Works Progress Administration (right) obtained work for artists. What other New Deal agencies helped specific groups of people?

Administration (NRA). With help from the NRA, each industry was to set up codes of fair competition. This meant that industries could agree to limit production and not cut prices. In this way, more companies could stay in business and keep people working.

The passage of the National Industrial Recovery Act marked President Roosevelt's first 100 days in office. During that time, 15 major laws had been passed to help people overcome the effects of the depression. The new laws showed Americans that the federal government felt responsible for their welfare.

1. Why did President Roosevelt declare a bank holiday?
2. What programs were started to put people to work?
3. How did the Farm Credit Administration help farmers?

3. The New Deal: Long-Range Planning

The New Deal also was aimed at reform. Changes were to be made through long-range planning aimed at improving American life and making sure there would be no more depressions. Most of the long-range reforms did not come into being until 1934 or later. Because of this, they were part of the "Second New Deal."

The members of Roosevelt's Cabinet strongly backed many of the reforms. Some of the strongest backing came from Secretary of Labor Frances Perkins. Perkins was the first woman to be a member of the Cabinet. The reforms also were strongly supported by a group of Roosevelt's advisors known as the "Brain Trust." They were given that name because they were people with college backgrounds. The group first worked with Roosevelt when he was a candidate for President. Three important members of the group were Raymond Moley, an economist and law professor, Rexford Tugwell, an economist, and Adolf Berle, Jr., an attorney.

Who was the first woman to serve on the Cabinet?

3.1 The Twentieth Amendment. Before 1933, American Presidents were elected in November and took office in March of the following year. This was true in Roosevelt's case. During the four months after Roosevelt's election, Hoover remained in office. Presidents who are still in office after a new President is elected are called *lame duck* Presidents. Since they are about to leave office, they tend not to make important decisions or be strong leaders.

What were lame ducks?

Many people felt that this practice was dangerous, especially during an emergency like the one in the 1930's. For this reason, the

Twentieth Amendment was ratified in 1933. It said that in the future, newly-elected Presidents and Vice-Presidents would take office on January 20 of the year following their election. It also said that newly elected members of Congress would start their terms on January 3 instead of March 4. This would cut down on the amount of time federal offices were held by lame ducks.

3.2 The Tennessee Valley Authority. One of the boldest programs of the New Deal was the Tennessee Valley Authority (TVA). Set up in May 1933, it was the government's first and largest attempt at regional planning. The TVA was to help develop the Tennessee Valley area, which took in parts of Tennessee, Kentucky, Alabama, Georgia, Mississippi, North Carolina, and Virginia. Much of the land in this area had been affected by *erosion*—the process of being slowly worn away by wind and water.

Why was TVA necessary?

The TVA built dams in the area to make electricity. It also ran power stations, helped control floods and soil erosion, and worked to help farming and industry grow. The electricity from the dams was sold to the people who lived in the area. Between 1933 and 1944, nine major dams and many smaller ones were built. People in the area were hired to help build the dams. This helped them raise their standard of living. The improvements made in the area helped bring more industry there.

3.3 Public Housing. During the New Deal, the federal government also took steps to help the housing industry and to improve housing for the poor. In June 1934, the National Housing Act was

The Tennessee Valley Authority was created to develop the valley cut by the Tennessee River. By 1945, how many dams were built? What was accomplished by building dams?

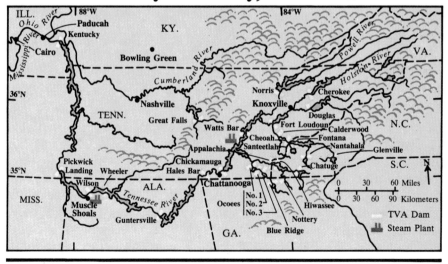

Tennessee Valley Authority, 1933–1945

passed. It set up the Federal Housing Administration (FHA). It guaranteed home improvement and mortgage loans made by banks and other businesses that loaned money. Under the act, the government hoped to bring about more home building and to build a strong home-financing system.

How did the New Deal aid the housing industry?

This was followed by the Wagner-Steagall Act, also called the National Housing Act of 1937. It set up the United States Housing Authority, which provided money for better housing for low-income people. Under the Wagner-Steagall Act, some of the worst areas in large cities were cleaned up. New homes were built with federal money.

3.4 Strengthening Labor Unions. For years, the United States government had backed business in its stand against unions. This changed under the New Deal. President Roosevelt and his advisors felt that without the backing of the workers, the New Deal could not work. Roosevelt felt the workers would support the New Deal if it gave them the chance to organize and bargain to raise their incomes. Then the workers would have more money to spend which, in turn, would help the rest of the economy. The first move came in June 1933 with the National Industrial Recovery Act (NIRA). Part of the act gave workers the right to organize. But workers could decide whether they wanted to join a union. After the act was passed, more workers joined unions.

Business, however, was still against labor organizing. For this reason, many labor leaders felt that a stronger law was needed. In 1934, Senator Robert Wagner of New York sponsored a bill to help workers and unions become stronger. It became the National Labor Relations Act, also called the Wagner-Connery Act. Passed in July 1935, it defined certain unfair labor practices so business would know what they could and could not do in relation to unions. The act also set up the National Labor Relations Board (NLRB). The board's job was to watch over employers and look into complaints. It also was to certify trade unions and settle disputes between business and labor.

What did the National Labor Relations Act provide?

Because of the Wagner Act, unions spread and grew in the late 1930's. The American Federation of Labor began to work to organize many different industries. This did not work well, however, because the AFL was made up of craft unions. There were many workers, such as those on factory assembly lines, who did not need to be skilled and could not join craft unions. So a group was formed to organize these workers. It was led by John L. Lewis and was called the Committee for Industrial Organization (CIO). Lewis' group organized all workers in the same industry into one union.

Who organized the CIO?

In 1938, the AFL and CIO parted ways. Members of the CIO formed a separate national union known as the Congress of Industrial

Unemployment, 1929–1943

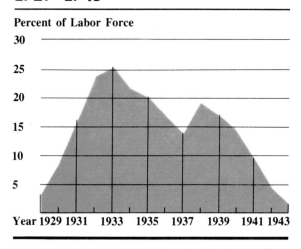

Percent of Labor Force

Despite New Deal efforts, there was still about 10 million people, or 20 percent of the labor force, unemployed in 1935. Unemployed schoolteacher Alice Conniffe shined shoes to make money. When did unemployment begin to decrease?

Organizations. By 1941, it had 2.8 million members. The AFL at that time had 4.5 million members.

The same year the AFL and CIO split, another important act was passed that helped workers. It was the Fair Labor Standards Act. It set up a 40-hour week and set a minimum wage. It also said that workers were to be paid for certain kinds of overtime work. The act also stopped child labor.

What did the Fair Labor Standards Act provide?

3.5 Social Security. Still another major New Deal reform was put into action in August 1935, when the Social Security Act was passed. *Social security* provided unemployment insurance for workers who were laid off their jobs. It made payments to older people who had retired or needed help. It gave federal aid for the care of crippled children, the blind, and dependent children (those who had no means of support).

Who pays for social security?

Money for the program was to come from taxes on business payrolls and workers' earnings. Although the funds came from the federal government, each state was to set up and run its own program.

1. What change did the Twentieth Amendment make in the Constitution?
2. What was the purpose of the TVA?
3. What were the two major labor groups after 1938?
4. What did the Social Security Act do?

Mary McLeod Bethune (1875–1955)

═══PROFILE═══

Mary McLeod Bethune was one of 17 children of former slaves. She began life as a sharecropper's child and ended up an important leader.

In 1903, Bethune opened a school for women in Daytona Beach, Florida. It was a poor school at first. The students used charcoal for pencils and crushed elderberries for ink. The school survived, however, and in 1923, it joined with a school for men. Bethune-Cookman College had Bethune as its first president.

By the 1930's, Bethune was gaining a national reputation. She set up the National Council of Negro Women and served as President

Franklin Roosevelt's official advisor on minority affairs. She used her influence to make sure that the government gave education and job training to young black people.

President Roosevelt invited Bethune to a White House party in 1937. She was the only black person there, and she wrote:

While I felt very much at home, I looked about me longingly for other dark faces. . . . I know so well why I must be here, must go to tea at the White House. To remind them always that we belong here, we are part of this America.

4. Problems and Critics of the New Deal _____

From the beginning, Americans could not agree about the New Deal. Some liked the programs and felt they were doing a lot of good. Others felt they were not doing what they should do. Still others thought the New Deal went against American principles. In time, some of the programs became the subjects of court cases that tested their constitutionality and threatened the New Deal.

Why was there controversy over the New Deal?

4.1 The New Deal and Civil Rights. Until 1933, most blacks favored the Republican party. A majority of blacks had voted for Herbert Hoover in the election of 1928. But when Roosevelt took office, many blacks began to turn to the Democratic party. They hoped the New Deal would bring them benefits that would help them through the depression. Their hopes were raised when President Roosevelt met with a number of black leaders and when First Lady Eleanor Roosevelt asked for support for programs to aid blacks. Blacks were pleased that many New Deal laws had clauses against racial discrimination.

How were blacks treated under the New Deal?

When the New Deal laws were put into effect, however, blacks did not always receive equal treatment. For example, CCC camps in many parts of the country were segregated. WPA programs in some areas did not give jobs to blacks. Few blacks in farming got help from the AAA. The AAA favored people who owned a lot of land, and most blacks owned small farms or were sharecroppers. Further, most blacks were not covered by social security. For these reasons, the New Deal brought few economic changes for most black Americans.

Why were Indians disappointed with the New Deal?

American Indians were also disappointed by the New Deal. In 1934, Congress passed the Indian Reorganization Act. It gave Indians the right to form corporations to hold land. Under the act, the federal government set aside money for Indians to buy back land they had lost under the Dawes Act of 1887. Most Indians, however, did not feel that they should have to buy back land which they thought was theirs in the first place. While they got back some land, their living conditions improved very little.

The Indian Reorganization Act also gave Indians the right to govern their people as a group through a council. The government hoped this would help the Indians gain back some of their traditional ways of life. But under the act, council members were to be elected by the adult members of each Indian group. This was not the way their leaders had been chosen in the past. So, many Indians would not take part in the elections. Even with the councils, final decisions were made by the Bureau of Indian Affairs.

4.2   Critics of the New Deal.   The New Deal also was criticized for other reasons. Many Americans felt the New Deal did not go far enough in what it did to help the poor. Others felt it involved the federal government more than it should in the economic system.

What were some of the proposals made by critics of the New Deal?

Senator Huey Long of Louisiana was one of the New Deal's strongest critics. He called for a $2,500 minimum income and a $5,000 homestead for all Americans. Long called his program "Share Our Wealth." Another critic was Dr. Francis E. Townsend of California. He believed the federal government could help both the economy and older people by giving Americans over 60 years of age $200 each month. Townsend's plan faded after the Social Security Act was passed.

Still another person who spoke out against the New Deal was Father Charles Coughlin, a Catholic priest from Michigan, whose radio program had some 10 million listeners. At first, Coughlin supported the New Deal. He wanted the federal government to take over the banks, utility companies, and natural resources. When this did not happen, Coughlin turned against the New Deal.

The strongest opposition to the New Deal came from business. After the TVA was started, many business leaders attacked the New Deal as socialism. The power companies said they could not compete with the federal government, since they did not control taxes or have huge amounts of money to spend. Small businesses said that the NRA favored Big Business. And both large and small businesses attacked government support of the unions.

Who posed the strongest opposition to the New Deal? Why did it oppose the New Deal?

4.3   The Courts and the New Deal.   Before long, some of the people unhappy with the New Deal took their cases to court. In 1935, in *Schechter Poultry Corp.* v. *United States,* the Supreme Court ruled the National Industrial Recovery Act unconstitutional. The Court said the Constitution gave the power to make laws (the industrial codes) to the legislature. Congress could not pass its power to the President.

The Court also ruled against the AAA. In January 1936, in the case of *United States* v. *Butler,* the Court said the tax used under the AAA was not really a tax. It was a system to control farm production. As such, it went beyond the powers allowed by the Constitution.

What New Deal programs were declared unconstitutional? Why?

Responses to the New Deal varied. Some people praised it. Others criticized it. How did this cartoonist see the New Deal programs?

Understanding Editorial Cartoons
SKILL

Not all newspaper cartoons appear on the comic pages. Some are found with editorials. An editorial cartoon blends pictures with words to comment on some subject in the news.

Editorial cartooning was popular in England in the middle 1700's. William Hogarth, a member of Parliament, published exaggerated drawings of his fellow politicians. Benjamin Franklin reportedly drew the first American editorial cartoon in 1754. The subject was colonial unity. Since that time, the editorial cartoon has been a regular part of most newspapers.

Historians use editorial cartoons as a way of looking into the past. Cartoons show how a character or an event was viewed at the time that it was drawn.

To begin to understand an editorial cartoon, ask these general questions.

1. What seems to be the subject?
2. What action is shown?
3. Who is the main actor?
4. What symbols appear, and what do they seem to mean?

During the 1930's, Franklin Roosevelt and the New Deal were favorite subjects for editorial cartoonists. On March 9, 1937,

Clifford K. Berryman published this cartoon in the *Washington Star*. The caption read: "Thus ended the Era of Good Feeling." Study the cartoon, and answer the following questions.

1. What is the subject of the cartoon?
2. What is happening in the picture?
3. Who is the main character?
4. How is the main character reacting?
5. Why does the main character appear not to be able to see through the eyeglasses?
6. What are some advantages of creating a cartoon over writing about this same subject?
7. What are some disadvantages?

The Supreme Court rulings angered Roosevelt. They also led to the fear that the Court soon would rule against other New Deal laws. But Roosevelt was reelected in 1936 by a landslide vote. He took his victory to mean that the American people wanted him to push ahead with the New Deal. He was determined to get around the Supreme Court, whose members he felt had fallen behind the times.

In February 1937, Roosevelt presented a plan to overhaul the federal court system. Part of the plan was to add up to a total of 15 members to the Supreme Court, one for each Justice who did not retire at age 70. Roosevelt hoped the new members would support the New Deal. The plan, however, led to a storm of debate. Many people felt that Roosevelt was trying to "pack the Court" because he wanted to get more power for himself.

What was Roosevelt's Court plan?

Before Congress could decide formally on the Court plan, events turned in favor of the New Deal. In April 1937, the Supreme Court ruled that the Wagner-Connery Act was constitutional. The following month, it ruled in favor of the Social Security Act. In the next few years, several members of the Supreme Court retired. This allowed Roosevelt to appoint seven new members in four years. Congress passed new laws to replace the AAA. The NRA codes, which did not work, died out.

Why did the Court plan not get passed?

1. Who were the major critics of the New Deal?
2. What brought about the controversy between Roosevelt and the Supreme Court?
3. What New Deal measures were upheld by the Court?

5. Conclusion

The New Deal did not end the depression. But it did give millions of Americans some relief and hope. Some of the New Deal reforms, such as social security, worked so well that they are still a part of the American system. The New Deal also helped change the role of labor unions in the American economic system.

Most important of all, however, is that for the first time millions of Americans began to look to the federal government for their well-being. Because of this, the government, and most of all the Presidency, began to play a larger part than ever before in the economy. This change would be carried on long after both the depression and the New Deal came to an end. The New Deal did not come to a sudden halt. It ended because new events captured the attention of the American people. Once again, events taking place in other parts of the world began to demand greater attention from the United States.

Chapter 23 Review

Main Points

1. The Great Depression began in 1929 and lasted through the 1930's.
2. Many Americans were affected by the depression as thousands of people lost their jobs.
3. President Hoover's attempts at recovery did include aid to businesses but not direct aid to the people.
4. In 1932, Democrat Franklin Roosevelt was elected President by a large majority.
5. Roosevelt's New Deal included emergency measures to help the economy and long-range measures to prevent future depressions.
6. Major New Deal legislation included the Agricultural Adjustment Act, the National Industrial Recovery Act, the National Labor Relations Act, and the Social Security Act.
7. The New Deal took minor steps to support civil rights for blacks and Indians, but little was accomplished.
8. Some critics of the New Deal did not think that the New Deal went far enough. Others thought it went too far.

Building Vocabulary

1. Identify the following:

Great Depression	PWA	Tennessee Valley Authority
Hoovervilles	AAA	NLRB
RFC	NRA	John L. Lewis
Franklin D. Roosevelt	Frances Perkins	Mary McLeod Bethune
CCC	"Brain Trust"	Indian Reorganization Act
Harry Hopkins		Huey Long

2. Define the following:

installment plan	dust bowl	lame duck
stockbrokers	fireside chats	erosion
"on margin"		social security

Remembering the Facts

1. What were the conditions existing in the 1920's that caused the depression?
2. How were American people affected by the depression during the 1930's?

3. What did President Hoover do to help the country recover?
4. Why did Congress repeal the Eighteenth Amendment?
5. What emergency measures did Roosevelt take to combat the depression?
6. What New Deal measures helped farmers? What measures helped labor and industry?
7. Who was helped by the Social Security Act?
8. What did blacks and Indians gain from the New Deal?
9. Why did critics oppose what the New Deal had done?
10. What was the conflict between the New Deal administration and the Supreme Court?

Understanding the Facts

1. Why did people greatly support the actions of business in the 1920's?
2. What problems in the operation of the stock market led to its crash in 1929?
3. How did Roosevelt's plan to help the country recover from the depression differ from Hoover's plan?
4. How did the New Deal try to help all parts of the economy?
5. What were the major differences between the AFL and the CIO?
6. Why did President Roosevelt want to add more members to the Supreme Court?

Using Maps

Regional Maps. The smaller the area covered by a map, the more detail the map can show. If two maps are of equal size, a map of one region of the United States can be more detailed than a map for the entire country. Regional maps drawn to larger scale are used to show detailed features.

The map on page 552 shows the region developed by the Tennessee Valley Authority. Read the legend, and study the map carefully. Then answer the following questions.

1. What states or parts of states are included on this map?
2. In what part of the country is this region located?
3. What is the main feature of the land in which the TVA project was built?
4. What is the main river of the TVA project?
5. On what other major rivers were dams built for the TVA?
6. What cities appear to have been most affected by the TVA project?
7. How far is it from Norris Dam to Kentucky Dam?
8. Where does the water from the TVA project join the Ohio River?

World War II   24

On the morning of December 7, 1941, most of battleship row at Pearl Harbor was aflame. This scene shows *West Virginia* and *Tennessee*. On *Arizona* alone, over 1,000 sailors died. Why was involvement in World War II welcomed by many Americans?

During much of the Great Depression, most Americans were too busy with the troubles facing the United States to worry about what was going on elsewhere. But the depression did not hurt the United States alone. It also brought about problems in many other countries. In Japan, Italy, and Germany, new leaders came to power. They built strong armies and navies and were threatening world peace with their plans to expand. Because of this, Americans found they had to pay greater attention to foreign affairs.

Why did Americans begin paying greater attention to foreign affairs in the late 1930's?

1. Foreign Affairs in the New Deal Years _____

Americans did not ignore all foreign affairs during the New Deal years. There were many important problems with which President Franklin D. Roosevelt had to deal. But for the most part, he followed the lead set by Herbert Hoover. The United States kept trying to work for better relations with Latin America and for friendship with Europe without becoming involved in either place. It also kept a close watch on Japan's growing power in the Far East.

1.1 The Good Neighbor Policy.   In his first inaugural address, President Roosevelt told Americans how he felt about the country's foreign policy. "In the field of world policy I would dedicate this nation to the policy of the good neighbor—the neighbor who . . . respects himself, and because he does so, respects the rights of others."

What was the Good Neighbor Policy?

The Good Neighbor Policy was followed most strongly in Latin America. President Hoover's goodwill tour and the Clark memorandum had been the first steps in showing that the United States wanted to change its policy toward Latin America. The Roosevelt administration took several more steps during the New Deal years.

First, Secretary of State Cordell Hull said that the United States no longer would use force to settle problems in Latin America. In 1933, American marines left Nicaragua. The following year, American soldiers left Haiti. That same year, fighting broke out in Cuba over control of the government. Ambassador Sumner Welles helped work out a treaty which brought an end to the United States' right to intervene in Cuba under the Platt Amendment. When the Mexican government took over American and British-owned oil companies in 1938, the United States did not make threats. Instead, it asked that both governments work together to settle American claims. In the end, Mexico paid the American companies for the holdings it had taken over.

How was the policy followed in Latin American relations?

Between 1933 and 1938, the United States also took part in meetings with several Latin American countries. During these, it was agreed that no country had the right to intervene in the affairs of another. It was also decided that the United States and Latin American countries would work together if threatened by war.

1.2 The Rise of Dictatorships. The United States wanted to be on good terms with Latin American countries. The reason for this had to do with changes taking place in the governments of some other countries. The United States was afraid that the time might come when all the nations of the Western Hemisphere would have to band together against one or more of these countries. Italy and Germany, for example, each was ruled by a *dictatorship*—a form of government in which one person (a dictator) or a small group of people hold all power.

In what countries did dictatorships arise in the 1920's and 1930's?

Both Italy and Germany were ruled by single dictators. After World War I, the Italian economy was in a depression. Many Italians felt that their country had not been rewarded properly for what it had done in the war. Benito Mussolini and his Fascist party promised to restore the economy and make Italy a great world power. Many Italians were willing to support them. By 1922, Mussolini had taken over the Italian government. He wanted Italy to have the power and glory it had had as the center of the Roman Empire. Mussolini set out to build an Italian empire in the Mediterranean and Africa. In 1935, the Italian army invaded and took over the African country of Ethiopia.

What was Mussolini's goal?

Two years before Italy took over Ethiopia, Adolf Hitler and the National Socialist party (or Nazi party) had gained control of the government of Germany. Hitler had become *chancellor,* or prime minister, of Germany. He had taken advantage of the country's economic problems and the bitter feeling about the Versailles Treaty to win over the people and become dictator. He promised to make Germany strong and to build it again into a great military power. He also promised to get back land Germany had lost after World War I.

What was Hitler's goal?

Hitler blamed Germany's problems on the Jews. He told the German people that Jews controlled the banks and had caused the depression. Under Hitler, laws were passed that took away most legal rights of German Jews. All Jews had to wear yellow stars on their clothing so everyone would know they were Jews. In time, the Nazis began to round up Jews and put them, as well as others, into prison camps, called *concentration camps.* More than 6 million Jews were killed. Hitler's long-range plan was to get rid of all Jews in Europe.

Who did Hitler blame for Germany's problems? What did he do to them?

In 1936, the German army marched into the Rhineland, an area between France and Germany. This went against the terms of the Versailles Treaty. It was the first step in Hitler's plan to rule Europe.

Nazi soldiers round up Jewish women and children to send them off to prison camps. The Nazis blamed Jews for Germany's defeat in World War I and for Germany's economic problems. What was Adolf Hitler's solution to this Jewish situation?

By the time Hitler's army entered the Rhineland, Japan was well on its way to becoming a military dictatorship. Japan still had an emperor, but Hirohito had no power. Politicians no longer were very important in Japan, especially among the Japanese peasants. The army and, to some degree, the navy were dominating the government. Trade and industry were growing, and Japan wanted more sources of raw materials. It also wanted to become a world power. Japan was trying to expand its territory by taking over land in Asia, especially in China.

Who controlled the government in Japan?

1.3 The Desire for Neutrality.   Leaders in the United States knew what was happening in Europe and Asia but did not want to get involved. Americans had very strong feelings against being drawn into another war. The desire to avoid the kind of trouble that had brought the United States into World War I led to the passage of three neutrality acts.

How did the United States try to avoid foreign involvement in the mid-1930's?

The first act was passed in 1935. It said that the President, after announcing that there was a state of war, had the power to stop shipments of arms to countries at war. It also warned Americans that if they traveled on ships belonging to countries at war, they did so at their own risk.

The second act, passed in 1936, made it illegal to make loans or to extend credit to countries at war. The third act came in 1937. It gave the President the power to name goods other than arms that could not be shipped to countries at war. It also made it illegal to travel on ships of countries at war.

1.4 The Beginning of World War II.   While the United States was trying to avoid war, Japan, Italy, and Germany went ahead with their plans to take over more territory. As early as 1931, Japan invaded Manchuria. Then in 1937, Japan began a major war against China. The Japanese army took over large areas of land and many major Chinese cities. Meanwhile, Italy attacked and then annexed the nearby country of Albania in 1939.

When and where did Japan begin its aggression?

Germany began its *aggression,* or attacks on others, in 1938. That year, the German army occupied Austria, which then became a part of

The Axis Powers reached the height of their expansion by 1942. German and Italian conquests included parts of Europe and Africa. What areas were conquered by the Japanese?

Axis Expansion, 1942

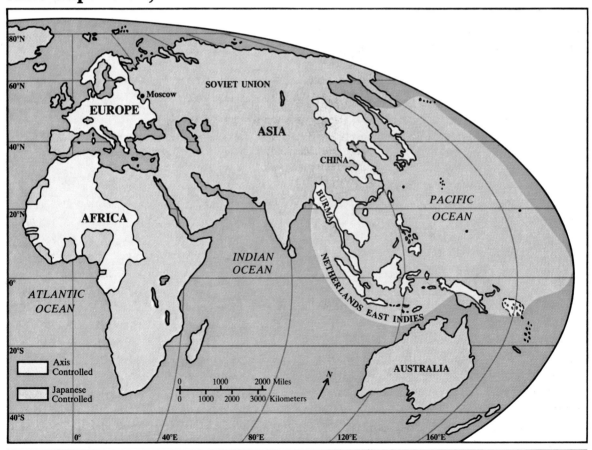

Adolf Hitler used rallies to whip up feelings of national pride, racism, and a sense of destiny for the German people. Many Germans, young and old, believed that Hitler could make their country strong again. Where else did dictators have a similar effect on people?

Germany. Hitler's goal was to unite all German-speaking people into one nation. The same year, Hitler demanded that the Sudetenland, the part of Czechoslovakia which had a German-speaking population, be made part of Germany.

Neville Chamberlain, the British prime minister, asked Hitler to meet with him, Mussolini, and Édouard Daladier, the French premier, to talk about the Sudetenland. The meeting took place in September 1938 in Munich. From this meeting came the Munich Pact. In it, the British and French agreed to Hitler's takeover of the Sudetenland. In return, Hitler gave his word that Germany would not take any more territory. Many people saw the agreement as *appeasement*—the act of giving in to an aggressor in order to keep peace. The pact convinced Hitler that both France and Great Britain were weak. He believed that neither of them could stop him from taking what he wanted. In less than six months, Hitler broke his word and took over the rest of Czechoslovakia.

Who took part in the Munich Conference? What agreement was reached?

In 1939, Germany signed a treaty with the Soviet Union in which they agreed not to attack each other. This left Germany free to attack Poland. On September 1, 1939, the Germans launched a *blitzkrieg,* or lightning war, against Poland. On land, they attacked with tanks. In the air, they used planes to bomb cities, roads, and communication lines. Poland was taken over in two weeks. Great Britain and France were still smarting from Hitler's takeover of Czechoslovakia. They went to Poland's aid and declared war on Germany. With this act, World War II began.

Why did Great Britain and France declare war on Germany?

World War II   567

For several months, things were quiet. Then in early 1940, the Germans launched large-scale attacks on countries in western Europe. Both Denmark and Norway fell to the Germans. In May, the Germans swept through Belgium and the Netherlands and on into France. The French had not expected the Germans to attack from the north. Their army remained grouped at their Maginot Line. This was a line of fortifications built along the eastern border of France. Even though the French army was large, it was beaten by June. Some of the French and British forces in France managed to escape. More than 300,000 British and French were *evacuated,* or withdrawn, from Dunkirk to England.

1.5 Lend-Lease and Defense Preparations. By 1939, Americans had become alarmed at the German, Italian, and Japanese victories. On September 8, President Roosevelt asked Congress to allow the United States to ship arms to countries at war. Two months later, the Neutrality Act of 1939 was passed, repealing part of the 1935 act. It allowed the United States to supply arms to countries at war.

The United States and Great Britain worked out an agreement the following year. In it, the United States agreed to give Great Britain 50 destroyers. In return, Great Britain gave the United States the right to lease certain British-controlled naval and air bases in the Caribbean.

The United States also began to build up its own armed forces. President Roosevelt and Congress wanted the country to be ready in case of enemy attack. To make sure there were enough soldiers, Congress passed a bill in September 1940 creating the first peacetime draft in the history of the United States. The American army which had only 170,000 soldiers in 1939 soon grew to over 1 million.

By this time, Americans were divided over the question of giving aid to the countries at war. General Robert E. Wood organized the America First Committee. It spoke out against American involvement. This and several others like it were supported by such well-known Americans as Charles Lindbergh and Henry Ford. Other Americans did not agree with them. They backed groups such as the Committee to Defend America by Aiding the Allies. It had been founded by Kansas newspaper editor William Allen White.

Against this background, the election of 1940 took place. In it, the Democrats nominated Roosevelt for a third term. The Republicans chose Wendell Willkie, a lawyer from Indiana. Roosevelt easily won the election. In his message to Congress in January 1941, Roosevelt suggested a policy he called Lend-Lease. He wanted the United States to give more aid to Great Britain. But the British were running out of money to buy war materials, and the Neutrality Acts said the United States could not make loans to countries at war. In March 1941, the

What countries did Germany conquer in 1940?

What did the Neutrality Act of 1939 permit?

How did the United States build up its own forces?

Who was opposed to giving aid to countries at war? Why?

What was the purpose of Lend-Lease?

President Roosevelt and Prime Minister Churchill met on a British battleship in August 1941. At that time, they signed the Atlantic Charter. What was the purpose of the charter?

Lend-Lease Act was passed. It allowed the President to transfer, lease, exchange, or sell arms or other war supplies to any country he felt was important to the security of the United States.

In August 1941, Roosevelt met secretly with British Prime Minister Winston Churchill off the coast of Newfoundland. They drew up a statement of war aims known as the Atlantic Charter. It said, among other things, that neither the United States nor Great Britain would seek new territory. Both countries would work to help bring about a lasting world peace.

What was the Atlantic Charter?

1.6 Trouble in the Pacific.   While the United States was trying to help Great Britain, the Japanese were on the move in Asia and the Pacific. After the Germans took France in 1940, a new government had been set up in the French city of Vichy. Several months later, the Vichy government agreed to allow Japan to occupy bases in French Indochina. Today this area contains Laos, Cambodia, and Vietnam. At about the same time, Japan formed a military and economic alliance with Germany and Italy. The three countries became known as the Axis Powers.

Who permitted Japan to occupy bases in Indochina?

The United States feared that Japan's expansion into Indochina would threaten the Philippines. President Roosevelt announced that starting October 16, 1940, no scrap iron or steel would be sent to any country outside the Western Hemisphere except Great Britain. The ban was aimed at Japan, which depended on American supplies. When the Japanese military moved into Indochina in July 1941, Roosevelt froze Japanese *assets*—property that belonged to Japan or its citizens—in the

What steps did Roosevelt take to counter Japan's moves in Asia?

World War II   569

United States. This act stopped American trade with Japan. Efforts to settle the differences between Japan and the United States failed.

1.7 Pearl Harbor. While the talks between the United States and Japan were going on, Japanese military leaders were making plans for a war against the United States. The Japanese wanted certain areas in Southeast Asia and the Pacific. They did not think they could do this without first weakening the United States. On December 7, 1941, Japanese naval and air forces attacked the large American naval base at Pearl Harbor, Hawaii. They caught the American forces there completely by surprise. Japanese planes sank or damaged 19 warships at Pearl Harbor and destroyed some 175 planes at Hickam Airfield. More than 2,000 sailors and soldiers and 68 civilians were killed, and over 1,000 people were wounded.

The day after the attack, President Roosevelt spoke to Congress:

> *Yesterday, December 7, 1941—a date which will live in infamy—the United States of America was suddenly and deliberately attacked by naval and air forces of the Empire of Japan. . . .*
>
> *I ask that the Congress declare that since the . . . attack by Japan . . . a state of war has existed between the United States and the Japanese Empire.*

Congress declared war on Japan the next day. Three days later, when Germany and Italy declared war on the United States, Congress recognized a state of war with those nations as well.

1. What was Roosevelt's foreign policy during the 1930's?
2. What event was the start of World War II in Europe?
3. Whom was Lend-Lease intended to aid?
4. What event brought the United States into the war?

2. The Critical Years _____

Late 1941 and 1942 brought hard times for the Allies—the United States, Great Britain, the Soviet Union, China, and many smaller countries. The Japanese attack had brought the United States into the war. But the Axis Powers were winning many victories.

2.1 The War in the Pacific. On the same day the Japanese attacked Pearl Harbor, they also attacked the Philippines, Guam, Midway Island, and Hong Kong. On December 8, they invaded Malaya and Thailand. In January 1942, they moved to the Netherlands East Indies (present-day Indonesia). In March, they took Burma. With the

Why did Japan attack Pearl Harbor?

What did Roosevelt say about December 7?

What advances did Japan make in 1942?

surrender of American and Filipino forces on the island of Corregidor in May, the Philippines fell to the Japanese. Japan also took control of huge areas of China and Southeast Asia, and many Pacific islands.

Two important naval battles, however, stopped the Japanese from taking over more areas. The Battle of the Coral Sea was fought on May 7 and 8, 1942. It was the first naval battle in which ships did not fight each other. The entire battle was fought by airplanes launched from aircraft carriers. Both sides had losses, and there was no real winner in the battle. But the Japanese were stopped from heading south toward Australia, as they had planned. The Battle of Midway took place about a month later in the Central Pacific. There American naval and air forces defeated a much larger Japanese force on its way to invade Midway Island. The battle stopped the Japanese advance across the Central Pacific and ended the Japanese threat to Hawaii.

What was different about the Battle of the Coral Sea?

Why was the Battle of Midway important?

2.2   The Eastern Front and North Africa.   While the Japanese were pushing forward in the Far East, other Axis forces were making gains in Europe and Africa. In the spring of 1941, the Germans overran Yugoslavia and Greece, although *partisans* (resistance fighters) continued to fight back in isolated mountain areas. This gave Germany control of the Balkans. In late June, the Germans broke their 1939 treaty with the Soviet Union and invaded that country. By the middle of November, the Germans were outside the Soviet capital of Moscow.

World War II was a global war. It was fought over a wide area and in various climates, from the deserts of North Africa (left) to the jungles of New Guinea (right). How was this war different from World War I?

At the same time, some German forces were fighting in eastern Europe, others were helping the Italians fight in North Africa. There German and Italian forces under General Erwin Rommel launched a major offensive against British forces at Tobruk. Rommel's troops took the Libyan city in June 1942. That month, the British finally stopped Rommel's offensive at El Alamein, near Alexandria, Egypt.

1. What battle stopped the Japanese advance across the Central Pacific?
2. How far did the Axis forces advance in eastern Europe?

3. The Home Front

World War I had seemed like a big war, but World War II was even bigger. This time the United States had to prepare to fight a war on many fronts. Americans had to fight Germany and Italy in Africa and Europe at the same time they were fighting Japan in the Pacific. Once again, the United States was called upon for much-needed supplies not only for Americans, but for soldiers and sailors of many Allied countries as well. Just as the effects of World War I were felt by nearly every American on the home front, so were those of World War II.

3.1 Mobilizing for War. Even before the attack on Pearl Harbor, the United States government had begun taking steps to ready the American economy for war. Once the country was in the war, agencies were set up to order the economy and to see that war materials were produced. In January 1942, the War Production Board (WPB) was set up. Headed by Donald M. Nelson, it decided which war materials would be produced. It also made sure war industries received the supplies they needed.

That same month, the Emergency Price Control Act was passed. It formed the Office of Price Administration (OPA) to set prices on all goods except those from farms. The OPA also set controls on the cost of rents in areas where there were defense plants. The OPA also began *rationing,* or setting limits on the amount of certain goods people could buy. Automobile tires had been rationed the year before by another agency. The OPA rationed sugar, coffee, gasoline, and fuel oil in 1942. In 1943, it added meat, fats and oils, butter, cheese, and processed foods to the list. A year later, it added shoes.

Besides setting up agencies to take care of the economy, the federal government also took other steps to prepare for war. One of the first things it did was to provide more people for the armed services. Thousands of young men were drafted under the 1941 law. In

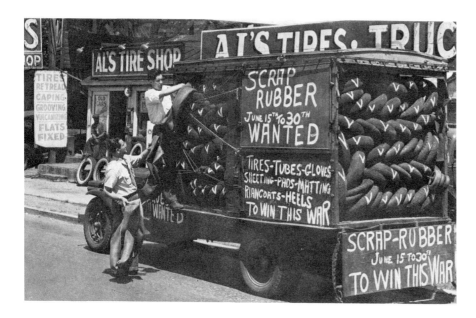

Wartime shortages led to rationing. Tires, for example, were salvaged in a drive to collect and reuse rubber. What other goods were rationed for the war effort?

November 1942, the Selective Service Act was changed so that men between the ages of 18 and 45 could be drafted.

More than 16 million Americans served in the armed forces during World War II. Over 11 million served in the army, some 4 million in the navy, over 600,000 in the marines, and about 241,000 in the Coast Guard. Women served in **noncombat jobs** (those not in the fighting). They made maps, operated radios, drove ambulances, and worked at office jobs or in hospitals. Some women, trained as pilots, flew airplanes from the factories where they were made to different airfields in the United States and England.

How many Americans served in the armed forces?

3.2 Producing for Victory. The huge amount of goods and war materials made by American industry during the war gave the Allies an edge over the Axis countries. Three years after the United States entered the war, American factories were making more products than those of all the Axis countries. American-built airplanes, ships, tanks, helmets, rifles, and munitions went to all the Allies.

How much did production increase during the war?

In nearly every industry, production jumped. In 1939, the United States had built fewer than 6,000 airplanes. In 1944, it built close to 96,000. In 1939, the gross tonnage of merchant ships built in American shipyards was just over 390,000. In 1943, the number jumped to over 10 million. New industries such as **synthetic** (artificial) rubber, nylon, and plastics also grew rapidly.

The great demand for production during the war ended the depression in the United States. There were enough jobs, because so many men were in the armed services. There was no shortage of workers, either. Thousands of women began working as welders, riveters, and in many other jobs.

How much did World War II cost the United States?

3.3 **Financing the War.** Like World War I, World War II cost the United States a great deal of money—over $300 billion. Ways had to be found to raise the money. The government got about 40 percent of it by increasing taxes. Citizens and businesses both had to pay higher taxes. The government also held a series of bond sales much like those of World War I. These sales brought in nearly $100 billion.

What Americans were hurt most by intolerance during the war?

3.4 **Problems for Japanese Americans.** The success of the Axis countries did more than make Americans prepare for war. It also led many Americans to fear and hate people from Axis countries who were living in the United States. Hurt most by this were people of Japanese background.

More than 100,000 Japanese Americans lived on the West Coast of the United States. Many people there, some of them public officials, were afraid that the Japanese Americans would help Japan if it attacked the United States. These people began to demand that people of Japanese background be moved from the West Coast.

In February 1942, President Roosevelt ordered the army to move some 110,000 people of Japanese ancestry from their homes to **relocation centers** (camps) in California, Arizona, Wyoming, Utah, Arkansas, and Idaho. They had to sell their homes and belongings, often at a loss. A great many of those relocated were American citizens.

What did the Supreme Court rule in Korematsu v. United States?

In a 1944 case, *Korematsu* v. *United States,* the Supreme Court held that the relocation program was constitutional under the war powers of the President. However, the Court later ruled that a person whose loyalty had been proved could not be held. During the war, more than 17,000 Japanese Americans fought for the United States. Japanese Americans formed the 442nd Regimental Combat Team. With their motto "Go for Broke," they were the most decorated combat force in the United States Army.

1. What was the purpose of the War Production Board?
2. How did the United States pay for the war?
3. What action was taken against Japanese Americans?

4. The Road to Victory

By late 1942 and early 1943, the huge industrial production of the United States began to have an effect. The tide of the war began to turn in favor of the Allies. Slowly, American and other Allied forces went on the offensive. By 1944, they were well on the road to victory.

4.1 Striking Back. In 1942, the Allies began striking back at the Axis countries. In August of that year, the Americans took the offensive in the southwest part of the Pacific. American marines landed on Guadalcanal in the Solomon Islands. After much fierce fighting on land and at sea, they took control of the island in February 1943. The victory at Guadalcanal was only the beginning of the Allied plan to hop from one island to another toward Japan.

What did the invasion of Guadalcanal signal?

In October 1942, the British under General Bernard Montgomery launched a counterattack against Rommel's German and Italian forces in North Africa. In November, the British won a second victory at El Alamein. They forced the Axis troops to retreat toward the west. This ended the Axis threat to the Suez Canal.

That same month, American and British forces under General Dwight Eisenhower landed on the west and north coasts of Africa. The Allied armies had the Axis forces in North Africa caught on both sides. One battle followed another until May 13, 1943. On that day, more than 250,000 Axis soldiers surrendered to British and American forces.

In November 1942, the Soviets made one of their most important moves on the eastern front. The Soviet city of Stalingrad had been under attack by the Germans since the summer. No matter what the

Allied forces led by American generals moved through French Morocco and Algeria while the British Eighth Army moved west from Egypt. They met in Tunisia for an invasion of Sicily and Italy. Why was Rome an important objective for the Allies?

The War in North Africa and Italy, 1942–1944

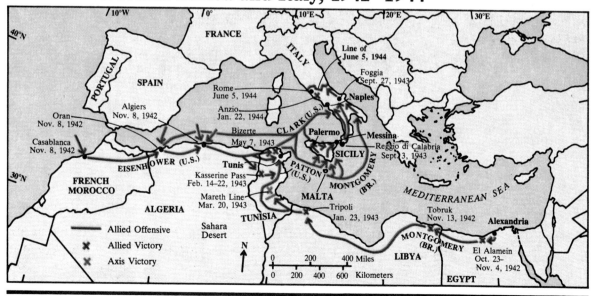

Germans did, they could not drive the Soviet forces out of the city. Instead, the Soviets attacked the Germans and surrounded the entire German Sixth Army. It surrendered in February 1943. This greatly weakened the position of the German forces on the eastern front.

4.2 The Invasion of Europe.   The Soviet Union had been urging the United States and Great Britain to open a second front. If the Allies could land somewhere in western Europe, Germany would have to send troops there to stop them. This would take some of the pressure off the Soviet army.

Where did the
Allies first invade
mainland Europe?

For this reason, the Americans and the British decided to attack Italy from North Africa. In July 1943, American forces led by General George Patton and British forces led by General Montgomery crossed the Mediterranean and landed on the island of Sicily. Together they forced the German troops on Sicily to retreat to Italy. Once the Allies had taken Sicily, they attacked the Italian mainland on September 3, 1943. Five days later, the Italian government accepted Allied surrender terms. Mussolini, who had been removed from the government, escaped on September 12 to a part of Italy still held by the Germans. Heavy fighting went on across Italy for several months until June 4, 1944, when the Americans took Rome.

At the same time the Allies were fighting in Italy, they also were planning for another invasion. Called Operation Overlord, it was to be the main attack against Germany in the west. Allied forces in southern England would cross the English channel and land on the coast of France in an area called Normandy. The United States had been storing tons of supplies for the Normandy invasion. Some 11,000 airplanes, 4,000 invasion craft, and 600 ships were ready in England. The invasion, led by General Eisenhower, would involve 176,000 troops. It would be the largest *amphibious,* or water to land, operation of the war.

American, British, and Canadian troops began landing on the beaches of Normandy on June 6, 1944. The date is known as D-Day. There they caught the Germans somewhat by surprise. Allied *paratroopers* (soldiers trained to use parachutes) were dropped behind German lines. After a short period, Allied forces broke through German defenses and began moving inland. By July, the Allies had about 1 million troops in France. More Allied forces landed on August 15. They pushed north up the valley of the Rhone River. By the end of August, the Allies had freed Paris from the Germans.

4.3 The Defeat of Germany.   At the same time the Allied attacks were taking place in the west, the Soviets were pushing the Germans back in the east. The first Soviet troops entered Poland on

Decision Making
=CONCEPT=

Profound decisions faced military planners during World War II. Choices of where and when to attack affected many lives and the course of the war.

After the Allied decision was made to land on the Normandy peninsula in France, it became General Dwight Eisenhower's responsibility to decide when to begin the invasion. Eisenhower was commander of all Allied forces in western Europe. The following selection is from his book, *Crusade in Europe*.

In order to obtain the maximum length of good . . . weather, the earlier the attack could be launched the better. Another factor in favor of an early attack was the continuing . . . efforts of the German to strengthen his coastal defenses. Because of weather conditions in the [English] *Channel, May was the earliest date that a landing attempt could be successfully undertaken. . . .*

Two considerations . . . combined to postpone the target date from May to June. The first and most important one was our insistence that the attack be on a larger scale than that originally planned. . . .

Another factor that made the later date [better was the plan for] *the air force. An early attack would provide*

the air force with only a minimum opportunity for [planning] *pinpoint bombing of* [important] *transportation centers. . . .*

Experience in Mediterranean warfare had [shown] *that each of our reinforced divisions . . .* [used] *about 600 to 700 tons of supplies per day. . . . On top of all this we had to provide for bringing in the heavy engineering and construction material needed to . . . refit captured ports, to repair railways, bridges, and roads, and to build airfields. A further feature of the . . . plan, and a most important one, provided for the speedy removal of wounded. . . .*

At three-thirty the next morning our little camp was shaking and shuddering under a wind of almost hurricane [strength]. *. . .*

[The weather staff announced] *that by the following morning a period of . . . good weather, heretofore completely unexpected, would* [begin], *lasting probably thirty-six hours. . . .*

. . . I quickly announced the decision to go ahead with the attack on June 6. The time was then 4:15 a.m., June 5.

1. What things did Eisenhower have to consider in making a decision?
2. Why was the first date postponed?
3. What other decision could the general have made?

Landing ships bring trucks and supplies to support the Allied invasion on D-Day. Balloons float overhead to protect the ships from low-flying enemy planes. When was the Normandy invasion?

What was the last German offensive?

Where did American and Soviet troops meet?

When did Germany surrender?

January 3, 1944. In the months that followed, the Soviets pushed into Rumania and the Balkans and on toward Germany.

The tide was turning against the Germans. The Allies were everywhere, and the Germans were finding it harder to keep up their defense. In December 1944, the Germans made one last try to prevent defeat. They sent a large attack against the Allies in the Ardennes, an area between France and Belgium. They hoped to split the American and British armies and then defeat them. In the Battle of the Bulge, the Americans finally were able to defeat the Germans, but at great cost. Nearly 8,000 Americans were killed, and thousands more were wounded, captured, or missing.

The German defeat in the Battle of the Bulge allowed the Americans to cross the Rhine into Germany. On April 25, 1945, American and Soviet troops met at Torgau on the Elbe River. Most of Germany was in Allied hands, and Soviets had entered Berlin.

By May 1, both Mussolini and Hitler were dead. Mussolini had been killed the month before while trying to escape to Switzerland. Hitler had killed himself in an underground bunker in Berlin. Berlin fell to the Soviets on May 2, and German military leaders asked to surrender. On May 8, 1945, the Allies accepted the German surrender. The day was called V-E Day for "Victory in Europe." The war in Europe was formally over.

4.4 Offensive in the Pacific. The war against the Japanese was still being fought in the Pacific and the Far East. Americans there were joined by Allied soldiers from Australia, New Zealand, and Great

Britain. Through late 1943 and into 1944, the American and Allied forces attacked Japanese-held islands. Islands that were heavily defended often were not attacked. Instead, American and Allied warships and planes kept them from getting supplies.

By August 1944, American forces in the Central Pacific had taken the Gilbert, Marshall, and Mariana islands, as well as Guam and New Guinea. Americans in the southwest Pacific under General Douglas MacArthur pushed toward the Philippines. They invaded the island of Leyte in October 1944 and then attacked the rest of the islands.

The Battle of Leyte Gulf was the last and largest naval battle of the war. The Japanese defeat there marked the end of their naval power. In

What was the last important naval battle of the war?

The end of Nazi Germany came in the spring of 1945 as Soviet and Allied forces overran Germany. Sweeping west, the Soviets surrounded Berlin and met their Western allies at the Elbe River. When was V-E Day?

The War in Europe, 1944–1945

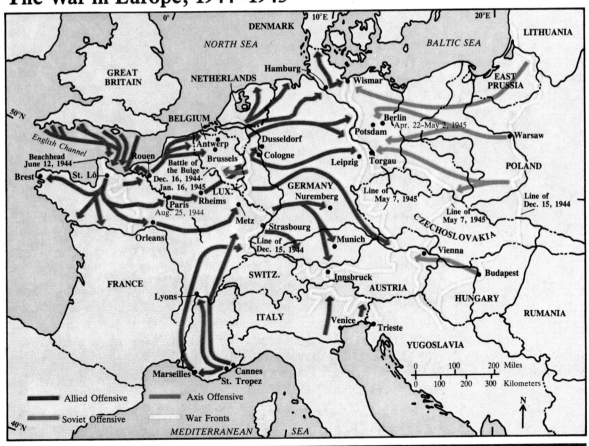

The War in the Pacific, 1942–1945

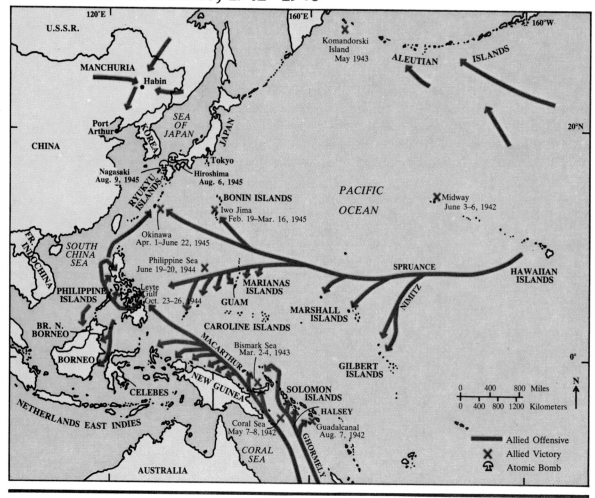

After Midway, the Allies attacked the Japanese empire primarily from the east and south. This strategy involved the process of island hopping slowly toward Japan. What decision was made by President Truman to end the war sooner?

Why were Iwo Jima and Okinawa important?

February 1945, the Americans invaded Luzon, the chief island of the Philippines. With the help of Filipino soldiers, they went on to take control of Manila. That same month, American marines landed on Iwo Jima, an island 750 miles (1,200 kilometers) from Tokyo. In April, the Americans invaded Okinawa, an island 360 miles (576 kilometers) southwest of Japan. Although the Americans won the battles, both Iwo Jima and Okinawa were costly. More than 4,000 Americans were killed at Iwo Jima and over 11,000 at Okinawa. But the victories gave the Americans bases from which bombing raids on Japan could be made.

4.5 A Change of Command. In 1944, presidential elections were held in the United States. Franklin Roosevelt was elected President for a fourth term. But the pressures of the office took their toll. On April 12, 1945, Roosevelt died while vacationing in Warm Springs, Georgia. He had served as President longer than any other leader in the country's history. When Roosevelt died, Vice-President Harry Truman became President. It was up to Truman to end the war.

How did Harry Truman become President?

4.6 The Defeat of Japan. Allied leaders began to plan the final defeat of the Japanese. Although the Allies were bombing Japan from the air regularly, they hesitated to invade the country. The battles of Iwo Jima and Okinawa had shown Allied leaders how costly such an invasion could be.

In July 1945, President Truman called upon the Japanese government to surrender or face "prompt and utter destruction." It had been decided that if the Japanese would not surrender, a new weapon would be used. The first *atomic bomb* had been tested successfully at Alamogordo, New Mexico, that year. It was the most powerful bomb ever developed.

Where was the atomic bomb tested?

The Japanese turned down the offer to surrender. President Truman then gave the order to drop an atomic bomb. The bomb was dropped on August 6, 1945, on the Japanese city of Hiroshima. This city was an important center for army supplies, shipbuilding, and railroad yards. The bomb destroyed almost all of the city. It killed between 60,000 and 70,000 people and wounded close to 100,000 others. The Japanese government, however, still would not surrender. Three days later, another atomic bomb was dropped, this time on the city of Nagasaki, an important industrial center. More than 35,000 people were killed. On August 14, 1945, the government of Japan agreed to surrender. On September 2, known as V-J Day, the formal surrender was signed on board the battleship *Missouri* in Tokyo Bay.

How destructive were the atomic bombs dropped on Japan?

4.7 Planning for War and Peace. The Allies had met many times to discuss plans for war and for peace. Both President Roosevelt and Prime Minister Churchill had taken part in many of these meetings. So had other Allied leaders and foreign ministers.

One important meeting took place in Tehran, Iran, in late 1943. There Roosevelt and Churchill met with Joseph Stalin, the Soviet leader, for the first time. The three made plans for the Normandy invasion and talked about setting up an organization of nations to keep the peace once the war was over.

Why was the meeting of Tehran important?

During the late summer and fall of 1944, another major meeting was held. Representatives from the United States, Great Britain, the Soviet Union, and China met at Dumbarton Oaks near Washington,

Albert Einstein (1879–1955)

When Albert Einstein was 26 years old, he wrote several papers for a German science magazine. In them, Einstein explained his theories about space and time, light, and energy. His equation, $E = mc^2$ (energy equals matter times the speed of light squared) is the keystone to the modern concept of the atom. In 1915, Einstein wrote another paper. This one was about his general theory of relativity. This theory changed ideas about gravity held since Sir Isaac Newton's time in the late 1600's.

During the 1930's, scientists began to apply Einstein's theories. They discovered how to break the atom into parts, giving off energy. In 1939, while working at the Institute for Advanced Study at Princeton, New Jersey, Einstein wrote a letter to President Franklin Roosevelt. He stressed the importance of research on a nuclear bomb. He warned Roosevelt that it was possible to build such a bomb and that the Nazi government in Germany was probably already working to make one.

During World War II, Germany failed to make a nuclear bomb, but the United States was successful. Einstein regretted his work on the bomb after he heard of the loss of life and the destruction caused by the bombs in Japan in 1945. Until his death in 1955, Einstein spoke to people and wrote articles about the continuing dangers of nuclear war.

Where were plans for the United Nations first drawn up?

D.C. They drew up plans which later served as a basis for the charter of the United Nations, an international organization much like the League of Nations.

Roosevelt, Churchill, and Stalin met again in February 1945 in the Soviet town of Yalta. They agreed that eastern European countries that had been held by the Germans should hold elections to form new governments. They also decided to hold a meeting in San Francisco in April to work on the charter for the United Nations.

What was decided at Potsdam?

In July and August of 1945, American, British, and Soviet representatives met at Potsdam, a town in Germany near Berlin. Many decisions were reached at the Potsdam Conference. It was the first meeting of heads of state in which President Truman took part. It was at Potsdam that he made the decision to use the atomic bomb against

At Yalta, Winston Churchill of Great Britain, Franklin D. Roosevelt of the United States, and Joseph Stalin of the Soviet Union (seated from left to right) met for their last major conference of the war. When was this meeting? What was achieved at the meeting?

Japan. It was also at Potsdam that the decision was made to follow a plan to divide Germany into four occupational zones. The United States, Great Britain, France, and the Soviet Union would occupy one zone each. The city of Berlin, which was located in the Soviet zone, would also be divided and shared by all four Allied powers.

1. What was Operation Overlord?
2. What caused the Japanese to surrender?
3. What was decided at the Yalta Conference?

5. Conclusion

The United States came out of World War II as the world's leading economic and military power. It had taken the lead in the defeat of the Axis Powers, and it was the only country in the world to have the atomic bomb. But the war did more than mark the beginning of the United States' role as a superpower. It also was the end of American noninvolvement. World War II had brought the United States new responsibilities in almost every area of the world. In the years ahead, however, American leadership would be challenged by the Soviet Union in many of those areas.

Chapter 24 Review

Main Points

1. During the New Deal, the United States became involved in foreign affairs in all parts of the world.
2. The Good Neighbor Policy sought to improve relations with Latin America.
3. The United States declared neutrality when the Axis Powers invaded other countries, starting World War II.
4. Success of Axis forces caused the United States to strengthen its own military forces and to supply Great Britain through Lend-Lease.
5. A Japanese attack on Pearl Harbor in Hawaii brought the United States into World War II.
6. Through a military draft and regulation of the economy, the United States mobilized to fight the war.
7. In several major battles in 1942 and 1943, the Allies stopped Axis expansion in Europe, Asia, and the Pacific.
8. Allied invasions of Europe led to Germany's surrender in May 1945.
9. The dropping of two atomic bombs led to Japan's surrender in August 1945.
10. Allied leaders planned war and peace during several wartime conferences. At one meeting, they agreed to establish the United Nations.

Building Vocabulary

1. Identify the following:

Franklin D. Roosevelt
Good Neighbor Policy
Benito Mussolini
Adolf Hitler
Maginot Line
Lend-Lease Act
Winston Churchill
Atlantic Charter

Axis Powers
December 7, 1941
Erwin Rommel
War Production Board
Bernard Montgomery
Dwight Eisenhower
Normandy

D-Day
V-E Day
Harry Truman
V-J Day
Hiroshima
Albert Einstein
Joseph Stalin
Potsdam Conference

2. Define the following:

dictatorship
chancellor
concentration camps
aggression
appeasement
blitzkrieg

evacuated
assets
partisans
rationing
noncombat jobs

synthetic
relocation centers
amphibious
paratroopers
atomic bomb

Remembering the Facts

1. What geographic area was the subject of the Good Neighbor Policy?
2. Who were the dictators that controlled Italy, Japan, and Germany?
3. What limitations did the neutrality acts place on America and Americans?
4. When and where did the Japanese attack the United States?
5. What did the United States do on the home front to mobilize for war?
6. What part did women play in the war?
7. What countries were allied with the United States in World War II?
8. Which Axis power surrendered first? Which Axis power surrendered last?
9. Who were the American Presidents during the war? Who were the important generals?
10. When and where were atomic bombs used during the war?

Understanding the Facts

1. Why did nations become involved in a second world war?
2. What did Germany under Adolf Hitler do to Jewish people?
3. How was Lend-Lease an effort to get around the restrictions of the United States neutrality acts?
4. Why were Japanese-Americans placed in relocation centers?
5. What part did the United States play on the warfronts in Europe, Asia, and the Pacific?
6. Why did the United States decide to drop atomic bombs on Japan?

Using Maps

Mollweide Projection. Mapmakers attempt to project the surface of a round earth on a flat map by using various systems. The map exercise for Chapter 21 concerned the Mercator Projection. The map on page 566 shows a Mollweide Projection. With a Mollweide Projection, meridians of longitude are equally-spaced, oval-shaped lines. Parallels of latitude are shown as horizontal lines.

Study the map on page 566. Compare it to the map on page 487. Using both maps, answer the following questions.

1. What same areas on the two maps appear to have different sizes? Why?
2. What are the advantages of using one map over the other map?
3. How successful were the Axis Powers in expanding control over other countries?
4. What countries were taken over by the Axis Powers?
5. What areas were taken over by the Japanese?
6. Where did neither Japan nor the Axis Powers gain territory?

Muncie 1920~1935

Muncie is located on the White River in the rich farmlands of east central Indiana. Deposits of natural gas were discovered there in the 1880's, and industries came to the area to use the gas for fuel. These industries caused Muncie to change from a farming community to an industrial city in the early 1900's. It was like many other small cities at that time.

Middletown

In the 1920's, the supply of goods from mass production caused changes in American customs. People had new ideas about ways to earn their livings, keep house, and enjoy more free time. Sociologists, or those people interested in recording the way others live and work together in groups, were studying these changes. In 1925, two sociologists named Robert and Helen Lynd decided to study one city in America. By studying a "typical" city, the Lynds hoped to record a general picture of what most American cities were like. Muncie was chosen for their study because it had "many features common to a wide group of communities." They called their study of Muncie *Middletown*.

Earning a Living

By 1920, Muncie was an industrial city of almost 37,000 people. Over 300 different products were made by over 100 different companies. These products included glass jars, auto parts, batteries, wire, and other metal products.

The Lynds noted that this production caused changes in the way people earned their livings in Muncie. Skilled artisans were often replaced by machines which did similar jobs but at faster speeds. The Lynds said:

And in modern machine production it is speed and endurance that are [needed]. A boy of nineteen may, after a few weeks of experience on a machine, turn out an amount of work greater than that of his father of forty-five. . . . It is not uncommon for a father to be laid off during slack times while the son continues to work.

So more young people were beginning to take jobs in the factories. Many people left farms in the area to take jobs in the city.

In the 1920's, families worked hard to earn money to buy the new machines which made life easier and more enjoyable. The Lynds discovered:

This [desire for] *the dollar appears in the . . . growing tendency among younger* [workers] *to* [trade future job interests] *for immediate "big money."*

Home Life

Home life in Muncie was also changing in the 1920's. The Lynds wrote:

It is not uncommon to observe [old] *and* [new] *habits . . . side by side in a family with primitive back-yard water or sewage habits, yet using an automobile, electric washer, electric iron, and vacuum cleaner.*

The use of prepared foods, canned goods, and refrigerators meant a change in eating habits. More fruits and vegetables were eaten during the winter months. Families started buying bread instead of making their own. Meat was eaten at least twice a day in many homes. A greater variety of foods could be bought and kept for longer periods of time without spoiling.

There was a clear difference in the traditional activities of men and women in Muncie. The Lynds wrote:

This is especially marked in the . . . activities known as "housework," which have always been almost exclusively performed by the wife, with more or less help from her daughters. In the growing number of . . . families in which the wife helps to earn the family living, the husband is beginning to share directly in housework. Even in [other] *families . . . activities of the wife in making a home are being more and more replaced by goods and services* [supplied] *by other agencies in return for . . . money . . . throwing ever greater emphasis upon the money-getting activities of the husband. . . .*

Smaller houses, easier to "keep up," labor-saving [machines], *canned goods, baker's bread, less heavy meals, and ready-made clothing are among the places where . . . time* [is] *saved today. . . .* [Homemakers] *repeatedly speak, also, of the use of running water, the* [change] *from wood to coal fires, and . . . linoleum on floors as time-savers.*

Education

One of the biggest changes noted by the Lynds was the sharp increase in the number of students in higher education. Only a few Muncie children went to high school before the 1900's. By the 1920's, most of them went to high school, and some of those went to college. The most important reason given for dropping out of school was lack of family money. Yet parents often gave up "extra things" to afford more education for their children. One mother said:

If children don't have a good education they'll never know anything except hard work. Their father wants them to have just as much schooling as he can afford.

The Ball Corporation was one of many industries in Muncie. What goods did factories in this industrial city produce by the 1920's?

The schools in Muncie changed to meet the needs of the people of the community. Classes were added in the high school to train students for specific jobs in homes, offices, and factories.

The city also had a community college. The owners of the Ball Corporation, which made glass canning jars, bought a private school on the edge of the city. They gave it to the state, and it then became a part of the state college system.

Free Time

When asked to comment on the changing times, one lifelong resident of Muncie said, "Why on earth do you need to study what's changing this country? I can tell you what's happening in just four letters: A-U-T-O!"

About two out of every three families in Muncie had an automobile. Some families bought automobiles before they bought bathtubs. The automobile was making free time enjoyment an everyday happening rather than an occasional event. As one woman said, "We just go to lots of things we couldn't go to if we didn't have a car." To have a picnic in a park or nearby woods could be decided in a moment.

Automobiles also were influencing the practice of vacations as part of free time activities. People could go farther away from home in automobiles, so they were interested in a shorter working time. Owners of companies began taking more time off, especially in the summers. Slowly, they also began allowing managers and supervisors to take vacations with pay. But factory workers, if allowed vacations, took them without pay.

Effects of the Depression

In 1935, the Lynds returned to Muncie to study it again. They wanted to see how the

A family enjoys a picnic along a roadside in Indiana. How did the automobile affect the way people in Muncie used their free time?

national depression of the 1930's had affected the lives of the people. The Lynds found that the depression had shaken the city, but not shattered it. By the time they arrived to begin their new study, business leaders of Muncie were saying that the depression was over. But many merchants had lost their businesses, and others were still doing poorly. Many workers had lost their jobs. Young people were very hard hit. They often could not afford to continue in college or to marry. Many could not find jobs.

City money for aid to the poor and unemployed had been only a small problem in Muncie in the 1920's. But during the depression, relief payments completely used up funds from private groups and were a heavy drain on city funds. During the worst of the depression, relief payments had to be cut because of the lack of funds. One woman wrote to the newspaper:

Our slip called for two dollars a week and [those in charge] *thought* [anyone] *could prepare forty-two meals a week on a dollar-fifty for two people. So we got fifty cents taken from the two dollars.*

. . . We haven't had a tube of toothpaste in weeks and have to check off some item of needed food when we get soap. I can only do my washing every two weeks, because that is as often as I can get oil for the oil stove to heat wash water and laundry soap with which to do my washing.

But the people of Muncie had less trouble than many people in other American cities. Ball Corporation, one of the largest industries in the city, had been able to keep up the sales of their glass canning jars. Throughout the depression, the increase in gardens and home canning had created a bigger market for their product. They tried to keep as many workers on the payroll as possible.

Radio brought the people of Muncie into contact with ideas and events from around the rest of the nation. How did radio influence the way people thought?

The people of Muncie had had to face some important questions about their values during the depression. The Lynds wrote:

A city [used to] *the question, "How fast can we make even more money?" was startled by being forced to shift its central concern for a period of years to the stark question, "Can we manage to keep alive?" . . .*

A city living by the faith that everyone can and should support himself lived through a period of years in which it had to confess that at least temporarily a quarter of its population could not get work. . . .

Nevertheless, the Lynds found that the depression had done little to change the basic views of most Muncie people:

On the surface [Muncie] *is meeting such present issues and present situations as it cannot escape by attempting to* [go back] *to the old* [ideas]: *we must always believe that things are good and that they will be better. . . . The system is fundamentally right and only the persons wrong; the cures must be changes in personal attitudes, not in the institutions themselves.*

The people of Muncie had been through a bad time, but they thought of it as temporary. They had only been "interrupted" in their race to make more money in order to buy more things. Muncie was a growing American city.

1. Explain the study called "Middletown."
2. How did the citizens of Muncie use their free time?
3. What company continued to grow during the depression? What effect did this have on Muncie?
4. What changes had taken place in Muncie from 1925 to 1935?

Los Angeles 1940-1955

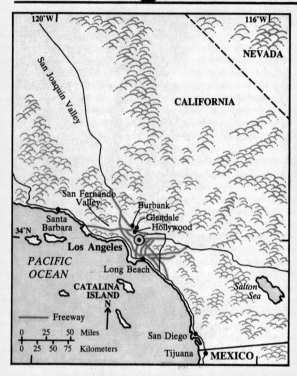

To many [newcomers in the 1950's], *Los Angeles is a modern Promised Land. It amazes and delights* [them], *and thaws* [them] *out physically and spiritually.*

These feelings of Los Angeles as a "Promised Land" seem to date back to the founding of the city. Spanish Catholic priests under Father Junipero Serra chose the site of a Shoshoni Indian village for their San Gabriel Mission in 1771. By 1800, 350 people made up the farming community there of *Nuestra Señora la Reina de Los Angeles,* or Our Lady the Queen of the Angels. Their main business was raising cattle. But their town soon developed into the trading, shopping, and social center of southern California. Huge *ranchos* (ranches) run by Spanish *dons* (nobles) grew around the town.

With the discovery of gold in northern California, the demand for beef from Los Angeles ranches rose. Many Spanish and Mexican ranchers became rich. However, during the mid-1800's, the price of beef dropped. A drought in the area caused many cattle to die. The Spanish and Mexican ranchers soon were in debt. Much of their land was bought by the Anglo-Americans arriving from the East and Middle West. By the 1860's, much of the *rancho* life around Los Angeles was ending.

American Control

California had become a state in 1850. Its first Anglo-American legislature divided the state into counties, established county governments, passed new laws, and set up new courts. The Spanish town of Los Angeles gradually took on the look of an Anglo-American city. Houses made of adobe gave way to houses made of red brick or wood. Formal gardens and white picket fences also appeared. By 1870, horse-drawn streetcars and carriages had taken the place of Mexican wagons. By 1885, the Santa Fe Railroad also reached Los Angeles. Its $1 fare from Kansas City brought people to the area in great numbers.

A real estate boom in the 1880's caused land prices to rise. New communities like Hollywood, Burbank, Glendale, and Long Beach appeared around the city of Los Angeles. The citrus fruit, olive, walnut, and grape industries in the area grew rapidly. Another real estate boom occurred in the

1920's, and half a million more Americans came to Los Angeles, many of them by automobile. Houses began to fill the valleys and climb the hillsides.

During the depression, droughts, and dust storms of the 1930's, thousands of people moved to California from central, southern, and eastern states. Many of them hoped that Los Angeles would be their "Promised Land." Some of these people found work in the oil and shipping industries. Sunkist, one of California's citrus fruit industries, offered jobs to others.

A Mixture of Backgrounds

By 1940, more than 1.5 million people lived in Los Angeles. Most of them were "newcomers."

Only a handful of the inhabitants are descended from pioneer Mexican and American families. Only a small number of adult Angelenos [citizens of Los Angeles] *were born in the city. The majority of the inhabitants have come here in recent years, mostly from the Middle West. . . . In addition to American settlers, Los Angeles has attracted immigrants of many races. . . . Mexicans, Japanese, Chinese, Filipinos.*

More black Americans were also seeking that "Promised Land" found in the job market of Los Angeles. The wartime prosperity that brought more people to the city uncovered old problems of prejudice and created new ones. There were pressures of competition for jobs and for housing.

Japanese Americans

When the Japanese bombed Pearl Harbor on December 7, 1941, feelings for the Japanese American population in Los Angeles changed. The Anglo-American citizens became frightened. They began to distrust all Japanese. Editorials in local newspapers referred to California as a "danger zone."

The Japanese were rounded up from their homes and moved to relocation camps. After the war, many of them returned to find their homes and businesses gone. A few received some government payment for what they had lost. Full repayment, however, was never made. S. J. Oki, a Japanese American who had been moved to a camp, reported:

Objectively, and on the whole, life in a relocation center is not unbearable. There are dust-storms and mud. Housing is inadequate, with families of six living in single rooms in many cases. Food is below the standard set for prisoners of war. In some of the camps

Los Angeles is known to many as a city of freeways. How has the automobile affected the environment and growth of the city?

Beginning in April 1942, about 110,000 Japanese Americans—half of them under 20 years old—were ordered to relocation centers. Why did this happen?

Mr. Yokida was a 65-year-old farmer who had lived in California for 40 years. He said:

For forty years I worked in central and southern California. I can remember when Los Angeles was only a small town. . . . This country never gave me citizenship, but I never went back to Japan and I have no interests there. The evacuation has worked a hardship on me and my family, but I suppose in time of war you have to stand for a lot of hardships. . . .

The Zoot-Suiters

The Japanese were not the only group facing discrimination. Some Mexican Americans were having problems with the Los Angeles police. They were being characterized as a violent people and were not permitted into many of the public parks, swimming pools, theaters, dance halls, and restaurants.

Some Mexican American young people joined together into groups. Their symbol of unity was an outfit called a "zoot suit." It included a flat hat with a wide brim and a long, loose, wide-shouldered coat worn over pants that were pleated and high-waisted with pegged or tight cuffs. A long key chain hanging from the pocket of the pants was usually part of the outfit.

In the spring of 1943, riots broke out between these "zoot-suiters" and soldiers who were waiting to go overseas. The federal government feared that the riots were being used as propaganda against the United States. It insisted that military police settle the trouble quickly. Military passes were cancelled, and strict controls were placed on soldiers and sailors. The street fighting gradually stopped, and order was restored.

hospitals are at times understaffed and supplies meager. . . .

What is not so bearable lies much deeper. . . .

Their faces look bewildered as they stare at the barbed-wire fences and [guard] towers that surround the camp. Their eyes ask: Why? Why? What is all this?

Kats Ento, who had been a farmer, wrote:

I am an American citizen. I was born and brought up in California. I have never been outside the United States, and I don't know Japan or what Japan stands for. But because my parents [did not give] me blue eyes, reddish hair, and a high nose, I am here in camp [held] without the formality of a charge, to say nothing of a trial. Does the Constitution say only white men are created equal?

A citizen's committee was set up by California Governor Earl Warren to investigate the cause of these riots. The committee reported that the riots had been caused mostly by racial prejudice against Mexican Americans. Poor police actions and bad newspaper reporting had added to the problem. As one young man said, "We are Americans for the draft, but Mexicans for jobs and police."

The Good Life—But Problems

In the 1950's, many people still came to Los Angeles to find the "good life." This meant having homes in the suburbs, owning cars, having swimming pools in backyards, and having jobs that allowed enough money to enjoy weekend free time.

Los Angeles was proud of its beautiful sunny, blue skies. It also was proud of its

During World War II, many women worked at aircraft plants. They inspired the song, "Rosie the Riveter." How many planes did Los Angeles plants produce?

efforts to help win World War II. Los Angeles aircraft plants produced one third of the planes being built in the United States during the war. All the "big four" rubber companies—Goodyear, Goodrich, Firestone, and United States Rubber—operated plants in the city. The city had become industrialized.

Smoke, microscopic dust, nauseating gases, and chemical fumes of various hues [colors] poured forth from thousands of newly built plants, and nobody gave the question of pure air a thought. Men had only one feverish purpose—to win the war.

Scientific research showed that the millions of automobiles owned by the Los Angeles citizens were beginning to have a great effect on the environment. Pollution was becoming a major problem. The climate, with its sunny skies and months without rainfall, was another cause of the problem. There were no strong winds to move the stale air out of the city. Smog alerts became common. City officials feared that the tourist trade would be hurt, especially after a headline in the St. Louis *Globe-Democrat* read:

Beautiful, Sunny California, Eh?
Los Angeles Now No. 1 Smog Town.

1. Who came to Los Angeles to find the "Promised Land"?
2. Compare the feelings of Kats Ento and Mr. Yokida.
3. Who were the "zoot-suiters"?
4. What caused the smog problem in Los Angeles?
5. How did events in the nation as a whole affect the economies of Muncie and Los Angeles?

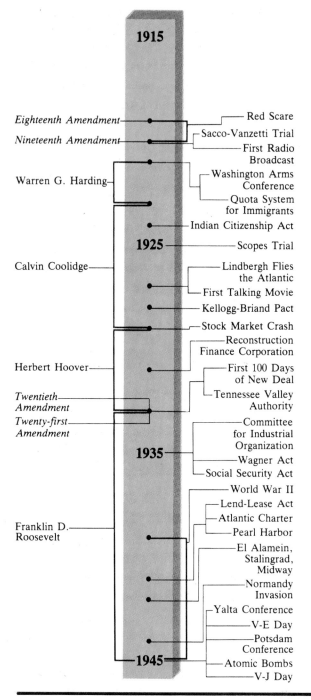

1915

Eighteenth Amendment — Red Scare
Nineteenth Amendment — Sacco-Vanzetti Trial
— First Radio Broadcast
Warren G. Harding — Washington Arms Conference
— Quota System for Immigrants
— Indian Citizenship Act
1925 — Scopes Trial
Calvin Coolidge — Lindbergh Flies the Atlantic
— First Talking Movie
— Kellogg-Briand Pact
— Stock Market Crash
— Reconstruction Finance Corporation
Herbert Hoover — First 100 Days of New Deal
— Tennessee Valley Authority
Twentieth Amendment
Twenty-first Amendment
— Committee for Industrial Organization
1935 — Wagner Act
— Social Security Act
— World War II
— Lend-Lease Act
— Atlantic Charter
— Pearl Harbor
— El Alamein, Stalingrad, Midway
Franklin D. Roosevelt — Normandy Invasion
— Yalta Conference
— V-E Day
— Potsdam Conference
1945 — Atomic Bombs
— V-J Day

Summary

1. American involvement in World War I left the people with a strong desire for peace, and the United States took steps to reduce armaments and improve relations with other countries.

2. The decade of the 1920's was a period of strong contrasts at home, with such gains in rights as women's suffrage, yet with much intolerance toward blacks, immigrants, and anyone considered different.

3. The boom economy, helped by policies of three Republican Presidents, hid such dangers as problems in agriculture and the overuse of credit buying.

4. The stock market crash of 1929 signaled the beginning of the Great Depression, which lasted throughout the 1930's.

5. New Deal laws, passed under President Franklin D. Roosevelt, attempted to provide relief and recovery from the depression as well as long-range reforms in the economy.

6. The policies of the New Deal brought about greater government involvement in the economy than at any earlier time in American history.

7. The policies of expansion by military dictatorships in Japan, Germany, and Italy brought about World War II, with the United States entering the war after Pearl Harbor in 1941.

8. American factories turned out materials for all the Allied nations, and American soldiers and sailors helped bring victory in both Europe and the Pacific.

Unit Questions

1. What were the feelings of Americans toward the results of World War I? What effects did this have on foreign policy and on the people at home?
2. What were the problems between the United States and Japan from 1900 to the beginning of World War II?
3. What were the policies of the federal government toward labor unions during the 1920's? How did those policies change during the 1930's and why?
4. What were some of the arguments and criticisms of the New Deal?
5. In what ways were the actions of the federal government alike during World War I as during World War II?
6. How did the actions of the dictatorships differ from the ideals of Americans?
7. What were some of the differences between the two world wars?
8. What major agreements were made by Allied leaders during World War II?
9. How was the position of the United States in foreign affairs different following World War II from its position after World War I?

Suggested Activities

1. Collect and play for the class recordings of music which was popular in the period from the 1920's to the 1940's. Compare the music of each period.
2. Locate and interview someone who remembers the Great Depression. Make comparisons with the interviews of other class members.
3. Make lists of the Americans who took part in the 1932 Olympics and their accomplishments. Compare them with the accomplishments of Americans in more recent Olympic games.
4. Make a study of the treatment of blacks, Mexican Americans, Japanese Americans, and women in the armed forces during World War II. What opportunities did they have and what problems did they face? Also determine how their treatment has changed.

Suggested Readings

Bonham, Frank. *The Ghost Front.* New York: E. P. Dutton, 1968. A story about twin brothers fighting in World War II.

Evans, Mark. *Scott Joplin and the Ragtime Years.* New York: Dodd, Mead, & Co., 1976. Traces the activities of the jazz musician who wrote many popular songs during the 1920's.

Meltzer, Milton. *Violins and Shovels: The WPA Arts Project.* New York: Delacorte Press, 1976. Describes efforts of the WPA to provide work for artists.

Uchida, Yoshiko. *Journey Home.* New York: Atheneum, 1978. Story of the return home from a detention center of a Japanese American girl and her family.

AMERICA
IS
Change

Change has been a factor throughout the history of American people. When people from the Old World moved to the New World, they changed where and how they lived. Over the centuries, the United States has changed politically, economically, and socially. The action of change contributed to the nation's growth and continuing development. The United States adjusted to change and directed change in a way that provided for a free and democratic society for American citizens.

Cold War and Crisis   25

The Brandenburg Gate in Berlin is a symbol of cold war division. It is on the main route between the two sectors of the divided German city. How did the situation in Germany after World War II affect the United States?

After World War II, most Americans realized that it was no longer possible for the United States to stay out of world problems. There were challenges to be faced that would take the cooperation of all the great powers. Before long, however, growing tension between the United States and the Soviet Union made cooperation difficult.

1. Changes in the Postwar World_____

The postwar world was a changed world. Germany and Japan had been defeated and were no longer a threat to other countries. Large areas of Europe and Asia lay in ruins, however, and much of the world had to be rebuilt.

1.1 The Situation in Europe. After the war, one of the most important things the Allied Powers had to decide was what to do with Germany. First, however, they had to rid the country of Nazis. When the Allies invaded Germany during the war, they found the Nazi concentration camps where some 12 million people, 6 million of them Jews, had been killed. The Allies were shocked and were determined to try the Nazis for their war crimes. In 1945, the International Military Tribunal was set up in Nuremberg, Germany. There, 24 top Nazi leaders were tried. Of these, ten were hanged. Most of the rest were given prison sentences. Later, other Nazis were also tried.

Why did the Allies put Nazi leaders on trial after the war?

Once the trials were under way, the Allies could turn their attention to setting up a new government for Germany. With the defeat of Hitler, no German government remained. The United States, Great Britain, France, and the Soviet Union each controlled part of Germany. These four powers, however, had to decide on a way to unify the country's government. Over time, this proved to be nearly impossible.

1.2 The Situation in the Far East. Japanese leaders also were tried for their war crimes. The International Military Tribunal for the Far East sentenced six top government leaders to be executed. Among them was former Premier Hideki Tojo. A number of army and navy officers also were tried in Japan and in countries taken over by Japan during the war.

The situation in the Far East was different from the one in Germany, however. Japan was not divided into occupational zones, as was Germany. An Allied Council was set up, and under the direction of the United States, a new constitution was written. It made Japan a

How was the situation in Japan different from that of Germany?

International Cooperation
CONCEPT

Before 1945, the United States limited its relations with other countries. International agreements were based usually on specific treaties. There were trade treaties and a treaty for building the Panama Canal. On two occasions, the United States joined with other nations to fight a war. Most often, the United States avoided becoming involved in the affairs of other countries.

During World War II, the United States realized that the best chance for remaining at peace was to try to prevent future wars. This could be done only by cooperating with other nations to keep the peace. In 1945, the United States joined in a major effort at international cooperation by helping to set up the United Nations. On June 26, 1945, a United Nations charter was signed by a United States representative.

We the peoples of the United Nations determined to save succeeding generations from the scourge of war, which twice in our lifetime has brought untold sorrow to mankind, and

to reaffirm faith in fundamental human rights, in the dignity and worth of the human person, in the equal rights of men and women and of nations large and small, and to establish conditions under which justice and respect for the obligations arising from treaties and other sources of international law can be maintained, and

to promote social progress and better standards of life in larger freedom, and for these ends

to practice tolerance and live together in peace with one another as good neighbors, and

to unite our strength to maintain international peace and security, and

to ensure, by the acceptance of principles and the institution of methods, that armed force shall not be used, save in the common interest, and

to employ international machinery for the promotion of the economic and social advancement of all peoples, have resolved to combine our efforts to accomplish these aims.

1. According to the aims of the United Nations, what were areas of cooperation?
2. What were the reasons for creating this international organization?
3. What was international cooperation to accomplish?

democracy. It also gave women legal and political rights for the first time in that country's history.

The Allies also occupied Korea after the war. Japan had ruled Korea since 1910. When the Japanese surrendered, American and Soviet soldiers moved into Korea. The country was divided at the 38th parallel into two occupational zones. The northern one was controlled by the Soviet Union, and the southern one by the United States.

How did Korea become divided?

In 1948, each zone in Korea set up its own government. The southern part was called the Republic of Korea. It formed a representative government. The northern part became the People's Republic of North Korea with a Communist government.

1.3 The United Nations.   After World War II, people had to face some problems. But in general, they looked forward to a peaceful future. They based their hopes, in part, on a new world organization— the United Nations (UN). Its charter had been written in San Francisco by delegates from 50 different countries. Signed on June 26, 1945, the charter laid out the general plan of the United Nations.

The charter called for a General Assembly with representatives from each of the member countries. Each country had one vote, which it could use to help decide UN policy. The charter also called for a Security Council of 11 members. It would work to keep world peace. Five members—the United States, the Soviet Union, Great Britain, France, and China—held permanent seats. The other six members served two-year terms. Each permanent member had the power to veto a decision by the Security Council.

What nations hold permanent seats on the Security Council?

The charter also set up four other *organs,* or parts of the organization. The Economic and Social Council would deal with questions of human welfare and rights. The International Court of Justice would hear cases brought to it by member countries. The Trusteeship Council would take charge of the *trust territories*. These were areas of the world not under a national government but under the care of the UN. The Secretariat would handle the organization's day-to-day business. It was headed by the Secretary-General.

What are the six major organs of the UN?

In 1946, the United Nations set up its headquarters in New York City on land given to it by the Rockefeller family. The UN soon found that its job of keeping the peace was becoming more and more difficult because of growing tension between the Western powers (the United States, Great Britain, and France) and the Soviet Union.

1. How did the Allies control Germany after the war?
2. What happened to Japan after World War II?
3. What was the purpose of the United Nations?

2. The Cold War in the West_____

The United States, Great Britain, France, and the Soviet Union had joined together to fight Germany. But cooperation among these countries began to break down after the war. The Western powers feared Soviet expansion and the spread of communism. Growing conflicts between the Western powers and the Soviet Union soon led to a *cold war*. This is a war in which there is no fighting, but where each side uses means short of military action to expand its influences.

What is cold war?

2.1 Promises and Problems. Some of the tension between the Western powers and the Soviet Union grew out of the failure of the Soviet Union to live up to agreements made during the war. For example, the Allies at Yalta had agreed to allow free elections in Eastern Europe. When the Soviets freed these areas, however, they helped set up Communist governments that were loyal to the Soviet Union. British Prime Minister Churchill warned that the Soviets had put up an "iron curtain" between Eastern Europe and the West.

What led to the cold war?

Events took place in Greece and Turkey in the late 1940's that added to the growing problems between the United States and the Soviet Union. Communists and Nationalists had been fighting a civil war in Greece since 1945. The Nationalists went to the UN for help in 1947. In Turkey, the Soviet Union wanted to share control of the Dardanelles, a strait which connects the Black and Mediterranean seas. The Soviets also wanted to build naval bases in Turkey. Turkey would not give in to Soviet demands. In 1947, it turned to the United States for support.

2.2 Containment in Europe. It seemed that the Soviets wanted to spread their power in all directions. They were doing this by forming *satellite nations,* or countries controlled by the Soviet Union. President Truman and other American leaders decided that the United States had to take a strong stand against the Soviet Union. In 1947, the United States turned to a policy of *containment*. Under it, the United States worked to contain, or limit, Soviet expansion and the spread of communism.

What was the Truman Doctrine? the Marshall Plan?

This change in American thinking was shown in the Truman Doctrine of 1947. In it, Truman said that the United States would aid countries in danger of being taken over by Communists. Congress agreed and ordered $400 million in military aid sent to Greece and Turkey. In June 1947, Secretary of State George Marshall set forth a plan to help restore Europe's economy and stop the spread of communism. It was known as the Marshall Plan, or European Recovery

A visible sign of the occupation of Germany appears at "Unity Bridge" between East Germany and West Berlin. What countries occupied Germany after its defeat in World War II?

Program. It offered aid to all European countries, including the Soviet Union. Under the plan, $17 billion would be spent over four years. The plan went into effect in 1948.

The Soviets refused to take part in the Marshall Plan and pressured other countries to follow them. They formed their own plan to help the Eastern European countries they controlled. The Soviets, however, had lost so much during the war that they could give little aid to others. Because of this, their plan did not have the impact of the Marshall Plan.

2.3 The Berlin Blockade. The chief struggle between the Western powers and the Soviet Union came over Germany. The Western powers had slowly moved toward forming a self-governing, economically strong German state. The Soviets were not in favor of this idea. They wanted to keep control over their zone in Germany.

Matters came to a head on June 7, 1948. The Western powers stated that they were going to set up a new government in West Germany. The Soviets said that this went against the 1945 agreement made at Potsdam. On June 24, they began a tight blockade of all land

and water routes into Berlin. They hoped that this would force the Western powers out of the city.

To avoid the blockade, the Western powers organized an *airlift*—a system of bringing in supplies by airplane. American and British pilots made over 272,000 flights to Berlin, delivering 2.3 million tons of supplies. In May 1949, the Soviet Union lifted the blockade. In the same year, two separate governments were set up in Germany. West Germany became the German Federal Republic with its capital in Bonn. East Germany became the German Democratic Republic.

How did the Western powers counteract the Berlin blockade?

2.4 The NATO Alliance.   The Berlin blockade alarmed Western leaders. They believed the Truman Doctrine and the Marshall Plan would not provide a strong enough defense against the Soviet Union. In April 1949, the United States and 11 other countries signed a treaty setting up the North Atlantic Treaty Organization (NATO). NATO's first members, besides the United States, were Canada, Great Britain, France, Norway, Denmark, Iceland, the Netherlands, Luxembourg, Belgium, Italy, and Portugal. Greece, Turkey, and West Germany joined later. The members of NATO supported the United Nations and agreed to settle differences through peaceful means. They also agreed that an attack on one of them would be seen as an attack against them all. Such an attack would be met with armed force, if necessary.

What nations belong to NATO?

1. Where did Nationalists and Communists clash in Europe?
2. What was the American policy of containment?
3. Why did the Soviets blockade Berlin?
4. What was the purpose of NATO?

3. Troubles in the Far East

Troubles in the postwar world were not found only in Europe. As the United States was seeking to stop the Soviets in the West, Communists made efforts to expand in the Far East. This added to the growing tension between the East and the West.

3.1 Communist China.   China came out of World War II a divided country. The Nationalist party, under Chiang Kai-shek, headed the government. At the same time, the Chinese Communist party, led by Mao Tse-tung, controlled nearly one fourth of the country's population. The two parties had been fighting for control of China since

Who led the Chinese Communists?

Communism, 1955

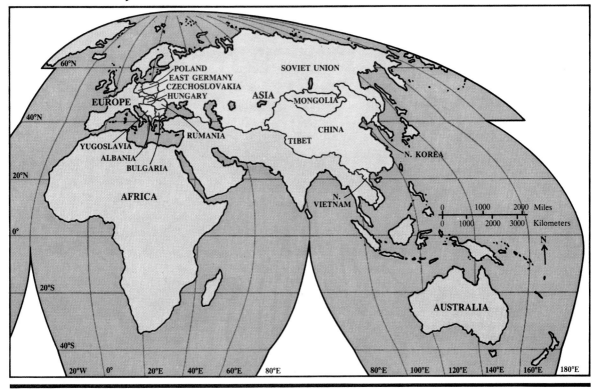

In 1955, communism was confined to Europe and Asia. What European countries had Communist governments? What Asian countries had Communist governments? How did the United States hope to stop the spread of communism in the world?

1927. During World War II, they had stood together against the Japanese. With Japan's surrender, however, civil war broke out again in 1947.

In this war, the Soviet Union backed the Communists, while the United States aided the Nationalists. However, the Nationalists steadily lost ground. By 1949, the Communists had driven them from the mainland to the island of Formosa (Taiwan).

On October 1, 1949, the People's Republic of China was set up under Mao Tse-tung. Great Britain, France, the Soviet Union, and several other countries recognized Mao Tse-tung's new government. The United States, however, refused to do so and continued to recognize Chiang Kai-shek's government. The Soviet Union wanted Mao Tse-tung's government to represent China in the UN. When the United States blocked this, the Soviet Union boycotted the Security Council.

When was Communist China established?

Cold War and Crisis   605

How did the war in Korea start?

3.2 The Korean War. East-West relations grew even worse over events in Korea. On June 25, 1950, the North Korean army attacked South Korea. They wanted to join all of the country under Communist rule. On June 27, President Truman ordered American naval and air forces to support South Korea.

At the UN, the Security Council called on all members to aid South Korea. Because of its boycott, the Soviet Union was not present to veto the UN action. About 15 countries, along with the United States and the Republic of Korea, sent soldiers. However, Americans made up about 48 percent and South Koreans about 43 percent of the fighting force. It was led by General Douglas MacArthur.

For a time, it seemed that the North Koreans would overrun the South. They took Seoul, the capital of South Korea, on June 28. By early August, they had pushed the UN troops back to a small area around Pusan on the southern coast. The tide began to turn in

With an armistice established in Korea in 1953, most of the fighting ended, and prisoners of war were exchanged. What was the farthest Communist advance? What was the farthest United Nations advance? Where was the armistice line?

War in Korea

September. General MacArthur staged a landing at Inchon, behind North Korean lines. Seoul was quickly recaptured, and UN forces drove the North Koreans back across the 38th parallel.

What occurred militarily in Korea?

Late in November, UN forces had pushed the North Koreans back to the Yalu River. Victory seemed at hand. Then 250,000 Chinese troops entered the fighting on the side of North Korea. They quickly drove the UN forces back south of the 38th parallel. MacArthur wanted to attack China itself. But President Truman decided against this as it would mean an all-out war that could involve the Soviet Union. He wanted to maintain a *limited war policy* and not risk potential nuclear war. When MacArthur objected to Truman's decision, the President replaced him with General Matthew Ridgway. In the spring of 1951, UN troops again drove the Communists north across the 38th parallel.

Peace talks began at Kaesong in July 1951. But they soon broke down. Talks began again at Panmunjom in October and lasted until July 1953, when an armistice was signed. In three years of fighting, American casualties numbered 54,000 killed and 103,000 wounded. The fighting ended almost where it began—at the 38th parallel. Many Americans were upset that no clear victory had been won. Communist expansion into South Korea, however, had been checked.

Where were peace talks held?

1. Why was China a divided country?
2. What caused the war in Korea?
3. Where was Korea divided?

4. The Postwar Years at Home

After World War II, the United States faced problems at home as well as abroad. American men and women in the armed forces had to be returned to civilian life. The economy had to be changed from wartime to peacetime purposes. There was also the question of the continued growth of government and the role it would play in postwar America.

4.1 From War to Peace. One of the first tasks of the government after World War II was to cut the size of the armed forces. The army had over 8 million people in August 1945. At the outbreak of the Korean War in 1950, it was down to about 600,000.

The Servicemen's Readjustment Act of 1944, or G-I Bill, helped members of the armed forces. Under this act, the government granted money to former service people to go to college, open businesses, or receive further job training.

What did the G-I Bill provide?

A second task facing the United States after the war was to change industry over to peacetime production. To do this, the government sold many of its war plants to private companies. Factories which had made military supplies began making consumer goods again. By the end of 1945, 93 percent of all the war plants had been changed or shut down.

Many people thought the change to peacetime production would bring a depression. However, most Americans enjoyed greater prosperity after the war, although minority groups did not share it fully.

What economic problem developed after World War II?

One problem during these years was inflation. By the end of the war, Americans had saved over $130 billion and were eager to spend this money. For a time, goods were still scarce. Prices began to rise in spite of government controls. For more than a year after the war, Truman kept controls on prices. In late 1946, however, they were ended by Congress. After that, prices rose rapidly.

4.2 Labor After the War. Rising prices led to demands for higher pay. In the years after the war, a growing number of labor strikes took place. In many cases, industry met the demands of workers. But prices of goods were then raised to cover higher costs. This led to a new rise in the cost of living which, in turn, led to demands for even higher wages.

Why did a number of labor strikes take place after World War II?

Strikes after World War II led to growing demands for stronger government controls over labor. In 1947, the Taft-Hartley Act was passed. It outlawed the ***closed shop,*** where workers had to join a union before being hired. The act gave the President the power to call for an 80-day ***"cooling-off" period*** when a strike threatened the country's welfare. This meant that workers could not strike for 80 days. The new law also stopped unions from giving money to political candidates.

The Taft-Hartley Act alarmed the unions. It made it harder for them to organize new workers. In spite of this, the number of members grew from 14.7 million in 1945 to over 15 million in 1950. Unions had come to be an accepted part of the American economy.

Why were unions against the Taft-Hartley Act?

4.3 The Election of 1948. When Harry Truman took office in 1945, he wanted to carry on the programs of the New Deal. This proved to be difficult, as many people were moving away from the idea of big government. The Republicans won control of Congress in 1946, and things became even harder for Truman. Republicans wanted the government to play a less active role in the economy. They worked to block many of Truman's ideas.

As the presidential election of 1948 drew nearer, the Republicans were sure they would win. Truman was running for another term, but the Democratic vote would be divided three ways. A group of southern Democrats known as Dixiecrats were against the party's stand on civil

Election of 1948

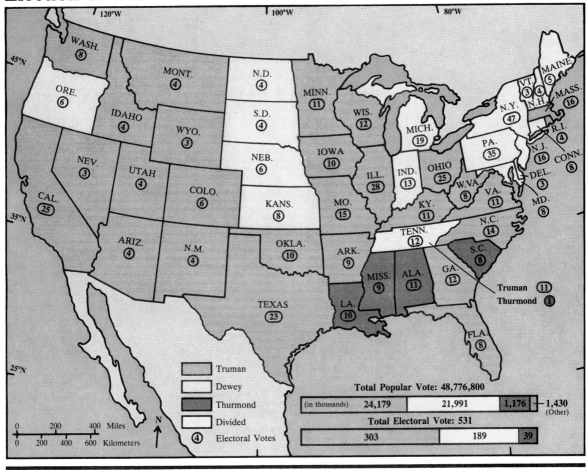

In the 1948 presidential election, what political parties did each candidate represent? What section of the United States did the Dixiecrat candidate seem to have the strongest support?

rights. They broke away from the party and supported Governor Strom Thurmond of South Carolina for President. A small group of liberals felt that Truman did not push hard enough for new reforms. They formed a new Progressive party and backed former Vice-President Henry Wallace.

Why did the Democratic party become split in 1948?

Truman refused to admit defeat. He traveled thousands of miles around the country and gave hundreds of speeches. Truman won a surprise victory over Governor Thomas Dewey of New York, the Republican choice. Truman received 24.1 million to Dewey's 22 million popular votes. He won 304 to Dewey's 189 electoral votes.

Who was favored to win the election of 1948? Who won?

Harry Truman (left) is shown smiling over an early announcement of the 1948 election outcome that was wrong. Dwight Eisenhower (right) is shown on the campaign trail in 1952. Whom did each candidate defeat to become President?

4.4 The Fair Deal. After his victory, Truman set forth a broad plan of reform, known as the Fair Deal. It called for new programs in education, health care, and housing. Truman also wanted to extend social security and to stop discrimination in employment.

Republicans and southern Democrats in Congress joined together to defeat much of the Fair Deal. In 1949, however, the National Housing Act was passed. It gave the government power to clear slums and build low-income housing. In August 1950, Congress extended social security to 10 million more workers.

How did the Fair Deal work?

In 1952, Truman stated that he would not run for office again. The Democrats then chose Governor Adlai Stevenson of Illinois as their candidate. The Republicans chose General Dwight Eisenhower. Eisenhower won by 33.9 million to 27.3 million popular votes and 442 to 89 electoral votes. His election marked the return of the Republican party to the White House after 20 years.

1. How were World War II veterans aided?
2. What did the Taft-Hartley Act attempt to do?
3. What was President Truman's Fair Deal?

5. The Eisenhower Years

When Eisenhower took office in 1952, the United States was prosperous. President Eisenhower was a popular figure, and the American mood was positive. At the same time, there was much tension about the cold war.

5.1 The Cold War at Home. Americans feared communism not only abroad but also at home. They saw the Communist victory in China and the testing of the Soviet Union's first atomic bomb. They watched the trial of Julius and Ethel Rosenberg, who were accused of passing atomic secrets to the Soviets. All of these things added to Americans' tension. They also led some Americans to question the loyalty of other Americans.

What things caused some Americans to begin questioning the loyalty of other Americans?

The Smith Act had been passed in 1940. This act made it illegal to support the violent overthrow of the government or to belong to any group that did so. In 1950, the McCarran Act was passed. It said that all Communist groups had to register with the Attorney-General. It stopped people who were Communists from entering the country. It also stated that *subversives*—people who secretly work inside a country to overthrow its government—could be jailed by the President in a national emergency.

What were the provisions of the Smith Act? the McCarran Act?

Under President Eisenhower, two new laws were passed. In 1952, the McCarran-Walter Act allowed the Attorney-General to deport people whose actions were thought to be against the country's interests. Two years later, the Communist Control Act outlawed the Communist party.

Besides passing laws, the government also took other steps to defend itself from communism. During and after World War II, Presidents Roosevelt and Truman ordered government workers checked to be sure they were not Communists. Eisenhower, too, tried to remove Communists from government jobs.

Although many Americans favored such steps, some people felt that they violated citizens' rights. Concern grew in the early 1950's. During that time, Senator Joseph McCarthy of Wisconsin charged that there were Communists in the State Department and in the military. These charges were never proved. But many Americans were frightened by what they heard.

What did Senator McCarthy do?

In 1954, a Senate committee was formed to look into McCarthy's charges against the army. Millions of Americans watched the hearings on television. McCarthy had little or no evidence to back up his charges. Many Americans were angered over the manner in which he treated

Senator Joseph McCarthy tries to make a point at a Senate committee hearing in 1954. Millions of Americans watched McCarthy at the hearing on television. What was McCarthy attempting to prove?

witnesses. Because of his actions, McCarthy lost most of his support. The Senate voted to condemn his actions, and the public turned against him.

What was the Eisenhower approach?

5.2 The Eisenhower Approach.   Eisenhower did not support McCarthy, but he took no direct action to stop him. Eisenhower also used this "middle-of-the-road" approach in dealing with other issues. Not all members of his party agreed with this way of doing things.

Some Republicans wanted to end many New Deal and Fair Deal measures. President Eisenhower made no move to do so. Instead, he supported those that expanded social security and low-cost housing programs. Eisenhower also favored the support of Big Business and named business people to his Cabinet. He generally favored private enterprise. In 1955, for example, Eisenhower tried to have a private company (instead of TVA) build a power plant for Memphis, Tennessee. The plan was defeated by Congress.

5.3 A New Beginning in Civil Rights.   Events during Eisenhower's years in office caused him to take steps that made a new start for government support of civil rights. In 1954, the Supreme Court ruled on the case of *Brown* v. *Board of Education of Topeka*. The Court overturned the "separate but equal" idea set forth in the 1896 case of *Plessy* v. *Ferguson*. In the Brown case, the Court held that segregation in the public schools denied black students equal protection under the Fourteenth Amendment. Chief Justice Earl Warren wrote:

[Education] *is the very foundation of good citizenship. Today it is a principal instrument in awakening the child to cultural values, in preparing him for later professional training, and in helping him to adjust normally to his environment. In these days, it is doubtful that any child may reasonably be expected to succeed in life if he is denied the opportunity of an education. Such an opportunity . . . is a right which must be made available to all on equal terms.*

In 1955, the Supreme Court ordered *desegregation*—the ending of segregation—of public schools. This order upset many whites, especially in the South where most public schools were segregated by law. Southern leaders tried many ways to prevent desegregation of the schools. In 1957, Governor Orval Faubus of Arkansas used the National Guard to keep black students from entering Central High School in Little Rock. President Eisenhower acted to back up the Court's order by sending federal troops to Little Rock.

When did desegregation begin?

It soon became clear that court action alone would not end segregation. A number of blacks turned to more direct action. On December 1, 1955, in Montgomery, Alabama, Rosa Parks refused to leave her seat on a bus so a white man could sit. Parks was arrested. Blacks in Montgomery, led by the Reverend Martin Luther King, Jr., boycotted buses in the city for over a year. During this time, the homes of several blacks were bombed. Finally, the Supreme Court ruled that

What took place in Montgomery, Alabama?

Rosa Parks (right) sits in the front of a Montgomery city bus after a Supreme Court ruling which banned segregation on the city's buses took effect on December 21, 1955. On December 1, Mrs. Parks was arrested for sitting in a bus area reserved for white passengers. How did blacks in Montgomery react to Parks' arrest?

the Montgomery law, which segregated seating on buses, was unconstitutional.

In addition, Congress moved to end restrictions on voting. It passed the Civil Rights Acts of 1957 and 1960. The 1957 act allowed the Attorney-General to bring suit for blacks who were denied their right to vote. The 1960 act allowed federal judges to appoint an officer to supervise voter registration. It also set penalties for bombing and bomb threats.

What did the Civil Rights Acts of 1957 and 1960 permit?

What were sit-ins?

In the late 1950's, blacks began working for their rights in many areas of the South. Voter registration drives were held. Some students began *sit-ins*. The students would sit in a section reserved for whites at a lunch counter or other business. They would not leave until they were served. More and more blacks joined in working to end segregation. Many whites resisted them. Often violence was directed against blacks. The struggle for civil rights would go on long after the Eisenhower years.

1. Why did Senator McCarthy investigate the State Department and the military?
2. How did the *Brown* v. *Board of Education of Topeka* decision affect the civil rights of blacks?
3. What did the Montgomery bus boycott accomplish?

6. Changing Foreign Policy

The struggle against communism lasted through the Eisenhower years. However, during this time, a change in the nature of the cold war took place. The late 1950's were marked by *oscillation*—a hardening and softening in attitudes and relations—on the part of the United States and the Soviet Union.

What change took place in the cold war in the late 1950's?

6.1 Commitment to Southeast Asia. President Eisenhower believed that it was necessary to stop the spread of communism in Southeast Asia. In the spring of 1954, Secretary of State John Foster Dulles put forth the *domino theory*. This said that the countries of Southeast Asia were like dominoes. If one fell to communism, the countries next to it would soon do the same. Eisenhower and Dulles were interested chiefly in Vietnam, which had been part of French Indochina. After World War II, the French were defeated by the Viet Minh, a nationalist group. The group was led by Ho Chi Minh and was made up largely of Communists.

Ralph Bunche (1904–1971)
═══ PROFILE ═══

Ralph Bunche was a peacemaker. At the United Nations, he, naturally enough, worked as a mediator.

In 1949, Bunche negotiated a peace settlement in the Middle East between Israelis and Egyptians. For that work, he received the Nobel Peace Prize. Throughout the 1960's, Bunche worked for peace in the Congo and in Cyprus. He also guided many African countries toward independence.

Bunche wanted to develop understanding among nations and to encourage international harmony. It seemed odd that the international peacemaker and mediator found one of the greatest challenges to peace in his own country. Harmony in the United States was unsettled by racial discrimination and segregation.

In 1959, Bunche became involved in an issue concerning his son and a private club's unwritten rule against admitting blacks. Bunche made the club's discrimination a broad issue for racial peace in the United States. He wrote, "No [black] American can be free until the lowliest [black]. . . is no longer disadvantaged because of . . . race."

As Undersecretary of the United Nations, Ralph Bunche saw a close connection between good will and harmony. He knew it helped in foreign conflicts, and he hoped it would be tried in conflicts at home.

A conference was held in Geneva, Switzerland, in 1954. Delegates from the United States, France, Great Britain, the Soviet Union, Communist China, Cambodia, Laos, and two groups from Vietnam attended. In the agreement which came out of the meeting, Vietnam was to be divided at the 17th parallel. A Communist government would be in control of the north and a non-Communist government in the south. In 1956, elections would be held to unite the country. Neither the Americans nor the South Vietnamese signed the agreements made at Geneva. They felt that these agreements gave the Communists a base of operation in Southeast Asia.

What were the 1954 Geneva Accords?

Following the Geneva talks, the United States supported the idea of an alliance like NATO for Southeast Asia. In September 1954, the

United States, Great Britain, France, Australia, New Zealand, Pakistan, Thailand, and the Philippines formed the Southeast Asia Treaty Organization (SEATO). These countries promised to aid each other in case of attack. They also agreed to protect South Vietnam and other countries in Indochina.

What nations belonged to SEATO?

6.2 Tensions in the Middle East.

Much of the Middle East was controlled by Great Britain and France until after World War II. Weakened by the war, both countries gave up most of their power there. The United States and the Soviet Union took great interest in the area. Both needed the area's oil. The Soviets also hoped to gain a naval base on the Mediterranean Sea.

Why was the Soviet Union interested in the Middle East?

When did Israel become an independent nation?

In 1948, the Jewish state of Israel was formed on part of the land of Palestine. Arab and Muslim people made up most of the population of Palestine. They fought the Jews over this land for many years. The Jews were able to defend their new state and took more land in these wars.

Egypt, an Arab country, began to build up its armed forces in the early 1950's. In 1956, Egypt took over the Suez Canal, which had been held by the British and the French. The Egyptian actions angered Great Britain and France because the canal was important for their trade. When Israel attacked Egypt in 1956, France and Great Britain also attacked. Although allied with Great Britain and France, the United States decided not to enter the fighting. Eisenhower had the matter brought before the UN, and the countries agreed to withdraw from Egypt.

What was the Suez crisis?

The United States feared that the Soviet Union would move into the Middle East to take the place of France and Great Britain. In 1957, the President put forth the Eisenhower Doctrine. It promised aid to any Middle Eastern country in danger of Communist attack. This meant both economic aid and military support. In this way, containment was extended to another area of the world.

Where was the Eisenhower Doctrine put to use?

In 1958, Eisenhower put his doctrine into practice. The Lebanese government asked for American help to stop a takeover by forces backed by Egypt and the Soviet Union. Eisenhower sent American marines to Lebanon. Because of this aid, Lebanon remained independent.

6.3 A New Interest in Latin America.

The United States was also interested in Latin America in the 1950's. When a government favoring communism came to power in Guatemala, the American Central Intelligence Agency (CIA) took action. It backed an anti-Communist group. With CIA help, this group gained control of the Guatemalan government in 1954.

Who helped to put down a Communist takeover in Guatemala?

Secretary of State Dulles (left) meets with Soviet Party Chief Khrushchev (right) and Soviet Premier Bulganin (center). In the cartoon, President Eisenhower asks Dulles, "You Sure Everything's All Right?" What was Dulles' policy toward the Soviets?

In the late 1950's, fighting also broke out in Cuba over control of the government. In January 1959, Fidel Castro seized power from Fulgencio Batista. Batista had been dictator of the country since 1933. The United States recognized Castro's government and hoped for good relations with Cuba. Castro, however, set up a Communist government and began building close ties with the Soviet Union.

In February 1960, Castro signed a trade agreement with the Soviets. It allowed them to get Cuban sugar at a low price. The United States then said that it would no longer import Cuban sugar. Many Cuban businesses owned by American companies were taken over by the Cuban government. Relations grew worse, and the United States became more alarmed at the Communist-controlled government in the Western Hemisphere. As one of his last acts before leaving office, Eisenhower ended diplomatic relations with Cuba.

What led to trouble between the United States and Cuba?

6.4   The Course of Coexistence.   There was a great deal of tension between the United States and the Soviet Union in the 1950's. Relations between the two countries improved under Eisenhower, however. By the late 1950's, *coexistence*—each country recognizing the others' right to exist in peace—was becoming the accepted policy. This change came about after the death of Joseph Stalin in 1953. Soviet

What is coexistence?

leaders who took over after Stalin were more willing to work with Western leaders.

One of the first signs of a change in the cold war came in 1955. In July of that year, President Eisenhower, Soviet Premier N. A. Bulganin, and other world leaders met in Geneva, Switzerland. They held a *summit conference*—a meeting of the heads of government of the major world powers. The leaders talked over such problems as unifying Germany and disarmament. No specific agreements were reached. But the *"spirit of Geneva,"* or willingness of the top leaders to work together, renewed hopes for peace.

As tensions eased between the United States and the Soviet Union, there was more contact between the two countries. In 1959, the new Soviet Premier, Nikita Khrushchev, visited the United States. Shortly after this visit, plans were made for a second summit conference in Paris in mid-May 1960.

What caused the breakup of the 1960 Paris summit meeting?

On May 1, 1960, a special high-altitude American plane, called a U-2, was shot down by the Soviets. It had flown 1,200 miles (1,880 kilometers) inside their country. The plane had been photographing Soviet military bases. At the Paris meeting on May 16, 1960, Khrushchev spoke out against the spying. He demanded that the United States stop such flights. He also called for an apology from Eisenhower and a postponement of the meeting, which then broke up. The end of the summit meeting showed that coexistence had not ended the tension between the United States and the Soviet Union.

1. Why did the United States become interested in Vietnam?
2. How did President Eisenhower respond to troubles in the Middle East?
3. Who seized control of Cuba in 1959?
4. What was the "spirit of Geneva"?

7. Conclusion

By the end of the 1950's, Americans were becoming more concerned with the direction their country was taking, both at home and abroad. Some gains were made in the area of civil rights during the 1950's. At the same time, the federal government continued to look after the welfare of its people. Because of nuclear weapons and long-range missiles, the United States realized that its security was no longer protected by its geography. American leaders made greater efforts to work with other countries to keep the peace.

Chapter 25 Review

Main Points

1. After World War II, the United States became involved in the affairs of other countries in many parts of the world.
2. The United States helped to organize the UN and was a permanent member of the Security Council.
3. After fighting as allies, conflicts developed between the Soviet Union and the United States.
4. The United States attempted to prevent the expansion of communism in Europe, Asia, Latin America, and within the United States.
5. The United States became involved in a military conflict to prevent North Korea from taking over South Korea.
6. Many Americans faced problems shifting from a wartime to a peacetime economy at home.
7. Democratic President Harry Truman's programs for economic and social reform were opposed by Republicans and southern Democrats.
8. Fear of the spread of communism in the United States led to a period of support for the actions of Senator Joseph McCarthy.
9. During the middle 1950's, the civil rights movement became more active.
10. President Eisenhower's policy toward the Soviet Union was peaceful coexistence.

Building Vocabulary

1. Identify the following:

Nuremberg	38th parallel	Ho Chi Minh
United Nations	G-I Bill	Ralph Bunche
Truman Doctrine	Taft-Hartley Act	SEATO
Marshall Plan	Joseph McCarthy	Eisenhower Doctrine
NATO	Rosa Parks	Fidel Castro
Mao Tse-tung	Martin Luther King, Jr.	Nikita Khrushchev

2. Define the following:

organs	limited war policy	sit-ins
trust territories	closed shop	oscillation
cold war	"cooling-off" period	domino theory
satellite nations	subversives	coexistence
containment	desegregation	summit conference
airlift		"spirit of Geneva"

Remembering the Facts

1. What actions were taken against German and Japanese military leaders?
2. How were Germany and Japan governed by the Allies?
3. What was the purpose of the UN?
4. What did the Marshall Plan seek to do?
5. How did the Western powers react to the Soviet Union stopping all land and water transportation into Berlin?
6. How did the United Nations deal with the conflict in Korea?
7. What reform plans did President Truman have for the United States?
8. What was done to prevent subversion within the United States?
9. What was the Supreme Court's decision in the *Brown* v. *Board of Education of Topeka* case?
10. How did blacks attempt to gain civil rights?
11. What caused tensions in Southeast Asia, Cuba, and the Middle East?

Understanding the Facts

1. Why was the United States more interested in joining the United Nations than it had been in joining the League of Nations?
2. How did the United States become involved in the war in Korea?
3. Why did a fear of communism in the United States develop? What dangers did it cause for constitutional rights?
4. How was *Brown* v. *Board of Education of Topeka* a step toward the aims of the Fifteenth Amendment?

Using Maps

Goode's Projection. Besides the Mercator and Mollweide Projections, mapmakers use other systems for reproducing the round earth as a flat map. Another projection is Goode's Interrupted Projection. Only the full continents of the Mollweide Projection are used, and oceans are cut. This makes an equal-area map with little distortion of land shapes. This projection is commonly used for world or hemispheric maps.

The map on page 605 is drawn using Goode's Projection. Compare it to the Mollweide Projection map on page 566 in Chapter 24. Study both maps, and answer the following questions.

1. What areas are the same on both maps?
2. How are the maps different? Why?
3. What are the advantages of using one map over the other map?
4. How successful was the Soviet Union in expanding its influence in Europe?
5. How did the land area influenced by the Soviet Union compare to the area held by the People's Republic of China?

Years of Hope
and Tension

26

John F. Kennedy won the Democratic nomination for President on the first ballot at the 1960 convention in Los Angeles. How did his New Frontier plan for government action offer a spirit of hope for many Americans?

The 1960's opened with a spirit of hope and unity among the American people. They seemed willing to face new problems both at home and elsewhere. But by the end of the decade, many tensions challenged the American spirit.

1. The New Frontier

President Eisenhower's second term ended in 1960. Eisenhower was as popular as ever, but there were signs that the policies of his party were not. Democrats had gained seats in the House of Representatives in 1956 and 1958. The 1960 presidential election promised to be a close one.

1.1 The Election of 1960. In 1960, Republicans chose Vice-President Richard Nixon to run for President. Nixon had served in the Senate and the House of Representatives. He had been Vice-President for eight years. The Democrats chose Senator John Kennedy of Massachusetts.

What was unique about the election of 1960?

In the fall of 1960, Kennedy's advisors set up four hour-long television debates between Nixon and Kennedy. Many Americans were impressed by Kennedy in the debates. In the election, he defeated Nixon by just over 100,000 popular votes—one of the smallest margins since the 1800's—and only one tenth of a percentage point. Kennedy became the first Catholic and the youngest person ever to be elected President of the United States.

1.2 The Program at Home. Once he took office, Kennedy made clear his feelings about a President's role. Unlike Eisenhower, he felt a President should play an active part in meeting the country's needs. In his inaugural address, Kennedy told the American people:

Let the word go forth from this time and place, to friend and foe alike, that the torch has been passed to a new generation of Americans—born in this century, tempered by war, disciplined by a hard and bitter peace, proud of our ancient heritage—and unwilling to witness or permit the slow undoing of those human rights to which this nation has always been committed. . . .

And so, my fellow Americans: ask not what your country can do for you—ask what you can do for your country.

What was the New Frontier?

Kennedy offered a program for government action which he called the New Frontier. Only a few of his plans were passed by Congress while he was in office, however. The minimum wage was raised from $1.00 to

$1.25 an hour over two years. More people were covered by social security. In May 1961, the Area Redevelopment Act was passed. It provided for loans and federal grants to areas of the country with many poor people and few jobs. In June 1963, the Higher Education Facilities Act was passed. It gave colleges money to improve their buildings or construct new ones.

One area in which Congress was very interested was the space program. Americans began to think more about outer space in 1957. That year, the Soviet Union launched the first successful *satellite*—a small object circling a planet—to orbit the earth. It was called Sputnik I. This was a blow to the United States. It led many Americans to fear that the Soviet Union had more scientific knowledge than did the United States. Because of this, the National Defense Education Act was passed in 1958. It gave colleges and college students federal money for studies in science and languages. That same year, the National Aeronautics and Space Administration (NASA) was set up to direct the American space program.

What Soviet achievement was a blow to American prestige?

When President Kennedy took office, he announced that he wanted Americans to land a person on the moon before 1970. That goal was reached by Neil Armstrong and Edwin Aldrin in 1969. On July 20, Armstrong became the first human to step on the moon. As he did so, he said "That's one small step for a man, one giant leap for mankind." Millions of people around the world watched the event on live television.

Who was the first person on the moon?

1.3 The Growth of Black Civil Rights. When Kennedy took office, he hesitated to push hard for civil rights for blacks. He thought that if he did, he would lose support for other important programs.

Still, while Kennedy was in office, some steps were taken that helped blacks. In 1962, against the wishes of the governor of Mississippi, the Supreme Court ordered that James Meredith, a black student, be allowed to enter the University of Mississippi. That year, Kennedy banned discrimination in housing built or bought with federal aid. With the backing of both the President and his brother, Attorney-General Robert Kennedy, the Department of Justice worked to carry out the Civil Rights Laws of 1957 and 1960. It brought 50 court suits in four southern states to get voting rights for blacks.

What gains in civil rights were made during the Kennedy administration?

The actions taken by Kennedy and the government came about in large part because of pressure from blacks. Black leaders wanted Congress and the American people to know they opposed segregation and discrimination. They organized and held *demonstrations*—public displays of feelings by a group toward a policy, a cause, or a person—in several cities. In August 1963, Martin Luther King, Jr., and other black

Martin Luther King, Jr., spoke to a crowd of nearly 200,000 people who had marched on Washington in 1963. Why did these people come to Washington? About what did King speak?

leaders led a march on Washington, D.C. Some 200,000 people gathered near the Lincoln Memorial. They heard King speak of his dreams for American blacks.

1.4   The Program Abroad.   At the same time the government was busy with civil rights at home, it was also working on foreign policy. Like Eisenhower, Kennedy planned to take a hard stand against communism. But he also wanted better American relations with the other countries of the world. To do this, the Peace Corps was formed in 1961. It trained Americans and sent them to countries in need of skilled workers. There, they helped the people with public health, education, agriculture, and other areas. More than 13,000 Americans took part in the program in its first year.

What steps did Kennedy take to improve relations abroad?

That same year, the Alliance for Progress was formed. Under it, the United States and Latin American countries agreed to work together during the next ten years. They would help industry grow and improve education, agriculture, and public services in Latin America. One fifth of the $100 billion it had to spend came from the United States.

Freedom

Freedom and liberty are two important American ideals. When the Stamp Act was at issue in 1775, Patrick Henry of Virginia said, "I know not what course others may take; but as for me, give me liberty, or give me death!" In 1851, Ernestine Rose, a women's rights activist, asked, "For what is life without liberty, and what is liberty without equality of rights?"

In the early 1960's, some people in the United States were not free to vote or to enjoy other rights as American citizens. It was this liberty without equality of rights that led to an organized civil rights movement.

On August 28, 1963, over 200,000 people took part in a march on Washington, D.C. They wanted to show the nation's lawmakers that there was broad support for needed civil rights legislation. Near the Lincoln Memorial, Martin Luther King, Jr., foremost leader of the movement, spoke to the crowd. He stated many of his own hopes for the future of the United States.

I say to you today, my friends, so even though we face the difficulties of today and tomorrow, I still have a dream. . . . I have a dream that one day this nation will rise up and live out the true meaning of its creed, "We hold these truths to be self-evident, that all men are created equal." I have a dream that one day on the . . . hills of Georgia, sons of former slaves and the sons of former slave owners will be able to sit down together at the table of brotherhood. . . . I have a dream that my four little children will one day live in a nation where they will not be judged by the color of their skin, but by the content of their character. . . .

And when this happens . . . we will be able to speed up that day when all God's children, [black and white], Jews and gentiles, Protestants and Catholics, will be able to join hands and sing in the words of the old Negro spiritual: "Free at last. Free at last. Thank God Almighty, we are free at last."

1. Based on this speech, what does freedom mean to Martin Luther King, Jr.?
2. Was King only concerned with freedom for people in the South?
3. Who did King think should benefit from freedom?
4. What prevented blacks from enjoying the freedom and liberty that was available to other American citizens?

President Kennedy (left) wanted the Peace Corps to stress personal contact more than any other foreign aid program. A medical clinic in Guatemala (right) cared for local health needs. For what other needs did Peace Corps workers care?

1.5 The Cuban Missile Crisis. Meanwhile, trouble was brewing in Cuba. When Fidel Castro took over the government of Cuba, many Cubans fled to the United States. Some wanted to return to overthrow Castro. In March 1960, President Eisenhower told the CIA it could train and supply them for such an invasion. Later President Kennedy decided to go ahead with the plan.

What was the Bay of Pigs? What was the outcome?

In April 1961, Cuban refugees began making air strikes against airfields in Cuba. On April 17, more than 1,000 of them landed at the Bay of Pigs, about 90 miles (144 kilometers) from Havana. They hoped the people of Cuba would rise up against Castro. When this did not happen, the invasion failed. This greatly embarrassed the United States and at the same time helped Castro. Some Latin Americans felt the United States had no right to interfere in Cuba's affairs. They spoke out against the United States.

What occurrence in Cuba alarmed Americans?

After the Bay of Pigs, Cuba developed closer ties with the Soviet Union. The Soviet Union sent military advisors and supplies to the island. The advisors began to set up guided missile sites there. This alarmed President Kennedy and the American military. They felt that to have offensive missiles so close was a threat to the security of the United States. Some of President Kennedy's advisors wanted to bomb the missile sites, but he refused. He felt such a step might lead to a nuclear war with the Soviet Union.

On September 13, 1962, Kennedy warned that if Cuba became a military base for the Soviet Union, the United States would do "whatever must be done" to protect its security. Kennedy appeared on television on October 22. He told people that he had ordered "a strict quarantine of all offensive military equipment under shipment to Cuba." He said that he had alerted the American armed forces.

Under the *quarantine* (a type of blockade), the American navy was to stop and inspect all ships bound for Cuba from Soviet-controlled countries. It went into effect on October 24. The first Soviet ship was stopped the following day. Since the ship carried only oil, it was allowed to go on to Cuba. But the United States had shown the Soviet Union it meant what it said. On October 26, President Kennedy heard from Soviet Premier Khrushchev. In a few days, they had come to terms on Cuba. The Soviet Union agreed to remove the missiles. The United States agreed to end the quarantine and not to invade Cuba. On November 20, 1962, President Kennedy announced that the missile sites had been removed.

How was the Cuban missile crisis settled?

1.6 The Berlin Wall. In addition to the problems over Cuba, the United States and the Soviet Union still did not agree about postwar Germany. A month after the invasion at the Bay of Pigs, President Kennedy and Premier Khrushchev met in Vienna. Khrushchev told Kennedy that they should come to terms that year on a new government for Berlin. If not, the Soviet Union would sign a separate peace treaty with East Germany.

Kennedy believed that the Soviet Union wanted to drive the Western powers out of Berlin. He felt that the United States had to show the Soviets it was prepared to deal firmly with such a move. So he asked Congress for more money to buy weapons and equipment. Then he announced plans to double the draft and call up more reserves.

In August, the East Germans, with Soviet support, built a fence to seal off the border between East and West Berlin. Then they replaced the fence with a concrete wall topped with barbed wire. President Kennedy's answer to this was to send more American troops to Berlin. In October, Khrushchev agreed that the German problem did not have to be solved that year. He also said that all the Soviet Union really wanted was for the Western powers to show they were ready to settle the matter. The Berlin Wall, however, stayed up. When President Kennedy visited Berlin in 1963, he stood near the wall and told the people of West Berlin gathered there that the United States was prepared to defend their freedom.

When was the Berlin Wall built?

1.7 Heading Off War. The Berlin Wall and the Cuban missile crisis made it clear how far apart the United States and the Soviet Union were on many issues. This led many people to fear that the two powers might be heading for war. Such a war would most likely be a nuclear war. These people were strongly opposed to the A-bomb. They were worried about what nuclear testing was doing to the atmosphere. Many Americans began to favor efforts to stop the nuclear arms race.

In July 1963, the United States, the Soviet Union, and Great Britain signed the Limited Nuclear Test Ban Treaty. In it, the three powers agreed not to test nuclear weapons in the atmosphere, outer space, or underwater. Although both France and the People's Republic of China were working on their own nuclear weapons, neither of them signed the treaty. Most people in the United States were pleased with the treaty. But some Americans felt that it did not do enough because it did not stop underground testing. In a few months, however, their worries turned to an event at home which had nothing to do with war.

What step was taken in 1963 to lessen the arms race?

1.8 The Assassination of the President. In November 1963, an event in Dallas, Texas, captured American attention and shocked the nation. On November 22, President Kennedy rode in a Dallas parade with Governor John Connally and Vice-President Lyndon Johnson. As the cars moved through the city, the President was shot and killed. Within hours after his death, Judge Sarah Hughes swore in Lyndon Johnson as President.

Where was President Kennedy assassinated?

Lyndon Johnson takes the oath of office aboard the presidential airplane after President Kennedy's assassination. Lady Bird Johnson (left) and Jacqueline Kennedy (right) stand beside the new President as Judge Sarah Hughes administers the oath. When was the Kennedy assassination?

Later, Lee Harvey Oswald was caught and accused of killing Kennedy. Before Oswald could be brought to trial, he was shot and killed by Jack Ruby, a Dallas nightclub owner. There was much debate about whether Oswald had acted alone or had been part of a **conspiracy**, or group plot, to kill the President. A commission under Chief Justice Earl Warren investigated the case. After much study, it decided that Oswald had acted on his own. Over the years, doubts still remained, however. Finally, the House studied the report of the Warren Commission and held that it was not conclusive.

Why is the Kennedy assassination a subject of controversy?

1. Who were the presidential candidates in 1960?
2. What was the purpose of the 1963 march on Washington?
3. What action did the United States take to prevent Soviet missiles from being delivered to Cuba?
4. Why did the Soviet Union build the Berlin Wall?

2. The Great Society

At the time of Kennedy's death, only a small part of his programs had been passed. When Johnson took office, he was able to put through more of them. In 1964, Johnson ran for President against Barry Goldwater, a Republican Senator from Arizona. Johnson won the election by an overwhelming majority. He took it to mean that the American people agreed with his ideas. A skilled politician who had served in Congress for nearly 25 years, Johnson moved beyond the New Frontier. He presented his own program—the "Great Society."

Who were the candidates in the election of 1964?

2.1 Carrying on the Program. Not long after Kennedy's death, President Johnson called for a "war on poverty." He made it clear that like Kennedy, he wanted laws passed which would help the poor people of America lead better lives. Johnson wanted to see that many of the programs proposed by Kennedy were, in some form, put into effect.

In August 1964, Johnson was able to get the Economic Opportunity Act passed. Its goal was to fight the causes of poverty by setting up programs to help people improve their job skills and get a better education. To run the programs, the act set up the Office of Economic Opportunity (OEO). One program was the Job Corps. It trained young people for jobs. Another was Volunteers in Service to America (VISTA). Under it, teachers and social workers volunteered to work with low-income and other groups. Still another was Head Start. It helped young children from low-income families prepare for school.

What was the purpose of the Economic Opportunity Act? What did the act provide?

President Johnson also worked to pass Kennedy's civil rights law. In 1964, he succeeded. The Civil Rights Act of 1964 made it illegal to discriminate against people in the use of such public places as hotels, eating places, and parks. It also outlawed discrimination in any program that received money from the federal government. The act further said that a person could not be refused a job because of race, color, religion, national origin, or sex. To check into and judge complaints, the act set up the Equal Employment Opportunity Commission (EEOC).

2.2 The Changing Black Rights Movement. The federal government was working to help blacks through legislation. At the same time, the black movement itself was changing. During the 1950's, blacks had been concerned mostly with voting rights and school segregation in the South. In the 1960's, they began to turn their attention to the North. Many blacks there felt that the civil rights movement was doing little for them.

How did the civil rights movement change in the 1960's?

As northern blacks became more frustrated, riots broke out in black neighborhoods. In 1964, there were riots in the Harlem area of New York City and in the Watts area of Los Angeles. The Watts riot lasted for six days. During that time, 35 people were killed, and 800 were hurt. Buildings were looted and set on fire. Businesses were attacked. Many blacks, as well as whites, lost all they owned. Before long, riots also broke out in other large northern cities. In Detroit, Michigan, one left 40 people dead, 2,000 hurt, and 5,000 without homes.

What was the Kerner Commission? What were its findings?

President Johnson set up a commission headed by Illinois Governor Otto Kerner. It was to find out what was causing the riots. The Kerner Commission reported that they were brought on by frustration over bad housing, crowded conditions, not enough jobs, and the general lack of opportunity. It also said that instead of moving toward equality, the gap between whites and blacks was growing wider.

Black leaders differed on the way to deal with the situation. In March 1965, Martin Luther King led blacks and whites in a five-day march from Selma to Montgomery, Alabama. They were protesting violence and discrimination against blacks. In 1966, King began a drive for open housing in Chicago.

What new approach was advocated by some black leaders in the 1960's? How did it differ?

Some other black leaders tried a different approach to improve conditions. Stokely Carmichael, head of the Student Non-Violent Coordinating Committee, coined the phrase *"black power."* It became a popular slogan, expressing an increased push for full rights. Black power, however, did not mean the same things to all people. To some, it meant electing black officials, having a greater voice in community decisions, and teaching and learning more about black culture and

Chien Shiung Wu (1912–   )
Graciela Olivarez (1928–   )

============================PROFILE============================

More women worked outside the home during the 1950's and 1960's than during any previous decade. Job discrimination based on sex lessened. Yet, it was still rare to find many women in specialized fields. Chien Shiung Wu in physics and Graciela Olivarez in government were two people who overcame restrictions on women and on members of minority groups.

Chien Shiung Wu was born in Liu Ho, China. When she was 24, she moved to the United States. At the University of California at Berkeley, Wu earned a doctorate in physics. She taught at Smith College and Princeton University before going to Columbia University in 1952.

Wu won many distinctions for her research in nuclear forces. She was recognized, in particular, for her work in disproving the principle of parity. Accepted as a universal principle for 30 years, parity maintained that in nature, there is no difference between a right and a left side.

In 1976, Wu became president of the American Physical Society. Her awards have come from the National Academy of Sciences and from 12 universities.

Graciela Olivarez was born in Phoenix, Arizona. Her father was Spanish, and her mother was Mexican. Olivarez quit school at age 15 to take a job. She was a secretary for a short time before becoming a radio announcer. Her "action line" program helped people who had problems with government and businesses. This work led her into community service work as state antipoverty director in Arizona.

Olivarez recognized that she needed further education to be more effective in helping other people. Even though she did not finish high school, Notre Dame University offered her a scholarship. In 1970, Olivarez became the first woman graduate of Notre Dame Law School.

For a while, Olivarez taught law and directed the Institute of Social Research and Development at the University of New Mexico. In March 1977, President Jimmy Carter appointed Olivarez head of the national Community Services Administration.

The successes of Wu and Olivarez show the possibilities that exist for the United States to use the skills and talents of all its people.

history. It also meant more black-owned businesses and more black influence in schools and neighborhood groups. To others, however, it meant the setting up of all-black communities.

In 1968, Martin Luther King went to Memphis, Tennessee, to support a sanitation workers' strike. While there, he was shot and killed by James Earl Ray. Without King's leadership, the civil rights movement began to lose its unity and effectiveness.

2.3 The Mexican American Rights Movement. Mexican Americans also began to push for more rights in the 1960's. Along with others of Spanish origin, they made up the second largest minority group in the country. In the 1950's, the Community Service Organization (CSO) had worked to get Mexican Americans in the Los Angeles area to register to vote. Other groups, such as the Mexican-American Political Association, worked to elect Mexican Americans to political offices.

What group did César Chávez organize? for what purpose?

César Chávez was an early leader of the CSO. In 1963, Chávez helped organize the National Farm Workers' Association. The group joined the AFL-CIO in 1966 and became known as the United Farm Workers. Its members wanted the right to bargain for higher pay and better working conditions. They led strikes and boycotts against large companies that grew lettuce and grapes.

Other groups also were formed by Mexican Americans during the 1960's. The Alianza was begun in New Mexico by Reies López Tijerina. It worked mostly to gain back deeds to Spanish and Mexican lands lost to the federal government. The Crusade for Justice was formed in Colorado by Rodolfo Gonzales. It tried to gain more civil rights for

César Chávez leads a group of people in support of the National Farm Workers' Association. The farm workers' motto was "huelga," a Spanish word for strike. They marched in groups to show their unity and strength. What did Chávez help to accomplish for Mexican American farm workers?

Mexican Americans. In 1970, a new political party called La Raza Unida was set up in Texas by José Angel Gutiérrez.

2.4 Expanding the Program. While Mexican Americans and other groups were trying to help themselves, President Johnson was working to make life better for all Americans. Between 1965 and 1968, he was able to get many new programs through Congress. One was the Elementary and Secondary School Act of 1965. It gave $1.3 billion to schools on the basis of the number of needy children in each district. This was the first large-scale federal aid ever given to schools. The Higher Education Act of 1965 allowed federal money for college scholarships for the first time.

How was education helped under the Johnson administration?

The Voting Rights Act of 1965 did away with literacy tests as a means of deciding who could vote. It also gave federal officers the power to register people to vote in areas where local authorities were keeping them from doing so. A new medical insurance was added to the social security program in 1965. One part, called Medicare, helped people 65 and over pay their medical bills. Another part, called Medicaid, helped low-income families pay theirs.

A new Cabinet office was also set up in 1965. Called the Department of Housing and Urban Development (HUD), it was headed by Robert Weaver. He was the first black Cabinet Secretary in the federal government. The Model Cities Act of 1966 gave cities money to rebuild run-down areas and to pay for city planning. The Open Housing Law of 1966 made it against the law to discriminate in the sale or rental of housing.

Who was the first black Cabinet Secretary?

More acts were passed in 1968. They gave the states money to improve their law enforcement and criminal justice agencies. They provided low-income families with places to live. They also set aside land for national parks and called for the cleaning up of polluted air and water. In three years, President Johnson had pushed through more programs than any other President before him except Franklin Roosevelt.

2.5 New Directions in Immigration. As President, Johnson also turned his attention to the country's immigration policy. Immigration patterns had been changing in the United States since the end of World War II. At that time, several special acts had been passed to allow *displaced persons*—those who have been forced to leave their country because of political reasons—to enter the United States.

Some 400,000 Europeans came into the country under the Displaced Persons Act of 1948. In 1952, the McCarran-Walter Act lifted the ban against Asian and Pacific peoples. That same year, Puerto Rico became a United States *commonwealth*—a country with local self-government but united under another country. In time, nearly

What major groups of people came into the United States in the late 1940's and 1950's?

500,000 Puerto Ricans entered the United States. The next year, the Refugee Relief Act was passed. Under it, hundreds of thousands of refugees from Communist areas came to the United States. Over 20,000 Hungarians came in under the act in 1956. They fled their homeland after a Soviet invasion put down a revolt against the Hungarian Communist government in power.

The new immigration law passed in 1965 under Johnson changed the old quota system which favored western and northern European immigrants. It limited the number of people who could enter the United States each year from the Western Hemisphere to 120,000. It also did away with the limit for each country. It set the number of people who could enter from the Eastern Hemisphere at 170,000. No more than 20,000 could enter from any eastern country.

1. How did Lyndon Johnson become President?
2. What were the main provisions of the Civil Rights Act of 1964?
3. What groups were organized to work for the civil rights of Mexican Americans?
4. According to revised immigration laws, how many people could enter the United States each year?

3. The Strain of Intervention

When President Johnson took office, American foreign policy still was aimed at keeping communism from spreading. Because of this, the United States became involved in many different parts of the world during the Johnson years. This, in turn, put a great strain on American relations with other countries and on the unity of the American people.

3.1 Intervention in the Caribbean. One area where the United States became involved was the Caribbean. In April 1965, there was a revolt in the Dominican Republic. President Johnson ordered more than 20,000 American troops into the area. He claimed that Communists were trying to set up a Communist dictatorship there. This, he felt, gave the United States the right of *intervention*—to interfere in the affairs of another nation. Many people in the United States, as well as most Latin Americans, did not agree. They said the United States should not have acted without first talking it over with Latin American leaders. Also, many people felt there was not enough evidence of Communist involvement to make such an action necessary.

Why did the United States intervene in the Dominican Republic in 1965?

The revolt in the Dominican Republic ended in August 1965. A government friendly to the United States was set up, and the next year, free elections were held. A short time later, American soldiers in the Dominican Republic were called home.

3.2 Conflict in the Middle East.   In 1967, American attention turned from the Caribbean to the Middle East. War had broken out there in June between the Arabs and the Israelis. The United States announced that it was neutral. The Soviet Union said it would not intervene unless the United States did.

On June 10, six days after the war had begun, a *cease-fire* went into effect. This was a temporary agreement to stop fighting. By this time, the Israelis had taken part of Syria and Jordan, including the Old City of Jerusalem. Both the Arabs and the Israelis needed more weapons and supplies. The Soviet Union began to supply the Arab air forces. Israel turned to the United States for help. After much debate, the United States agreed to sell Israel jet fighter-bombers. It became Israel's chief source of military supplies.

How did the Six-Day War involve the United States and the Soviet Union?

The Six-Day War did not settle the Arab-Israeli conflict. However, it did involve both the United States and the Soviet Union in the Middle East. This worried many people. They feared that the Arab-Israeli conflict could lead to world war.

3.3 Buildup in Vietnam.   While the Arabs and Israelis were in conflict in the Middle East, the South Vietnamese and Communists were at war in Southeast Asia. In 1955, the first American advisors were sent to South Vietnam to train their army. Both Eisenhower and Kennedy sent more troops and military supplies between 1956 and 1962.

When did Americans first become involved in Vietnam?

By the time Johnson became President, a group of Vietnamese Communists called the Vietcong were well established in South Vietnam. They fought as *guerrillas*—bands who make war by harassment and sabotage. The Vietcong were getting help from North Vietnam.

In August 1964, after an attack on American warships by North Vietnamese gunboats, President Johnson asked Congress to allow him to take steps to prevent any future attacks. Congress replied by passing the Gulf of Tonkin Resolution. It allowed the President, as commander in chief, to use any measures necessary to halt an attack on American forces, stop North Vietnamese aggression, and aid any SEATO member who asked for help defending its freedom.

What event caused the American build-up in Vietnam?

In February and March 1965, Vietcong attacks killed several Americans. This led President Johnson to order air strikes against targets in North Vietnam. He also sent more troops to South Vietnam.

War in Vietnam

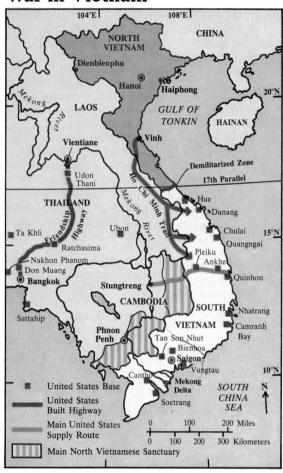

As fighting in Vietnam went on, many refugees (right) fled their homes. What elements on the map highlight factors that affected military operations and contributed to spread the fighting to other countries in Southeast Asia?

By 1968, there were more than 500,000 American troops there. The war was thought to be costing the United States about $25 billion a year.

3.4 The Antiwar Movement. As the number of Americans wounded and killed in Vietnam grew, so did the number of Americans against the war. College students especially were against it. All over the country, demonstrations took place. In 1967, more than 100,000 people took part in an antiwar parade in New York City. That same year, more than 50,000 paraded in San Francisco, and some 55,000 marched from the Lincoln Memorial to the Pentagon in Washington, D.C.

What did the war in Vietnam bring about in the United States?

The war in Vietnam caused a split among the American people. Many felt the war was necessary to stop communism. Others felt that it was a civil war which should be settled by the Vietnamese. Still others felt the money spent on the war could be put to better use at home. Congress also was divided between *"hawks"*—those who favored greater military effort—and *"doves"*—those who wanted the war effort to be lessened.

3.5 The Election of 1968. As the 1968 presidential election drew near, the war in Vietnam became more of an issue. On March 31, 1968, President Johnson announced that he would not run for another term. This left Vice-President Hubert Humphrey, Senator Eugene McCarthy of Minnesota, and Senator Robert Kennedy of New York as the three leading Democratic candidates. Both McCarthy and Kennedy came out strongly against the war. This won them the favor of many young Americans. But on June 5, 1968, while attending a California primary election victory celebration in Los Angeles, Kennedy was shot to death by Jordanian immigrant Sirhan Sirhan.

Who sought the Democratic nomination in 1968?

When the Democrats met in Chicago in August to pick a candidate, the atmosphere was tense. The war in Vietnam was the major issue. During the convention, antiwar protestors demonstrated. Chicago Mayor Richard Daley sent in the police to break up the demonstrations. The clashes that resulted made the situation at the convention worse. The Democrats finally chose Hubert Humphrey as their candidate. Earlier that month, the Republicans picked former Vice-President Richard Nixon. Both Humphrey and Nixon said they would end the war in Vietnam. But Humphrey lost support because many people linked him with President Johnson's policies on the war.

What occurred during the Democratic convention?

Nixon won the election of 1968 with 31.7 million to Humphrey's 31.2 million popular votes. Nearly 10 million Americans, however, voted for neither Humphrey nor Nixon. Instead, they cast their votes for George Wallace of the American Independent party. Wallace had been governor of Alabama. He was in favor of strong "law and order" measures and supported the war in Vietnam. Wallace also felt the federal government was involved in too many parts of American life. Some of these, he felt, should be handled by the states.

What third party candidate was strong in 1968?

1. Where did the United States send troops in the 1960's?
2. Where did the United States try to settle problems using diplomacy rather than troops?
3. Why were many Americans against United States' involvement in the war in Vietnam?
4. Who won the election of 1968?

Election of 1968

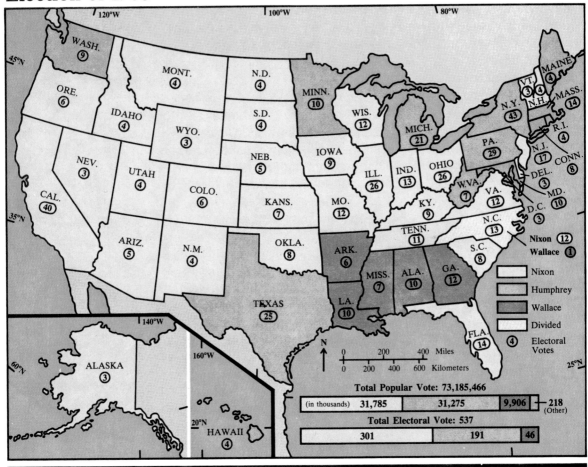

In the 1968 presidential election, George Wallace campaigned as a third party candidate. Where did Wallace win electoral votes? How was this election similar to the 1948 presidential election?

4. New Directions in Foreign Affairs

As President, Richard Nixon was faced with a great many problems in foreign affairs. The war was still going on in Vietnam, and trouble was brewing again in the Middle East. Nixon worked to do something about these problems. He also tried to improve relations with the Soviet Union and the People's Republic of China. His efforts in this area soon gave the United States new directions in foreign affairs.

4.1 The Search for Peace. During his campaign, Nixon had promised to get the United States out of Vietnam. He said he would bring about a peace with which Americans could live. He promised a peace with honor. In June 1969, Nixon said that 25,000 American troops would leave Vietnam by the end of August. In March, he announced *Vietnamization.* This was a program in which American troops would equip and train the South Vietnamese to take over the fighting so that Americans could withdraw. In November, Nixon announced that all American troops would be pulled out slowly from Vietnam.

What did Nixon promise regarding Vietnam?

The peace talks which had begun under President Johnson dragged on, and so did the war. In March 1970, matters grew worse. A new leader in Cambodia asked President Nixon for aid against Communists in his country. In April, Nixon said that American and South Vietnamese troops had gone into Cambodia to attack Communist strongholds. This angered many Americans, who already were against the war. They felt Nixon was following the same course as Johnson.

What action prompted renewed protests?

Huge demonstrations to protest the Cambodian invasion broke out at many American colleges. Four students were shot and killed during a demonstration at Kent State University in Ohio. Two were killed at Jackson State College in Mississippi. These killings angered some Americans even more. Protest against the war became stronger.

Almost three years passed before any agreement was reached on the war. In late January 1973, the United States, South Vietnam, North Vietnam, and the Vietcong's Provisional Revolutionary Government finally came to terms. The United States agreed to withdraw all its military forces from Vietnam. The North Vietnamese and Vietcong agreed to return all American prisoners of war. It also was agreed that elections would be held in South Vietnam to decide its government.

What were the terms of the agreement reached on the Vietnam War in 1973?

By the end of March, the last American troops left Vietnam. But the war there still went on. While many Americans were saddened by this, they were glad that the United States was out of the war. During its involvement, some 46,000 Americans had been killed, and more than 300,000 others had been wounded.

4.2 Detente With the Soviet Union. Even as the United States was fighting the Vietnam War, relations with the Soviet Union had begun to improve. In 1969, the United States and the Soviet Union were among some 60 countries that signed the Nuclear Nonproliferation Treaty. In it, countries with nuclear weapons promised not to help other countries to build them. That same year, the two powers began talks on limiting defensive nuclear weapons. Out of these talks came the Strategic Arms Limitation Treaty (SALT). In it, the United States and the Soviet Union agreed to limit production of certain missiles.

What multination treaty was signed in 1969?

Drawing by Richter; © 1974 The New Yorker Magazine, Inc.

Bill Mauldin's cartoon (left) is titled "The Odd Couple." Mischa Richter's cartoon (right) has an official saying "Detente" to explain unusual additions to a Soviet military parade. How did each cartoonist view detente?

In June 1969, President Nixon went to Moscow to sign the SALT agreement. He was the first American President to visit there. Nixon said that the United States and the Soviet Union should have closer economic and business ties. A few months later, the United States agreed to sell American wheat and other grains to the Soviet Union. It was the largest export grain order the United States had ever received. All of this was part of a new policy toward the Soviet Union formed by President Nixon and Secretary of State Henry Kissinger. Called *detente,* it meant a relaxing of cold war tensions between the United States and the Soviet Union.

What new policy was developed by the Nixon administration in regard to the Soviet Union?

That detente was working was shown in 1973 when Soviet Premier Leonid Brezhnev visited Washington, D.C. He met there with President Nixon, members of Congress, and some American business leaders. During the visit, it was agreed that both the United States and the Soviet Union would work on another SALT agreement. In addition, both leaders agreed that their nations should avoid actions which might lead to nuclear war. There was also agreement for the two countries to work together in the areas of business, science, and culture.

4.3 A New China Policy.   At the same time, President Nixon was also trying to improve relations with the People's Republic of China. The Chinese invited an American ping-pong team to visit the People's Republic of China in April 1971. Three months later, Nixon announced that he would visit that country the following year. He said he was going there to seek *normalization*—a return to normal conditions—of relations between the two countries. In September, the United States recommended to the United Nations that the People's Republic of China be allowed to become a member. The People's Republic of China took over the seat in the United Nations which had been held by the Republic of China (Taiwan).

How did American policy toward China change?

On February 21, 1972, President Nixon became the first American President to visit the People's Republic of China. He met with Premier Chou En-lai and Chairman Mao Tse-tung. They agreed to set up closer trade and other relations between the two countries. Nixon signed a declaration that said Taiwan was legally part of mainland China. It also said that in time, American forces would leave there, and that Taiwan's future would be decided by the Chinese themselves. This, more than anything, showed how much United States policy toward China had changed under President Nixon. This policy was continued in the

When did Nixon first visit China? What was accomplished by the visit?

President Nixon stands on the Great Wall of China, not far from Peking, during his 1972 visit to the People's Republic. With him is Chinese Deputy Premier Li Hsien-Nien (to the immediate left of the President). What did President Nixon hope to accomplish with this trip?

1970's. In January 1979, the United States formally recognized the People's Republic of China.

4.4 Time Bomb in the Middle East. Meanwhile, another Arab-Israeli war broke out in the Middle East. On October 6, 1973, the eve of the Jewish holy day of Yom Kippur, Egyptian and Syrian soldiers crossed into Israeli lands. The United States said that the Soviets were sending military supplies to Egypt, so America would send them to Israel. This led some Arab countries to stop oil sales to the United States. In late October, to avoid further trouble, the United Nations called for a cease-fire and said it would send in a force to keep the peace. This helped calm both the United States and the Soviet Union.

How was the 1973 Arab-Israeli war stopped?

Meanwhile, Secretary of State Kissinger began what was called **shuttle diplomacy**. He flew from one Middle Eastern capital to another to arrange peace terms. In this way, he was able to work out a cease-fire agreement between Israel and Egypt, and between Israel and Syria. Kissinger also helped set up peace talks. A few weeks after the agreements made at the peace talks were signed, President Nixon visited several Arab countries in the Middle East. The visit pointed up a change in American policy toward better relations with the Arab nations.

1. What action did Nixon take concerning Vietnam?
2. What was the purpose of the Strategic Arms Limitation Treaty?
3. How did American foreign policy toward the Soviet Union change?
4. What caused some Arab countries to stop oil supplies to the United States?

5. Conclusion

During the 1960's and early 1970's, there was a great deal of tension in the United States. At the same time, there was hope. The unity of the American people was tested by such issues as poverty, civil rights, and war. The civil rights movement was bringing about change. While it did not bring about total equality, it did draw attention to the poverty and lack of opportunity faced by many Americans. The war in Vietnam showed that the United States could not be expected to solve all problems in every area of the world. Tension also was eased by the new and better relations with the Soviet Union and the People's Republic of China. Many people felt this would lead to better cooperation among the great powers of the world.

Chapter 26 Review

Main Points

1. In 1960, John Kennedy became the first Catholic and youngest person to be elected President.

2. Congress failed to pass most of Kennedy's programs before he was assassinated in November 1963.

3. Under President Johnson, more programs were passed by Congress than under any other President since Franklin Roosevelt. These included legislation on civil rights, education, urban development, and immigration.

4. Frustration with the lack of progress for civil rights led to changes in the black rights movement.

5. Blacks and Mexican Americans organized to elect public officials to gain more control over public affairs.

6. Problems in Southeast Asia, the Caribbean, and the Middle East faced Presidents during the 1960's and 1970's.

7. President Nixon attempted to improve relations with the Soviet Union and the People's Republic of China.

Building Vocabulary

1. Identify the following:

John Kennedy	Lyndon Johnson	Six-Day War
Sputnik I	César Chávez	Vietcong
Neil Armstrong	Chien Shiung Wu	Richard Nixon
James Meredith	Graciela Olivarez	SALT
Peace Corps	Medicare	Leonid Brezhnev
Bay of Pigs	Robert Weaver	Chou En-lai
Berlin Wall		

2. Define the following:

satellite	commonwealth	"doves"
demonstrations	intervention	Vietnamization
quarantine	cease-fire	detente
conspiracy	guerrillas	normalization
"black power"	"hawks"	shuttle diplomacy
displaced persons		

Remembering the Facts

1. What programs from Kennedy's New Frontier did Congress pass?

2. What problems did the United States have with the Soviet Union over Cuba?

3. What major laws were passed during the Johnson administration?

4. Where did riots occur in the 1960's? What caused them?

5. What did Mexican Americans do to gain their rights as citizens?

6. How did the United States' immigration policy change?

7. How did the United States try to bring peace to the Middle East?

8. How did relations between the United States and the People's Republic of China change during the Nixon administration?

9. What three national figures were assassinated during the 1960's?

Understanding the Facts

1. How did President Kennedy deal with the Cuban missile crisis?

2. Why was it necessary to pass laws such as the Civil Rights Act of 1964 and the Voting Rights Act of 1965?

3. What was the aim of the Great Society?

4. Why did some people favor and some people oppose the idea of "black power"?

5. Why did the United States get involved in Southeast Asia, the Caribbean, and the Middle East?

Using Maps

Direction and Distance. Americans often have been far removed from the centers of world conflict. News from reporters and from those fighting helped to describe distant scenes. With television and other advances in communications, however, Vietnam became a familiar place. Names such as Saigon, Hue, and the Mekong Delta were as well known as many places in the United States.

The map on page 636 is of Vietnam between 1961 and 1975. Study it for direction and distance. Using the scale and the direction indicator, answer the following questions.

1. How far was Hanoi from Saigon?

2. Where was Hanoi, the capital of the North, in relation to Saigon, the capital of the South?

3. How far was each capital city from the demilitarized zone?

4. What was the nearest United States air base to Haiphong? How far was it?

5. What direction did an airplane fly from Tan Son Nhut Air Base to the nearest base in Cambodia?

6. What was the greatest length of the Ho Chi Minh Trail?

7. With North Vietnamese in Cambodia, what was the shortest distance for an attack from Cambodia to Saigon?

A Time of Discontent   27

Chicago is aglow in this view of a city that was typical of a growing and sprawling urban America. How does this scene also illustrate one of the major challenges that faced all Americans in the 1970's?

The confidence of the American people, shaken in the 1960's, was further damaged in the 1970's. Events shattered their trust in government at home and American power abroad. During these years, Americans could not agree on solutions to problems that faced them. The 1970's was a time of discontent and disillusion for many people.

1. The Search for Consensus

What did Nixon promise in his 1968 campaign?

President Nixon had promised in his 1968 campaign to bring the people together—to unify the country. Nixon said he would follow policies that would heal the wounds of war abroad and violence at home. This represented a search for *consensus,* or general agreement.

1.1 Nixon and the Economy. One of the most important problems facing the country in the late 1960's was inflation. Prices rose higher and higher each year, mostly because of the cost of the Vietnam War. To stop inflation, Nixon first called for a tight money policy. This would make less money available for people to spend. To do this, interest rates were raised. As people stopped borrowing and buying, businesses began to cut back, and unemployment rose. Prices, however, kept on rising, causing *stagflation* (a stalled economy in a period of inflation).

Why did Nixon call for wage and price controls?

In August 1971, Nixon announced his New Economic Policy. It called for a 90-day freeze on wages and prices. This was to be followed by a system of wage and price controls. This new plan went against Nixon's belief in free enterprise, but it did slow inflation for a time. The controls did little to help the economy grow or lower unemployment. In January 1973, when Nixon removed the government controls, prices rose again.

Another part of Nixon's plan to restore the economy was to cut government spending. Nixon did not want to reduce spending for the military. So most of the cuts he planned were for domestic areas. One of these was the welfare system. In 1969, Nixon offered a *minimum-income plan* to replace many welfare programs. Under this plan, the government would make direct money payments to the poor to bring their incomes to a certain minimum. Many people were against the Family Assistance Plan because they felt the payments were too low. So the plan was never passed.

What was Nixon's Family Assistance Plan?

In the same year, Nixon also announced his New Federalism. This was a plan to cut the federal government's role in the economy by turning over many of its tasks to state and local governments. On January 22, 1971, Nixon described New Federalism:

> The time has come in America to reverse the flow of power and resources from the states and communities in Washington, and start power and resources flowing back from Washington to the states and communities and, more important, to the people, all across America. . . . We have made the federal government so strong it grows muscle-bound and the states and localities so weak they have no power. If we put more power in more places, we can make government more creative in more places. That way we multiply the number of people with the ability to make things happen—and we can open the way to a new burst of creative energy throughout America. . . .

To help state governments take over their new tasks, Nixon proposed a ***revenue-sharing plan.*** Under this plan, the federal government would give part of its revenues to state and local governments. In 1972, Nixon's plan was passed as the State and Local Fiscal Assistance Act. It granted state and local governments $30 billion over five years to use as they saw fit.

What was revenue sharing?

Many people were against revenue sharing. Mayors of large cities pointed out that their governments would receive less aid than under old programs. Many Americans feared that without federal rules, the money would not be used to help all people equally. On the whole, Nixon's economic policies did little to bring about consensus.

Why were some people against revenue sharing?

1.2 Nixon and Desegregation.   The Nixon administration was not active in desegregating schools. Early efforts at ending segregation had begun in the South, where schools were segregated by law. In the North, there were no such laws. However, school district lines were often drawn along racial lines. As a result, whites usually attended school with whites, and blacks with blacks. By the late 1960's, efforts were underway to end this form of separation.

What caused school segregation in the North? What method has been used to end it?

The NAACP and the Congressional Black Caucus, as well as some civil rights leaders and some parents, favored the use of busing to end segregation. However, many people were against busing. Many parents did not want their children to go to school outside their own neighborhoods. Others thought that busing was too costly. Still others did not want to desegregate the schools.

In 1972, President Nixon asked Congress to pass a law which would stop federal courts from issuing orders for busing. Congress, however, did not do so. The courts continued to order busing as a means of ending segregation.

Patricia Harris (1924–)
Herman Badillo (1929–)

==PROFILE==

The passage of the Voting Rights Act increased the political participation of minority group members in the United States. As a result, they began to be elected and appointed to more positions in government. Two such people were Patricia Harris and Herman Badillo.

Patricia Harris attended Howard University and the University of Chicago graduate school. After working for the Young Women's Christian Association and the American Council on Human Rights, Harris attended law school at George Washington University. For a year, she worked as a lawyer with the Justice Department, but she left to teach law at Howard University.

In 1965, President Lyndon Johnson appointed Harris ambassador to Luxembourg. She was the first black woman to hold such a position. In 1976, President Jimmy Carter appointed Harris head of the Department of Housing and Urban Development. She later became Secretary of Health and Human Services.

Herman Badillo grew up in Puerto Rico. When he was 11 years old, he moved to New York City to live with an aunt. Badillo moved to Chicago, Los Angeles, and back to New York, working to pay his way through school.

Badillo studied accounting at City College of New York. He got an accounting job after graduation and went to the Brooklyn Law School at night. In 1954, Badillo became a lawyer and entered politics. During the racially-tense 1960's, Badillo won the support of Puerto Ricans as well as black and white people to become borough president of the Bronx.

In 1970, Badillo was elected to the House of Representatives from a mostly Puerto Rican district in the Bronx. Badillo was the first person of Puerto Rican birth to sit in Congress. He gained national recognition as one of the observers at the Attica, New York, prison riot in 1971. Badillo was brought there at the request of the rebelling inmates to hear their demands.

Minority group members are still underrepresented in positions in government. But their political participation is the beginning of their greater political influence.

1.3 The Women's Movement. The subject of women's rights became more and more an issue in the 1970's. During Nixon's years in office, American women stepped up a long-time struggle against discrimination against them. By 1970, women made up nearly 40 percent of the work force. Yet, like members of minority groups, women faced discrimination both in the kinds of jobs they could get and in the amount of money they were paid. For example, in 1970, women earned only 60 percent as much as men. Women often were not only limited to lower-paying jobs but were paid less for the same job.

What caused the women's movement?

To end such discrimination, the National Organization for Women (NOW) was formed in 1966. At first, its members worked to make women see the difficulties they faced. After that, NOW directed its attention largely to social and economic matters. One of its major areas of concern was job discrimination. Laws, such as the Civil Rights Act of 1964 and the Equal Employment Opportunity Act of 1972, aided the group as it worked for equal jobs and equal pay. The 1964 act had set up the Equal Employment Opportunity Commission to look into cases of job discrimination. The 1972 act gave the EEOC the power to enforce the 1964 law through the courts.

What groups have women formed to work for women's rights?

There were also other groups formed to work for women's rights. Many of them turned their attention to politics. The National Women's Political Caucus (NWPC) was set up to help women get elected to public office. Women in this group felt that in this way, they would be better able to make policy changes. Representative Barbara Jordan of Texas, for example, offered a bill to add homemakers to the social security plan.

Many people felt that a constitutional amendment was needed to guarantee women's rights. This idea led to a heated debate. Some people said that the amendment was not needed—that there were already enough laws. They claimed that women might have to serve in combat if such a law was passed. Many people felt that it could weaken family life.

In 1972, Congress voted to submit an Equal Rights Amendment (ERA) to the states. It said that equal rights under the law could not be denied any citizen because of sex. After ten years, however, the drive to win ratification for the ERA ended in failure in July 1982. The ERA had been approved by 35 states, but this was three short of the 38 states needed for ratification. ERA supporters said they would reintroduce the measure in Congress, and then start a new drive for ratification.

What is the status of ERA?

1.4 The Space Program. Another area of conflict in the 1970's was the space program. In 1969, the United States had reached

Astronaut James Irwin appears with a lunar rover in the shadow of the lunar module (foreground) which landed Irwin and Astronaut David Scott on the moon. Irwin commanded the 1971 Apollo 15 mission that landed near Mt. Hadley (background). Besides moon landings, what other feats did Americans accomplish and hope to accomplish in space?

What were some major achievements in the space program in the 1970's?

Kennedy's goal of landing on the moon. By the end of 1972, the United States had made five more moon landings. Although most people admired such feats, some thought that the money could be better used elsewhere. They felt that greater efforts should be made to solve the problems on earth. In spite of this, Nixon was able to get support for Skylab, which was launched in 1973. This was an orbiting laboratory to test the ability of humans to live and work in outer space.

In 1975, the United States and the Soviet Union carried out a joint space mission. An American Apollo and a Soviet Soyuz spacecraft docked together while orbiting the earth. This docking symbolized the spirit of detente between the two powers. After 1975, both the United States and the Soviet Union began sending probes into outer space. The United States also began work on a *space shuttle*. This was a spaceship which would carry people to and from space. Unlike earlier spacecraft, this one could be used many times.

1.5 Nixon and Presidential Power.   Nixon faced some difficulties in getting his programs passed. This was because the Democrats

Progress

CONCEPT

Progress means moving forward. It implies moving forward for some good purpose. The people who formed the United States in 1776 believed that their work was progress. By it, they wanted to establish justice and ensure liberty. Progress, however, had a price. A war had to be fought before progress was realized.

Throughout the twentieth century, industrial and technological development continued to move forward, establishing the United States as the leading industrial nation in the world. By 1969, technological advances made it possible for people to travel to and walk on the moon.

Many people questioned whether the price of technological progress was worth it. Some people asked if the money used for space exploration could not have been better spent to improve social conditions.

In 1971, David Scott and James Irwin became the fourth crew of astronauts to explore the moon. Scott later expressed these thoughts about his experience and the purpose of the space program.

We feel a sense of pride in . . . our program, yet we cannot escape a sense of deep concern for the fate of our planet and [its people].

This concern has led us to add certain items to the equipment we are leaving on the moon. . . .

. . . A plaque of aluminum affixed to the deserted [lunar module shows] *the two hemispheres of our planet; upon it are engraved the name of our spacecraft, the date of the mission, and a* [list] *of the crew. From these data, the equipment, and even the* [size] *of our footprints, intelligent beings will readily* [tell] *what kind of creatures we were and whence we came.*

In a little hollow in the moon dust we place a . . . figurine of a [person] *in a space suit and beside it another metal plaque bearing the names of the 14 . . . Russians and Americans . . . who have given their lives so that* [people] *may range* [through space]. . . .

Occasionally, while strolling on a crisp autumn night . . . I look up at the moon . . . . I do not see a hostile, empty world. I see the radiant body where [we have] *taken* [our] *first steps into a frontier that will never end.*

1. What concerned Astronaut Scott beyond the accomplishment of getting to the moon?
2. Why were missions to the moon viewed as progress?

How did Nixon try
to increase presi-
dential power?

controlled Congress during his years in office. To get around this, Nixon tried in a number of ways to concentrate power in the White House. For one thing, he often vetoed bills. He *impounded* funds, or refused to spend money voted by Congress for certain programs. Nixon often refused to enforce a measure if he did not favor it. He also claimed *executive privilege* as a constitutional right. This allowed a President to keep information from Congress.

1. What controls did President Nixon place on the economy?
2. What discrimination in jobs did women and minority groups face?
3. How did the Soviet Union and the United States cooperate in space exploration?
4. How did Nixon try to concentrate power in the Presidency?

2. Crisis in the Presidency

The fact that the American people could not come to a consensus over important issues caused tension in the country. Matters grew worse when news of scandal among the country's top leaders reached the people. This led to a crisis in the Presidency. It became a test of the American constitutional system.

2.1 The Election of 1972. Although there was little consensus among the American people, President Nixon enjoyed solid support as the election of 1972 neared. This was based largely on the success of his foreign policy. His campaign was highly organized and backed by more than $50 million in contributions. Nixon's position was made even stronger by the fact that the Democratic party was divided. In November, Nixon won a huge victory over the Democratic candidate, Senator George McGovern of South Dakota. Nixon received 46 million to McGovern's 28.5 million popular votes. The electoral vote was 520 to 17.

How did 1972 differ
from previous elec-
tions in which
Nixon was involved?

2.2 The Watergate Scandal. Early in 1973, Americans learned of a scandal involving the President and members of his staff. In June 1972, five people had been arrested for breaking into the headquarters of the Democratic National Committee in Washington, D.C. The office was in the Watergate Hotel, and the scandal that followed was called Watergate. It was soon discovered that the burglars

Election of 1972

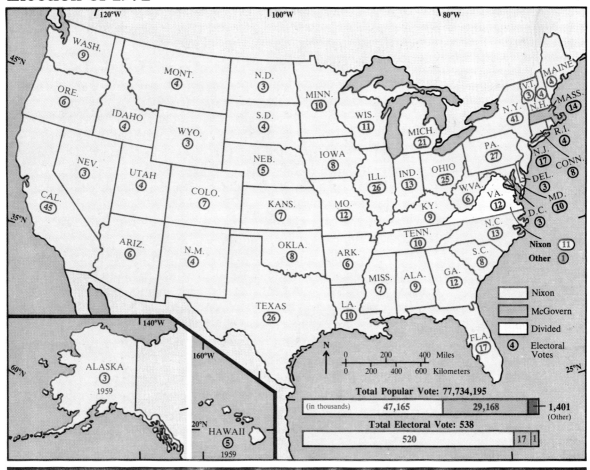

An organized campaign and a divided Democratic party contributed to Richard Nixon's landslide victory in 1972. How did this victory compare with the 1960 and 1968 elections in which Richard Nixon campaigned to be President?

were connected to the White House and the Committee to Reelect the President. The five had been directed by White House consultant E. Howard Hunt and G. Gordon Liddy, who worked for the committee.

This association was pointed out by *Washington Post* reporters Carl Bernstein and Robert Woodward in the first of many stories dealing with Watergate. Even so, the event did not draw a great deal of attention until January 1973. At that time, the burglars along with Hunt and Liddy went on trial before Judge John Sirica. Five of them pleaded guilty, the other two were found guilty by a jury and sentenced to prison.

What things did the Senate hearings uncover about Watergate?

In February 1973, the Senate set up a committee to look into charges of corruption in the 1972 election. It was headed by Senator Sam Ervin of North Carolina. In May 1973, the Senate committee began hearings, which were shown on television. White House Counsel John Dean told the Senate committee in June that President Nixon knew of the break-in shortly after it happened. Nixon had not reported the crime, which meant that if the charges were true, he was guilty of an illegal act. Dean said that *executive clemency,* or the lessening of punishment by order of the President, had been promised to the Watergate burglars. Over $200,000 had been raised to pay them off.

In July 1973, it was learned that President Nixon had made tape recordings of everything that had been said in his office. Nixon repeatedly had said that he had not known about the break-in nor had he used his powers to cover it up. The Senate committee hoped that his tapes would bring out the truth. Nixon, however, refused to give up the tapes, claiming executive privilege.

In October, Special Prosecutor Archibald Cox issued a *subpoena,* or a written legal order, for some of the tapes. Nixon had Cox fired, causing a storm of public protest. Nixon named Leon Jaworski to replace Cox. He also turned over some of the tapes in question. However, 18 minutes had been erased from one of the tapes. More and

How did more and more Americans lose faith in Nixon?

more Americans lost faith in the President, and there were growing demands for impeachment.

In the middle of Watergate, the American people had received another blow to their faith in government leaders. In October 1973, Vice-President Spiro Agnew resigned from office. He had been charged with accepting bribes as governor of Maryland and as Vice-President.

Why did Vice-President Agnew resign from office?

These charges were dropped in exchange for his resignation and an agreement not to contest an income tax evasion charge. After Agnew left office, Nixon named House Minority Leader Gerald Ford of Michigan as Vice-President. Ford was the first person to become Vice-President under the Twenty-fifth Amendment, which had been ratified in 1967. It set up rules for filling the office of President or Vice-President if a person holding either office was unable to carry out official duties.

2.3 Nixon's Resignation. Ford's position became more important as demand grew for Nixon's impeachment. In late 1973, the Judiciary Committee, which acts for the House in cases of impeachment, began to investigate Nixon. It also issued subpoenas for the tapes, and pressures on Nixon mounted. In March 1974, White House staff members H. R. Haldeman and John Ehrlichman, as well as former Attorney-General John Mitchell, were charged with conspiracy,

Senator Sam Ervin of North Carolina headed a select Senate committee to investigate the Watergate scandal. Here the Senator questions a White House aide. What information did the committee learn about President Nixon's involvement in the scandal?

obstruction of justice, and *perjury,* or lying under oath. They were later convicted of these charges and sent to prison.

In April 1974, Nixon agreed to turn over written copies of some of the tapes to the House Judiciary Committee. It turned out that some of the material from the tapes had been left out. Still, they seemed to suggest his guilt. In July, the Committee held hearings, which were seen on television. The Committee voted three articles of impeachment against the President. The charges were obstructing justice, misusing presidential power, and defying the Committee's subpoenas.

What were the impeachment charges voted against Nixon?

About the same time, the Supreme Court ruled that Nixon must turn over more tapes to Jaworski. When he did so, one of them strongly suggested that Nixon had ordered a cover-up. On August 9, certain that he would be removed from office, Nixon resigned, becoming the first President to do so. That same day, Gerald Ford became the 38th President of the United States. He was the first person to serve as President who had not been elected to either the Presidency or the Vice-Presidency.

2.4   A Difficult Time.   Ford became President in a time of crisis. People were very upset over Watergate and had lost faith in

When Gerald Ford became President, one of his most difficult tasks was to renew Americans' faith in their government officials. How did Ford make the task more difficult for himself?

On assuming office, what did Ford try to do?

What caused Ford to lose favor with some people?

government. Ford hoped to restore that faith. When he took office, he told the American people: "Our long national nightmare is over. Our Constitution works. Our great Republic is a government of laws and not of men. Here, the people rule."

At first, Americans greeted Ford favorably. Shortly after taking office, however, he lost some of those good feelings. In September, Ford pardoned Nixon for any crimes which he might have committed while in office. This meant that Nixon would not have to face criminal charges for his part in Watergate. Ford hoped that pardoning Nixon would help heal the wounds of Watergate. Most Americans, however, were angered by the pardon.

Ford's act hurt the Republican party, which already had been badly damaged by Watergate. In the congressional elections of 1974, Democrats added to their majority by winning many Republican seats. President Ford and the Democratic Congress were often at odds. Ford had promised a balanced budget, along with cuts in social spending. The Democrats were against these ideas. They called for spending increases to aid the economy. So Ford made changes in his budget that would bring it more in line with Congress' views.

On the subject of energy, too, Ford had to modify his plans. In the 1970's, production of oil, gas, and coal in the United States declined, while demand grew. This led the country to depend on oil imports, especially from the Middle East. In November 1973, a number of Arab countries had stopped selling oil to the United States because of the country's support of Israel. When this embargo was lifted in March 1974, the price of crude oil was nearly four times higher than it had been.

This pointed up the country's energy problem and led to a number of measures to correct it. In his last months in office, Nixon had offered a program that was supposed to make the United States self-sufficient in energy by 1980. This would be done, in part, by spending money to find new forms of energy. Congress, however, passed only some of Nixon's measures.

Under Ford, there was much disagreement over how to make America self-sufficient in energy. Ford favored *deregulation*. This meant removing price controls on gas and oil. Prices would then rise, and because of this, people would use less fuel. Higher profits from higher prices would aid companies in developing new forms of energy. Ford was not able to get Congress to pass this measure. However, Congress did pass the Energy Policy and Conservation Act. This act dealt with saving fuel and finding new forms of energy.

Along with the energy crisis, Ford had to face rising inflation. Although he generally did not favor price controls, Ford used them to hold prices down. However, he was not able to do much more than Nixon had done to slow inflation.

In foreign affairs, Ford followed Nixon's lead. He carried on detente with the Soviet Union and worked toward closer relations with China. He also went on working for nuclear arms control. Ford visited the Soviet Union where, in December 1974, he signed the Vladivostok Accord with Soviet Premier Leonid Brezhnev. This helped lay the basis for a SALT II treaty.

President Ford wanted to continue American aid to South Vietnam. Congress, however, would not agree to this. In April 1975, the Communists defeated the South Vietnamese and gained control of the whole country. Although the war was finally over, large areas of Vietnam had been destroyed, and more than 1 million Vietnamese had died. Thousands more fled after the Communist victory. Over 100,000 of these people eventually settled in the United States.

What helped to cause an energy crisis in the United States in the early 1970's?

What was Ford's foreign policy?

1. What events were part of the Watergate scandal?
2. Which White House staff members went to jail for their roles in the Watergate scandal?
3. What actions did Nixon take to keep the truth about Watergate from the American people?
4. How did Gerald Ford become President?

3. The Carter Administration

What were some of Carter's campaign promises?

In the election of 1976, Ford ran against Democratic candidate Jimmy Carter, former governor of Georgia. Carter won with 40.3 million to Ford's 38.5 million popular votes. The electoral vote was 297 to 241. During the campaign, Carter made a number of promises. He said that he would balance the budget and cut military spending. He stated that he would create jobs to lower unemployment. Carter also planned to "clean up" the government and make certain changes in foreign policy.

Once in office, however, Carter had little more success than Ford in dealing with Congress. This was due partly to the fact that Carter had not previously served in the federal government. Conflicts between Carter and Congress stemmed from differences on a number of issues. The search for consensus continued.

Televised political debates became popular in the 1960 election when Kennedy debated Nixon. Here Gerald Ford (right) debates campaign issues with Jimmy Carter (left) in 1976. What do you think seems to be the purpose of a televised debate?

3.1 Carter's Human Rights Policy. One area of conflict was Carter's new foreign policy. He wanted the United States to place more emphasis on human rights. Carter thought that the country could do this in two ways. It could set an example of behavior for other countries. The United States could also use its power to uphold human rights all over the world.

One way in which the United States could uphold human rights was to cut off military and economic aid to governments which violated these rights. Carter, for example, favored withdrawing aid from Chile, Argentina, Uruguay, and Ethiopia. These were countries ruled by dictators who jailed people opposing them. Carter also urged the white-minority governments of South Africa and Rhodesia (Zimbabwe) to share power with their black-majority populations.

How did Carter think the United States could stress human rights?

President Carter singled out the Soviet Union on the issue of human rights. He condemned its government for violating the rights of Soviet Jews. He also listened to Soviet *dissidents,* or people who speak out against their government. The Soviets were angered by Carter's policy. In March 1977, they held up a new round of SALT talks, partly because of it. Soviet Foreign Minister Andrei Gromyko said that Carter's support for human rights in the Soviet Union had "poisoned the atmosphere" of the meeting. It would be another two years before an agreement was reached.

What nation did Carter single out on the issue of human rights? What problems did it cause?

Relations between the two countries grew worse when, in late 1979, the Soviet Union attacked Afghanistan. Carter saw this as a violation of human rights. In protest, he asked the United States Olympic team to boycott the 1980 Summer Olympics in Moscow. Partly because of the Soviet attack on Afghanistan, Congress failed to approve the SALT II treaty.

Carter's policy had critics at home as well. Many people felt that another country's treatment of its citizens was its own business. Others were against cutting off aid to countries on the basis of human rights. They felt that this weakened those countries in their fight against communism.

Why were some people against Carter's policy on human rights?

3.2 The Panama Canal. The lack of consensus over human rights was evident in Carter's Panama Canal policy. For many years, the people of Panama had demanded an end to American control of the canal. In 1964, anti-American riots had broken out in Panama. Presidents Johnson, Nixon, and Ford had all favored some change in policy. Each feared possible war over control of the canal.

On September 7, 1977, President Carter and General Omar Torrijos Herrera of Panama signed two new treaties in Washington, D.C. The first guaranteed the neutrality of the canal. The United

After the signing of a peace treaty, Egyptian President Anwar Sadat (left) shakes hands with Israeli Prime Minister Menachem Begin (right). What was President Carter's role in bringing about this peace treaty?

What were the terms of the Panama Canal treaties?

Why was Carter's Panama Canal policy opposed?

Who met at Camp David in September 1978?

States, however, would share the right to defend it. The second provided for the United States to turn over control of the canal to Panama by the year 2000.

The ceremony to sign the treaty was attended by representatives of 26 countries of the Western Hemisphere. Most of them agreed that the treaties were a sign of goodwill on the part of the United States. There were many Americans, however, who were against Carter's Panama Canal policy. They saw it as a sign of weakness on the part of the United States. In spite of this, the treaties were approved by the Senate in March and April of 1978.

3.3 Middle East Diplomacy.   From Central America, Carter turned to the Middle East. In November 1977, Egyptian President Anwar Sadat had gone to Israel to talk with Prime Minister Menachem Begin about the problems between the two countries. Later Begin returned the visit. But the talks broke down.

In September 1978, President Carter invited both leaders to come to the United States. The three went to Camp David, Maryland. There Sadat and Begin worked out a number of agreements which promised to lead to peace. President Carter's role in helping bring about these "Camp David Accords" received praise from many world leaders.

In March 1979, Egypt and Israel signed a treaty ending over 30 years of war. Egypt became the first Arab country to recognize Israel.

Still, problems remained. The Palestinian Arabs did not like the treaty. They claimed the right to a homeland in Palestine and refused to recognize Israel. They were backed by other Arab countries. The Arab-Israeli conflict continued.

Who was opposed to the peace treaty between Egypt and Israel? Why?

3.4 A Troubled Economy. Carter's successes in foreign affairs often were dimmed by troubles with the economy. Because of rising inflation and the great number of people out of work, Carter had to give up his plans for a balanced budget. Inflation, which had slowed a little under Ford, climbed during Carter's years in office. Between 1977 and 1979, it rose from 6 to more than 10 percent. By 1980, it had reached over 12 percent. Although unemployment went down from 9.2 percent in May 1975 to around 7 percent in 1980, it was still high.

What economic problems existed under Carter?

President Carter refused to use wage and price controls to fight inflation. Instead, he asked business and labor to hold down prices and wages voluntarily. This did not work. Both business and labor tried to keep up with ever-rising prices.

One reason for inflation was the greater cost of oil and other forms of energy. To meet this problem, Carter outlined an energy plan. It was designed to make the United States depend less on foreign oil. Carter

What was Carter's energy plan?

The Consumer Price Index shows how inflation has influenced the overall costs of goods and services over a period of time. Trends for specific areas are also shown, using 1975 as a starting point. How have prices changed since 1975?

Consumer Price Index

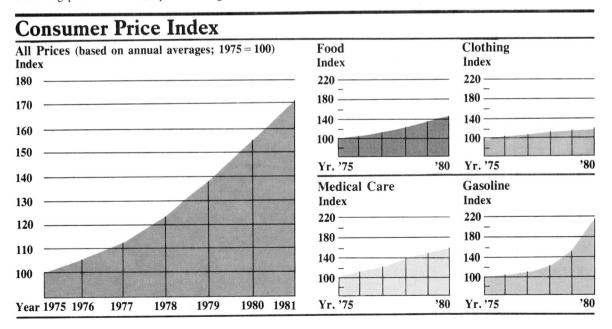

All Prices (based on annual averages; 1975 = 100)

called for conservation measures as well as deregulation of gas and oil. He also called for using coal and developing new forms of energy.

Carter's plan was to go into effect under the direction of a new Department of Energy. Congress set up the department in August 1977. However, there was a long battle over the rest of Carter's plan. In October 1978, the Energy Act was passed. It provided for removing price controls on natural gas by 1985. It also promoted the use of coal.

Less than a year later, Carter decided to lift price controls on oil by October 1981. He also proposed a *"windfall profits" tax,* which was passed by Congress in March 1980. This was a tax on the extra profits that oil companies would make as government price controls were lifted. Consumers were against removing controls. They feared that they would have to pay for the tax in the form of higher prices for gasoline and heating oil.

3.5 The Crisis in Iran.   As economic problems mounted at home, the United States faced a serious crisis in Iran. For many years, the United States had backed the government of Shah Mohammed Reza Pahlevi in Iran. This was because the United States wanted a buffer against the Soviet Union in the Persian Gulf area. Under the Shah's rule, Iran took steps to modernize its economy. However, the use of secret police and the denial of political and civil rights turned many Iranians against the Shah. He was overthrown in January 1979. A month later, Muslim Ayatollah Ruhollah Khomeini came to power. The new government of Iran was strongly anti-American.

What led to the Iranian crisis?

In October 1979, President Carter allowed the Shah to enter the United States for medical treatment. Iranians wanted the Shah returned to their country to be tried for crimes against the government. The United States refused to do this. On November 4, 1979, revolutionary students in Iran seized the American embassy in Tehran, taking a number of hostages. Months of negotiations failed to bring about the release of the hostages. In late April 1980, Carter authorized a rescue attempt. Because of mechanical breakdowns, it failed. Negotiations continued with the help of the Algerian government.

1. Why did Carter want to withdraw American aid to Chile, Argentina, Uraguay, and Ethiopia?
2. When will the United States turn over control of the Panama Canal to Panama?
3. With what two countries did Carter work to reduce tension in the Middle East?
4. Why did Iranians seize hostages at the American embassy in Tehran?

4. A Change
of Direction _____

By 1980 many Americans had become dissatisfied with the policies of the Carter administration. Some critics thought President Carter was too weak in his dealings with the Soviet Union. They also believed he was too soft in the handling of the Iranian hostage crisis. Others thought there was too much government regulation and were upset with financial policies that were pushing up inflation and causing widespread unemployment. Many people were leaning to *conservatism*—a belief that government should be less involved in local affairs and economic matters, and that social changes should be slow and gradual.

Why were Americans dissatisfied with Carter's policies?

4.1 Campaigns and Candidates. The political campaigns of 1980 reflected the country's changing mood. Although President Carter's popularity had declined he was able to defeat a challenge by Senator Edward Kennedy of Massachusetts at the Democratic convention in New York. Carter won renomination on the first ballot. Vice President Mondale was renominated as the President's running mate.

Who was the Democratic presidential candidate?

Ronald Reagan, the Republican nominee for President in 1980, was a vigorous campaigner. Although Reagan's call for a return to conservative values was popular throughout the country, analysts considered the election too close to call. Why was the outcome difficult to predict?

Who was the Republican presidential candidate? The independent candidate?

Ronald Reagan, former governor of California, was nominated for President on the first ballot at the Republican convention in Detroit. George Bush, a former Representative and UN ambassador, was chosen as Reagan's running mate. John Anderson of Illinois, a dissident Republican member of Congress, entered the contest as an Independent candidate. This made the election of 1980 a three-person race. Most pollsters believed the presidential election was too close to predict the outcome.

Ronald Reagan dominated the 1980 election across the United States. Reagan, a conservative, won many traditionally liberal states. How does Reagan's performance compare with that of other postwar Republican candidates?

Election of 1980

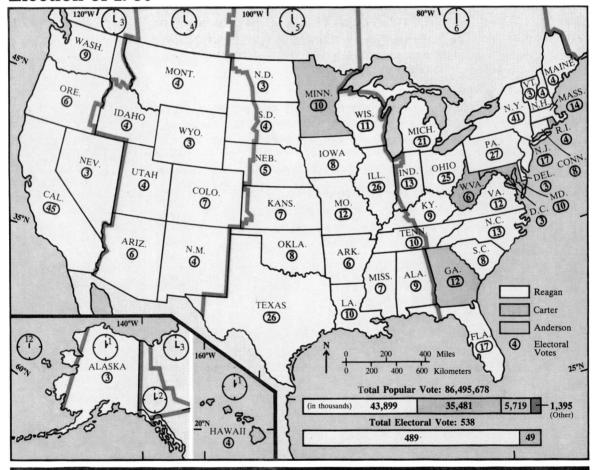

4.2 The Election of 1980. Reagan, the conservative candidate, swept to a landslide victory. The 69-year-old Republican became the nation's fortieth, and oldest, President. He won 44 states, with a total of 489 electoral votes. He carried the entire Plains state area, the Southwest, and the West. He lost only Georgia in the South and Minnesota in the Midwest. Most surprisingly, he made a strong showing in the Northeast, carrying such large industrial states as New York, Pennsylvania, New Jersey, and Massachusetts.

Who won the election of 1980?

Jimmy Carter, by contrast, won only six states (Georgia, Minnesota, West Virginia, Maryland, Rhode Island, and Hawaii) and the District of Columbia, and 49 electoral votes. Except for strong support among blacks, the usual Democratic supporters—blue-collar workers, labor union members, and ethnic and minority groups—failed to cast their votes for Carter. John Anderson, the Independent candidate, won no states or electoral votes, though he received over 5.7 million popular votes.

The Republican party also gained control of the United States Senate for the first time since 1955. Although the House of Representatives remained under Democratic control, the Republicans won more than twenty new seats. Thus, things looked very hopeful for the plans and programs of the newly-elected Republican administration. The size of Reagan's victory signalled that the American people desired a change in governmental direction. To what degree they would support Reagan's policies remained to be seen.

Who gained control of the Senate?

1. Why did many American voters become dissatisfied with the policies of the Carter administration?
2. What is meant by a policy of conservatism?
3. What was the outcome of the election of 1980?

5. Conclusion

The Vietnam War had torn the country apart, and Watergate had been a strain on the nation's political system. However, the fact that the country had survived these crises helped many people recover some of their confidence. Although there was still no clear consensus on solutions to the nation's problems, certain trends were appearing. Whether the movement away from big government would be a lasting trend remained to be seen.

Chapter 27 Review

Main Points

1. School desegregation was a major domestic issue during the Nixon years.
2. Action by the women's rights movement led to efforts to pass the Equal Rights Amendment.
3. Scandal in the Nixon administration involved the President's cover-up of his ties to a break-in at Democratic National Committee headquarters.
4. When it was clear that Nixon would be impeached, he resigned. Gerald Ford became President.
5. Ford's pardon of Nixon caused Ford to lose favor with many people.
6. An Arab oil embargo caused problems for the United States which consumed more oil than it produced.
7. In 1976, Jimmy Carter defeated President Ford in the election.
8. The Carter administration played a part in negotiating a peace treaty between Israel and Egypt.
9. President Carter lost much popular support because of mounting inflation and the hostage crisis in Iran.
10. In 1980, Ronald Reagan's election as President marked a shift to a more conservative mood in the nation.

Building Vocabulary

1. Identify the following:

New Federalism	Skylab	Jimmy Carter
Patricia Harris	Watergate	"Camp David Accords"
Herman Badillo	Sam Ervin	Energy Act
Equal Rights Amendment	Gerald Ford	Ronald Reagan

2. Define the following:

consensus	impounded	perjury
stagflation	executive privilege	deregulation
minimum-income plan	executive clemency	dissidents
revenue-sharing plan	subpoena	"windfall profits" tax
space shuttle		conservatism

Remembering the Facts

1. How did Nixon plan to bring about a consensus among Americans?
2. What laws helped a woman gain equal pay with a man doing the same job?

3. What measure did some people want passed to protect the equal rights of men and women?
4. What was the Watergate scandal?
5. Why did Nixon resign from office?
6. How did President Ford attempt to solve energy problems?
7. What was the basis of President Carter's foreign policy?
8. How did revolution in Iran affect its relations with the United States?
9. What had been Ronald Reagan's experience before becoming President of the United States?

Understanding the Facts

1. Why was peace in the Middle East important to the United States?
2. How did Presidents Nixon, Ford, and Carter try to control inflation?
3. Why did some people feel a need for the Equal Rights Amendment?
4. What effect did the Watergate scandal have on the American people?
5. Why was it difficult to establish a national consensus in the United States?
6. How did Reagan's election show a change in governmental direction?

Using Maps

Time Zones. Because of its rotation, one side of the earth has day while the other side has night. It is necessary to adjust time so that the sun is at approximately the same position in an area at approximately the same time each day. To do this, the earth has been divided into 24 time zones. Each zone is about 15 degrees of longitude.

Standard time is figured from the Prime Meridian which is in the center of the initial time zone. Local time there is called Greenwich Time. To establish local time, each zone to the west of Greenwich subtracts one hour for each zone. Those to the east of Greenwich add one hour for each zone. Near where the zones meet on the opposite side of the world is the International Date Line.

The map on page 663 shows the United States divided into time zones. It also shows the results of the presidential election of 1980. Study the map, and answer the following questions.

1. When Eastern polls opened at 6 A.M., what time was it on the West Coast?
2. As voting stopped in Ohio at 7:30 P.M. local time, what time was it in Oregon?
3. As voting stopped in Missouri at 7 P.M. local time, what time was it in Nevada?
4. As voting stopped in Oregon at 8 P.M. local time, how long had the voting places been closed in Ohio?
5. With projections for Ronald Reagan's victory announced by 8 P.M. eastern time, how might voter turnout in the western states have been affected?

The New Federalism   28

Ronald Reagan promised a new direction for the United States when he was sworn in as President. The policies of the past, Reagan believed, had failed to solve the problems that the United States faced at home and abroad. What problems must the Reagan administration confront in the 1980's?

Ronald Reagan was sworn in as the 40th President of the United States on January 20, 1981. Only minutes after taking the oath of office, the new President was able to announce that the 53 Americans held captive in Iran had been set free. After 444 days of captivity, the hostages finally arrived back in the United States on January 25. Their release added further to the popularity of President Reagan after his sweeping victory at the polls, even though the arrangements had been worked out by President Carter just before leaving office.

What did Reagan announce shortly after the inauguration?

1. A New Beginning _____

Reagan's personal popularity helped him make some important changes in government policy during the first few months of his administration. Reagan believed that from the days of the New Deal the Democrats had made the federal government too big. He also wanted his New Federalism to go into effect. First proposed by President Nixon, the plan was to cut the federal government's role in the economy by turning over many of its tasks to state and local governments. By strengthening state governments, he hoped to reduce federal spending and build up national defense.

What did Reagan believe?

1.1 The Reagan Style. Not only did President Reagan set out to change the direction of government, but he also changed presidential style. He no longer followed the tiring 12-hour days of previous Presidents. Instead, he operated on a 9-to-5 routine, with Wednesday afternoons off for relaxation.

What was Reagan's style?

Reagan's style of governing was built on the Cabinet model, similar to that used by President Eisenhower. He delegated significant authority to his aides and department heads. Reagan called himself "chairman of the board." His job was to chart overall policies, while his executives were to carry them out.

1.2 Cutting Bureaucracy. As he promised in his campaign, President Reagan began at once to make changes. Only minutes after being sworn into office, he ordered a freeze on federal hiring. He wanted to cut down the size of the government work force of nearly 5 million people. He then ordered a reduction in government travel, filmmaking, and consulting contracts. He felt the federal government was spending too much money on unnecessary programs.

President Reagan brought many changes to the White House. He preferred to work in a relaxed and informal atmosphere. He relied on the advice of his Cabinet and aides more than any President since Eisenhower. How did Reagan see his job?

In addition to checking hiring and spending, the President called for a 3-month delay on all new government regulations, and then created a Task Force on Regulatory Relief headed by Vice President Bush to review federal regulations. He also created the Council on Integrity and Efficiency to attack waste and fraud in government.

What campaign pledge did President Reagan honor?

The President honored another campaign pledge when, on July 7, 1981, he nominated Sandra Day O'Connor to fill the seat of retiring Justice Potter Stewart on the Supreme Court. Judge O'Connor was the first woman appointed to the highest court of the land.

1.3 Energy and the Environment. The Reagan administration proposed similar policy changes regarding energy and conservation. On January 28, 1981, the President himself put an end to all remaining government controls on oil and gasoline prices. In his executive order, Reagan said that such controls had held down American oil production. He also claimed that federal controls had boosted energy consumption and stifled the development of new technology. Reagan saw ending price controls as a "positive first step" toward a "balanced energy program."

What steps did the President take regarding energy conservation?

At the same time, Secretary of the Interior James Watt believed there had been too much protection of the nation's natural resources. Watt, too, wanted to reduce federal regulations as much as possible. He urged more mining, grazing, drilling, and prime development of government-owned resources.

Sandra Day O'Connor (1930-)

PROFILE

A little more than 100 years ago Justice Joseph Bradley denied a woman a license to be a lawyer because, he said, a woman should fulfill her mission in life as a wife and mother. Sandra Day O'Connor must have believed that a woman could fulfill her mission and also be a lawyer. She went to Stanford University and graduated with high honors in law.

O'Connor became a deputy attorney in California and later, with her husband returned to her home state, Arizona, to become Assistant Attorney General. While raising a family of 3 boys, she served as a state senator from 1969 to 1974, and was the first woman to be voted as the leader of a state legislature in the United States.

Five years later, after deciding to return to law, O'Connor was appointed to the Superior Court in Maricopa County. In 1979 she was appointed by the governor to the Arizona Court of Appeals.

President Ronald Reagan, in September 1981, appointed Sandra Day O'Connor to the Supreme Court of the United States. Her appointment as the first female Justice broke a tradition 191 years old. It also marked the end of the fight for full equality for women in American legal circles.

During 1981 the Department of the Interior allowed private companies to search for oil in nearly 1 billion acres (405 million hectares) of coastal waters. The Department also allowed searches for oil and coal in protected wilderness areas. The first land lease opened up about 9,000 acres (3,642 hectares) in the Capitan Wilderness Area of southwestern New Mexico.

The shift in conservation policy met with strong opposition from environmentalists and outdoor groups. These people felt the opening of protected areas to *resource exploration* (the search for new sources of natural resources) could result in dangerous oil spills in coastal waters and destruction of much of the nation's scenic natural environment. Watt, on the other hand, believed his policies would not only supply

Who opposed the conservation policy of the Reagan administration?

Secretary of the Interior James Watt angered many environmentalists with his plans to open previously protected federal lands to development and to reduce regulations. What did Watt believe these policies would accomplish?

enough sources of energy to make the nation much less dependent upon foreign imports, but also would create new opportunities for increasing employment. When Watt proposed to open up all wilderness lands for exploitation over an 18-year period, however, his plan was overwhelmingly rejected by the House of Representatives in August, 1982.

1.4   Assassination Attempt.   On March 30, 1981, just over two months after he had taken office, an assassination attempt was made on President Reagan. Emerging from a Washington hotel after a speaking engagement, the President was struck in the chest by a bullet fired by 25-year old John Hinckley, Jr. Hinckley was immediately subdued and arrested, and eventually tried and judged to be insane. Also wounded in the attack on the President were Secret Service agent Timothy McCarthy and city patrolman Thomas Delahanty. Most critically injured was presidential press secretary James Brady.

What caused added confusion?

While a shocked nation awaited reports on the condition of the President, Secretary of State Alexander Haig added to the confusion by announcing to the nation over television that "I am in control here in the White House." Proper constitutional procedure places the Vice President in authority when something happens to a President. Meanwhile, Vice President Bush hurriedly returned to Washington from a speaking trip in Texas.

The President made a remarkable recovery from his wound, as did press secretary Brady. After that, increased precautions were taken to safeguard the President's life. The steps were considered especially necessary when a series of attacks were made on other world leaders. For example, on May 13 Pope John Paul II was shot and seriously wounded in Rome by a Turkish terrorist, and on October 6 Egyptian President Anwar Sadat was gunned down while reviewing a military parade.

1.5   The PATCO Strike.   Members of the Professional Air Traffic Controllers Organization (PATCO) went on strike on August 3, 1981. The controllers walked off their jobs after their chief negotiator, union president Robert Poli, turned down the federal government's final offer on a new contract. PATCO sought a $575 million-a-year contract that called for a 4-day, 32-hour work week; a $10,000 across-the-board salary increase; and more liberal retirement provisions. The government had offered a package estimated at $50 million in wages and benefits.

What did PATCO members want? What did the government offer?

Federal law forbids strikes by federal employees. When the air traffic controllers walked off the job, President Reagan deemed the strike illegal and threatened to fire all PATCO members who did not return to work within 24 hours. When 11,500 controllers did not return to work, they were fired. They also became ineligible to be rehired at a later date.

During the early days of the strike, people traveling by air suffered delays and disruptions in service. Soon, however, the airlines found

Seconds after the attempted assassination of President Reagan, secret service agents and police surround and subdue would-be assassin John Hinckley (at far left). The President was wounded along with three others, including Press Secretary James Brady. According to the Constitution, who assumes the duties when something happens to the President?

The New Federalism   673

Members of PATCO went on strike in the summer of 1981 for better pay, shorter hours, and improved retirement benefits. Not long after the strike began, striking PATCO members were fired from their jobs. Why did President Reagan consider the PATCO strike illegal?

ways of handling about 75 percent of normal traffic. They worked with the 5,700 air traffic controllers who had remained on the job. The airlines and the government also set up special programs to train new controllers for the future.

1.6 The AWAC Controversy. During the spring of 1981 the Reagan administration announced it planned to sell $8.5 billion in military equipment, including 5 highly sophisticated reconnaissance airplanes called AWACs, to Saudi Arabia. Early polls showed that there was strong opposition to the sale in Congress. Some members felt that such equipment might be dangerous to the security of Israel. Others were concerned that the equipment could fall into the hands of hostile powers.

Why was the sale of AWACs to Saudi Arabia opposed?

President Reagan again demonstrated great skill in using political pressure and personal persuasion to win the support of key congressional leaders. On October 28, 1981, the Senate voted 52 to 48 against a resolution that would have blocked the sale.

1. What changes did President Reagan make in government operations upon taking office?
2. What steps did the Reagan adminstration take to solve the energy problem?
3. What crises arose during the first year of the Reagan adminstration?

2. The Reagan Economic Program

Calling upon Americans to "begin an era of national renewal" in his inaugural address, President Reagan outlined his economic program as "a new beginning." In the weeks that followed, he urged Congress to support this program. It called for decreases in taxes, reduced federal regulations, and sharp cuts in federal spending—all designed to stimulate the economy and to curb "double-digit" inflation.

2.1 The Federal Budget. On February 18, 1981, President Reagan spelled out the details of his economic program to a joint session of Congress. The plan called for a $41.4 billion cut in the $739.3 billion budget for 1982 proposed earlier by President Carter. Reagan also asked for a 30 percent reduction in individual income taxes to be spread over a 3-year period.

What did the President propose?

Though some compromises had to be made, the President got most of what he wanted. Congress approved budget cuts of $35.2 billion for 1982 and income tax reductions of 25 percent spread over three years. The tax cut was the largest ever enacted. Reagan signed the measures into law on August 13, saying they marked an end to "excessive growth"

The economic programs of the Reagan administration have been successful in some areas. The rate of inflation has slowed dramatically (left). On the other hand, the federal government operated at the largest deficit in history in 1982. What has been the trend of the inflation rate since 1979? Of the budget deficit?

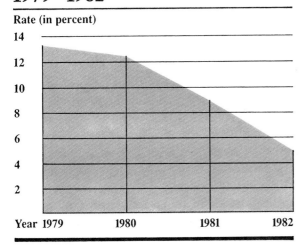

Rate of Inflation, 1979–1982

Rate (in percent)

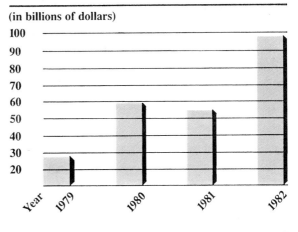

Budget Deficit, 1979–1982

(in billions of dollars)

in government spending and taxing. Five weeks later, however, the President called for $8.2 billion additional cuts in federal spending for 1982 because of concern over the estimated **budget deficit** (the excess in spending in regard to revenues received).

Democratic leaders, like House Speaker Thomas "Tip" O'Neill, strongly opposed Reagan's economic program. They called it **Reaganomics**—policy designed to increase production or favor supply. They pointed out that less money would be taken in by the federal treasury because of the tax cuts, and complained that most of the budget cuts would have to be made in social programs since Reagan proposed to increase spending on national defense.

Why did Democratic leaders oppose the President's economic program?

2.2 Reducing Social Services. The Reagan administration, supported by conservative members in Congress, sought to make cuts in the amount of federal money being spent for public health, education, and welfare. It also wanted to reduce the influence of government on non-political activities. This approach was opposed by liberal members of Congress, as well as by the aged, poor, and unemployed who felt the cuts would cause greater hardship for them.

Nevertheless, major cuts in social services went into effect October 1, 1981. These cuts affected nearly all programs funded by the federal government. Requirements were tightened for receiving benefits, particularly for those on the Food Stamp program and Aid to Families with Dependent Children (AFDC). Congress ordered a 3 percent reduction in federal Medicaid payments to the states during 1982. It also made changes requiring elderly and disabled persons to pay more for their medical care. Unemployment insurance benefits were reduced from 39 to 26 weeks in most states. Public service jobs funded under the Comprehensive Employment and Training Act (CETA) were completely eliminated. The Reagan administration believed that private groups and volunteer agencies should play a greater role in providing social programs and charitable assistance.

What cuts were made in social services?

2.3 Tax Increase. Despite the severe cuts in the federal budget, the Reagan administration was unable to achieve all of the results it sought. Although Reagan's policies did bring about a significant reduction in the rate of inflation, the President had said his economic program would promote business and produce a balanced budget. Instead, the nation continued to face rising unemployment, high interest rates, serious economic recession, and record budget deficits. In fact, federal spending, especially increased military expenditures, produced a 1982 deficit of more than $100 billion.

Thus, in the summer of 1982, Reagan had to ask Congress for a 3-year increase in federal taxes. Unwilling to alter the cut in individual

What caused the need for a tax increase?

income taxes passed the year before, the President called for numerous changes in tax laws that would provide the government with an estimated $98.3 billion in additional revenues. Critics called the tax proposals the largest tax increase in American history. The President called it "tax reform."

The tax bill itself was worked out by Senate Finance Chairman Robert Dole of Kansas. Among the major provisions included in the bill were a 10 percent withholding tax on interest and dividend payments; an increase in the excise taxes levied on cigarettes, telephone service, and air travel; a reduction in the allowances allowed for medical expense and casualty losses in itemizing deductions on income tax returns; and a reporting system on the money earned in tips by restaurant workers and the like.

What were the provisions of the tax bill?

Blaming the need of a tax increase on the deficit and the "big-spending" policies of previous administrations, President Reagan put the strength of his office behind passage of the bill. He used television and newspaper ads to gain public support, and political pressure and personal contacts to obtain bipartisan support in Congress. With the aid of liberal Democrats like Senator Edward Kennedy and Speaker O'Neill, the bill finally was passed by a slim margin in Congress in late August.

Who helped to pass the tax bill?

As the leader of the Democratic-controlled House of Representatives, Speaker Tip O'Neill (at far right) has led the opposition to many of the Reagan administration's economic programs. Why has O'Neill opposed Reagan's programs?

2.4 Legislative Setback. Within weeks of the tax victory, however, the President suffered his first major legislative defeat. He opposed passage of a $14.2 billion supplemental funding bill, calling it a "budget buster." Most Democrats and a number of prominent Republicans on the other hand believed the appropriations were needed to fund a number of social, education, and defense programs, as well as aid for farmers and elderly persons and government salaries. When President Reagan vetoed the bill, both the Republican-controlled Senate and the Democratic-controlled House overrode his veto by the necessary two-thirds vote. People waited to see whether this was just a temporary setback for the President or a serious split in the ranks of the Republican party.

Why did members of Congress support more spending?

Meanwhile the administration's attempt to control the budget deficit plus a gradual but steady decline in interest rates produced a positive reaction on the stock market. Throughout the fall months of 1982, the Dow-Jones stock average climbed to new highs, and several days saw record trading in shares of stock. Many people hoped it signaled an upturn in the economy and the end to the nation's recession. Some warned, however, that it was just a temporary improvement in a generally dismal economic picture, particularly since the unemployment rate continued to rise well above 10 percent nationally—the highest since the Great Depression.

What led people to hope the economy was turning around?

1. What specific things did President Reagan call for in his economic program?
2. Why was it necessary for the President to seek a tax increase in 1982?
3. What legislative setback did the President receive in 1982?

3. Reagan's Foreign Policy

Throughout the 1980 political campaign, Ronald Reagan had said that the United States had fallen behind the Soviet Union in military power. He saw the Iranian hostage crisis as one of many signs that the nation had become weak. He believed that other countries no longer held the United States in high esteem. He promised to change this after his election.

3.1 U.S.-Soviet Relations. After his inauguration, President Reagan announced he would pursue a tougher foreign policy. Amerian foreign policy, he said, would concentrate less on human rights and more on fighting *terrorism,* or the use of fear to gain power. He announced that any future acts of terrorism would be met swiftly and severely. His choice of Alexander Haig, Jr., a professional soldier and former commander of NATO forces, as Secretary of State reflected this.

Although Reagan took a tough stand against communism, he also expressed the hope for peaceful relations. In April 1981, he ended the ban on grain exports to the Soviet Union, an action favored by American farmers. And in September, Secretary of State Haig met with Soviet Foreign Minister Andrei Gromyko to discuss relations between the United States and the Soviet Union.

On November 18, 1981, President Reagan called upon the Soviet Union to dismantle its medium-range nuclear missiles. He promised that if the Soviets would do this, the United States would cancel its plan to supply nuclear missiles to NATO forces in Europe. Reagan was responding to mass demonstrations in Europe opposing nuclear weapons and to a growing movement in the United States advocating a nuclear arms "freeze." His policy aimed to show that it was up to the Soviet Union to reduce the "threat of nuclear war."

What did the President propose regarding arms?

3.2 The Arms Program. In September 1981, President Reagan announced that any new SALT (Strategic Arms Limitation) treaty with the Soviet Union must include ways to see that it was being carried out. He also warned that unless arms were limited, the Soviet Union would be in an arms race "which it could not win." To back up his words, the President announced in October a 6-year national defense program that would cost more than $180 billion.

There were five major parts to the new arms program: (1) Construction of 100 MX missiles to be placed in underground silos. The MX missile is a 4-stage rocket equipped with 10 nuclear warheads, each of which can be fired at a separate target. (2) Development of 100 four-engine intercontinental B-1 bombers, to replace the B-52 bombers. Each B-1 bomber can carry 32 air-to-ground nuclear missiles. (3) A program to develop a new "Stealth" bomber, invisible to enemy radar. (4) Construction of 6 giant Trident nuclear-powered submarines equipped with 7 new D-5 missiles carrying 8 nuclear warheads each. (5) Strengthening of the defense communications network in case other communications systems are knocked out in a nuclear attack.

What were the elements of the new arms program?

In outlining the arms program to Congress, Secretary of Defense Caspar Weinberger emphasized its main objective is to prevent nuclear war. It is intended to show other powers that they cannot threaten or defeat the United States.

Development of the MX (left) and the Hawk (right) missiles are part of Reagan's arms and national defense program. Reagan insists he favors an arms limitation treaty, but only if the Soviet Union consents to inspection. What is the objective of the arms program according to administration officials?

Why was Reagan against the western powers helping to build the Soviet pipeline?

3.3 The Pipeline Controversy. In the summer of 1982, President Reagan became upset when he learned that American, British, French, and Italian companies were providing supplies to the Soviets to be used in the construction of a 3,000-mile pipeline to carry natural gas from Siberia to Western Europe. He thought it was wrong for the western powers to help build a Soviet pipeline for two reasons: (1) The pipeline would provide the Soviet Union with $10 billion of western money. (2) The pipeline would make this nation's European allies too dependent on the Soviet Union for their energy supplies.

In addition, the President wanted to penalize the Soviet Union for supporting the martial-law regime in Poland which had placed stringent controls on the new Polish union, Solidarity, and had arrested many of its leaders. When the western countries refused to give up supplying the

Soviets, Reagan took action to prevent the Soviet Union from buying American goods, services, or technology. Although he agreed to remove these sanctions in November 1982 after the death of the Soviet leader, Leonid Breshnev, the pipeline controversy caused a serious split between the United States and several of its important NATO allies.

3.4 Latin-American Relations. Ever since Cuba aligned itself with the Soviet Union in the 1960's, the United States feared that the Castro regime might try to establish Communist governments in other parts of Latin America. The various republics of Central America, with large populations of landless peasants and wealth concentrated in the hands of a small upper class, seemed likely targets. In an effort to stop the spread of communism, the United States gave military and financial aid to governments headed by groups of military officers called *juntas.*

What did the United States fear regarding the Castro regime?

By the late 1970's many of the juntas, particularly those in Nicaragua and El Salvador, were opposed by large numbers of their own people. Although there were communists and other "leftists" among the opponents, many were members of the middle class or peasants who wanted land reform and social change. To maintain power, the juntas resorted to a variety of suppressive tactics, including mass arrests and executions.

Why have many of the juntas in Central America been opposed?

Though the United States expressed sorrow over these violent tactics, it did not want to aid the possibility of communist expansion by

President Reagan was angered when he learned that American and western companies were helping the Soviet Union build a gas pipeline between Siberia and Western Europe. Why did Reagan oppose this project?

weakening the juntas. Nevertheless, it put pressure on several governments to introduce land reforms and improve the living conditions for peasants. Some changes were made, but in general the plight of the poor in most Latin American countries remained a major problem.

When Reagan became President, new steps were taken to stop the spread of communism. With the administration claiming that Cuba was arming leftist groups, the United States resumed the sale of weapons to El Salvador in January 1981. At the same time, it stopped economic aid to Nicaragua because of evidence that indicated the Nicaraguan junta was aiding leftist guerrillas in El Salvador.

Meanwhile, there was little evidence that the juntas had stopped using terror against their opponents. Archbishop Oscar Romero, an

What steps did the Reagan administration take to stop the spread of communism?

Hot Spots of Latin America

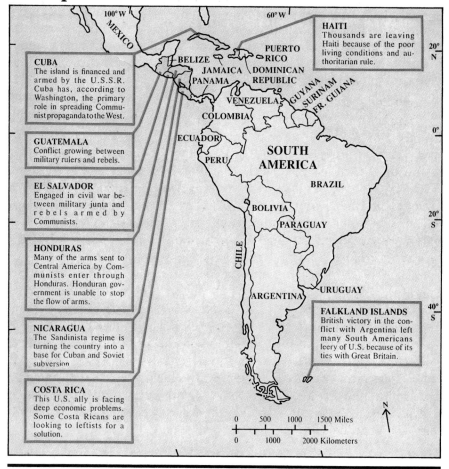

CUBA
The island is financed and armed by the U.S.S.R. Cuba has, according to Washington, the primary role in spreading Communist propaganda to the West.

GUATEMALA
Conflict growing between military rulers and rebels.

EL SALVADOR
Engaged in civil war between military junta and rebels armed by Communists.

HONDURAS
Many of the arms sent to Central America by Communists enter through Honduras. Honduran government is unable to stop the flow of arms.

NICARAGUA
The Sandinista regime is turning the country into a base for Cuban and Soviet subversion.

COSTA RICA
This U.S. ally is facing deep economic problems. Some Costa Ricans are looking to leftists for a solution.

HAITI
Thousands are leaving Haiti because of the poor living conditions and authoritarian rule.

FALKLAND ISLANDS
British victory in the conflict with Argentina left many South Americans leery of U.S. because of its ties with Great Britain.

outspoken critic of the junta in El Salvador, was shot while saying mass in March 1981. In December, three American nuns and an aide were brutally murdered by government soldiers. Many Americans thought that military and economic aid should be stopped until conditions improved. The Reagan administration, however, continued to support the juntas as the only way of preventing communist expansion in Latin America.

3.5 The Falklands War.   While attempting to deal with the problems of Central America, the Reagan administration suddenly was confronted with a serious problem in South America. On April 2, 1982, several thousand Argentine troops invaded the British-held Falkland islands off the Argentine coast and seized control. Argentina justified its invasion on the basis the islands had been stolen by the British in 1833. Though rightful ownership of the islands had been disputed for years, it was not until rumors of possible major offshore oil deposits came to light that the tension between Argentina and Great Britain began to mount over the issue.

How did the Falklands War begin?

The British government responded immediately to the Argentine invasion. Prime Minister Margaret Thatcher ordered a naval task force to set sail for the South Atlantic and threatened that the islands would be retaken by force if the Argentines refused to withdraw.

The actions of both nations placed the United States in a dilemma. On the one hand, British military action could be interpreted as violating the principles of the Monroe Doctrine and the Rio Pact. On the other, Great Britain was this nation's closest ally. Faced with the dilemma, Secretary of State Haig used *shuttle diplomacy* flying between London and Buenos Aires for several weeks in an attempt to work out a settlement. When negotiations failed, the United States announced it would support Great Britain. Along with other members of NATO, it agreed to impose economic sanctions against Argentina.

The Falklands War was brief. Combining sea power with effective air cover, the British landed troops brought from Europe. The British forces swiftly overpowered the Argentine defensive positions forcing Argentina to surrender and return the Falklands to British rule. The war, however, created bitter feelings on the part of the Argentines toward the United States. Not only did the United States in their eyes fail to uphold the principles of the Monroe Doctrine, but they believed it played a major role in their defeat by providing military aid to the British. It was obvious that it would take a long time to heal the breach caused by the Falklands War.

Who won the Falklands War?

3.6 The Lebanon Crisis.   No sooner had the Falklands War wound down than trouble erupted in the Middle East. Hope that the

The Middle East

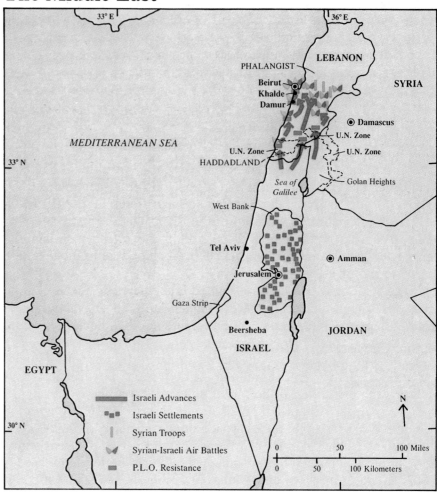

The Middle East was again the scene of turmoil when Israeli forces invaded Lebanon to assault PLO outposts. In what cities did the PLO put up resistance? In what part of Lebanon were Syrian troops grouped?

Why did Israel invade Lebanon?

Camp David accords could in time bring peace to that region was badly shaken when Israeli forces crossed into Lebanon in June 1982. The massive assault was designed to crush the strongholds of the Palestine Liberation Organization (PLO). The PLO had used its Lebanese bases to launch frequent artillery bombardments against Israel's northern settlements.

Moving quickly through South Lebanon, the Israeli armored columns converged on the capital city of Beirut and set seige to the western section where most of the PLO forces were located. For nearly 10 weeks West Beirut was under constant air and rocket attack as Israel demanded the surrender of the PLO defenders.

Meanwhile, special U.S. envoy Philip Habib worked unceasingly to arrange for a cease-fire. Finally in late August an agreement was reached whereby the PLO fighters were permitted to leave West Beirut safely for such Arab countries as Syria, Jordan, Algeria, Tunisia, and Egypt. The evacuation was monitored by a small peace-keeping force made up of French, Italian, and American troops.

What agreement did Habib arrange?

With a break in the figthing in Lebanon, President Reagan announced a new proposal to ease Arab-Israeli tensions. Reaffirming this nation's commitment to Israel's security, the President suggested "self government for the Palestinians living in the West Bank and Gaza Strip in association with Jordan." He also called for Israel to cease setting up new settlements in those areas. The President's plan neither supported the establishment of an independent Palestinian state nor continued Israeli control over the West Bank and Gaza Strip. It basically outlined a 5-year transition period during which the Palestinian inhabitants of those areas would have "full autonomy over their own affairs."

Efforts to gain support for the plan were undertaken by George Shultz, who had replaced Alexander Haig as Secretary of State. The Israeli government immediately rejected the plan, and Prime Minister Begin angrily denounced it as an "affront to Israel." Several Arab nations on the other hand expressed initial support. They saw it as an indication that the United States was becoming more understanding of the Arab point of view.

What was the reaction to Reagan's proposal?

American troops helped evacuate PLO troops from West Beirut during the August, 1982 cease-fire. President Reagan formulated a plan to break the dispute between the Arab nations and Israel. How did the Arab nations react to the President's plan?

1. What changes occurred in U.S.-Soviet relations during the Reagan administration?
2. What problems did the United States face in Latin America during the Reagan administration?
3. What initiative did President Reagan take to ease Arab-Israeli tensions in the Middle East?

4. Holding the Conservative Line _____

The sweeping Reagan victory in the 1980 election was largely due to the collection of different political groups Reagan was able to pull together. Their support made it possible for Reagan to change the direction of government during his first year in office.

4.1 Big Business. The Reagan victory marked a return to earlier ideas of free enterprise and the policies of laissez-faire. President Reagan and his advisers thought that American business would grow faster, make more money, and employ more people if government removed controls and lowered taxes. Reagan himself found other ways to help business and industry. He lifted controls on oil to allow American oil companies to raise their prices. He permitted cutbacks in safety regulations to help auto manufacturers to save expenses. He persuaded Japan to reduce its export of cars into the United States.

How did Reagan help business?

American business leaders were generally pleased with Reagan's point of view and supported most programs he proposed. Though they became angry over the 1982 tax increase, they made up an important part of the conservative coalition. Critics of the administration, however, accused Reagan of supporting business and favoring the well-to-do at the expense of labor and the poor.

4.2 The Moral Majority. Another important group of Reagan supporters were conservatives who believed that American society had become too liberal and materialistic. They thought that Americans needed to return to supporting such old-fashioned values as patriotism and Christian ethics. Led by a number of fundamentalist preachers, like Reverend Jerry Falwell, they formed a political action group known as the Moral Majority.

What did the Moral Majority want?

The Moral Majority wanted to reshape American politics. Members of the Moral Majority wished to have prayer reinstituted in school classrooms, prevent federal funds from being used for abortions, and reduce sex and violence on television. They formed a powerful

Conservatism and Liberalism
CONCEPT

How much should we try to keep the present the same as the past? How fast should we adjust to new social and technological developments? How much should government be involved in our lives? These questions illustrate the basic differences between conservatives and liberals.

Conservatism is defined as the desire to conserve or keep that which exists. Conservatives want change to occur slowly, if at all. They generally are opposed to large-scale government involvement in local affairs and economic matters. On the other hand, liberals accept a larger government role as a necessity to promote freedom, equal justice, and equal opportunity. They are less attached to tradition, and are willing to make changes more quickly. Both conservatism and liberalism have made important contributions to the American political tradition.

Since the 1968 election of Richard Nixon, conservatives have gained more influence in American politics. In 1980 conservatives supported Ronald Reagan for President. President Reagan's speeches and policies show that he is in agreement with a conservative philosophy. Read the following excerpt from a speech made by President Reagan on July 13, 1982, and see if you can identify expressions of conservatism within it.

Together you and I are involved in an epic struggle to restore the governmental balance intended in our Constitution and desired by our people. We're turning America away from yesterday's policies of big brother government. We're determined to restore power and authority to states and localities, returning as much decision making as possible to the [local] level of government where services are delivered. . . . We in this administration have taken another look at the Constitution, and are applying it to the America of today. We will restore the 10th Amendment to the Constitution, which says that the Federal Government shall do only those things provided in the Constitution, and all other powers shall remain with the states and with the people.

1. Does President Reagan want the government to do more or less in the lives of the American people?
2. Does the President think that some Americans have taken actions that are changes from what the Constitution intended?
3. What attitude toward change is shown in the President's statement?
4. How would a liberal be expected to answer the President?

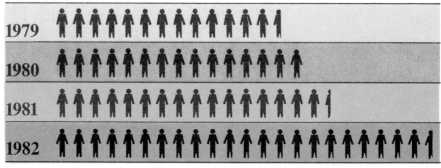

Unemployment, 1979–1982

Year

1979	
1980	
1981	
1982	

Based on Annual Average

equals 500,000 persons

The problem of unemployment has troubled both the Carter and Reagan administrations. What groups have been hardest hit by unemployment?

political lobby to push their ideas in Congress and worked to defeat liberal candidates running for office. By 1982, however, many members were not completely satisfied with the President's performance. They felt Reagan had not worked hard enough to satisfy their demands.

How did most blue-collar workers normally vote?

4.3 The Blue-Collar Vote. Before 1980 most industrial workers and white ethnic groups had usually voted Democratic. These lower-middle- and middle-class voters, however, had been hard hit by high taxes, rising inflation, and growing unemployment in the late 1970's. Many felt that the Democrats had spent too much on social programs. They also wanted more emphasis placed on patriotism and national defense. Thus, they supported Reagan in 1980.

But after two years, many blue-collar workers were no longer happy with Reaganomics. Unemployment had become a serious problem. Certain valued social programs had been scrapped, educational benefits reduced, and unemployment coverage lowered. There was even talk that social security was in serious difficulty. Thus, there was widespread dissatisfaction among blue-collar workers.

Who was hard hit by Reaganomics?

4.4 Minority Groups. Blacks and Hispanics were among the hardest hit by Reaganomics. Black unemployment was twice that of non-blacks, and in some cities unemployment of males between the ages of 16 and 35 was over 30 percent. Because many blacks and Hispanics were poor, the cuts in social programs also hurt them.

Black members of Congress, as well as other minority group leaders, spoke out against the reduction of social services to little avail.

Though some conservative black appointees remained loyal to the policies of the administration, it was clear by 1982 that support for Reagan among the black and Hispanic communities was minimal.

4.5 The Election of 1982. People looked closely at the congressional elections of 1982. They wanted to see whether the groups which had supported the Republicans in 1980 would vote the same way in 1982. The election results showed a definite setback for President Reagan and his conservative policies. Though the Republicans maintained their control in the Senate, the Democrats gained 26 seats in the House, in addition to 7 governorships. The election showed that the Republican party had lost significant support among several groups that had formed their winning combination in 1980. Many blue-collar workers, Southerners, and elderly voters had returned to the Democratic party.

Who made gains in the 1982 election?

Republican losses were serious, but not critical. By increasing Democratic control in the House, voters indicated they wanted changes in Reaganomics. They wanted to try different methods to end recession and increase employment. At the same time, by leaving the Republicans in control of the Senate, they showed support for the administration's overall goals of reducing federal spending and controlling inflation. How the Republicans responded to these election results would determine their presidential prospects in 1984.

What did the 1982 election results show?

1. Who made up the major groups responsible for Reagan's victory in 1980?
2. What were their attitudes toward the administration in 1982?
3. What were the results of the 1982 election?

5. Conclusion_____

The Reagan administration marked the first major change of American political, social, and economic policy in nearly forty years. Since the days of the New Deal, the emphasis had been on large-scale government spending for social programs. With strong popular support, President Reagan set out to reverse the trend of big government spending. But when his budget cuts affected programs upon which many lower- and middle-class Americans depended, Reagan's support began to dwindle. The election of 1982 showed that while voters wanted to reduce waste, graft, and inefficiency, they did not want to lose social programs completely.

Chapter 28 Review

Main Points

1. The policies of the Reagan administration called for a reduction of the role the federal government played in the lives of the American people.

2. During his first two years in office, President Reagan faced a number of domestic crises including an unsuccessful assassination attempt.

3. Reagan's economic program sought to curb inflation through decreased federal spending and tax cuts.

4. Despite a sharp drop in the inflation rate, huge budget deficits continued to affect the nation's recovery from deep recession and forced the necessity for a tax increase in 1982.

5. Concerned with the need to strengthen national defense, President Reagan took a firmer stance in dealings with the Soviet Union.

6. Conflict in the Falkland islands and Lebanon created difficult diplomatic problems for the Reagan administration.

7. Members of several groups who had supported Reagan in 1980 became dissatisfied with Reaganomics because of continuing recession and mounting unemployment.

8. The Democrats made significant gains in the House of Representatives and in state legislatures and governorships in the 1982 election.

Building Vocabulary

1. Identify the following:

New Federalism	PATCO	Solidarity
Sandra Day O'Connor	AWAC	Margaret Thatcher
James Watt	Thomas O'Neill	Philip Habib
Alexander Haig	Robert Dole	Moral Majority

2. Define the following:

resource exploration	Reaganomics	juntas
budget deficit	terrorism	

Remembering the Facts

1. What did President Reagan believe about the Democrats' control of the federal government?

2. What was Reagan's presidential style?

3. What were the Reagan administration's energy and conservation policies?

4. What important world leaders had assassination attempts made on their lives in 1981?
5. Why were the air traffic controllers fired when they went on strike?
6. Why did Reagan want to decrease federal spending and cut taxes?
7. What social services were reduced or eliminated by the Reagan administration?
8. What were points of conflict between the Soviet Union and the United States in the early 1980's?
9. What problems did this nation face in Central America?
10. What action did the United States take to help settle the crises in the Falkland islands and Lebanon?
11. Which political party gained the most in the election of 1982?

Understanding the Facts

1. How did President Reagan change the direction of government?
2. What did President Reagan see as the root cause of the nation's economic problems?
3. What problems did the Falkland and Lebanon crises cause for the United States?
4. How successful was Reagan's economic program?
5. What groups had a change of attitude regarding the Reagan administration? Why?
6. How can the 1982 elections results be interpreted regarding the attitude of the American people toward the Reagan administration?

Using Graphs

Reading Picture Graphs. The illustration on page 688 is called a picture graph. In picture graphs, a varying number of symbols or symbols of varying size are used to express the amount or level of the thing being shown. In this graph a number of symbols are reproduced for each year to show the number of people receiving unemployment compensation in each of the years from 1979 to 1982. To read the graph, consult the key to determine the number of people each symbol represents. Simply multiply the number of symbols by the number shown in the key to determine the total. Using this approach, read the graph and answer the following questions.

1. What year had the highest unemployment? The lowest?
2. What was the largest number of people unemployed in each of the years?
3. Was unemployment higher in 1982 than it was in 1979?
4. Based on the graph, is the 4-year trend toward higher or lower unemployment?
5. Since 1979, which year shows the greatest increase in unemployment?

Challenges
for America

Countries around the world sent "tall ships" to the United States during the Bicentennial in 1976. Many American boaters also joined the celebration in New York harbor. How has the United States changed in 200 years?

As it moved into the 1980's, the United States was just over 200 years old. In that time, the country, the people, and the ways of life had changed greatly. The story of the United States has been one of change and of meeting new challenges. In the years to come, there will be more changes—in society, in culture, and in the economy. These changes will continue to bring new challenges to America and Americans.

1. A Changing American Society

Much has happened in the United States since the 1950's, and American society has had to change with the times. This can be seen in the wealth and well-being of the people, as well as in their problems. It also can be seen in their levels of education and their ideas. The very makeup of the people is different in the 1980's from the recent past.

1.1 The American People. The people of the United States always have been a mixed group, coming from every area of the world. This was still true as the nation entered the 1980's. According to the 1980 census, there were about 226.5 million Americans. Making up that number were 180.5 million whites, 26.5 million blacks, about 14.6 million Hispanics, 3.5 million Asian Americans, and about 1.4 million American Indians.

Into what groups is the American population broken down by the Census Bureau?

As a whole, the American people make up one of the most prosperous nations in the world. The *median family income* of Americans was $3,319 a year in 1950. This means that one half of the families in America made more and one half made less than $3,319 that year. By 1980, the figure had risen to about $18,000. The *gross national product* (GNP)—the value of all goods and services produced in one year—also rose. In 1950, the GNP was $286 billion. In 1980, it was $2.5 trillion.

How much did median family income increase between 1950 and 1980?

Education is another area of change. The number of Americans able to go to college has grown greatly. Only 1.1 percent of people 18 to 24 years old were able to go to college in 1870. That year 52,000 Americans were working toward college degrees. In 1970, more than 32 percent could go to college, and close to 8 million were working toward degrees. At the same time, hundreds of thousands more were taking college courses for which they would receive no degree.

How many more people go to college today than did 100 years ago?

1.2 Population Change and Mobility. Americans as a people not only have become more prosperous and more educated, they also have changed in other ways. Even though the population has kept growing, its rate of growth has declined. For every ten Americans born

What is happening to the rate of population growth? Why?

Population by State, 1980

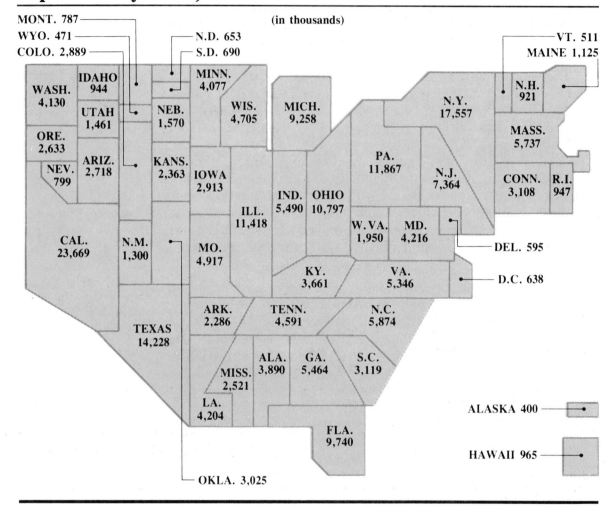

(in thousands)

MONT. 787
WYO. 471
COLO. 2,889
N.D. 653
S.D. 690
VT. 511
MAINE 1,125

WASH. 4,130
IDAHO 944
UTAH 1,461
ORE. 2,633
NEV. 799
ARIZ. 2,718
N.M. 1,300
CAL. 23,669
NEB. 1,570
KANS. 2,363
MINN. 4,077
WIS. 4,705
MICH. 9,258
IOWA 2,913
ILL. 11,418
IND. 5,490
OHIO 10,797
MO. 4,917
KY. 3,661
N.Y. 17,557
PA. 11,867
N.J. 7,364
W. VA. 1,950
MD. 4,216
VA. 5,346
N.H. 921
MASS. 5,737
CONN. 3,108
R.I. 947
DEL. 595
D.C. 638
TEXAS 14,228
ARK. 2,286
TENN. 4,591
N.C. 5,874
MISS. 2,521
ALA. 3,890
GA. 5,464
S.C. 3,119
LA. 4,204
FLA. 9,740
OKLA. 3,025

ALASKA 400
HAWAII 965

In 1980, which states had the largest number of people? Which states had the smallest? Which section of the United States was most populated? Which section was least populated?

in 1915, only eight were born in 1960, only six in 1970, and only five in 1980. As far as experts can tell, the rate will keep on going down in the years ahead.

As the birthrate has gone down, so has the proportion of young people. In 1970, the median age of Americans was just over 28. In 1979, it rose to 30. By the year 2000, it is expected to be about 35.

Some of the changes in population are due to a change in immigration. In America's early years, a great many people came to

How has immigration changed in recent years?

694 Challenges for America

settle. Since quotas on immigration were passed in the 1920's, fewer immigrants have entered the country. So immigrants have contributed less to population growth. In the 1970's, for example, over 80 percent of all Americans had been born in the United States, and so had their parents.

The home countries of more recent immigrants are different, too. In the past, most immigrants came from Europe. In the 1970's, the largest number came from Mexico and the Philippines. Many also came from the West Indies and India, as well as Vietnam and other areas of Southeast Asia.

Another factor that has made a difference in American society is the people's *mobility,* or ability to move or be moved. Americans always have been a people on the move. During the 1800's, they moved in great numbers from east to west and from rural to urban areas. In the 1950's, people began moving from the cities to the suburbs in search of more space, better schools, less crime, and lower taxes. By 1980, more Americans lived in suburbs than in central city areas.

Why did people move to the suburbs?

The movement to the suburbs has caused hardships for many cities. Most of the people who left the cities were white and had good incomes. When they moved away, they left the central cities occupied mostly by the poor, the aged, and minorities, many of whom could not find jobs. They needed the social services provided by the cities. But as the need

What problems were caused by the move to the suburbs?

How did total American population change from 1930 until 1980? What percent of the total population does each foreign nationality group make up? What can account for the size of the total foreign-born population?

Population Growth, 1930–1980

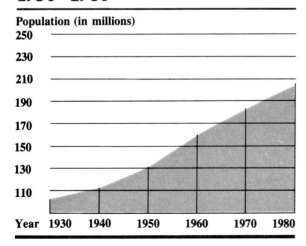

Population (in millions)

| Year | 1930 | 1940 | 1950 | 1960 | 1970 | 1980 |

Total Estimated Population, 1980

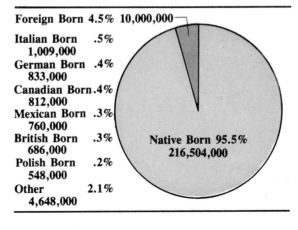

Foreign Born 4.5% 10,000,000

Italian Born .5%
1,009,000
German Born .4%
833,000
Canadian Born .4%
812,000
Mexican Born .3%
760,000
British Born .3%
686,000
Polish Born .2%
548,000
Other 2.1%
4,648,000

Native Born 95.5%
216,504,000

for these services grew, the cities found that they were less able to provide them. What to do about this is one of the most important questions facing the United States.

Hardest hit by the movement to the suburbs are the industrial cities of the Northeast and Middle West, such as New York, Philadelphia, Cleveland, and Detroit. The entire northeast part of the country also has been losing people to the *sun belt*—the southeast and southwest parts where the weather is sunny and warm much of the time. In the 1960's, California moved ahead of New York as the state with the most people. By 1980, Los Angeles, San Diego, Houston, Dallas, and San Antonio were among the ten largest cities in the United States. At present, it is believed that the number of people in the sun belt will continue to grow.

1.3 The Problem of Poverty.   Although the United States is a very prosperous nation, poverty is one of its major problems. More than 10 percent of the population (over 22.5 million Americans) live in poverty. In many cases, the poor are concentrated in certain areas of the country. One such area is Appalachia, a mountain region that stretches from New York to Georgia and Mississippi. Thousands of people there need better housing, medical treatment, and other services. The federal government has tried to help these people, and in some ways, it has succeeded. But much still remains to be done.

Much poverty also exists among minority groups. The incomes of American Indians, blacks, and Hispanics as a whole are lower than that of whites. As a group, American Indians still are the poorest and least educated of all Americans. Blacks, too, have been hit hard. Throughout the 1970's, twice as many blacks as whites were unemployed. Most poor blacks lived in the inner cities where housing was bad, crime rates were high, and services were poor.

1.4 Seeking Equality.   An awareness of the differences between their lives and those of other Americans led some groups to push for equality. During the 1960's and 1970's especially, minority groups and women organized and worked to achieve this goal.

One group of people who stepped up their efforts during these years were American Indians. In 1968, they formed the American Indian Movement (AIM) to work for Indian rights. They wanted the Bureau of Indian Affairs to do more to end discrimination in jobs and in housing. They also wanted the Bureau to do more to protect water rights on Indian reservation land. In 1976, the Indians went a step further. More than 20 groups joined together to form a council. They hoped that by acting as one, they would have more say about the use of their land.

How many Americans are poor?

On the whole, what group of Americans are the poorest?

Why was AIM formed?

Although women in the United States had had the right to vote since 1920, they still had to work for equal educational and vocational opportunities in the 1970's. What other groups also organized to achieve the goal of equality?

The efforts of American Indians are just one part of a drive for greater equality and participation by all members of society that has been going on for many years. This move has brought about increased voting rights and greater opportunities for education for many people. It also has helped put an end to some discrimination. Still, much remains to be done. Issues such as poverty and minority rights will keep on challenging the United States and its people in the years ahead.

What has the movement for equality accomplished?

1. Based on the 1980 census, what was the total population for the United States?
2. Which sections of the United States grew fastest?
3. What groups worked for equality?

2. American Cultural Trends _____

Cultural trends, like other things in American life, have undergone changes. Each new group of people entering the United States has brought its own heritage, beliefs, and ideas. Over the years, this has

What has helped to make American culture so diverse?

helped to make American culture one of the most mixed in the world. This variety is seen in what Americans do with their free time. In recent years, they have had more free time than ever before. More and more people are using this time to read, watch television, listen to or make music, and attend or take part in sporting events. These new ways of spending free time also have affected American culture.

2.1 Trends in Literature, Art, and Music. In the 1970's, Americans read more books than ever before. These books were different from those read in the past. Most were in paperback, which meant they cost less to buy. Many were written to appeal to the greatest number of people possible. Among the more popular were novels about science fiction, international intrigue, and romance. Just as popular were novels that took an actual event or case history and built a story around it. Truman Capote's *In Cold Blood*, for example, detailed a chilling murder that took place in the Midwest.

How is American literature different today from that of the past?

If American literature since the 1950's had to be described in one word, that word would be *diversity,* or having lots of differences. In recent times, racial and ethnic groups, as well as women, have tried to bring greater attention to their needs. In 1952, Ralph Ellison told how blacks were viewed by whites in his book, *Invisible Man.* In 1963, Betty Friedan asked women to recognize what society was doing to them and to demand equal rights in her book, *The Feminine Mystique.* In 1976, Alex Haley traced the history of his family from its beginnings in Africa to its present life in America in *Roots.* Isaac Bashevis Singer wrote many books about Jewish life in New York City and in his boyhood home of Warsaw, Poland.

What developments have occurred regarding American music?

Some of the same trends that affected American literature also influenced American music. Music, too, became Big Business, with records and tapes being sold by the millions. During the 1900's, Americans grew to be great fans of *popular music*—music well-liked by the general public. In the 1950's, rock and roll came into its own with such hits as Bill Haley and the Comets' "Rock Around the Clock," Paul Anka's "Diana," Chuck Berry's "Johnny Be Good," and Elvis Presley's "You Ain't Nothin' But a Hound Dog." The Beatles, a British rock group, brought a new kind of rock and roll to the United States in the 1960's. They thrilled American teenagers with such hits as "I Want to Hold Your Hand," "Help!", and "Hard Day's Night."

What forms of music enjoy great popularity?

Two other kinds of music also were popular with Americans during much of the 1900's. They are jazz and country-western. Jazz has remained popular since the 1920's, when it was the rage. It has gone through many changes. In recent years, it has gained a new popularity among younger Americans. In the 1970's, country-western music,

Rachel Carson (1907–1964)

PROFILE

When Rachel Carson entered college, she wanted to become a writer. After a few courses in biology, however, she changed her mind. Carson continued to study biology in graduate school, and she taught biology for several years. In 1936, she began work with the United States Fish and Wildlife Service where she stayed for 15 years.

In 1951, Carson published a book, *The Sea Around Us*. Reviewers praised it with enthusiasm for both its scientific content and its readable style. With this book, Carson showed an ability to present scientific facts in a simple way so that they could be easily understood.

Carson's best-known book was *Silent Spring*, published in 1962. It pictures a time when chemicals used to control insects would destroy not only the insects but many birds and fish as well.

Silent Spring awoke many people to the possible dangers of pesticides and chemicals. As one of the most widely read nonfiction books of its time, *Silent Spring* influenced some state legislatures to vote on pesticide control.

Rachel Carson wrote and lectured about the way people affect nature. She contributed much to the increased attention given to the environment since the 1960's.

which had been a favorite of many Americans for years, captured the attention of a great many more people. Country-western stars like Johnny Cash, Loretta Lynn, Dolly Parton, Kenny Rogers, and Charlie Pride drew large crowds wherever they appeared.

In many cases, the music of the late 1970's and the 1980's is a blend of several of these forms. It has been greatly influenced by the use of electronic instruments and sound systems, too. Electronics have made new sounds possible and have put a new feeling of energy into popular music.

Like literature and music, American painting came in many different styles and treated many different themes in the 1900's. One style was called Abstract Expressionism. It was created by New York artists after World War II. It was the first American style of painting to have an impact around the world. Paintings done in this style do not try

What are some of the new forms of American art?

Challenges for America   699

to show a scene in a realistic way. Instead, more attention is paid to the act of creating the painting. This was best explained by Jackson Pollack, one of the style's creators. He said, "I want to express my feelings, rather than to illustrate them."

During the late 1950's, another new American style of art appeared. Called Pop Art, its subjects were common, everyday things like soup cans and highway signs. These were painted with vivid colors and bold lines. Pop artist Andy Warhol became famous for his paintings of huge Campbell Soup cans. Another Pop artist, Roy Lichtenstein, gained fame for his comic-strip paintings.

In the middle 1960's, still other American styles of art appeared. One called Minimal Art used designs and shapes to make colors seem like what they were not. Another was Super-Realism. Its subjects were painted in such a realistic way that it was easy to mistake the paintings for photographs.

For what purposes have black and Hispanic artists used painting in recent years?

After the 1960's, many American artists began to use their paintings as a form of social protest. Black and Hispanic artists in particular created paintings that pointed out people's problems or

Some people thought that Jackson Pollock (left) showed the rhythm and power of American life in his painting. Norman Rockwell's conservative gentleman (right) examines an abstract canvas. What is Abstract Expressionism?

showed scenes from their own past. Sometimes their works were painted as murals on outside walls in large cities.

2.2 Movies and the Mass Media.   Still another American art form is motion pictures. As such, they have been an important source of entertainment for Americans for many years. The movies of the early 1900's were black and white silent films, shown on small screens. In more recent times, however, more subjects are treated, and color, wide screens, and better sound have made movies more exciting than before.

Since the late 1940's and early 1950's, the attraction of movies has been challenged by television. When television sets first became available, they had small screens. They offered a limited number of programs, all in black and white. The sets also were expensive. For these reasons, very few American homes had televisions. By 1980, this was no longer the case. About 98 percent of American homes had at least one television set. Television has become America's most important form of *mass media*—a means of communication which reaches a great many people.

How has television changed since the early 1950's?

Today most people agree that television has a greater impact on the American people and culture than any other single factor. This impact, however, has led to disagreement over the role of television. Some people feel that many television programs are of poor quality or in poor taste. They accuse the television networks of caring more about drawing large audiences to please their advertisers than about the quality of their shows. Other people do not like what television is doing to American politics. They point out that only candidates with money are able to buy advertisement time. This, they say, is not fair because it gives those candidates a better chance to reach more people. Still other critics of television say that it is not good for children. These people feel that because many children spend so much time watching television, they no longer read or have other interests.

Even with these arguments, nearly everyone agrees that television can do a lot for the American people. This was shown in the 1960's and 1970's when public television became more important. It offered educational programs and shows for children, pleasing many critics of network television. Then, too, in the 1970's, push-button boxes for responses to questions asked on television programs were available in some areas. This opened the possibility of doing a wide variety of programs that asked viewers their opinions. So, despite the mixed feelings about television, it appears that it will continue to have a great impact on the American people in the future.

Newspapers and radio are two other forms of mass media. At one time, newspapers were the American people's most important source of

Principal Interstate Highways

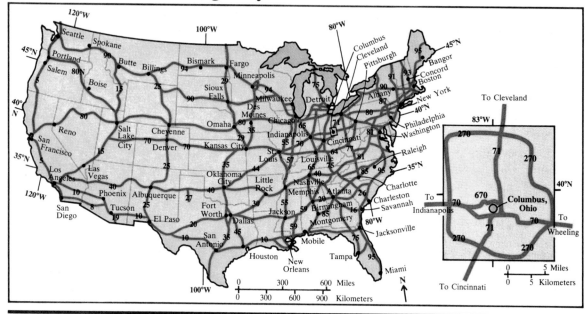

Most major cities are connected by the United States Interstate Highway System. Many cities have beltways that carry interstate traffic around downtown areas. Why are more highways located in the East than in the West?

What changes have occurred regarding newspapers in recent times?

information. Some large cities had as many as four daily papers. While newspapers are still an important source of news, many large cities now have only one daily paper. Most present-day newspapers receive much of their news from *wire services*—national and international organizations which gather news to pass on to newspapers. Some people fear that this could make it easy for a person or group to control the news and keep Americans from getting more than one opinion or version of news events.

Like newspapers, radio still is important in the United States. Many people depend on it for news and for entertainment. New inventions, like portable radios and car radios, have helped to ensure that radio will remain important in years to come.

2.3 The Role of Sports.   During the 1970's, Americans not only were using their spare time to enjoy reading and the arts. They were also using it for some athletic activity. Over 80 million Americans were jogging; bowling; riding bicycles; playing softball, tennis, or golf; or taking part in some other sport. At the same time, millions each year watched high school, college, or professional sports teams. By 1975, there were three times as many professional sports teams as there had been in 1965. Attendance at sports events was up by 33 percent.

Today, sports is Big Business. This is due in large part to television. The networks pay for the rights to televise sports events. Many sports teams receive more income from television rights to their games than they receive from the sale of tickets.

1. Who were some leading writers, artists, and musicians?
2. What has become the most important form of mass media?
3. How have films changed in recent years?
4. How have professional sports changed?

3. Energy, Economy, and Environment

As the American people entered the 1980's, they faced a challenge in the economy. But the problem of the economy did not stand alone. Woven into it were problems of energy and the environment. Because these problems are so closely related, they are considered together.

What problems are connected with the economy?

3.1   The Impact of Technology.   One of the greatest influences on the present American economy is *technology*—the application of ideas, methods, and tools to the production of goods. Technology has helped Americans make more goods with less work. It also has helped

How has technology affected American life?

Advances in technology have helped many persons with handicaps. Recent innovations, such as the robotic arm and the home robot, have made it possible for those paralyzed to lead more active lives. In what other ways has technology changed the way Americans live?

Technological advances in the auto industry include this automated welder. Automation has often replaced human workers with machines where a job has been too dangerous or too boring. What problems have automated industries created?

Americans to raise their standard of living, and it has given them more free time.

One example of the new technology is *automation*—the making of products by machines controlled electronically. For example, machines can be used to weld parts of cars and to print newspapers. Machines run by one or two people can roll and shape steel. But automation ends the need for certain jobs. This makes fewer jobs and puts people out of work.

What problems has technology created?

Technology has brought about other problems, too. Because industry is producing more, it is using natural resources at a rapid rate. It also is using many chemicals that are polluting the air and water. Many of the chemical fertilizers used by farmers are adding to the pollution. In many areas of the country, mining is destroying land. Because of technology, Americans are using more and more energy.

What is the nation's energy problem?

3.2 The Energy Issue. As early as 1947, the United States imported more oil than it sold to other countries. Thus, American industry came to rely heavily upon foreign nations for its energy needs. In the mid-1970's, the Organization of Petroleum Exporting Countries (OPEC) raised oil prices very high. This put a great strain on the American economy. As a result of high gas prices, smaller cars, and energy-saving programs, the country built a surplus of petroleum. In 1981 the OPEC nations agreed not to raise oil prices further. But oil continues to be one of the nation's most critical needs.

Recognizing Trends
SKILL

Decisions are usually made by evaluating available information on a subject and by examining past events to see what can be learned. Decision makers also try to recognize trends—how other people have decided similar issues over a period of time.

The following selection is from a November 1980 article in *The New York Times*. It is a report on a meeting called to plan future energy policy.

The state government can and should play a crucial role in New Jersey's energy future, according to eight [people] who are heavily involved in the energy industry or in legislation, regulation or research affecting it. They disagree, however, on which fuel sources the state should lean on.

"The most significant problem I see is our increasing dependence on . . . unreliable sources of oil," said . . . the state's Commissioner of Energy. "All our problems stem from that."

Like the others—the presidents of two utility companies, two Princeton University energy experts, an Assemblyman, a Sierra Club officer and an aide to a United States Senator—[the Commissioner of

Energy] *said he felt that the oil future looked bleak.*

Conservation [and] solar energy . . . should be encouraged. . . .

. . . Disagreements were clearly evident about coal and nuclear power. . . . [The] energy aide to [the Senator from Hawaii] said that New Jersey and Hawaii were alike in a number of ways, among them:

Hawaii imports about 90 percent of its oil, and has no known fossil-fuel deposits.

Hawaii is about the same size as New Jersey, and Oahu, the main island, has about the same population density.

The energy-consumption patterns of the two states are similar.

However . . . Hawaii, unlike New Jersey, had decided to marshal its natural resources—sun, wind, and ocean power—to try to achieve energy self-sufficiency.

"I don't see that happening in New Jersey," said [the president of the utility company]. . . . "With no [energy] *sources of any significance, I think we've got to share the wealth with other states. . . .*"

1. What trend in energy use is reflected in this article?
2. What are the trends in efforts to solve energy problems?

Many Americans in the 1980's have been looking for other ways to meet energy needs. The United States has one fourth of the world's supply of uranium, which is used to make fuel for nuclear power plants. It also has one fourth of the world's coal reserves. There is enough oil to fill millions of barrels inside *oil shale*, a kind of rock found in the Rocky Mountain area.

What arguments are voiced against nuclear energy?

In each of these cases, however, there is a problem. Many people are afraid of nuclear energy. They say it is dangerous and that there is too much of a chance for accidents at nuclear power plants. For this and other reasons, only about 70 plants had been built by 1981. They provided only 3 percent of the country's supply of electricity.

What arguments are raised against increased use of coal?

Many people do not want to use coal or oil shale, either. They have pointed out that when coal is burned, it pollutes the air. The method of *strip mining*—getting coal by scraping off soil and rocks covering it—destroys the land. While some people have said that the land can be reclaimed, others have said that the damage will take hundreds of years to repair. The same arguments have been applied to oil shale. It, too,

Uranium (left) and coal (right) are being used to produce energy in order to lessen the need to depend on expensive imported oil. Why are these two energy sources alternatives to oil for meeting America's energy needs?

has to be dug out of the earth. As yet, no inexpensive method is available to get oil from oil shale.

3.3 The Changing American Economy. The need to import huge amounts of oil is only part of the changing American economy. Americans have come to realize that they are faced with shrinking natural resources. Oil is not the only resource that has to come from other countries. The same is true of such important metals as copper and iron ore.

Imports make up America's foreign trade, and resources are only one part of that trade. Another part is the growing number of manufactured goods Americans have been buying from other countries. Cars, radios, cameras, and hundreds of other items made in other countries are sold to Americans every year. So much has been sold that the United States has a poor **balance of trade**. This means Americans have been paying more for goods from other countries than they have been receiving for the American goods sold to other countries.

What is the country's problem regarding foreign trade?

Another problem of the changing economy has to do with the growth of some American businesses. The size of some American companies has been growing since the late 1800's. In some cases, this means that fewer companies were making the same product. This, in turn, means less competition, which usually means higher prices. By 1980, four companies made all new American cars. Four companies provided 98 percent of America's phone service. And four companies made 89 percent of all computers in the United States.

What changes in business have affected the economy?

Many very large businesses have become **conglomerates**—groups of companies that produce many different kinds of products. For example, a business may have begun as an oil company. Over time, it may have bought several other companies, including one that makes toys, another that makes clothes, and still another that makes furniture. The size and wealth of such large companies raises serious issues. Some Americans think these companies have too much control over the country's resources. Others feel that by eliminating their competition, these companies have too much control over the prices of goods.

What is a conglomerate?

One point on which most Americans do agree is that the federal government will continue to play an important role in the American economy in the 1980's. But different groups of Americans have different ideas about what the federal government should do. Many want it to work to develop new sources of energy. Some want it to set quotas to limit foreign imports. Others want it to do something to limit the size and power of Big Business. Still others want it to cut back on certain rules so that businesses can make more goods for less money.

What things do Americans want the federal government to do regarding business and the economy?

Challenges for America 707

How has the job
market changed in
recent years?

3.4   The Condition of Labor.   The changes taking place in the economy have affected American workers, too. For one thing, the kind of work done by Americans is changing rapidly. New technology has cut down on the need for *blue-collar workers*—people who do manual labor in industry. By 1980, only 32 percent of nonfarm American workers were in blue-collar jobs. Over 48 percent were *white-collar workers*—people who work in professional or in office jobs. This means that more Americans are offering some kind of service than are making goods.

The kinds of work Americans do is important to labor unions. As more people go into white-collar jobs, the percentage of labor union members decreases. In 1955, union workers made up 33 percent of nonfarm workers. By 1980, they made up only about 24 percent. Unions are afraid that in the years ahead, they will lose influence and workers will have to lower their standards of living.

What problems do
workers face? How
might they be
solved?

All American workers have been faced with high inflation, which has cut into their earnings. For many people, prices have been going up faster than wages. Automation and competition from other countries also have been threatening jobs.

Some people feel that one way to solve these problems is to have American workers do more work in less time and at less cost. In this way, they would produce more and also would meet foreign competition. Some critics also feel that if workers would accept lower raises, inflation could be slowed down.

3.5   The Condition of Farming.   The part of the American economy that has gone through the most changes is farming. In 1790, more than 90 percent of all Americans earned their living as farmers. By 1980, only about 2 percent earned their living in this way. Between 1960 and 1980, the number of farms declined from 3.9 to 2.3 million.

Even though there are fewer farms and farmers, farm production has grown greatly. This has been due in part to machinery and fertilizers. They have made it possible for fewer people to produce more crops to meet the needs of Americans and to send surplus products to other countries. Although there are fewer farms, those which remain are larger and more efficient. In 1960, the average farm was 297 acres. In 1980, it was over 450 acres.

Most farms in the past were owned and run by individual farmers. In the 1980's, many are controlled by corporations. Some control tens of thousands of acres of land. They take charge of everything from planting seeds to selling crops.

Not all farmers or other Americans are in agreement about corporations in farming. Many people think corporations soon will control so much land that they will have the final say on what Americans

Technological advances in farming can be seen in the use of a solar-heated barn (left) and a mechanical tomato harvester (right). How has farming benefited from modern machinery?

pay for food. Others feel that the large farms will help keep prices down. They can produce more crops at lower cost than many small farms.

Farmers, like other Americans, face many challenges in the years ahead. Many farmers feel they are not getting enough money for their products. They say that fuel and equipment prices have been rising so rapidly that they cannot keep up with them. Many farmers feel the federal government should do more to help them.

What problems do farmers face?

1. What is automation?
2. What are the major energy sources available to most Americans?
3. What caused inflation in the economy?
4. What was the average size of a farm in 1980?

4. Conclusion

As they entered the 1980's, Americans faced a great many challenges. These ranged from social issues, such as poverty, to economic ones, such as the growth of conglomerates. Many of these things were not new. For example, the United States always has had many different ethnic groups. The challenge of the 1980's is for the nation to accept all of its different groups equally and give each the same chance to share fully in American life. On the other hand, some issues, such as the energy crisis, are newer. These challenges point up the need for change. But since the country's beginnings, Americans have lived with change and have adjusted to it.

Chapter 29 Review

Main Points

1. Changing to meet new challenges has been a part of American history.
2. Varied groups have continued to make up the growing American population.
3. The major move of population from cities to suburbs began in the 1950's.
4. The shifting population has produced more rapid growth in the South and West than in the Northeast.
5. Changing cultural trends have occurred in literature, music, and painting.
6. Television has become an important form of mass media.
7. Americans have begun to see how the environment has been used and misused.
8. The high cost of energy has made the problem of inflation in the economy more severe.

Building Vocabulary

1. Identify the following:

Appalachia
American Indian Movement
Truman Capote

Betty Friedan
Alex Haley

Beatles
Rachel Carson
Pop Art

2. Define the following:

median family income
gross national product
mobility
sun belt
diversity
popular music

mass media
wire services
technology
automation
oil shale

strip mining
balance of trade
conglomerates
blue-collar workers
white-collar workers

Remembering the Facts

1. What percent of the population is composed of blacks, Hispanics, and Indians?
2. How were Americans more mobile between 1950 and 1980?
3. What efforts were made to use sources of energy other than oil?
4. Where in the United States do people most suffer from poverty?
5. What objections to television programming have been raised?
6. How has television helped sports become Big Business?
7. How has automation both created and solved problems?
8. What has been a major trend in union membership since 1955?
9. How has farming changed?

Understanding the Facts

1. Why did some people continue to be poor when the average standard of living improved?
2. How did the movement of people to suburbs create new challenges for cities?
3. What things influenced the ways Americans spent their free time?
4. What caused an energy crisis in the United States?
5. What were advantages and disadvantages to a few large farms producing most of the food?
6. What trends in American life are likely to influence the future?

Using Maps

Highway Maps. New methods of transportation—car, bus, and truck—have replaced railroad and riverboat as major means of moving people and goods in the United States. Throughout the country, a network of highways connects centers of trade with areas of recreation. In spite of high fuel costs, the use of automotive vehicles is likely to increase.

The map on page 678 shows the principal sections of the United States Interstate Highway System. The insert map shows a more detailed view of the highway system for Columbus, Ohio. Study the maps, and answer the following questions.

1. Which interstate highway connects Denver with Kansas City? Which connects Butte with Salt Lake City?
2. What do all east-west highways have in common other than direction? What do all north-south highways have in common?
3. What is the approximate distance from Miami to Washington, D.C., along the interstate highway?
4. Which highways cross the United States from coast to coast?
5. How can someone driving Interstate 71 from Cleveland to Cincinnati avoid downtown Columbus?

Houston 1960-1985

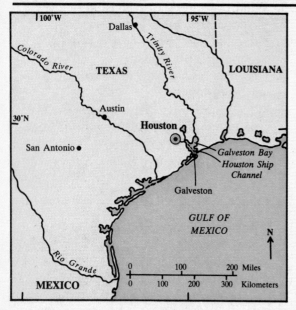

Located 50 miles (80 kilometers) inland from the Gulf of Mexico, Houston has grown from a small ranch town into a large American city. Once green with trees and grass, it has become a mass of concrete, steel, and glass in just a short time. Old buildings stand in the shadows of new high-rise apartments, stores, and offices. The city has grown outward in all directions.

The Beginning

John and Augustus Allen founded Houston in 1836. They named the new town after Sam Houston, commander of the Texas forces and president of the Republic of Texas. For a while, the town was the capital of Texas.

Houston, like other towns, had large areas of rich land where cotton could be grown. Nearby forests were good sources for building materials. Narrow marshy channels of water called bayous surrounded Houston, making water transportation possible. Later, when railroads were built, the city was on the main route between New Orleans and the West.

A Seaport

Realizing a need for better transportation of goods, business people early in the twentieth century started a campaign to collect funds to widen the Buffalo Bayou. This was a channel of marshy land leading to the Gulf of Mexico. Over many years, business people gradually gained what they wanted—a deeper waterway. This waterway was called the Houston Ship Channel. Beginning in 1914, large oceangoing vessels could load and unload in Houston.

The Houston Ship Channel has been widened and deepened twice since its opening. Walter Farnsworth was captain of the first oceangoing ship to go through the channel. He looked at it 40 years later:

Over there was a cemetery. . . . They must have moved it to straighten the channel. And see that sugar and molasses plant [factory], *that was all red clay. And when we got into port they had to tie up our lines to trees, and took eight days to unload our cargo. It's all a little hard to believe now.*

From Houston, ships carried cargoes of cotton, lumber, and sometimes rice to many countries. With the discovery of oil in fields near the city, petroleum and products made from it became the largest cargo.

Other industries producing metals, electronic equipment, machinery, and foods, moved to Houston. The costs of fuel, raw materials, and transportation were lower there than in many other areas of the country. Wages were also lower, but so was the cost of living. For these reasons, both workers and business leaders moved to Houston in large numbers.

Space City, U.S.A.

In 1961, Houston was chosen by the National Aeronautics and Space Administration (NASA) to be the site for a new center for the government program for putting astronauts into space. The city was chosen because it had excellent land, air, and sea transportation available. The seaport "provided an excellent means of transporting bulky space vehicles to other NASA locations, especially Cape Canaveral." The airport offered all-weather jet service. The warm climate of southeastern Texas permitted year-round outside work. Many local industries could

provide needed supplies, and engineers, scientists, and other skilled workers already lived in the area. There were many universities and research laboratories in the city.

President John Kennedy visited the Space Center after construction began in 1962. He said:

[During the next five years] *your city will become the heart of a large scientific and engineering community. . . . [In that time] the National Aeronautics and Space Administration expects to double the number of scientists and engineers in this area. . . .*

His prediction came true. Rice University became the first school in the nation to have a department of Space Science. Many more industries and science firms moved to the city. New jobs were created. NASA workers

Houston registered a 31 percent population gain in the 1960's. Its growth, however, has been constant since its founding in 1836. What industries and improvements have contributed to Houston's growth?

Technicians at the Johnson Space Center follow the progress of a spacecraft on their monitors. When was Houston selected as the site for the space center?

and others moved into the area. Houston became known as "Space City, U.S.A."

The People of Houston

A large number of the people living in Houston have come from other parts of Texas and the United States. Some have come from other countries. Since so many people of different cultures live in the city, organizations have been formed to help them. One example is the League of United Latin American Citizens (LULAC). It was founded in the 1950's to help Mexican Americans, Latin Americans, and other Spanish-speaking citizens adjust to life in the United States.

The major goal of the LULAC is to help stop discrimination and prejudice against these citizens. This is partly done by helping people find jobs and helping them learn English. The "School of 400" was started to help Spanish-speaking children learn at least

400 English words. The LULAC also gives scholarships to students going to college or technical school.

Blacks in Houston in the 1960's and 1970's still worked at less-skilled, lower-paying jobs and lived in the poorest housing in the city. But the growing awareness of the civil rights movement helped to improve people's lives in many ways. In 1980, two women and a Mexican American man were elected to Houston's city council for the first time. Two new black members were also elected to the council. Although there were still barriers, blacks and other minority groups began to advance professionally and politically.

Taking the Opportunity

The rise of Barbara Jordan to national prominence was one example of the new opportunities for women and blacks in the 1960's and 1970's. Born in Houston in 1936, Jordan is the daughter of a Baptist minister who also worked as a warehouse clerk. Jordan went through the segregated schools of Houston. She was an outstanding student at Texas Southern University and then attended Boston University Law School. Looking back on her childhood, Jordan said:

When I was growing up, we didn't focus on being poor and black. Segregation was there. It was the way of life, and if you were fortunate and would just drive hard enough, you might be able to break out of it a little bit.

In 1962, Jordan ran for the Texas House of Representatives and lost. She learned that "It was necessary to be backed by money, power, and influence." She commented:

I considered abandoning the dream of a political career in Texas and moving to some section of the country where a black woman

candidate was less likely to be considered a novelty. I didn't want to do this. I am a Texan; my roots are in Texas. To leave would be a cop-out. So I stayed, and 1966 arrived.

In 1966, Jordan had gained the needed support and was elected to a seat in the Texas Senate. Barbara Jordan was the first black to be elected to such a seat since 1883. She was a hardworking member of the state senate and won election to the United States House of Representatives in 1972. Looking back, she said, "I'm glad I stayed in Texas."

Always Growing

Constant building has been the chief characteristic of Houston. New people meant more building, and the city was always growing. When the city's population reached 1 million in the 1950's, Jesse Jones, a Texas millionaire who helped to build Houston, commented:

I always said that someday Houston would be the Chicago of the South and it is. Railroads built this town, the port made it big, cotton and cattle kept it rich, oil boomed it, and now we're the chemical capital of the world. Growing, growing, growing, that's Houston.

Houston continued to grow into the 1980's. One news magazine reported:

It's Boomtown, U.S.A.—the fastest-growing city in the country and a dazzling

The oil industry in Texas began not far from Houston at Spindletop Spring in 1901. Today, oil refineries continue to be built in the area. How has oil made Houston a boomtown?

monument to free enterprise. It has low taxes, low unemployment and a high-rise downtown that has turned Houston into the industrial and cultural capital of the Sun Belt. Every week, more than 1,000 new residents stream into this Klondike-on-the-bayou, and it may soon pass Philadelphia as the nation's fourth largest city. But some Texas-size headaches are developing in Houston. "The '70's were boom years and we were able to keep booming without many problems," says city-council member Ben Reyes. "Now, we'll either have to act or let the city start deteriorating."

The city and other nearby local governments helped attract industry to the Houston area through favorable tax policies. They also made it easier for people to build in Houston by not having any zoning laws. Anyone could put up buildings, shopping centers, or factories wherever they could buy land. Houston has been the only large American city without zoning laws.

No zoning means little, if any, planning, and this has caused problems for Houston. Every year, floods cause millions of dollars worth of damage. There is no city-wide plan to control such flooding. There are no city or state income taxes, and property taxes are very low. With little money and a city sprawling in every direction, city services such as fire and police protection are spread very thin. City officials admit that 25 percent of Houston's streets are unlighted, 400 miles (640 kilometers) are unpaved, and 29 percent of the poor live in substandard housing.

The Astrodome is the world's first all-purpose, air-conditioned, domed stadium. It rises 208 feet above the flat plains and is surrounded by more than 30,000 parking spaces. How has the automobile affected Houston?

Houston's skyline is mostly the result of recent construction. How do these clean-lined skyscrapers contrast with conditions in other parts of the city that have resulted from Houston's rapid physical growth?

Welfare payments are $40 per child per month.

Traffic is another major problem for Houston in the 1980's. "This is not a city for pedestrians," an economist wrote. "It was built for people on wheels." Public transportation service has been poor because 95 percent of the people in Houston use cars. Despite efforts to improve service, city buses carry fewer and fewer passengers as they move slowly among the many automobiles. A newspaper writer said, "A kingly elephant hemmed in by a flood of . . . mice could feel no more helpless than a bus driver in downtown traffic."

Many attempts have been made to solve Houston's traffic problems. One solution is called "CarShare." Drivers with similar schedules and needs are matched by a computer so they can form car pools.

As a rapidly growing city of the space age, Houston has had many problems. But it also has many advantages. Its economy is very strong and the resources to solve the problems are available. It is truly "Boomtown, U.S.A."

1. How was Houston started?
2. What helped industry to grow in Houston?
3. Why was the city selected for the Space Center?
4. What has caused problems for Houston?
5. What are some of the problems Houston must face?
6. Why is Houston called "Boomtown, U.S.A."?

Unit IX Review

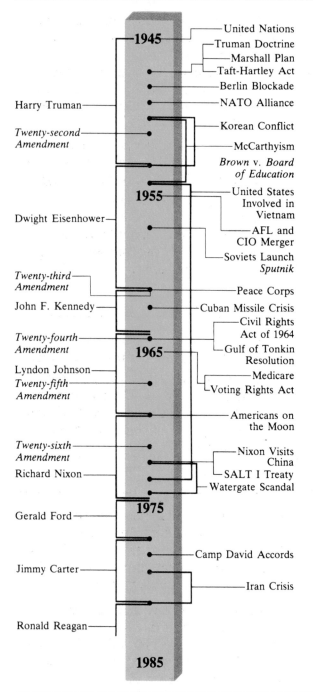

1945 — United Nations
— Truman Doctrine
— Marshall Plan
— Taft-Hartley Act
— Berlin Blockade
— NATO Alliance

Harry Truman

Twenty-second Amendment
— Korean Conflict
— McCarthyism
— *Brown* v. *Board of Education*

1955 — United States Involved in Vietnam

Dwight Eisenhower
— AFL and CIO Merger
— Soviets Launch *Sputnik*

Twenty-third Amendment
— Peace Corps

John F. Kennedy
— Cuban Missile Crisis

Twenty-fourth Amendment
— Civil Rights Act of 1964

1965 — Gulf of Tonkin Resolution

Lyndon Johnson
Twenty-fifth Amendment
— Medicare
— Voting Rights Act

— Americans on the Moon

Twenty-sixth Amendment

Richard Nixon
— Nixon Visits China
— SALT I Treaty
— Watergate Scandal

1975

Gerald Ford

— Camp David Accords

Jimmy Carter
— Iran Crisis

Ronald Reagan

1985

Summary

1. The establishment of the United Nations after World War II offered hope for world peace, but the emergence of a cold war between the United States and the Soviet Union brought a lengthy period of tensions and conflicts.

2. As the world's most powerful nation, the United States committed itself to helping other nations all over the world fight against the spread of communism.

3. Following World War II, the nation entered a long period of general prosperity, although large numbers of Americans lived in poverty.

4. The black civil rights movement made important progress against the segregation which had existed since Reconstruction, but many problems in the areas of economic and social equality remained.

5. In addition to blacks, women, Mexican Americans, Indians, and other groups struggled for equality.

6. Such issues as poverty, civil rights, war, and Watergate split the American people, testing their ability to solve national problems.

7. Compared to the agricultural nation 200 years ago, the United States of the 1980's is a greatly changed nation in its social, cultural, and economic life.

8. Despite change and the many new problems of the 1980's, there were many signs of hope that Americans would meet present-day challenges as they had met challenges in the past.

Unit Questions

1. What have been the major changes in the policy of the United States toward the Soviet Union since World War II?
2. What have been the causes of inflation since World War II? What problems has this caused for Americans?
3. What were the similarities in the programs at home of Presidents Truman, Kennedy, and Johnson? How were they different in their views of the role of the federal government from those of Presidents Eisenhower and Nixon?
4. What changes took place in the black civil rights movement from the 1950's into the 1970's?
5. What other groups took part in movements for increased rights and what were their aims?
6. What have been the changes in the policy of the United States toward the People's Republic of China since the end of World War II?
7. How were the foreign policy aims of President Carter different from previous Presidents? How did President Reagan seek to change that policy?
8. What have been the major changes in population in the United States since World War II? Which of those changes is shown by the case of Houston?

Suggested Activities

1. Find out information about the American space program in the late 1970's and 1980's. What have been its goals? What new information has been learned from the program?
2. Make a report about some sporting activity in which you take part. What is the history of the activity, and how many other Americans take part in it?
3. Identify the major changes you think will take place in the United States in your lifetime. Explain why and whether the country will be better or worse because of them.

Suggested Readings

Batterberry, Arianne, and Batterberry, Michael. *The Pantheon Story of American Art: For Young People*. New York: Pantheon Books, 1976. Illustrations of American art from the time of the Indians to the present.

Cox, John. *Overkill: Weapons of the Nuclear Age*. New York: Thomas Y. Crowell Co., 1978. Discusses the growing number of nuclear weapons.

Hilton, Suzanne. *Who Do You Think You Are? Digging For Your Family Roots*. Philadelphia: Westminster Press, 1976. The book involves students in historical work tracing their family background.

Pringle, Laurence. *City and Suburb: Exploring an Ecosystem*. New York: Macmillan, 1975. Discusses the way living systems in the environment are interrelated and dependent on each other.

Epilogue

For nearly 400 years, Americans experienced periods of political, economic, and social change. In spite of enormous challenges, they adapted to preserve a spirit of independence and to protect an ideal for democratic government.

During the 1600's and 1700's, most Americans lived on farms of varying size scattered along the Atlantic coast of North America. Colonial life centered around small villages and towns. Only a few larger cities served as trade centers. From this rural, agrarian society came one nation in 1776. With the Constitution, life in America reorganized around federal and state capitals, and concerns slowly became more national.

By the early 1800's, not only was American political life changing but also American economic life was changing. Labor that had been done mostly by hand or animal power was being done with the force of steam. By the 1900's, electricity and gasoline power provided the force to drive machines. Steamboats, trains, automobiles, and airplanes became the products of a continuing industrial revolution in the United States.

As the United States aged, it grew dramatically. The lure of the country's natural resources—land, lumber, water, minerals—drew more people to the United States and across the continent that the country occupied. Total population rose, the number of cities increased, and American life continued to change. From a small, rural republic, the United States grew into an industrial giant with worldwide influence and concerns.

The attitudes of the American people kept pace with the physical expansion of the country. Americans believed progress and opportunity were unlimited. By the twentieth century, Americans called for equality for all people. Many thought that it was within the power of the United States to abolish poverty, wipe out hunger and disease, and see that all people were secure in their old age. They sought an American dream for the world.

But continued opportunity had its challenges. Midway through the twentieth century, perhaps signaled by the explosion of the atomic bomb in 1945, the United States entered a new phase. After a history of plenty, Americans began to experience scarcity. Once again the American people have had to adapt to preserve and protect their ideals and principles to the realities of a changing world.

Appendix

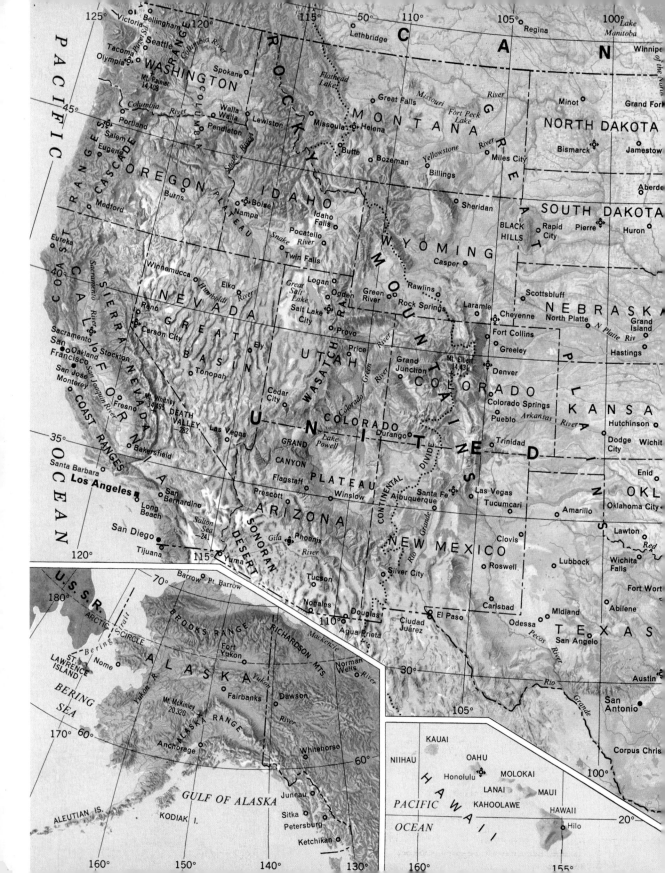

The Declaration of Independence

In Congress, July 4, 1776
The Unanimous Declaration of the Thirteen
United States of America

When in the course of human events, it becomes necessary for one people to dissolve the political bands which have connected them with another, and to assume among the powers of the earth, the separate and equal station to which the laws of nature and of nature's God entitle them, a decent respect to the opinions of mankind requires that they should declare the causes which impel them to the separation.

We hold these truths to be self-evident, that all men are created equal, that they are endowed by their Creator with certain unalienable rights, that among these are life, liberty, and the pursuit of happiness. That to secure these rights, governments are instituted among men, deriving their just powers from the consent of the governed; that whenever any form of government becomes destructive of these ends, it is the right of the people to alter or to abolish it, and to institute new government, laying its foundation on such principles, and organizing its powers in such form, as to them shall seem most likely to effect their safety and happiness. Prudence, indeed, will dictate that governments long established should not be changed for light and transient causes; and accordingly all experience hath shown, that mankind are more disposed to suffer, while evils are sufferable, than to right themselves by abolishing the forms to which they are accustomed. But when a long train of abuses and usurpations, pursuing invariably the same object, evinces a design to reduce them under absolute despotism, it is their right, it is their duty, to throw off such government, and to provide new guards for their future security. Such has been the patient sufferance of these colonies; and such is now the necessity which constrains them to alter their former systems of government. The history of the present King of Great Britain is a history of repeated injuries and usurpations, all having in direct object the establishment of an absolute tyranny over these states. To prove this, let facts be submitted to a candid world.

He has refused his assent to laws, the most wholesome and necessary for the public good.

He has forbidden his governors to pass laws of immediate and pressing importance, unless suspended in their operation till his assent should be obtained; and when so suspended, he has utterly neglected to attend to them.

He has refused to pass other laws for the accommodation of large districts of people, unless those people would relinquish the right of representation in the legislature, a right inestimable to them and formidable to tyrants only.

He has called together legislative bodies at places unusual, uncomfortable, and distant from the depository of their public records, for the sole purpose of fatiguing them into compliance with his measures.

He has dissolved representative houses repeatedly, for opposing with manly firmness his invasions on the rights of the people.

He has refused for a long time, after such dissolutions, to cause others to be elected; whereby the legislative powers, incapable of annihilation, have returned to the people at large for their exercise; the state remaining in the meantime exposed to all the dangers of invasion from without and convulsions within.

He has endeavored to prevent the population of these states; for that purpose obstructing the laws for naturalization of foreigners, refusing to pass others to encourage their migrations hither, and raising the conditions of new appropriations of lands.

He has obstructed the administration of justice, by refusing his assent to laws for establishing judiciary powers.

He has made judges dependent on his will alone, for the tenure of their offices, and the amount and payment of their salaries.

He has erected a multitude of new offices, and sent hither swarms of officers to harass our people, and eat out their substance.

He has kept among us, in times of peace, standing armies without the consent of our legislatures.

He has affected to render the military independent of and superior to the civil power.

He has combined with others to subject us to a jurisdiction foreign to our constitution, and unacknowledged by our laws; giving his assent to their acts of pretended legislation:

For quartering large bodies of armed troops among us;

For protecting them, by a mock trial, from punishment for any murders which they should commit on the inhabitants of these states;

For cutting off our trade with all parts of the world;

For imposing taxes on us without our consent;

For depriving us, in many cases, of the benefits of trial by jury;

For transporting us beyond seas to be tried for pretended offenses;

For abolishing the free system of English laws in a neighboring province, establishing therein an arbitrary government, and enlarging its boundaries so as to render it at once an example and fit instrument for introducing the same absolute rule into these colonies;

For taking away our charters, abolishing our most valuable laws, and altering fundamentally the forms of our governments;

For suspending our own legislatures, and declaring themselves invested with power to legislate for us in all cases whatsoever.

He has abdicated government here, by declaring us out of his protection and waging war against us.

He has plundered our seas, ravaged our coasts, burned our towns, and destroyed the lives of our people.

He is at this time transporting large armies of foreign mercenaries to complete the works of death, desolation, and tyranny, already begun with circumstances of cruelty and perfidy scarcely paralleled in the most barbarous ages, and totally unworthy the head of a civilized nation.

He has constrained our fellow citizens taken captive on the high seas to bear arms against their country, to become the executioners of their friends and brethren, or to fall themselves by their hands.

He has excited domestic insurrections among us, and has endeavored to bring on the inhabitants of our frontiers, the merciless Indian savages, whose known rule of warfare is an undistinguished destruction of all ages, sexes, and conditions.

In every stage of these oppressions we have petitioned for redress in the most humble terms: our repeated petitions have been answered only by repeated injury. A prince, whose character is thus marked by every act which may define a tyrant, is unfit to be the ruler of a free people.

Nor have we been wanting in our attentions to our British brethren. We have warned them from time to time of attempts by their legislature to extend an unwarrantable jurisdiction over us. We have reminded them of the circumstances of our emigration and settlement here. We have appealed to their native justice and magnanimity, and we have conjured them by the ties of our common kindred to disavow these usurpations, which would inevitably interrupt our connections and correspondence. They too have been deaf to the voice of justice and consanguinity. We must, therefore, acquiesce in the necessity which denounces our separation, and hold them, as we hold the rest of mankind, enemies in war, in peace friends.

We, therefore, the representatives of the United States of America, in General Congress, assembled, appealing to the Supreme Judge of the world for the rectitude of our intentions, do, in the name and by authority of the good people of these colonies, solemnly publish and declare, that these united colonies are, and of right ought to be, free and independent states; that they are absolved from all allegiance to the British Crown, and that all political connection between them and the State of Great Britain is and ought to be totally dissolved; and that as free and independent states, they have full power to levy war, conclude peace, contract alliances, establish commerce, and to do all other acts and things which independent states may of right do. And for the support of this declaration, with a firm reliance on the protection of Divine Providence, we mutually pledge to each other our lives, our fortunes, and our sacred honor.

John Hancock, **President**

New Hampshire
Josiah Bartlett
William Whipple
Matthew Thornton

Massachusetts
Samuel Adams
John Adams
Robert Treat Paine
Elbridge Gerry

New York
William Floyd
Philip Livingston
Francis Lewis
Lewis Morris

New Jersey
Richard Stockton
John Witherspoon

Francis Hopkinson
John Hart
Abraham Clark

Pennsylvania
Robert Morris
Benjamin Rush
Benjamin Franklin
John Morton
George Clymer
James Smith
George Taylor
James Wilson
George Ross

Delaware
Caesar Rodney
George Read
Thomas M'Kean

Maryland
Samuel Chase
William Paca
Thomas Stone
Charles Carroll
*   of Carrollton*

Rhode Island
Stephen Hopkins
William Ellery

Connecticut
Roger Sherman
Samuel Huntington
William Williams
Oliver Wolcott

Virginia
George Wythe
Richard Henry Lee

Thomas Jefferson
Benjamin Harrison
Thomas Nelson, Jr.
Francis Lightfoot Lee
Carter Braxton

North Carolina
William Hopper
Joseph Hewes
John Penn

South Carolina
Edward Rutledge
Thomas Heyward, Jr.
Thomas Lynch, Jr.
Arthur Middleton

Georgia
Button Gwinnett
Lyman Hall
George Walton

The Constitution of the United States

Preamble

We the People *of the United States, in order to form a more perfect union, establish justice, insure domestic tranquillity, provide for the common defense, promote the general welfare, and secure the blessings of liberty to ourselves and our posterity, do ordain and establish this CONSTITUTION for the United States of America.*

The Preamble is an introduction that explains why the Constitution is necessary and lists the purposes and goals to be achieved.

Article 1   Legislative Branch

Section 1 Congress

All legislative powers herein granted shall be vested in a Congress of the United States, which shall consist of a Senate and House of Representatives.

Section 1 grants Congress the sole power to make law at the national level. It also established a bicameral legislature.

Section 2 House of Representatives

1. The House of Representatives shall be composed of members chosen every second year by the people of the several states, and the electors in each state shall have the qualifications requisite for electors of the most numerous branch of the state legislature.

2. No person shall be a representative who shall not have attained to the age of twenty-five years, and been seven years a citizen of the United States, and who shall not, when elected, be an inhabitant of that state in which he shall be chosen.

Section 2 set the House term at two years, provided for the popular election of Representatives, and set the qualifications which must be met to hold the office.

3. Representatives and direct taxes shall be apportioned among the several states which may be included within this Union, according to their respective numbers, which shall be determined by adding to the whole number of free persons, including those bound to service for a term of years, and excluding Indians not taxed, three fifths of all other persons. The actual enumeration shall be made within three years after the first meeting of the Congress of the United States, and within every subsequent term of ten years, in such manner as they shall by law direct. The number of representatives shall not exceed one for every thirty thousand, but each state shall have at least one representative; and until such enumeration shall be made, the State of New Hampshire shall be entitled to choose three; Massachusetts, eight; Rhode Island and Providence Plantations, one; Connecticut, five; New York, six; New Jersey, four; Pennsylvania, eight; Delaware, one; Maryland, six; Virginia, ten; North Carolina, five; South Carolina, five; and Georgia, three.

In regard to income taxes, the direct tax requirement was voided by the 16th Amendment. The 3/5 reference to slaves was cancelled by the 13th and 14th Amendments.
A census has been taken every 10 years since the first in 1790. The current size of the House—435 members—was established by law in 1929. Since then, there has been a reapportionment of seats based on population shifts rather than an addition of seats because of population growth.

4. When vacancies happen in the representation from any state, the executive authority thereof shall issue writs of election to fill such vacancies.

A vacancy in the House is filled through a special election called by the state's governor.

5. The House of Representatives shall choose their Speaker and other officers; and shall have the sole power of impeachment.

Only the House may impeach, or charge, federal officials with not carrying out their duties.

Section 3 Senate

1. The Senate of the United States shall be composed of two senators from each state, chosen by the legislature thereof, for six years; and each senator shall have one vote.

2. Immediately after they shall be assembled in consequence of the first election, they shall be divided as equally as may be into three classes. The seats of the senators of the first class shall be vacated at the expiration of the second year, of the second class at the expiration of the fourth year, of the third class at the expiration of the sixth year, so that one third may be chosen every second year, and if vacancies happen by resignation, or otherwise, during the recess of the legislature of any state, the executive thereof may make temporary appointments until the next meeting of the legislature, which shall then fill such vacancies.

Section 3 set the Senate term at six years and provided for one third of the membership to be selected every two years. In addition, a state's governor can fill a vacancy by temporary appointment until the next general election. State legislative selection of Senators was ended with ratification of the 17th Amendment.

3. No person shall be a senator who shall not have attained to the age of thirty years, and been nine years a citizen of the United States, and who shall not, when elected, be an inhabitant of that state for which he shall be chosen.

Like those for the House, the only constitutional requirements that must be met for membership in the Senate deal with age, citizenship, and residency.

4. The Vice-President of the United States shall be President of the Senate, but shall have no vote, unless they be equally divided.

The Vice-President is the presiding officer of the Senate. The Vice-President may (but is not required to) vote only when there is a tie vote on a bill or issue.

5. The Senate shall choose their other officers, and also a President *pro tempore,* in the absence of the Vice-President, or when he shall exercise the office of President of the United States.

6. The Senate shall have the sole power to try all impeachments. When sitting for that purpose, they shall be on oath or affirmation. When the President of the United States is tried, the Chief Justice shall preside; and no person shall be convicted without the concurrence of two thirds of the members present.

Only the Senate may try persons impeached by the House. The Chief Justice presides in the trial of a President. Conviction requires a two-thirds vote of "guilty" by the members present.

7. Judgment in cases of impeachment shall not extend further than to removal from office, and disqualification to hold and enjoy any office of honor, trust, or profit under the United States; but the party convicted shall nevertheless be liable and subject to indictment, trial, judgment, and punishment, according to law.

Punishment is limited to removal from office and, if the Senate chooses, barring of future office-holding; but a person impeached can still be tried in court and held accountable under the law for any crimes committed.

Section 4 Congressional Elections and Meetings

1. The times, places, and manner of holding elections for senators and representatives shall be prescribed in each state by the legislature thereof; but the Congress may at any time by law make or alter such regulations, except as to the places of choosing senators.

Although the time, place, and manner of holding elections is left to the states, Congress can set regulations. In 1872, Congress set the first Tuesday after the first Monday in even numbered years as the date for congressional elections.

2. The Congress shall assemble at least once in every year, and such meeting shall be on the first Monday in December, unless they shall by law appoint a different day.

Congress must meet at least once a year. The opening date was changed to January 3 by the 20th Amendment.

Section 5 Congressional Powers and Duties

1. Each house shall be the judge of the elections, returns, and qualifications of its own

members, and a majority of each shall constitute a quorum to do business; but a smaller number may adjourn from day to day, and may be authorized to compel the attendance of absent members, in such manner, and under such penalties, as each house may provide.

Each house has the power to exclude, or to refuse to seat, a member elect. This power was limited in 1969 to judgment of constitutional qualifications only by a Supreme Court ruling in *Powell* v. *McCormack*. Technically to conduct business, 218 members must be present in the House and 51 in the Senate. The quorum rule is seldom enforced, however, in handling of routine matters.

2. Each house may determine the rules of its proceedings, punish its members for disorderly behavior, and, with the concurrence of two thirds, expel a member.

Each house sets its own rules. There are a few unique ones. Under the "seniority" rule, committee chairmanships go to the majority party member who has served the longest on the committee. Under "senatorial courtesy," the Senate will refuse to confirm a presidential appointment if a Senator from the appointee's state and of the same party as the President objects to the appointment. One notable difference between the two houses in rules governing proceedings concerns debate. Debate is limited to one hour per member in the House, whereas in the Senate, a member can hold the floor indefinitely.
Though both houses can censure (rebuke) or expel members for misconduct, both have rarely been used.

3. Each house shall keep a journal of its proceedings, and from time to time publish the same, excepting such parts as may in their judgment require secrecy; and the yeas and nays of the members of either house on any question shall, at the desire of one fifth of those present, be entered on the journal.

In addition to the journals, a complete official record of everything said on the floor, as well as the roll call votes on all bills or issues, is available in the *Congressional Record* published daily by the Government Printing Office.

4. Neither house, during the session of Congress, shall, without the consent of the other, adjourn for more than three days, nor to any other place than that in which the two houses shall be sitting.

Neither house may recess for more than 3 days without consent of the other, nor may it conduct business in any place other than the Capitol.

Section 6 Privileges and Restrictions of Members

1. The senators and representatives shall receive a compensation for their services, to be ascertained by law, and paid out of the Treasury of the United States. They shall in all cases except treason, felony, and breach of the peace, be privileged from arrest during their attendance at the session of their respective houses, and in going to and returning from the same; and for any speech or debate in either house, they shall not be questioned in any other place.

To strengthen the federal government, the Framers set congressional salaries to be paid by the U.S. Treasury rather than by members' respective states. Originally, members were paid $6 per day. In 1981, salaries are $79,125 for the Speaker, $65,000 for the President pro tem and floor leaders, and $60,663 for regular members. Members also receive numerous monetary benefits such as travel allowances, free postage ("franking" privilege), and a special tax exemption for maintaining a second home in Washington, D.C.
The "immunity" privilege is of little importance today. The Framers included it as a safeguard against the British colonial practice of arresting legislators to keep them from performing their duties. More important is immunity from slander or libel for anything said on the floor or published in official publications.

2. No senator or representative shall, during the time for which he was elected, be appointed to any civil office under the authority of the United States, which shall have been created, or the emoluments whereof shall have been increased, during such time; and no person holding any office under the United States shall be a member of either house during his continuance in office.

A person cannot serve in Congress and hold another government position at the same time.

Section 7 The Legislative Process

1. All bills for raising revenue shall originate in the House of Representatives; but the Senate may propose or concur with amendments as on other bills.

All money bills must originate (begin) in the House. Money bills include two types—tax bills for raising revenues and appropriation bills for spending funds.

2. Every bill which shall have passed the House of Representatives and the Senate shall, before it become a law, be presented to the President of the United States; if he approve he shall sign it, but if not he shall return it, with his objections, to that house in which it shall have originated, who shall enter the objections at large on their journal, and proceed to reconsider it. If after such reconsideration two thirds of that house shall agree to pass the bill, it shall be sent, together with the objections, to the other house, by which it shall likewise be reconsidered, and if approved by two thirds of that house, it shall become a law. But in all such cases the votes of both houses shall be determined by yeas and nays, and the names of the persons voting for and against the bill shall be entered on the journal of each house respectively. If any bill shall not be returned by the President within ten days (Sundays excepted) after it shall have been presented to him, the same shall be a law, in like manner as if he had signed it, unless the Congress by their adjournment prevent its return, in which case it shall not be a law.

Paragraph 2 of Section 7 outlines the basic requirements for enacting legislation. These are (1) bills must be approved in like form by both houses, (2) be submitted to the President for his signature, and (3) be approved (signed) by the President. Vetoed bills must be returned to Congress with objections for reconsideration. They can be enacted into law by a two-thirds vote of both houses. Should the President fail to sign a submitted bill within 10 days, it automatically becomes law unless Congress has adjourned. If Congress has adjourned, then the bill fails to become law (pocket veto). Unlike some governors, the President cannot veto certain items. He must veto a bill in its entirety.

3. Every order, resolution, or vote to which the concurrence of the Senate and House of Represen-

tatives may be necessary (except on a question of adjournment) shall be presented to the President of the United States; and before the same shall take effect, shall be approved by him, or being disapproved by him, shall be repassed by two thirds of the Senate and House of Representatives, according to the rules and limitations prescribed in the case of a bill.

The Framers included this paragraph to prevent Congress from passing joint resolutions instead of bills to avoid the possibility of a presidential veto. A bill is a draft of a proposed law, whereas a resolution is a formal expression of opinion, on a matter. There are 3 types of resolutions—simple, concurrent, and joint. Only joint resolutions, which have the same effect as bills when passed, require the President's signature.

Section 8 Legislative Powers

Almost all of Congress' legislative powers are found in this section.

The Congress shall have power:

1. To lay and collect taxes, duties, imposts, and excises, to pay the debts and provide for the common defense and general welfare of the United States; but all duties, imposts, and excises shall be uniform throughout the United States;

Congress may tax only for public purposes, and it must exercise its power with respect to all other constitutional provisions. Taxes must be uniform—the same rate—throughout the country. That is, the federal excise on whiskey must be the same in Florida as it is in Illinois.

2. To borrow money on the credit of the United States;

When need arises, Congress can borrow funds. The most common means of borrowing is through the sale of bonds. There is no constitutional limit on the amount Congress can borrow, though Congress has placed a ceiling (which it periodically revises) on the amount the federal government can go into debt.

3. To regulate commerce with foreign nations, and among the several states, and with the Indian tribes;

Congress has exclusive power to control foreign and interstate commerce. Like its taxing power,

Congress' commerce power has expanded over time and today is quite broad. Congress can exercise control over not only the exchange of goods (buying, selling, and transporting) but also the means (the carriers) by which they are traded. And it can use its power to encourage, promote and protect, as well as to prohibit, restrain, and restrict.

4. To establish a uniform rule of naturalization, and uniform laws on the subject of bankruptcies throughout the United States;

Naturalization is the process by which immigrants become citizens. Bankruptcy is the process by which debtors are relieved of debt obligations when they cannot pay in full.

5. To coin money, regulate the value thereof, and of foreign coin, and fix the standard of weights and measures;

The U.S. monetary system is based on the decimal system, with dollars as the base unit. In setting standards of weight and measures, Congress adopted the English system in 1838 and the French metric system in 1866.

6. To provide for the punishment of counterfeiting the securities and current coin of the United States;

Counterfeiting is punishable by a fine up to $5000 and/or imprisonment up to 15 years.

7. To establish post offices and post roads;

Since colonial times, the postal service has been a government monopoly. Until 1970, it operated as an executive department. That year Congress established it as an independent agency, headed by an 11-member board of governors.

8. To promote the progress of science and useful arts, by securing for limited times to authors and inventors the exclusive right to their respective writings and discoveries;

The works of authors (writers, poets, composers, dramatists, artists) are protected by copyrights. Today a copyright extends for the life of an author plus 50 years. The works of inventors are protected by patents which vary in length of protection from 3 1/2 to 17 years. Patents are obtainable on processes as well as products.

9. To constitute tribunals inferior to the Supreme Court;

This clause gave Congress the power to create the federal court system under the Supreme Court.

10. To define and punish piracies and felonies committed on the high seas, and offenses against the law of nations;

Federal law extends to those traveling on American ships on the high seas.

11. To declare war, grant letters of marque and reprisal, and make rules concerning captures on land and water;

Only Congress can declare war. But the President, as commander in chief, can use the armed forces as much as he chooses.
Letters of marque and reprisal, authorizing private parties to attack enemy vessels in time of war, have been forbidden under international law since 1856.

12. To raise and support armies, but no appropriation of money to that use shall be for a longer term than two years;

The restriction on funding was intended to ensure the army would always be subject to civilian control.

13. To provide and maintain a navy;

Rules and procedures for the navy are similar to those for the other armed services.

14. To make rules for the government and regulation of the land and naval forces;

Under this provision, Congress has established the uniform Code of Military Justice.

15. To provide for calling forth the militia to execute the laws of the Union, suppress insurrections, and repel invasions;

Militia refers to the National Guard. It may be federalized (called into federal service) by either Congress or the President.

16. To provide for organizing, arming, and disciplining the militia, and for governing such part of them as may be employed in the service of the United States, reserving to the states respectively

the appointment of the officers, and the authority of training the militia according to the discipline prescribed by Congress;

When federalized, the National Guard is subject to the same rules and regulations that Congress has set for the armed services.

17. To exercise exclusive legislation in all cases whatsoever over such district (not exceeding ten miles square) as may, by cession of particular states, and the acceptance of Congress, become the seat of the government of the United States, and to exercise like authority over all places purchased by the consent of the legislature of the state in which the same shall be, for the erection of forts, magazines, arsenals, dock-yards, and other needful buildings;—and

In order to check state interference and to avoid interstate jealousy, the Framers provided for a national seat of government outside of any state. The District of Columbia was the result of a compromise over Hamilton's plan on the assumption of state debts. Washington himself marked out the exact 10-mile square, which was reduced to 69 square miles when Congress returned to Virginia its portion of donated land in 1846.

18. To make all laws which shall be necessary and proper for carrying into execution the foregoing powers, and all other powers vested by this Constitution in the government of the United States, or in any department or officer thereof.

This provision is the basis of Congress' implied powers. Any implied power, however, must be related to an expressed power and must be constitutional in all other respects.

Section 9 Powers Forbidden the United States

1. The migration or importation of such persons as any of the states now existing shall think proper to admit, shall not be prohibited by the Congress prior to the year one thousand eight hundred and eight, but a tax or duty may be imposed on such importation, not exceeding ten dollars for each person.

Paragraph 1 contains the agreement the Framers reached regarding regulation of the slave trade in

exchange for Congress' exclusive control over interstate commerce.

2. The privilege of the writ of habeas corpus shall not be suspended, unless when in cases of rebellion or invasion the public safety may require it.

The writ of habeas corpus is a court order to release or to bring an individual before the court to determine if that person should be charged with a crime. It is intended to prevent persons from being imprisoned for no reason. The writ may be suspended only during wartime. It was suspended twice—during the Civil War and during World War II in Hawaii. The Hawaiian suspension was later held unconstitutional in *Duncan v. Kahanomoku*.

3. No bill of attainder or ex post facto law shall be passed.

A bill of attainder is a law that is directed against an individual or group and provides punishment without a trial. An ex post facto law is one which prescribes punishment for an act committed before the law's enactment.

4. No capitation, or other direct, tax shall be laid, unless in proportion to the census or enumeration herein before directed to be taken.

A capitation tax is a direct tax imposed on individuals. The income tax, authorized by the 16th Amendment, is the exception to this prohibition.

5. No tax or duty shall be laid on articles exported from any state.

The prohibiting of the taxing of exports was part of the Commerce Compromise.

6. No preference shall be given by any regulation of commerce or revenue to the ports of one state over those of another; nor shall vessels bound to, or from, one state, be obliged to enter, clear, or pay duties in another.

This prohibition prevents Congress from favoring one state or region over another in the regulation of trade.

7. No money shall be drawn from the treasury, but in consequence of appropriations made by law; and a regular statement and account of the receipts

and expenditures of all public money shall be published from time to time.

8. No title of nobility shall be granted by the United States: And no person holding any office of profit or trust under them, shall, without the consent of the Congress, accept of any present, emolument, office, or title, of any kind whatever, from any king, prince, or foreign state.

Section 10 Powers Forbidden the States

1. No state shall enter into any treaty, alliance, or confederation; grant letters of marque and reprisal; coin money; emit bills of credit; make any thing but gold and silver coin a tender in payment of debts; pass any bill of attainder, ex post facto law, or law impairing the obligation of contracts, or grant any title of nobility.

2. No state shall, without the consent of the Congress, lay any imposts or duties on imports or exports, except what may be absolutely necessary for executing its inspection laws; and the net produce of all duties and imposts, laid by any state on imports or exports, shall be for the use of the treasury of the United States; and all such laws shall be subject to the revision and control of Congress.

3. No state shall, without the consent of Congress, lay any duty of tonnage, keep troops, or ships of war in time of peace, enter into any agreement or compact with another state, or with a foreign power, or engage in war, unless actually invaded, or in such imminent danger as will not admit of delay.

Article 2 Executive Branch

Section 1 President and Vice-President

1. The executive power shall be vested in a President of the United States of America. He shall hold his office during the term of four years, and, together with the Vice-President, chosen for the same term, be elected, as follows:

2. Each state shall appoint, in such manner as the legislature thereof may direct, a number of electors, equal to the whole number of senators and representatives to which the state may be entitled in the Congress: but no senator or representative, or person holding an office of trust or profit under the United States, shall be appointed an elector.

3. The electors shall meet in their respective states, and vote by ballot for two persons, of whom one at least shall not be an inhabitant of the same state with themselves. And they shall make a list of all the persons voted for, and of the number of votes for each; which list they shall sign and certify, and transmit sealed to the seat of the government of the United States, directed to the President of the Senate. The President of the Senate shall, in the presence of the Senate and House of Representatives, open all the certificates, and the votes shall then be counted. The person having the greatest number of votes shall be the President, if such number be a majority of the whole number of electors appointed; and if there be more than one who have such majority, and have an equal number of votes, then the House of Representatives shall immediately choose by ballot one of them for President; and if no person have a majority, then from the five highest on the list the said house shall in like manner choose the President. But in choosing the President, the votes shall be taken by states, the representation from each state having one vote; a quorum for this purpose shall consist of a member or members from two thirds of the states, and a majority of all the states shall be necessary to a choice. In every case, after the choice of the President, the person having the greatest number of votes of the electors shall be the Vice-President. But if there should remain two or more who have equal votes, the Senate shall choose from them by ballot the Vice-President.

Coupled with the previous paragraph, Paragraph 3 outlines the original method of selecting the President and Vice-President. It has been replaced by the method outlined in the 12th Amendment. It should be noted, however, that there has been considerable change in the machinery created by the Framers. For example, the Framers did not envision the rise of political parties, the development of nominating systems (primaries and conventions), or the broadening of democracy whereby electors would be elected rather than chosen by state legislatures.

4. The Congress may determine the time of choosing the electors, and the day on which they shall give their votes; which day shall be the same throughout the United States.

Congress set the first Tuesday after the first Monday in November of every fourth year (leap year) as the general election date for selecting presidential electors in 1845.

5. No person except a natural-born citizen, or a citizen of the United States, at the time of the adoption of this Constitution, shall be eligible to the office of President; neither shall any person be eligible to that office who shall not have attained to the age of thirty-five years, and been fourteen years a resident within the United States.

The only constitutional qualifications to be President are provided here. Though not expressly stated, the qualifications to be Vice-President are the same, since the Vice-President could succeed to the office of President.

6. In case of the removal of the President from office, or of his death, resignation, or inability to discharge the powers and duties of the said office, the same shall devolve on the Vice-President, and the Congress may by law provide for the case of removal, death, resignation, or inability, both of the President and Vice-President, declaring what officer shall then act as President, and such officer shall act accordingly, until the disability be removed, or a President shall be elected.

Until the adoption of the 25th Amendment, the succession of the Vice-President was based on a precedent set by John Tyler in 1841. In 1947, Congress established an official line of succession when there is no Vice-President to qualify. First in line is the Speaker of the House.

7. The President shall, at stated times, receive for his services a compensation, which shall neither be increased nor diminished during the period for which he shall have been elected, and he shall not receive within that period any other emolument from the United States, or any of them.

Originally, the President's salary was $25,000 per year. In 1981, it is $200,000. Like members of

8. Before he enter on the execution of his office, he shall take the following oath or affirmation:—"I do solemnly swear (or affirm) that I will faithfully execute the office of President of the United States, and will, to the best of my ability, preserve, protect, and defend the Constitution of the United States."

The oath of office is generally administered by the Chief Justice, but can be administered by any official authorized to administer oaths. All President-elects except Washington have been sworn into office by the Chief Justice. Only Vice-Presidents Tyler, Coolidge, and Lyndon Johnson in succeeding to the office have been sworn in by someone else.

Section 2 Powers of the President

1. The President shall be commander in chief of the army and navy of the United States, and of the militia of the several states, when called into the actual service of the United States; he may require the opinion, in writing, of the principal officer in each of the executive departments, upon any subject relating to·the duties of their respective offices, and he shall have power to grant reprieves and pardons for offenses against the United States, except in cases of impeachment.

As commander in chief, the President exercises broad military power. All military personnel is subordinate to the President.
The provision the President "may require the opinion. . ." is the constitutional base for the Cabinet.
Like his other powers, the President's judicial powers are limited. Presidential clemency is limited to those accused or convicted of federal crimes. A reprieve is a delay in carrying out a sentence. A pardon is a legal absolution of responsibility for a crime. The President can also commute (reduce) and parole (suspend the completion of) an imposed sentence.

2. He shall have power, by and with the advice and consent of the Senate, to make treaties, provided two thirds of the senators present concur; and he shall nominate, and by and with the advice and consent of the Senate, shall appoint ambassadors, other public ministers and consuls, judges of the Supreme Court, and all other officers of the United States, whose appointments are not herein otherwise provided for, and which shall be established by law; but the Congress may by law vest the appointment of such inferior officers, as they think proper, in the President alone, in the courts of law, or in the heads of departments.

The President is the chief architect of American foreign policy. He alone is responsible for the conduct of foreign relations, or dealings with other countries. Though requiring Senate approval, a treaty is ratified (signed upon approval) by the President. If it is not ratified or made public, an approved treaty is voided, and Congress cannot override the President's decision to kill it. A treaty has the same legal force as an act of Congress. In addition to treaties, the President can make binding agreements (executive agreements) with other countries under his ordinance power. Executive agreements do not require Senate approval.
Most federal positions today are filled under the rules and regulations of the civil service system. Most presidential appointments serve at the pleasure of the President. Removal of an official by the President is not subject to congressional approval, but the power can be restricted by conditions set in creating the office.

3. The President shall have power to fill up all vacancies that may happen during the recess of the Senate, by granting commissions which shall expire at the end of their next session.

Presidential appointments requiring Senate approval are made on a temporary basis if the Senate is in recess.

Section 3 Duties of the President

He shall from time to time give to the Congress information of the state of the Union, and recommend to their consideration such measures as he shall judge necessary and expedient; he may, on extraordinary occasions, convene both houses, or either of them, and in case of disagreement between them with respect to the time of adjournment, he may adjourn them to such time as he shall think proper; he shall receive ambassadors and other public ministers; he shall take care that the laws be faithfully executed, and shall commission all the officers of the United States.

Today the President is the chief designer of the nation's major legislative program. Presidential recommendations are put forth in the State of the Union address, the Budget Report, and special messages dealing with specific proposals.

The provision to "receive ambassadors . . . " is the constitutional basis of the President's power to extend and to withdraw diplomatic recognition of a foreign government.

All military commissions (appointments as officers in the armed forces) require presidential authorization and congressional approval.

Section 4 Impeachment

The President, Vice-President and all civil officers of the United States, shall be removed from office on impeachment for, and conviction of, treason, bribery, or other high crimes and misdemeanors.

Presidential appointees can be removed by the impeachment process as well as by presidential request of resignation.

Article 3 Judicial Branch

Section 1 United States Courts

The judicial power of the United States shall be vested in one Supreme Court, and in such inferior courts as the Congress may from time to time ordain and establish. The judges, both of the Supreme and inferior courts, shall hold their offices during good behavior, and shall, at stated times, receive for their services, a compensation, which shall not be diminished during their continuance in office.

Section 1 created a national judiciary. Congress established the national court system in 1789. Today there are 10 judicial circuits, with a Court of Appeals in each, and 90 judicial districts. At least one district with a District Court is in every state. Other constitutional courts include: (1) the Court of Claims,

established in 1855; (2) the Customs Court, established in 1890; and (3) the Court of Customs and Patent Appeals, established in 1910. There is also various special, or legislative, courts that handle cases arising out of the exercise of particular congressional powers but do not exercise the judicial power of the United States.

Federal judges are appointed by the President with Senate approval, and nearly all hold office during good behavior for life.

Originally, judges' salaries were $3500 ($4000 for the Chief Justice). In 1981, Supreme Court Justices are paid $75,960 (the Chief Justice $79,125); Court of Appeals judges $60,663; and District Court judges $57,528.

Section 2 Jurisdiction

1. The judicial power shall extend to all cases, in law and equity, arising under this Constitution, the laws of the United States, and treaties made, or which shall be made, under their authority;—to all cases affecting ambassadors, other public ministers, and consuls;—to all cases of admiralty and maritime jurisdiction;—to controversies to which the United States shall be a party;—to controversies between two or more states;—between a state and citizens of another state;—between citizens of different states;—between citizens of the same state claiming lands under grants of different states; and between a state, or the citizens thereof, and foreign states, citizens or subjects.

Jurisdiction is the right of a court to try a case. Federal courts have jurisdiction over a case because of its subject matter or the parties involved. In regard to subject matter, federal courts try cases that: (1) arise under the Constitution, acts of Congress, or treaties, or (2) are part of admiralty law (matters that arise on the high seas or navigable waters within the country) or maritime law (matters that arise on land but are directly related to water). Since adoption of the 11th Amendment, a state cannot be sued in federal court by a foreign citizen or a citizen of another state.

The judicial power of the United States includes civil cases (private wrongs that arise under common law or equity) as well as criminal cases. Common law is the rules and principles that developed in England from decisions made on the basis of custom. Equity is a branch of law that provides legal remedy when strict application of common law results in an injustice. The main difference is that common law deals with wrongs that have occurred, whereas equity seeks to prevent them from occurring.

2. In all cases affecting ambassadors, other public ministers and consuls, and those in which a state shall be party, the Supreme Court shall have original jurisdiction. In all other cases before mentioned, the Supreme Court shall have appellate jurisdiction, both as to law and fact, with such exceptions, and under such regulations as the Congress shall make.

The Supreme Court has both original and appellate jurisdiction. Original jurisdiction refers to cases to be tried for the first time. Appellate jurisdiction refers to cases to be reviewed after being tried in a lower court. The vast majority of cases the Supreme Court hears are on appeal. Its decisions are by majority opinion.

3. The trial of all crimes, except in cases of impeachment, shall be by jury; and such trial shall be held in the state where the said crimes shall have been committed; but when not committed within any state, the trial shall be at such place or places as the Congress may by law have directed.

All people accused of committing a crime for which they can be tried in federal court are guaranteed the right of trial by jury in the state where the crime takes place.
   This provision makes it possible for there to be jury trials in the Supreme Court in cases of original jurisdiction. To date, there has been only one jury trial, however—that of *Georgia* v. *Brailsford* in 1794.

Section 3 Treason

1. Treason against the United States shall consist only in levying war against them, or in adhering to their enemies, giving them aid and comfort. No person shall be convicted of treason unless on the testimony of two witnesses to the same overt act, or on confession in open court.

Treason is the only crime specifically defined in the Constitution, and Congress cannot alter or amend the criteria for conviction. The charge can be levied against American citizens at home or abroad and resident aliens.

2. The Congress shall have power to declare the punishment of treason, but no attainder of treason shall work corruption of blood, or forfeiture except during the life of the person attainted.

Congress has set the punishment for treason to be from a minimum of 5 years imprisonment and a $10,000 fine to a maximum of death. No person convicted of treason has ever been executed by the United States. John Brown was executed by Virginia for treason against that state.

Article 4   Relations Among the States

Section 1 Official Acts

Full faith and credit shall be given in each state to the public acts, records, and judicial proceedings of every other state. And the Congress may by general laws prescribe the manner in which such acts, records, and proceedings shall be proved, and the effect thereof.

States must honor the laws, records, and court decisions of other states. Regarding judicial proceedings, there are two exceptions. (1) One state does not have to enforce another state's criminal code, and (2) one state does not have to recognize another state's grant of a divorce if legitimate residence was not established by the person obtaining the divorce.

Section 2 Privileges of Citizens

1. The citizens of each state shall be entitled to all privileges and immunities of citizens in the several states.

A state may not deny to its citizens or the citizens of another state the rights enjoyed by citizens of the United States. In other words, a resident of one state may not be discriminated against unreasonably by another state.

2. A person charged in any state with treason, felony, or other crime, who shall flee from justice, and be found in another state shall, on demand of the executive authority of the state from which he fled, be delivered up, to be removed to the state having jurisdiction of the crime.

The process of returning a fugitive to the state where a crime has been committed is known as extradition. Most requests are routinely processed, but the Constitution does not absolutely require that a fugitive be surrendered. A governor can refuse to honor the request for extradition if it will result in an injustice to the fugitive.

3. No person held to service or labor in one state, under the laws thereof, escaping into another, shall, in consequence of any law or regulation therein, be discharged from such service or labor, but shall be delivered up on claim of the party to whom such service or labor may be due.

This provision applied to fugitive slaves. It was cancelled by the 13th Amendment.

Section 3 New States and Territories

1. New states may be admitted by the Congress into this Union; but no new state shall be formed or erected within the jurisdiction of any other state; nor any state be formed by the junction of two or more states, or parts of states, without the consent of the legislatures of the states concerned as well as of the Congress.

Only Congress can admit states to the Union. New states are admitted on the basis of equality with older states. The general process, as outlined by the Northwest Ordinance of 1787, is: (1) a territory seeking statehood petitions Congress, (2) Congress passes an enabling act directing the drafting of a state constitution, (3) a territorial constitutional convention drafts a constitution which is approved by popular vote and submitted to Congress, and (4) Congress passes an act of admission.

Though a new state cannot be carved out of an existing state without its consent, there has been one unusual exception—West Virginia, which was admitted in 1863 after Virginia had seceded.

Texas provides another interesting case. It was the only state that was an independent republic at the time of its admission and the only state admitted by joint resolution rather than by an act. In addition, by terms of its admission, Texas could subdivide itself into 5 states, if it so chooses.

2. The Congress shall have power to dispose of and make all needful rules and regulations respecting the territory or other property belonging to the United States; and nothing in this Constitution shall be so construed as to prejudice any claims of the United States, or of any particular state.

Congress has the power to control all property belonging to the United States. It can set up governments for territories, establish national parks

and forests, authorize reclamation projects, and exercise eminent domain (taking of private property for public use through condemnation).

Section 4 Protection of the States

The United States shall guarantee to every state in this Union a republican form of government, and shall protect each of them against invasion; and on application of the legislature, or of the executive (when the legislature cannot be convened) against domestic violence.

Though the Constitution does not define "republican form of government," the Supreme Court has held it to mean one in which the people choose their own representatives to run the government and make the laws in accord with delegated power.

The federal government can use whatever means are necessary to prevent foreign invasion and to put down domestic violence.

Article 5 The Amendment Process

The Congress, whenever two thirds of both houses shall deem it necessary, shall propose amendments to this Constitution, or, on the application of the legislatures of two thirds of the several states, shall call a convention for proposing amendments, which, in either case, shall be valid to all intents and purposes, as part of this Constitution, when ratified by the legislatures of three fourths of the several states, or by conventions in three fourths thereof, as the one or the other mode of ratification may be proposed by the Congress; provided that no amendment which may be made prior to the year one thousand eight hundred and eight shall in any manner affect the first and fourth clauses in the ninth section of the first article; and that no state, without its consent, shall be deprived of its equal suffrage in the Senate.

There are 4 methods for amending the Constitution—2 of proposal and 2 of ratification. To date, all amendments have been proposed by Congress and only the 21st has been ratified by convention instead of by state legislature. There is one prohibition against change—that is, no state can be denied its equal representation in the Senate.

Article 6   General Provisions

1. All debts contracted and engagements entered into, before the adoption of this Constitution, shall be as valid against the United States under this Constitution, as under the Confederation.

This provision assured the nation's creditors that the new federal government would assume the existing financial obligations (debt) of the country.

2. This Constitution, and the laws of the United States which shall be made in pursuance thereof; and all treaties made, or which shall be made, under the authority of the United States, shall be the supreme law of the land; and the judges in every state shall be bound thereby, anything in the Constitution or laws of any state to the contrary notwithstanding.

The Supremacy Clause guarantees federal law will take priority over state law in cases of conflict. To be valid, however, any law must be constitutional.

3. The senators and representatives before mentioned, and the members of the several state legislatures, and all executive and judicial officers, both of the United States and of the several states, shall be bound by oath or affirmation to support this Constitution; but no religious test shall ever be required as a qualification to any office or public trust under the United States.

Almost all government officials must affirm or take an oath to uphold the Constitution. No religious qualification can be set as a requirement for holding public office.

Article 7   Ratification

The ratification of the conventions of nine states shall be sufficient for the establishment of this Constitution between the states so ratifying the same.

To become operable, 9 states were required to ratify. Delaware was first and New Hampshire ninth, but not until Virginia (10th) and New York (11th) ratified, was the Constitution assured of going into effect.

Done in convention by the unanimous consent of the states present the seventeenth day of September in the year of our Lord one thousand seven hundred and eighty-seven, and of the independence of the United States of America the twelfth. In witness whereof we have hereunto subscribed our names.

Of the 55 delegates who attended the Constitutional Convention, only 38 signed the document. The 39th signature—that of John Dickinson—was written by George Read at Dickinson's request. Elbridge Gerry of Massachusetts and Edmund Randolph and George Mason of Virginia refused to sign. 13 delegates left the convention prior to its end. Rhode Island sent no delegates to the convention.

George Washington, **President and Deputy from Virginia**

New Hampshire
John Langdon
Nicholas Gilman

Massachusetts
Nathaniel Gorham
Rufus King

Connecticut
William Samuel
*   Johnson*
Roger Sherman

New York
Alexander Hamilton

New Jersey
William Livingston
David Brearley
William Paterson
Jonathan Dayton

Pennsylvania
Benjamin Franklin
Thomas Mifflin
Robert Morris
George Clymer
Thomas Fitzsimons
Jared Ingersoll
James Wilson
Gouverneur Morris

Delaware
George Read
Gunning Bedford, Jr.
John Dickinson
Richard Bassett
Jacob Broom

Maryland
James M'Henry
Daniel of St. Thomas
*   Jenifer*
Daniel Carroll

Virginia
John Blair
James Madison, Jr.

North Carolina
William Blount
Richard Dobbs
*   Spaight*
Hugh Williamson

South Carolina
John Rutledge
Charles C. Pinckney
Charles Pinckney
Pierce Butler

Georgia
William Few
Abraham Baldwin

Attest: *William Jackson,* **Secretary**

The first 10 amendments are known as the Bill of Rights. They were proposed by Congress during its first session and were adopted in body in 1791. Originally, the prohibitions limited only the federal government. But many of the guarantees have been extended against state action by the Due Process Clause of the 14th Amendment.

Amendment 1 Freedoms of Expression

Congress shall make no law respecting an establishment of religion, or prohibiting the free exercise thereof; or abridging the freedom of speech, or of the press; or the right of the people peaceably to assemble, and to petition the government for a redress of grievances.

The 1st Amendment protects 5 basic civil liberties—freedom of religion, of speech, and of the press and the rights to assemble peacefully and to petition for redress of grievances. Like all civil rights, however, these liberties are not absolute; they must be exercised in a manner relative to the rights of others.

Under the guarantee of religious freedom, the government cannot establish an official religion or place restrictions on religious beliefs. Though the 1st Amendment does create a separation of church and state, the amendment does not prohibit the government from expressing a friendly attitude toward or encouraging religion.

Freedoms of speech and of the press guarantee to all individuals the right to express themselves freely, both orally and in writing, and to free and unrestricted discussion of public affairs. However, one can still be held accountable under the law for false and malicious use of words—whether oral (slander) or written (libel). Then, too, some forms of censorship for national security or the public good are permissible, even though Congress and the states cannot censor ideas before they are expressed.

The rights to assemble and petition guarantee the means to protest, including the right to demonstrate. Without them, free expression would be limited. But notice that these rights, too, are limited. Public meetings and picketing must be peaceable. Ones that result in violence can lawfully be broken up.

Amendment 2 Right to Keep Arms

A well-regulated militia being necessary to the security of a free state, the right of the people to keep and bear arms shall not be infringed.

The right to keep and bear arms is not free from government restriction. The federal government and the states can and do regulate the possession and use of firearms, such as requiring the licensing of guns and prohibiting the carrying of concealed weapons.

Amendment 3 Quartering of Troops

No soldier shall, in time of peace, be quartered in any house, without the consent of the owner, nor in time of war, but in a manner to be prescribed by law.

Like the 2nd Amendment, this amendment was designed to prevent what had been common practice by the British during the colonial period. It is of little importance today, even though Congress could authorize the boarding of troops in private homes during wartime.

Amendment 4 Searches and Seizures

The right of the people to be secure in their persons, houses, papers, and effects, against unreasonable searches and seizures, shall not be violated, and no warrants shall issue, but upon probable cause, supported by oath or affirmation, and particularly describing the place to be searched, and the persons or things to be seized.

This amendment prohibits unreasonable searches and seizures. However, the police do not need a warrant for a search and seizure if they are a witness to a crime or are in hot pursuit of a criminal. Nor do they need one to search a movable object, such as a car, since it could vanish while a warrant is sought.

There are two types of unreasonable searches and seizures—(1) those made without warrants when warrants are required, and (2) those that do not comply with the elements of the warrant. For it to be proper, a warrant must be issued by a court (judge), there must be good reason for its use, and it must describe in specific terms the place to be searched and the person or thing to be seized. Evidence secured by an improper search and seizure is inadmissible in any court.

Amendment 5 Rights of the Accused

No person shall be held to answer for a capital, or otherwise infamous crime, unless on a presentment or indictment of a grand jury, except in cases arising in the land or naval forces, or in the militia, when in actual service in time of war or public danger; nor shall any person be subject for the same offense to be twice put in jeopardy of life or limb; nor shall be compelled in any criminal case to be a witness against himself, nor to be deprived of life, liberty, or property, without due process of law; nor shall private property be taken for public use, without just compensation.

The 5th Amendment protects the legal rights of people in criminal proceedings.

No person may be brought to trial for a felony without first being charged with a specific crime by a grand jury. Since a grand jury action is not a trial, but hearing to determine if a crime has been committed and if there is sufficient evidence to have the accused stand trial, a grand jury's decision does not have to be unanimous. And since they are not trials, grand jury hearings are not made public.

No person may be tried for the same crime twice. But there are exceptions to the prohibition against double jeopardy. For example, if a person commits an act which violates both federal and state law, that person can be tried for that crime in both federal and state courts. Also, in a recurring crime, like bigamy, double jeopardy does not apply.

People may not be forced to give testimony against themselves. However, the prohibition against self-incrimination does not bar voluntarily testifying against one's self. The protection applies to any proceedings where testimony is legally required.

Due process involves the "how" and "what" of government action. Thus, there are two forms—procedural and substantive. In procedural due process, the government must act fairly in its relations with people. In substantive due process, it must proceed under fair laws in its dealings with people.

Government cannot take private property for public use without payment of a fair market price.

Amendment 6 Criminal Proceedings

In all criminal prosecutions, the accused shall enjoy the right to a speedy and public trial, by an impartial jury of the state and district wherein the crime shall have been committed, which district shall have been previously ascertained by law, and to be informed of the nature and cause of the accusation; to be confronted with the witnesses against him; to have compulsory process for obtaining witnesses in his favor, and to have the assistance of counsel for his defense.

The 6th Amendment protects the procedural rights of people in criminal proceedings.

The right to a speedy and public trial was to prevent a person from languishing in jail or being tried by a secret tribunal. But a trial must not be so speedy as to prevent time for preparing an adequate defense nor so public that mob rule prevails.

A trial can be moved from the district where the crime was committed (a motion for a change in venue) if public prejudice might affect the impartiality of the trial.

A person must be informed of the charges for an arrest. After being arrested, an accused is brought before a judge for arraignment, a determination if formal charges by a grand jury will be sought.

The right to confront witnesses guarantees an accused the right to cross-examination (direct rebuttal to testimony given). Though testimony can be given by deposition when witnesses for legitimate reasons cannot be present in court, it carries less weight because it is not subject to cross-examination.

A witness can be compelled to testify by means of a subpoena, a writ commanding that person to appear in court. Failure to comply with a subpoena will result in being held in contempt of court.

Though one can act as one's own counsel, all people are entitled to counsel. If one cannot afford counsel, the government must provide one from the public defender's office. The right to counsel includes police interrogation as well as trial.

Amendment 7 Jury Trial

In suits at common law, where the value in controversy shall exceed twenty dollars, the right of trial by jury shall be preserved, and no fact tried by a jury shall be otherwise re-examined in any court of the United States than according to the rules of common law.

Civil suits involve parties contesting private matters. Unlike criminal cases in which it is always the prosecutor, the government may or may not be a party in a civil suit. When a party, it can be either the plaintiff (the party wronged) or the defendant (the party being held accountable).

Amendment 8 Excessive Punishments

Excessive bail shall not be required, nor excessive fines imposed, nor cruel and unusual punishments inflicted.

Bail is security (money) put up to obtain the release of an accused from jail pending trial. Bail is set by the court at the time of arraignment. Failure to appear for trial is ground for forefeiture of the bail to the government.

For it to be unconstitutional, a punishment must be both cruel and unusual. Like bails and fines, a punishment must not be unreasonably severe in relation to the crime. Rarely have bails, fines, and punishments been contested as violating the 8th

Amendment 9 Rights of the People

The enumeration in the Constitution of certain rights shall not be construed to deny or disparage others retained by the people.

The Constitution does not specifically list all rights of the people. This amendment protects the peoples unenumerated rights.

Amendment 10 Reserved Powers

The powers not delegated to the United States by the Constitution, nor prohibited by it to the states, are reserved to the states respectively, or to the people.

The 10th Amendment safeguards the reserved powers of the states. But with the adoption of the 14th Amendment, a state's reserved powers, particularly its police powers, are subject to closer scrutiny. State practices that infringe upon personal liberty will be viewed as violating the guarantee of due process against arbitrary or unreasonable state action.

Amendment 11 Suits Against States

The judicial power of the United States shall not be construed to extend to any suit in law or equity, commenced or prosecuted against one of the United States by citizens of another state, or by citizens or subjects of any foreign state.

Adopted in 1798, the 11th Amendment changed a provision in Article 3, Section 2. It resulted from strong opposition to the Supreme Court's ruling in *Chisholm* v. *Georgia* in which the Court held that if a state could bring suit against citizens of another state, then certainly citizens of another state could bring suit against a state. The ruling was seen as weakening state sovereignty.

Under the 11th Amendment, foreign citizens or citizens of another state must sue a state in its courts in accordance with its law.

Amendment 12 Election of President and Vice-President

The electors shall meet in their respective states and vote by ballot for President and Vice-President, one of whom, at least, shall not be an inhabitant of the same state with themselves; they shall name in their ballots the person voted for as President, and in distinct ballots the person voted for as Vice-President, and they shall make distinct lists of all persons voted for as President, and of all persons voted for as Vice-President, and of the number of votes for each, which lists they shall sign and certify, and transmit sealed to the seat of the government of the United States, directed to the President of the Senate;—the President of the Senate shall, in the presence of the Senate and House of Representatives, open all the certificates and the votes shall then be counted;—the person having the greatest number of votes for President, shall be the President, if such number be a majority of the whole number of electors appointed; and if no person have such majority, then from the persons having the highest numbers not exceeding three on the list of those voted for as President, the House of Representatives shall choose immediately, by ballot, the President. But in choosing the President, the votes shall be taken by states, the representation from each state having one vote; a quorum for this purpose shall consist of a member or members from two thirds of the states, and a majority of all the states shall be necessary to a choice. And if the House of Representatives shall not choose a President whenever the right of choice shall devolve upon them, before the fourth day of March next following, then the Vice-President shall act as President, as in the case of the death or other constitutional disability of the President.—The person having the greatest number of votes as Vice-President, shall be the Vice-President, if such number be a majority of the whole number of electors appointed, and if no person have a majority, then from the two highest numbers on the list, the Senate shall choose the Vice-President; a quorum for the purpose shall consist of two thirds of the whole number of senators, and a majority of the whole number shall be necessary to a choice. But no person constitutionally ineligible to the office of President shall be eligible to that of Vice-President of the United States.

Adopted in 1804, the 12th Amendment changed the procedure for electing the President and Vice-President as outlined in Article 2, Section 1, Paragraph 3.

Amendment 13 Slavery

Section 1. Neither slavery nor involuntary
servitude, except as a punishment for crime
whereof the party shall have been duly convicted,
shall exist within the United States, or any place
subject to their jurisdiction.

Section 2. Congress shall have power to enforce
this article by appropriate legislation.

Amendment 14 Rights of Citizens

Section 1. All persons born or naturalized in the
United States, and subject to the jurisdiction
thereof, are citizens of the United States and of the
state wherein they reside. No state shall make or
enforce any law which shall abridge the privileges
or immunities of citizens of the United States; nor
shall any state deprive any person of life, liberty, or
property, without due process of law, nor deny to
any person within its jurisdiction the equal
protection of the laws.

Section 2. Representatives shall be apportioned
among the several states according to their
respective numbers, counting the whole number of
persons in each state, excluding Indians not taxed.
But when the right to vote at any election for the
choice of electors for President and Vice-President
of the United States, representatives in Congress,
the executive or judicial officers of a state, or the
members of the legislature thereof, is denied to
any of the male inhabitants of such state, being
twenty-one years of age, and citizens of the United
States, or in any way abridged, except for
participation in rebellion, or other crime, the basis
of representation therein shall be reduced in the
proportion which the number of such male citizens
shall bear to the whole number of male citizens
twenty-one years of age in such state.

Section 3. No person shall be a senator or
representative in Congress, or elector of President

or Vice-President, or hold any office, civil or military, under the United States, or under any state, who, having previously taken an oath, as a member of Congress, or as an officer of the United States, or as a member of any state legislature, or as an executive or judicial officer of any state, to support the Constitution of the United States, shall have engaged in insurrection or rebellion against the same, or given aid or comfort to the enemies thereof. But Congress may by a vote of two thirds of each house, remove such disability.

Section 3 was aimed at punishing the leaders of the Confederacy. By 1872, most were permitted to return to political life, and in 1898, amnesty was granted to all still living.

Section 4. The validity of the public debt of the United States, authorized by law, including debts incurred for payment of pensions and bounties for services in suppressing insurrection or rebellion, shall not be questioned. But neither the United States nor any state shall assume or pay any debt or obligation incurred in aid of insurrection or rebellion against the United States, or any claim for the loss or emancipation of any slave; but all such debts, obligations and claims shall be held illegal and void.

Like Section 3, Section 4 dealt with matters directly related to the Civil War. It validated the debt of the United States, prohibited assumption of any of the Confederate debt, and prohibited payment for any loss resulting from freeing of the slaves.

Section 5. The Congress shall have power to enforce, by appropriate legislation, the provisions of this article.

Amendment 15 Black Suffrage

Section 1. The right of citizens of the United States to vote shall not be denied or abridged by the United States or by any state on account of race, color, or previous condition of servitude.

Section 2. The Congress shall have power to enforce this article by appropriate legislation.

Adopted in 1870, the 15th Amendment replaced Amendment 14, Section 2 in guaranteeing blacks the right to vote. Yet, despite its prohibition against both the federal government and the states, blacks were disfranchised by many states following Reconstruction. By such means as poll taxes, literacy tests, "grandfather clauses," and white primaries, blacks were successfully prevented from participating in political life in much of the South until well into the 20th century. Not until the 1960's did Congress take firm action to enforce the guarantee of the 15th Amendment and end voter discrimination.

Amendment 16 Income Tax

The Congress shall have power to lay and collect taxes on incomes, from whatever source derived, without apportionment among the several states, and without regard to any census or enumeration.

Adopted in 1913, the 16th Amendment provided an exception to the restrictions placed on direct taxation by Article 1, Section 2, Paragraph 3, and Section 9, Paragraph 4. Like the 11th Amendment, it was adopted to reverse a Supreme Court ruling. Although there had been a temporary income tax during the Civil War, the tax's constitutionality was not tested until it was reinstated by the Wilson-Gorman Tariff Act of 1894. The Court held that it was unconstitutional since it was a direct tax imposed without apportionment or regard to enumeration in *Pollack* v. *Farmer Loan and Trust Company.*

Under the amendment, Congress has levied a tax on income derived from all sources, including wages, salaries, interest, dividends, rents, royalties, commissions, bonuses, and tips. The income tax applies to business income as well as personal income. It is a "progressive" tax—that is, the rate increases as income increases. In addition to its power to levy taxes on income, Congress has the authority to provide for its enforcement. It has provided stiff penalties for both tax evasion and tax fraud.

Amendment 17 Election of Senators

Section 1. The Senate of the United States shall be composed of two senators from each state, elected by the people thereof, for six years; and each senator shall have one vote. The electors in each state shall have the qualifications requisite for electors of the most numerous branch of the state legislatures.

Section 2. When vacancies happen in the representation of any state in the Senate, the executive authority of such state shall issue writs of election to fill such vacancies: Provided, that the legislature of any state may empower the executive thereof to make temporary appointments until the people fill the vacancies by election as the legislature may direct.

Section 3. This amendment shall not be so construed as to affect the election or term of any senator chosen before it becomes valid as part of the Constitution.

Amendment 18 National Prohibition

Section 1. After one year from the ratification of this article the manufacture, sale, or transportation of intoxicating liquors within, the importation thereof into, or the exportation thereof from the United States and all territory subject to the jurisdiction thereof for beverage purposes is hereby prohibited.

Section 2. The Congress and the several states shall have concurrent power to enforce this article by appropriate legislation.

Section 3. This article shall be inoperative unless it shall have been ratified as an amendment to the Constitution by the legislatures of the several states, as provided in the Constitution, within seven years from the date of the submission hereof to the states by the Congress.

Amendment 19 Woman Suffrage

Section 1. The right of citizens of the United States to vote shall not be denied or abridged by the United States or by any state on account of sex.

Section 2. Congress shall have power to enforce this article by appropriate legislation.

Amendment 20 Change of Terms, Sessions, and Inauguration

Section 1. The terms of the President and Vice-President shall end at noon on the 20th day of January, and the terms of senators and representatives at noon on the 3rd day of January, of the years in which such terms would have ended if this article had not been ratified; and the terms of their successors shall then begin.

Section 2. The Congress shall assemble at least once in every year, and such meeting shall begin at noon on the 3rd day of January, unless they shall by law appoint a different day.

Section 3. If, at the time fixed for the beginning of the term of the President, the President-elect shall have died, the Vice-President-elect shall become President. If a President shall not have been chosen before the time fixed for the beginning of his term, or if the President-elect shall have failed to qualify, then the Vice-President-elect shall act as President until a President shall have qualified; and the Congress may by law provide for the case wherein neither a President-elect nor a Vice-President-elect shall have qualified, declaring who shall then act as President, or the manner in which one who is to act shall be selected, and such person shall act accordingly until a President or Vice-President shall have qualified.

Section 4. The Congress may by law provide for the case of the death of any of the persons from whom the House of Representatives may choose a President whenever the right of choice shall have devolved upon them, and for the case of the death of any of the persons from whom the Senate may choose a Vice-President whenever the right of choice shall have devolved upon them.

Section 5. Sections 1 and 2 shall take effect on the 15th day of October following the ratification of this article.

Section 6. This article shall be inoperative unless it shall have been ratified as an amendment to the Constitution by the legislatures of three fourths of the several states within seven years from the date of its submission

Amendment 21 Repeal of National Prohibition

Section 1. The eighteenth article of amendment to the Constitution of the United States is hereby repealed.

Section 2. The transportation or importation into any state, territory, or possession of the United States for delivery or use therein of intoxicating liquors, in violation of the laws thereof, is hereby prohibited.

Section 3. This article shall be inoperative unless it shall have been ratified as an amendment to the Constitution by conventions in the several states, as provided in the Constitution, within seven years from the date of the submission hereof to the states by the Congress.

Amendment 22 Presidential Tenure

Section 1. No person shall be elected to the office of the President more than twice, and no person who has held the office of President, or acted as President, for more than two years of a term to which some other person was elected President shall be elected to the office of the President more than once. But this article shall not apply to any person holding the office of President when this article was proposed by the Congress, and shall not prevent any person who may be holding the office of President, or acting as President, during the term within which this article becomes operative from holding the office of President or acting as President during the remainder of such term.

Section 2. This article shall be inoperative unless it shall have been ratified as an amendment to the Constitution by the legislatures of three fourths of the several states within seven years from the date of its submission to the states by the Congress.

Amendment 23 Presidential Electors for D.C.

Section 1. The District constituting the seat of government of the United States shall appoint in such manner as the Congress may direct:

A number of electors of President and Vice-President equal to the whole number of senators and representatives in Congress to which the District would be entitled if it were a state, but in no event more than the least populous state; they shall be in addition to those appointed by the states, but they shall be considered, for the purposes of the election of President and Vice-President, to be electors appointed by a state; and they shall meet in the district and perform such duties as provided by the twelfth article of amendment.

Section 2. The Congress shall have power to enforce this article by appropriate legislation.

Adopted in 1961, the 23rd Amendment provided for the choosing of electors for the District of Columbia. Until its adoption, residents of the District were excluded from presidential elections.

By the wording of the amendment, the District is limited to 3 electors, the same number as the least populous state. If the District was a state, it would be entitled to 4 electors based on its probable representation in Congress.

Amendment 24 Prohibition of Poll Tax

Section 1. The right of citizens of the United States to vote in any primary or other election for President or Vice-President, for electors for President or Vice-President, or for senator or representative in Congress, shall not be denied or abridged by the United States or any state by reason of failure to pay any poll tax or other tax.

Section 2. The Congress shall have power to enforce this article by appropriate legislation.

Adopted in 1964, the 24th Amendment prohibits both the federal government and the states from denying a qualified voter the right to vote in federal elections for failure to pay any tax. The amendment did not prohibit states from imposing a poll tax as a voting qualification in state and local elections. However, the Supreme Court held the poll tax to be a denial of the Equal Protection Clause of the 14th Amendment and, therefore, unconstitutional in *Harper* v. *Virginia State Board of Elections* in 1966.

Amendment 25 Presidential Succession and Disability

Section 1. In case of the removal of the President from office or his death or resignation, the Vice-President shall become President.

Section 2. Whenever there is a vacancy in the office of the Vice-President, the President shall nominate a Vice-President who shall take the office upon confirmation by a majority vote of both houses of Congress.

Section 3. Whenever the President transmits to the President pro tempore of the Senate and the Speaker of the House of Representatives his written declaration that he is unable to discharge the powers and duties of his office, and until he transmits to them a written declaration to the contrary, such powers and duties shall be discharged by the Vice-President as Acting President.

Section 4. Whenever the Vice-President and a majority of either the principal officers of the executive departments, or of such other body as Congress may by law provide, transmit to the President pro tempore of the Senate and the Speaker of the House of Representatives their written declaration that the President is unable to discharge the powers and duties of his office, the Vice-President shall immediately assume the powers and duties of the office of Acting President.

Thereafter, when the President transmits to the President pro tempore of the Senate and the Speaker of the House of Representatives his written declaration that no inability exists, he shall resume the powers and duties of his office unless the Vice-President and a majority of either the principal officers of the executive departments, or of such other body as Congress may by law provide, transmit within four days to the President pro tempore of the Senate and the Speaker of the House of Representatives their written declaration that the President is unable to discharge the powers and duties of his office. Thereupon Congress shall decide the issue, assembling within 48 hours for that purpose if not in session. If the Congress, within 21 days after receipt of the latter written declaration, or, if Congress is not in session, within 21 days after Congress is required to assemble, determines by two thirds vote of both houses that the President is unable to discharge the powers and duties of his office, the Vice-President shall continue to discharge the same as Acting President; otherwise, the President shall resume the power and duties of his office.

Adopted in 1967, the 25th Amendment clarifies Article 2, Section 1, Paragraph 6. Until its adoption, the assumption of the office of the President by the

Vice-President because of vacancy was based upon the precedent set by John Tyler following the death of William Henry Harrison in 1841. The 25th Amendment clearly states the Vice-President assumes the office of President should it become vacant. Nine times in American history it has become vacant—four times because of natural deaths (Harrison in 1841, Taylor in 1850, Harding in 1923, and Franklin Roosevelt in 1945); four times because of assassinations (Lincoln in 1865, Garfield in 1881, McKinley in 1901, and Kennedy in 1963); and once because of resignation (Nixon in 1974).

The amendment also provides for the Vice-President becoming acting President should the President become disabled. There are two procedures covering presidential disability—(1) the President can voluntarily declare to the Speaker and President pro tem in writing that he (or she) is unable to discharge the duties of the office; or (2) the Vice-President and the Cabinet can do so when the President cannot.

The 25th Amendment also provides for filling the office of the Vice-President by presidential appointment and congressional approval should it become vacant. Eighteen times in American history there has been a vacancy—9 times because of assumption to the Presidency (Tyler in 1941, Fillmore in 1850, Andrew Johnson in 1865, Arthur in 1881, Theodore Roosevelt in 1901, Coolidge in 1923, Truman in 1945, Lyndon Johnson in 1963, and Ford in 1974); 7 times through death (Clinton in 1812, Gerry in 1814, King in 1853, Wilson in 1875, Hendricks in 1885, Hobart in 1899, and Sherman in 1912); and 2 times by resignation (Calhoun in 1832 and Agnew in 1973).

Gerald Ford is the first and only person to be appointed Vice-President by a President. Ford also became President following Nixon's resignation. Thus, he is the only person to hold both offices having never been elected to either.

Amendment 26 Eighteen-Year-Old Vote

Section 1. The right of citizens of the United States, who are eighteen years of age or older, to vote shall not be denied or abridged by the United States or by any state on account of age.

Section 2. The Congress shall have power to enforce this article by appropriate legislation.

Adopted in 1971, the 26th Amendment lowered the voting age to 18. Note, however, that the amendment does not prohibit any state from allowing citizens less than 18 to vote if it so chooses. Thus, the amendment does not, in fact, establish a minimum voting age.

Presidents and Vice-Presidents

No.	Name	Born	Died	Yrs. in Office	Party	State*	Vice-Pres.	State*
1	George Washington	1732	1799	1789–1797	None	Va.	John Adams	Mass.
2	John Adams	1735	1826	1797–1801	Federalist	Mass.	Thomas Jefferson	Va.
3	Thomas Jefferson	1743	1826	1801–	Dem.-Rep.	Va.	Aaron Burr	N.Y.
	Thomas Jefferson	1743	1826	–1809	Dem.-Rep.	Va.	George Clinton	N.Y.
4	James Madison	1751	1836	1809–	Dem.-Rep.	Va.	George Clinton	N.Y.
	James Madison	1751	1836	–1817	Dem.-Rep.	Va.	Elbridge Gerry	Mass.
5	James Monroe	1758	1831	1817–1825	Dem.-Rep.	Va.	Daniel D. Tompkins	N.Y.
6	John Quincy Adams	1767	1848	1825–1829	Nat.-Rep.	Mass.	John C. Calhoun	S.C.
7	Andrew Jackson	1767	1845	1829–	Democratic	Tenn.	John C. Calhoun	S.C.
	Andrew Jackson	1767	1845	–1837	Democratic	Tenn.	Martin Van Buren	N.Y.
8	Martin Van Buren	1782	1862	1837–1841	Democratic	N.Y.	Richard M. Johnson	Ky.
9	William H. Harrison	1773	1841	1841	Whig	Ohio	John Tyler	Va.
10	John Tyler	1790	1862	1841–1845	Whig	Va.		
11	James K. Polk	1795	1849	1845–1849	Democratic	Tenn.	George M. Dallas	Pa.
12	Zachary Taylor	1784	1850	1849–1850	Whig	La.	Millard Fillmore	N.Y.
13	Millard Fillmore	1800	1874	1850–1853	Whig	N.Y.		
14	Franklin Pierce	1804	1869	1853–1857	Democratic	N.H.	William R. King	Ala.
15	James Buchanan	1791	1868	1857–1861	Democratic	Pa.	John C. Breckinridge	Ky.
16	Abraham Lincoln	1809	1865	1861–	Republican	Ill.	Hannibal Hamlin	Maine
	Abraham Lincoln	1809	1865	–1865	Republican	Ill.	Andrew Johnson	Tenn.
17	Andrew Johnson	1808	1875	1865–1869	Democratic	Tenn.		
18	Ulysses S. Grant	1822	1885	1869–	Republican	Ill.	Schuyler Colfax	Ind.
	Ulysses S. Grant	1822	1885	–1877	Republican	Ill.	Henry Wilson	Mass.
19	Rutherford B. Hayes	1822	1893	1877–1881	Republican	Ohio	William A. Wheeler	N.Y.
20	James A. Garfield	1831	1881	1881	Republican	Ohio	Chester A. Arthur	N.Y.
21	Chester A. Arthur	1830	1886	1881–1885	Republican	N.Y.		
22	Grover Cleveland	1837	1908	1885–1889	Democratic	N.Y.	Thomas A. Hendricks	Ind.
23	Benjamin Harrison	1833	1901	1889–1893	Republican	Ind.	Levi P. Morton	N.Y.
24	Grover Cleveland	1837	1908	1893–1897	Democratic	N.Y.	Adlai E. Stevenson	Ill.
25	William McKinley	1843	1901	1897–	Republican	Ohio	Garret A. Hobart	N.J.
	William McKinley	1843	1901	–1901	Republican	Ohio	Theodore Roosevelt	N.Y.
26	Theodore Roosevelt	1858	1919	1901–	Republican	N.Y.		
	Theodore Roosevelt	1858	1919	–1909	Republican	N.Y.	Charles W. Fairbanks	Ind.
27	William H. Taft	1857	1930	1909–1913	Republican	Ohio	James S. Sherman	N.Y.
28	Woodrow Wilson	1856	1924	1913–1921	Democratic	N.J.	Thomas R. Marshall	Ind.
29	Warren G. Harding	1865	1923	1921–1923	Republican	Ohio	Calvin Coolidge	Mass.
30	Calvin Coolidge	1872	1933	1923–	Republican	Mass.		
	Calvin Coolidge	1872	1933	–1929	Republican	Mass.	Charles G. Dawes	Ill.
31	Herbert Hoover	1874	1964	1929–1933	Republican	Cal.	Charles Curtis	Kans.
32	Franklin D. Roosevelt	1882	1945	1933–	Democratic	N.Y.	John Garner	Texas
	Franklin D. Roosevelt	1882	1945		Democratic	N.Y.	Henry Wallace	Iowa
	Franklin D. Roosevelt	1882	1945	–1945	Democratic	N.Y.	Harry Truman	Mo.
33	Harry Truman	1884	1972	1945–	Democratic	Mo.		
	Harry Truman	1884	1972	–1953	Democratic	Mo.	Alben Barkley	Ky.
34	Dwight Eisenhower	1890	1969	1953–1961	Republican	N.Y.	Richard Nixon	Cal.
35	John F. Kennedy	1917	1963	1961–1963	Democratic	Mass.	Lyndon Johnson	Texas
36	Lyndon Johnson	1908	1973	1963–	Democratic	Texas		
	Lyndon Johnson	1908	1973	–1969	Democratic	Texas	Hubert Humphrey	Minn.
37	Richard Nixon	1913		1969–	Republican	N.Y.	Spiro Agnew	Md.
	Richard Nixon	1913		–1974	Republican	N.Y.	Gerald Ford	Mich.
38	Gerald Ford	1913		1974–1977	Republican	Mich.	Nelson Rockefeller	N.Y.
39	Jimmy Carter	1924		1977–1981	Democratic	Ga.	Walter Mondale	Minn.
40	Ronald Reagan	1911		1981–	Republican	Cal.	George Bush	Texas

*State of residence at election

749

States in the United States

Name	Year of Admission	Population (1980 Census)	No. of Representatives	Area in Square Miles	Capital
Alabama	1819	3,890,061	7	51,609	Montgomery
Alaska	1959	400,481	1	586,412	Juneau
Arizona	1912	2,717,866	5	113,909	Phoenix
Arkansas	1836	2,285,513	4	53,104	Little Rock
California	1850	23,668,562	45	158,693	Sacramento
Colorado	1876	2,888,834	6	104,247	Denver
Connecticut	1788	3,107,576	6	5,009	Hartford
Delaware	1787	595,225	1	2,057	Dover
Florida	1845	9,739,992	19	58,560	Tallahassee
Georgia	1788	5,464,265	10	58,876	Atlanta
Hawaii	1959	965,000	2	6,450	Honolulu
Idaho	1890	943,935	2	83,557	Boise
Illinois	1818	11,418,461	22	56,400	Springfield
Indiana	1816	5,490,179	10	36,291	Indianapolis
Iowa	1846	2,913,387	6	56,290	Des Moines
Kansas	1861	2,363,208	5	82,264	Topeka
Kentucky	1792	3,661,433	7	40,395	Frankfort
Louisiana	1812	4,203,972	8	48,523	Baton Rouge
Maine	1820	1,124,660	2	33,215	Augusta
Maryland	1788	4,216,446	8	10,577	Annapolis
Massachusetts	1788	5,737,037	11	8,257	Boston
Michigan	1837	9,258,344	18	58,216	Lansing
Minnesota	1858	4,077,148	8	84,068	St. Paul
Mississippi	1817	2,520,638	5	47,716	Jackson
Missouri	1821	4,917,444	9	69,686	Jefferson City
Montana	1889	786,690	2	147,138	Helena
Nebraska	1867	1,570,006	3	77,227	Lincoln
Nevada	1864	799,184	2	110,540	Carson City
New Hampshire	1788	920,610	2	9,304	Concord
New Jersey	1787	7,364,158	14	7,836	Trenton
New Mexico	1912	1,299,968	3	121,666	Santa Fe
New York	1788	17,557,288	34	49,576	Albany
North Carolina	1789	5,874,429	11	52,586	Raleigh
North Dakota	1889	652,695	1	70,665	Bismarck
Ohio	1803	10,797,419	21	41,222	Columbus
Oklahoma	1907	3,025,266	6	69,919	Oklahoma City
Oregon	1859	2,632,663	5	96,981	Salem
Pennsylvania	1787	11,866,728	23	45,333	Harrisburg
Rhode Island	1790	947,154	2	1,214	Providence
South Carolina	1788	3,119,208	6	31,055	Columbia
South Dakota	1889	690,178	1	77,047	Pierre
Tennessee	1796	4,590,750	9	42,244	Nashville
Texas	1845	14,228,383	27	267,338	Austin
Utah	1896	1,461,037	3	84,916	Salt Lake City
Vermont	1791	511,456	1	9,609	Montpelier
Virginia	1788	5,346,279	10	40,817	Richmond
Washington	1889	4,130,163	8	68,192	Olympia
West Virginia	1863	1,949,644	4	24,181	Charleston
Wisconsin	1848	4,705,335	9	56,154	Madison
Wyoming	1890	470,816	1	97,914	Cheyenne
District of Columbia		637,651		69	

Glossary

Glossary

A

abolish put an end to something

abolitionists people who wanted to put an end to slavery

acquittal verdict of not guilty

administration major offices in the executive branch of government

adobe sun-dried brick

aggression attacks on others

agriculture planned growing of food

airlift system of bringing in supplies by airplane

alien person who is not a citizen of the country in which he or she lives

alliances unions for specific purposes

amendment change in, or addition to, a document

amnesty general pardon by the government

amphibious water to land

anarchists people who want to do away with government

annexed added new land to a territory

appeal review of a lower court's findings by a higher court

appeasement act of giving in to an aggressor in order to keep peace

arbitration hearing and deciding of a disagreement by a third party

armada fleet of warships

armistice agreement to stop fighting

arsenal place where weapons are kept

artisans skilled workers

assassinated killed by sudden or secret attack

assets property or things that have value

assume take over a debt

atomic bomb bomb that uses the splitting of atoms to cause a powerful explosion

auctions public sales where goods or slaves were sold to the persons who offered the most money for them

automation making of a product by machines controlled electronically

aviation air transportation

B

balance of trade condition when a nation is making at least as much money from goods exported as it is from goods imported.

bicameral two-house

big stick diplomacy foreign policy based on the idea that the United States would be willing to use force to protect American interests

bimetalism policy of backing paper money with gold and silver

black codes laws which limited the rights of blacks, passed by the southern states during Reconstruction

blacklist list of people who are not allowed to work in an industry

"black power" movement among blacks for full rights and a greater voice in their political affairs

blitzkrieg very fast attack, usually using both ground and air forces

blockade closing off an area to prevent certain things from going in or coming out

blockade runners people who slipped goods into or out of a blockaded port

blue-collar workers people who do manual labor in industry

bonds certificates bearing a written promise to repay with interest in a certain length of time an amount of money borrowed

border states states located between the North and South in the Civil War in which sentiment about slavery was divided

bounties payments of money to a person for entering the armed services

boycott refusal to buy or use certain products as a means of protest

budget deficit the excess in spending in regard to the revenues received

C

capital money used in operating a business

carpetbaggers name given to people from the North who moved to the South during Reconstruction, usually for the purpose of gaining money through political power

casualties persons wounded or killed

caucuses meeting of members of a political party or group to make plans or select candidates

cease-fire temporary agreement to stop fighting

cede yield or grant land

celebrities well-known people from the world of sports and entertainment

census count of the number of people in a place

chancellor prime minister

charter official paper giving permission for settlements and trade in a certain area

checks and balances system written into the Constitution which allows each branch of government to check on, or balance, the power of the other branches

city-manager form type of government in which a professional manager is hired by the city council to take care of city business

closed shop company in which workers must join a union before being hired

coexistence countries recognizing the rights of each other to live in peace

cold war war in which there is no fighting, but each side uses means short of military action to expand its influences

colonies settlements in other lands made by people still tied to the rule of their home countries

commission form type of city government which allows each person on the commission to take care of one area of government

commonwealth country with local self-government but united under another country

communism economic system based on ownership of all property by society

compact agreement

compromise settlement of differences by each side giving up part of what it wants

compulsory attendance laws laws requiring that children attend school part of the year

concentration camps prison camps, especially those of the Nazis during World War II

concurrent powers powers which are shared by the federal and state governments

conductors persons who secretly helped runaway slaves escape on the Underground Railroad

confederation loose union of peoples or groups for shared support and action

conglomerates groups of companies that produce many different kinds of products

conquistador Spanish conqueror in the Americas in the 1500's

consensus general agreement

conservation saving of natural resources

conservatism a belief that government should be less involved in local affairs and economic matters, and that changes that take place should be slow and gradual

conspiracy group plot

constitution written plan of government

consumer goods products made for individual use

consumers people who buy and use food, clothing, or any article a producer makes

containment policy of limiting Soviet expansion and the spread of communism

convoy system system in which warships travel along with supply ships for protection

"cooling-off" period time during which workers are ordered not to strike when it might affect the nation's welfare

cooperative business owned and operated by the people who use its services

corollary statement or policy which adds to an earlier statement or policy

corporations businesses in which groups of investors own shares of stock

corrupt bargain agreement influenced by bribes

cotton gin machine which is used to remove seeds from cotton

coureurs de bois early French settlers who hunted and trapped alone in the deep forests of North America, often following Indians' ways of life

cowhands workers who care for and move cattle

cultures ways of life

D

defensive war war fought by a country remaining in its own territory and defending it from attack

delegated powers powers given to the federal government by the Constitution

demonstrations public displays of feelings by a group toward a policy, a cause, or a person

deport force a person to leave a country

depression period of slow economic activity with prices low and many people out of work

deregulation removing price controls

desegregation ending of segregation

deserters soldiers or sailors who run away from their duty

destroyers small, fast warships

detente relaxing of cold war tensions between the United States and the Soviet Union

dictatorship form of government in which one person (a dictator) or a small group of people hold all power

direct primary nominating election

direct representation representation in which members represent only the people in the area from which they were elected

direct tax tax which must be paid to the government and is not included in the price of goods

disarmament reduction of weapons, military supplies, and armed forces by a government

displaced persons those who have been forced to leave their country because of political reasons

dissidents people who speak out against their government

diversity having lots of differences

dividends shares of a company's profits which are paid to its stockholders

dollar diplomacy foreign policy of investing American money in foreign countries in an attempt to maintain economic power in those countries without using force

domestic internal or within a country

domino theory idea that countries bordering a country which falls to Communist control will soon also fall

"doves" those who want a decrease in military action as a solution to world conflict

draft selection of people who would be forced to serve in the military

dry-farming type of farming using deep plowing into the soil to bring up underground moisture

dust bowl Great Plains area which experienced a long drought and dust storms

duties taxes on imports

E

elect certain number of people chosen by God to be saved and go to heaven

electors persons chosen by the voters to vote for President and Vice-President

emancipated set free

embargo law stopping all ships except foreign ships without cargo from leaving the country for foreign ports

empire many different peoples and lands ruled by one government or leader

empresarios people who organize and take the risk for business deals

entrenched set up in a strong position

environment surrounding land, water, and air

erosion process of land being slowly worn away by wind and water

evacuated withdrawn

excise tax tax on goods made and sold inside the country

exclusive powers powers that belong only to the federal government

executive clemency lessening of punishment by the order of the President

executive privilege the constitutional right of the President to keep information from Congress

expansionists people who wanted to expand the land area of the United States

exporting sending goods for foreign sale.

expressed powers powers of the federal government stated in the Constitution

F

factory system system in which workers in buildings known as factories made goods with power-driven machines

famine general lack of food in an area causing starvation

federal having to do with the central government in a system where states are joined under one central control but keep some governing powers

federalism division of power between a central government and a number of state governments

fireside chats talks on the radio made by President Franklin Roosevelt

foreclosures taking away of property due to failure to make payments on its debt

"forty-niners" name given to the people who left the East to move to California during the 1849 gold rush

freedmen men, women, and children who had been slaves and were freed after the Civil War

freedom of the seas right of merchant ships in peace or war to move in any waters, except those belonging to a country

free verse poems which do not rhyme

frontier new area to explore or develop

fugitive runaway

G

gag rule law preventing the reading of antislavery petitions in the House

gauge distance between the rails on railroad tracks

ghost towns empty, lifeless towns left behind by gold miners

"gilded age" name given the late 1800's because many Americans thought that society was not what it appeared to be

glaciers heavy, giant sheets of solid ice that move slowly across the land

gold rush movement of people from the eastern United States to California after gold was discovered there

gold standard money system in which paper money is backed by gold alone

"gospel of wealth" idea that part of the wealth from Big Business should be used for the good of society

graduated income tax tax system in which people with more money pay higher taxes.

"grandfather clauses" laws allowing people to vote if they, their fathers, or their grandfathers had voted on or before January 1, 1867

greenbacks paper money that was not backed by gold or silver

gross national product value of all goods and services produced in a country in one year

guerrillas bands who make war by harassment and sabotage

H

"hawks" those who want an increase in military action as a solution to world conflict

heritage background

hogans small, round houses of the Navaho Indians, made of mud and logs

holding company company that owns controlling interest in other companies

homesteaders people who settled on land with plans to farm it

I

immigrated came to live in a country

impeach charge a person with a crime while that person is holding a government office

imperialism spreading the rule of one country over that of another

implied powers powers of the federal government not directly stated in the Constitution but implied by the wording

importing bringing in goods from other countries to sell

impounded refused to release

impressment stopping of American ships and forcing of American sailors to work on British ships

inauguration ceremony of installing a person in office

indentured servants people who bound themselves to work for others for a certain time

indigo vegetable dye used on cloth

industry making and selling of goods

infantry groups of soldiers who fight on foot

inflation increase in money supply with a resulting rise in prices

inherent powers powers of the federal government which belong to it because it is a national government

initiative method by which citizens can propose new laws at any time

injunctions court orders preventing an action

installment plan plan which allows people to buy goods on credit and make monthly payments

intendant head of the sovereign council of New France

interchangeable parts parts that are exactly alike

intercollegiate involving two or more colleges

internal improvements programs that are used to make a country better, such as the building of roads, bridges, and canals

"international police power" responsibility for preserving order and protecting life and property around the world

interstate trade trade between two or more states

intervention act of interfering in the affairs of another nation

intolerant not willing to respect the beliefs, practices, or behavior of others

investors people who buy shares in a company

ironclad kind of battleship covered with thick iron plates

isthmus narrow strip of land between two larger bodies of land

J

jazz kind of music which has syncopated rhythms and developed from ragtime and blues music during the early 1920's

joint occupation agreement between Great Britain and the United States that people from both nations could settle in the Oregon territory

joint stock companies companies formed by a group of people for the purpose of selling stock to raise money for a business venture

judicial review power to judge whether or not acts of Congress and actions of the President are constitutional

judiciary branch of government responsible for the court system

juntas governments headed by groups of military officers

jurisdiction authority of a court to hear certain cases

K

kayak small, canoelike boat used by the Arctic Indians

kiva round underground room used by the Pueblo Indians for ceremonies, meetings, and work

L

labor unions organized group of workers that act as bargaining agents

laissez-faire French term that refers to an economy in which the government does not make rules for business

lame duck official who is still in office after a new official has been elected

land bridge narrow strip of land between Asia and North America in the Ice Ages

land speculation buying up land to sell at a profit

lease rent

legislature lawmaking body

liberalism a belief that government should take as large a role as necessary to promote freedom, equal justice, and equal opportunity

limited government idea that a government may exercise only those powers granted to it by the people

limited war policy plan to avoid a major war that might involve nuclear weapons

literacy test test to prove that a person could read and explain a part of a state's constitution before being allowed to vote

long drive annual drive of cattle from Texas to the railroad lines in Abilene

long houses large, rectangular homes of the Iroquois Indians, made of wood poles and bark

loose construction broad interpretation of the Constitution to mean more than what it says

lottery chance drawing

loyalists American colonists who remained loyal to England during the Revolution

M

manifest destiny certain fate of the United States to stretch from ocean to ocean

manufacturing making goods by hand or machine

mass media means of communication which reaches a great number of people

mass production system of producing large numbers of an item quickly using interchangeable parts

median family income income figure with half the families making more than it and half making less than it

meeting houses Puritan places of worship

mercantilism economic policy to increase a country's wealth by increasing its manufacturing and exports, by taxing imports, and by establishing colonies to provide raw materials and new markets

mergers joining together of two or more companies to form a larger company

756

mesas flat tops of high hills

migrated moved from one place to settle in another

minimum-income plan plan in which the government would make direct money payments to the poor to bring their incomes to a certain minimum

minutemen patriot soldiers who could be ready for duty at a moment's notice

missionaries church workers sent to teach Christianity to non-Christians

mobility ability to move or be moved

monopoly exclusive control of trade

mounds large hills of earth which were part of the religion of some Eastern Woodlands Indians

muckrakers authors who criticized Big Business and government in the early 1900's

munitions war materials

N

national anthem song of praise and patriotism

nationalism feeling of pride in the nation as a whole and loyalty to its goals

negotiating discussing in order to reach an agreement or to work out terms

neutrality position of taking no side in a conflict

"new" immigration movement of immigrants to the United States from southern and eastern Europe after 1880

night watches people who lit street lamps and called out the hour of the night

noncombat jobs jobs in the military that are not part of the fighting

normalization return to normal conditions

null and void not binding

nullification idea that a state may cancel a federal law within its own borders

O

oil shale kind of rock containing oil found in the Rocky Mountain area

"old" immigration movement of immigrants to the United States from northwestern Europe before the early 1880's

"on margin" buying stocks by paying 10 percent of the purchase price with the rest as a loan

open range unclaimed public grasslands

operettas light operas

ordinances rules or laws

organs parts of an organization

oscillation hardening and softening of attitudes and relations

P

pacifists people who are against violence and war as a way of settling problems

paratroopers soldiers trained to use parachutes

partisans supporters of a person, party, or cause

patents licenses to make, use, or sell new inventions

patriots those who love their country and strongly support its authority and interests

"peculiar institution" name given slavery by Southern whites, meaning that it was a way of life unique to the South

perjury lying under oath

perpetual everlasting

persecuted treated cruelly by others

personal liberty laws laws to stop state and local officials from obeying the federal fugitive slave laws

pet banks name given to state banks that received money President Jackson withdrew from the Bank of the United States

philosophy set of ideas

planters owners of large farms known as plantations

platform statement of the policies of a political party

pocket veto veto of a bill that occurs when the President fails to sign one presented to him by Congress within ten days of its recess

"police powers" powers set aside for the states that safeguard individual well-being

poll tax tax to be paid before being allowed to vote in an election

pool agreement to divide up the market and control prices

popular music music well-liked by the general public

popular sovereignty idea that a government receives its authority from the people; used before the Civil War to allow settlers in a new area to decide whether or not slavery would be allowed in their territory

potlatch special feast of the Northwest Coast Indians in which the chief proved how rich he was

precedents acts that serve as examples in later situations

prejudice attitude or opinion about a person, group, or race which is formed without taking time or care to judge fairly

preparedness idea that a nation should always be ready to defend itself from enemy attack

proclamation official anouncement

prohibition forbidding by law of the manufacture, shipping, and sale of alcoholic beverages

propaganda information designed to help or harm a cause

proprietary colonies type of colony operated under a charter granted to the proprietor by the king

proprietors friends of the king that were given grants to start colonies in America

protective tariff heavy tax on imported goods, protecting goods made at home by making imported goods more expensive

pueblos apartmentlike buildings in which whole villages of Pueblo Indians lived

Q

quarantine form of isolation of disease or blockade of an area

quartered given a place to live

quota certain number assigned to a group for certain purposes, such as immigration

R

radical extreme or sudden changes from the usual; a person who favors extreme changes in beliefs, habits, or institutions

ratify give formal approval to a law

rationing setting limits on the amount of certain goods people can buy

Reagonomics government economic policy designed to increase production or favor supply

rebates refunds

recall way for citizens to vote on removing elected officials from office

reconstruction rebuilding, especially the Union after the Civil War

redeemed paid off a loan or a bond

red scare fear of communism and its spread to the United States

referendum method that allowed citizens to vote to approve or defeat any bill brought up by the legislature

refinery plant where crude oil is refined or changed into usable products

regulatory commission supervising agency set up by the government

relocation centers camps in the United States in which people of Japanese ancestry were kept during World War II

renaissance time when there is much artistic and intellectual activity

renounce give up claims

repealed withdrawn, usually referring to a law

reservations separate areas set aside or reserved for the Indians by the United States government

reserved powers powers that are not given to the federal government but are reserved to state governments

reserve requirement requirement that banks chartered by the federal government must put a certain amount of money into the Federal Reserve bank in its district

reservoirs places where water is collected and stored for use

resource exploration search for new sources of natural resources

revelations special messages from God

revenue bills tax bills for raising money and bills authorizing the spending of money

revenue-sharing plan plan in which the federal government gives part of its revenues to state and local governments

revivals meetings to make people more interested in religion

rituals forms of service or ceremonies

royal colony type of colony under the direct control of the king

rural country

S

sachems chiefs of the Iroquois Indians

satellite small object circling a planet

satellite nations small, weak countries which are controlled by a stronger country

scalawags name given to southern whites who supported the Republican party after the Civil War

secede withdraw from an organization, a group, or the Union

secession withdrawing from the Union

sectionalism rivalry based on the special interests of different areas in a country

sedition use of language to stir up rebellion against a government

segregate set apart or separate

separation of powers division of power among the three branches of government

settlement houses places established in the late 1800's and early 1900's as meeting centers or places of education for the poor, immigrants, minorities, and others

sharecropping system in which people farm land they do not own in return for a share of the crop

shuttle diplomacy negotiations to settle disputes between nations by a third party flying back and forth to discuss issues with each nation

sit-ins a form of protest, especially against segregation when blacks occupied sections in lunch counters and restaurants reserved for whites and would not leave until they were served

slave codes laws which controlled the lives of slaves

slaves people who are the property of their owners

social Darwinism idea that life is a struggle and only the fittest survive

social security program of government aid for older, disabled, or unemployed citizens

space shuttle spaceship that would be used several times to carry people to and from space

speakeasies nightclubs that sold liquor illegally during Prohibition

specie gold or silver coin

speculators people who buy stocks, bonds, or land for the purpose of selling it for a profit later when prices rise

spheres of influence areas of control over trade

"spirit of Geneva" willingness of world leaders to work together for world peace

spoils system practice of giving government jobs to political supporters

stagflation stalled economy in a period of inflation

states' rights idea that each state could decide if an act of the government is unconstitutional

station safe places that were part of the Underground Railroad

stockbrokers people who sell stocks

strict construction narrow interpretation of the Constitution to mean just what it says

strikes refusals by workers to work until the company's owners agree to their demands or offer an acceptable compromise

strip mining method of getting coal by scraping off soil and rocks covering it

subpoena written legal order

subversives people who secretly work inside a country to overthrow its government

suffrage right to vote

summit conference meeting of the heads of government of the major world powers

sun belt southeast and southwest parts of the United States where the weather is sunny and warm much of the time

supremacy of civilian authority principle that the military is subject to civilian authority

supremacy of national law principle that national law is superior to state law

surveyed examined and measured land

symbolism use of one thing to stand for something else

synthetic artificial

T

tariffs taxes on imported goods

technology application of ideas, methods, and tools to the production of goods

temperance self-control, usually in the use of alcoholic beverages

tenements apartment houses generally without sanitation, comfort, and safety

tenure of office length of time that a person can stay in office

terrorism use of fear to get power

textile woven fabric; cloth

tipis cone-shaped homes of the Western Plains Indians, made of poles and buffalo hides

totem poles large wooden posts carved with figures of faces and animals, showing the family history and titles of the family leader of some Northwest Coast Indians

town meeting gathering of all eligible voters in a town to debate political issues and pass laws

trail boss leader of a cattle drive

transcendentalism idea that people could go beyond their limitations and perfect themselves and their society

transcontinental crossing a continent

travois small platforms fastened to two poles, used by the Western Plains Indians

trenches ditches

trench warfare war that is fought by soldiers forming defensive lines of trenches to slow down the enemy

triangular trade triangular pattern of trade of molasses from the West Indies, rum from New England, and slaves from Africa

trust organization of several companies which are run as one company

trust territories areas of the world not under a national government but under the care of the United Nations

turnpike road built by a private company that charged a fee for using it

U

umiak a large, canoelike boat used by the Arctic Indians

urban city

utopias ideal communities

V

vetoed refused to approve

viceroys persons ruling colonies as direct representatives of the home country

Vietnamization program in which American troops equipped and trained the South Vietnamese to take over the fighting so that Americans could withdraw

virtual representation representation in which members represent all people in an area or country

vocational relating to a career or job

vulcanization process which makes rubber able to stand great heat or cold

W

wards people under the care of a guardian

white-collar workers people who work in professional or office jobs

wickiups homes of the Apache Indians made from frames of thin poles covered with animal skins

wigwams small, rounded homes of some Eastern Woodlands Indians

"windfall profits" tax tax on the extra profits that oil companies would make as government price controls were lifted

wire services national and international organizations which gather news to pass on to newspapers

workman's compensation law law giving payments to workers hurt in industrial accidents

Y

yellow-dog contracts agreements in which workers had to sign that they would not join a union before they took a job

yellow fever disease caused by a kind of mosquito

yellow journalism attempt by newspapers to appeal to the emotions of readers in an attempt to sell more papers

Index

Index

Birney, James, G., 250
black codes, 361
Black Hawk, Chief, 228
Black Hawk's War, 228
Black Hills, South Dakota, 394
blacklist, 532
"black power," 630
blacks, 236, 248, 250, 251, 301,
    302, 317, 319, 359, 360, 361,
    362, 365, 366, 368, 369, 373,
    377, 378, 379, 383, 390, 398,
    399, 400, 401, 410, 423, 432,
    438, 494, 497, 511, 521, 522,
    524, 525, 526, 534, 555, 556,
    613, 614, 623, 624, 625, 630,
    632, 647, 659, 688, 693, 696,
    700 (see also slavery, slaves)
Black Sea, 602
Bladensburg, Maryland, 202
"Bleeding Kansas," 324, 325
blitzkrieg, 567
blockade, 197
blockade runners, 339, 343
blue-collar workers, 688, 708
Bolsheviks, 498
Bonaparte, Napoleon, 187, 191,
    198, 202
bonds, 179
Bond, Thomas, 170
boom-bust cycle, 510
Booth, John Wilkes, 352
Borah, William E., 517
border states, 336
Boston, Massachusetts, 56, 57,
    62, 67, 76, 88, 109, 110, 112,
    116, 258, 265, 273, 277, 324,
    345, 401, 428
Boston Massacre, 109
Boston Red Sox, 433 (see also
    baseball)
Boston Tea Party, 110
bounties, 345
Bowie, Jim, 289
Bowler, Jack, 317
Boxer Rebellion, 474
Boxers, 472
boxing, 535; Dempsey, Jack,
    535; Tunney, Gene, 535
boycott, 107
Boyd, Belle, 343
Braddock, Edward, 101
Bradford, Cornelia, 167
Bradford, William, 55, 74, 75,
    76, 77
Bradstreet, Anne, 88

Brady, James, 672
"Brain Trust," 551
Brazil, 30, 31, 45, 316, 481, 525
Brazos River, 288
"Bread Colonies," 93 (see
    Middle Colonies)
Breckenridge, John C., 328
Breed's Hill, Massachusetts, 116
Brest-Litovsk, Russia, 498
Brezhnev, Leonid, 640, 657, 681
Briand, Aristide, 518
Bridenbaugh, Carl, 168
Bridger, Jim, 281
British Parliament, 107, 108,
    109, 110, 112, 148
British West Indies, 133
Bronx, New York, 376, 648
Brook Farm, 247, 256
Brooklyn, New York, 376
Brown, John, 325, 327, 328
Brown v. Board of Education of
    Topeka, 612
Bruce, Blanche K., 366
Bryant, William Cullen, 211
Bryan, William Jennings, 423,
    436, 438, 444, 491
Buchanan, James, 325, 326
budget deficit, 676, 678
Buena Vista, Battle of, 292
buffalo, 6, 268, 296, 394, 396
Buick, 507
Buick, David D., 507, 529
Bulganin, N. A., 618
Bulgaria, 402
Bulge, Battle of the, 578
Bull Moose party, 446
Bull Run, Battles of, 337, 338,
    341, 343
Bunche, Ralph, 615
Bunker Hill, Battle of, 116, 135
Bureau of Indian Affairs, 556,
    672
Burgoyne, John, 117
Burma, 570
Burnham, Daniel, 455
Burnside, Ambrose, 347
Burr, Aaron, 186, 189, 236
Bush, George, 664, 670, 672
Butler, Nicholas Murray, 436,
    518

C

Cabinet, 177, 221, 612, 633
Cabot, John, 49

Cabral, Pedro Alvarez, 30
Cadillac, 507
Cahokia, Illinois, 119
Calhoun, John C., 200, 217,
    223, 224, 315
California, 16, 36, 38, 45, 281,
    282, 285, 286, 287, 288, 291,
    292, 293, 294, 295, 304, 321,
    322, 346, 389, 394, 404, 405,
    441, 495, 544, 556, 574, 664,
    696
California Trail, 287
Calvert, George, 58
Calvinists, 63
Cambodia, 569, 615, 639
Cambridge, Massachusetts, 91
"Camp David Accords," 660,
    684
Canada, 14, 18, 38, 39, 40, 41,
    61, 101, 117, 122, 125, 184,
    198, 200, 201, 202, 204, 300,
    304, 318, 395, 421, 533
Canal Age, 268, 269, 270, 277
canals, 206, 207, 218, 224, 302,
    477
Canary Islands, 27, 29
Cape Cod Bay, 55
Cape Cod, Massachusetts, 74,
    77
Cape Horn, South America, 36
Cape Verde Islands, 30
capital, 413
capital city, 202, 213, 234, 235,
    237, 238, 413, 545
Capone, Al, 533
Capote, Truman, 698
Cardozo, Francis L., 366
Caribbean, 29, 31, 34, 38, 191,
    316, 466, 475, 476, 480, 481,
    568, 634, 635
Caribbean Indians, 35
Carmichael, Stokely, 630
Carnegie, Andrew, 415, 416,
    419
Carolinas, 61, 288
carpetbaggers, 366, 367
Carranza, Venustiano, 481
Carson, Rachel, 675
Carteret, Sir George, 61
Carter, Jimmy, 631, 648, 658,
    659, 660, 661, 662, 663, 665
Cartier, Jacques, 38
Cash, Johnny, 698
Cass, Lewis, 322
Castro, Fidel, 617, 626

Comanche Indians, 297
commission form, 439
Committee for Industrial
  Organization (CIO), 553
Committee on Public
  Information, 496
Committee to Defend America
  by Aiding the Allies, 568
Committee to Reelect the
  President, 653
Common Sense, 114, 116
commonwealth, 633
communism, 520, 521, 614, 624,
  634, 637, 659, 679, 681
Communist China, 615
Communist Control Act, 611
Communist party, 520
Communists, 498, 520, 601, 602,
  604, 605, 606, 611, 634, 639,
  657, 681
Community Service
  Organization, 632
compact, 55
Company of New France, 40
Company of the Hundred
  Associates, 40
compromise, 138
Compromise of 1850, 322, 323,
  324
Compromise of 1877, 372, 373
compulsory attendance laws,
  432
Comstock Lode, 389, 397
concentration camps, 564
Concord, Massachusetts, 112,
  113, 116
concurrent powers, 160
conductors, 318
Confederacy, 334, 335, 336,
  337, 341, 342, 346, 347, 348,
  350, 351, 356, 357, 358, 366
Confederate, 334, 335, 336, 337,
  338, 339, 340, 342, 343, 346,
  347, 348, 350, 351, 352, 356,
  357, 358, 359, 362, 368, 369,
  370, 381, 388
Confederate congress, 329, 344
Confederate States of America,
  328, 329, 334, 344
confederation, 96
conglomerates, 707, 710
Congo, 615
Congregational church, 57, 90
Congregationalism, 67, 90, 91

Congress, 139, 148, 149, 150,
  151, 152, 154, 155, 156, 157,
  158, 161, 162, 177, 178, 179,
  180, 181, 182, 185, 186, 187,
  188, 189, 191, 198, 200, 204,
  205, 206, 208, 221, 222, 223,
  224, 226, 228, 234, 235, 236,
  237, 238, 254, 265, 289, 290,
  291, 315, 320, 321, 322, 324,
  326, 346, 356, 357, 358, 360,
  361, 362, 363, 369, 371, 372,
  397, 406, 419, 422, 423, 436,
  444, 445, 447, 467, 468, 469,
  475, 490, 491, 492, 494, 495,
  496, 499, 503, 522, 523, 544,
  545, 547, 548, 552, 556, 557,
  559, 568, 570, 602, 608, 610,
  612, 613, 622, 623, 627, 629,
  633, 635, 637, 640, 647, 648,
  649, 652, 656, 657, 658, 659,
  662, 674, 675, 676, 677
Congressional Black Caucus,
  647
Congress of Industrial
  Organization, 553-554
Connally, John, 628
Connecticut, 57, 61, 64, 96,
  114, 142; Hartford, 254
Connecticut River, 96
conquistador, 34
consensus, 646, 647, 652, 658,
  659
conservation, 444, 445
conservatism, 663, 687
conservative, 445
conspiracy, 629, 654
Constantinople, 26
constitution, 132
Constitution, 201
Constitution of the United
  States, 137, 139, 140, 141,
  142, 143, 147–163, 177, 181,
  182, 183, 189, 192, 193, 197,
  204, 208, 217, 220, 222, 223,
  224, 249, 329, 403, 490, 523,
  557; text, 727–748
consumer goods, 529
consumers, 411
Continental Army, 112, 116,
  117, 118, 119, 120, 121, 124
Continental Association, 112
Continental Congress, 110, 111,
  117, 122, 125
Constitutional Convention, 142,
  157

Constitutional-Union party, 328
containment, 602
Convention of 1800, 187, 188
convoy system, 497, 498
Cook, James, 283
Coolidge, Calvin, 528
"cooling-off" period, 608
cooperative, 422
Cooper, James Fenimore, 211
Cooper, Peter, 270
Copley, John Singleton, 212
Coral Sea, Battle of the, 571
Cornwallis, Charles, 121
corollary, 479
corporate system, 416
corporations, 416, 417, 419
Corregidor, 571
corrupt bargain, 218
Cortés, Hernando, 33, 34
cotton, 263
cotton gin, 266
Coughlin, Father Charles,
  556–557
Council for New England, 54, 55
Council of National Defense, 491
Council of the Indies, 35
country-western music, 698–699
coureurs de bois, 42
courts, 156, 525
cowhands, 390, 391
Cowpens, South Carolina, 120,
  121
Cox, Archibald, 654
Crane, Stephen, 428
Crawford, William, 217
Crazy Horse, Chief, 395
creativity, 257
Crédit Mobilier, 371
Cree Indians, 17
Creek Indians, 227, 228
Creel, George, 496
Creoles, 301
Crèvecoeur, Michel Guillaume
  Jean de, 97
Crisis, The, 116
Crockett, Davy, 289
Cromwell, Oliver, 59
Croton Dam, 274
crude oil, 414, 419
Crusade for Justice, 632
Crusades, 25
Cuba, 31, 33, 468, 469, 470,
  471, 475, 476, 518, 563, 617,
  626, 627, 681; Bay of Pigs,
  626, 627; Havana, 518

Cuban Missile Crisis, 626, 627
Cubans, 468, 469, 471, 475, 476, 626
Cullen, Countee, 534
cultures, 6
Cumberland River, 338
Cumberland Road, 206 (see also National Road)
Curtis, Charles, 523
Cushing, Caleb, 463
Custer, George, 395
Cuzco, 11, 34
Cyprus, 615
Czechoslovakia, 567
Czolgosz, Leon, 441

D

Dakotas, 390, 391, 423
Dakota Territory, 346
Daladier, Edouard, 567
Daley, Richard, 637
Dallas, Texas, 628, 629, 696
Dare, Virginia, 50
Dartmouth College, 91, 366
Daugherty, Harry, 527
Davis, Henry Winter, 356
Davis, Jefferson, 329, 335
Davis, John, 50
Davis, Richard Harding, 470
Dawes Act, 397, 523, 556
Dawes, William, 112
Daytona Beach, Florida, 555
Dayton, Jonathan, 136
D-Day, 576
Dean, John, 654
decision making, 577
Declaration of Independence, 114, 124, 136, 249, 251, 256; text, 724–726
Declaratory Act, 108
defensive war, 337
Delaware, 49, 63, 93, 133, 142, 236, 336, 342
Delaware River, 44, 45, 61, 62, 117, 166, 267, 269
delegated powers, 158
de Lesseps, Ferdinand, 476
de Lôme, Enrique Dupuy, 468
Democratic National Committee, 652

Democratic party, 219, 223, 328, 357, 369, 378, 398, 555, 637, 652, 658, 663
Democratic-Republicans, 182, 186, 187, 188, 189, 190, 197, 204, 205, 217, 219
Democrats, 219, 230, 231, 320, 322, 325, 326, 327, 358, 362, 369, 371, 372, 373, 378, 419, 423, 437, 438, 447, 473, 491, 503, 529, 546, 547, 568, 610, 622, 637, 650, 656, 669, 676, 677
demonstrations, 623
Dempsey, Jack, 535
Denmark, 25, 402, 480, 568
Department of Energy, 662
Department of Housing and Urban Development, 633, 648
Department of Justice, 520
Department of Navy, 470
deport, 188
depression, 230, 559
deregulation, 657, 662, 670
desegregation, 613
deserters, 197
destroyers, 497
detente, 640
Detroit, Michigan, 201, 272, 506, 507, 508, 509, 510, 511, 526, 534, 630, 664
Dewey, George, 469
Dewey, Thomas, 609
Dias, Bartolomeu, 28
Dicey, Edward, 327
dictatorship, 564
Dinwiddie, Robert 100
direct primary, 440
direct representation, 107
direct tax, 107
disarmament, 501, 517
discrimination, 319, 623, 630, 631, 633, 714
displaced persons, 633
Displaced Persons Act, of 1948, 633
dissidents, 659
District of Columbia, 234, 236, 239, 323
diversity, 698
dividends, 416
Dix, Dorothea, 254, 343
Dixiecrats, 608
Dole, Robert, 667
Dole, Sanford B., 466, 467

dollar diplomacy, 479
domestic, 179
Dominican Republic, 31, 479, 480, 634, 635
Dominion of New England, 67
domino theory, 614
Dorchester Heights, Massachusetts, 116
Doubleday, Abner, 433
Doughty, Thomas, 212
Douglass, Frederick, 250, 319, 386
Douglas, Stephen, 324, 326, 327, 328,
Dove, David, 169
"doves," 637
Dow, Neal, 255
draft, 345, 378, 497, 573, 627
Drake, Edwin, 410
Drake, Sir Francis, 50
Dred Scott case, 325, 326
dry-farming, 393
Duane, James, 112
DuBois, William E. B., 401
due process of law, 422
Dulles, John Foster, 614
Dumbarton Oaks, Washington, D.C., 581
Durant, William, 507
Duryea, Charles, 529
Duryea, Frank, 529
dust bowl, 543
Dutch, 43, 44, 45, 61, 84, 92, 93, 376, 379, 463
Dutch East India Company, 43
Dutch West India, Company, 76, 376
duties, 181, 191

E

East, 206, 212, 268, 281, 296, 297, 304, 338, 340, 341, 347, 350, 390, 391, 393, 394, 395, 405, 407
East Berlin, 627
Eastern Hemisphere, 634
East Germany, 604, 627
East India Company, 110
East St. Louis, Illinois, 522
Economic Opportunity Act, 629
economy, 529–530, 540, 544, 675–676, 703, 704, 707, 708
Ecuador, 525

767

Edison, Thomas, 411–412
Egypt, 36, 615, 616, 642, 660, 685
Ehrlichman, John, 654
Eighteenth Amendment, 532, 547
Einstein, Albert, 582
Eisenhower Doctrine, 616
Eisenhower, Dwight, 575, 576, 577, 610, 611, 612, 613, 614, 617, 618, 622, 624, 626, 635
El Alamein, Egypt, 572, 575
"Elastic Clause," 158
Elbe River, 578
El Caney, Cuba, 470
election, of 1789, 177; of 1796, 186–187; of 1800, 189; of 1824, 217–218; of 1828, 219–220; of 1836, 230; of 1840, 231; of 1844, 290; of 1848, 322; of 1856, 325; of 1860, 328; of 1868, 369; of 1876, 371–372; of 1896, 435–438; of 1912, 446; of 1916, 491–492; of 1932, 545–547; of 1948, 608–609; of 1952, 610; of 1960, 622; of 1968, 637; of 1972, 652; of 1976, 658; of 1980, 665; of 1982, 689
electoral college, 156, 177
elect, the, 245
Elementary and Secondary School Act of 1965, 633
Elizabeth I, 88
Elk Hills, California, 527
Ellicott, Andrew, 234
Ellison, Ralph, 698
El Salvador, 681, 682, 683
emancipated, 320
Emancipation Proclamation, 341, 342, 378
embargo, 198
Embargo Act of 1807, 198
Emergency Price Control Act, 572
Emerson, Ralph Waldo, 246, 256, 257
empire, 8
empresarios, 288
Energy Act, 662
energy crisis, 710
energy policy, 670–672, 705
Energy Policy and Conservation Act, 657

England; bill of rights, 163; colonies, 83, 84, 86, 92–94, 99, 107, 110, 112, 170; exploration, 27, 45, 49–62, 64, 67, 70, 169, 210, 225, 319, 376, 411; immigration, 402; in Falklands War, 683; industrial revolution, 263; involvement in Civil War, 337, 341, 348, 350, 370; involvement in World War I, 486, 488, 489, 492, 498, 568; involvement in World War II, 567–569, 573, 576, 578–579, 581–583; post World War II, 599, 601, 602, 605, 615, 616, 628; Revolutionary War, 114–125; slave trade, 315; War of 1812, 200–205, 209, 238
English, channel, 486, 489
Ento, Kats, 592
entrenched, 347
environment, 12, 670, 699
Episcopal church, 94
Equal Employment Opportunity Commission, 630, 649
Equal Rights Amendment, 649
"Era of Good Feelings," 217
Ericson, Leif, 25
Erie Canal, 268
erosion, 552
Ervin, Sam, 654
Eskimos, 18
Espionage Act, 497
Estonia, 402
Ethiopia, 564, 659
Europe, 5, 25, 26, 27, 28, 29, 49, 50, 51, 99, 101, 125, 166, 246, 256, 263, 266, 281, 295, 300, 304, 391, 402, 404, 405, 434, 438, 542, 599, 602, 604, 679, 680, 695
European immigrants, 302
European Recovery Program, 602-603
Europeans, 31, 33, 36, 43, 49
evacuated, 568
Everglades, Florida, 229
excise, tax, 181
exclusive powers, 160
executive branch, 139, 147, 151, 154, 156, 191, 235, 237
executive clemency, 654
executive privilege, 652
expansionists, 282

exporting, 94
expressed powers, 158

F

factories, 247, 268, 272, 277, 278, 524, 540, 553, 573, 608
factory system, 264, 266
Fair Deal, 610
Fair Labor Standards Act, 554
Fairmount Waterworks, 274
Falklands War, 683
Family Assistance, Plan, 646
famine, 276
Far East, 25, 26, 27, 33, 38, 571, 578, 599
Farm Credit Administration (FCA), 550
farmers, 41, 43, 85, 86, 135, 166, 181, 206, 252, 266, 268, 288, 305, 344, 391, 393, 394, 421–424, 427–428, 435, 436; black, 399; plight of, 421; revolt, 421; white, 398, 399
Farmers' Alliances, 423
farming, 36, 91, 93, 94, 266, 523, 572, 708; changes, 708; corporations, 708; groups, 421; organizations, 435
Farnsworth, Walter, 712
Farragut, David, 339
Far West, 389, 501
Fascist party, 564
Faubus, Orval, 613
federal, 141
federal budget, 675–676
Federal Emergency Relief Administration (FERA), 549
Federal Farm Loan Act, 449
Federal Farm Loan Bank, 449
Federal Housing Administration (FHA), 553
federalism, 148
Federalist Papers, The, 141, 150, 156, 157
Federalist party, 217
Federalists, 141, 142, 182, 186, 188, 189, 190, 191, 204, 205
Federal Reserve Act, 447
Federal Reserve bank, 448
Federal Reserve Board, 448
Federal Reserve System, 447
Federal Trade Commission (FTC), 448

Federal Trade Commission Act, 448
Ferdinand, 29
Ferdinand, Archduke Franz, 485
Fifteenth Amendment, 369, 399
Fifth Amendment, 162, 326
Filipino, 467, 471, 472, 473, 495, 544, 571, 580, 591
Finland, 402
Finney, Charles, 245, 249
Finns, 84, 92
fireside chats, 548
Firestone, 593
First Continental Congress, 111, 112
Fisk, Jim, 371
Fisk University, 401
Fitzgerald, F. Scott, 534
Five-Power Pact of 1922, 517, 519
Florida, 31, 35, 36, 43, 61, 63, 122, 125, 186, 203, 208, 328, 366, 371
Florida Territory, 229
Floyd, John, 221
football, 433; Grange, Harold "Red," 535; Thorpe, Jim, 535
Foraker Act, 475
Forbes, Charles R., 527
Force Act, 369
Force Bill, 224
Ford, Gerald, 654, 655, 656, 657, 658, 659, 661
Ford, Henry, 507, 508, 509, 511, 529, 568
Ford Motor Company, 507, 508, 509
Fordney-McCumber Tariff, 530
foreclosures, 135
Forest Reserve Act of 1891, 444
Formosa (Taiwan), 605
Fort Astoria, 283
Fort Atkinson, 297
Fort Boise, 285
Fort Bridger, 288
Fort Christina, 44
Fort Donelson, 338
Fort Duquesne, 100, 101
Forten, Charlotte, 370
Fort Gunnybags, 307
Fort Hall, 285
Fort Henry, 338
Fort Laramie, 285
Fort Laramie Treaty, 297

Fort Leavenworth, 292
Fort McHenry, 202
Fort Sumter, 334
"forty-niners," 295
Foster, Stephen, 213
Fourteen Points, 499, 501, 502, 517
Fourteenth Amendment, 362, 363, 399, 400, 422, 612
Fox Indians, 19, 228
Fox River, 41
Framers of the Constitution, 147, 148, 149, 151, 152, 154, 155, 156, 162, 163, 178, 193
France, 27, 38, 39, 41, 42, 43, 63, 99, 101, 105, 116, 117, 136, 183, 184, 186, 187, 189, 191, 197, 198, 200, 203, 300, 302, 337, 341 348, 452, 464, 472, 473, 485, 486, 497, 498, 501, 517, 518, 519, 564, 567, 568, 569, 576, 578, 583, 599, 601, 602, 605, 615, 616, 628
Francis I, 38
Franklin, Benjamin, 100, 114, 117, 136, 137, 139, 141, 142, 167, 168, 169, 170, 185, 558; Plan of Union, 100
Fredericksburg, Virginia, 347, 348
freedmen, 360, 361, 370, 373
Freedmen's Bureau, 360, 361, 368, 369
freedom, 625
freedom of the seas, 197
Freeport, Illinois, 326
Free-Soil party, 322, 325
free verse, 259
Frémont, John C., 292, 325
French, 84, 92, 100, 101, 105, 183, 186, 187, 188, 191, 192, 197, 202, 234, 281, 300, 301, 403, 472, 476, 478, 486, 489, 498, 502, 568, 614, 680; settlements, 40–43, 45
French and Indian War, 97, 100, 101, 105, 125
French Indochina, 569, 614
French West Indies, 99
Friedan, Betty, 698
Frobisher, Martin, 50
frontier, 95, 389, 393
Frost, Robert, 534
Fuel Administration, 494
fugitive, 323

Fugitive Slave Act, 323, 324, 325
Fuller, Margaret, 256
Fulton, Robert, 269
Fundamental Orders of Connecticut, 57
fur traders, 39, 41, 42, 43, 44, 45, 281, 287

G

Gadsden Purchase, 293
Gage, Thomas, 112
gag rule, 320
Gallaudet, Thomas, 254
Galloway, Joseph, 112
Galveston, Texas, 390, 439
Gannet, Deborah, 119
Garfield, Harry, 494
Garrison, William Lloyd, 249, 259
Garvey, Marcus, 525, 526
gauge, 272
Gaza strip, 685
Gehrig, Lou, 535
General Court, 57
General Motors Company, 507
Geneva, Switzerland, 615, 618
Genoa, Italy, 25
Gentlemen's Agreement, 523
George II, 63
George III, 88, 99, 101, 105, 108, 112, 114
George, David Lloyd, 501
George, Henry, 428
George Town, Maryland, 234, 235, 236
George Washington University, 648
Georgia, 35, 63, 111, 125, 129, 142, 152, 186, 217, 228, 229, 288, 300, 321, 328, 330, 351, 370, 380, 381, 552, 658, 696; Atlanta, 272, 350, 351, 380–383, 400
German Democratic Republic (see East Germany)
German Federal Republic (see West Germany)
Germans, 84, 92, 93, 472; during World War I, 491–492, 497, 501, 503; during World War II, 563–578; immigration, 276, 277, 377, 402–403, 453

769

Germany, 63, 86, 464, 465, 472-473; Berlin, 578, 582, 583, 604, 627; Berlin Wall, 627; East, 604, 627; divided, 583; during World War II, 563–578; Nuremberg, 599; post World War II, 599, 602, 603, 618, 627; West, 604; World War I, 480, 485–489, 491, 492, 498, 501, 503, 511, 519

Geronimo, Chief, 396

Gettysburg Address, 349

Gettysburg, Pennsylvania, 348, 349, 356

Ghana, 28

Ghent, Belgium, 204

Ghost Dance, 396

ghost towns, 389

Gibbons v. *Ogden*, 208

Gibbs, Jonathan, C., 366

G-I Bill, 607

Gila River, 293

Gilbert Island, 579

Gilbert, Sir Humphrey, 50

"gilded age," 420

glaciers, 5

Glorious Revolution, 67

gold, 33, 35, 38, 50, 52, 227, 230, 295, 346, 371, 389, 407, 436, 438, 590; mining camps, 295; rush, 295, 304–305, 307

gold reserves, 438

gold rush, 404

gold standard, 436–438

Goldwater, Barry, 629

golf, 536

Goliad, Texas, 289

Gompers, Samuel, 426

Gonzales, Rodolfo, 632

Good Neighbor Policy, 563

Goodrich, 593

Goodyear, 593

Goodyear, Charles, 266

Gorgas, William, 478

"gospel of wealth," 419

Gould, Jay, 371

graduated income tax, 424, 440, 447

Grand Canyon, 35

"grandfather clauses," 399

Grange, 421–423

Grange, Harold "Red," 535

Granger laws, 422–423

Grant, Ulysses S., 338, 348, 350, 351, 352, 369, 371, 382

Great Basin, 15, 389

Great Britain (see England)

Great Compromise, 138, 139, 152

Great Depression, 540, 563; causes, 540, 546

Great Lakes, 19, 20, 41, 42, 125, 201, 204, 228, 269, 410, 416, 506

Great Northern Railroad, 412

Great Plains, 14, 281, 285, 295, 297, 389, 391, 393–394, 421, 452, 543

"Great Society," 629

Greece, 36, 129; ancient, 129; immigration, 402, 403, 453, 455; post World War II, 602; World War I, 486; World War II, 571

Greek, 213, 403

"Greek Revival," 213

Greeley, Horace, 342

greenbacks, 346

Greenhow, Rose O'Neal, 343

Greenland, 18, 50

Grenville Acts, 106, 107

Grenville, George, 105, 106

Grimké, Angelina, 248

Grimké, Sarah, 248

Grinnell, Moses, 324

Gromyko, Andrei, 659, 679

gross national product (GNP), 669

Guadalcanal, Battle of, 575

Guam, 471, 570

Guatemala, 7, 616

guerrillas, 635

Guiana, 466

Guilford Court House, North Carolina, 121

Gulf of Mexico, 19, 34, 35, 41, 45, 133, 300, 688

Gulf of Saint Lawrence, 38, 45

Gulf of Tonkin Resolution, 635

Gutiérrez, José Angel, 633

H

Habib, Philip, 685

Hagan, Walter, 536

Haida Indians, 16

Haig, Alexander, 672, 679

Haiti, 31, 191, 479, 480, 563

Haldeman, H. R., 654

Haley, Alex, 698

Haley, Bill, 698

Half Moon, 43

Hall, Oakey, 300

Hamilton, Alexander, 133, 134, 141, 150, 156, 177, 179, 180, 181, 182, 184, 189

Hamilton, Dr. Alexander, 62

Hammer v. Dagenhart, 449

Hammond, Octavia, 381

Hanover, New Hampshire, 91

Harding, Warren G., 503, 517, 526–528

Hariot, Thomas, 70, 73

Harlem, 534, 630

Harlem Renaissance, 534

Harpers Ferry, Virginia, 327

Harrisburg, Pennsylvania, 348

Harrison, William Henry, 199, 231, 444

Harris, Patricia, 648

Harte, Bret, 434

Hartford, Connecticut, 57, 204

Hartford Convention, 204, 223, 315

Harvard College, 91, 256, 257, 265, 401

Hat Act of 1732, 99

Haughery, Margaret Gaffney, 275

Havana Conference, 518

Havana, Cuba, 468, 626

Hawaii, 281, 463–467, 495, 523, 705

Hawkins, Sir John, 50

"hawks," 637

Hawthorne, Nathaniel, 256

Hay-Bunau-Varilla Treaty, 477

Hayes, Rutherford B., 371, 372

Hay, John, 472

Haymarket Square, 426

Hayne, Robert, 223, 315

Head Start, 629

Hearst, William Randolph, 468

Hearth, John, 267

Helena, Montana, 389

Hemingway, Ernest, 534

Henry IV, 39

Henry VIII, 49

Henry, Patrick, 107, 112, 136, 142, 625

Henry Street Settlement, 428

Hepburn Act, 442, 445

Herbert, Victor, 434

heritage, 313
Herrera, Omar Torrijos, 659
Higher Education Act, 633
Higher Education Facilities Act, 623
Hinckley, John, Jr., 672
Hirohito, 565
Hiroshima, Japan, 581
Hispanics, 688, 693, 696, 700
Hitler, Adolf, 564, 566, 578, 599
Ho Chi Minh, 614
hogans, 14
Hogarth, William, 558
Hohokam, 13
holding company, 441
Holland, 55, 63, 99, 117
Holmes, Oliver Wendell, 497
Homestead Act of 1862, 346, 391
homesteaders, 391, 393, 394, 397
Honduras, 7, 479
Hong Kong, 570
Honolulu, Hawaii, 467
Hooker, Joseph, 347, 348
Hooker, Thomas, 57
Hoover, Herbert, 494, 518, 526–527, 529, 531, 544, 547, 551, 563
Hoovervilles, 542–543
Hopewell Indians, 20
Hopi Indians, 13
Hopkins, Harry, 549
Horseshoe Bend, Battle of, 203
House Judiciary Committee, 655
House of Burgesses, 54
House of Representatives, 138, 139, 152, 153, 156, 157, 177, 185, 189, 200, 218, 237, 238, 320, 321, 364, 372, 492, 622, 629, 648, 654, 665, 689, 715
Houston, Sam, 289, 712
Houston Ship Channel, 712
Houston, Texas, 522, 696, 712, 717
Howard, W. P., 381
Howe, Elias, 266
Howe, Samuel, 254
Howe, William, 116
Hudson Bay, 101
Hudson Bay Company, 283
Hudson, Henry, 43, 93
Hudson River, 43, 45, 61, 84, 117, 211, 213, 268, 269

"Hudson River School," 212, 213
Huerta, Victoriano, 480, 481
Hughes, Charles Evans, 491, 492, 526
Hughes, Sarah, 628
Huguenots, 63, 92
Hull, Cordell, 563
Hull House, 428, 436, 455
Humphrey, Hubert, 637
Hungary, 402, 403, 639
Hunt, E. Howard, 653
Hunter, Jane Edna, 428
Huron Indians, 39, 40
Hutchinson, Anne, 57

I

Ice Ages, 5
Iceland, 25
Ickes, Harold, 549
Idaho, 282, 389, 395, 574
Illinois, 120, 228, 246, 277, 324, 326, 366, 422, 436, 610, 630
Illinois River, 41
immigrants, 85, 188, 252, 276, 277, 278, 302, 313, 389, 402, 403, 404, 405, 410, 428, 432, 436, 453, 454, 455, 495, 521–524, 530, 544
immigrated, 83
immigration, 402, 403, 633–634, 694–695
impeach, 153
impeachment process, 153, 154, 364, 654, 655
imperialism, 464, 473
implied powers, 158
importing, 94
impounded, 652
impressment, 183
inauguration, 190
Incas, 10–12, 34; artists, 11–12; capital city, 11; farming, 10; government, 11, 12; religion, 11
Inchon, Korea, 607
income tax, 445
indentured servants, 86, 87, 89
Independence, Missouri, 284, 285
India, 25, 28, 99, 101, 495, 695
Indiana, 199, 247, 269, 324, 568
Indianapolis, Indiana, 207

Indian Ocean, 28, 31
Indian Removal Act, 228
Indian Reorganization Act, 556
Indians, 12–21, 29, 33, 35, 36–40, 42–43, 52–53, 70, 74, 76, 95–97, 100–101, 105–106, 117, 119, 129, 133, 178, 199, 200–203, 212, 221, 227–229, 232, 287–288, 295–296, 362, 370, 376, 390, 394–397, 407, 438, 470, 523–524, 556, 673, 693, 696; Apache, 14, 296, 396; Arapaho, 297, 394–395; Blackfoot, 14; Blackhawk, 228; Cayuga, 20; Choctaw, 19; Cherokee, 19, 228–229; Cheyenne, 14, 394–395; Chickasaw, 19, 228; Comanche, 14, 297; Cree, 17; Creek, 19, 227–228; Crow, 14; Dakota, 14; Fox, 19, 228; Hopewell, 20; Hopi, 13; Huron, 19, 39, 40; Iowa, 228; Kaw, 523; Mandan, 14; Menominee, 228; Miami, 19; Mohawk, 20, 39, 110; Narragansett, 57; Natchez, 19; Navaho, 14; Nez Percé, 16, 395; Oneida, 20; Onondaga, 20; Osage, 14, 523; Ottawa, 17, 228; Paiute, 397; Pawnee, 14; Pequot, 97; Plains, 14–15, 394, 396; Potawatomi, 452; Powhatan, 19, 52–53, 70; Sac, 228; Sauk, 19; Seminole, 19, 229; Seneca, 20; Shawnee, 19, 199; Shoshoni, 192; Sioux, 14, 228, 394, 396; Ute, 16; Wampanoag, 55, 96; Winnebago, 19, 228; Zuñi, 13, 35
indigo, 94
Indochina, 495, 616
industrialization, 410, 424, 432, 463
Industrial Revolution, 263
industry, 263, 266, 278, 529, 565, 573
infantry, 486
inflation, 436, 657, 661, 676
inherent powers, 159
initiative, 424, 441
injunctions, 448
installment plan, 540

Know-Nothings, 277
Knox College, 366
Knox, Philander, 479
Knoxville, Tennessee, 522
Korea, 474, 475, 601, 606
Korean War, 606–607
Korematsu v. *United States,* 574
Ku Klux Klan, 367, 368, 369, 522
Ku Klux Klan Act of 1871, 369

L

labor, 410, 424, 536, 708; blue-collar workers, 688, 708; unskilled, 404; white-collar workers, 708
labor unions, 425, 426, 448, 530, 608
Labrador, 42, 50
Lafayette, Marquis de, 121
Laffite, Jean, 203
La Follette, Robert, 440, 446
La Follette Seamen's Act, 449
laissez-faire, 419, 428
Lake Champlain, 202
Lake Erie, 41, 202
Lake Huron, 40, 410
Lake Michigan, 41, 452, 456
Lake of the Woods, 284
Lake Ontario, 40, 41, 117
Lake Superior, 410
lame duck, 551
Lancaster, Pennsylvania, 84
land bridge, 5
Land Ordinance of 1785, 130, 131
land speculation, 227
Lanusse, Armand, 302
Laos, 569, 615
La Raza Unida, 633
La Salle, 41, 42
Latin America, 208, 210, 466, 478–480, 518, 563, 564, 616, 624, 634, 681–683, 714
Latvia, 402
Lawrence, Amos, 324
Lawrence, Kansas, 325
Law, Thomas, 236
League of Nations, 517, 523
League of the Iroquois, 20–21, 39
League of United Latin American Citizens (LULAC), 690

lease, 475
Leaves of Grass, 259
Lebanon, 616, 684–685
Lee, Jason, 284
Lee, Richard Henry, 114
Lee, Robert E., 327, 335, 337, 341, 346, 347, 348, 350, 351, 352, 356, 382
legislative branch, 147, 151, 152, 153, 191, 235
Lehigh Valley, 267
Leland, Henry N., 507
Lend-Lease Act, 568–569
L'Enfant, Pierre Charles, 234
Lenin, 498, 520
Leopard, 197
levees, 300, 302
Lever Food and Fuel Act, 494
Lewis and Clark Expedition, 193, 281, 283
Lewis, John L., 553
Lewis, Meriwether, 192, 193
Lewis, Sinclair, 534
Lexington, 112, 113, 116, 224
Leyte Gulf, Battle of, 579
liberalism, 687
Liberator, The, 249
Liberia, 249
Liberty Loan Act, 496
Liberty party, 250, 251, 322
Library of Congress, 237
Libya, 572
Lichtenstein, Roy, 700
Liddy, G. Gordon, 653
Liliuokalani, 466, 467
limitations on power, 160
limited government, 147
Limited Nuclear Test Ban Treaty, 628
limited war policy, 607
Lincoln, Abraham, 326, 327, 328, 330, 334, 335, 338, 340, 341, 342, 347, 348, 349, 352, 356, 357, 358, 360, 378, 379
Lindbergh, Charles, 529, 568
Line of Demarcation, 30
literacy test, 399, 403
literature, 88, 113, 114, 116, 210, 211, 212, 213, 245, 248, 256, 257, 258, 259, 275, 285, 324, 352, 359, 428, 434, 438, 439, 464, 533, 534, 577, 698 (see also individual titles)
Lithuania, 402
Little Bighorn, Battle of, 395

Liu Ho, China, 631
Livingston, Robert, 114
Lloyd, Henry Demarest, 428
Lodge, Henry Cabot, 403, 501
London Company, 53, 54
London, England, 75, 251, 428
Long Beach, California, 590
long drive, 390
Longfellow, Henry Wadsworth, 113, 259
long houses, 20
Long, Huey, 556
Long Island, 117, 212
long-range missiles, 618
Long, Stephen, 281
loose construction, 182
Los Angeles, California, 287, 412, 590–593, 630, 632, 637, 648; Japanese, 591–592; Mexican, 592; smog, 593; World War II, 593; zoot suiters, 592–593
lost colony, 50
lottery, 497
Louisiana, 41, 42, 191, 192, 197, 281, 288, 300, 301, 329, 357, 367, 371, 400, 556
Louisiana Purchase, 191, 281, 283
Louisville, Kentucky, 273, 412, 425
L'Ouverture, Toussaint, 191
Lovejoy, Elijah, 250
Lowell, Massachusetts, 264, 266
Lowell Offering, The, 264
loyalists, 109, 120
Lusitania, 489, 491
Lutheran, 63, 92, 166
Luxembourg, 648
Lynd, Helen, 586–587
Lynd, Robert, 586–587
Lynn, Loretta, 699
Lyon, Mary, 253
Luzon, Philippines, 473, 580

M

McAdoo, William Gibbs, 494
MacArthur, Douglas, 545, 579, 606, 607
Macarthy, Cecee, 301–302
McCarran-Walter Act, 611, 633
McCarthy, Eugene, 637
McCarthy, Joseph, 611–612

McClellan, George B., 340, 341, 347
McCormick, Cyrus, 266, 267
McCoy, Joseph, 390
McCullough v. *Maryland,* 208, 226
Macdonough, Thomas, 202
McDowell, Irwin, 338, 343
McDowell, Mary, 454
McGovern, George, 652
McGuffey, William, 254
McKay, Claude, 534
McKinley Tariff, 465, 466
McKinley, William, 438, 441, 444, 468, 471, 472, 473
McLoughlin, John, 283
Macon's Bill Number 2, 198
Macrae, David, 359
Madero, Francisco, 480
Madison, Dolley, 238
Madison, James, 133, 137, 139, 141, 157, 189, 191, 198, 200, 204, 205, 223
Magellan, Fernando, 31, 33
Maginot Line, 568
Mahan, Alfred Thayer, 464
Maine, 468
Maine, 59, 62, 67, 129, 255–256, 322
Malaya, 570
Manassas, Virginia, 338
Manchuria, 474, 566
manifest destiny, 282, 463
Manila, 473, 580
Manila Bay, 469
Mann-Elkins Act, 445
Mann, Horace, 252, 253, 254
manufacturing, 50
Mao Tse-tung, 604, 605, 641
Marbury v. *Madison,* 191, 208
Marbury, William, 191
Marcy, William, 222
Mariana Islands, 579
Marion, Francis, 120
Marne, Battle of the, 486, 498
Marquette, Father Jacques, 41
Marshall, George, 602
Marshall Island, 579
Marshall, James, 295
Marshall, John, 157, 191, 208, 229
Marshall Plan, 602, 603, 604
Martineau, Harriet, 270
Maryland, 57, 58, 61, 64, 100, 133, 180, 202, 208, 234, 269, 275, 336, 341, 342, 356, 525, 654

Mason, George, 137, 142
Mason, John, 59
Massachusetts, 57, 59, 88, 109, 110, 112, 114, 125, 135, 142, 177, 211, 217, 220, 223, 246, 247, 252, 253, 254, 259, 315, 322, 356, 403, 622, 637
Massachusetts Bay Colony, 56, 57, 59, 64, 67, 77, 88, 96
Massasoit, Chief, 55, 75
Massey, Kate, 381
mass media, 677–678
mass production, 266
Mayas, 7–8
Mayflower, 55, 74
Mayflower Compact, 55, 163
Maysville Road bill, 224
Meade, George, 348
Meat Inspection Act, 442
meat-packing industry, 416, 439, 452, 453
median family income, 693
Medicaid, 633
Medicare, 633
Mediterranean Sea, 25, 492, 564, 576, 577, 602, 616
meeting houses, 56
Mellon, Andrew, 526, 530
Melville, Herman, 258
Memphis, Tennessee, 339, 612, 632
Menominee Indians, 228
mercantilism, 96, 99
Meredith, James, 623
mergers, 530
Merrimac, 339 (see also *Virginia*)
Mesabi Range, 410, 416
mesas, 13
Methodists, 92, 166, 302
Meuse-Argonne, 498
Mexia, Ynes, 525
Mexican-American Political Association, 632
Mexican Americans, 438, 494, 524, 591, 592, 632, 714
Mexican War, 304, 313, 321, 322, 492
Mexico, 7, 21, 33, 35, 36, 286, 287, 288, 292, 293, 295, 302, 304, 321, 322, 390, 480, 481, 492, 495, 524, 525, 533, 544, 563, 695
Michigan, 344, 410, 452, 511, 556, 654

Middle America, 38
Middle Colonies, 92-93
Middle East, 25, 26, 486, 616, 635, 638, 641, 642, 656, 660, 683–685
Middle Kingdoms, 28
Midway, Battle of, 571
Midway Island, 463, 570
migrated, 5
Miles, Nelson A., 471
Millay, Edna St. Vincent, 534
Millerites, 246
Miller, William, 246
Milwaukee, Wisconsin, 277
miners, 295, 304, 389, 390, 394, 442
Minimal Art, 700
minimum-income plan, 646
mining towns, 390
Minneapolis, Minnesota, 412
Minnesota, 637
Minuit, Peter, 43
minutemen, 112
missionaries, 36
missions, 35–37, 40, 288
Mississippi River, 14, 19, 20, 35, 41, 42, 101, 119, 122, 125, 133, 184, 191, 192, 193, 227, 228, 230, 269, 272, 288, 295, 300, 328, 330, 336, 338, 339, 348, 366–367, 494, 552, 623, 639, 696
Mississippi Valley, 35, 41, 42, 119, 120, 122, 203, 282, 297, 303
Missouri, 581
Missouri, 193, 200, 212, 244, 246, 247, 320, 322, 324, 326, 336, 342, 389, 391, 412, 422, 423, 441
Missouri Compromise, 320, 322, 324, 326
Mitchell, John, 654
Mittelberger, Gottlieb, 86
mobility, 294, 695
Model Cities Act of 1966, 633
Modoc Indians, 16
Mohawk Indians, 39, 110
Molasses Act of 1733, 99
Moley, Raymond, 551
Mondale, Walter, 663
Monitor, 339
monopoly, 25, 226, 419, 435, 448, 449, 530

Monroe Doctrine, 208, 210, 466, 479, 518
Monroe, Elizabeth, 238
Monroe, James, 205, 207, 208, 210, 217, 238
Montana, 282, 295, 297, 389, 390, 391, 394
Montcalm, Louis, 101
Montenegro, 486, 502
Monterey, California, 287
Montezuma, 33, 34
Montgomery, Alabama, 329, 335, 613–614, 630
Montgomery, Bernard, 575, 576
Montreal, Canada, 42, 101, 201
Moral Majority, 686
Moran, George "Bugs," 533
Morgan, J. P., 416
Mormons, 245
Morrill Act, 432
Morris, Nelson, 416
Morris, Robert, 117
Morse, Samuel F. B., 266
Moscow, U.S.S.R., 571, 640
Mott, Lucretia, 251
mounds, 20
Mount Holyoke Female Seminary, 253
Mount, William Sidney, 212
movies, 534, 535, 701
moving assembly line, 508, 509, 511
muckrakers, 439
Muncie, Indiana, 586–589
munitions, 487, 573
Munn v. *Illinois*, 422
music, 212, 213, 434, 439, 532, 567, 698; "Babes in Toyland," 434; Cash, Johnny, 699; country-western, 698–699; Jazz Age, 534, 698; Joplin, Scott, 434; Lynn, Loretta, 699; "Maple Leaf Rag," 434; "My Old Kentucky Home," 213; "O Susanna," 213; Parton, Dolly, 699; popular music, 698; Pride, Charlie, 699; ragtime, 434, 532; rock and roll, 698; Rogers, Kenny, 699; "Stars and Stripes Forever, The," 434; "Star-Spangled Banner, The," 202; "Student Prince," 434
Muslims, 25, 26, 28, 616

Mussolini, Benito, 564, 566, 576, 578
MX missile, 679

N

Nagasaki, Japan, 463, 581
Naismith, James, 433
Narragansett Indians, 57
Nashville Railroad, 412
National Aeronautics and Space Administration (NASA), 623, 713
national anthem, 202
National Association for the Advancement of Colored People (NAACP), 401, 526, 647
National Broadcasting Company (NBC), 534
National Defense Act, 491
National Defense Education Act, 623
National Farm Workers' Association, 632
National Guard, 491, 613, 627
National Grange of the Patrons of Husbandry, 421
National Housing Act, 552–553
National Industrial Recovery Act, 550–551, 553, 557, 559
nationalism, 205, 208–209, 297
Nationalist party, 604, 605
National Labor Relations Act, 553
National Labor Relations Board (NLRB), 553
National Labor Union, 425
National League, 433
National Organization for Women (NOW), 649
National Origins Act, 53
National Progressive Republican League, 446
National Recovery Administration (NRA), 550–551
National-Republicans, 219, 230
National Road, 206, 224, 268
National Security League, 491
National Shipping Board, 491
National Socialist party (Nazi party), 564, 599
National Urban League, 402

National Women's Political Caucus, 649
Nativists, 277
Nauset, Massachusetts, 77
Navaho Indians, 14
Navigation Acts, 96, 106
Nazi (see National Socialist party)
Nebraska, 324, 390-391, 423
negotiating, 178
Nelson, Donald M., 572
Netherlands, 568
Netherlands East Indies (Indonesia), 570
neutrality, 183, 486, 490, 492
neutrality acts, 565, 568
Nevada, 293, 295, 346, 389, 397, 404
Nevins, Allan, 97
New Amsterdam, 44, 61, 376
New Bedford, Massachusetts, 319
Newcomen, Thomas, 269
New Deal, 547–559, 608, 612, 669; Agricultural Adjustment Act (AAA), 550, 551, 559; Brain Trust, 551; Civil Conservation Corps (CCC), 549; Fair Labor Standards Act, 554; Farm Credit Association (FCA), 550; Federal Emergency Relief Administration (FERA), 549; Federal Housing Administration (FHA), 553; Indian Reorganization Act, 556; National Housing Act, 552–553; National Industrial Recovery Act (NIRA), 550–551, 553, 557, 559; National Labor Relations Board (NLRB), 553; social security, 554, 556, 610, 623, 633; Tennessee Valley Authority (TVA), 552, 557; Wagner-Connery Act, 553; Wagner-Steagall Act, 553; Works Progress Administration (WPA), 550
New Economic Policy, 646
New England, 52, 55, 64, 86, 100, 116–117, 200, 204, 217, 256, 259, 263–264, 272, 283, 287, 434
New England Colonies, 90–91

New England Confederation, 96
New England Federalists, 223
New Federalism, 646, 669,
New France, 40, 41, 42
New Freedom, 447, 479
New Frontier, 622, 629
New Guinea, 579
New Hampshire, 59, 64, 67,
   125, 142
New Haven, Connecticut, 57,
   62, 91, 96
"new" immigration, 402
New Jersey, 61, 67, 93, 117,
   133, 136, 138, 142, 208, 269,
   441, 447, 705
New Jersey Plan, 138
Newlands Act, 444
New Mexico, 12, 14, 35, 281,
   286, 291, 293, 321, 322, 323,
   389, 396, 481, 492, 632
New Nationalism, 446, 447
New Netherland, 43, 44, 45, 61
New Orleans, Battle of, 203
New Orleans, Louisiana, 133,
   184, 191, 204, 205, 275,
   300–303, 339, 390, 412, 712;
   blacks, 301; education,
   302–303; people, 301;
   religion, 302; slave market,
   301
Newport, Rhode Island, 464
New Sweden, 44–45, 61
New World, 30, 34, 36, 38, 40,
   43, 49, 50, 85, 316
New York, 39, 61–62, 67, 93,
   100, 114, 133, 142, 178, 189,
   201, 208, 210, 211, 213, 219,
   222, 245–247, 249–250, 258,
   269–270, 300, 320, 371, 416,
   428, 441, 529, 546, 609, 696,
   699
New York Central Railroad,
   412
New York City, 92, 93, 107,
   112, 117, 177, 225, 268–269,
   272, 274–275, 277, 324, 344,
   346, 376–379, 412, 428, 443,
   468, 518, 531, 534, 551, 553,
   601, 630, 636, 648, 698
New York Yankees, 535 (see
   also baseball)
New Zealand, 578, 616
Nez Percé Indians, 16, 395
Niagara Falls, 41
Niagara River, 201

Nicaragua, 479, 563, 681, 682
night watches, 274
Nillin, Margrett, 383
Niña, 29
Nine-Power Pact, 519
Nineteenth Amendment, 23
Nixon, Richard, 622, 637, 638,
   639, 640, 641, 642, 646–647,
   649–650, 652, 654–657, 659,
   687
noncombat jobs, 573
Non-Intercourse Act, 198
Nootka Indians, 16
Norfolk, Virginia, 336, 339
normalization, 641
Normandy, 576, 581
North, 180, 234, 250, 269, 272,
   313–315, 318–328, 330,
   334–339, 341–346, 348, 352,
   356, 358–360, 362, 366, 369,
   370, 376, 399, 400, 423, 425,
   630, 647
North Africa, 571, 572, 575
North Atlantic Treaty
   Organization (NATO), 604,
   615, 679, 683
North Carolina, 38, 52, 61, 70,
   95, 143, 335, 358, 528, 552,
   654
Northeast, 217, 219, 432
Northern Pacific Railroad, 412
Northern Securities Company,
   441
North Korea, 606, 607
Northup, Solomon, 316
North Vietnam, 635, 639
Northwest Alliance, 423
Northwest Ordinance, 130, 131,
   132
Northwest Passage, 38, 41, 43,
   50
Northwest Territory, 130, 131,
   132, 133, 183, 199
Norway, 25, 402, 568
Nova Scotia, 38, 122
nuclear arms race, 628
nuclar energy, 706
Nuclear Nonproliferation
   Treaty, 639
nuclear war, 626, 628, 641
nuclear weapons, 582, 618, 628,
   679
Nugent, John, 306
null and void, 189, 223
nullification, 223, 224, 232, 315

nullify, 224
Nuremberg, Germany, 599

O

O'Banion, Dion, 533
Oberlin College, 366
Oberlin, Ohio, 253
O'Connor, Sandra Day, 670,
   671
Office of Economic
   Opportunity, 629
Office of Price Administration,
   572
Oglethorpe, James, 63
Ohio, 41, 199, 213, 224, 231,
   246, 249, 269, 270, 324, 356,
   366, 371, 410, 419, 438, 503,
   639
Ohio River, 41, 42, 130, 131,
   207, 269, 318
Ohio Valley, 19, 20, 95, 99, 110
oil boom, 414
oil shale, 706
Okinawa, Japan, 580
Oki, S. J., 591–592
Oklahoma, 35, 396, 543
"old" immigration, 402
"Old Ironsides," 201
Oldsmobile, 507
Olds, Ransom E., 507, 529
Old World, 85, 88
Olivarez, Graciela, 631
Olive Branch Petition, 112
Olney, Richard, 466
Omaha, Nebraska, 346, 423,
   522
"on margin," 541
O'Neill, Thomas "Tip," 676,
   677
Ontario, Canada, 199
Open Door policy, 472, 474,
   519
Open Housing Law of 1966, 633
open range, 390
Operation Overlord, 576
operettas, 434
Order of the Sons of America,
   524
ordinances, 130
Oregon, 221, 281–286, 290, 291,
   313, 371, 394, 441
Oregon Trail, 285, 288, 297
organs, 601
Orlando, Vittorio, 501

Osage Indians, 523
Osceola, 229
oscillation, 614
Oswald, Lee Harvey, 629
Ottawa Indians, 17, 228
Ottawa River, 40
Ottoman Empire, 486, 502
overgrazing, 390
Owen, Chandler, 497
Owen, Robert, 247

P

Pacific Ocean, 16, 28, 31, 38, 41, 193, 281, 282, 304, 324, 467
Pacific Railroad, 390
pacifists, 491
Packard Motor Company, 510
Page, George, 267
Pago Pago, 465
Pahlevi, Shah Mohammed Reza, 662
Paine, Thomas, 114, 116
painting, 212–213, 699–701
Paiute Indians, 16, 397
Palestine Liberation Organization (PLO), 684–685
Pakenham, Sir Edward, 203
Pakistan, 616
Palestine, 616, 661
Palmer, A. Mitchell, 520
Panama, 31, 34, 476, 477, 659, 660
Panama Canal, 476, 477, 478, 600, 659, 600
Panic of 1837, 231
Panmunjom, Korea, 607
paratroopers, 576
Paris, France, 122, 301, 471, 486, 497, 500, 501, 529, 576, 618
Paris Peace Conference, 519
Parker, Josiah, 185
Parkman, Francis, 285
Parks, Rosa, 613
partisans, 571
Parton, Dolly, 699
patents, 266
patriots, 109
Patterson, William, 138
Patton, George, 576
Pawtucket, Rhode Island, 263, 264, 265
Pawtuxet Indians, 55
Payne-Aldrich Tariff, 444
Peace Corps, 624

Pearl Harbor, Hawaii, 570
"peculiar institution," 315
Peking, China, 472
Peninsula Campaign, 341
Pennsylvania, 61–63, 84, 93, 95, 96, 100, 112, 114, 116, 133, 136, 142, 152, 166, 181, 182, 212, 219, 221, 257, 267, 269, 318, 321, 322, 325, 348, 356, 368, 410, 416, 442, 525
Pennsylvania Dutch, 84
Pennsylvania Railroad, 494
Penn, William, 61, 62, 63, 96, 166
Pensacola, Florida, 203
People's party, 423
People's Republic of China, 605, 628, 638, 641, 642
People's Republic of North Korea, 601
Pequot Indians, 96
perjury, 655
Perkins, Frances, 551
Perkins Institute, 254
perpetual, 334
Perry, Matthew, 463
Perry, Oliver Hazard, 201
persecuted, 246
Pershing, John, 481, 497, 498
Persia, 36
Persian Gulf, 662
personal liberty laws, 324
Peru, 10, 33, 34, 525
pet banks, 227
Petersburg, Virginia, 351
Philadelphia College (University of Pennsylvania), 93
Philadelphia, Pennsylvania, 62, 63, 92, 93, 111, 112, 116, 117, 134, 136, 166, 167, 168, 169, 170, 171, 180, 185, 225, 226, 235, 248, 269, 270, 272, 274, 277, 370, 411, 427, 716
Philippines, 31, 35, 467, 469, 471, 472, 473, 475, 523, 544, 569, 570–571, 579, 616, 694, 695, 696
philosophy, 246
Phoenix, Arizona, 631
Pickens, Andrew, 120
Pierce, Franklin, 254
Pike, Zebulon, 281
Pilgrims, 55, 74, 77
Pinchot, Gifford, 444, 445
Pinckney, Thomas, 184, 186

Pinckney Treaty, 184, 186
Pine Ridge reservation, 396
Pinta, 29
Pittsburgh, Pennsylvania, 100, 273, 274, 338, 344, 410, 416, 428, 534
Pittsburgh Pirates, 433 (see also baseball)
Pittsburg Landing, 338
Pitt, William, 101
Pizarro, Francisco, 34
Plains Indians, 14–15, 394, 396
Plains of Abraham, 101
Plan of Union, 100
plantations, 83, 213, 300, 316, 523
planters, 83, 94
platform, 231
Platt Amendment, 475, 563
Platte River, 281, 285
Plessy, Homer, 400
Plessy v. *Ferguson,* 400, 612
pluralism, 403
Plymouth Company, 52, 54, 75
Plymouth, Massachusetts, 55, 56, 57, 59, 64, 67, 74–77, 96
Pocahontas, 53
pocket veto, 357
Poe, Edgar Allen, 258–259
poets, 256–259
Poland, 402, 403, 502, 567, 576, 680
"police powers," 160
political parties, 186, 545; American Independent, 637; Anti-Federalist, 141–142; Bull Moose, 446; Communist, 520; Democratic, 219, 223, 328, 357, 369, 378, 398, 555, 637, 652, 658, 663, 689; Democratic-Republican, 182, 186–190, 197, 204–205, 217, 219; Fascist, 564; Federalist, 217; Free-Soil, 322, 325; Know-Nothing, 277; La Raza Unida, 633; Liberty, 250–251, 322; Nationalist, 604–605; National-Republicans, 219, 230; National-Socialist (Nazi), 599; People's, 423; Populist, 424, 437–438; progressive, 609; Republican, 325–326, 328, 366, 371, 445, 447, 503, 526, 528, 546, 555, 608–610, 656, 664, 689;

Southern-Democratic, 398;
Whigs, 230–231, 320, 322, 325, 328, 366
Polk, James K., 290, 291, 293
Pollack, Jackson, 700
poll tax, 399
Pomo Indians, 16
pool, 417
Pop Art, 700
Pope Alexander VI, 30
popular music, 698
popular sovereignty, 147, 322, 326
population, 273, 276, 278, 288 305, 389, 402, 693, 695, 696
populism, 423
Populists, 424, 437, 438
Portland, Maine, 255
Portsmouth, New Hampshire, 474
Portugal, 27–30, 38, 99
Portuguese, 45, 92, 463
Potawatomie Creek, 325
Potawatomi Indians, 452
potlatch, 16, 17
Potomac River, 58, 133, 207, 234
Potsdam Conference, 582
Potsdam, Germany, 582, 603
poverty, 696, 704
Powderly, Terence, 426
Powhatan, Chief, 52, 53
Powhatan Indians, 52–53, 70
Preamble, 147
precedents, 177
prejudice, 250
preparedness, 491
Presbyterians, 62, 92, 93, 166
President, 139, 149, 150, 151, 153, 154, 156, 162, 177, 178, 187–189, 202, 217, 220, 222, 226, 228, 236, 652, 654–655, 669
Presley, Elvis, 698
Pride, Charlie, 699
priest, 36, 304, 556, 590
Princeton, New Jersey, 117, 433
Princeton University, 93, 631, 705
prison reform, 254
proclamation, 342
Proclamation of 1763, 106
Proclamation of Neutrality, 183
Professional Air Traffic Controllers Organization (PATCO), strike, 673–674

progress, 651
Progressive Era, 431, 449, 526, 536
progressive literature, 438
Progressive party, 609
progressives, 438, 447
prohibition, 255, 533, 547
Promontory Point, Utah, 412
propaganda, 488
Prophet, the, 199
proprietary colonies, 57, 64
proprietors, 57, 59, 61, 64
proslavery, 325
Prosser, Gabriel, 317
protective tariff, 181, 205, 218
Protestant, 49, 58, 62, 83, 277, 625
Providence, Rhode Island, 57–62
public education, 252, 432, 529
public housing, 552
Public Works Administration (PWA), 549
Pueblo, Colorado, 501
Pueblo Indians, 13–14, 35
pueblos, 13
Puerto Ricans, 471, 634, 648
Puerto Rico, 468, 471, 475, 633, 648
Pulaski, Tennessee, 368
Pulitzer, Joseph, 468
Pure Food and Drug Act, 442
Puritans, 55, 56, 57, 59, 88, 90, 250
Pusan, Korea, 606

Q

Quakers, 62, 92, 96, 166, 168–171, 248, 263
quarantine, 627
quartered, 110
Quebec, Canada, 39, 41, 99, 101
Quincy, Josiah, 265
quota, 522

R

radical, 356
Radical Republicans, 356
Radicals, 356, 357, 358, 360, 362, 364, 366, 369, 370, 373
radio, 534, 548, 556, 701

ragtime, 434, 532
railroad regulation, 445
railroads, 224, 270, 272, 273, 277, 278, 316, 324, 337, 344, 346, 351, 367, 371, 380, 390, 391, 394, 407, 411, 412, 415, 421, 422, 435, 442, 494, 712
ranchers, 390, 394
Randolph, A. Philip, 497
Randolph, Edmund, 136, 177
Rappahannock River, 351
ratify, 140
rationing, 572
Ray, James Earl, 632
Reagan, Ronald, 664–665, 669–670, 672, 674–681, 685–689
Reaganomics, 676, 688
rebates, 415, 435, 448
recall, 424
Reconstruction, 356, 357, 358, 360, 362, 365, 366, 368–370, 372, 373, 398, 407
Reconstruction Acts, 362, 365
Reconstruction Finance Corporation (RFC), 545
Red Cloud, Chief, 394
Red Cloud War, 394
redeemed, 179
"Redeemers," 373
red scare, 520
Reed, Walter, 476
referendum, 424, 441
refinery, 414
refining companies, 417
reform, 255, 256, 397, 427, 432, 444, 449
reformers, 249, 251, 255, 397, 436, 438
Refugee Relief Act, 634
regulatory commission, 435
Relief and Construction Act, 545
religion, 8, 49, 54, 58, 61, 62, 67, 92, 245–246, 247, 251, 252; Aztecs, 10; colonial, 90; Eastern Woodlands, 20; Incas, 11; Mayas, 8; Navahos, 14; non-Christian, 302; Pueblo, 14; revivals, 245
relocation camps, 591–592
relocation centers, 574
"Remember Goliad," 289
"Remember the Alamo," 289
"Remember the *Maine*," 468

space program, 623
space shuttle, 650
Spain, 27, 29, 30, 31, 33, 34, 35, 38, 43, 49, 50, 51, 117, 122, 133, 184, 191–200, 208, 282, 286, 287, 300, 467, 468, 469, 471, 473
Spaniards, 31, 33, 34, 35, 40, 45, 63
Spanish, 36, 92, 281, 286, 302, 304, 431–432, 463, 467–471, 714
Spanish-American War, 468, 469, 470, 471, 473, 475, 476
Spanish Armada, 51
Spanish West Indies, 99
speakeasies, 533
specie, 227
"Specie Circular," 227, 230
Speckled Snake, 227
speculators, 179, 230
spheres of influence, 472
"spirit of Geneva," 618
"Spirit of St. Louis," 529
spoils system, 221, 222
sports, 433, 535, 536, 698, 702–703; Big Business, 703; bowling, 702; golf, 702; jogging, 702; professional teams, 702; riding bicycles, 702; softball, 702, tennis, 702
Spotsylvania Courthouse, Virginia, 351
Springfield, Illinois, 334
Springfield, Massachusetts, 135, 433
Sputnik I, 623
Squanto, 55, 75
stagflation, 646
Stalingrad, U.S.S.R., 575
Stalin, Joseph, 581, 582, 617–618
Stamp Act, 88, 107, 625
Stamp Act Congress, 107
Standard Oil Company, 414, 415, 417, 419, 428, 441
Standish, Miles, 55, 74, 77
Standish, Rose, 74
Stanton, Edwin, 363, 364
Stanton, Elizabeth Cady, 251
Stark, George, 506
State and Local Fiscal Assistance Act, 647
states' rights, 189, 222, 223, 224, 226, 227, 232

station, 318
Staunton, Virginia, 440
Stealth bomber, 679
steamboats, 208, 213, 269, 270, 273, 300
steam engine, 269, 270
steel, 266, 410, 411, 415, 416
Steffens, Lincoln, 439
Stephens, Alexander, 330
Stephenson, George, 270
Stephens, Uriah, 425
stevedores, 300
Stevens, John, 466
Stevenson, Adlai, 610
Stevens, Thaddeus, 356, 370
stock, 419, 541
stockbrokers, 540
stockholders, 416, 419
stock market, 540, 541, 542
Stowe, Harriet Beecher, 324
Strait of Magellan, 50, 525
Strategic Arms Limitation Treaty (SALT), 639, 679
Strauss, Levi, 305
strict construction, 182
strikes, 426, 427, 530, 608
strip mining, 706
Strong, George Templeton, 378, 379
Stuart, Gilbert, 212
Student Non-Violent Coordinating Committee, 630
submarines, 488, 489, 492, 497
subpoena, 654
suburbs, 695
subversives, 611
Sudetenland, Czechoslovakia, 567
Suez Canal, 575
suffrage, 220
Sugar Act of 1764, 106
summit conference, 618
Sumner, Charles, 356
Sumter, Thomas, 120
sun belt, 696, 716
Sun Dance, 15
Super-Realism, 700
supremacy of civilian authority, 151
supremacy of national law, 150
Supreme Court, 149, 156, 157, 162, 178, 189, 191, 208, 222, 223, 226, 227, 229, 237, 326, 362, 372, 399, 400, 419, 422, 441, 449, 491, 497, 557, 559, 574, 612, 613, 623, 655, 670, 671

surveyed, 130
Susquehanna Valley, 84, 93, 267, 412, 415
Sussex, 489
Sussex Pledge, 489, 492
Sutter, John, 287, 295
Sweden, 25, 44, 45, 402
Sweet, O. H., 526
Swift, Gustavus, 416, 453
Switzerland, 129, 344, 486
symbolism, 258
synthetic rubber, 573
Syracuse, New York, 254
Syria, 635, 642, 685

T

Taft-Hartley Act, 608
Taft-Katsura Agreement of 1905, 474
Taft, William Howard, 444–447, 472, 479
Taiwan, 641
Tallmadge, James, 320
Talon, Jean, 41
Tanaina Indians, 17
Taney, Roger B., 326
Tarbell, Ida M., 439
tariff act, 181
Tariff Act of 1828, 218, 222, 224
Tariff of 1816, 206
tariff reform, 447
tariffs, 139, 206, 314, 329, 346
Taylor, Zachary, 291, 322
Tea Act, 110
Teapot Dome, Wyoming, 527
technology, 703, 704
Tecumseh, 199, 202
Tehran, Iran, 581, 662
telegraph, 266, 272, 380, 411
telephone, 411
television, 611, 698, 701
Teller Amendment, 469
temperance, 255
Temperance Crusade, 255
tenements, 274, 436, 453
Tennessee, 130, 131, 203, 227, 328, 335, 339, 357, 358, 362, 381, 552
Tennessee River, 338
Tennessee Valley Authority (TVA), 552, 557
Tenochtitlán, 8, 10, 33, 34

Vietcong, 635, 639
Viet Minh, 614
Vietnam, 569, 614, 615, 635–639, 657, 695
Vietnamization, 639
Vietnam War, 162, 639, 646, 665
Vikings, 25
Villa, Francisco (Pancho), 481
Vincennes, 120
Virginia, 339, 340
Virgina, 54, 55, 57, 58, 61, 70, 71, 73, 74, 95, 100, 107, 112, 114, 119, 133, 136, 137, 142, 157, 177, 189, 202, 220, 221, 231, 258, 269, 288, 335, 336, 341, 347, 348, 351, 552, 625
Virginia and Kentucky Resolutions, 315
Virginia City, Nevada, 389
Virginia Plan, 136, 138
Virgin Islands, 480
virtual representation, 107
V-J Day, 581
Vladivostok Accord, 657
vocational training, 400–401
Volunteers in Service to America (VISTA), 629
Voting Rights Act of 1965, 633, 648
vulcanization, 266

W

Wabash River, 199
Wabash, St. Louis, and Pacific Railroad Company v. *Illinois*, 422
Wade, Benjamin, 356, 370
Wade-Davis Bill, 357
Wagner-Connery Act, 559
Wagner, Robert, 553
Wagner-Steagall Act, 553
Walden, 256
Wald, Lillian, 428
Wallace, George, 637
Wallace, Henry, 609
Walla Walla, Washington, 284
Wallowa Valley, Oregon, 395
Wampanoag Indians, 55, 96
war bonds, 496
War Department, 343
wards, 396
War Hawks, 200
Warhol, Andy, 700

War Industries Board, 494
War of 1812, 199, 200, 205–206, 208–210, 212–213, 217, 263, 314, 315
"war on poverty," 629
War Production Board (WPB), 572
Warren, Earl, 593, 612–613, 629
War Revenue Act, 496
Warsaw, Poland, 698
Wars of the Roses, 49
Washington, 282, 291
Washington, Booker T., 400, 402
Washington Conference on Limitations of Armaments, 517, 519
Washington, D.C., 202, 204, 213, 220, 234–239, 266, 334, 338, 348, 448, 501, 518–519, 525, 545, 581, 624–625, 636, 640, 647, 652, 659
Washington, George, 100, 112, 116–118, 121, 124, 136–137, 141–142, 177–180, 182–183, 186–187, 222, 234, 276
Watergate, 652, 653, 654, 655, 656, 665
Watson, Mary Jane, 209
Watson, Thomas, 423
Watt, James, 269
Watt, James, Secretary of Interior, 670–672
Watts, California, 630
Weaver, James B., 424
Weaver, Robert, 633
Webster, Daniel, 223, 224, 315
Webster-Hayne debates, 223
Webster, Noah, 253–254
Weinberger, Caspar, 679
Weld, Theodore, 249
West, 200, 206, 217, 219, 223–224, 226, 232, 234, 269, 273, 277, 281–282, 285, 293–295, 297, 346, 350, 370, 389, 391, 393–395, 399, 404, 405, 407, 423, 434, 444, 463, 495, 712
West Africa, 302
West, Benjamin, 212
West Berlin, Germany, 627
Western Hemisphere, 466, 467, 634, 660
West Indies, 29, 35–36, 61, 96, 99, 101, 122, 183–184, 197, 203, 300, 302, 316, 695

West Virginia, 327, 336, 356, 410
Weyler, Valeriano, 468
Wheatley, Phillis, 88
Whigs, 230, 231, 320, 322, 325, 328, 366
Whiskey Rebellion, 181, 182
"Whiskey Ring," 371
whiskey tax, 191
white-collar workers, 708
White House, 202, 217, 230–231, 235, 237–239, 473, 555, 610, 652–653
White, John, 70
White, William Allen, 568
Whitman, Marcus, 284
Whitman, Narcissa, 284
Whitman, Walt, 259
Whitney, Eli, 266, 315
Whittier, John Greenleaf, 259
wickiups, 14
wigwams, 19
Willard, Emma Hart, 253
William and Mary, College of, 94
Williamsburg, Virginia, 94
Williams, Roger, 57
Willkie, Wendell, 568
Wills, Helen, 535
Wilmot, David, 321, 322
Wilmot Proviso, 322
Wilson, Woodrow, 447–449, 479–481, 485–486, 488–489, 490–491, 494, 499–503, 517, 520, 523
"windfall profits" tax, 662
Winnebago Indians, 19, 228
Winnemucca, Sarah, 397
Winthrop, John, 57
wire services, 702
Wisconsin, 277, 422, 440, 452, 611
Wisconsin Territory, 228
Wolfe, James, 101
women, 264, 305, 532, 573–574; colonial life, 89–90; Iroquois, 20; Pueblo, 14; *Women in the Nineteenth Century*, 256; women in wartime, 118–119, 343, 494, 573; Women's Building, 456; Women's Christian Temperance Union, 533; women's movement, 649; women's rights, 248, 250–251, 253, 256, 523; women's suffrage, 436, 490, 523

Wood, Leonard, 476
Woodward, Robert, 653
Woolen Act of 1699, 99
Working Girl's Home
   Association, 428
workmen's compensation law,
   440
World's Columbian Exposition,
   455
World Series, 433
World War I, 436, 486,
   489–491, 493, 495, 498,
   501–503, 511, 517, 519–524,
   529–531, 540, 564, 572, 574
World War II, 599–601,
   604–605, 607, 614, 616, 633;
   beginning, 566–567; financing,
   574; Los Angeles, 593; Pearl
   Harbor, 570; war in the
   Pacific, 570
Wounded Knee Creek, 396

Wright, Orville, 529
Wright, Wilbur, 529
writ of habeas corpus, 147
Wu, Chien Shiung, 631
Wyoming, 15, 282, 293, 390,
   394, 574

X

XYZ Affair, 187

Y

Yale College, 91
Yalta, 582, 602
Yap Island, 519
yellow-dog contracts, 532
yellow fever, 302, 478

yellow journalism, 468
Yokut Indians, 16
Yom Kippur, 642
York (Toronto), Canada, 202
Young, Brigham, 246
Young, James Sterling, 238
Young Men's Christian
   Association (YMCA), 427
Young Women's Christian
   Association (YWCA), 427,
   648
Yucatán Peninsula, 7
Yugoslavia, 571

Z

Zimbabwe, 659
Zimmermann, Arthur, 492
Zimmermann note, 492
Zuñi Indians, 13–14, 35

Acknowledgements

Thanks are due to the following authors and publishers for the material quoted on the pages indicated: **p. 31:** Adapted from Major, R. H. (trans. and ed.). *Select Letters of Christopher Columbus*. London: The Hakluyt Society, 1870. **p.55:** Adapted from *The Mayflower Compact*. **pp. 70–73:** Lorant, Stefan (ed.). *The New World*. New York: Duell, Sloan & Pearce, 1946. Reprinted by permission. **pp. 74–76, 77:** Bradford, William. *Of Plymouth Plantation 1620–1647*. Ed. Samuel Eliot Morison. New York: Alfred A. Knopf, Inc., 1952. Reprinted by permission. **p. 76:** Pory, John, Altham, Emmanuel, and DeRasieres, Isaack. *Three Visitors to Early Plymouth*. Ed. Sydney V. James, Jr. Plimoth Plantation, Inc., 1963. Reprinted by permission. **p. 87:** Mittelberger, Gottlieb. *Journey to Pennsylvania*. Ed. and trans. Oscar Handlin and John Clive. Cambridge, Massachusetts: The Belknap Press of Harvard University Press, 1960. **p. 88:** Ellis, John Harvard (ed.). *The Works of Anne Bradstreet*. Gloucester, Massachusetts: Peter Smith, 1867. **p. 88:** Wheatley, Phillis. *Poems and Letters*. Ed. Chas. Fred. Heartman. Miami, Florida: Mnemosyne Publishing Co., Inc., 1969. **p. 97:** Crèvecoeur, J. Hector St. John. *Letters from an American Farmer*. New York: Albert & Charles Boni, 1904. **p. 97:** Nevins, Allan. *The Emergence of Modern America 1865–1878*. New York: The Macmillan Company, 1927. **p. 113:** Longfellow, Henry W. *Paul Revere's Ride*. Portland, Maine: L. H. Nelson Company, 1905. **p. 113:** Adapted from O'Brien, Harriet E. (comp.). *Paul Revere's Own Story*. Privately printed by Perry Walton, 1929. **p. 116:** Fast, Howard. *The Selected Works of Tom Paine*. New York: The Modern Library, 1943. **p. 123:** Adapted from Butterfield, L. H. (ed.). *Adams Family Correspondence*. Vol. I. Cambridge, Massachusetts: The Belknap Press of Harvard University Press, 1963. **pp. 137, 139–140:** Donovan, Frank. *The Benjamin Franklin Papers*. New York: Dodd, Mead & Company, 1962. **p. 137:** Schrag, Peter. *The Ratification of the Constitution and the Bill of Rights*. Boston: D. C. Heath and Company, 1964. **p. 150:** Hamilton, Alexander, Madison, James, and Jay, John. *The Federalist Papers*. New York: The New American Library, 1961. **p. 166:** Adapted from Birket, James. *Some Cursory Remarks*. New Haven: Yale University Press, 1916. **pp. 168, 169–170:** *The Life and Letters of Benjamin Franklin*. Eau Claire, Wisconsin: E. M. Hale & Company. Reprinted by permission. **p. 168:** Bridenbaugh, Carl and Jessica. *Rebels and Gentlemen*. New York: Oxford University Press, 1942. **pp. 168–169:** Van Doren, Carl. *Benjamin Franklin*. New York: The Viking Press, 1938. **p. 185:** Wansey, Henry. *The Journal of an Excursion to the United States of North America in the Summer of 1947*. London, 1796. **p. 186:** *Washington's Farewell Address*. **p. 209:** Cobbett, William. *The Emigrant's Guide*. London: Mills, Jowett, and Mills, 1829. **p. 211:** Bryant, William Cullen. *Thanatopsis*. New York: G. P. Putnam's Sons, 1878. **p. 221:** Ambler, Charles H. *The Life and Diary of John Floyd*. Richmond: Richmond Press, Inc., 1918. **p. 225:** Adapted from Kemble, Frances Anne. "Boat, Stage, Railroad, and Canal (1832-1833)." As quoted in Bushnell, Albert Hart. *American History Told by Contemporaries*. New York: Macmillan Co., 1901. **pp. 227–228:** Armstrong, Virginia Irving (comp.). *I Have Spoken*. Chicago: The Swallow Press Inc., 1971. **pp. 235–236:** Adapted from Mitchell, Stewart (ed.).

New Letters of Abigail Adams. Boston: Houghton Mifflin Company, 1947. **p. 236:** Adapted from Beston, Henry. *American Memory*. New York: Farrar & Rinehart, 1937. **pp. 237, 238:** Adapted from Smith, Mrs. Samuel Harrison. *The First Forty Years of Washington Society*. Ed. Gaillord Hunt. New York: Charles Scribner's Sons, 1906. Reprinted by permission. **p. 238:** Young, James Sterling. *The Washington Community 1800–1828*. New York: Columbia University Press, 1966. **p. 249:** *The Liberator*, Vol. I, No. 7, page 1, February 12, 1831. Boston, Massachusetts. **p. 251:** *History of Woman Suffrage*, Elizabeth C. Stanton *et al.*, eds., Vol. I, New York, 1881. **p. 257:** Emerson, Ralph Waldo. *Nature, Addresses, and Lectures*. Boston: Houghton Mifflin and Company, 1855. **p. 265:** Quincy, Josiah. "Travel Journal (June 1801)" *Massachusetts Historical Society Proceedings* (May 1888). **p. 271:** Martineau, Harriet. *Society in America*. New York: Saunders and Otley, 1837. **p. 285:** Parkman, Francis. *The Oregon Trail*. Chicago: The John C. Winston Company, 1931. **p. 294:** Colton, Rev. Walter. *Three Years in California*. New York: A. S. Barnes & Co., 1850. **pp. 300, 303:** Hall, A. Oakey. *The Manhattaner in New Orleans*. New York: J. S. Redfield, 1850. **p. 302:** Quoted in Searight, Sarah. *New Orleans*. New York: Stein and Day, 1973. **pp. 302–303, 303:** Ripley, Eliza. *Social Life in Old New Orleans*. New York: D. Appleton and Company, 1912. **pp. 304, 305, 306:** Soulé, Frank, Gihon, John H., and Nisbet, James. *The Annals of San Francisco*. New York: D. Appleton and Company, 1845. **p. 306:** Bancroft, Hubert Howe. *Popular Tribunals*. Vol. I. San Francisco: The History Co., 1887. **p. 316:** Northup, Solomon. *Twelve Years a Slave*. Eds. Sue Eaken and Joseph Logsdon. Baton Rouge: Louisiana State University Press, 1968. **p. 321:** U.S. *The Congressional Globe*. 29th Cong., 2d Sess., 1847. **p. 321:** U.S. *The Congressional Globe*. 31st Cong., 1st Sess., 1850. **p. 342:** From a public letter in 1862 to Horace Greeley of the New York *Tribune*. **p. 349:** *The Gettysburg Address*. **p. 352:** *Lincoln's Second Inaugural Address*. **p. 359:** From *The Americans at Home* by David Macrae. Published in 1952 by E. P. Dutton, and reprinted with their permission. **pp. 360–361:** Trowbridge, J. T. *The South: A Tour of Its Battle-fields and Ruined Cities*. New York: Arno Press, Inc., 1969. **p. 370:** Billington, Ray Allen (ed.). *The Journal of Charlotte Forten*. London: Collier-Macmillan Ltd., 1953. **p. 376:** Russell, William Howard. *My Diary North and South*. Vol. II. London: Bradbury and Evans, 1863. **p. 377:** Dicey, Edward. "Three Weeks in New York." *Macmillan's Magazine*, (April 1862), pp. 458, 461–463. **p. 379:** Nevins, Allan, and Thomas, Milton Halsey (eds.). *The Diary of George Templeton Strong*. New York: The Macmillan Company, 1952. **p. 379:** Skinner, John E. Hilary. "After the Storm." As quoted in Still, Bayard. *Mirror for Gotham*. Washington Square: New York University Press, 1956. **p. 381:** Coulter, E. Merton. *Georgia, A Short History*. Chapel Hill: University of North Carolina Press, 1947. **p. 381:** From the *Macon Daily Telegraph and Confederate*, December 12, 1864. As quoted in Garrett, Franklin M. *Atlanta and Environs*. Vol. I. Athens: University of Georgia Press, 1954. **p. 381:** Massey, Kate. "A Picture of Atlanta in the Late Sixties." *The Atlanta Historical Bulletin*, 1940–41. **pp. 381–382:** From a letter on file at the Atlanta Historical Society. As quoted in

Garrett, Franklin M. *Atlanta and Environs*. Vol. I. Athens: University of Georgia Press, 1954. **p. 382:** Thompson, C. Mildred. *Reconstruction in Georgia*. New York, 1915. As quoted in Garrett, Franklin M. *Atlanta and Environs*. Vol. I. Athens: University of Georgia Press, 1954. **pp. 382–383:** From the *Daily Intelligencer*, September 13, 1865. As quoted in Garrett, Franklin M. *Atlanta and Environs*. Vol. I. Athens: University of Georgia Press, 1954. **p. 383:** Adapted from Rawick, George P. (ed.). *American Slave*. As quoted in Litwack, Leon F. *Been in the Storm So Long*. New York: Alfred A. Knopf, Inc., 1979. **p. 396:** Fee, Chester Anders. *Chief Joseph*. New York: Wilson-Erickson Inc., 1936. **p. 400:** Washington, Booker T. *The Story of My Life and Work*. Toronto: J. L. Nichols & Company, 1901. **p. 403:** *Congressional Record*. 54th Cong., 1st Sess., p. 2817 (March 16, 1896). **p. 403:** Richardson, J. D. (ed.). *Messages and Papers of the Presidents*. Vol. IX, 1897. **pp. 425–426:** *Autobiography of Mother Jones*. 1925 **p. 437:** Bryan, William J. *The First Battle*. Chicago: W. B. Conkey Company, 1896. **p. 443:** Stein, Leon. *The Triangle Fire*. Philadelphia: J. B. Lippincott Company, 1962. **p. 454:** *Transactions of the Illinois State Historical Society for the Year 1920*. Springfield, 1920. **p. 455:** *Transactions of the Illinois State Historical Society for the Year 1906*. Springfield: Illinois State Journal Co., 1906. **p. 456:** Ralph, Julian. *Harper's Chicago and the World's Fair*. New York: Harper & Brothers, 1893. **p. 456:** "Good-by to the Fair," *Chicago Tribune*, Nov. 1, 1893. **p. 470:** Davis, Richard Harding. *Notes of a War Correspondent*. New York: Charles Scribner's Sons, 1910. **p. 473:** Olcott, Charles S. *The Life of William McKinley*. Vol. II. Boston: Houghton Mifflin Company, 1916. **p. 492:** U.S. 65th Congress, 1st Sess.. *Senate Document 5*. **p. 502:** *Supplement to the Messages and Papers of the Presidents Covering the Second Administration of Woodrow Wilson*. **p. 506:** Glazier, Captain Willard. *Peculiarities of American Cities*. Philadelphia: Hubbard Brothers, Publishers, 1883. **p. 506:** Stark, George W. *Detroit at the Century's Turn*. Detroit: Wayne University Press, 1951. **pp. 508–509:** Ford, Henry. *My Life and Work*. Garden City, New York: Doubleday, Page & Company, 1922. **p. 509:** *Colliers*, 4 July 1914, pp. 9, 10. As quoted in Holli, Melvin G. (ed.). *Detroit*. New York: New Viewpoints, 1976. **p. 510:** *Detroiter 7* (17 January 1916). As quoted in Holli, Melvin G. (ed.). *Detroit*. New York: New Viewpoints, 1976. **pp. 510–511:** *New Outlook* (27 September 1916). As quoted in

Holli, Melvin G. (ed.). *Detroit*. New York: New Viewpoints, 1976. **p. 511:** Parkins, Almon Ernest. *The Historical Geography of Detroit*. Lansing: Michigan Historical Commission, 1918. **p. 517:** Lentz, Andrea D. (ed.). *The Warren G. Harding Papers*. Columbus: Ohio Historical Society, 1970. **p. 531:** *The New Day: Campaign Speeches of Herbert Hoover*. California: Stanford University Press, 1928. **p. 543:** Allen, Frederick Lewis. *Since Yesterday*. New York: Harper & Brothers Publishers, 1939. **p. 555:** Holt, Rackham. *Mary McLeod Bethune*. Garden City, New York: Doubleday & Company, Inc., 1964. **p. 570:** *President Roosevelt's Message Asking for War Against Japan*. December 8, 1941. **p. 577:** Eisenhower, Dwight D. *Crusade in Europe*. Garden City, New York: Doubleday & Company, Inc., 1948. **pp. 586–587:** Excerpted by permission of Harcourt Brace Jovanovich, Inc. from *Middletown* by Robert S. and Helen M. Lynd, copyright 1929 by Harcourt Brace Jovanovich, Inc.; copyright 1957 by Robert S. and Helen M. Lynd. **p. 589:** Excerpted by permission of Harcourt Brace Jovanovich, Inc. from *Middletown in Transition* by Robert S. and Helen Merrell Lynd, copyright 1937 by Harcourt Brace Jovanovich, Inc.; copyright 1965 by Robert S. and Helen M. Lynd. **pp. 590, 591:** *Los Angeles, A Guide to the City and Its Environs*. Comp. Workers of the Writers' Program of the Work Projects Administration in Southern California. New York: Hastings House, Publishers, 1941. **pp. 591–593:** Quoted in Caughey, John and Laree. *Los Angeles, Biography of a City*. Berkeley: University of California Press, 1976. **p. 600:** From the Charter of the United Nations. **p. 613:** *Brown* v. *Board of Education of Topeka*, 1954. **p. 622:** *John F. Kennedy's Inaugural Address*. January 20, 1961. **p. 625:** From a speech given by Martin Luther King, Jr., on August 28, 1963. **p. 647:** Richard M. Nixon, *State of the Union Address*. January 22, 1971. **p. 651:** Scott, David R. "What Is It Like to Walk on the Moon?" *National Geographic*, September 1973. Reprinted by permission. **p. 681:** Wholey, Janet. "Experts Agree: Oil Has a Bleak Future." Sunday, November 23, 1980. copyright © 1980 by The New York Times Company. Reprinted by permission. **pp. 688, 691:** "Greater Houston Its First Million People—and Why" *Newsweek*. July 5, 1954, p. 39. **p. 689:** Oates, Stephen B. *Visions of Glory*. Norman, Oklahoma: University of Oklahoma Press, 1970. **pp. 690, 690–691:** Jordan, Barbara. "How I Got There." *Atlantic Monthly*, March 1975. **pp. 691–692:** "A City's Growing Pains." *Newsweek*. January 14, 1980, p. 45.

Photo Credits

Unit 6

Page 386, Museum of the City of New York; 387, Thomas Gilcrease Institute of American History & Art, Tulsa, Ok.; 388, The Granger Collection; 391, Thomas Gilcrease Institute of American History & Art, Tulsa, Ok.; 393, Library of Congress; 395, The Taft Museum, Cincinnati, Ohio; 398, Thomas Gilcrease Institute of American History & Art, Tulsa, Ok.; 401 (lt.), Courtesy of the NAACP; 401 (rt.), 405, Historical Pictures Service; 409, Courtesy of the Bethlehem Steel Corp.; 411, Library of Congress; 414, Rockefeller Archive Center; 415, Carnegie Library, Pittsburgh; 422, The Granger Collection; 425, Library of Congress; 427, Collection, The Museum of Modern Art, N.Y.; 431, Museum of the City of New York; 433, New York Historical Society; 437, The Granger Collection; 439, Library of Congress; 440, Historical Society of Wisconsin; 442, Library of Congress; 445, Eastman Kodak Co.; 448, 453, 454, Library of Congress; 455, Chicago Historical Society; 456, 457, Historical Pictures Service.

Unit 7

Page 461 (top), George Luks, *Armistice Night*, 1937, Collection of the Whitney Museum of American Art; 461 (bot.), National Archives; 462, 464, The Granger Collection; 465, The Bishop Museum; 469, Library of Congress; 474, Peabody Museum of Salem; 477, Library of Congress; 478 (lt.), The Granger Collection; 478 (rt.), Historical Pictures Service; 484, The Granger Collection; 488, Historical Pictures Service; 493, National Archives; 495 (lt.), The Granger Collection; 495 (rt.), 496 (lt.), National Archives; 496 (rt.), Bishop Museum; 500, The Bettmann Archive; 503, Bildarchiv Preussischer Kulturbesitz; 507, Library of Congress; 508, Ford Motor Co.; 509, Library of Congress; 510, Henry Ford Museum.

Unit 8

Page 514, U.S. Department of Energy; 515, Collection of Everson Museum of Art, Syracuse, N.Y.; 516, New School for Social Research, New York; 519, File Photo; 521, Historical Pictures Service; 522, Library of Congress; 524 (lt.), Historical Pictures Service; 524 (rt.), Courtesy of the New York Historical Society; 533, Historical Pictures Service; 535, Schomburg Center for Research in Black Culture, New York Public Library, Astor, Lenox and Tilden Foundations; 536, George Bellows, *Dempsey and Firpo*, 1924, Collection of the Whitney Museum of American Art; 539, Isaac Soyer, *Employment Agency*, 1937, Collection of the Whitney Museum of American Art; 542, Wide World Photos; 543, Historical Pictures Service; 544, Library of Congress; 549, National Archives; 549, UPI; 550 (lt.), Franklin D. Roosevelt Library; 550 (rt.), National Museum of American Art, Smithsonian Institution, Gift of Mr. and Mrs. Soyer; 554, UPI; 557, © 1935 (renewed 1963) by the Conde Nast Publications, Inc.; 558, Franklin D. Roosevelt Library; 562, UPI; 565, Yivo Institute for Jewish Research; 567, 569, Historical Pictures Service; 571 (lt.), UPI; 571 (rt.), PHOTRI; 573, The Bettmann Archive; 578, U. S. Coast Guard; 583, Franklin D. Roosevelt Library; 587, Ball Corporation; 588, Brown Brothers; 589, Kansas State Historical Society; 591, File Photo; 592, 593, Library of Congress.

Unit 9

Page 596, J. R. Eyerman/Black Star; 597, NASA; 598, M. Scheller/Black Star; 603, 606, 610, UPI; 612, Wide World Photos; 613, UPI; 617 (lt.), Carl Mydans Life Magazine, © Time Inc.; 617 (rt.), Historical Pictures Service; 621, 624, UPI; 626 (lt.), Wide World Photos; 626 (rt.), Nicholas Sapieha/Stock, Boston; 628, Lyndon B. Johnson Library; 632, George Ballis/Black Star; 636, Magnum; 640 (lt.), By permission of Bill Mauldin and Wil-Jo Associates, Inc.; 640 (rt.), Drawing by Richter; © 1974 The New Yorker Magazine, Inc.; 641, UPI; 645, James Westwater; 650, NASA; 655, B. Alpert/Keystone; 656, Wide World Photos; 658, UPI; 660, D. B. Owen/Black Star; 663, Michael Evans/Liason Agency; 665 (lt.), PHOTRI; 665 (rt.), UPI; 668, Burt Glinn/Magnum; 668, Steve Liss/Gamma-Liason; 670, Dirck Halstead/Liason Agency; 672, Newsweek; 673, Dirck Halstead/Liason Agency; 673, Martin A. Levick/Black Star; 674, Yvonne Hemsey/Liason Agency; 676 (lt.), Hans Namuth; 676 (rt.), Reprinted from *The Saturday Evening Post* © 1962 The Curtis Publishing Company; 677, Newsweek; 679, Jay Lurie/FPG, 680. Young/Hoffhines Photography; 680, (lt.), Liason Agency; 680 (rt.), Hires/Liason Agency; 681, Gamma-Liason; 682 (lt.), U.S. Department of Energy; 682 (rt.), Phil and Loretta Hermann for Tom Stack and Associates; 685 (lt.), U.S. Department of Agriculture; 685 (rt.), Tracy Borland; 685, Roland Neveu/Liason Agency; 689, File Photo; 690, NASA; 691, UPI; 692, Texas Department of Highways; 693, Gerald D. Hines Interest, Inc; 703, Dan Connolly/Liason Agency

Unit Openings

Front cover, Peter Gridley/Freelance Photographers Guild
Back cover, Brian Parker/Tom Stack & Associates